Fourth Edition

Agricultural Statistics in India

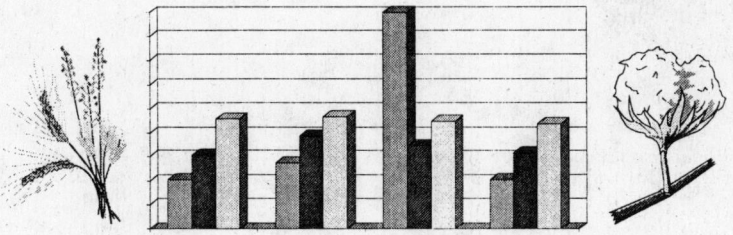

Techno Economic Research Institute Publication

Fourth Edition

Agricultural Statistics in India

P.C. Bansil

Techno Economic Research Institute
New Delhi

CBS Publishers & Distributors Pvt. Ltd.

NEW DELHI • BANGALORE • PUNE • COCHIN • CHENNAI (INDIA)

ISBN : 81-239-0793-1

First Edition : 1970
Second Revised Edition : 1974
Third Revised Edition : 1984
Fourth Edition : 2002
Reprint : 2011

Published by Satish Kumar Jain and produced by V.K. Jain for
CBS Publishers & Distributors Pvt. Ltd.,
CBS Plaza, 4819/XI Prahlad Street, 24 Ansari Road, Daryaganj,
New Delhi - 110002, India.   • Website: www.cbspd.com
e-mail: delhi@cbspd.com, cbspubs@vsnl.com, cbspubs@airtelmail.in
Ph.: 23289259, 23266861, 23266867   • Fax: 011-23243014

Branches:
• *Bengaluru:* Seema House, 2975, 17th Cross, K.R. Road,
  Bansankari 2nd Stage, Bengaluru - 560070   Ph.: +91-80-26771678/79
  Fax: +91-80-26771680   • E-mail: cbsbng@gmail.com,
  bangalore@cbspd.com
• *Pune:* Bhuruk Prestige, Sr. No. 52/12/2+1+3/2,
  Narhe, Haveli (Near Katraj-Dehu Road By-pass), Pune - 411051
  Ph.: +91-20-64704058/59, 32342277   • E-mail: pune@cbspd.com
• *Kochi:* 36/14, Kalluvilakam, Lissie Hospital Road,
  Kochi - 682018, Kerala   • Ph.: +91-484-4059061-65
  Fax: +91-484-4059065   • E-mail: cochin@cbspd.com
• *Chennai:* 20, West Park Road, Shenoy Nagar, Chennai - 600030
  Ph.: +91-44-26260666, 26208620   • Fax: +91-44-42032115
  E-mail: chennai@cbspd.com

Printed at :
India Binding House, Noida (UP)

vi

Preface to the Fourth Edition

India today has achieved the rare distinction of having a stock of some 60 million tonnes of foodgrains. This is something which would be beyond the comprehension of those who witnessed the mid-sixties drama of India living from ship to mouth. A sea change has taken place in the agricultural scene during the past 17 years or so since the third edition of this book was released in 1984. Along with these changes, needs for agricultural data base have become all the more demanding.

With such a long gap obviously there was the need to completely rewrite a major part of the publication which alone will, at least, partly explain the delay in bringing out this edition. Besides revising the existing text, some chapters have been deleted and new ones added. The present volume consists of 31 chapters.

Although significant progress has been made to improve agricultural data base so far, there are still large gaps, both qualitative and quantitative, particularly with regard to livestock. All these have been highlighted at appropriate places. Every possible effort has been made to present the latest available information on different aspects of the complicated agricultural statistical system.

I do hope that the book in its updated form will prove useful to students of agricultural economics, researchers, educated farmers, administrators, policy makers and bankers alike. I shall very much welcome any comments for further improvement of the volume.

While a number of friends have helped me in providing the latest material on the subject, I have taken the liberty of using some of the papers read by a few experts at various seminars which have been duly acknowledged in the text at appropriate places. My special thanks are due to my colleagues Mr. K.R. Dasgupta and Mr. C.P. Sharma, without whose help it would not have been possible for me to complete the arduous job of major revision of the text and data. Two of our senior faculty members, Mr. S.P. Malhotra and Dr. P. N. Radhakrishnan, were available for guidance during the preparation of this volume. Mr. Y.N. Arjuna was actually the real motivator to bring the book to its final shape. But for his patience to cope with the frequent changes made in the various drafts of the book and his editorial improvements, this edition of the book would not have seen the light of the day. Many thanks to him.

Dr **P.C. Bansil**
Techno Economic Research Institute
J-7, Saket, New Delhi 110017

October 2001

Preface to the Third Edition

For the first time in her long history, India has succeeded to disprove Malthus and has attained her cherished goal of self-sufficiency in food. This has attracted the attention of politicians and scholars worldwide. To enable one to appreciate the depth of the problem, there is the need for various types of agricultural data. This work, the third edition of which is being released, has grown along with India's agriculture and is intended to be a source of reliable information on the subject.

The present edition has not only been completely rewritten and updated, but also expanded to cover important topics like agricultural census. While the first edition contained only 16 chapters and the second 24, the present one has 28 chapters. Every possible effort has been made to incorporate the latest available information as to-date.

There are two more areas—cost of production of livestock products and crop losses—which deserve special mention. IARSI has done a lot of work on the cost of production of milk and other products. The methodology is being finalized. We have, however, not included any aspect on these issues, in this edition. Similarly crop losses, although an important issue, has not been discussed fully because of lack of adequate information. But a section on important issues like feed, seed and wastage rates and marketed surplus have been added in the chapter dealing with miscellaneous statistics.

It is hoped that the book will be useful to students of economic problems of Indian agriculture, in particular, and educated farmers, political leaders, bank managers and planners, in general, within and outside the country.

While a number of friends have helped to provide various types of materials and information, I would like to thank Dr. M.S. Bhatia, Ministry of Agriculture, for this help. The responsibility for the views expressed here, any errors of omission or commission is only mine and not of the official agencies with whom I have been associated.

New Delhi　　　　　　　　　　　　　　　　　　　**P.C. Bansil**
December 1983

Preface to the Second Edition

The first edition of the study was released some time in the end of 1970 and was finished in about one and a half years. There has been in recent years a sharp increase in the number of agricultural students which has risen from 1.4 thousand in 1947 to 12.8 thousand in 1972. The number of agricultural institutions increased to 93 by September 1972 from only 17 in 1947 and there are at present 18 agricultural universities in the country. The number of postgraduate agricultural colleges has also increased from a meagre 5 in 1951 to 42 in 1971. There are 20 veterinary postgraduate colleges today as compared to only one in 1955. The total enrolment of students for agricultural and animal sciences has multiplied 16 times since 1960. During 1971 alone as many as 9.3 thousand bachelor's and 1.5 thousand postgraduate degrees were awarded in agriculture and veterinary sciences. Even otherwise in a developing country like India whose economy is predominantly agricultural in character, agricultural statistics call for special importance. With all this, an increasing need has been felt to revise the first edition of the study and enlarge its scope so as to make it useful to a wider section of the student population.

The present edition consists of 24 chapters as against only 16 in the earlier one. Besides rewriting the existing material, the new chapters concern population, irrigation, agricultural labour—employment and wages, commodity statistics, national sample surveys, consumption and stocks of foodgrains, cost of production studies, index numbers relating to agricultural economics and world agricultural statistics. An effort has also been made to keep the size of the book to a reasonable level so that its price does not reach beyond the level of an average student. This has been made possible by deleting some of the Appendices. A few Appendices which the present volume contains will be of great value for students of agricultural economics and statistics.

Thanks are due to my friends Mr. R.S. Chadha and Mr. P.P. Singh who were kind enough to go through the manuscript and gave many valuable suggestions. The responsibility for any errors of either omission or commission, however, is mine.

Lusaka   **P.C. Bansil**
December, 1973

Preface to the First Edition

With the emphasis on economic planning, of which agricultural development is an essential constituent and the rising demand for agriculturally trained personnel for employment, the number of agricultural colleges and students has appreciably increased in the country during recent years. So much so that each State is planning to have an agriculture university of its own.

Setbacks in agricultural extension programmes and lack of adequate success on the agricultural front in the country with an essentially technical approach have drawn attention to the need for agricultural economic studies and integration of economic and technical approach in agricultural planning and extension. Such studies, if they have to come to any meaningful results, must necessarily depend upon a sound and comprehensive statistical framework.

There is, at present, no study available which can serve as a guide to all those interested to know about the nature and scope of agricultural statistics and use them for their day to day purposes. With the ushering in of the 'Green Revolution' and 'New Strategy' there is an increasing awareness of agricultural statistics in India. As a consequence of the nationalization of 14 major banks in the country and Government schemes to expand agricultural credit, the need for knowledge about agricultural statistics and limitations from which they suffer has grown for the vast banking community.

This book has been organized to overcome these difficulties. It should be useful and of interest to students of economic problems of Indian agriculture in particular, educated farmers, political leaders, bank managers and planners in India as well abroad in general.

The study discusses at length the nature, scope, development and availability of various types of agricultural statistics in India. The information consolidated here is otherwise so scattered that credit can rightly be taken for bringing it together, for the first time in a study on agricultural economics. Obviously a good deal of material presented has been obtained from numerous books and official publications which it is difficult to acknowledge individually. Much of the information is from the Directorate of Economics and Statistics, Ministry of Agriculture, the help of which is gratefully acknowledged herewith.

Quite a number of colleagues have spent time and offered valuable comments to improve the study. Dr. G.D. Agrawal who has been associated with teaching, examining and formation of syllabi as well as with research in agricultural economics and is at present holding a senior post in the Food and Agriculture Organisation (FAO) of the United Nations provided valuable guidance and comments on an earlier draft. Dr. Vidya Sagar who also is now with the FAO, undertook the laborious task of going through an earlier draft of the manuscript while he was in the Planning Commission, Government of India. I owe a debt of gratitude to them and other friends.

No one is more conscious of the need for improvements in this book than me, but the main intention in bringing it out is that once the framework has been soundly designed, it is easy to take care of details even later. The responsibility for the views expressed, and also any omission or commission is mine alone and not of any official agencies with which I have been associated.

New Delhi
August, 1970

P.C. Bansil

Contents

Agricultural Statistics in India

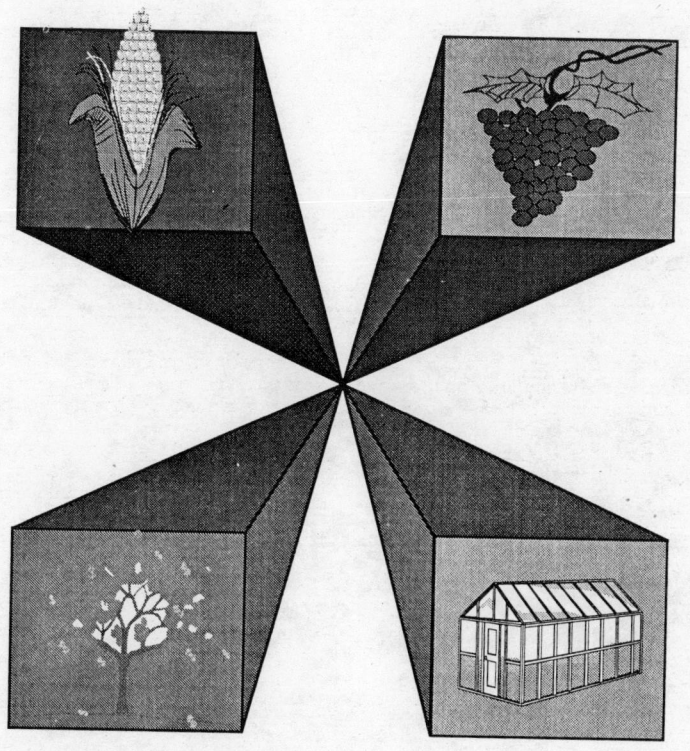

1

Agricultural Statistics and their Development in India

EARLY DEVELOPMENTS IN STATISTICS

Collection and use of statistics for administrative purposes in India has a very long and well-known history, spread over many centuries. However, it was only in the nineteen thirties that Prasanta Chandra Mahalanobis (PCM) put statistical practice on a scientific basis in India. The other pioneer was Pandurang V. Sukhatme (Sukhatme), who specialised in the application of statistical methods in agriculture-related subjects and nutrition. PCM demonstrated that statistics is an essential tool for rational decision-making based on fallible information in any activity—science and industry, business and trade, government and administration. He called statistics the *key technology* of the age. With fanatical zeal, PCM pursued the development of statistics in India in all directions. His own theoretical research covered many areas of statistics—sample surveys, multivariate analysis, developmental planning—to mention a few. In each of these areas, he made path-breaking advances. Most of his research was motivated by logical and operational problems of collection and interpretation of fallible data and substantiated through large-scale applications.

He established the Indian Statistical Institute (ISI) in 1931 as a scientific society for theoretical and applied research in statistics. A brilliant group of researchers—Raj Chandra Bose, Samarendra Nath Roy, C. Radhakrishna Rao, K.R. Nair, Kanwar Kishen and many others joined him at the ISI. *Sankhya*, the research journal of ISI, soon won international recognition. It is interesting to note that K.R. Nair brought his academic excellence into the official statistical system of India first as the Senior Statistician of the Forest Research Institute and then as the Director of the Central Statistical Organisation. So did K. Kishen as the Director of the Statistical Bureau of Uttar Pradesh. A strong relation between academicians and practitioners of statistics was thus initiated.

Even in the midst of the struggle for independence, the Indian National Congress had started thinking about strategies for economic development of the country after independence. It was at that time that PCM offered

1

Pandit Jawaharlal Nehru his full assistance in all statistical aspects of developmental planning. Thus began an association which lasted till Panditji's death.

NATURE OF AGRICULTURAL STATISTICS

Agricultural statistics refer to information presented quantitatively, i.e. in figures, on various aspects of agriculture with reference to a country or region. Obviously, they can be used only in respect of those items and attributes which are amenable to some sort of measurement. For example, the surface of land is measurable in area units—acres or hectares; farm products can be measured in units of weight or volume and the income from a crop can be measured in terms of the currency. Certain attributes, on the other hand, cannot be expressed in figures, e.g. the quality of management. Hence, they are not amenable to statistical expression. Once statistics on an item or feature of farming are available, they have to be so compiled and organized as to be useful.

A description of various statistical techniques of collecting agricultural information or their analysis, better known as analytical statistics, is outside the scope of their study which is concerned only with the nature of agricultural statistics available, or those that should be made available, their role and their development. If there is a discussion on the assembling of certain information, such as on prices, it refers mainly to a description of the method of collection and obvious weaknesses in it in order to understand the extent to which they are usable for certain purposes and the direction in which improvements are required. For sampling techniques, statistical analysis, etc., the reader has to refer to books on mathematical or analytical statistics.

In order to understand the nature of agricultural statistics more fully, they may be classified into the following broad groups:

1. Land utilization and irrigation.
2. Forestry.
3. Agricultural production—arable, plantations, livestock and fisheries.
4. Agricultural prices and wages.
5. Agricultural organisation and farming structure, e.g. persons employed in agriculture, their status, land held under various tenures, size of holding, number of draught cattle, implements, machines, farm buildings, etc.
6. Economics of production and marketing, i.e. cost of production, inputs, input-output ratios, marketing charges, marketing spread over, etc.
7. General, such as, literacy among those employed in agriculture, health, sanitation, etc. Rainfall and its distribution, temperature and its range, etc.
8. Forecasts—weather, crops, prices.

Each of the groups mentioned above is fully dealt with in respect of their present position, drawbacks, role and improvements needed in the following chapters. Some general idea may, however, be formed from what is stated below.

The total area of land surface is recorded according to various uses, i.e. forests, farming, fallow waste land, roads, buildings, mines, etc.; where land statistics are advanced each area has detailed classification according to soil type, quality and grade. Further, area statistics have a breakdown for each crop—under pasture, double cropped, irrigated, rainfed, etc.

Yields are given crop-wise per unit of area and production per crop is given for various geographical units. The production figures refer to field crops, livestock, fishery, poultry, etc. In forestry they refer to various forest products, e.g. timbers, grasses, resins.

Irrigation statistics give information on area irrigated—gross and crop-wise, source of irrigation, method of irrigation, number of wells and tanks, those fallen in disuse, etc. With emphasis on agricultural planning, statistics on farm labour, wages, size of farms, tenure relationship, farm inputs, e.g. fertilizer, insecticides and equipment, contribution to national income, etc., are gaining importance. So are the forecasts relating to weather, production and prices. Outlook studies on prices are not advanced yet.

Scope Agricultural statistics have a wide coverage and their scope is ever widening. Detailed statistics are needed for agricultural policy decisions, planning agricultural development and for estimates of national income. The chapters that follow deal with different aspects of the subject in detail.

DEVELOPMENTS IN INDIA

Agricultural statistics in India has a long tradition. The tasks they were assigned to perform varied from time to time. The development of agricultural statistics in India can be described with reference to different periods as follows:

1. Statistical set-up in ancient India.
2. Statistical organization during 19th century.
3. Statistical organization up to World War I (1901-18).
4. Growth of statistical organization during inter-war period (1919-39).
5. War-period development (1939-45).
6. Post-war period (1946 onwards).
7. Present-day organization of
    (i) the Central Government and (ii) State Governments.

Ancient India

In ancient India, mention may be made of the *Ramayana* period during which statistics of employment, unemployment and taxes were collected during the reign of king Bharat. Kautilya's *Arthashastra* makes mention of the statistical agency maintained by the State. It contains details of the economic condition of the Indian people during this period (cf. 325 B.C.). Statistics of land area, agricultural production, population and taxes were collected through an organized State machinery during the reigns of Mauryan kings, Gupta dynasty and the Kushans.

Statistics of prices of agricultural and other products are available in detail in Administration Reports of Alauddin Khilji (14th century A.D.). Statistics relating to the cost of constructing roads, bridges, tanks, hospitals, schools and other buildings of public welfare are available in the State Papers of Sher Shah. His State Papers also contain statistical information regarding cost of building materials like lime and mortar, wages to labourers and architects, details of crimes in the country and punishments awarded by the State.

Statistics of acreage and yield are also available in historical records of the Moghul period. Among the prominent records of this period, mention may be made of *Tuzk-a-Babri* and *Ain-i-Akbari*. The latter contains elaborate statistical information about land, production, population, famines and other economic details during A.D. 1556-1605. This monumental work of Akbar's time also contains details of army personnel, arms and ammunitions used, coins manufactured, state properties and policies on the fixation and collection of land revenue which were based on agricultural production. Acreage details of land along with the method of its measurement are also given in it.

After the downfall of the Moghul Empire, the East India Company maintained full accounts of exports and imports. With the extension of the Company's suzerainty over the country, statistical data began to be collected in greater detail.

Later, during the 18th century, when the ryotwari system was introduced in some parts of India, land revenue officers were appointed by the Company to collect figures of land revenue, cost of cultivation and price of agricultural produce. Land revenue under this system was based on agricultural production and fertility of the soil. However, during this period of the statistics of acreage and production of crops were not collected for the entire country. At places where the Government introduced the system of permanent land settlement, the collection of revenue was entrusted to agents known as revenue farmers. The Company was, therefore, interested in acreage and production statistics of these areas. During this period no separate statistical organization existed, even though statistical information had accumulated through the administrative activities of the Company.

The Nineteenth Century

It was during the latter half of the Nineteenth century that need was felt for proper collection of statistics, especially in the field of agriculture, due to the occurrence of famines. The famine of 1860 was a very severe one and the government had to take steps to save the population from starvation and death. Up to this time no census of population for the country as a whole had been attempted. The decennial census was introduced in 1872, but its coverage was limited and did not include the whole of India. The first decennial census in its proper form was conducted in 1881. Even at this stage, the census organization was ad hoc and after the census was over, the entire organization was liquidated immediately. This practice continued up to the census of 1941. The census organization was made permanent as late as 1949 during the post-independence period. The appointment of the Registrar General was, however, made for the period of the census only.

The first Indian Famine Commission, 1880, recommended the appointment of a Director of Agriculture and a few statistical officers in each province to assist him in the collection of statistics and maintenance of detailed records of acreage and production. The recommendations of this Commission were accepted by the Government of India and the Central Department of Agriculture was established in 1871. Later, Departments of Agriculture were also established in various provinces to assist the Central Department.

Prior to 1860, the statistics which were collected as a need to assist the administration suffered much in quality and lacked comprehensiveness. The first significant development to overcome this shortcoming was the setting up of a Statistical Committee in 1862 for the preparation of model statistical forms for the compilation of a uniform system of Imperial Statistics. The forms of statistics recommended by the Committee related to the collection of data on industry, trade, finance, education, judiciary, population, agriculture, livestock and mining, and the local administrators were asked to adapt statistics already possessed by them or available to them to these uniform forms. This led to the publication in 1868 of the *Statistical Abstract of British India*, based on the returns of the local administrations, and containing useful statistical information for all the British provinces. It was started mainly for the benefit of industrialists and traders in London and continued to be published from England as an annual feature till 1923 when its publication was transferred to India.

In 1874, Sir John Strachey, the then Governor of North West Province (now Uttar Pradesh) wrote to the Government suggesting the creation of a department for collecting statistical information regarding trade and agriculture. He also suggested the appointment of a Director of Agriculture and Commerce. Accordingly, in 1875 a Department of Agriculture and Commerce come into existence. Its functions were to collect trade statistics, improve the quality of agricultural statistics and improve the system of agriculture. This was then the first government department, having something to do with the collection of basic data, although this was not its only function. Statistics of agricultural wages began to be collected in 1873 on half yearly basis and were published in the *Provincial Gazettes*. They were also published on annual basis in the *Prices and Wages*.

The preparation of the Gazetteers of India, containing a mass of useful economic statistics relating to each province, which started in 1866 with a study relating to the Madras Presidency, marked another important stage in the development of statistics. An ad hoc Director General of Statistics was appointed under the Department of Agriculture, Revenue and Commerce, for organizing this work on uniform lines. *The Imperial Gazetteer of India* was published for the first time in 1881. This official publication contained detailed statistical records relating to economic conditions of different parts of the country.

In 1883, a statistical conference was held at Calcutta. The conference recommended the setting up of an institution of all-India crop forecasts, and conducting the quinquennial livestock census. Both these recommendations were accepted by the Central Government which directed the Provincial Governments to cooperate in the matter. Accordingly, the first crop forecast of wheat production was started in 1884 and many other crops were added to the list later on. By 1900, the crops included in the forecasts besides wheat, were rice, oilseeds, cotton, jute and sugarcane. The Revenue and Agriculture Department of the Government of India published for the first time in 1886 *Agricultural Statistics of British India*. It continued to appear annually. The first livestock census was conducted in 1887-88.

The Finance and Commerce Department of the Government of India compiled and published figures of foreign trade, exports and imports till the end of the 19th century. In 1895 the Government established a Statistical Bureau at the Centre to deal with agricultural and foreign trade statistics of the country. This Bureau functioned till 1922 under the guidance and supervision of the Director General of Statistics.

Notwithstanding these sporadic efforts, the fact remains that during the 19th century no serious efforts were made by the Government of India to collect economic statistics.

Pre-World War I Period (1901-1918)

The beginning of the twentieth century witnessed far reaching improvements in the statistical set-up of the country. The establishment of the Department of Commercial Intelligence and Statistics at Calcutta in 1905 proved beyond doubt the seriousness of the Government in the collection of statistical data, The main purpose of this new department was to maintain a link between the Government of India and the business community. It was also entrusted with the task of compiling business and trade statistics of the country for public use. The Statistical Bureau under the guidance of the Department of Commercial Intelligence and Statistics, Calcutta, published for the first time the *Indian Trade Journal* in 1906. This monthly publication still continues and provides valuable statistical information pertaining to trade and business.

The main functions of the Department of Commercial Intelligence and Statistics were:

   (i) to collect commercial statistics to help trade and business;

  (ii) to provide a link between Indian and foreign businessmen;

 (iii) to compile and publish statistical information in journals and ad hoc bulletins; and

 (iv) to compile and publish statistical data previously published by the Government of India on subjects of commercial, judicial, administrative and agricultural importance.

Immediately after 1912, the year when the headquarters of the Indian Government were shifted from Calcutta to Delhi, it was decided to separate the Statistics section from the Commercial Intelligence, but the separation was temporary. In 1922, the Statistics section was again amalgamated with the Department of Commercial Intelligence. This new Department was named as the Office of the Director General of Commercial Intelligence and Statistics and was located at Calcutta.

The following journals were published by this office.

Annual

1. Review of Trade in India.
2. Statement of the Foreign Sea-borne Trade and Navigation of British India.
3. Statistical Abstract for British India.
4. Estimate of Area and Yield of Principal Crops in India.
5. Agricultural Statistics of British India.

Quinquennial

1. Index Number of Indian Prices.

Quarterly

1. Wholesale Prices of Certain Staple Articles of Trade at Selected Stations in India.

Monthly

1. Monthly Statistics of the Production of Certain Selected Industries of India.
2. Monthly-Statistics of Cotton Spinning and Weaving in Indian Mills.
3. Monthly Survey of Business Conditions in India.
4. Monthly Accounts Relating to the Sea-borne Trade and Navigation of British India.
5. Accounts Relating to the Coastal Trade and Navigation of British India.
6. Kathiawar and Travancore Trade Statistics.
7. Indian Customs Revenue Statement.
8. Trade at Stations Adjacent to Land Frontier Routes.
9. Raw Cotton Trade Statistics.
10. Monthly Accounts Relating to the Inland (Rail and River-borne) Trade of India.

Inter-War Period (1919-1939)

Even after this progress in the collection of statistics, the Government of India found them inadequate during World War I. It was considerably handicapped in the successful execution of the war efforts on account of paucity of data regarding the production of various raw materials in the country. However, the Government was unable to improve the statistical organization during the war.

The Government of India, with a view to developing industries and improving the statistical organization of the country, announced the appointment of the Industrial Commission in 1916. The Commission made thorough observations regarding the responsibility of the Government for collection, compilation, careful analysis and judicious distribution of commercial and industrial statistics and intelligence, both in peace and war. The Commission also recommended the appointment of a Director of Commercial Intelligence to deal with:

(i) statistics of foreign trade;
(ii) production and industrial statistics; and
(iii) statistics of trade of India and foreign countries, tariff, and industrial policy.

The recommendations of the Commission in this respect were, however, not accepted by the Government.

Immediately after the winding up of the Industrial Commission, the Indian Economic Enquiry Committee was appointed in 1924 under the chairmanship of the late Sir M. Visvesvaraya. The report of the Committee to enquire into "the question of adequacy of the statistical data available and the desirability and possibility of supplementing it, and of undertaking an economic enquiry was out after a year." The Committee concluded that if statistics in India were to be maintained on a satisfactory basis, all work relating to it should be coordinated and centralized as in the Dominions; in other worlds, the statistics of all departments, both of the Central and Provincial Governments, should come under the supervision of one central authority who would act as the adviser to the Government in all statistical matters. The Committee supported the placing of the entire statistical organization on a statutory basis by enacting a Census and Statistics Act. The Committee identified fields where statistics collected were either incomplete or were totally wanting. Among the valuable findings of the Committee were that (i) statistics of finance, population, trade, transport, communications, migration and vital statistics were 'more or less complete', (ii) production statistics, i.e. statistics of agriculture, pasture and dairy farming, forests, fisheries, minerals, large-scale industries, and cottage industries were complete in some respects but incomplete and wanting, in many others, and (iii) statistics relating to income, wealth, cost of living index, indebtedness, wages and prices were entirely unsatisfactory and the Government had not made any genuine efforts to improve the position in this respect.

The Committee made a number of recommendations for the improvement of statistics, mainly industrial statistics by conducting quinquennial wage censuses in large industries and collecting statistics of output of raw materials consumed in cottage industries. In brief, the main recommendations of the Committee regarding the improvement of statistical organization of the country were for the establishment of the Central Statistical Bureau and Provincial Statistical Bureau in each province to assist the central statistical authority. The recommendations of the Committee were implemented only partially.

Immediately after the conclusion of he Indian Economic Enquiry Committee, the Report of the Royal Commission on Agriculture (India) was out in 1928. One of the responsibilities of the Imperial Council of Agricultural Research proposed by it was to compile and distribute statistical information concerning agriculture and animal husbandry. The Council was also to take over the publication work from the Central Agriculture Department. A Statistical Research Bureau was set up at Delhi in 1933 to analyse and interpret economic statistics. One of the most important events in the development of statistics in India was the appointment of the Bowley-Robertson Committee in 1934 by the Government of India. The Committee was called upon to:

(i) facilitate the further study of economic problems of India;
(ii) give views on existing statistical information and organization with special reference to the gaps;
(iii) suggest means for filling them;
(iv) recommend about the organization of a Central Statistical Department to collect and coordinate statistical enquiry for the whole of India;
(v) discuss the practicability and scope of a census of production;
(vi) give a critical review of the material available for measuring national income; and
(vii) give recommendations on the construction of index numbers of prices, wages and production.

The recommendations of the Bowley-Robertson Committee are a landmark in the development of Indian statistics, rural and urban surveys, census of production and Government publications, their most important recommendations were those pertaining to the measurement of national income. A brief summary of some of their recommendations relevant to agriculture is given below.

Organization of Statistics In matters pertaining to organization of statistics, the Committee felt the need for a coordinating agency. It recommended the appointment of a statistician for each province to coordinate provincial statistics and to conduct supplementary population census in the middle of the decennium, mainly devoted to information regarding members of the family, their age, sex and occupation.

Rural and Urban Surveys The Committee recommended the adoption of a random sample method for rural surveys. For cities, complete census was recommended.

Government Publications. Regarding government publications, the Committee recommended the publication in India of a book on the lines of *Guide to Official Statistics* published in Britain. It would enable any person to know the names of government and other publications giving statistics pertaining to any field and also giving information regarding the nature and quality of such statistics.

Regarding the current government publications, the Committee observed that these were usually released after a very long interval and were of little use to the public. Instead, it would be better if early publication of popular and easily available publications were encouraged.

National Income. Recommendations regarding statistics of national income are discussed in a separate chapter. All the recommendations of the Committee were not accepted by the Government, but some of those which were accepted were immediately implemented. It was the result of the recommendations of the Committee that the office of the Economic Adviser to the Government of India was created in 1938 to collect and analyse economic statistics. The Statistical Research Bureau was merged with this office. Soon after the establishment of this office, World War II broke out.

War Period Development (1939-1945)

During World War II, the Government of India again found itself face to face with the same difficult plight as it did during World War I, i.e. the lack of a well-developed statistical organization to cope with the various problems of war emergency such as control over prices, rationing of food supplies, allocation of funds and goods for defence purposes, imports of food, etc. As a result of this emergency, small statistical organizations were hurriedly established in various departments of the Government of India and also in State Governments to collect the required statistics. It was in 1944 that the Economics and Statistics Section was created in the Central Department of Agriculture. As an aid to the collection of industrial statistics, the Industrial Statistics Act was passed in 1942. Later the Directorate of Industrial Statistics was established in 1945. This Directorate conducted the first Census of Manufactures in 1946.

In the same year, an inter-departmental committee with the Economic Adviser to the Government of India as its Chairman was set up. It considered the statistical material available and made recommendations for filling up gaps and for improvement in the existing organization. Among the organizational recommendations was a scheme for the decentralization of primary responsibility for departmental statistics coupled which the formation of a Central Statistical Office for coordination, institution of a statistical cadre, establishment of statistical bureaus at the headquarters of State Governments and the preparation of overall statistics for the entire country.

Thus, during the British period statistical development was limited, depending mainly on the requirements for administration of the country.

A proper statistical organization in the country was not built up, although many committees gave thoughtful consideration to this problem and made valuable recommendations.

Post-War Period

After the war, significant developments took place in the field of collection and analysis of statistics in India. One of the main reasons for this had been the urge for the rapid economic development of the country after independence and the realization by the Government that economic planning cannot take place without adequate knowledge of the existing resources.

Immediately after Independence in 1947, the Economic Adviser's office started the publication of 'General Purpose Wholesale Price Index Numbers'. This substituted the Economic Adviser's sensitive Wholesale Price Index Number of 29 articles. The Labour Bureau also started constructing the Cost of Living Index Numbers for certain rural and urban areas with the base year 1939 and Retail Price Index Numbers at certain rural centres with 1944 as the base year. All these index numbers have later been revised and the base year shifted to more recent years.

In 1948, the Directorate of Economics and Statistics was set up under the Ministry of Food and Agriculture. It took over from the Directorate General of Commercial Intelligence the collection of statistics relating to land utilization, crop production, plantations, agricultural prices, agricultural wages, forests, food distribution, and the Grow Food campaign.

In 1949, the Reserve Bank of India started a new publication called *Annual Report on Trend and Progress of Banking in India*. This annual publication gives detailed statistics pertaining to all kinds of banking institutions operating in India. Later, the Reserve Bank of India published an ad hoc volume *Monetary and Banking Statistics of India*. This comprehensive volume provides at one place all monetary, banking and insurance statistics of India from 1900 to 1952.

In the same year, 1949, the Government of India appointed for the first time the National Income Committee to prepare an estimate regarding the national income of India and to suggest a technique for its measurements every year on a regular basis. The Committee prepared estimate of India's national income for a number of years and also pointed out difficulties in its measurement by the social accounting method. Since 1854 a National Income Unit has been permanently attached to the Central Statistical Organization of India for the purpose.

Again in 1949, a statistical unit was established at the Centre to coordinate all statistical activities in the country. In 1951 this unit developed into a full-fledged Central Statistical Organization (CSO) of the Government of India. In the same year, the Census Act was made permanent and the offices of the Census Commissioner and Registrar General of India were set up at New Delhi. Simultaneously statistical bureaus were also set up in the states.

The Directorate of National Sample Surveys was set up in 1950 under the Ministry of Finance, Government of India, with a view to compiling and collecting statistics on economic and social aspects of life in the country.

In 1951, an International Statistical Conference was held at Calcutta to discuss the common statistical problems of different nations and to suggest improvements with a view to bringing uniformity in the concepts and terms used in collection and compilation of statistical data.

The Collection of Statistics Act, passed in 1953, empowered the State Governments as well as the Central Government to collect all economic and commercial statistics in the country. The All India Rural Credit Survey was conducted in 1951-52 to collect statistics of rural indebtedness and other problems of rural finance. As a result of the recommendations of the Survey, the Imperial Bank of India was nationalized on July 1, 1955. All India Agricultural Labour Enquiries were conducted in 1950-51 and 1956-57.

WORLD AGRICULTURAL CENSUS

The decennial World Census of Agriculture sponsored by the Food and Agriculture Organization of the United Nations consists of a series of National Agricultural Censuses taken all over the world in or around the same year within a world framework. The first step towards a World Census of Agriculture was initiated in 1924 by the International Institute of Agriculture, Rome which persuaded member-countries to carry out a general agricultural census on a comparable uniform pattern evolved by the Institute. The object was to obtain from these various countries internationally comparable information on the structure of agriculture through holding-wise enumeration of crop areas and livestock in one operation. Sixty-three countries and territories participated in the first census in 1930 and of these, only forty-six took it by holdings, the rest indicated aggregates at various levels of geographical areas. The intention of the Institute was to repeat the census at an interval of ten years. However, due to World War II, the 1940 Census either could not be undertaken or, if undertaken, could not be completed.

The next World Census of Agriculture was carried out in 1950 under the guidance of the Food and Agriculture Organization of the United Nations which had replaced the International Institute of Agriculture in 1945 and had taken over its responsibilities. One hundred and six countries and territories participated in this census. The Third World Census of Agriculture was carried out in 1960. It was more comprehensive and its coverage wider than the 1950 Census. The Fourth World Agricultural Census was again due around 1970 and the FAO had suggested that depending upon the preparedness of the member countries, the reference for the census could be fixed by the individual countries. This reference year was to be as close to the year 1970 as possible.

AGRICULTURAL CENSUS IN INDIA

1950-1960 Census

In India, both in the 1950 and 1960 censuses, data required by the World Agricultural Census was collected through sample surveys carried out by the National Sample Survey Organization during the 8th, 16th and 17th rounds respectively; and these gave estimates for the country as a whole and for a group of States. Such estimates were of limited value for micro-level planning, say, for a district or lower regional levels.

The schedules adopted for the 1961 survey (16th round of NSS) collected information on the following items:

   (i) holder, holding and tenure particulars giving details of area owned, area leased in and leased out, terms of leasing in and leasing out, etc.;

  (ii) land utilization particulars;

 (iii) area under crops;

 (iv) demographic particulars of the members of the sample households;

  (v) irrigation and drainage facilities on the farm;

 (vi) use of fertilizers and soil dressings; and

(vii) number of livestock and poultry and agricultural implements and machinery.

The survey was repeated during the 17th round (September 1961 to July 1962) of the National Sample Survey and the coverage was extended to urban areas also. Estimates for the various characteristics under study for the States and the country as a whole have been given in the 17th round report on land holdings[*]

Agricultural planning in India has hitherto been on an overall programme basis and that too for relatively larger administrative units, due mainly to lack of sufficiently comprehensive data. As more emphasis is now being laid on district and block level planning envisaging detailed programmes and targets for districts and blocks, elaborate data at the level of these administrative and planning units are necessary for realistic planning and successful implementation of development programmes and realization of targets.

1970 Census

With a view to examining the scope and methodology of 1950 Census of Agriculture in India, a Technical Committee on Coordination of Agricultural Statistics was set up in the Ministry of Food & Agriculture in 1949. In view of the imperative need for detailed data on the structure of agricultural holdings for planning purposes and for the purpose of placing agricultural statistics on sound footing, this Committee recom-

---

[*]NSS Report No. 162. Tables with notes on some results of Land Holdings in Rural India—17th Round (September 1961 to July 1962).

mended that the census should be undertaken on a complete enumeration basis. Due to various reasons, in 1950 and 1960 the required data were collected through sample surveys by the National Sample Survey Organization and not by the method of complete enumeration. This gave estimates at the all-India level and for States, which were not always reliable.

In the context of the new strategy for agricultural development which the Government of India launched in 1966-67, reliable information regarding structure and characteristics of agricultural holdings became imperative for effective and efficient planning and its implementation. For the above purpose, data about operational holdings as distinct from ownership holdings were needed. An operational holding is defined as all land which is used wholly or partly for agricultural production and is operated as one technical unit by one person alone or with others without regard to title, legal form, site or location. Since an operational holding is a fundamental unit of decision-making in agriculture and consequently for development of programmes aimed at improving the lot of individual cultivators, a census of operational holdings providing data on their number, tenure relationships, size, type of farming and farming practices, assumed special importance.

To meet the data requirements for planning at the lower levels, 1970 Agricultural Census was conducted on a complete enumeration basis by retabulation of basic land records. In the States of Kerala, Orissa and West Bengal where such records did not exist, data were collected by Sample Surveys. NSS also collected information on fertilizers, pesticides, area under high yielding varieties, livestock, agricultural machinery and employment, etc., in their 26th Round as a part of the Census of Holdings.

The field work for complete enumeration which was completed in December, 1971 required the services of over one lakh village accountants who were involved in collecting the required data. The data provided valuable information about the type of farmers who had adopted the high yielding varieties programme, type and size of land involved, multiple cropping programmes and production, distribution, marketing and credit required in respect of fertilizers. Information regarding the size and characteristics of holdings on which chemical fertilizers are being used has also become available. The data collected is helpful in the formulation of policies in respect of special area programmes, agricultural machinery and implements, strengthening and streamlining of extension services and effective planning in respect of schemes like the Small Farmers Development Agency and the Marginal Farmers and Agricultural Labourers as well as tribal projects. The information would also be useful for compiling national income statistics and making further refinements in it.

INDIAN STATISTICAL SERVICE

Realizing the role which statistics will have to play in a developing economy, the Government of India constituted a cadre of professional statisticians known as the Indian Statistical Service (ISS) in November 1961 by pooling together posts in Statistical discipline existing in various Ministries which were offered for inclusion in the ISS. For entrants at various levels 'In-Service Training Programmes' were drawn up by an ad hoc committee of expert statisticians and approved by the Government of India for implementation.

INDIAN STATISTICAL SYSTEM AND THE CONSTITUTION

India being a federation of States, there is a dichotomy of responsibility for government between the Union or Central Government on the one hand, and the State Governments on the other. Under the Indian Constitution, the responsibility is divided on the basis of a three-fold classification of all subjects, viz., Union List, State List and Concurrent List, the last category representing the areas where both the Union and State Governments could operate. At the Central as also the State levels, there is a further division of responsibility, subject-wise or group-wise, among the different ministries and departments. The authority and responsibility for collection of statistics relating to particular subject-fields is determined by the overall responsibility for the subject under the Constitution. However, appropriate to the federal set-up, the Central Government acts as the coordinating agency for presentation of statistics on an all-India basis, even in fields where the States have the primary authority and responsibility for collection of statistics. The Department of Statistics (of which the Central Statistical Organization is the technical wing), located in the Cabinet Secretariat, is charged with the important function of coordinating all statistics at the State and Central levels. The State statistical bureaus, attached to different departments in different State Governments, are charged with the responsibility of coordination of all statistics at the State level and keeping liaison with the Central Statistical Organization for the purpose of coordination at the all-India level.

At the Centre most ministries have either a full-fledged statistical department, or a division or a section depending upon their needs and upon the stage of development of statistics in the relevant field. At the State level the collection and compilation of statistics relating to the particular field have been assigned to different units, big or small, of various government departments as shown in Table 1.1.

INTERNATIONAL COLLABORATION

The department of statistics and programme implementation have recently signed an MoU with the Australian Bureau of Statistics for the development of an extensive and integrated communications network for the Indian statistical system. Both the governments have agreed to exchange professional knowledge and experiences in a wide range of national statistical activities and programmes. The important areas, wherein collaborative endeavours would be undertaken include price statistics, especially the development of a cohesive statistical framework for inflation related studies. As for agricultural statistics, experiences regarding the methodology of collection of various types of farm statistics would be shared. In industrial statistics, experiences on aspects relating to collection, processing and estimation of industrial parameters and timely indices of industrial production will be shared.

Table 1.1 Compilation of Statistics at the State Level

Area	Department
1. Agricultural Department/ Economic and Statistics Department/Planning, Health and Social Welfare/General Administration Department/ Finance/Land Record/Revenue Departments.	State Statistical Bureau.
2. Department of Agriculture	Statistics Unit, Directorate of Agriculture.
3. Department of Cooperation	Office of the Registrar, Co-operative Societies.
4. Labour Department	(a) Office of the Labour Commissioner. (b) Office of the Chief Inspector of Factories. (c) Directorate of Employment Services.
5. Industries Department	Directorate of Industries.
6. Finance Department	Office of the Commissioner of Excise.

THE PLAN REQUIREMENTS

The new responsibilities for wider social and economic functions of the Government have led to a further demand for and impetus to the development of comprehensive statistics. More important was the emphasis, from the point of view of overall economic policy, on a single synoptic picture of the information field, and consequently on proper coordination and control. The need for new types of statistics for judging the progress of the Plan schemes. Overall assessment of the Plans and evaluation surveys was, therefore, felt and suitable orientation of the existing statistical system both at the Centre and States was attempted. An additional stimulus was provided by the growing statistical requirements of international organizations, such as the United Nations and its specialized agencies, and their attempts to promote suitable standards of international comparability with a view to developing an integrated statistical system.

During the last two decades, considerable progress has been made in securing increasingly reliable, comparable and comprehensive agricultural statistics to meet the growing needs of formulation and execution of agricultural development plans and their periodic assessment and evaluation. Improvements brought out in the sphere of the agricultural statistics since independence have been many and far reaching, the principal one being the extension of the coverage of land utilization statistics from 69% of the total area of the country before the First Plan to about more than 94% currently. The coverage of crop forecast has also increased considerably, the number of crops covered currently being 37 compared to only 10 before the First Plan. Objective procedure for crop estimation has been introduced gradually covering more areas and more crops with a view to having reliable estimates of crops production. At present, 95% of the production of cereals and 73% of the production of pulses are based on crop estimation surveys. In respect of commercial crops these percentages are high, being 94 for groundnut, 75 for cotton, 99 for jute and 94 for sugarcane. Considerable progress has also been achieved in introducing uniform and agreed concepts and definitions of land utilization, crop areas and other related topics. Steps had also been taken to evolve a systematic procedure for the collection and compilation of farm harvest, wholesale and retail prices as also market arrivals of agricultural commodities.

With the formulation of each Plan, the economy has become more complex calling for detailed and comprehensive data relating to the agricultural sector. Some of the deficiencies of the existing system of agricultural statistics relate to the lack of provision for central supervision over area enumeration done by the State Governments, inadequate quantum of central supervision over field work of crop estimation surveys, considerable time lag in the availability of firm estimates of area and production of principal crops, non-availability of objective estimates of area and production of fruits, vegetables and minor crops and lack of comprehensive data of cost of production of principal crops required for regulating prices of agricultural commodities.

During the Fifth Plan a number of efforts were initiated for bridging some of the above gaps. Schemes for timely reporting of estimates of area and production of principal crops, improvement of crop statistics, establishment of an agency for reporting agricultural statistics by complete enumeration in Kerala, Orissa and West Bengal were undertaken.

In relation to certain items of work such as collection of data on area and production of fruits and vegetables and minor crops, improvement in irrigation statistics and improving the scope and coverage of market intelligence, preliminary efforts have been made, although concrete work in respect of these items has still to be undertaken. Inconsistencies in figures collected by various sources in respect of production and utilization of commodities like cotton, tobacco, jute, tea, coffee, rubber, etc. need reconciliation. Substantial improvements are called for in the collection of data on area, production, yield, wholesale and retail prices, market arrivals, etc. in respect of North-Eastern region and remote areas such as different parts of Jammu & Kashmir, Himachal Pradesh, Hill areas of Uttar Pradesh and Sikkim. Since the terms of reference of the Agricultural

Prices Commission have been considerably widened by the Government and there is ever growing interest on the problems concerning cost of production, indices of input costs, etc. and farm economy as a whole, the schemes relating to these subjects would have to be considerably strengthened. With increasing outlays being provided by the Government for agriculture and allied sectors, problem-oriented and policy-oriented research studies command great relevance. More varied and more indepth agro-economic studies and research are called for. The programmes included in the Sixth and subsequent Five Year Plans are directed primarily towards filling the lacunae mentioned above and to meet other needs connected with development of India's agricultural economy.

INFORMATION TECHNOLOGY

In pursuance of the Government's decision to give a boost to Information Technology, Department of Agriculture and Cooperation has formulated Information Technology Vision (IT) 2020 and a programme for the Ninth Five Year Plan. The main features are:

- All information relating to agriculture sector would be available to the ultimate users, the farmers for optimizing their productivity and income.
- The extension and advisory services making use of Information Technology would be available to the farmers on a round the clock basis.
- The tools of Information Technology will provide networking of agriculture sector not only in the country but also globally and the Centre and State Government Departments will have reservoirs of database for data mining and warehousing.
- The long term Vision on "Information Technology in Agriculture Sector" is to bring farmers, researchers, scientists, and administrators together by establishing "Agriculture-online" through exchange of ideas/information.

Information Technology Scheme for Ninth Five Year Plan Period

Ninth Plan outlay Rs. 180,00,00 (Rs. in thousands) for Information Technology Schemes to strengthen/promote the use of Informatics in Agriculture. The Schemes include:

Operationalising e-governance

In the year 1999-2000, Local Area Network (LAN) had been established in the Headquarters of the Department and all officers of the rank of Section Officers and above had been provided with Personal Computers and Internet connections. Website of this Department has been launched on 13th April 1999 and can be visited on the following address: <http://www.nic.in/agricoop>. Officers are now using e-mail in their day-to-day working and the Department of Agriculture and Cooperation has also been given the following centralized e-mail address: agrindia@krishi.delhi.nic.in <mailto:agrindia@krishi.delhi.nic.in>. Separate ICONs on the website has been provided for all e-mail addresses of the Department of Agriculture and Cooperation including Public Sector Undertakings, Autonomous bodies and field units. This will facilitate use of e-mail extensively. Training in computers for the officers and staff of the Department is being provided on all working days on programmes including office procedure automation. The effort is to move towards paperless office and e-governance.

Information Technology Scheme for States and Union Territories

A new Central Sector Scheme proposed for networking of States/Union Territories is to be implemented during the Ninth Plan. it is envisaged to establish AGRISNET as an overlay network on NICNET in a cost effective manner, covering 23 Functional Divisions of the Department of Agriculture and Cooperation, 4 Attached Offices, 25 Subordinate Offices, 2 Public Sector Undertakings, 5 Autonomous Organizations, all the State/ Union Territories Agriculture Departments and about 500 District Agriculture Offices. The objective of this scheme is to make 'Agriculture on line' in India.

Scheme for Field Units of Department of Agriculture and Cooperation

A Central Sector Scheme for strengthening of Informatics in the field offices/units of the Department of Agriculture and Cooperation has been approved. The scheme will be implemented by NIC through NICNET and the main field offices will be linked with Department of Agriculture and Cooperation Headquarters through VSAT communications. The rest of the field units will have dial-up connections. The VSAT technology has been selected keeping in view the future requirements, quantum of traffic and ultimate reach to the village level. Once the offices become computerized and functional, their software needs will be assessed by them keeping in view their specific requirements. Further, the common software requirements will be met from the Department of Agriculture and Cooperation headquarters scheme.

2

Statistical Organizations of Central and State Governments

INTRODUCTION

In India, collection of statistical data which were of use to the sovereign was practised even in ancient times. More recently, the Mughals had a system of collection and compilation of crop statistics to help them in land revenue collection. With the progress of British rule these systems died out; the British, in course of time, created their own data-generating systems to serve their specific ends. These system of data collection did not develop into an integrated or well-coordinated statistical system during colonial rule and their coverage was largely limited to a few specific fields like trade and commerce, production of selected industries, population, some basic crop statistics and livestock. At the time of independence, India inherited a statistical system in the shape of independent statistical units attached to different ministries and offices, each using its own concepts and definitions and procedures, relying by and large on common sense and intuition for interpretation of collected data. Data were obtained primarily as a by-product of administration and in a few cases through periodical complete enumeration. There was little or no assessment of the reliability of data, and little or no attempt to make logical use—as distinct from intuitive use—of statistics in decision making.

The demarcation of functions between the Centre and the States in the Constitution of India provides for a broadly decentralized statistical system for the country, the demarcation being done partly on the functional basis and partly on the regional basis. For example, statistics of items like foreign trade, banking and currency and census are wholly allocated to the Centre. On the other hand, subjects like agriculture and education are assigned to the States. There is also a common category of what is known as concurrent subjects, for example, industry, where both the Centre and the States can operate simultaneously to meet their respective requirements. Nevertheless, items 45 in the concurrent list of subjects in the Constitution provides that enquiries and statistics relating to State subjects as well as concurrent subjects shall be a concurrent responsibility; although census is a Central subject, item 30 of the concurrent list provides in particular that vital statistics is a concurrent subject with which both the Centre and the States are concerned. The Indian Constitution, therefore, recognizes that the functions of planning and policy making cannot be confined to water-tight compartments on a subject-wise or regional basis and that the statistics relating to State subjects in the State may be of vital importance and concern to the Government of India and the country as a whole. This may be due to reasons connected with the nature and importance of the subject itself or because of the need for a certain amount of uniformity in the quality and the pattern of statistics relating to the parts, to enable them to be compared or to be aggregated into all-India statistics.

The Central Government thus has an equal jurisdiction over the items in the concurrent list which includes vital statistics, economic and social planning, trade unions, social insurance, labour welfare, relief and rehabilitation, price control, etc. The Central Government can also frame laws and issue directives regarding the state list to State Governments for bringing uniformity in statistics collected by them. In fact, the Central Government works as a coordinating agency for the statistics, collected by the various State Governments and publishes the statistical information on an all-India basis. To carry on their coordination activity, the Central Government established the Central Statistical Organization in 1951 which has a Standing Committee to advise the State Governments in matters pertaining to collection, analysis and interpretation of various statistics.

Independence in 1947 ushered in an era of economic planning and emphasised the necessity of a strong database covering a variety of social and economic topics. The system of data collection left behind by the colonial rulers was found to be far from adequate to meet this immediate demand. It did not even provide the basic data required for estimation of national income which was so vital for assessing performance and progress of the economy. Data reflecting the condition of the vast majority of the population languishing in a state of chronic hunger were hard to come by. There was no provision for generating employment statistics for the large section of population engaged in agriculture and other unorganised sectors of the economy. The immediate task, therefore, was to set up a statistical system capable of filling the large gaps in the data essential for formulating effective economic plans.

Since independence, there has been tremendous progress in all directions overcoming many difficulties. Under our federal structure, statistics is the concern of the States as well as of the Central government. Allocation of resources from the Central government to the States depends on statistics reflecting socio-economic conditions and performance of the States. It is not unlikely that statistics collected by individual States may be biased in favour of the respective States. It is absolutely essential at the Central level to standardise concepts, definitions, and procedures of collection of statistics so as to get rid of this likely bias.

At the instance of Prime Minister Jawaharlal Nehru, a modest beginning was made in 1949. The National Income Committee was appointed by the Government of India to work out a reliable method of estimating national income. On its recommendation, the Directorate of National Sample Survey was set up in 1950 to collect essential statistics relating to socio-economic characteristics and agricultural production. In the following year (May 1951), the Central Statistical Organisation was formed. In short, the foundations of a modern statistical system were laid in those early years of Independence. Since then, the sustained efforts of academics and official statisticians have seen the collection of statistics in India gradually mature into one of the most comprehensive statistical systems of the developing world.

CENTRAL STATISTICAL ORGANISATION (CSO)

CSO coordinates statistical activities of the different Ministries of the Government of India and the State governments and for promotion of statistical standards. Since its inception, CSO has been coordinating the statistical activities in the country, including laying down and maintenance of statistical norms and standards and providing liaison with Central, State and international statistical agencies. The CSO also shoulders the responsibility of preparation of national accounts, compilation and publication of industrial statistics, conducting economic census and surveys, middle class family income and expenditure surveys, training, compilation of price statistics, human development statistics, environment statistics and dissemination of statistics on various socio-economic aspects of national life.

Today, the Department of Statistics(DoS) of the Government of India is the apex body in the official statistical system of the country. It comprises the Central Statistical Organisation (CSO), the National Sample Survey Organisation (NSSO) and the Computer Centre (CC) of the Department. The Department is also responsible for all policy matters of the Indian Statistical Institute (ISI), an autonomous body of international repute, whose contributions in the development of statistical theory and practice are acclaimed worldwide.

The number of statistical agencies at the Centre was only 102 with an expenditure of about Rs. 4.7 million in 1966. The corresponding number of agencies is now exceeds 360 in all the States/Union Territories. The largest number of statistical units (19) are attached to the Ministry of Agriculture. Major statistical organizations in the various Central ministries are as shown in Table 2.1.

At the Centre, most of the ministries collect or use statistics in some manner or other and have their own statistical units. Some of them located in the administrative departments are engaged in the processing of data which are purely by-products of administration. Examples of such agencies are, Officers of Income-tax Department, Central Board of Revenue, Railways, Posts and Telegraphs and the Directorate General of

Table 2.1 Major Statistical Organizations in the Various Central Ministries

Central ministries	Major statistical organizations
1. Cabinet Secretariat	(a) Central Statistical Organization
	(b) Directorate of National Sample Survey
2. Commerce	(a) Office of the Director General of Commercial Intelligence and Statistics
	(b) Office of the Economic Adviser
	(c) Statistics Division, Office of the Chief Controller of Imports and Exports
	(d) Economic and Statistics Branch, Office of the Textile Commissioner
3. Defence	Army Statistical Organization
4. Finance	(a) Statistics and Intelligence Branch (Central Excise)
	(b) Statistics Branch, Directorate of Inspection (Income-tax)
	(c) Department of Statistics, Reserve Bank of India
5. Food, Agriculture, Community Development and Cooperation	(a) Directorate of Economics and Statistics
	(b) Statistics Section, Department of Animal Husbandry
	(c) Directorate of Marketing and Inspection
	(d) Institute of Agricultural Research Statistics (IARS)
6. Health and Family Planning	Statistical Bureau, Directorate General of Health Services
7. Ministry of Food Processing	Statistical wing
8. Ministry of Rural Development	Monitoring and Evaluation Section.
9. Home	Office of the Registrar General, India
10. Labour and Employment	Labour Bureau
11. Planning Commission	Programme Evaluation Organization
12. Railways	(a) Statistics Directorate, Railway Board
	(b) Statistics Office, Zonal Railways

Supplies and Disposals. There are again some statistical units in organizations set up for control of production and distribution of products in short supply, and these maintain statistics which are of value alike to government organizations and public. Examples of these are Textile Commissioner's Office, Iron and Steel Controller, etc. There are also various organizations established by the Government specifically for the function of collecting and compiling statistical data.

The statistical units in various ministries may be divided into the following four categories according to their functions:

(i) Organizations possessing data collected in the usual course of official administration and execution of laws. In this category are included statistical sectors of the Central Board of Revenue,

Railways, Posts and Telegraphs, Directorate of Supply and Disposal, etc.

(ii) Organizations associated with control agencies entrusted with the production and distribution of commodities. The examples are: statistical sections attached to the Textile Commissioner, Controller of Iron and Steel, Electrical Commissioner to the Government of India and Controller of Imports and Exports in India.

(iii) Organizations specially set up for the purpose of collecting and publishing data. Mostly it is such organizations which collect statistics in India. They include the Census Organization; Department of Commercial Intelligence and Statistics, Directorate of Industrial Statistics; Labour Bureau; Directorate of Economics and Statistics in the Ministry of Agriculture, etc.

(iv) Research organizations such as Statistical Division of the Indian Council of Agricultural Research; the Research Department of Reserve Bank of India, etc.

CENTRAL ORGANIZATIONS

The statistical units attached to a few important Central Ministries and others, are described below. The publications issued by the units attached to the Ministry of Agriculture are given in Appendix B.

Department of Statistics and Central Statistical Organization

For meeting the growing needs of statistical data for the purpose of planning and administration and for ensuring that scientific and standard methods of collection of statistical data are employed by various agencies under the Central and State Governments, a Department of Statistics has been set up in the Cabinet Secretariat. This department is responsible for bringing about the necessary coordination between the various statistical agencies, setting up agreed standards and norms and promoting the collection and compilation of statistics on scientific lines. Before issuing general directions on statistical standards and norms and methods of collection of data, the Department attempts to arrive at agreed conclusions. The Department has an advisory body consisting of statistical experts in the Government of India including experts from the States. The body is called 'Central Technical Advisory Council on Statistics' and consists of: (a) the Director, Central Statistical Organization; (b) one expert to represent each of the State Governments and Union Territories/ Administrations; (c) one expert representing each of the Central ministries/ departments; and (d) expert(s) nominated by the Government from non-governmental organizations dealing with the statistics. The council meets at least once a year. A similar body designated as Standing Advisory Committee on Statistics composed of: (a) The Director, Central Statistical Organization; (b) Five representatives from Central Government; (c) Five representatives from the State Governments also act as Standing

Committee to advise the Department of Statistics. The Central Statistical Organization set up in 1951 works as an attached technical office of the department of statistics for statistical matters.

New National Statistical Commission Constituted

A new National Statistical Commission has been set up by the Government under the Chairmanship of Andhra Pradesh Governor, Dr. C. Rangarajan to go into deficiencies of the present statistical system and recommend measures for revamping it.

The Commission, with a tenure of 12 months is being, assisted by a secretariat, headed by a full-time Secretary in the rank of an Additional Secretary to the Central Government. The Commission, including the chairman, would be working part-time.

According to an official note, the Commission membership includes Mr. V.R. Rao, former director of the Central Statistical Organisation. Mr. S.M. Vidhwans, former Director (Economics and Statistics), Government of Maharashtra, Prof. J. Roy of the Indian Statistical Institute, Dr. Prem Narain of the Indian Agricultural Research Institute, Dr. Rakesh Mohan, Director-General of the National Council for Applied Economic Research, Dr. V.R. Panchmukhi, Director-General of Research and Information Systems for Non-aligned and other Developing Countries, Dr. Y. Venugopal Reddy, Deputy Governor of the Reserve Bank of India, Dr. K. Srinivasan, Executive Director of the Population Foundation of India, Prof. Suresh Tendulkar of the Delhi School of Economics, Dr. A.B.I. Srivastava, Chief Consultant with Educational Consultants India Limited and Mr. Fredie Ardeshir Mehta, noted economist.

The Commission's main task is to examine critically the deficiencies of the present statistical system in terms of timeliness, reliability and adequacy and to recommend corrective measures in a bid to generate timely and reliable statistics for the purpose of policy and planning in Government and other levels of the administration. The Commission has also been asked to recommend permanent and effective coordination mechanism for integrated development of the decentralised statistical system in the country.

The Commission will also review the existing legislation for gathering statistical information and recommend amendments, if necessary, to ensure collection and dissemination of timely, reliable and adequate statistics.

During its tenure, the Commission will review the existing organisations of the Ministry of Statistics and Programme Implementation and other statistical units of the Government and make recommendations on their staffing and training requirement to enable them to cope with the increase and development of statistical services.

The Commission will also examine the need for instituting statistical audit of the range of services provided by the Government and local bodies and make necessary recommendations for improving them.

Ministry of Agriculture

The important Statistical units of this Ministry are:

(i) *Directorate of Economics and Statistics* This Directorate collects all agricultural statistics which were previously collected by: (a) the Department of Intelligence and Statistics, Calcutta, (b) the Agricultural Marketing Adviser to the Government of India, (c) the Department of Food, and (d) the Department of Agriculture. The main function of the Directorate is to advise the Ministry of Agriculture, Government of India on current issues of agro-economic policies arising out of its day-to-day work. While the Secretariat of the Ministry is responsible for taking economic policy decisions on various matters in the sphere of both agriculture and food and implementing these decisions, the work which requires special technical knowledge or detailed examination and analysis from the economic policy angle is done in the Directorate. For this purpose, the Directorate has undertaken to collect, compile, process and maintain agro-economic data and publish standard blue books on them. The nature of data available in the Directorate is indicated below.

Rainfall, land utilization, irrigation, area and production of crops, yield per acre, food statistics (procurement, imports, distribution and stocks on Government account), agricultural prices (wholesale, harvest and retail), market arrivals, forest statistics, livestock statistics, number of agricultural implements, agricultural wages, cotton ginned and pressed, index numbers relating to agricultural economy, cost of cultivation, bank advances against stocks pledged/hypothecated, progress reports regarding foodgrains production schemes, allocation for the agricultural sector under the successive Five Year Plans, etc.

Directorate of Marketing and Inspection The Directorate collects data and issues ad hoc reports on production, transport and marketing of agriculture, livestock and fishery products including rice, wheat, gram, barley, groundnuts, fish, milk and milk products etc. The statistics thus collected are being used by the Government of India in the formulation of their policy regarding the production and distribution of agricultural products, economic controls, and the fixation of tariff values for agricultural commodities.

Indian Agricultural Statistics Research Institute of the Indian Council of Agricultural Research (ICAR) The objective of this Institute is to promote and conduct research and training in *Agricultural Statistics* in the country for improving the planning and evaluation of agricultural research and development. To achieve this objective, the functions of the Institute are:

(a) To conduct research in experimental designs, sampling methods, statistical genetics and computer programming and data processing;

(b) To conduct postgraduate courses for training professional statisticians and in-service training for agricultural scientists;

(c) To provide advisory service to agricultural scientists and agricultural organisations; and

(d) To provide consultancy service for data processing.

The Institute made a modest beginning in 1933 as the 'Statistical Section' of the ICAR and made efforts to apply statistical methods in agricultural and animal husbandry research in India. The activities of this Section entered a new phase towards the end of 1943 when following the Bengal famine, the Government of India directed it to undertake research to develop objective and reliable methods for collecting yield statistics of principal food crops. This led to the development of the crop cutting survey technique for estimation of yield whose efficiency and practicability was subsequently demonstrated in different States. The success which this method attained was such that in the course of few years, this method was extended practically to the entire country and to all principal food crops. The 'Statistical Branch' of the Council was reorganized in 1945 into Agriculture and Animal Husbandry Units and was headed by a Statistical Adviser to the Council. The Council then instituted regular postgraduate training courses for professional statisticians willing to specialize in agricultural statistics and for research workers in the field of agriculture and animal husbandry who were desirous of acquiring knowledge in statistical methods for ultimate use in their research work.

In 1953, according to the decision of the Government of India, the work of large scale sample surveys on food crops was transferred from the ICAR to the National Sample Survey Organization. The activities of this Branch expanded subsequently in several directions and in 1955 it was renamed as 'Statistical Wing' of the ICAR.

Since 1956, suitable sampling methodologies for estimating production of principal livestock products and number were evolved. In recognition of its important role as a Training and Research Institution, the Wing was redesignated by the Government of India as the Institute of Agricultural Research Statistics (IARS) in June, 1959. Since then sampling methods were evolved for estimation of fruits and vegetables production in the country. The Institute also undertook surveys for the assessment of agricultural development programmes like Intensive Agricultural District Programme (IADP), High Yielding Varieties Programme (HYVP), etc. It also developed suitable sampling methodology for estimation of cost of production of principal crops as well as livestock products like milk, wool, egg and poultry.

The Institute was declared as a full-fledged Institute under the administrative control of ICAR with effect from April 1, 1970 and is since then headed by a Director. It is equipped with the two Computer Systems: (i) IBM 1620 Model II; and (ii) a third generation Burroughs B-4700. Since January 1, 1978, the name of the Institute has been changed to Indian Agricultural Statistics Research Institute (IASRI).

Statistical Section of the Forest Research Institute This section performs the following functions:

(a) Preparation of experimental designs and statistical analysis and interpretation of results for all research branches of the Institute;

(b) Advice to State silviculturists on experimental designs and assistance to them on a limited scale in the analysis of data;

(c) Advice to State Forest Departments on sampling techniques for surveys of forest resources;

(d) Conducting statistical training courses for forest officers, deputed from States and students of the Indian Forest College;

(e) Research on designs of experiments; and

(f) Research on sampling techniques.

Central Rice Research Institute, Cuttack The Institute has one statistician, who compiles all data which are presented in ad hoc publications.

Department of Community Development and Cooperation in the Ministry of Agriculture Within the Department, there exists an Administrative Intelligence Unit which is charged with the maintenance of progress of various developmental measures *inter-alia* connected with the increase in agricultural production. The Department in association with the State Statistical Bureaus conducts: (a) sample surveys for estimating the area benefited by improved agricultural practices, and (b) survey of primary agricultural credit cooperative societies. The Department is also taking steps in studies in regard to village and block agricultural production programmes and preparation of block level indices of agricultural production.

The other statistical units are *Statistical Units of the Central Marine Fisheries Research Station*, Mandampam, and *Statistical Unit of Sugar and Vanaspati*.

The Commodity Committees (now Regional Development Offices) have also Economics and Statistics Units, particularly the Cotton and Jute Development Regional Offices.

Ministry of Irrigation and Power

The Central Water and Power Commission in the Ministry has two statistical sections, one dealing with statistical problems relating to waterways, irrigation and navigation, and the other with the collection of comprehensive data relating to electricity undertakings.

SET UP BELOW CENTRAL LEVEL

Collection of agricultural statistics is beset with several difficulties in view of the fact that these relate to small units scattered all over the country and have to be collected within a limited period of time. Farmers being mostly illiterate, enquiry method cannot be relied upon and direct observation and physical measurement have to be resorted to for collecting reliable information. With the gradual increase in the requirements of data for policy, administration and planning, collection of agricultural statistics has become all the more difficult. For proper development of agricultural statistics, sound and comprehensive organization is needed at different levels. Questions regarding the agency for collection of area statistics, strengthening of primary agencies for crop-cutting surveys, institution of central supervision over the work of area enumeration, strengthening of State and Central supervision over the conduct of crop cutting surveys, setting up of statistical units in State Irrigation Departments, organizational set-up, for animal husbandry, forestry and fisheries statistics and strengthening of the wholetime technical reporting agencies for market intelligence have already been discussed in the relevant sections. The organizational set-up for agricultural statistics especially basic statistics of land utilization, area and production, etc. at tehsil, district, State and Central levels is discussed below.

At the primary level, the Patwari has to continue to collect the basic agricultural statistics relating to land utilization, area under crops and irrigation based on complete enumeration of all fields. For a radical improvement in agricultural statistics, it is necessary to have a professionally competent fully trained and unified statistical organization from the level just above the Patwari and/or Kanungo right up to the State and Central levels. In many States, statistical staff at the district level dealing with agricultural statistics exclusively exist. In a few States, Taluk Statistical Assistants dealing mostly with agricultural statistics have been recently appointed. What is needed is that the statistical staff at different levels should be fully qualified and given adequate training and their services should be utilized exclusively for agricultural statistics.

Tehsil Level Staff

Tehsil is an important link in the flow of agricultural statistics. It is, therefore, necessary to ensure that the statistics flowing through that level are properly checked and scrutinized. At present, in most of the States there is no provision for technical staff to look after this type of work at the tehsil level. It is necessary to provide one Statistical Supervisor in each tehsil to supervise field work of different censuses and surveys to the extent of about 10 per cent, to scrutinize the basic returns like crop abstracts, etc., received from Patwaris, Revenue Inspectors, etc. to check village totals in the basic village forms or *Khasra* registers for at least one village per Patwari and to collect other development statistics on selected items. This Supervisor will work under the Tehsildar. To improve the accuracy of tabulation, one hand operated calculating machine should be provided for each tehsil. The firms manufacturing the calculating machines should be induced to set up maintenance centres at convenient locations.

District Level Staff

A statistical unit consisting of a District Agricultural Statistics Officer assisted by one Statistical Supervisor/Assistant and one Junior Clerk Computer should be provided at district level to supervise and coordinate agricultural statistics work at the district level. He will work under the Chief Agricultural Development Officer (CADO) proposed by us at the district level in Chapter 62 on Administration. He will help the district authorities in the compilation scrutiny and analysis of agricultural statistics and submission of returns to the State and Central Organisations. One hand operated calculating machine should be provided to ensure accuracy in the computational work done at the district level.

State Headquarters

The set up for agricultural statistics at the State level differs from State to State. In most of the States, this work is handled by the Bureaus of Economics and Statistics, which deal with statistics in different sectors of the economy. In some States like Uttar Pradesh, Maharashtra, Madhya Pradesh, Punjab, Haryana and Gujarat, the work of agricultural statistics is handled by the Agricultural Statistician under the Director of Agriculture/Land Records. In view of the diversity of the administrative set up in different States, broad guidelines for a uniform pattern for agricultural statistics organization at the State level can be laid down and the final decision has to be left to the administrative convenience of the State Governments. However, it has to be ensured that an adequate organization, irrespective of where it is located, should be built up at the State level to organize collection, compilation, analysis and processing of agricultural statistics according to a minimum programme and making available the final results to all concerned including the Central Government according to an agreed time schedule. The existing organizations at the State level should be suitably strengthened to enable them to effect necessary improvements in the data being collected at present and to organize collection of additional information if required. The Head of the State agricultural statistics organization should be a qualified statistician with adequate experience in any one or more fields of agricultural statistics, viz., crop statistics, animal husbandry statistics, fisheries statistics and agricultural research statistics. If this organization forms part of the Bureau of Economics and Statistics, the officer in over-all charge of agricultural statistics should have the status of Additional Director of Statistics (Agriculture). The Agricultural Statistician though belonging to the cadre of the Bureau, should be administratively under the Agricultural Production Commissioner (APC) and be physically located in the same building so that the APC could have the benefit of his advice and assistance in the day-to-day affairs. If the organization is located in the State Agriculture/Land Records Department, the officer should have the rank of Additional/Joint Director of Agriculture/Land Records (Statistics). It should be the duty of this officer to advice the APC, Secretary and Director of Agriculture and other concerned officers at the State level on all statistical matters relating to agriculture. He should be assisted by adequate number of Statisticians and Assistants Statisticians in appropriate scales and lower technical and ministerial staff. The organization should also have a few qualified economists to take charge of economic investigations in the field of agriculture. The statistical organizations in the fields of agriculture, animal husbandry and fisheries in States where these are in the Bureaus should belong to the general State Statistical Cadre, so that the career prospects of the statisticians working in separate units are not adversely affected. In States where these organizations are not in the Bureaus the statisticians in the fields of agriculture, animal husbandry and fisheries statistics should form a separate common cadre.

OTHER ORGANIZATIONS

National Sample Survey

The difficulties in the way of expeditious collection of data on a comprehensive basis and the limitations of cost and manpower brought to the fore the sampling approach. The Directorate of National Sample Survey under the Department of Statistics (Cabinet Secretariat) was created to collect statistical data on a random sampling basis in the various sectors of national economy such as socio-economic surveys. The data which are collected on a random sampling basis over demographic and socio-economic conditions such as composition of households, pattern of expenditure and income, employment and unemployment; agricultural prices, cost of cultivation, output of livestock products, land utilization, crop cutting experiments, agricultural holdings, livestock number, livestock products, etc.

The surveys are conducted on behalf of the Government of India. The field work, i.e. data collection of the survey and primary scrutiny, is the responsibility of the Directorate of National Sample Survey (NSS), which is an attached office of the Department of Statistics, Government of India, except in West Bengal and Bombay City, where it is the responsibility of the Indian Statistical Institute (ISI). The technical work which includes planning, survey, processing of the data, tabulating the results and preparing the final report, is done by the ISI. A programme Committee consisting of representatives of various Central ministries concerned, State Governments, the Central Statistical Organization (CSO), NSS Directorate and ISI, advises the Government of India (Department of Statistics) on the general plan of the survey, the items of information to be collected in each round and the tabulation programme. Most of the States have started participating on matching basis with the Central Programme of the NSS.

To ensure rapid processing and systematic analysis of socio-economic data, collected regularly through the National Sample Survey (NSS) it has now been decided to bring all aspects of work relating to NSS under one unified control. It will be entrusted to a single Government organization located in the Department of Statistics, Cabinet Secretariat. This organization will be responsible for designing, field work and tabulation.

There exists a Crop Survey Wing within the Directorate of NSS which provides technical guidance to the States in conducting sample surveys for estimating yield rates of principal crops and is also closely associated with training of field staff, inspection of field work and consolidation of results at the all-India level. This wing also keeps itself engaged with various developmental work, e.g. extension of sampling techniques to new crops and new areas, application of sampling technique to other related fields like Grow More Food Activities, etc.

Reliable and timely data on crop production are of crucial importance for agricultural planning and management of food distribution. The present system of reporting of crop areas and production does not adequately meet the needs of the Government for purposes of policy. With a view to improving crop statistics and building advance estimates of area and production a scheme for timely reporting of crop areas based on a complete plot-to-plot enumeration in respect of sample of villages with proper checks on the complete enumeration work of the primary reporting agency has been introduced in eleven States. It is proposed to be extended to other States gradually.

The scope of crop surveys in the NSS will be expanded to provide estimates of acreage under all major food and non-food crops by enumeration of crop averages in a sample of 5,000 villages with the help of Central staff and in the other 5,000 villages by State staff and centralized tabulation of data collected by NSS and the States which collaborate in these programmes. There surveys will be integrated with the State crop estimation work so that the NSS sample of villages will form a part of the State sample for the scheme of timely reporting of crop areas. The sample villages for crop cutting will also be sub-samples of TRS samples. These arrangements are expected to provide independent estimates at the national level and improve the reliability of estimates at the State level.

Ministry of Commerce

Out of seven Statistical units in the Ministry, the following three have some relation with agriculture.

(i) Statistical Section of the office of the Textile Commissioner, Bombay—1953.
(ii) Department of Commercial Intelligence and Statistics.
(iii) Office of the Economic Adviser.

The Statistical Section of the office of the Textile Commissioner collects statistics of production of cotton textile and consumption, and statistics of raw cotton and coal used by cotton factories, textile machinery, etc. and publishes, *Monthly Statistics of Cotton Spinning and Weaving in India*.

The Department of Commercial Intelligence and Statistics is responsible for the compilation and publication of India's internal and foreign trade statistics.

The Office of the Economic Adviser compiles and publishes the weekly index numbers of wholesale prices popularly known as the Economic Adviser's Index or the Official Index.

Ministry of Finance

The Reserve Bank of India has set up a full-fledged Research Department which collects different types of statistics. Special mention may be made of the All-India Rural Credit Survey conducted by the Bank in 1951-52. The All-India survey is followed up by the Rural Credit Follow-up Surveys. The Fourth Follow-up Survey had been conducted in July 1960-June 1961 with 1959-60 as the reference period.

The Division of Rural Economics, like the Economic Department of the Reserve Bank of India of which it is a part, has been so organized as to provide the nucleus of a research counterpart to the operational activities undertaken by the Bank in the field of rural credit. It has, therefore, a sphere of study and work complementary mainly to the Agricultural Credit Department. The Division was set up in August 1945 with a programme of research which embraces "a study of problems relating to the finance for the production, storage and marketing of agricultural output of all kinds, output of cottage industries income from which helped to supplement income from agriculture and of the output of industries closely alike or complementary to agriculture, such as dairy farming." To undertake this programme, it was envisaged at that time that the Division would be studying: (1) the role played by Central Banks in other countries in the development of rural economy, (2) the part played by several financial agencies including the Reserve Bank of India in providing credit to the rural sector, (3) rural indebtedness, (4) agriculture and its terms of trade, (5) problems relating to agricultural marketing, and (6) trends in rural incomes including the study of problems relating to farm business, size of the holdings, tenure and tenancy, techniques of cultivation, etc. The Division was also expected to conduct periodical surveys which would be "in the nature of economic X-ray photographs, so to speak, of the economy."

Broadly speaking, the development of activities of the Division has taken place in three stages. The first stage covers the period from the Division's inception in August 1945 up to the initiation of the All-India Rural Credit Survey in 1951 to 1955, which marks the second stage of development, the Division was fully occupied with the work relating to the All-India Rural Credit Survey. The third stage of development of the activities in the Division followed the publication of the Report of the Committee of Direction of the All-India Rural Credit Survey which devoted a chapter to the follow-up, publicity, review and research. In pursuance of the recommendations of the Committee, the Division was reorganized, creating two sections, namely, the General Section and the Survey Section in 1955-56. The former deals with problems in agricultural economics and agricultural finance.

Ministry of Labour and Employment

An Agricultural Labour Enquiry Branch was originally created in this Ministry in 1950-51 for maintaining detailed statistical records emerging out of the proceedings of the Agricultural Labour Enquiry Committee (1950-51). It published a number of ad hoc reports in connection with proceedings, witnesses and recommendations of the Enquiry Committee. The unit could not finally wind up its functions of the first enquiry when the appointment of the Second Agricultural Labour Enquiry Committee was announced in 1956. Now this unit is working more or less on a quasi-permanent basis with the Labour Ministry. Since 1955 it is constructing consumer price index number for agricultural labour in India.

Labour Bureau—Ministry of Labour and Employment

The Labour Bureau of the Ministry is responsible for the collection and dissemination of labour statistics and intelligence. It undertakes family budget enquiries and compiles cost of living index numbers. Survey of agricultural labour conducted on an ad hoc basis is also one of the activities of the Bureau. It also compiles the consumer price index numbers of agricultural labourers on the basis of weighting diagrams obtained with the National Sample Survey of agricultural labourers.

Ministry of Home Affairs

In the Ministry of Home Affairs the most important statistical unit is the office of the 'Census Commissioner and Registrar General of India' with its counterparts in the Census Regions. This department maintains detailed records of vital statistics in India and conducts the decennial census of population in the country. The Census Reports are published by the department after each census and the vital statistics are recorded on a permanent basis. Further, it also prepares and maintains the National Register of Citizens at the headquarters of every district in India.

Office of the Registrar General. For the 1961 population census the following categories were included for agriculture in the classification adopted for the working population:

  (i) cultivation;
 (ii) agricultural labour; and
(iii) mining, quarrying, livestock, forestry, fishing, hunting, plantation, orchards and allied activities.

One of the salient features of the 1961 census was to supplement the data collected by information on the economic activities of the household as an entity. This information was collected through the household schedule which provided for data on the chief economic activities of the household, viz. cultivation and household industry. Information was collected in respect of family workers and hired workers.

The appointment of the Registrar General was made for each census before 1961. This created a big lacuna in a period of development.

Requirements of planning need annual forecasts of population. This is possible only if the appointment is made permanent and some sort of a sample survey is also conducted annually. It has now been decided that the office as well as the post of the Registrar General will continue throughout in interperiod. The work of population projections, vital registration and sample census will continue during this period.

Beginning with 1881, the census has since been taken once every ten years. The census operation is of immense magnitude carried out with the help of about 6 million honorary enumerators including government employees, employees of local bodies and teachers. Plans have been worked out by the Registrar General and Census Commissioner for evolving an integrated system of demographic and vital statistics on a continuing basis and these are under implementation. A fuller discussion of the census is given in an independent chapter.

Statistical Organizations in the States

Statistical organizations in the States like those in the Government of India are also generally of a decentralized type. Different Departments in the States collect, maintain and issue statistics relating to their respective subjects. Some of the States have already set up statistical units in the Departments of Agriculture or Land Records while in a few the Statistical Bureaus are in charge of agricultural statistics. The State Statistical Bureaus are responsible for effecting coordination in statistical matters between the different Governments of their respective States to provide technical guidance to these department and to recommend improved methods for the collection of primary statistics by them.

Non-Governmental Organizations

Besides the official agencies, a number of semi-official and private organizations exist and have contributed to the progress of agricultural statistics in India. Some of them worth mentioning are:
1. The Indian Statistical Institute, Calcutta.
2. National Council of Applied Economic Research, New Delhi.
3. Indian Society of Agricultural Economics, Bombay.
4. Indian Society of Agricultural Statistics, New Delhi.
5. Indian Institute of Management, Ahmedabad.
6. Universities and educational institutions.
7. Indian Dairy Association.
8. East India Cotton Association Ltd.
9. Indian Jute Mills Association.
10. Indian Sugar Mills Association.
11. National Federation of Cooperative Sugar Factories Ltd.
12. Vanaspati Manufacturers Association.
13. State Trading Corporation of India.
14. Agricultural Universities (Appendix 2.1).
15. Tea, Coffee, Rubber, Tobacco and Lac Boards.

Appendix 2.1

List of State Agricultural Universities (SAUs) and their Addresses

Name and Address of SAUs	Head
Acharya N.G. Ranga Agricultural University (APAU) Rajendranagar, Hyderabad: 500 030 Andhra Pradesh E-mail : root@apau.ap.nic.in : drapau@hdl.vsnl.net.in : vc_apau@hotmail.com	Dr I.V. Subba Rao Vice-Chancellor
Agricultural University Udaipur (AUU) University Campus, Udaipur: 313 001 Rajasthan	Dr A.S. Faroda Vice-Chancellor
Assam Agricultural University (AAU) Jorhat: 785 013 Assam E-mail : vc@aau.ren.nic.in	Dr. G.L. Kaul Vice-Chancellor
Bidhan Chandra Krishi Vishwa Vidyalaya (BCKVV), Haringhatta P.O. Mohanpur: 741 252 West Bengal E-mail : root@bckv.wb.nic.in : spsarkar@hotmail.com : drbckv@cal.vsnl.net.in	Dr S.P. Sarkar Vice-Chancellor
Birsa Agricultural University (BAU) Kanke, Ranchi: 834 006 Bihar E-mail : root@bau.bih.nic.in : bau@bih.nic.in	Dr R.P. Roy Sharma Vice-Chancellor
CCS Haryana Agricultural University (HAU) Hissar: 125 004 Haryana E-mail : root@hau.pnp.nic.in : vc@hau.hry.nic.in	Sri Vinay Kumar Vice-Chancellor
Central Agricultural University (CAU) IROISEMBA, Imphal: 795 004 Manipur	Dr S.S. Baghel Vice-Chancellor
Chandra Shekhar Azad University of Agriculture & Technology (CSAUA&T) Kanpur: 208 002 Uttar Pradesh E-mail : gps_dr@hotmail.com : aksinghal@hotmail.com	Dr. S.B. Singh Vice-Chancellor

List of State Agricultural Universities (SAUs) and their Addresses (Contd.)

Name and Address of SAUs	Head
Govind Ballabh Pant University of Agriculture & Technology (GBPYA&T) Pantnagar: 263 145 Uttar Pradesh E-mail : root@gbpuat.ernet.in : vc@gbpuat.ernet.in	Dr J.B. Choudhary Vice-Chancellor
Gujarat Agricultural University (GAU) Dantiwada, Sardar Krishi Nagar: 385 506 Banaskantha Gujarat E-mail : vc@gauskn.guj.nic.in Web site://www.gau.guj.nic.in	Dr M.H. Mehta Vice-Chancellor
Himachal Pradesh Krishi Vishwa Vidyalaya (HPKVV) Palampur: 176 062 Himachal Pradesh E-mail: root@hpkv.cbd.nic.in	Dr P.K. Kohla Vice-Chancellor
Indira Gandhi Krishi Vishwa Vidyalaya (IGKVV) Krishak Nagar, Raipur: 492 012 Madhya Pradesh E-mail : adr@zrcmp01.mp.nic.in : asastri@yahoocom	Dr Ved Prakash Kashirao Patil Vice-Chancellor
Jawharlal Nehru Krishi Viswa Vidyalaya (JNKVV) Jabalpur: 482 004 Madhya Pradesh E-mail : root@jnau.mp.nic.in	Dr A.S. Tiwari Vice-Chancellor (Acting)
Kerala Agricultural University (KAU) Vellanikkara, Trichur: 680 656 Kerala E-mail : kauhqr@ren.nic.in	Dr. Shyamasundaran Nair Vice-Chancellor
Konkan Krishi Vidyapeeth (KKV) Dapoli: 415 712, Ratangiri Maharashtra E-mail : root@kkv.ren.nic.in : kkv.dapoli@mailcity.com	Dr S.S. Magar Vice-Chancellor (Officiating)
Mahatma Phule Krishi Vidyapeeth (MPKV) Rahuri-413 722, Ahmednagar Maharashtra E-mail : kvmp@ren.nic.in	Dr S.N. Puri Vice-Chancellor
Marathwada Agricultural University (MAU) Parbhani: 431 402 Maharashtra E-mail : mau@ren.nic.in : ve@mau.ren.nic.in : vcmau@123india.com	Dr V.M. Pawar Vice-Chancellor

List of State Agricultural Universities (SAUs) and their Addresses (Contd.)

Name and Address of SAUs	Head
Narendra Dev University of Agriculture & Technology (NDUA&T) Faizabad: 224 229 Uttar Pradesh E-mail : nduat@up.nic.in	Prof R. Yamdagni Vice-Chancellor
Orissa University of Agriculture & Technology (OUA&T) : 751 001 Orissa E-mail : root@uat.ori.nic.in : snp@uat.ori.nic.in	Dr. Rajkishore Bhujabal Vice-Chancellor
Punjab Agricultural University (PAU) Ludhiana: 141 004 Punjab E-mail : root@pau.chd.nic.in : jssohal@pau.chd.nic.in : gskalkat@panchd.nic.in	Dr Gurucharan Singh Kalkat Vice-Chancellor
Dr Panjabrao Desmukh Krishi Vishwa Vidyalaya Krish Nagar, Akola: 444 104 Maharashtra E-mail : vc@pdkv.mah.nic.in : root@pdkv.mah.nic.in : root@pkv.ren.nic.in	Prof. M.L. Madan Vice-Chancellor
Rajasthan Agricultural University (RAU) Bikaner: 334 002 Rajasthan E-mail : vc@raub.raj.nic.in : root@raub.raj.nic.in	Dr C.P.S. Yadav Vice-Chancellor
Rajendra Agricultural University (RAU) Pusa, Samstipur: 848 125 Bihar E-mail : rau@bih.nic.in : mail-rau@bih.nic.in : aktiwari@rau.bih.nic.in	Dr V.P. Gupta Vice-Chancellor
Sher-e-Kashmir University of Agricultural Sciences & Technology (SKAS&T, Kashmir) Post Box 262, GPO Srinagar Shcampus: 191 121 Srinagar, Kashmir Jammu & Kashmir E-mail : root@skuast.jk.nic.in : yusufkamal@hotmail.com	Dr M. Yusuf Kamal Vice-Chancellor
Sher-e-Kashmir University of Agricultural Sciences & Technology (SKAS&T, Jammu) Camp Office, Railway Road, Jammu: 180 004 Jammu & Kashmir	Mr H.U. Khan Vice-Chancellor

List of State Agricultural Universities (SAUs) and their Addresses (Contd.)

Name and Address of SAUs	Head
Tamil Nadu Agricultural University (TNAU) Coimbatore: 641 003 Tamil Nadu E-mail : root@unau.tn.nic.in : drtnau@md3.vsnl.net.in : vctnau@vsnl.com : skannaiyan@hotmail.com	Dr S. Kannalyan Vice-Chancellor
Tamil Nadu Veterinary & Animal Sciences University (TNV&ASU) Madras: 600 007 Tamil Nadu E-mail : root@tnvasu.tn.nic.in : tanvvas@md2.vsnal.net.in : biointn@iitm.ernet.in : btismvc@giasmd01.vsnl.net.in Web site://www.tnau.edu/	Dr R. Prabaharan Vice-Chancellor
University of Agricultural Sciences (UAS) GKVK, Banglore: 560 065 Karnataka E-mail : vc@uasblr.kar.nic.in	Dr S. Bisaliah Vice-Chancellor
University of Agricultural Sciences (UAS) Krishi Nagar, Dharwad: 580 005 Karnataka E-mail : root@uasd.kar.nic.in : root@zrckarp8.kar.nic.in	Dr M. Mahadevappa Vice-Chancellor
West Bengal University of Animal & Fishery Sciences (WBUA&FS) 68, Khudiram Bose Sarani, Belgachia Calcutta: 700 037 West Bengal	Dr Ashim K. Bhattacharya Vice-Chancellor
Yashwant Singh Parmar University of Horticulture & Forestry (YPUH&F) Solan: 173 230 Himachal Pradesh E-mail : yspuhf@ren.nic.in : vc@yspuhf.hp.nic.in	Dr R.P. Awasthi Vice-Chancellor

3

Population Census

Of Roman origin, the world 'census' is derived from 'censors' or the magistrates in ancient Rome who prepared a register of population for the purpose of taxation and fixation of liability of adult males for compulsory military service. The measure adopted was, however, unpopular with the people and the project was given up by the authorities in the medieval period. But the fund of details that the census provided became very necessary for multifarious purposes in a modern welfare state. With the ushering in of the democratic system of governments, the need for reliable data became all the more important for purposes such as demarcation of electoral areas, scientific development planning and administration of educational, health and other social welfare programmes.

The census itself has a hoary tradition dating back to the third millennium before Christ. The Roman census was popular but with the fall of the Empire their system of census also perished. Despite its antiquity, people seem to have maintained some superstition about census. There was a long gap in the history of census until the middle of the 17th century. Fears were expressed in the British House of Commons even in 1753, that numbering of people would be followed by some public misfortune or epidemic distemper. Canada and the Scandinavian countries were among the earliest to have attempted a proper population enumeration, though decennial census in Canada started only in 1851. The USA had regular decennial population counts from 1790. The United Kingdom went through its regular census in 1801. As early as the East India Company administration estimates of population of some of its local possessions were made from the middle of the 17th century.

ANCIENT PERIOD

Some three to seven thousand years ago there were people possessing a technology sufficiently advanced to support a dense population and they found for the soil and climate of India favourable conditions for the application of this technology. As early as third century B.C. Kautilya's *Arthashastra* had prescribed the collection of population statistics as a measure of state policy for the purpose of taxation.

Rigveda makes it clear that population was scanty and spread over wide areas in small villages. The Brahmana literature around 800-600 B.C. reveals that some of the villages had grown into towns and capitals within urban mode of life. Ashoka's edicts show that a rough census known as 'Khanashumari' was instituted by Indian princes from very ancient days. The Buddhist literature indicates that between the 7th and 4th centuries B.C. the economy of northern India was comparable to that of the later middle ages in Europe.

Some idea of the total population in the country could also be formed from the records left by India's first real empire under the sway of Chandragupta (321-297 B.C.). They indicate a standing army of approximately 700 thousand men. Under Ashoka (274-236 B.C.) this empire achieved one of the highest points of Indian civilization based on efficient administration, the use of written commands, abundant commerce, intensive agriculture and the use of metals.

With the consideration to all these factors, first ever estimate of the population of ancient India around 300 B.C. was placed at 100-140 millions by Pran Nath. No population estimates are available for a period of nearly two thousand years after that.

It was then left to Moreland who has given an estimate of 100 million as the population of India for 1600. For a numerical basis of calculation, Moreland relies in the south on the strength of armed forces and in the north on the land under cultivation, on both of which subjects contemporary figures are available. Assuming a ratio of 30 people to one fighting man (a ratio like that of France and Germany in 1914), he estimates that the southern part of India had about 30 million people. From Akbar's records of land under cultivation together with con- temporary accounts of densely and sparsely settled areas, he concludes that the middle Ganges and the Punjab had close to 40 million persons. Adding together thickly settled areas, such as Bengal and Gujarat, and the thinly occupied areas not included in the contemporary empires, he concludes that the total population was around 100 million. Kingslay Davis considers that the actual figures for 1600 should be 125 million. Similar estimates have been made by various authorities for 1800, 1834, 1845, 1855 and 1867 before the regular census of 1871 (Table 3.1).

THE FIRST CENSUS

In India census on modern lines was in vogue in Travancore. The first census in Fort Saint George and surrounding villages in Madras was taken as early as 1687. However, the first systematic attempt to obtain information regarding the population of India based on actual counting of heads was made between 1867 and 1872 during the Vice-royalty of Lord Mayo who followed a policy of 'vigorous expansion' in the country.

Table 3.1 Estimates of India's Population, 300 B.C. to A.D. 1871

Date	Millions	Average annual per cent growth during preceding period
300 B.C.	100-140[1]	—
A.D. 1600	100[2]	—
1800	120[3]	0.09
1834	130[4]	0.24
1845	130[5]	—
1855	175[6]	2.97
1867	194[7]	0.86
1871	255[8]	6.84

[1]Pran Nath, A Study in the Economic Condition of Ancient India (London; Royal Asiatic Society, 1929) Chapter 5.

[2]W.H. Moreland, India at the Death of Akbar (London: Macmillan, 1920), pp. 9-22.

[3]Wm. Playfair, The Statistical Breviary (London: J. Wallis et al., 1801), p. 58. The figure of 120 million is not the one given by Playfair. He gives 41 million for what he calls the total British Interests in India. The area he gives for this territory, however, is less than a third the area of India today, so for our purpose his estimate has been roughly tripled. This is not entirely justified, because the British held the more populous area, but since Playfair's population figure is obviously too low there is some reason to raise it in the manner followed.

[4]J.R. M'Culloch, A Dictionary: Practical, Theoretical and Historical of Commerce and Commercial Navigation, Vol. 1, 2nd ed. (London: Longman, Rees, et al., 1834), pp. 546-47.

[5]Ibid., American Edition, 1835, Vol. 1, pp. 1108-09.

[6]Great Britain, Statistical Abstract for the Several Colonial and Other Possessions of the United Kingdom, 1854-68, Sessional Papers, Cmd. 146, Sixth Number (London: Her Majesty's Stationery Office, 1870), P. 5 only an estimate—124 million—for British India is given, but by assuming that non-British India then constituted 29 per cent of all-India population (somewhat above the present 24 per cent), we arrive at the figure given.

[7]Great Britain, Parliamentary Papers, Statistical Tables Relating to the Colonial and Other Possessions of the United Kingdom, Part 13, 1867 (London: Her Majesty's Stationery Office, 1869, p. 1.

[8]This is the 1871-72 census figure corrected for territory omitted and for defective methods.

It may be said that the first of the series of decennial censuses was in effect only a compilation of enumeration spread over between 1867 and 1872. This did not cover the entire country. However, there was a uniform schedule and it did encompass the basic demographic, social and economic characteristics. This largely laid the foundation for the decennial census conducted in the country.

The total population of India according to the first ever census of India was placed at 203 million. It, however, omitted the native States entirely as well as provinces of Oudh, Berar and the Punjab because they had taken a census only a few years before. The census was held in Oudh in 1869, Berar in 1867 and Punjab in 1868. In presenting the total population for 1871-72, the authorities incorporated these provincial census data. This means that the census period really extended over 5 to 6 years from 1867 to 1872, instead of only two years. This census also omitted certain other territories that total population of which in 1881 was 33 million.

In addition, because of poor methods and adverse conditions it failed to count an estimated 12 million population even in the area covered. With due consideration to all these facts, the population of India was later declared as 236 million. Even this would seem to be on the lower side. Applying certain corrections. Kingslay Davis has estimated India's population for 1871-72 as 255 million. By applying similar corrections to the later censuses up to 1941 the estimated figures are given in Table 3.2.

Table 3.2 Census Returns and Estimated Populations, 1872-1941

Year	Census population[1] (000's)	Estimated Population[2] (000's)
1871	203415	255165
1881	250160	257380
1891	279593	282134
1901	283870	285288
1911	303041	302985
1921	305730	305879
1931	338171	*
1941	388998	**

[1]Census of India, 1931, Vol. I, Part-1 p. 5; Vol. II (Burama) Part 2, p. 6; 1921, Vol. I, Part 2, p. 6.

[2]Made by adjusting the territory of all censuses to that of 1931 and 1941, and by allowing for under-numeration officially said to have occurred in the first three censuses.

* Burma is, of course, omitted throughout.

**The censuses of 1931 and 1941 were accepted as representing the population of India. Hence no estimates for these years were required. Doubtless there is undernumeration in India, so that all figures are lower than they should be; but further correction would be hazardous and would not significantly change the trend.

The first census of 1872 was just the forerunner of the decennial censuses carried out since February 1881. Thus, first simultaneous count covered almost all regions except Kashmir and certain forest areas. The third census taken in February 1891 included Kashmir and Sikkim as also Upper Burma which had by then been acquired by the British. The 1872 census returned a population of 206.2 million, which increased to

287.3 million in 1891. Much of the increase was due to additions to areas.

The 1901 Census embraced for the first time the Baluchistan Agency, the Bhil country in Rajputana, Andaman and Nicobar Islands and certain outlying areas in the confines of Burma, Punjab and Kashmir. A code of census procedure was newly drawn up by the Census Commissioner, Sir Richard Temple. The first enumeration of the aborigines of Andamans and Nicobar was also taken during that year. Special parties toured the islands in boats and the report described an encounter the enumerators had with the hostile Jarawas resulting in the death of a Jarawa. The new tribe of Tabo was also located during the operations in North Andaman. The 1901 Census put the population at 294.4 million. The India Report that year published the first linguistic survey by George. A. Grierson and this was strengthened by the 5th and 6th enumeration conducted in March 1911 and 1921.

Lack of comparability of geographical coverage remains the major difficulty in establishing a population series covering, say, the last hundred years. The difficulty is most acute in the pre-census era, i.e. prior to 1871. However, one should also expect lower levels of general accuracy in earlier periods apart from the coverage question. Since 1871, census population estimates are available for India. Earlier censuses suffered from considerable under-coverage. This has, however, been corrected by Kingslay Davis[1] and his series suits our purpose satisfactorily for the period 1871-1951. Davis's series is for undivided India excluding Burma. Estimates of population for the Indian Union or British India could be derived from this series by applying the ratio available for particular years. The pre-census period is, therefore, the most difficult one for our purpose. Davis gives the following figures for population of this period:[2]

Year	In million
1855	175
1867	194
1871	255 (adjusted for under-coverage)

---

[1]Kingslay Davis, The Population of India and Pakistan, Princeton, New Jersey, 1951.

[2]The figure relating to 1855 in respect to British India is taken from Statistical Abstract for Several Colonial and other possessions of the United Kingdom, 1854-68, Sessional Papers, CMd 146, Sixth number, Great Britain, Her Majesty's Stationery Office, London, 1870, p. 5 and is multiplied by 1.2 to cover non-British India. The 1867 figure is taken from Statistical Tables relating to the Colonial and other possessions of the United Kingdom, Parliamentary Papers, Great Britain, part 13, 1867, p. 1.

None of the earlier estimates are very satisfactory and the rate of increase of 6.84 per cent per year between 1867. and 1971 is neither plausible nor possible. While Davis suspects considerable under-reporting in 1855 and 1867 figures, he has not attempted to improve these. A survey of the Indian official statistics gives a somewhat better figure for 1855 or there-about. For example, the Parliamentary Paper, 1857, give a return of the area and population of each division of each presidency of India for 1856. Figures for native states and foreign territories are included in the return and the total adds up to 181 million for 1856[3]. The figures for 1867 or thereabout are consistent with the figure of 194 million given by Davis for 1867. Under the circumstances, the figure of 181 million may probably be noted in this context that Naoroji[4] used a figure of only 170 million for 1867-68 and Atkinson[5] a figure of 188 million for 1875.

To work out annual population estimates for the pre-census period, Mukherjee[6] makes use of the following figures:

		(in million)
Year	As reported	As adjusted
1856	181	277
1871	203	255

Davis's corrected figure for 1871 is 25.5 per cent higher than the reported figure. To construct the adjusted series, it has been assumed that at least this proportion of under-reporting must have existed in the earlier figures also. The adjusted series is more plausible because the rise between 1867 and 1871 is now consistent, with a rise of less than 1 per cent per year between 1856 and 1867 and almost negligible rise between 1871 and 1881.

THE PERIOD 1871-1941

After 1870, because of the censuses, our knowledge of India's population growth rests on firm ground. Yet the actual census figures cannot be taken at face value for two reasons; first, additional territory was covered

---

[3]The same set to figures is also reproduced in the Annals of Indian Administration. 1856, pp. 523-530.

[4]Dadabhai Naoroji, Poverty and Un-British Rule in India, Swan Sonnenschien & Co., Ltd., London, 1871.

[5]F.J. Atkinson, A Statistical review of the income and wealth of British India, Journal of the Royal Statistical Society, Vol. LXV, Part II, June 1902, pp. 209-272.

[6]M. Mukherjee, National Income of India' Trends and Structures, 1966 p. 44.

by each new census; second, improvements in enumeration were made each time till 1901.

For example, the census of 1871-72, which gave a total of 203 million, omitted territories which, in 1881, totalled some 33 million.[7] It omitted the native states entirely, and committed the provinces of Oude, Berar, and the Punjab because these had taken censuses only a few years before.[8]

In addition, because of poor methods and adverse conditions, it failed to count an estimated 12 million people even in the area covered.[9] Nevertheless on the basis of this census and those taken in particular provinces in the 8160's together with estimates, the population of India proper in 1871-72 was announced as 236 million, considerably more than the 203 million actually enumerated.[10] The total figure (236 million) was obviously below reality, because for Oude, Berar, and the Punjab the census figures of earlier dates were utilized without change, and because for some of the native states the estimates were far too low. Yet, just because the bulk of the country had for the first time been actually enumerated, this all-India total based on the census plus estimates for uncovered territory was far above the guesses made only a few years previously, and it presumably came somewhere near the truth.[11]

If we are to get a truer picture of the population in 1871-72 the first census must be corrected on the basis of the 1881 Census, which was more reliable than the estimates for uncovered territory made at the earlier date. The problem does not end there, however, for in 1891 the territory covered was still greater and the techniques used were still better than in 1881. On the basis of the 1891 Census, then, the 1881 Census (1871-72) must be corrected a second time. In this way one must add corrections to each census on the basis of all subsequent censuses till 1931.

---

[7]Census of India, 1931, Vol. 1, Part I, p. 5.

[8]Oude in 1869, Berar in 1867, the Punjab in 1855 and 1868. In presenting the data on the population for 1871-72, the authorities incorporated these provincial censuses. This fact means that the censuses period really extends over five or six years, from 1867 to 1872, instead of over two years. In general we shall refer to the results as applying to 1871 this being what would appear to be the model year.

[9]Great Britain, Memorandum on the Census of British India of 1871-72, Sessional Papers, Cmd. 1349 (London: Her Majesty's Stationery Office 1875), pp. 5, 45, 47; General Report of the Census of India, 1901, Sessional Papers, Cmd. 2047 (London: His Majesty's Stationery Office 1904), p. 5.

[10]Great Britain, Memorandum on the Census of British India of 1871-72, op. cit., p. 5.

[11]To illustrate the superiority of a census we may take the case of Bengal. Prior to the census "no one knew exactly the population of a single district of Bengal. The census of 1872 suddenly disclosed the presence of 22 millions of British subjects whose existence had never previously been suspected. The population of Bengal and Assam, up to that time reckoned at 40 million, was ascertained to number $67\frac{3}{4}$ million of souls." Sir W.W. Hunter (ed.). The Imperial Gazetteer of India, Vol. I (London: Trubner, 1881), p. xx.

On the basis of these corrected figures it can be stated with some confidence that from 1871 to 1941 the average rate of increase of India's population was approximately 0.60 per cent per annum. This was slightly less than the estimated rate for the whole world (0.69) from 1850 to 1940.[12] India's growth, therefore, is not exceptional either way, but close to average. It is, however, less than that found in Europe, in North America, and in a good many other countries.

The total Indian increase during 1871-1941 was 52 per cent. The British Isles during the same period increased 57 per cent, and during the 70 year period from 1821 to 1891 (more comparable to India's recent history) they increased 79 per cent. Similarly Japan, during the 70 years from 1870 to 1940, experienced a growth of approximately 120 per cent, and the United States a growth of 230 per cent.

For the British Raj, the census operation was part of the politics of domination and rule. It was about 140 years ago when the Raj's drummers in the numerous towns and villages of the country announced the advent of the census enumerator for the first time in history. Like Wee Willie Winkie, he visited people at night in those days, and families were urged to chain their dogs and keep lanterns at the window in preparation for his arrival. Benedict Anderson, the British-born historian of Southeast Asia, defined the census as one of the three institutions of power of the colonial state, the other two being the map and the museum. As he put it in his book, *Imagined Communities*: "Together they profoundly shaped the way in which the colonial state imagined its domination—the nature of human beings it ruled, the geography of its domain, and the legitimacy of its ancestry."

It was a theme that political scientist Sudipta Kaviraj was to take a step further. For him, the census was part of the process of "colonial modernity". He argues that it was through census enumeration, that "mapped and counted identities", as against "fuzzy" ones, came into being. Concept like "majority" and "minorities" were the natural outcome of such an exercise. The process that Kaviraj talks about is still in many ways a continuing one to this day. But the census operations in post-independent India also witnessed a shift in its vantage point. It was not "them" who were being counted and analysed, it was "us". Data culled for the project of domination has necessarily to be distinguished from that collected for the project of national development, even though there may not be unanimity in what constitutes such development.

POST-INDEPENDENCE PERIOD

With the dawn of independence and adoption of a democratic system of government, the importance of authentic data on population was enhanced. The Indian census today is universally acknowledged as the most authentic

---

[12]Kingslay Davis, "The world demographic transition," *Annals of the American Academy of Political and Social Science*, Vol. 237 (January, 1945), p. 3.

and comprehensive source of information about our land and the people. The size of the legislatures as also the demarcation of electoral constituencies depended on the statistical information regarding the size of the population and its geographical distribution. These data are invaluable also for the implementation of constitutional provisions like the welfare of the socially and economically backward classes.

The advent of the five-year plans added a new dimension to the census operations. It is formulated to yield information regarding such a variety of aspects of the nation's economy like population, urbanization, manpower, employment, literacy, migration, housing and other welfare measures. The planners as well as the research scholars look for detailed and sophisticated data on the trends in occupational and industrial affiliations of the working population, fertility patterns, age and educational levels, etc. Census has to meet this increasing hunger for data.

There is another aspect. In the process of planning, data collection and decision making are two inseparable and interdependent aspects. Census forms an important link in this strategic task. During the last 100 years, this machinery has met the varied demands of changing times. During this period, a greater degree of sophistication has come into our methods of collection, tabulation and analysis of statistical data.

One more step was taken in 1948. A permanent census law was placed on the Statute Book. The entire census organization is created by the Census Act which authorizes census-takers to ask the prescribed questions and legally compel all persons to answer the queries truthfully. The law guarantees that the information collected at the census will be used only for statistical purposes, that the information on individuals will be kept confidential and cannot be used as evidence in a court of law. The Act provides a legal backing to the entire census operations and gives extraordinary power to secure all types of assistance from the local bodies or any other persons in order to get through this extremely onerous task.

The 1961 Census

The second census after independence, held in 1961, was a comprehensive one and was conducted in the background of vast territorial changes that had taken place inside the country. A major revision on a linguistic basis took place in 1956. On October 1, 1953 the new Andhra State, including Telangana areas, was constituted. Chandannagore was merged in West Bengal and Bombay was bifurcated on May 1, 1960. The demarcation of the areas at different levels had to be done in the context of the new changes and enumeration blocks in urban and rural areas were created on the basis of about 600 persons in urban areas and 750 in rural areas.

Features One of the characteristic features of this census was the systematic mapping out of every village and every ward of block of a town showing the location of each and every census house. Apart from being valuable guides to locate every house during census enumeration, these maps served as basis for all types of surveys and are intended to meet various administrative needs. Listing of houses as a prelude to the major census operations was done for the first time during the census. Apart from individual slips, household schedule giving details of holdings and land rights of agricultural households besides providing particulars of household industry, was incorporated. Data on language census giving a most valuable picture of the actual linguistic situation in India, incorporating details of linguism and bi-linguism, have been brought out and these have been rated high.

The 1961 census has yielded a population figure of 439 million which was very much higher than the population estimated by experts. Data were collected on scientifically and technically qualified persons. Valuable socio-economic surveys relating to 800 villages were made. Information on handicrafts, fairs and festivals of the country were prepared. Studies about scheduled castes and scheduled tribes were specially made. While special reports on cities with a population of one million and above were prepared, detailed census reports for individual States and Union Territories were brought out by the concerned Census Superintendents. A unique contribution was the production of Atlas volumes depicting the census results with maps on physiography, rainfall, soil and agriculture. A number of valuable publications based on the data collected during the census were brought out.

While the British inducted petty revenue officials and school teachers to conduct the census on a 'voluntary' basis without any payments, a small honorarium to the enumerators was introduced for the first time at the 1961 Census. The amount has been gradually increased from census to census.

The 1971 Census

Elaborate preparations were made for the 1971 Census and for the first time computers were used to analyse the data. An army of enumerators visited every home in the country to collect valuable information. Each enumerator was incharge of a block and they were drawn from the class of school teachers or village patwari or some other village level official in rural areas. Each census supervisor guided five enumerators of whom there were two lakhs throughout the country working under the direction of 350 District Census Officers who worked part time.

Translation and printing of census schedules and instructions was a responsible work which had to be carefully undertaken. About 3,500 tonnes of paper had to be procured to print millions of schedules and instructions. The full printing capacity of a number of Government of India Presses had to be utilized in order to ensure that the schedules and instructions reached every enumerator well in advance.

The 1981 Census

Unlike prior to 1961, the census organization today has a core staff which has helped in avoiding the 'phoenix' approach in the former censuses. Planning for the 1981 census commenced around 1976 and a very active pace was built up by 1978. In every State and Union Territory the nucleus office was expanded and Directors of Census Operations came into position. The development of questionnaires was necessarily the first step in the organization of the 1981 Census. Draft questionnaires were developed on the basis of past experience, current needs and international recommendations and these were presented at the first Data Users Conference which was held from 13th to 15th February, 1978. The Data Users Conference was attended by representatives of the user Ministries of the Government of India, of the State governments, of universities and other expert bodies and research institutions, individual experts and others. Based on these discussions, certain questionnaires were developed which were later tested out in the field. The questionnaires were again exposed to consideration of a wealth of expertise at a second Data Users Conference held from December 21-23, 1978. Based on these discussions the following three questionnaires were finalized.

1. The houselist
2. The household schedule
3. The individual slip

The statutory framework for the census of India is the Census Act of 1948. Under this Act various census functionaries were appointed. The law guarantees confidentiality of information. The 1981 Census experience clearly indicated the urgent need for a hard look at the Census Act. Unlike the palmy days when the count was on one day or when the Collectors could order all dogs to be chained and lamps to be lit and placed in windows to help enumerators, in today's world it was found that constant vigilance was necessary at every stage merely to ensure that enumerators were available and carrying out the operations as required. No doubt, under the statute functionaries can be punished but the stipulations in the law are not firm enough with regard to this matter. If the census has to be carried out successfully next time it is clear that the law has to be considerably stiffened.

On an average, one enumerator canvassed the forms to about 600 to 750 people. A supervisor was appointed for every 5 enumerators and there was a reserve of both supervisors and enumerators. The total number of enumerators and supervisors who carried out the 1981 Census was about a million and a quarter and this entire army of personnel was given intensive training including practical work. A small honorarium was paid to these workers.

The census was followed by a Post Enumeration Survey and a Census Evaluation Study. These were evaluatory surveys which sought to determine the accuracy of the census and also the validity of the returns regarding certain characteristics of the population. These helped in estimating the content and coverage errors.

For the first time, separate Directorates of Census Operations were established in the State of Sikkim and Union Territories of Mizoram and Pondicherry and the census was conducted there independently. In former years the Directorate of West Bengal used to have some degree of technical control over the operations in Sikkim, Tamil Nadu Directorate conducted census in Pondicherry while Mizoram was part of Assam. In the case of Dadra & Nagar Haveli the operations were conducted by Directorate of Goa, Daman and Diu.

Position Upto 1991 Census

The five census operations that post-independent India conducted had several stories to tell. For one thing, population growth figures revealed the way various regions in the country inhabited different time zones: Tamil Nadu and Kerala, at one end of the spectrum, achieved replacement levels of fertility, Uttar Pradesh and Bihar, at the other, could take another 100 years to do so. Then take infant mortality levels in tribal districts. They indicated how tribal communities in this country were experiencing nothing short of a social haemorrhage, with loss of land and access to forests resulting in a people being steadily denied their dignity and way of life.

One of the biggest whodunits of the 1991 census figures was the mysterious disappearance of millions of women into the great unknown. In 1901, there were supposedly 1,072 women for every 1,000 men in the country. Ninety years later, the figure had fallen to 929, with states like MP, UP, Haryana and Rajasthan forming an almost unbroken belt where the sex-ratio was below 850.

It is by turning the torch on these problem areas that the census operation can, at its best, become a potent critique of state policy and a template for future strategies of change. But it cannot perform this function if it is just a mechanical exercise in counting heads. To be relevant, it has to be sensitive to social reality. The 1991 census was conducted under the shadow of the mounting environmental crisis and information on the kind of cooking fuel used within the household was elicited for the first time.

Another significant alteration made concerned the definition of literacy, which could not quite be gauged from the number of years a person spent at school. For the purposes of the census, a literate person came to be one who could read and write "with understanding".

Similarly, the definition of women's work was refined. This was provoked largely by the gross underestimation of women's participation in the work force—the 1981 census had actually held that women constituted only 16.5 per cent of the total work force! The problem lied in how "work" was being seen—at that point of time, even seasonal agricultural labour performed by women was not taken into account.

Enumerators in 1991 were therefore specifically asked to classify as "work", any service of a productive nature, even if it was not given monetary value. The result was startling: there was a 42 per cent increase in the female work force between 1981 and 1991.

As for the future, there are numerous areas that require closer scrutiny. But, clearly, one of the biggest themes of the next census will be urbanisation, because that's where a great deal of the action is going to be since at least a third of the country's total population now lives in cities. Surprisingly, the 1991 census indicated a slow down in urban growth levels. While, urban growth was put at 46 per cent in 1971, it had come down to 36 per cent by 1981, only to decline by another 10 per cent in 1991.

But a closer look at the figures indicated that while megacities like Mumbai and Delhi had grown at very rapid rates, medium and small towns did not quite keep pace. Something like 65 per cent of urban India—some 218 million—lived in 300 cities with a population of a lakh and above. Half this number lived in the 23 one-million plus cities and half of that, in the four metros of Mumbai, Delhi, Kolkata and Chennai.

Now it's the story of what happened to urbanisation after 1991 that the nation awaits. What changes did liberalisation bring in its wake? Did it increase urban growth in any way? And, if so, has that spread been even, or have only the larger cities continued to grow in a monstrous manner? Our burgeoning cities reveal more than just urban growth, they reflect life in the great rural hinterland as well, since migration to the big city is often from rural or semi-rural environs. So what causes people in modern India to leave the land of their birth? Which are the regions they leave and where do they go? And what does all this say about India's growth strategies? We would need to wait for the next census before we can even begin to understand this complex process.

In these uncertain times, when community is pitted against community, and visceral hatreds of every kind are being stoked for petty political ends, the great millennial head count should serve as a reminder of the numerous unfinished tasks of bringing a better life to the millions that make up India.

ONE BILLION AND MORE

While the exact date for scaling the billion mark can at best be an estimation, the office of the Registrar General and Census Commissioner of India zeroed-in on May 11, 2000 as D-day, when India's population crossed the one-billion rubicon. Amidst all the talk of dealing with India's security, the failure to come to grips with the burgeoning population has emerged as a foremost problem, one which is impinging on the country's economic, political, environmental and social security in far greater ways perhaps than any external threat.

Before India could embark on the millennium exercise, the country had already crossed the billion mark in 2000, occupying one sixth of the world population. Some of the facts are as given below.

- India's population crossed the one billion mark on May 11,2000-which was 16% of the world's population living on 2.4% of the globe's land area
- Global population increased three-fold in the last century, while India's grew nearly five times
- If the current trends continue, India will overtake China in 2045 to become the most populous country in the world
- If the National Population Policy 2000 is successfully implemented India's population will be 1,107 million in 2010 instead of the current projection of 1,162 million

Vital Statistics

Crude Birth Rate
From 40.8 in 1951 to 26.4 in 1998

Infant Mortality Rate
From 146 in 1951 to 72 in 1998

Crude Death Rate
From 25 in 1951 to 9 in 1998

Life Expectancy at Birth
Increased from 37 in 1951 to 62.9 in 1996-2001

Total Fertility Rate
From 6 in 1951 in 3.3 in 1997

**World
Population**

3 billion in 1960 (33 years later)	**6 billion in 1999** (12 years later)	**8 billion in 2028** (15 years later)
2 billion in 1927 (123 years later)	**5 billion in 1987** (13 years later)	**7 billion in 2013** (14 years later)
1 billion in 1804	**4 billion in 1974** (14 years later)	

CENSUS 2001

Its the 2001 Face Odyssey. The fourteenth Indian census, one of the largest administrative exercises in the world which has traced the contours of a nation called India. Falling as it has in a period when an old century and millennium has yielded place to the new, it cannot but be a way of reading the failures and successes of the Indian state, both before and after independence. Census 2001 is unique in several ways from the earlier censuses because several new, economic and social parameters have been added. And for the first time hundred per cent data will be fed into the computer and processed accordingly, so that it will be feasible to find out the interplay of various socio-economic indicators which could not be assessed/calculated in the past due to limitation of manual tabulation.

In order to act as a baseline survey of the affluence of the society— apart from the traditional questions related to housing, drinking water and electricity—, for the first time data has been collected on aspects like whether the households (family) owns a radio, TV, telephone, bicycle, scooter and car. It also provides first hand data about the availability of banking services and waste water disposal facility to the citizens of the country. For the first time a unique parameter of privacy available to the married couples has been collected in the form of number of couples of having independent sleeping room. These data has already been collected during the House-listing operations conducted between April-June 2000 and are being processed accordingly.

Special attention is being paid to slum areas, so that separate details/reports can be generated exclusively in relation to slum areas. The definition of slums used in the Census is very wide and encompasses not only the notified slums but also includes the areas which lack basic minimum facilities like drinking water, electricity, sewerage, etc. Hence it will be feasible to contrast indicators of affluence like percentage of slum households having access to TV, radio, scooter, car, etc., with the normal populace and similarly, it shall be feasible to contrast the affluence indicators of scheduled castes and scheduled tribes with the general populace.

Similarly, rural/urban comparisons can be made and one can get an idea of urban/rural divide. The type of building materials used in the construction of houses has also been collected, which will be a very good indicator of number of *kutcha* houses, *pucca* houses in various parts of country and along with other parameters like total number of rooms, will be able to give a projection of housing stock required to be built in future. The drinking water facilities have also been collected and can throw light on the severity of drinking water problem in the country.

The main Census operations took place between 9 and 28 February 2001. A lot of personal details were collected about everybody, which included the name, sex, age, age at marriage, SC/ST status, mother tongue, other languages known, disabilities, economic activities, families engaged in cultivation and plantations, land holding migration, fertility, amongst others. This a powerful data base will be ready which will be able to answer several questions related to socio-economic picture of the country. But the single most noticeable feature of census 2001 is the truly empowering provision in the schedule requiring respondents to affix their signatures or thumb impressions on completing the questionnaire. This, in addition to the signatures of the enumerators and supervisors, should ensure maximum coverage of the population in a given locality and accuracy of information provided.

From 1872 till 1941, every Census had questions related to infirmities of the population but these were dropped after independence except for the 1981 census. In 2001 these have been reintroduced and the definition of infirmity has been made fairly simple and covers five types of disabilities, viz., disability of speech, hearing, orthopedic, vision and mental. Such accurate figures will be highly useful in allocating sufficient resources for the development of disabled in the country. In the field of economic activity, a question has been introduced for the first time to find out the daily commuting done by persons to reach their place of work which happens to be substantial in the case of metros and major towns. This data will be extremely helpful in planning the urban transport facilities in these areas. The question related to economic activity include the complete details of industry in which the person is working (so that it can be classified as per National Industries Classification) and the detailed occupation of every worker (so that it can be classified as per the National Code of Occupation). For the first time concerted efforts have also been made to improve the recording of the women's work participation.

Manual as it is, the process of enumeration remains as tedious and long drawn as it was in 1901 when the total population was logged at 238,396,327. But what is different this time is the use of information technology in computing the figures. More than 24 lakh enumerators— men and women—have been commissioned by the Registrar-General and Census. Commissioner of India to reach each and every individual household both in urban and rural India. The preparation for this massive exercise was on for two years. Different processes are used in different countries. China, like India, also does manual enumeration through communes. But in the more developed countries such as the U.S. and the U.K., where the postal system is sound and literacy levels are high, census is done through the mail. Only Japan conducts a census every five years. It can afford to.

In short, this database shall prove to be a gold mine for planners, researchers, and private firms doing market research, apart from local self-governments. The 23 questions that being codified for each individual in a household will provide a variety of information for making policies and strategies for the growth and development of the nation. Religion is being codified as also Scheduled Castes and Scheduled Tribes which have been notified by respective States, though not OBCs. Curiously, there is no specific query on income levels, whereas this would have been an important index particularly when the Government was segregating the poor (below the poverty line population) from the non-poor (above the poverty line population) in targeting its benevolence in the food sector. Also, income levels would have given an index of the so-called middle class that is being wooed by multinationals as the largest chunk of consumers.

Several people in non-agriculture sector have been amused by a query on the distance of residence from place of work and the mode of travel. For the census officials, however, this all important question will provide information on the pressure on infrastructure, pollution, environment, roads etc. The mode of transport would indicate a development index and the pressure on individuals. This is a new query. The National Family Health Survey (NFHS-2), for instance, has recorded that the population density increased from 177 persons per kilometre raised to the power 2, in 1971 to 216 in 1981 and 267 in 1991, indicating increasing population pressure on land. Likewise, there are questions to indicate fertility rates, migration, unemployment and so on.

This census, however, is markedly different from the earlier ones in that it has made some attempt at being gender sensitive. In the category of work being done by individuals, the work carried on by a woman and a man have been recorded separately. Even cow milching by a woman for domestic use has to be coded. According to Ms. Prashar, an economically productive work has been defined as "any economically productive activity, with or without compensatory wages or profit, which may be physical or mental."

One of the most disturbing features of 2001 census is that some states, including Punjab, suffer from problem of the "missing girl child." In Punjab, where the girl child sex ratio has dipped to 793 per thousand boys, the Akal Takht issued an edict calling for ostracisation of those resorting to female foeticide.

The girl child in the country ratio now stands at a poor 927, compared to 934 ten years ago and 122 out of 591 districts have less than 900 daughters for 1000 sons.

Why the Concern?
- Sex ratio in India 2001: 933 females to 1,000 males (Fig. 3.1)
- In 0-6 years age group: 927:100
- The lowest in Daman and Diu: 709:1000
- Chandigarh 773:100
- Delhi 821:1,000
- Haryana 861:1,000
- Punjab 874:1,000

In the past 6 years, not a single doctor has been booked under Prenatal Diagnostic Techniques Act (IMA figures).

For the first time, perhaps, paid and unpaid women's work which is occasionally not reported has been included—labour on farm, rearing of goats, sale of farm produce, fish and vegetables, collection of tendu leaves, rice dehusking, grinding of masala, pottery, assisting in blacksmithy, family shops, manufacture of bamboo products, papad, pickles, products from embroidery, knitting, weaving, preparation of paper bags, book-binding, painting, poultry, rag-pickers, construction labour, running of beauty parlours and tuition at home.

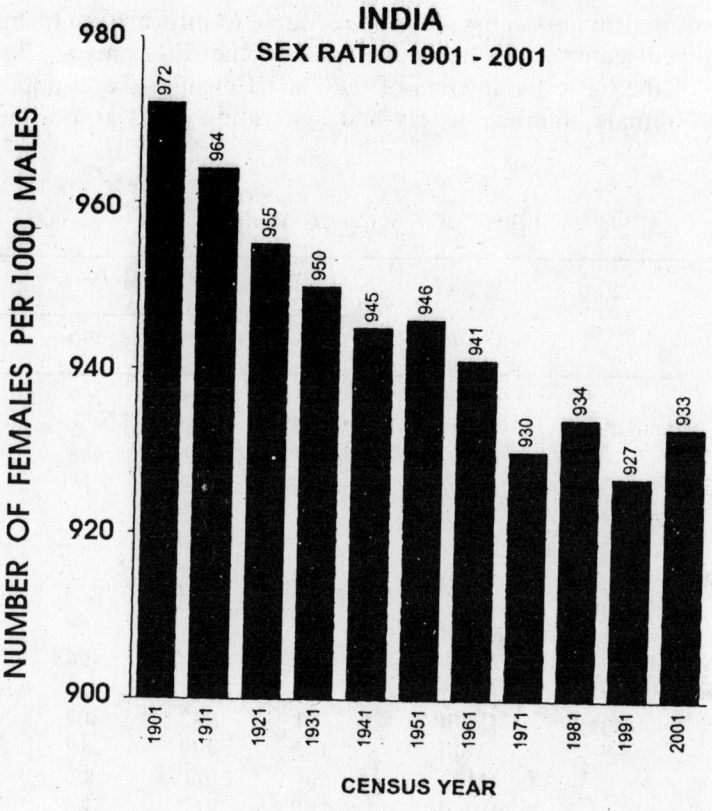

Fig. 3.1

The new millennium census of the biggest democracy, however, has shied away from the really gender-sensitive question of putting value to the unpaid domestic productivity of housewives. Raising children and doing household chores without a weekly off, which often results in lowering a woman's self-worth when children grow up and move away, is an issue women's groups have raised the world over. The Census India, however, said it was not possible to add value to the chores of a homemaker who was illiterate and to someone who was say, a doctor, doing the same work at home. With the claim it was not done anywhere in the world, they passed up an opportunity to be trendsetters.

While the Census department has been doing commendable work in translating raw data into a vast treasure house of information in the form of thematic and specialised reports, considerable effort needs to be directed at ensuring that private agencies and the average man derive the fullest benefit out of this mammoth operation. That could become a reality only if the data processed is disseminated far more rapidly than it has been in previous censuses. The recourse to information technology in the current census will hopefully make some difference.

Some of the basic parameters of the 2001 Census—Total population, male and female, literacy levels and sex ratios. This is presented in Table 3.3.

Table 3.3 Key Census Statistics

		1971	1981	1991	2001
Population	(Million)	548	683	846	1027
Density	(per mk^2)	177	216	267	324
Persons per household	(Number)	5.46	5.55*	N.A.	N.A.
Districts	(Number)	360	412	466	593
UAS/towns	(Number)	2,590	3,378	3,768	N.A.
Villages (inhabited)	('000s)	576	557*	N.A.	N.A.
Rural population	(Million)	439	524	629	N.A.
Urban population	(Million)	109	159	217	N.A.
Urban as % of total	(%)	19.9	23.3	25.7	N.A.
Male population	(Million)	284	353	438	531
Female population	(Million)	264	330	406	496
Female per 1,000 males	(Number)	930	934	929	N.A.
Workers*+	(Million)	181	242	307	N.A.
Male	(Million)	145	179	218	N.A.
Female	(Million)	36	63	89	N.A.
Birth rate	(per 1,000)	41.2	37.2	32.5	N.A.
Death rate	(per 1,000)	19.0	15.0	11.4	N.A.
Expectation of life at birth: (years		45.6	50.5	58.2	N.A.
Male	(Years)	46.4	50.9	57.7	N.A.
Female	(Years)	44.7	50.0	58.7	N.A.
Literacy rate	(%)	34.5	43.6*	52.1+	65.38
Male	(%)	46.0	56.4*	63.9+	75.85
Female	(%)	22.0	29.8*	39.4+	54.16

Note   :   1.   Birth rate and Death rate under 1991, 1981 & 1971 relate to 1981-90, 1971-80 and 1961-70 respectively; Expectation of life at birth to 1981-90, 1971-80 and 1961-70. Workers are total of main and marginal.

2.* Excluding Assam.

3.+ Excluding J&K

Source : Census of India, Registrar General & Census Commission, India.

SAMPLE REGISTRATION SCHEME

The utility of up-to-date and accurate demographic database hardly needs to be emphasized for the purposes of development planning. While decennial censuses conducted in India provide fairly adequate data on the population stock over time, data on the main population flows, namely, births, deaths and migration in a given period of time remain deficient and incomplete. Since 1970 onward the Sample Registration Scheme (SRS) has been able to provide comparatively good estimates of vital rates at the State and national levels for the rural and urban areas separately. Specific demographic surveys, on the other hand, have been conducted to throw light on the causes and consequences of changes in demographic processes over time, not only at the State and national levels but also at the levels of smaller areas.

In fact, demographic sample surveys covering larger areas have proved as an alternative to the Civil Registration System for providing estimates of the vital rates needed in evaluation of the on-going family planning programme in the country. Recently, National Family Health Survey (NFHS), the largest ever national representative sample survey covering 89,777 ever-married women aged 13-49 both in rural and urban areas provided a treasure-trove of information on fertility, family planning, child mortality, maternal and child health and immunization of children. The results of the survey are contained in 20 detailed reports giving the demographic and health scenario for 25 States and the nation.

The results of this survey have been widely disseminated and used in formulating population policies and programmes at the national as well the State level. Since in recent years the focus has been on decentralization of planning up to the level of district and block, it seems that we have to increase sample size and the coverage of various surveys to provide estimates at the district level. While the idea of conducting national-level comprehensive surveys is laudable to provide checks on the regular system of data flows, it must not be forgotten that repetition of such surveys before the lapse of 5 years is not advisable because of the time and cost involved. Moreover, analysis and utilization of data take some time. Much of the census data of 1991 is still not published for wider use. Collection of data through official systems has not only been found deficient but also has not been made available in time when most required for planning.

There is a need to strengthen the system on a regular basis. Already efforts are being made to improve the registration of births, deaths and marriages. Provision of electronic equipment at the grass-root level will certainly improve the collection and compilation of data as well as their onward transmission to higher levels. It will also facilitate the dissemination of information very fast at the district or even block level. Already the idea is being mooted to dispense with routine census-taking. However, we must ensure that a parallel system which is less cumbersome and less time-consuming should be evolved before we do away with the population census. In case civil registration is perfect, hundred per cent household surveys with less cost can be organised throughout the country with the help of health functionaries spread over the whole country in just two to three months with almost 100% accuracy to give the total number of households, their residents along with their ages and some basic characteristics. These household surveys will enable the health workers to assess also births, deaths and new marriages annually in the area. This is not at all difficult; in fact, in some States like Tamil Nadu, Madhya Pradesh and Rajasthan, such surveys have been conducted. All the eligible couples have been interviewed. Similarly, persons engaged in development and agriculture departments can be asked to conduct household inquiries on employment, occupation and persons engaged in organised activities. We have a large number of skilled and semi-skilled government servants in Central, State and local governments and the canvassing of schedules in the selected sectors will not be a difficult work. What is more required is to make them aware about the importance of data in effective provision of their services and encouragement for them to better equip them with skill for handling socio-economic data keeping in view the future prospect of their career improvement. This is a question worth pondering: how some non-governmental organisations are able to do better in collecting demographic data than the governmental agencies engaged in such jobs?

Strengthening of the official data system in the field of population, however, does not negate the need of the specific demographic surveys to study in detail the demographic behaviour of the population either at the national or at the sub-national level. However, development of new techniques in different fields of population studies can effectively help in bridging the data gaps. It is here that statistician demographers have to play their *role*. They must come out with better and improved techniques which do not depend on extraneous data needs and assumptions and rather depend on use of the indigenous data already available. Of course, this requires continuous research efforts, especially at the level of some well-known research organisations.

Estimation of Population Parameters

In any sample survey, our aim is to provide reasonable and acceptable estimates of various population characteristics based on the sample observations. These estimates are generally expressed in terms of averages and proportions, e.g. average number of children born/alive/desired/ideal, birth rate, death rate, infant mortality rate, etc. When the sample design is as simple as simple random sampling, the sample average or proportion can be safely used to obtain the estimates of the population parameters. In the complex sampling designs as adopted in various large-scale sample surveys like the NFHS where the units are considerably heterogeneous, the direct use of sample averages or proportions will provide considerably biased and misleading estimates.

In a large-scale sample survey with a complex sampling design, one has to give proper weightage to the sample estimates of various sections (or strata) so as to obtain acceptable estimates of the population characteristics for the whole domain of study.

A good deal of discussion regarding the use of appropriate sample weights can be found in the State-level reports of the NFHS. The interesting feature of the NFHS weights is that they provide adjustment factors (weights) for non-response in contrast to many other large-scale sample surveys conducted in India.

For the purpose of fruitful planning and policy-making pertaining to health and family welfare, it is necessary to have basic information at smaller regions within a State, such as districts or groups of districts. These data will be useful to chalk out requisite action programmes for the areas under study. For obtaining valid estimates of these smaller sub-divisions, it is necessary to increase the overall sample size which will definitely increase the work load and in turn may increase the non-sampling errors as mentioned earlier. Necessary precautions should be taken to minimize the non-sampling errors as much as possible either by reducing work load or by increasing field supervision during the data-collection and data-processing phases through the use of skilled and well-trained personnel.

In China, a one-in-thousand post-census sample survey was conducted in 1982 and it was found sufficiently representative to give estimates of important social, economic and demographic indicators even at country and State levels. In case of India, it would mean covering over 1.80 lakh households, almost double the number of households covered in the National Family Health Survey (NFHS). Further, every year, one-third of these households can be replaced to account for changes occurring in the population. Virtually, this much sample size scattered all over the country might be able to give estimates of major social, economic and demographic indicators even at the district level. As a matter of fact, some innovative survey technology has to be evolved to reduce data gap existing at the district level, on the one hand, and to standardize the data set, on the other hand. Probably, the sample size at the all-India level has to be almost triple of 1.80 lakh households to encompass both SRS and NSS coverages. If there is proper counselling, all data-collecting agencies at the national and State levels can pool their resources and streamline their efforts to collect relevant and most needed data by canvassing compact and less time-consuming shorter schedules. Even census-taking can be considered for only 10 per cent of the households and thereby time in conducting and processing the relevant data can be reduced considerably. There is an urgent need to reconsider new approaches to conducting population censuses and related surveys (Table 3.4).

INTERNATIONAL INCOME COMPARISONS

Allied with the population problems is an important issue relating to international income comparisons. A comparison of GNP and per capita income between countries is always problematic as exchange rates rarely reflect the true value of all incomes earned in a country. An alternative measure that is gaining acceptance is PPP. Inter-country comparisons are

Table 3.4 Agricultural Population and Population Economically Active in Agriculture as Estimated in 1997

(thousands)

Country	Total population	Agricultural population	Economically active population		
			Total	Agriculture	Percentage
WORLD	5848739	2564110	2827341	1301659	46.0
Algeria	29473	7263	9384	2348	25.0
Egypt	64465	24972	23928	8454	35.3
Sudan	27899	17773	10887	6936	63.7
Canada	29943	848	16019	419	2.6
Mexico	94281	23594	37538	8731	23.3
U.S.A.	271648	6615	138771	3174	2.3
Argentina	35671	3754	14100	1471	10.4
Brazil	163132	29365	75029	13876	18.5
Afghanistan	22132	15056	9196	6256	68.0
Bangladesh	122013	71551	61891	36294	58.6
China	1243738	851844	742843	508779	68.5
INDIA	960178	541391	420385	256358	61.0
Indonesia	203480	93884	95624	48206	50.4
Japan	125638	6010	66860	3236	4.8
Myanmar	46765	33273	24609	17509	71.2
Nepal	22591	21068	10492	9785	93.3
Pakistan	143831	75117	53013	25675	48.4
Bal-lux	10605	219	4385	90	2.1
France	58542	2278	26229	1021	3.9
Italy	57241	3521	25243	1553	6.2
U.K.	58426	1110	29179	555	1.9
Australia	18246	882	9240	447	4.8
Russian Fed	147708	16783	78276	8894	11.4

Source : 1. F.A.O. Production year book, 1977.
2. Indian Agriculture in Brief. 27th edition, 2000. Directorate of Economics and Statistics, Ministry of Agriculture, Government of India.

increasingly done on a PPP. Inter-country comparisons are increasingly done on a PPP basis, as this better evaluates the relative power of different currencies over equivalent goods and services.

The Gross National Product (GNP) of a country measured in conventional dollars differs considerably when compared with the purchasing power parity (PPP), a method adopted to evaluate real price levels between countries just as conventional price indices help calculate real values over time. The U.S. is taken as the standard and hence both normal and PPP values will be the same for that country.

The GNP of developing countries in PPP terms relative to the U.S. dollar is many times the GNP as measured on a conventional basis whereas the opposite is true of developed countries. In general, income differences between countries are narrower when measured on a PPP basis than with market exchange rates. The U.S. remains the largest economy by either measure, but the ranking of other countries changes.

An interesting finding is that Japan and Germany have lower GNPs in terms of PPP as compared to normal dollar values. But India, China and Mexico have their GNPs many times more than their conventional dollar values.

Indian Economy is Fourth Largest in the World

India has moved up from the fifth to fourth place in the world in purchasing power parity (PPP) terms, further enhancing its stature as an emerging economy with great potential.

India is now only behind the USA, China, which has moved up to the second place, and Japan in PPP calculations.

The figures for 1999, given in the World Bank's annual World Development Report, are: USA $8.351 billion, China $4,112.2 billion, Japan 3,042.9 and India 2,144.1 billion dollars.

Compared to the G-8 countries—the size of the Indian economy in PPP terms is ahead of six out of the eight G-8 powers, analysts said.

The figures for the G-8 other than the USA and Japan are: Germany $1,837.8 billion, France $1,293.8 billion, U.K. $1,234.4 billion, Italy $1,196.3 billion, Canada $726.1 billion and Russia $928.8 billion.

Pakistan has fallen significantly behind India in PPP terms despite the fact that the Pakistani per capita was ahead of India's both by conventional calculations and PPP.

The Indian per capita in PPP terms in 1999 was $2,149 and Pakistan's $1,757, though Pakistan is still ahead of India by $20 in conventional calculations—India $450 and Pakistan $470.

Per Capita Income

A clearer picture is now available about the various economies after the East Asian crisis of 1997-98. Per capita income levels in economies such as South Korea, Malaysia and Thailand have shown an upward move in 1999. Given the low base with which these countries growth levels are compared, advanced economies, with the exceptions of Sweden and the U.S, have only improved upon their incomes modestly. Switzerland, with an annual per capita of $38,350, tops the list. The U.S. with a per capita of $30,060, takes in the eighth position (Chart I).

The two economies which are in the international spotlight for the potential they hold out—China and India—registered growth rates of 6.3 per cent and 5.8 per cent respectively. Behind the seemingly comfortable position on per capita growth rates lies the realisation that the Indian per capita ($450) is still far below the threshold set for transcending the divide between low income and middle income economies ($755), in per capita income terms. China with a per capita income of $780, is at the lower and of the massive middle-income bracket ($755–$9,265).

Given this backdrop, a more realistic reflection could be gained from the GNP per capita based on the Purchasing Power Parity (PPP), which indicates the value of a dollar at the marketplace (Chart II), India with $2,149 on PPP terms occupies the 153rd position and China with $3,291 is 128th.

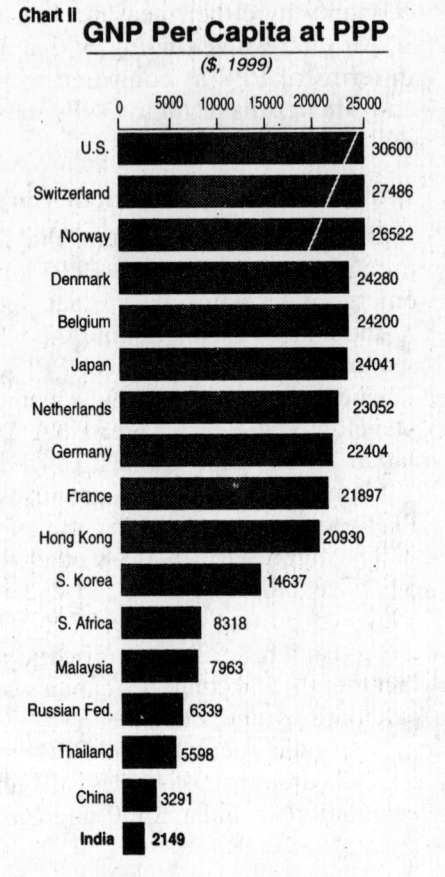

Chart II

GNP Per Capita at PPP
($, 1999)

U.S.	30600
Switzerland	27486
Norway	26522
Denmark	24280
Belgium	24200
Japan	24041
Netherlands	23052
Germany	22404
France	21897
Hong Kong	20930
S. Korea	14637
S. Africa	8318
Malaysia	7963
Russian Fed.	6339
Thailand	5598
China	3291
India	**2149**

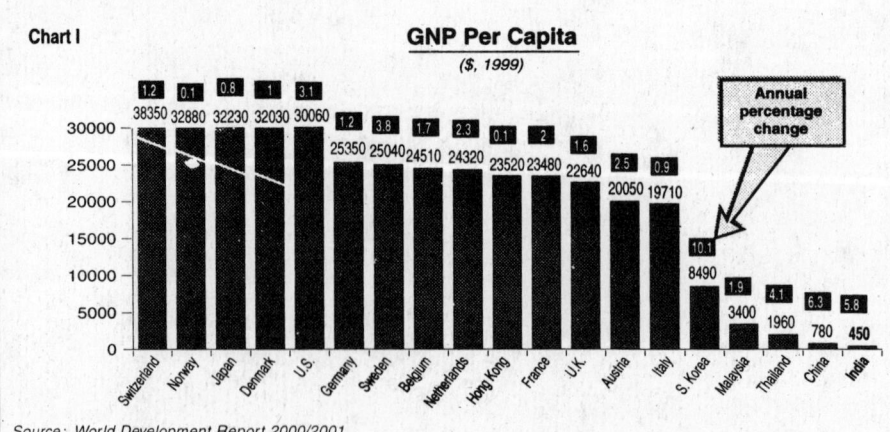

Chart I

GNP Per Capita
($, 1999)

Annual percentage change

Country	Value	Annual % change
Switzerland	38350	1.2
Norway	32880	0.1
Japan	32230	0.8
Denmark	32030	1
U.S.	30060	3.1
Germany	25350	1.2
Sweden	25040	3.8
Belgium	24510	1.7
Netherlands	24320	2.3
Hong Kong	23520	0.1
France	23480	2
U.K.	22640	1.6
Austria	20050	2.5
Italy	19710	0.9
S. Korea	8490	10.1
Malaysia	3400	1.9
Thailand	1960	4.1
China	780	6.3
India	450	5.8

Source: World Development Report 2000/2001

Urban Population

The urban population is exploding the word over. The growth of select cities with more than 10 million population is displayed in Chart I. Tokyo, Mumbai and Lagos are expected to grow faster than other cities listed here. Tokyo leads the chart with a population expected to rise to 30 million in 2015, nearly twice that of Delhi's projected population 15 years later. Mumbai in India had over five million in 1970 whereas its population shot up to 15 million in 1996 and may be nearly equal to Tokyo's by 2015.

The steepest growth is expected in Lagos. Its population which was 10 million in 1996 is projected to grow to 25 million 15 years from now. However, New York has been able to keep its population in check at around 16 million for three decades Shanghai's population has been growing less vigorously and is expected to exceed to 15 million in 2010 from 10 million in 1996.

Countrywise, (Chart II) China's urban population in nearly four times that of Japan and nearly a third of its total population live in urban agglomerates. Argentina, the Russian Federation, the U.K. the U.S. have nearly four-fifth's of their total population in urban places. India's urban population at 272 million (28 per cent of the total population) is also nearly three times that of Japan.

Chart II

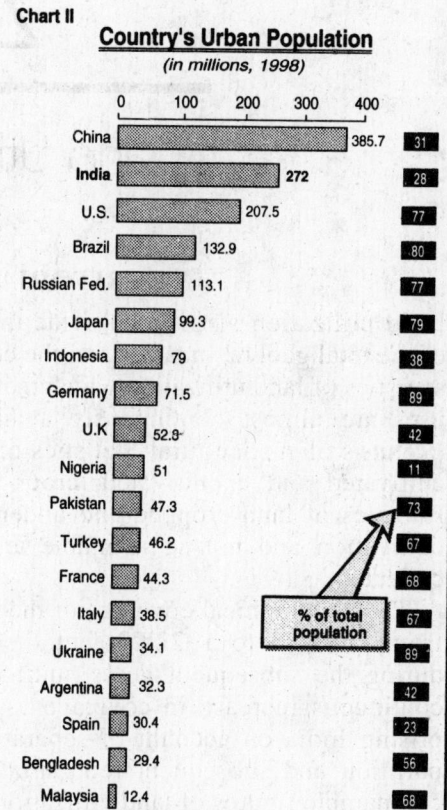

Country's Urban Population
(in millions, 1998)

Country	Urban Population (millions)	% of total population
China	385.7	31
India	272	28
U.S.	207.5	77
Brazil	132.9	80
Russian Fed.	113.1	77
Japan	99.3	79
Indonesia	79	38
Germany	71.5	89
U.K	52.9	42
Nigeria	51	11
Pakistan	47.3	73
Turkey	46.2	67
France	44.3	68
Italy	38.5	67
Ukraine	34.1	89
Argentina	32.3	42
Spain	30.4	23
Bangladesh	29.4	56
Malaysia	12.4	68

Chart I

The world's largest cities continue to boom

- ■ 1970
- ▨ 1996
- ▨ 2015

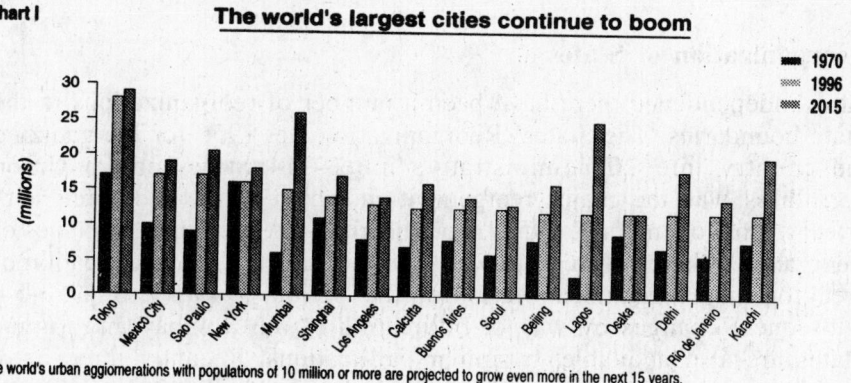

The world's urban agglomerations with populations of 10 million or more are projected to grow even more in the next 15 years.

Source: World Development Indicators, 2000

4

Land Utilization

TERRITORIAL DIVISION

Land utilization statistics provide the area figures showing distribution of the total geographical area of the country into its various uses. Detailed statistics of land utilization which mainly give area of land put to different uses are almost continuously available since 1884. In the year, the 'Returns of Agricultural Statistics of British India', gave details of area cultivated and uncultivated, crops cultivated and irrigation. Separate statistics of land cropped and under current fallows, land available for cultivation and not so available and of area under forests were also collected.

The geographical coverage of the statistics has continuously increased from 1884-85 to 1922-23, but there has been no substantial change during the subsequent years, until after the World War II. Due to the continuous increase in coverage as also changes in the territory comprising India on account of separation of Burma (now Myanmar), the partition and subsequent reorganizations of States from time to time, comparable figures of land utilization are not available over a long period of time.

Reorganization of States

After independence there have been a number of reorganizations in the State boundaries. The States' Reorganization Act 1956 for reorganizing the country into 20 administrative units—14 States and 6 Union Territories was the major reorganization which came into force with effect from November 1, 1956. A publication—Agricultural Statistics of Reorganized States—presents *inter alia* the statistics of classification of area for the reorganized States for the period 1949-50 to 1953-54. Subsequent changes by way of bifurcation of the Bombay and Punjab States are also available in similar publications. Recently three more states have been carved out of Uttar Pradesh, Madhya Pradesh and Bihar. Broad changes in this respect have been detailed in Appendix 1.

ADMINISTRATIVE SET-UP

Before examining suggestions in respect of improvements required in the compilation of agricultural statistics it is desirable to have a general idea of the administrative background through which the system of agricultural statistics in India has been operating. The collection of agricultural statistics is taken as a by-product of the normal departmental activities of the State Governments which are primarily responsible for the compilation of these statistics. The Government at the Centre functions only in an advisory capacity and is concerned with coordination, consolidation and timely publication of statistics furnished by the State Governments. Within the States, the collection of agricultural statistics is entrusted principally to the staff of the Department of Land Records. This organization is not, however, uniform in all the States. In fact, the States can be broadly divided into two classes, viz. (i) temporarily settled; and (ii) permanently settled. In the former, land revenue is fixed for a definite period of years and is subject to revision at the end of this period, while in the latter the rate has been fixed for perpetuity. An elaborate revenue agency extending to the remotest village exists in the temporarily settled States. In every village or a group of 3 to 4 villages, depending on their size there is a primary reporter[1] who resides locally and is well informed of the agricultural and economic conditions in the area under his jurisdiction. There are Revenue Inspectors, each incharge of a circle, and above them are the supervising officers at the level of tehsils/sub-divisions and districts which form principal administrative units of the States. This organization is mostly entrusted with the collection and compilation of agricultural statistics. There is no such elaborate official agency available in the permanently settled States. The only land records organization available in these States consists of officers at thanas/sub-divisions and each officer in charge of 100 to 150 villages. The responsibility of coordinating statistics within each State both temporarily and permanently settled, rest with the Director of land Records or the Director of Agriculture or in some State with both the organization.

CLASSIFICATION OF LAND UTILIZATION

Before 1950-51, the land utilization statistics were available under five categories, namely, (i) forests, (ii) area not available for cultivation, (iii) other uncultivated land excluding current fallows, (iv) fallow land, and (v) net area sown. This five-fold classification was found to be insufficient to meet the needs of agricultural planning. Based on the recommendation of in Technical Committee on Condition of Agricultural Statistics, 1949, a more detailed classification was introduced in 1950-51.

---

[1]The primary reporter is called 'Patwari' in Punjab, Haryana, Jammu & Kashmir, Himachal Pradesh, Delhi, Rajasthan and Madhya Pradesh; 'Lekhpal' in U.P.; 'Karnam' in Tamil Nadu and Andhra Pradesh; 'Shanbhog' in Karnataka; 'Karamchari' in Bihar; 'Mandal' in Assam; and 'Pravartiyar' in Kerala.

The existing nine-fold classifications with standard concepts and definitions adopted are given in Table 4.1.

Table 4.1

Classification	Definition
1. Forest	Area under forests include all lands classed as forests under any legal enactment dealing with forests or administrated as forests, whether state-owned or private, and whether wooded or maintained as potential forest land. The area where crops are raised in the forest and grazing lands and areas open for grazing within the forests should be included under the appropriate heading.
2. Area not available for cultivation:	
(a) Barren and unculturable land	This covers all barren and unculturable land like mountains, deserts, etc. Land which cannot be brought under cultivation unless at a high cost shall be classed as unculturable, whether such land is in isolated blocks or within cultivated holdings.
(b) Land put to non-agricultural use	All lands occupied by buildings, roads and railways or under water, e.g. rivers and canals and other lands put to uses other than agriculture.
3. Other uncultivated land excluding current fallow:	
(a) Permanent pastures and other grazing lands	These cover all grazing lands whether they are permanent pastures and meadows or not. Other common grazing lands at the village are included under this head.
(b) Miscellaneous treecrops and groves not included in the sown area	Under this class is included all cultivated land which is not included under 'net area sown' but is put to some agricultural use. Lands under casurina trees, thatching grass, bamboo bushes and other groves for fuel, etc. which are not included under orchards are classed under this category.
(c) Cultivable Waste	These include all lands available for cultivation whether not taken up for cultivation or taken up for cultivation once, but not cultivated during the current year and last five years or more in succession; such lands may be either fallow or covered with shrubs and jungles which are not put to any use (they may be assessed or unassessed and may be isolated blocks or within cultivated holdings), land once cultivated but not cultivated for five years in succession is also included in this category at the end of the five years.
4. Fallow lands:	
(a) Current fallow	This class comprises cropped areas which are kept fallow during the current year; for example, if any seeding area is not cropped again in the same year, it is treated as current fallow.

Table 4.1 *(Contd.)*

Classification	Definition
(b) Fallow land other than current fallows	This refers to all lands which were taken up for cultivation but are temporarily out of cultivation for a period of not less than one year but not more than five years, the reasons for keeping lands fallow may be either poverty of cultivators or inadequate supply of water or malarial climate or silting of canal and rivers or unremunerative nature of farming.
5. Net area sown:	This represents the area sown with crops and orchards, counting areas sown more than once in the same year only once.
Utilizing above information some additional statistics are worked out.	
6. Area sown more than once:	This refers to area on which crops are cultivated more than once during each agricultural year. This is obtained by deducting net area sown from the total cropped area.
7. Total cropped area:	This represents the area covered with crops. This is the sum total of the areas covered by all the individual crops, areas sown with crops for more than once during the year being counted as separate areas for each crop. This can also be obtained by subtracting total areas under classes 1 to 4 from the geographical area.

The total of these classes under each classification adds up to the reporting area according to village papers. The revised classification has been accepted in principle by all the States and has been adopted in the 1950-51 issue of the Indian Agricultural Statistics. The new classification has since been introduced by all the States except West Bengal and Manipur, in respect of which data are still presented on the basis of the old classification. The adoption of the revised classification has introduced an element of non-comparability in the land utilization statistics. For instance, 'current fallows' in the old classification in vogue up to 1949-50 has been broken up into 'other fallow lands' and 'current fallows' in the new classification. In the erstwhile Bombay State, lands lying fallow up to a period of ten years were till 1949-50 included under current fallows. In terms of the new classification, lands lying fallow for a period of two to five years are included under 'other fallow lands' and those lying fallow beyond a period of five years under 'cultivable waste' or even under 'miscellaneous tree crops and groves not included in the net area sown'. On the other hand, in Punjab, lands lying fallow up to a period of two years were included under 'current fallows' while those lying fallow for more than two years were included under 'other uncultivated land excluding current fallows'. Thus it is not possible to have comparable figures for 1950-51 onwards and those for the earlier years. It is now being proposed to have a twenty two fold classification (Table 4.2).

Table 4.2 Twenty-two Fold Classification

1. *Built up land*

    It is defined as an area of human habitation developed due to non-agricultural use and that which has a cover of buildings, transport, communication utilities in association with water vegetation and vacant lands.

    Agricultural land: It is defined as the land primarily used for farming and for production of food, fiber, other commercial and horticultural crops. It includes land under crops (irrigated and un-irrigated), fallow, plantation etc.

2. *Crop land*

    It includes those lands with standing crop (*per se*) as on the date of the satellite imagery. The crops may be of either kharif (June-September) or Rabi (October-March) or Kharif Rabi seasons.

3. *Fallow land*

    It is described as agricultural land which is taken up for cultivation but is temporarily allowed to rest un-cropped for one or more seasons, but not less than one year. These lands are particularly those which are seen devoid of crops at the time when the imagery is taken of both seasons.

4. *Plantations*

    It is described asn an area under agricultural tree crops, planted adopting certain agricultural management techniques. It includes tea, coffee, rubber, coconut, arecanut, citrus, orchards and other horticultural nurseries.

    Forest: It is an area (within the notified foest boundary) bearing an association predominantly of trees and other vegetation types capable of producing timber and other forest produce.

5. *Evergreen/Semi-evergreen forest*

    It is described as a forest which comprises of thick and dense canopy of tall trees which predominantly remain green throughout the year. It includes both coniferous and tropical broad leaved evergreen trees Semi-evergreen forest is a mixture of both deciduous and evergreen trees but the latter predominate.

6. *Decidous forest*

    It is described as a forest which predominantly comprises of deciduous species and where the trees shed their leaves once in a year.

7. *Degraded forest or Scrub*

    It is described as a forest where the vegetative (crown) density is less than 20% of the canops cover. It is the result of both biotic and abiotic influences. Scrub is a stunted tree or bush/shrub.

8. *Forest Blank*

    It is described as openings amidst forests without any tree cover. It includes openings of assorted size and shapes as seen on the imagery.

9. *Forest Plantations*

    It is described as an area of trees of species of forestry importance and raised on notified forest lands. It includes, eucalyptus, casuarina, bamboo etc.

10. *Mangrove*

    It is described as a dense thicker or woody aquatic vegetation or forest cover occurring in tidal waters near estuaries and along the confluence of delta in coastal areas. It includes species of the general Rhizophora and Aviccunia.

Table 4.2 Twenty-two Fold Classification (*Contd.*)

> *Wastelands:* It is described as degraded land which can be brought under vegetative cover with reasonable water and soil management or on account of natural causes. Wastelands can result from internet/imposed constraints such as, by location, environment, chemical and physical prosperities of the soil or financial or management constraints (NWDB 1987).

11. *Salt affected land*

    The salt affected land is generally characterized as the land that has adverse effects on the growth of most plants due to the action or presence of excess soluble or high exchangeable sodium. Alkaline land has an exchangeable sodium percentage (ESP) of about 15 which is generally considered as the limit between normal and alkali soils. The predominant salts are carbonates and bicarbonates of sodium Coastal saline goils may be with or without ingress or inundation by sea water.

12. *Waterlogged land*

    Waterlogged land is that land where the water is at/or near the surface and water stands for most of the year. Such lands usually occupy topographically low lying areas, It excludes lakes, ponds and tanks.

13. *Marshy/Swampy land*

    Marshy land is that which is permanently or periodically inundated by water and is characterized to vegetation which includes grasses and weeds. Marshes are classified into salt/brackish or fresh water depending on the salinity of water. These exclude Mangroves.

14. *Gullied/Ravenous land*

    The gullies are formed as a result of localized surface runoff affecting the friable unconsolidated material in the formation of perceptible channels resulting in undulating terrain. The gullies are the first stage of excessive land dissection followed by their networking which leads to the development of ravenous land. The word 'ravine' is usually associated not with an isolated gully, but a network of deep gullies formed generally in thick alluvium and entering a nearby river, flowing much lower than the surrounding high grounds. The ravines, are extensive systems of gullies developed along river courses.

15. *Land with or without scrub*

    They occupy (relatively) higher topography like uplands or high grounds with or without scrub. These lands are generally prone to degradation or erosion. These exclude hilly and mountainous terrain.

16. *Sandy area (coastal and desertic)*

    These areas which have stabilized accumulations of sand in-site or transported in coastal riverine or inland (desert) areas. These occur either in the form of sand dunes, beaches, channel (river/stream) islands, etc.

17. *Baren rocky/Stony waste/Sheet rock area*

    It is defined as the rock exposures of varying lithology often barren and devoid of soil cover and vegetation and not suitable for cultivation. They occur amidst hill forests as openings or scattered as isolated exposures or loose fragments of boulders or as sheet rocks on plateau and plains. It includes quarry or gravel pit or brick kilns.

    > *Water bodies:* It is an area of impounded water, area in extent and often with a regulated flow of water. It includes man-made reservoirs/lakes/tank/canals, besides natural lakes, rivers/streams and creeks.

Table 4.2 Twenty-two Fold Classification   (Contd.)

18. *River/Stream*
    It is a course of flowing water on the land along definite channels. It includes from a small stream to a big river and its branches. It may be perennial or non-perennial.

19. *Reservoir/Lakes/Tanks/Canal*
    It is a natural or man made enclosed water body with a regulated flow of water. Reservoirs are larger than tanks/lakes and are used for generating electricity, irrigation and for flood control. Tanks are smaller in areal extent with limited use than the former. Canals are inland waterways used for irrigation and sometimes for navigation.
    Others: It includes all those which can be treated as miscellaneous because of their nature of occurrence, physical appearance and other characteristics.

20. *Shifting Cultivation*
    It is the result of cyclic landuse practice of felling of trees and burning of forest areas for growing crops. Such lands are also known as Jhum lands. This result in extensive loss of soil leading to land degradation.

21. *Grassland/Grazing land*
    It is an area of land covered with natural grass along with other vegetation, often grown for fodder to feed cattle and other animals. Such lands are found in river beds, on uplands, hill slopes etc. Such lands can also be called as permanent pastures or meadows. Grazing land are those where certain pockets of land are fenced for allowing cattle graze.

22. *Snow covered/Glacial area*
    It is snow covered areas defined as a solid form of water consisting of minute particles of ice. It includes permanently as on the Himalayas. Glacier is a mass of accumulated ice occuring amidst permanently snow covered areas.

Geographical Area

Total geographical area according to Surveyor General of India relates to whole of Indian Union. The latest available figure for the State/Union Territory/a district as furnished by the Central Statistical Organization based on the data released by the Surveyor General of India is used.

Reporting Area for Land Utilization Purposes

The reporting area stands for the area for which data on land use classification are available. Where land utilization figures are based on land records, reporting area is the one according to village papers, i.e. the papers prepared by the village accountant. In some cases the village papers may not be maintained in respect of the entire area of the State. For example, such papers are not prepared for the forest area but the magnitude of such area is known: also there are tracts in many States for which no village papers exist but for which ad hoc estimates of classification of area, etc., are framed to complete the coverage. In such cases, this gives the summation of the area for which village papers actually exist and the area for which ad hoc estimates are available.

Out of total geographical area of 328 million hectares, land-use statistics are available for about 305 million hectares which constitute roughly 93.3 per cent of the total area (Table 4.3). Thus only for about 6.7 per cent of the geographical area these data are not available. Of the 23 million hectares for which land-use data are not available, 17.7 million hectares are located in Jammu and Kashmir. The non-reporting areas in other States largely consist of hill-tracts in Arunachal Pradesh, Nagaland, Manipur and Tripura. Besides, there are small tracts in some States covered either by forests or barren mountains which are not accessible. Efforts are being made to bring these non-reporting areas under 'reporting'.

Forest

Area under 'Forests' includes all actually forested areas or lands classed or administered as forests under any legal enactment dealing with forests whether state-owned or private. If any portion of such land is not actually wooded but put to some agricultural use, that portion is included under the appropriate head of cultivated or uncultivated land.

The figures of area under forests are collected by the Forest Departments in the States and published in Indian Forest Statistics. The two sets of figures had a discrepancy of 14.1 million hectares till recently because of the following means. There is, however, no such difference now.

(i) Certain lands not covered by forests but worked by Forest Departments, are counted as forests by the Forest Departments and included in the area under forests, while the same are not treated as forests by the Revenue or Agriculture Departments and are put under any of the heads according to their use such as 'other uncultivated land excluding fallow lands', if they are covered with shrubs, bamboos, or other grasses, and under 'net area sown' they are cultivated.

(ii) The forest areas deemed to be 'unprofitable' and some of the areas administered as forests by corporated bodies or private individuals are sometimes classified by some States as 'area not available for cultivation' or 'other uncultivated land excluding fallow lands.'

(iii) Difference in coverage both in respect of period and area.

(iv) Difference in the methods followed by the two Departments in the enumeration of forest areas.

Areas Not Available for Cultivation

(a) *Land put to Non-agricultural Uses*. This stands for all lands occupied by buildings, industrial undertakings, roads and railways or underwater, e.g. rivers and canals and all other lands put to any other non-agricultural uses.

Table 4.3 Land Use Classification in India

(million ha.)

Classification	1950-51	1960-61	1970-71	1980-81	1990-91	1991-92	1992-93	1993-94P	1994-95P	1995-96P	1996-97P
Geographical Area	328.71	328.71	328.71	328.71	328.71	328.71	328.71	328.71	328.71	328.71	328.71
I. Reporting Area for land utilisation statistics (1 to 5)	284.32	298.46	303.76	304.15	304.86	299.62	304.85	304.79	304.87	303.89	304.81
1. Forests	40.48	54.05	63.91	67.47	67.80	67.87	67.98	68.28	68.39	68.82	68.75
	(14.2)	(18.1)	(21.0)	(22.2)	(22.2)	(22.3)	(22.3)	(22.4)	(22.5)	(22.6)	(22.5)
2. Not available for cultivation (a+b)	47.52	50.75	44.64	39.62	40.48	40.74	40.89	40.90	41.28	41.38	41.54
(a) Non Agricultural Uses	9.36	14.84	16.48	19.66	21.09	21.47	21.77	22.21	22.51	22.37	22.45
	(3.3)	(5.0)	(5.4)	(6.4)	(6.9)	(7.0)	(7.2)	(7.2)	(7.4)	(7.3)	(7.4)
(b) Barren and uncultivable land	38.16	35.91	28.16	19.96	19.39	19.27	19.12	18.69	18.77	19.01	19.09
	(13.4)	(12.0)	(9.3)	(6.6)	(6.4)	(6.3)	(6.2)	(6.2)	(6.1)	(6.2)	(6.3)
3. Other uncultivated land (excluding fallow land (a+b+c))	49.45	37.64	35.06	32.31	30.22	30.05	29.47	29.08	29.08	28.64	28.48
(a) Permanent Pastures and other grazing land	6.68	13.97	13.26	11.97	11.40	11.30	11.10	10.97	11.24	11.06	11.04
	(2.3)	(4.7)	(4.4)	(3.9)	(3.7)	(3.7)	(3.6)	(3.6)	(3.6)	(3.6)	(3.6)
(b) Miscellaneous tree crops and groves	19.83	4.46	4.30	3.60	3.82	3.76	3.78	3.70	3.63	3.48	3.5
	(7.0)	(1.5)	(1.4)	(1.2)	(1.2)	(1.2)	(1.2)	(1.2)	(1.2)	(1.2)	(1.2)
(c) Cultivable Wasteland	22.94	19.21	17.50	16.74	15.00	14.99	14.59	14.41	14.21	14.10	13.94
	(8.1)	(6.4)	(5.8)	(5.5)	(4.9)	(4.9)	(4.8)	(4.7)	(4.7)	(4.6)	(4.6)
4. Fallow Land (a+b)	28.12	22.82	19.88	24.75	23.36	24.61	23.86	24.21	23.30	23.85	23.22
(a) Fallow land other than current Fallow	17.44	11.18	8.76	9.92	9.66	9.94	9.67	9.83	9.77	10.02	9.89
	(6.1)	(3.8)	(2.9)	(3.3)	(3.2)	(3.3)	(3.2)	(3.2)	(3.3)	(3.3)	(3.2)
(b) Current Fallow	10.68	11.64	11.12	14.83	13.70	14.67	14.39	14.38	13.53	13.83	13.33
	(3.8)	(3.9)	(3.5)	(4.9)	(4.5)	(4.8)	(4.7)	(4.7)	(4.3)	(4.5)	(4.4)

Table 4.3 Land Use Classification in India (Contd.)

(million ha.)

5. Net area sown (6-7)	118.75	133.20	140.27	140.00	137.76	141.63	142.65	142.42	142.82	141.20	142.82
	(41.8)	(44.6)	(46.3)	(46.0)	(46.9)	(46.5)	(46.8)	(46.7)	(46.9)	(46.7)	(46.8)
6. Gross cropped area	131.89	152.77	165.79	172.63	185.74	182.24	185.62	186.60	188.15	186.47	489.54
7. Area sown more than once	13.14	19.57	25.52	32.63	47.98	40.61	42.97	44.18	45.33	45.27	46.72
8. Cropping intensity*	111.10	114.70	118.20	123.30	129.88	128.67	130.12	131.74	131.28	131.28	132.70
III. Net irrigated area	20.85	24.66	31.10	38.72	47.78	49.87	50.30	51.34	53.00	53.40	55.14
IV. Gross irrigated area	22.56	27.98	38.19	49.78	62.47	65.68	66.76	68.25	70.64	71.35	73.28

Note : 1. P: Provisional, 2. *: Cropping intensity is obtained by dividing the gross cropped area by the net area sown

3. Figure in parenthesis indicate percentage to Reported area

Source : *Agricultural Statistics at a Glance, 2000*, Directorate of Economics and Statistics, Ministry of Agriculture, Government of India

(b) *Barren and Uncultivable Land*. This covers all barren and uncultivable lands like mountains, deserts, etc. Lands which cannot be brought under cultivation without incurring heavy expenditure on their development are classed as unculturable, such land could be outside or within cultivated holdings.

In Rajasthan, lands classified under this head lie mostly in the Thar desert, where the soil is sandy and rainfall is below 20 inches. In other States, they are generally in districts where the topography is hilly or is covered with laterites or such soils as are highly infertile, stony and coarse, and the rainfall is insufficient so that it is hardly possible to develop or cultivate these lands at a reasonable cost.

Other Uncultivated Land Excluding Current Fallows

(a) *Permanent Pastures and Other Grazing Lands*. These cover all grazing lands, whether they are permanent pastures and meadows or not, The common land in the village and grazing lands within the forest areas are included under this head.

(b) *Miscellaneous Tree Crops and Groves Not Included in the Net Area Sown*. All the culturable land put to some agricultural use but not included under 'net area sown' is included under this class. Lands under thatching grasses, bamboo bushes and other groves, trees for fuel, etc. which are not included under orchards are placed in this category.

(c) *Culturable Waste*. These include lands available for cultivation whether or not taken up for cultivation or abandoned after a few years for one reason or the other. Such lands may be either fallow covered with shrubs and jungles which are not put to any use. They may be assessed or unassessed and may be in isolated blocks or within cultivated holdings. Land once cultivated but not cultivated for five years in succession is included in this category. It is a sort of residual class which includes all uncultivated lands not accounted for by any other class.

It is a misnomer to assume that all the 17.36 million hectares of land under this head is available for cultivation as the definition of the term will suggest. A Waste Land Survey Committee went into this matter in 1959 and studied the position for 7 important States. Land available for cultivation in holdings over 100 hectares was estimated by them as 450 thousand hectares. Another survey for locating waste lands in smaller blocks was taken up during the Third Plan. An additional area of 2.2 million hectares was located which could be available for cultivation.

Fallow Lands

(a) Fallow Land Other than Current Fallows. This includes all lands which were taken up for cultivation but are temporarily out of cultivation for a period of not less than one year and not more than five years. The reasons for keeping such land fallow may be one of the following:

  (i) Inability of farmers to cultivate or lack of means.
 (ii) Inadequate water supply.
(iii) Malarial climate.
(iv) Silting of canals and rivers.
 (v) Soil erosion.
(vi) Unremunerative nature of farming.

(b) Current Fallow. This class comprises cropped areas which are kept fallow during the current year. For example, if any seedling area is not cropped again in the same year it is treated as current fallow.

There is, however, a close relationship between the 'fallow lands' and the 'net area sown' since there are frequent shift-overs from one to the other. Good and timely rainfall, weather conditions, prices, political stability, security of tenure and tenancy conditions help in increasing the area sown.

Net Area Sown

It represents the actual physical area under crops and orchards. Area cropped more than once is counted only once. The total cropped area represents the sum total of area under all crops. The difference between the total cropped area and net area sown is accounted for by the area sown more than once on the same land during the same year with the same or different crops.

It will be noted that the above details give the classification of land according to its actual use, but not according to its potential use. Thus, area under culturable waste does represent the area really cultivable as discussed later.

INDIAN AGRICULTURAL STATISTICS

The coverage for land utilization statistics which was restricted to 284.3 million hectares in 1950-51 from a total geographical area of 328.73 million hectares has gone up to 304.81 million hectares by now. These data are now being published in the annual publication entitled 'Indian Agricultural Statistics' Vols. I and II issued by the Directorate of Economics and Statistics, Ministry of Agriculture, Government of India.

'Indian Agricultural Statistics, Vol. I' is a continuing volume of the publication entitled 'British India Agricultural Statistics (provisional)' formerly published by the Department of Commercial Intelligence and Statistics with some changes in contents and rearrangement of tables. Between 1940-41 and 1948-49 combined issues giving data for more than one year were published. Besides, due to changes in the constitutional set-up, the scope of different issues was also different. For example, up to 1943-44, the British India Agricultural Statistics (provisional) gave figures in respect of the British Indian Provinces and Centrally Administered Areas of undivided India. For the years 1944-45 to 1946-47, this publication called 'Indian Agricultural Statistics, Summary Tables for Provinces' gave statistics in respect of former Provinces of Indian Union and Centrally Administered Areas. From 1947-48 onwards, this publication furnishes area statistics of all the reporting States, under the new administrative set-up. Further, statistics relating to livestock, harvest prices and land revenue which were published up to the year 1946-47 as part of Indian Agricultural Statistics, are being issued in separate publication, since 1947-48.

Indian Agricultural Statistics Vol. I (latest issue relates to the year 1996-97).

The all-India figures given in the Summary Table relate to 10 years while those for the individual States are given for 5 years.

Indian Agricultural Statistics Vol. II—Detailed Tables (latest issue relates to the year 1990-91) furnish State-wise and district-wise figures of classification of area, area irrigated and crops irrigated and area under crops. Summary Tables giving all-India figures contain data for 10 years. The State-wise figures are for.5 years and district-wise for 2 years.[2] As in the case of Vol. I, the information is based on returns received from the State Governments concerned. Volume II also gives an Introductory Note, dealing with the salient features of rainfall, land utilization, irrigation and cropping pattern of the year.

Volume II of Indian Agricultural Statistics is a continuation volume of Vols. I and II of Agricultural Statistics of India earlier published by the Department of Commercial Intelligence and Statistics up to 1938-39. From 1939-40 onwards there have been changes in the title and contents of these publications.

SEASON AND CROP REPORTS

While the all-India land utilization statistics are published in the Indian Agricultural Statistics, the individual States publish these statistics in respect of their States in the Season and Crop Reports, which besides land utilization statistics, give figures for area and production of crops, area irrigated and sources of irrigation, livestock statistics, prices, etc. Barring Rajasthan, Jammu & Kashmir and West Bengal all the States and the Union Territories of Delhi and Himachal Pradesh publish Season and Crop Reports. The scope of the Season and Crop Reports published by various States, however, differs. With a view to eliminating the wide disparity in the nature and mode of presentation of information, a model Season and Crop Report was prepared in the Directorate of Economics and Statistics and circulated to the States for adoption. All States except Orissa, Assam, Rajasthan and West Bengal have adopted the model Season and Crop Report.

---

[2]The combined issue for 1954-55 and 1955-56 of Indian Agricultural Statisics Vol. II gives District-wise figures for 4 years.

The statistics of land utilization published in the respective Season and Crop Reports generally agree with those published in the Indian Agricultural Statistics. In some cases, however, the Season and Crop Reports give the latest figures based on information received from some districts subsequent to the submission of the annual returns of agricultural statistics to the Central Government. In such cases the two sets of figures differ.

The utility of the land use statistics is further limited by the inordinate time-lag in their publication. The fully revised data on total cropped area and its distribution by specific crops is normally available with a lag of two years; though the latest estimates relate only to 1997-98. The lags in the publication of gross irrigated area by crops is even longer—latest available information pertains only to 1996-97. Even this estimate is provisional and subject to revision as more complete returns become available from the States.

In an effort to reduce the time-lag, the Ministry of Agriculture introduced some years ago a timely reporting scheme (TRS) by which each State was required to report the estimates of area sown soon after the completion of sowing on the basis of complete enumeration of plots in either one village from each Patwari circle or one village from out of every five villages. (It was also proposed as a means of checking the accuracy of TRS data, that the land use and crop cutting survey of the NSS should use a sub-sample of TRS villages as its sample.)

Apart from the question of time-lag, there are problems of conceptual nature. The lack of standardization in the forms used in recording cropped area by the primary reporting agency in different States and in the treatment of particular items, for example, are under mixed crops and source of irrigation, is a major problem. The efficiency of the primary reporting agency also seems to vary widely from State to State. In fact some States do not seem to maintain up-to-date record of irrigated area, a fact which is reflected in the non-reporting of some of the irrigated areas for several years. The problem has been discussed at considerable length in the past and an attempt has been made to define and evaluate uniform concept for recording. There is little information on the progress in implementing these suggestions.

Studies of changes in land use pattern and associated factors are helpful in locating imbalances in the utilization of land resources policies and in formulating to correct them. In view of considerable regional variations in utilization of land resources, such studies are more revealing and useful when carried out at the State and district level. This, however, becomes rather difficult on account of what may be termed as statistical changes that have taken place due to:

(a) variation in reporting area owing to (i) changes in district boundaries, and (ii) extension of reporting as a result of cadastral survey and institution of reporting agency;

(b) transfer of area from one category to another in the process of adoption of revised concepts, definitions and classifications in the same or different years in the different parts of the State; and

(c) changes made in the district boundaries and transfers to districts from one State to another consequent on States reorganization in 1956 and at other subsequent dates as discussed elsewhere.

WEAKNESSES OF THE LAND UTILIZATION STATISTICS

Detailed statistics of land use which mainly give area of land put to different agricultural uses are available almost continuously from 1887-88, although coverage of these statistics has been changing from time to time and their scope gradually expanding. Present coverage of land use and crop statistics is about 93 per cent[3] of the total area of the country, i.e. 77 per cent covered by complete enumeration, 5 per cent by sample surveys and another 11 per cent by conventional estimates. Since the remaining non-reporting area of 7 per cent is mainly covered by hills and forests and there is very little cultivation on it, the present position of land use in the country could be considered as quite satisfactory although there is still scope for improvement.

According to 'Wastelands Survey and Reclamation Committee,' although classification suggested by the Ministry of Agriculture had been adopted in all the States, the concept of the term 'Uncultivated lands excluding fallow lands' is not yet clearly understood. Lands which were classified as 'culturable waste' at the time of settlement, same areas are still continued to be shown as such in the Revenue Records even though they cannot be made culturable after incurring any reasonable expenditure. Similarly, some of the lands which are culturable, continue to be classified as barren and unculturable or pasture lands. In some other cases, pasture lands have been included in the category of culturable waste.[4]

In view of these considerations, the Committee expressed the view that the areas included in the two categories, viz. 'other uncultivated lands excluding fallow land' and 'fallow lands other than current fallows' may not fairly represent the actual extent of culturable wastelands in the country, and accordingly much reliance could not be placed on the statistics supplied by the State Government.[5]

The non-comparability of concepts and definitions creates a difficulty in the way of determining the land utilization trends over a period of time. Besides the changing definitions, another great difficulty in examining the trends for various land utilization categories is the fact

---

[3]This was 69 per cent before the First Five Year Plan.

[4](i) Report on Location and Utilization of Wastelands in India, Part VI, Madhya Pradesh, p. (ii) "Indian agriculturable statistics, a critical review," Agricultural Situation in India. Annual Number, August 1960, p. 531.

[5]Ib d., p. iii.

that the increase under any category may be solely or partly due to an increase in the reporting area.

The area statistics figures generally relate to the agricultural year ending 30th June, but in the case of Assam and Madhya Pradesh they relate to the years ending 31st March and 31st May respectively. Land utilization statistics for West Bengal are still collected under the old classification. The classification adopted for reporting the land utilization statistics of the State is not, therefore, as elaborate as in other States. A comparison of the data in this State with the other States is, therefore, untenable. Precision for the total area under these sub-heads thus is lost. Over-time non-comparability is augmented by the fact that prior to 1919-20, some of the former Provinces adopted the financial year, while others followed the agricultural year; for the former Princely States, the year to which the figures relate differ from State to State.

COLLECTION OF AGRICULTURAL STATISTICS IN KERALA, ORISSA AND WEST BENGAL

In Kerala, Orissa and West Bengal which are permanently settled in revenue collection, there is no field agency to collect agricultural statistics by field to field enumeration. Sample surveys are carried out for obtaining estimates of area under principal crops at district and State levels. The sample surveys have not been able to provide data on area sown to minor crops, complete land use statistics and area under irrigated crops for which there has been a pressing demand to meet the requirements for effective agricultural planning. It was with this end in view that the scheme for establishment of an agency for collection of agricultural statistics on complete enumeration basis was included in the Fifth Five Year Plan with 100 per cent Central Assistance. The objective of the scheme was to set up regular reporting agencies in the States of Kerala, Orissa and West Bengal in a phased manner to cover 20 per cent of villages by the end of the Fifth Plan period. The scheme was taken up for implementation in Kerala and Orissa during the year 1975-76. By the end of 1977-78, 20 per cent of the villages were covered with regular reporting agencies in Kerala, thereby achieving the target fixer for the Fifth Five Year Plan. In Orissa, by the end of 1978-79, 15 per cent of the villages were covered with regular reporting agencies.

For the latest position refer to chapter 6 on Area Statistics.

SCHEME FOR COMPUTERISATION OF LAND RECORD

Possession of land in India is an important status symbol. India is perhaps one of the few countries in the world where around 82% of the geographical area of the country is cadastrally surveyed and each field is numbered. Besides the village Shajra(Map), where each field is marked, the village official-Patwari is supposed to maintain and keep such records updated. He is the custodian of some of the important documents-Girdawari, Jamabandi, Field Book, Village map (Shajra), daily record book (Rose Namcha) and Mutation (Intkal). He is supposed to keep all these record books complete and update them in time. Every year, the patwari is required to complete the Girdawari which is to be certified/ counter signed by the Girdawar/Kanoongo. This book provides complete information about the ownership the actual cultivator (Kashtkar) and his status-tenant, sharecropper etc. While the village map is a complete record of all the fields, which are numbered, the field book provides the dimension of each numbered field. Both of these records are permanent and no change is allowed in them.

There are complaints of a good deal of corruption about the entries in the basic record particularly Girdawari. The final entries in the Girdawari are required to be a transferred to the Jamabandi, which has to be updated every four years. Experience however, shows that there are delays running into six to ten years when Jamabandi is completed. Such delays are quite often intentional, because under normal circumstances, revenue department officials have no authority to change the entries once made in the Jamabandi. Settlement in dispute in this respect falls under the jurisdiction of civil courts. Every land transfer (sale and purchase) is first entered in the Girdawari and after mutation (Intkal) transferred in Jamabandi. Since quite often mutations are not effected promptly, records of rights are invariably out of date.

Such land records which are a most authoritative source to establish ownership as well the name of the cultivator of a particular piece of land are most important to form the base for implementing various land reform measures. A regular periodical updating of such records is, therefore, a prerequisite for implementing various land reforms. This includes scientific survey of the remaining unmeasured lands and recording of the rights of tenants and share croppers which have remained unrecorded uptill now.

This manual system came under criticism and a Centrally Sponsored Scheme of Computerisation of Land Records (CLR) was launched in the year 1988-99 with a view to removing the problems inherent in the manual system of maintenance and updating of land records and meet the requirements of various groups of users. It was decided that efforts should be made to computerise CORE DATA contained in land records more accessible to people/planners/administrators. During the period from 1988-99 to 1991-92, pilot projects were taken up in some States. Subsequently, in 1993-94 it was decided to implement CLR as a full-fledged scheme. Recently, it has been decided that in those Tehsils, Talukas/Blocks, where data entry has been completed 100% or is nearing completion, the scheme should be operationalised so that the delivery of the computerised land record documents (ROR/RTC etc.) may be started early.

It was felt that in preparation, maintenance and updating of these land records, the Jamabandi in particular, accent should be on induction of modern technology for reducing the cost and time and minimizing in interpolation. One significant area of modernisation in the traditional field of revenue administration was the government decision to initiate computerisation of land record. Pilot Projects were taken up in the districts in each of the 21 States of the country for providing land holders easy excess to entries in land records and enable them to have copies of the land record quickly and accurately. It was envisaged that the application of computer techniques would be helping maintenance of land records more easily and neatly. Simultaneously, extension of computer techniques is also being encouraged in other area of land record administration such as Land Consolidation, Land Acquisition and Land Registration. At present the scheme is being implemented in 544 districts, leaving only those where there are no land records.

Once completed, CLR is expected to facilitate speedy completion of work for the district administration and help farmers. It will save them from unnecessary visits to various officials and offices. It is hoped that this will bring efficiency in department offices. During the implementation of the scheme in the last one decade, it has been observed that Data Entry Operations at the district level have not been at a very satisfactory pace, because of various reasons. It hardly needs to emphasise the significance of expediting the completion of Data Entry Operations under the CLR. In the absence of this, it is not possible to either give computerised documents to public/other users or to use the system for generating more advanced outputs or to integrate it with other computerised systems at the district level.

COMPUTERISATION OF OTHER AGRICULTURAL AND ANIMAL HUSBANDRY STATISTICS AT THE MICRO LEVEL

Availability of reliable statistics is a prerequisite for any sound policy formulation and for taking any economic decision at the macro or micro level. Undoubtedly the country has made a significant stride in systematic collection of various agricultural including horticultural statistics at the district level, but below that statistics are rarely available on a regular basis. Even if the basic data are collected below the district or subdivision level, these are not properly monitored. As a result, very few micro action plan can be formulated which have any reliable statistical foundation. Often many economic programmes are framed simply out of political expediency in the areas which have better economic status depriving the other more backward areas in the absence of reliable updated statistics. In fact, presently agricultural statistics have a wide coverage and their scope is ever widening. Detailed statistics are needed for agricultural policy decisions, planning agricultural development and for estimates of national income. The increasing responsibility have led to a further demand for and impetus to the development of comprehensive statistics.

The Role of Panchayats With the devolution of powers to the Panchayats, following the passage of the constitution (73rd Amendment) Act, 1992, the Panchayat Raj Institutions are to function as institutions of self Government. The Act provides responsibilities upon Panchayats at the appropriate level with respect to (a) the preparation of plans for economic development and social justice, and (b) the implementation of such schemes for economic development and social justice as may be entrusted to them. An important factor for the success of the Panchayati Raj System is the need for transparency in the functioning of these bodies. Panchayats being closer to the people, their right to information and accessibility to the Panchayats must be ensured. There should be an arrangement for making available to the public however, on payment of a nominal fee, documents on muster rolls, ownership of land, village resources, etc.

Agency for Collection of Area Statistics In India, the responsibility of collection of area statistics including ownership of land rests with village revenue agency, particularly in the former temporarily settled states. However, in the permanently settled states of West Bengal, Kerala, and Orissa there is no village revenue agency and the land utilisation and crop area statistics in states are based on sample surveys. In the area all fields have been cadastrally surveyed and mapped, the geographical area of each survey number and sub-numbers is accurately known and thus the area under the crop for a given region can be determined accurately. If, however, the whole field is not under the same crop or if there are patches included in the fields for which only the total geographical area known, the area under the crop is normally estimated approximately by the Patwari. Thus, as a system, the collection of data based on land records is the best provided the basic records are properly maintained. The land records being authoritative and legal documents, data based on them have certain statutory validity also. In actual practice, however, it has been found that due to a number of reasons the Patwari does not devote the time and attention that is needed to the collection of agricultural statistics, resulting in inaccuracies in recording and delays in submission of returns.

Micro Level Data Requirements The present collection of land records and area statistics have attained respectability to some degree though there are many leeways with regard to accuracy and timeliness resulting in long processed legal disputes on ownership of individual holdings and accruance of problems in micro-planning. But in respect of area and production of fruits and vegetables there is so far no firm estimates. The problem of recording the area under fruits and estimating their production is different from that of field crops. Fruit trees other than those grown in orchards, are scattered along the fields and as such an accurate determination of area under these scattered trees becomes difficult. Because of extensive mixed sowing, in the case of vegetables, difficulty arises in apportioning the area under various vegetable crops.

To overcome the problems there are suggestions like (i) making arrangements for collection of information regarding the area under each of the important fruit and vegetable crops in the normal agricultural statistics on the basis of complete enumeration done by the Patwaris, and (ii) in order to provide a sound basis for future planning, as well as supplying a reliable frame for conducting sample surveys for studying different aspects of fruit cultivation a census of fruit trees, which should include scattered trees also, should be conducted once in every five year throughout the country.

Extending the Coverage of Computerisation Programme   The need for updating and computerisation of land records has already been discussed in previous section. It has been pointed out that the implementation of the programme of computerisation of Land Record has so far been very unsatisfactory in most of the states. Moreover, wherever a little progress has been made, the computerisation of data is very limited being only related to size of holdings and their ownerships. As such, this limited computerisation of records is neither cost effective nor helpful in micro planning. The programme of computerisation should encompass, besides various parameters of land records, other agricultural and horticultural statistics at the individual farm level. The programme may also cover collection of information with regard to the possession of bovine animals and poultry at the household level. Once these detailed computerised information at the farm level in the villages are made available, various developmental agencies may make use of them for initiating developmental programmes at the grassroot level. The computerised data sheets may be supplied to the users at a reasonable price so that it can recover, at least partially, the cost of computerisation of these basic data.

Thus, the computerised village-wise sheets may possess the following information.

1. Size of holdings and their ownerships;
2. Size of area under each tenant cultivators;
3. Terms of tenancy
4. Crops grown on each holding during the kharif and rabi seasons and their production;
5. Holding wise area irrigated;
6. Source of irrigation-canal, well, deep tubewell, lift etc.
7. Number and area of each orchard and ownership of the orchards;
8. Number and kind of trees planted in each plot.
9. Approximate quantity of fruits produced in each plot.
10. Number and kind of fruit trees at the farm backyard or around the cultivated holding of each individual; the approximate annual produce of fruits from such trees;
11. Number and kind of bovine animals possessed by each villager.
12. Average quantity of milk produced by the milch cattle possessed by each villager

13. Number and owner of poultry farms in the village.
14. Number of poultry birds possessed by each owner and the average annual laying of eggs by each bird, and
15. Number of goats and sheep possessed by each villager.

Computerisation of Land Records as envisaged has a limited scope with regard to its utility at least for quite some time. But if various types of agricultural data listed above (this list can be expanded) can also be computerised, it will be useful to administrators, policy makers and researchers alike. For purposes of micro planning, the available data do not allow any micro level study below the district might be possible to do away with even a census like livestock as well as agriculture which are being carried out at every 5 year intervals.

Since all these changes will be recorded every year or even twice a year, computerised results will be available thereafter. Before implementing such a programme, there will be a need to conduct a comprehensive field study in some selected states with different systems of data reporting at the field level, examine the present technical level available and existing workload, etc. and then come up with clear recommendations for implementing the broad based computerised programme.

5

Forestry

INTRODUCTION

India has a long tradition of professional forestry with a history of forest legislation since 1865 when most of the forests became State property. Indian Forest Act, drafted first in 1865, was revised in 1878 and was consolidated again in 1927 to regulate laws relating to forests managed for production. Subsequently, several amendments of the Act were made and some of the States have promulgated their own Forest Act. After the adoption of the National Forest Policy, 1988, it was proposed to update and consolidate all forest laws and amendments made by the States from time to time to bring about a uniform law throughout the country in conformity with the provisions of the new forest policy. Forest (Conservation) Act, 1980 is another forest legislation amended in 1988. It stipulates concurrence of the Union Government for diversion of forest lands for non-forestry purposes with provisions of compensatory afforestation. Other related legislations are the Wildlife (Protection) Act, 1972 amended in 1991 and the Environment (Protection), Act, 1986.

ROLE OF THE FORESTRY SECTOR IN ECONOMY

Forests contributes 1.1 per cent to GDP of the country. However, this figure does not take into account its numerous non-market and external benefits and the vast amount of fuelwood and fodder collected or the fuelwood and the timber harvested illegally. Collection of various non-wood forest products (NWEPs) by villagers is also not recorded fully.

Besides its role in environmental stability and meeting the requirements of the people, forests maintain the soil fertility and provide critical support to development of agriculture.

Pressure on Forests

Due to the large human and cattle population and widespread rural poverty, the forests of the country are subjected to enormous pressures. These pressures are resulting in deforestation and forest degradation. The factors contributing to this phenomenon are given below.

Shifting Cultivation   It is estimated that about 10 million ha. of forest areas have been subjected to shifting cultivation is practiced in tribal dominant areas mostly in the northeastern States where shifting cultivation accounts for most of the forest degradation. Tribal population increased from 5.7% in 1971 to 8% in 1991. The increase in the population of shifting cultivators and the declining productivity of forest soils have resulted in the shifting cultivation cycle shortening from about 20 years of 4 years. Such intense farming on poor quality forest soils has made the system ecologically fragile. This system needs to be rationalised by settled cultivation with tree farming under various agroforestry systems.

Fuelwood   The consumption of fuelwood in India is about five times higher than what can be sustainably removed from forests. The bulk of wood consumed in India is for burning. Fuelwood meets about 40 per cent energy needs of the country. The estimated fuelwood consumption in the country is about 380 million cu.m. About 70 per cent of the fuelwood is accounted for by households and the rest by commercial and industrial units. Around 80 per cent of the rural people and some 48 per cent of urban people use fuelwood. In order to control demand for fuelwood there has to be some alternative and efficient source of energy. The practice of tree growing in homestead and all available land may be promoted to reduce pressure on forests. Another issue is the increasing trend of collection of fuelwood by tribal people for sale in nearby urban centres, leading to rapid depletion of forests. These issues need to be addressed in the rural energy policy.

Grazing   In the absence of adequate productive pasture lands and a grazing policy, forests have become the major source of grazing and fodder. It is estimated that around 60% of the live stock (about 270 million) graze in forests. These include traditional sedentary village livestock and migratory animals herded by ethnic graziers. Additionally, graziers collect about 175 million tonnes of green fodder annually, by lopping and harvesting grasses. This also adversely affects regeneration of forests. A sample survey by FSI estimates that the impact of grazing affects approximately 78 per cent of country's forests. Grazing occurs even in PAs. In another survey 67 per cent of the national parks and 83 per cent of the wildlife sanctuaries were found having grazing incidences. These issues may be addressed in the national fodder policy.

Forest Fire   Forest fires in India are generally ground fires. Annually about 35 million ha. of forest area is affected by fires. About 90 per cent of the forest fires are caused by human agencies to promote new flush of grasses, collection of fruits and honey or to prepare land for shifting cultivation. A sample survey conducted by FSI in 1995 found that fires affect around 55 per cent of the forest area annually.

In most cases fire protection in India is based on a system of fire lines and fire watchers, which is mostly ineffective. A centrally sponsored scheme 'Modern Forest Fire Control Methods' has introduced the use of improved hand tools but its use is at present restricted to only few areas.

Extension of these methods to other areas and establishment of a comprehensive fire plan is essential to check this menace.

Diversion of Forest Land   Other factors, leading to deforestation and/ or forest degradation are, transfer of forest lands for other land uses, encroachments on forest lands (at present 1.5 million ha.) for agriculture and other purposes and incidence of pests and diseases. The Forest (Conservation) Act, 1980 has reduced the average rate of diversion of forest lands for other uses from 150,000 ha./year between 1950 and 1980 to 25,000 ha./year after the implementation of the Act. The diversion rate during last five years is 15,500 ha./year. Involvement of encroachers in forestry programmes can, to some extent, reduce the severity of the problem. To control the impact of pests and diseases in forests, detailed study and research on these aspects are essential.

Deforestation

The per capita availability of forest land in India is one of the lowest in the world, 0.08 hectare, against an average of 0.5 hectare for developing countries and 0.64 hectare for the world.

The rate of deforestation in the country has been considerably reduced during the last few years. The average annual rate of deforestation fell from about 1.3 million hectares in the 1970s to 339,000 hectares in 1980s and to about 129,000 hectares during 1990-95. However, considering that an important objective of the National Forest Policy, 1988 is to increase the forest/tree cover to 33 per cent from the present level of 19.27 per cent, even the reduced level of deforestation is a negative achievement, though of lesser intensity.

Forest Degradation

Forest degradation is a matter of serious concern. While there has been improvement in controlling deforestation, forest degradation or qualitative loss of forests is continuing. The biomass and growing stock of wood in the natural forests of India is 93 ton/ha. and 47 cu.m/ha. respectively, as against an average of 169 ton/ha. and 113 cu.m/ha. for developing countries. This indicates that availability of forest biomass per capita in the natural forests of India is only about 6.0 ton as against an average of 82 ton in the developing world.

In the recent past efforts were concentrated mostly on social activities neglecting the natural forests. Immediate action is needed for rehabilitation and intensive protection of natural forests. Periodic inventory of forest resources to establish bench marks and treatment regimes, implement- ation of working plans, scientific studies on wood and non-wood resources and enhanced community participation need to be given special emphasis.

Forest Plantation

India's achievement in raising forest plantations, in terms of area, has been impressive. Till 1997-98 the total area of tree plantations, under different schemes, was 28.28 million ha. Of this, some 3.54 million ha. were raised before 1980; 13.51 million ha. during 1980s; and the rest during the 1990s. The current annual rate of planting is about 1.2 million ha. The quality of these plantations varies considerably.

There is a contention that forest plantations can, to some extent, compensate for the deforestation and forest degradation. Equally anchored is the view that forest plantations cannot compensate for environmental and conservation values of natural forests. It is to be stressed that forest plantations are a means to meet the increasing demand for industrial raw material or for direct consumption (e.g. fuelwood), but not to justify deforestation or claim restoration of biodiversity and other environmental services.

Moreover, the performance of forest plantations in India, in terms of survival, growth and yield, has been poor. Based on survival rate and stock density, effective area of forest plantation has been estimated to be about 11.0 million ha. 40 to 50 per cent of the reported/recorded total. The Mean Annual Increment (MAI) of forest plantations in India varies from about 2 cu.m/yr for valuable timber species to about 5 to 8 cu.m/ yr for Eucalyptus and other fast growing species. This may be compared to an MAI of over 10 cu.m/ha/yr generally and about 50 cu.m/ha/yr for good quality industrial plantations in different countries; over 70 cu.m/ ha/yr has been reported in certain cases. By any measure, the performance of forest plantations in India is far below the potential.

Inadequacies in site selection and site-species matching, poor planting stock, lack of proper maintenance and protection (from fire, grazing, pests and diseases), lack of timely tendings/thinnings, delays in fund allocation, and lack of adequately trained staff are some of the causes for the situation. Forest plantations being a major investment activity, the current low level of productivity is a cause of concern.

If forest plantations are adequately managed to achieve their potential productivity, India will be in a position to meet the future domestic demand, and will probably be able to achieve some surplus production for export. Forest plantation development should be undertaken on the basis of a master plan, specifying their categories, their management regimes, utilisation and investment needs. Each plantation unit should be covered by proper management plans. Emphasis should be placed on enhancing production qualitatively and quantitatively. They should be undertaken as enterprises, stressing efficiency.

Tree plantation activities have got much emphasis but at the same time the natural regeneration of forests have not been attended. Major portion of budgetary allocation, say about 70 to 80 per cent are being earmarked for social forestry without giving any attention to the regeneration of natural forests. The establishment of plantations at the expense of natural forests resulted in the loss of biodiversity.

Protected Area (PA)

In terms of the area declared as national parks, sanctuaries and other 'reserves' India's achievement in protected area development is significant. PAs in India cover about 14.8 million ha representing about 14 per cent of the forest area, consisting of 80 national parks, 441 wildlife sanctuaries and 8 biosphere reserves. However, the condition of several of the PAs are poor, because of fire, grazing, and inadequate management. Most of the PAs are not covered by comprehensive management plans. Some are below the minimum size required to be effective. People-wildlife interface in several cases are fraught with conflicts and tension.

The existing PAs should be assessed for their effectiveness, and they should be covered by appropriate management plan. Measures are to be properly planned and implemented for biodiversity conservation, buffer zone management, wildlife conservation and watershed protection. Potential for development of eco-tourism, participatory eco-development, other non-destructive uses of resources, and wildlife farming should be investigated and suitable programmes developed.

Private Forestry Initiatives

Though forestry activities are mainly with the government, rural people have been practising tree planting in their farms and homesteads, to meet household requirements for fuel, poles, timber, and medicinal plants. Tree plantation on community lands is also executed by the government. With the advent of social forestry, a promotional drive was launched for tree planting in wastelands, institutional lands, and non-forest public and private lands. Currently the area of private tree planting (under agroforestry, farm forestry in block and line plantations) covers an area of over six million hectares. The other non-forest sources of wood are rubber, coconut, cashew, and mango plantations. The non-forest sources together provide about 50 per cent of total wood supply in the country; and probably an equal or larger share of NWFPs. There are also a large number of small private nurseries, meeting the local demand for seedings.

These private initiatives are not adequately supported by the government through relevant research, extension, technological packages, input delivery, market information or credit facilities. In the interest of sustainable forestry development, it is necessary to encourage the small operators to keep up their interest and to ensure that these are adequately understood and addressed.

The private sector is, however, dominant in the area of harvesting and processing and the needs and problems relating to this area are different from those of the small-scale producers of wood in rural areas.

Development of Forests

Two immediate steps are required for the sustainable development of forests. One is to rehabilitate and increase the productivity of 31 million ha degraded forests and other is to increase the area under forest and tree cover to make it 33% of the total area of the country. Besides, the activities of institutional development, better input (finance and planting stock) and market facilities should also be given priority.

Land Use Classification and Availability for Forestry and Tree Planting   Out of 329 million ha of country's geographic area, 65 million ha are either under habitation (urban and rural), industries and infrastructure such as roads, rivers, canals, railway lines etc. or under permanent snow, rocks, desert or not available due to other reasons. But some of the areas under habitation and along roads, rails, canals and rivers etc. have the potential for tree plantation, mostly in strips.

Forest Policy

The first forest policy of 1894 was revised in 1952. National Commission of Agriculture (NCA) studied the forestry planning in the country in 1976 and made recommendations for future action. This led to the emergence of social forestry and the establishment of Forest Development Corporations (FDCs). However, the forest policy was again revised in 1988 as the National Forest Policy, 1988. The new policy accords highest priority to the environmental role of forests. The policy states that 'the principle aim of the Forest Policy must be to ensure environmental stability and ecological balance including atmospheric equilibrium, which are vital for the sustenance of all life forms, human, animal and plant. The derivation of direct economic benefit must be subordinated to this principle aim.'

The basic objectives of the National Forest Policy, 1988 are:
- Maintenance of environmental stability through preservation, and, where necessary, restoration of the ecological balance that has been adversely disturbed by serious depletion of the forests of the country.
- Conserving the natural heritage of the country by preserving the remaining natural forests with the vast variety of flora and fauna, which represents the remarkable biological diversity and genetic resources of the country.
- Checking soil erosion and denudation in the catchment areas of rivers, lakes, reservoirs in the interest of soil and water conservation, for mitigating floods and droughts and for the retardation of siltation of reservoirs. Also checking the extension of sand-dunes.
- Increasing substantially the forest/tree cover in the country through massive afforestation and social forestry programmes, especially on all denuded and degraded and unproductive lands.
- Meeting the requirements of fuelwood, fodder, minor forest produce and small timber of the rural and tribal population.

- Increasing the productivity of forests to meet essential national needs.
- Encouraging efficient utilisation of forest produce and maximising substitution of the wood.
- Creating a massive people's movement with the involvement of women, for achieving these objectives and to minimise pressure on existing forests.

The policy states that industrial wood requirements are to be met from the farm forestry and private area plantations.

The policy also sets a national goal to have a minimum of one-third of the total area of the country under forest or tree cover. In the hills and in mountainous regions, the aim should be to maintain two-third of the area under such cover in order to prevent erosion and land degradation and to ensure the stability of the fragile ecosystem.

In order to implement the policy prescription, the Ministry issued guideline on 1.6.1990 to involve the village communities in the development and protection of degraded forests on the basis of their taking a share of the usufruct from such areas. The concept of Joint Forest Management (JFM) was accordingly initiated and endorsed to all State and Union Territories for operationalising the same by developing appropriate mechanisms. Twentytwo States have issued their resolutios for Joint Forest Management (JFM). As on 1.1.2000 around 10.25 million sha. of degraded forests in the country were being managed and protected by 36,075 Village Forest Protection Committees. The activities under JFM programme are being monitored by a JFM Cell constituted by the Ministry.

Though the new policy is only 12 years old, its impact so far is satisfactory. More monitoring of its impact in various regions of the country is required. A new National Forestry Action. Programme (1999) has now been drawn. It provides statewise profile for 26 states (Table 5.1), a perspective for 20 years and is a storehouse of forestry data. Table 5.2 is a sample of available data for one state (Assam). Similar information is available for all the 26 states.

STATISTICS

Although forestry is a major land use next to agriculture, this is almost a neglected sector in the structure of Indian economy. Forest statistics are collected mainly as by-product of forest administration and management. In India, forests occupy 22.7 per cent of the total land area. Of late, forests have assumed much greater importance in their impact on environment, socio-economic conditions of the rural poor, the tribals and the planned development of wood based industry. The present proportion of forest area is rather low as compared to different regions in the world. The per capita forest area in India is only 0.8 ha. as compared to the world average 0.64 (*see* Table 5.3).

Collection of forestry statistics was initiated to meet the administrative needs of the State Forest Departments. Up to 1946-47 data on a small

Table 5.1 National Forestry Action Plan (1999): Index of Tables

number of items of forestry were collected and published in respect of British India alone. After independence, with the integration of the princely States, the coverage of statistics was gradually extended to the forests located in the former princely States also.

The principal forest statistics relate to area under forests, volume of standing timber and firewood, quantity and value of out-turn of timber, firewood and minor forest produce, employment in forestry and forest industries, foreign trade and data on revenue and expenditure. Miscellaneous information on the progress of working plans, breaches of forest rules and grazing of cattle in government forests is also collected. The scope of the forest statistics has been expanded since 1958-59 to include data on area afforested and deforested area surveyed, classification of forests by management status, silvicultural system and density, out-turn of logs and sleepers, and wholesale prices of forest produce. These data which are collected through the State Departments of Forests are compiled and published at the Centre by the DES which maintains close liaison with the Inspector General of Forests. The Central Forestry

Table 5.2 Assam State Statistical Profile

1. Geographical area	:	78,438 sq. km.
2. Population (1991)		
(a) Human	:	22.41 million (2.65% of Country)
(b) Scheduled Caste	:	1.66 million (7.40% of State)
(c) Scheduled Tribes	:	2.87 million (12.82% of State)
(d) Cattle (1991)	:	—
3. Literacy rate	:	52.89 per cent
(a) Male	:	61.87 per cent
(b) Female	:	43.03 per cent
4. Per capita forest area	:	0.11 hectare
5. Forest cover	:	23,824 sq. km. (30.4% of State)
(a) Dense forest	:	15,548 sq. km.
(b) Degraded forest (open)	:	8276 sq. km.
6. Scrub		635 sq. km.
7. Recorded forest area	:	30,708 sq. km. (39.15% of State)
(a) Reserved forest	:	18,242 sq. km.
(b) Protected forest	:	3,934 sq. km.
(c) Unclassed state forest	:	8,532 sq. km.
8. Protected area (FST 1995)	:	23,115 sq. km.
9. Forest cover in tribal districts	:	23,824 sq. km.
10. Forest cover in hilly areas	:	—
11. Growing stock	:	304.4 million cu.m.
12. Average annual per capita consumption of fuelwood (FSI 1996).	:	
(a) Rural population		338 kg
(c) Urban population	:	435 kg
13. Total annual consumption of fuelwood (1996)	:	4.7 million tonnes
14. Annual availability of fuelwood from forests (1996)	:	1.5 million tonnes
15. Projected annual consumption of fuelwood in		
(a) 2001	:	5.2 million tonnes
(b) 2006	:	5.8 million tonnes

Commission which was set up in 1965, collects data on certain aspects of forestry such as area under forests by ownership, legal status, composition, out-turn of forest produce, etc. in standardized forms referred to in Chapter 46 on Forest Planning, Research and Education. It also collects information on a few additional items required for planning in forestry.

Forest Statistics are by and large collected by the State Forest Departments and National estimates are worked out at the Centre on the basis of information received from the State Governments. State-wise data on various aspects of forestry like forest area, out-turn of timber, fuel wood and other minor forest products, revenue and expenditure of

State Forest Departments, employment generated in the Forestry Sector etc. are published in the India Forest Statistics annually.

Classification

Detailed data on the area under 'coniferous' or soft wood and 'non-coniferous' or broad leaved forests are reported by State Forest Departments according to types of ownership. The data are separately reported for forest area under State Forest Departments and other civil authorities, corporate bodies and private individuals. The emphasis on forestry development is on economic management or exploitation of the forests as sources of forest products. This calls for a further classification into 'merchantable forests' and 'others' as also 'unprofitable or inaccessible'. Data on area under forests according to legal status, i.e. 'reserved', 'protected' and 'unclassed' are also being collected for coniferous and non-coniferous forests separately. Some of the data are available according to species such as *deodar, chir, kail* and fir among coniferous trees, and *sal, teak, sisso* dipterocarps and others in non-coniferous species.

With regard to classification, the importance of the various types of wood varies from State to State. We recommend that while the State Governments may adopt a more detailed classification for collection of the information in their own State they should collect the data on the uniform classification so that compilation at all-India level becomes possible. Statistics should also be collected according to functional classification, viz. protection forests, production forests and social forests.

INDIAN FOREST STATISTICS

At the centre, the Directorate of Economics and Statistics, Ministry of Agriculture, had been coordinating and compiling the data on forest statistics, on the basis of annual returns received from State Forest Departments. The principal forest statistics of area under forests, out-turn of timber and other forest produce, employment in forests and forest industries, revenue and expenditure and foreign trade of forest products, etc. are published annually in the *Indian Forest Statistics* issued by the Directorate of Economics and Statistics and relates to the financial year ending 31st March. Up to 1946-47, data on forestry were issued through the annual returns of statistics relating to 'Forest Administration in India'. The scope of the publication was restricted to only State-owned forests in British India. No information was made available about the private forests in British India and those in the princely States.

From 1947-48, the scope of this publication was widened and the following information which was not included in the annual returns during the pre-independence period, was included:

(i) Classification of forest area according to type of wood.
(ii) Volume of standing timber and firewood and their increments in exploitable forests.

(iii) Employment of labour in forestry and forest industries.

(iv) Out-turn of logs, sleepers, etc.

(v) Out-turn of timber and firewood species-wise.

(vi) Out-turn of minor forest produce—quantity and value.

(vii) Foreign trade in forest produce.

Up to 1951-52, forests and forest product statistics used to be published in one volume. The issues for the subsequent three years were published in two volumes—Vol. I giving only all-India figures and Vol. II State-wise details. From the year 1955-56 again, the publication is being brought out in one volume and gives all-India data for 10 years and State-wise data for two years instead of 5 years as given in the previous publications. State-wise estimates of major forest produce as available in the above publication relate to the areas managed by the State Forest Departments, but do not cover forest areas under ownership rights of corporate bodies, civil authorities or private individuals. To that extent figures are incomplete.

Changes After 1958-59

Besides the extension of coverage of forest statistics, certain improvements were brought about in the proforma for collection of forest statistics from the year 1958-59. In addition to the amplification of the existing tables, the following new tables were added for collection of information regarding:

(i) Area afforested and deforested during the year.

(ii) Classification of forests according to use, management status, silvicultural system and density.

(iii) Quantity and value of manufacture of forest produce, e.g. plywood, pulp matches, etc.

(iv) Annual consumption and carry over of major and minor forest produce according to different categories of produce.

(v) Wholesale prices of major and minor forest produce at important centres.

(vi) Games shot.

(vii) Seasoning kilns and treatment plants.

Along with the amplification of the information as already mentioned, a revised set of proformae for the reporting of forest statistics has been finalized by the Directorate of Economics and Statistics in consultation with the State Forest Departments. A common definition for the term 'forest' has been adopted. All unwooded or other areas put to some agricultural or non-forest use would be left out from 'forest' areas and indicated separately. This would being about a greater agreement in the figures reported in the 'Indian Forest Statistics' and 'Agricultural Statistics.' The following additional information is also made available according to the revised proforma since the year 1958-59.

(i) Area of forests surveyed with topographical details.

(ii) Out-turn of logs, sleepers, etc.

(iii) Species-wise out-turn of timber and fuel wood.

(iv) Out-turn and volume of minor produce.

Forest statistics are compiled by the State Forest Departments. Censuses of industries and agriculture also include items on forests which are generally dealt with by the Industries and Revenue Departments of the States respectively. But for a few States, no separate statistical organization exists at the State level. One of the serious drawbacks in the publication—Indian Forest Statistics—is that there is a time-lag of about 5 years or even more in publishing data. After 1958-59, the publication relating to the period 1958-59 to 1960-61, for example, was released only in April, 1969.

Forests of India in Comparison to other Countries

The ability of the forest to satisfy demands in the aggregate relates, of course, to the extent of forests and forest productivity to the ratio of people to land. With 1,8 per cent of the total forest area in the world, the per capita forest area in India has decreased from 0.20 ha. in 1951 to 0.08 ha. in 1995. By comparison, India's forests rank is very low relative to other countries as shown in Table 5.3.

Table 5.3 Comparison of Per Capita Forest Land—1996-97

Country	Per Capita Forest Land in Ha.
1. India	0.08
2. Former U.S.S.R.	2.15
3. U.S.A.	0.84
4. U.K.	0.04
5. China	0.12
6. Thailand	0.24
7. Italy	0.12
8. Canada	9.32
9. Australia	2.33
10. Nepal	0.27
11. Sweden	2.85
12. Bangladesh	0.01
13. Indonesia	0.64
14. Malaysia	1.02
15. Brazil	3.76
16. Nigeria	0.14
17. Sudan	1.71
Average World	0.64
Developing Countries	0.50
Developed Countries	1.07

The mean annual increment (average annual volume growth per hectare of forest) of India's forest is 1.37 cu.m/ha. (87.6 million m^3 in 64 million ha. of forest cover [FSI-95]) whereas the world average is 2.1.

INDIAN AGRICULTURAL STATISTICS

Apart from the Indian Forest Statistics, another publication of the same Ministry also publishes estimates on area under forest in Vols. I and II of Indian Agricultural Statistics. These are based on Agricultural Statistics collected by the revenue agencies and relate to the year July to June. But the two sets of figures generally do not tally (vide Annexure I). The differences generally arise mainly from the differences in the geographical coverage, diversity of purposes for which the statistics are compiled by the two agencies and the differences in the references period.

A revised definition of forest area recommended by the Standing Committe on Improvement of Agricultural Statistics has been accepted for adoption in the Forest Statistics India and Indian Agricultural Statistics.

PLANNING AND STATISTICAL CELLS

A scheme for the establishment of Planning and Statistical Cells in the State Forest Departments was included in the Fourth Five Year Plan. Many of the States have already set up statistical cells others are in the process of doing so. A Forestry Statistical Cell has also been set up at the Centre under the Inspector General of Forests which enables compilation of data collected by the Chief Conservator of Forests within a reasonable period. As mentioned earlier, these publications are now being released without much delay.

With a view to reducing the time-lag in the dissemination of forestry statistics, a proposal to get the data computerized through the National Information Centre of Electronics Commission was under consideration. It is envisaged that the computerization of data will help in maintaining the data in a proper manner and also help greatly in timely dissemination.

MINISTRY OF ENVIRONMENT AND FORESTS

It was during 1987 that a new Ministry of Environment and Forests was created. The responsibility for research and data collection covering various aspects of forestry was transferred to this Ministry. Indian Forestry Statistics which was being published by the Directorate of Economics and Statistics, Ministry of Agriculture, was also transferred to this newly created Ministry Indian Council of Forestry Research and Education, Dehradun, is now beinging out an annual publication-Forest Statistics India. First issue (1988-94) was brought out in 1997 and latest issue of this publication for the year 2000 has already been released. This publication has improved both the quantitative and qualitative aspects of the data.

This issue covers information, on area, types of forests, legal status, composition, forests closed and open to grazing, working plans, afforested and deforested area, concentrated regeneration, etc.; volume of standing timber, fuel wood and annual growth; out-turn of fuel wood, logs, slippers and minor forest products; employment of labour in forestry and forest industries; revenue and expenditure; imports and exports of forest produce; wholesale prices of forest produce; breaches of forest rules; grazing of animals in Government forests; estimated value of forest produce given away free or at reduced rates, games shot in forest area and some international data on forestry. It is now being released by the Indian Council of Forest Bureau, Dehradun.

State of Forest Report

Since comprehensive assesment of the forest resources involves measurement of numerous parameters such as forest cover, growing stock, annual increment, species composition, bio-diversity, non-timber forest products etc. However, in the absence of adequate resource, the Forest Survey of India (FSI) is able to assess only the forest cover biennially at the national level, using remote sensing technology. The assessment of other parameters is done for only specific areas.

The first State of Forest Report (SFR) on the forest cover of the country was published in 1987 using Landsat data of US satellite on 1:1 million scale through visual method of interpretation. The resolution of the sensor was 80 m. From the second assessment, the resolution of the sensor improved to 30 m and the scale of interpretation to 1:250,000. The Indian Remote Sensing (IRS) satellite data, having a resolution of 36.25 m, has been used since the fifth assessment. The digital image processing was also simultaneously introduced to assess the forest cover of Madhya Pradesh and Maharashtra States. Seventh Report (1999) has now been published by the Forest Survey of India (FSI). Results of the past six assements are given in Table 5.4.

Table 5.4 Forest Cover Estimates from 1987 to 1997

Assessment	Year	Data period	Resolution of sensor (m)	Forest cover (sq.km)	Percentage of geographic area
First	1987	1981-83	80	640,819	19.49
Second	1989	1985-87	30	638,804	19.43
Third	1991	1987-89	30	639,364	19.45
Fourth	1993	1989-91	30	639,386	19.45
Fifth	1995	1991-93	36.25	638,879	19.43
Sixth	1997	1993-95	36.25	633,397	19.27

Methodology

The satellite imagery (data) used for the forest cover assessment is procured from the National Remote Sensing Agency (NRSA), Hyderabad in digital form as well as False Colour Composite (FCC) prints. For the present assessment, linear Imaging and Self-scanning Sensor (LISS) II data of Indian Remote Sensing Satellite (IRS-1B), with a resolution of 36.25 m, and LISS III data of IRS 1C and 1D satellites, with a resolution of 23.5 m, have been used.

The period of satellite data is of utmost importance. The reflectance from the forest is dependent on the growth of the crown and its chlorophyll content. A deciduous forest would, therefore, not give proper reflectance in leafless period. Thus, data of the spring/summer season(s) for such forests is not suitable for interpretation. During the rainy season, it is difficult to find cloud free data. Further, similar reflectance of agriculture and other areas poses problems in delineation of forest cover during the rainy season. Therefore, the data of rainy season is often not suitable for the assessment. The data period suitable for interpretation for most of the forest areas of our country is October to January. In the event of non-availability of data of this period, data of other periods is also used. There are two methods of interpretation; the visual and the digital.

In visual interpretation, satellite data is procured on a specified scale (1:2,50,000 scale in the present case) in the form of hard copy called FCC A base map is prepared on a tracing sheet (Mylar) using Survey of India (SOI) toposheet of corresponding scale. Selected details are taken from the toposheet. The interpretation of imagery is done using interpretation keys based on tone, texture, location, association, etc.

In the present assessment, visual method of interpretation has been used for the assessment of forest cover of the states of Bihar, Goa, Gujarat, Jammu and Kashmir, Karnataka, Kerala, Orissa, Punjab, Rajasthan, Tamil Nadu, Uttar Pradesh, West Bengal and Union Territories of Andaman and Nicobar Islands, Chandigarh, Dadara and Nagar Haveli and Daman and Diu.

In digital interpretation, satellite data is procured in digital form. Using Digital Image Processing (DIP) softwares, radiometric and stretch corrections are applied for improving visual impact of the FCC. Geometric rectification of the data is carried out with the help of scanned SOI toposheet for assigning geographical coordinates to the image.

For classification of the data, first the non-forest areas are masked out from the scene by delineating them. The SOI toposheets, forest cover maps of preceding cycle and ground truth information of the past assessments are used for masking. After masking out the non-forest areas, density classification of the forest cover is done by Normalised Difference Vegetation Index (NDVI).

In the present assessment, digital method of interpretation has been used for the assessment of the forest cover of the states of Andhra Pradesh, Arunachal Pradesh, Assam, Delhi, Himachal Pradesh, Madhya Pradesh, Maharashtra, Manipur, Meghalaya, Mizoram, Nagaland, Sikkim and Tripura. These states comprise 63% forest cover of the country.

The forest cover is broadly classified into 3 classes namely dense forest, open forest and mangrove. The other classes include scrub and non-forest. These classes are defined in Box 1.

Box 1
Forest Cover Classes

Dense forest	All lands with tree cover of canopy density of 40 per cent and above.
Open forest	All lands with tree cover of canopy density between 10 to 40 per cent.
Mangrove	Salt tolerant forest ecosystem found mainly in tropical and sub-tropical inter-tidal regions.
Scrub	All lands with poor tree growth mainly of small or stunted trees having canopy density less than 10 per cent.
Non-forest	Any area not included in the above classes.

There are certain cartographic and technological limitations in the assessment of forest cover. In visual interpretation, the minimum size in the imagery that can be mapped is 2 mm × 2 mm, which corresponds to 25 ha on the ground on 1:250,000 scale and ha on 1:50,000 scale. Considerable details on ground may be obscured in areas having clouds and shadows. The reflectance of young plantations with small crown and low chlorophyll content is not recorded by satellite sensors. Gregarious occurrence of bushy vegetation like lantana, tea and coffee poses problems in delineation of forest cover. Tonal variation, while generating photo prints, may cause variation in hue, affecting interpretation.

Forest Cover

The forest cover of the country as per 1999 assessment is estimated to be 637,293 sq.km, which is 19.39% of the geographic area of the country. Summary of the assessment is presented in Table 5.5 and Fig. 5.1.

Table 5.5 Forest Cover as per 1999 Assessment

Land use	Area in sq.km	Percentage
Dense forest	377,358	11.48
Open forest	255.064	7.76
Mangrove	4.871	0.15
Sub-total	637,293	19.39
Scrub	51.896	1.58
Non-forest	2,598.074	79.03
Total	3,287,263	100.00

It would be of interest to known that no firm data are available in respect of the extent of loss of forest cover in India or its annual rate of deforestation. It is generally believed that India lost its forest cover quite

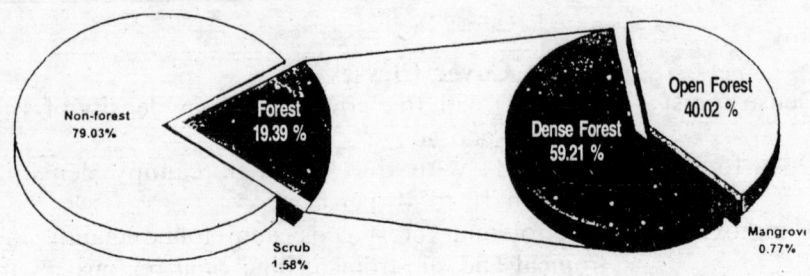

Fig. 5.1 Forest Cover in India

heavily during the 1070s, but the trend was reversed from 1980s onwards. In 1984 the NRSA published data for the years 1972-75 and 1980-82 showing that the country lost[1] 1.3 mha of dense forests (with crown cover of more than 40 per cent) every year, and its area fell from 46.42 to 36.02 mha during that period. However, the area of dense forests has remained almost stable since 1981-83, as Table 5.6 based on the data published by the FSI (Forest Survey of India) shows:

Table 5.6 Area of Dense Forest Cover in India as Reported by NRSA

(mha)

Year	Dense forest cover
(1)	(2)
1972-75	46.42
1980-82	36.14
1985-87	37.85
1987-89	38.50
1989-91	38.56
1991-93	38.58
1995-97	36.73

According to the FAO (1998), deforestation continued at the rate of 0.6 per cent during 1980-90 in India. It however defines deforestation as loss of natural forests, not counting plantations. According to the FAO, changes in the area of natural forests and plantations during the period 1980-90 were given in Table 5.7.

FSI vs.FAO-who is right? Part of the problem is definitional. The FSI data about tree cover includes plantations on farm and degraded lands (whatever can be observed by the satellite), whereas the FAO calculates the rate of deforestation only on natural forests, and discusses

[1]Indian Journal of Agricultural Economics, Conference No July-Sept. 2000.

Table 5.7 Changes in Tree Cover During the 1980s in India

(mha)

Particulars (1)	1980 (2)	1990 (3)	Annual rate of increase/decline (per cent) (4)
Natural forest cover	55.12	51.73	(-) 0.6
Plantations	3.18	13.23	(+) 14.0
Total tree cover	58.30	64.96[5]	(+) 1.0

the figures of plantations separately (these are based on government data and obviously do not accurately like into account mortality etc). When the area under plantations is added to that of natural forests, the FAO data show that the tree cover in India during 1980-90 has increased from 58.30 to 64,96 million ha!

One explanation of the improved scenario could be the general ban on green felling which many Indian states have clamped since the late eighties. How effective has been this ban, and what has been the impact of the Supreme Court order in January, 1977 on logging ban, is not very well known. The relative contribution of forests to state revenues has been falling dramatically since Independence, just as it has fallen for land revenue, because of expansion of economic activity outside land. This has enabled the states to forego incomes from logging. Other factors, such as liberalised wood imports (touching 1.3 billion US $ in 1997-98), natural spread of Prosopis juliflora shrubs, and the success of farm forestry have contributed in reducing pressure on forests. Finally, thesuccess of participatory policies may have led toimprovement in forest cover. Even when the forest cover has remained unaltered, little information is available on the species composition and changes in the total forest stock.

Demand, Availability and Prices of Fuelwood

Several estimates for fuelwood demand are available, but these are so disparate that a degree of agnosticism is in order. There are differences even in the figures of actual consumption estimated by different agencies. The National Forestry Action Plan, 1999 of the Ministry of Environment and Forestry estimated removal of fuelwood from forest lands alone as 270 million tonnes, whereas National Council of Applied Economic Research (NCAER) put the total figure of fuelwood consumption including all sources as 94.5 million tonnes in 1978-79 and Tata Energy Research Institute (TERI's) estimate for 1991 was 175 million tonnes (Ravindranath et al., 1996).

These differences arise perhaps for several reasons. First, it is difficult to be precise about the demand for an item which is mostly collected and where substitutions occur: smaller twigs and leaves can substitute for larger sticks and logs; and where fuelwood is easily accessible and opportunity cost of rural labour remains low, fuelwood can substitute for ohter non-commercial and commercial fuels, leading to higher estimates of needs. Second, there are difficulties in assessing direct and indirect impacts of various causal variables such as product price, prices of substitutes, size and location of user households, price and income elasticity of demands, and likely changes in the causal variables themselves.

Third, consumption of fuelwood is highly supply elastic and varies a great deal with availability. For instance, the annual amount of wood used in Raipur (Madhya Pradesh), which is surrounded by dense forests, was almost 1 tonne/household, whereas in Hyderabad (Andhra Pradesh), a metropolitan town, it was less than 0.5 tonne/household (Dunkerley et al., 1990). Variations in total consumption of cooking fuels by households and the mix of fuels used were influenced by household income, accessibility and prices of the different fuel supplies, climate, resource endowment, size of city, household fuel preference, social characteristics, food habits and regional cooking styles.

As for consumption, the Forest Survey of India (FSI, 1988, p. 46) estimated that there was a gap of 130 mt in demand and internal production of firewood in the country in 1987. Estimates for the year 2000 A.D. vary from 92 mt by the Working Group on Energy Policy of the Planning Commission to 300-330 mt by the Advisory Board on Energy. The demand projections of many such studies for future years have often not been matched by the figures of actual consumption in those years, and the predicted demand has been found to be exaggerated, often by a factor of 2to 4, as compared to actual consumption (Saxena, 1997). This suggests that the methodology followed in these studies for estimating demand should perhaps be put to critical scrutiny. Firstly, the term demand should be sharply defined and distinguished from the need or requirement. It is more precise to measure consumption than demand. Secondly, the discussion on quantification of demand should take into account the prevailing or anticipated price. The present estimation process make no reference to prices. Thirdly, the experience of glut of eucalyptus wood in several north Indian markets whereas shortage existed elsewhere shows that the gap between supply and demand cannot be bridged by simply enhancing production, other constraints may be equally relevant.

OTHER PUBLICATIONS

Some other useful publications on forest statistics are as follows:
1. India's Forests and the War.
2. Forestry in India.
3. Hundred Years of Indian Forestry, 1861-1961.
4. FAO/ECAFE Timber Trend Study for the Far East-Country Report for India.

5. Integration of Forests and Industries—J.A. Von Monrov Report.
6. NSSO[2].

The first two of these publications were brought out by the Directorate of Economics and Statistics and presented most of the available data at one place. The second publication, for example, was published at the time of the Fourth World Forestry Conference, 1954 and presented important facts and statistics relating to forestry. The third was issued on the occasion of the Celebration of Indian Forest Centenary by Forest Research Institute and Colleges, Dehra Dun. The Timber Trend Study Report, besides reproducing the data on area and out-turn of forest produce from the Indian Forest Statistics, supplies the following additional information::

1. Methods of logging operation and waste and losses incurred during logging.
2. Production costs at different stages of forest exploitation such as stumpage prices, felling costs, transport charges from stump to permanent lines of transport and transport charges along these permanent lines.
3. Supply and consumption of round wood, fuel wood and charcoal, bamboo and plam species.
4. State-wise movement of round wood and future supply of indigenous raw sources etc.

This study, published in 1958 by the Ministry of Food and Agriculture gives for the first time a fair appraisal of the future requirements of round wood and its products by end-uses in a detailed form. The Monrov Report which was completed in 1960 deals at length with the following points:

1. Characteristics of forests and forest industries.
2. Analysis of requirements and supply of forest produce—building material, mining, transport and communication, wood-working industries, packaging, paper, rayon and matches.
3. Present and potential requirements of industrial wood—fuel wood, tanning material, lac, rosin and terpentine, medicinal plants and essential oils.
4. Future lines of development, giving a tentative list of selected integrated and semi-integrated industries.

Valuable information is also contained in the following publications which deal comprehensively with different aspects of Indian Forestry:

1. Timber Trends and Prospects in India—1960-1975 (Prepared for the VII Session of 'Asia Pacific Forestry Commission—1962' by Forest Research Institute and Colleges, Dehra Dun).

---

[2]NSSO—The only source of data relating to the consumption of firewood and chips is available in various rounds of NSSO—27th, 32nd, 38th, 43rd, 50th and 55th rounds provide information on quantity and value of these species consumed.

3. Progress Report of India, 1960-65 (Prepared for the IX Commonwealth Forestry Conference, January, 1968).
4. Forestry in India—1967.

Data on forestry in respect of area, production and revenue are collected by the State Forest Departments as a by-product of the forest administration and management. Discrepancy, however, exists in respect of area under forests as given by the State Forest Departments and under land use statistics published in Indian-Agricultural Statistics. The fuel wood and timber production reported by Chief Conservators for Forests pertain to the recorded production from the forest area. During 1979-80, available information on forestry in the form of bulletin 'India's Forest 1980' was prepared. The forest bulletin on 'Exports and Imports of Forest Products' was up-dated.

The summary of India, State of Forest Reports are being released annually by the Indian Council of Forestry Research and Education, which is now in clearing house for data on Forestry. Forest Department is no longer with the Miny. of Agriculture. A new Miny.—Miny. of Environment and Forests—now looks after this subject.

RECONCILIATION OF DISCREPANCY

As already mentioned in Chapter 4, land utilization statistics (LUS) also provides data on area under forests. According to LUS, the total area under forests in 1996-97 is 69.0 Mha (Table 5.8). The areas as reported in Forest Statistics Indian aggregate to 76.5 Mha. The position has not improved since then. There is thus a wide difference of 5.8 Mha between the two sets of figures. The differences are large in some of the States and are in either direction. The question of reconciling the discrepancy between the two sets of figures has been receiving attention in the Ministry of Agriculture for quite a long time. At one time it was thought that the major part of the difference between the two sets of figures was due to differences in the definitions adopted for the two types of data. According to Forest Statistics, the recommended definition for forest is as follows:

"Area under forests includes all lands classed as forests in any legal enactment dealing with forests and administered as forests irrespective of whether these are State-owned or private and whether wooded or managed as potential forest land."

Uniform adoption of the definition for both LUS and forest statistics does not eliminate completely the sources of discrepancy between the two sets of figures. It is necessary that at the State level, the Chief Conservator of Forests and the crop reporting authority should get together and take steps to eliminate the differences. Clear-cut procedures should be laid down for updating of the records every year and publication of one set of figures by both the agencies. Perhaps, the reconciliation has to be attempted at the district level between the divisional Forest Officer and the officer in charge of agricultural statistics at district level.

(Area in sq.km)

Table 5.8 State/UT Wise Forest Area

S.No.	State/Uts	Geographic area	Reserved forests	Protected forests	Others	Total	% of forests to total Geographic area	Total forests area (LUS) (1000 hectares)
1.	Andhra Pradesh	275068	50479	12365	970	68314	23.20	6245
2.	Arunachal Pradesh	83743	15321	8	36211	51540	61.55	5154
3.	Assam	78438	18242	3934	8532	30708	39.15	1930
4.	Bihar	173877	5051	24168	7	29226	16.81	2949
5.	Goa	3814	165	NA	1259	1424	37.34	126
6.	Gujarat	196024	13819	887	4577	19393	9.89	1861
7.	Haryana	44212	247	1104	322	1673	3.78	115
8.	Himachal Pradesh	55673	1896	31473	2038	35407	63.60	1056
9.	Jammu and Kashmir	222235	20182	NA	NA	20182	9.08	2747
10.	Karnataka	191791	28611	3932	6181	38724	20.19	3062
11.	Kerala	38863	11038	183	NA	11221	28.87	1081
12.	Madhya Pradesh	443446	82700	66678	5119	154497	34.84	14215
13.	Maharashtra	307690	48373	9350	6119	63842	20.75	5274
14.	Manipur	22327	1463	4171	9520	15154	67.87	602
15.	Meghalaya	22429	981	12	8503	9496	42.34	935
16.	Mizoram	21081	7127	3568	5240	15935	75.59	1598
17.	Nagaland	16579	86	507	8036	8629	52.05	863
18.	Orissa	155707	27087	30080	17	57185	36.73	5606
19.	Punjab	50362	44	1107	1750	2901	5.76	290
20.	Rajasthan	342239	11585	16837	3278	31700	9.26	2476
21.	Sikkim	7096	2261	285	104	2650	37.34	257

Table 5.8 State/UT Wise Forest Area (Contd.)

(Area in sq.km)

S.No.	State/Uts	Geographic area	Reserved forests	Protected forests	Others	Total	% of forests to total Geographic area	Total forests area (LUS) (1000 hectares)
21.	Sikkim	7096	2261	285	104	2650	37.34	257
22.	Tamil Nadu	130058	19486	2528	614	22628	17.40	2141
23.	Tripura	10486	3588	509	2196	6293	60.01	606
24.	Uttar Pradesh	294411	36425	1499	13739	51663	17.55	5150
25.	West Bengal	88752	7054	3772	1053	11879	13.38	1195
26.	Andaman & Nicobar Island	8249	2929	4242	NA	7171	86.93	695
27.	Chandigarh	114	31	NA	NA	31	27.19	Meg.
28.	Dadra and Nagar Haveli	491	203	NA	NA	203	41.34	20
29.	Delhi	1483	42	NA	NA	42	2.83	1
30.	Lakshadweep	32	NA	NA	NA	NA	NA	NA
31.	Pondicherry	493	NA	NA	NA	NA	NA	NA
	Total	3287263	416516	223309	125385	765210	23.28	68750

Source: Forest Survey of India, The State of Forest Report 1997

India has 76-52 million hectares of recorded forest area. This accounts for 23.28% of total geographic area. Per Capita availability of forests in India is 0.08 ha which is much lower than the world average of 0.8 ha. Even if no further net deforestation takes place merely on considering the increase in population, the forest area has already been reduced to 0.07 as per capita by now 2000 (Government of India, 1993).

OUT-TURN OF MAJOR AND MINOR FOREST PRODUCE

Statistics of out-turn of major forest produce are at present available for timber, fuel, logs, sleepers, etc. both in terms of quantity and value. These data are classified into 'coniferous' and 'non-coniferous' wood. Separate data are also be reported for sawn timber, round wood, and fuelwood including charcoal wood and wood for distillation. Data on out-turn are available for selected species such as *deodar, chir, sal, teak, sisso, simul* and dipterocarps. In regard to minor forest produce, only statistics of value of production are available for bamboos and canes, drugs, fibers and flosses, fodder and grazing and grass other than fodder. Data are also available for lac, gums and resins, dye-stuffs, tanning materials, bidi leaves, vegetable oils and seeds, charcoal, ivory honey and bees wax. The basic defect with the data of forest produce is that they relate only to the forests under the control of State Forest Departments who report data with regard to authorized removals only, Secondly, there is considerable quantity of timber and fuelwood grown outside the forest lands. Suitable procedures have to be devised to frame estimates of unrecorded production through sample surveys or otherwise at least once in five years. The possibility of collecting data on timber and fuelwood from agricultural lands through the periodical agricultural censuses should be examined.

Generally forests are auctioned in a standing position and so the figures of produce removed by the contractors lack accuracy. Hence, there is need for varifying the reported figures through sample checks. In the case of minor forest produce, quantitative estimates of out-turn are not reported for several items. With greater emphasis on the exploitation of minor forest produce and better organization of the agencies for collection of these produce, the need for getting improved data on both quantity and value becomes obvious. Sometimes, when the rights for exploitation of minor forest produce are auctioned, it may be difficult to get actual figures. Special efforts are needed to get reliable estimates of minor forest produce both in terms of quantity and value. As an example of how better statistics will help in better administration it may be mentioned that in Madhya Pradesh after nationalization of trade in tendu leaves, the revenue from tendu leaves shot up from Rs. 86 lakhs in 1963-64 to Rs. 812 lakhs in 1968-69. This was largely due to complete reporting of all tendu leaves collected. For evaluating the out-turn of both major and minor forest products the question arises as to the point at which the value is to be reckoned. For ensuring inter-State uniformity and correct estimation of the contribution to the national income from the forestry sector, the concept of value of out-turn should be clearly defined and should relate to the value at the first point of sale by the Forest Departments.

PRICES AND COSTS

Data on annual average wholesale prices of various species of timber, sleepers, fuelwood, and plywood are reported for important assembling and marketing centres in different States. The scope of these statistics needs to be enlarged. Wholesale prices according to species and types of produce should be collected by size-classes at coup sites. Government depots and important assembling and marketing centres at intervals of a fortnight or a month. Wholesale prices of minor produce should be collected by size-classes at forest sites. Government depots and important assembling and marketing centres at intervals of a fortnight or a month. Wholesale prices of minor forest produce should also be collected regularly on a monthly basis to start with. For a study of the trends in prices of forest produce, compilation of index numbers of wholesale prices of timber, fuelwood and other forest produce should be initiated. Forestry items should also be included in the scope of the All-India Index Number or Wholesale Prices.

For indicating the lines on which improvement in the efficiency of forest management can be achieved a careful analysis of the costs of various operations from the stage of plantations to the actual marketing of timber is necessary. As these forest operations and management are done through departmental agencies, it should be possible to work out these costs on the basis of available data. What is important is to bring in the economic concepts and the usual principles of costing and making the data available either as part of administration reports or as a regular series. Similarly compilation of data on cost of collection of minor forest produce together with the data in prices received for them would throw light on the measures necessary for improving the efficiency of collection pf minor forest produce.

EMPLOYMENT IN FORESTRY

The State Forest Departments report at present the number of persons employed annually in management, extraction and primary and secondary industries under various categories. Data on permanent and temporary labour force are also reported by some States. The available data, however, are incomplete and lack uniformity. In view of the highly labour intensive nature of the forestry sector, we recommend that regular data on labour employed in activities such as forest plantations, silvicultural operations, communications, tree-felling, transport, collection of forest produce and primary and secondary industries should be collected according to uniform concepts and definitions. Separate data for skilled and unskilled labour, source of labour—whether local or migrant and status of labour—whether wholly or partly dependent on forest occupations, should also be collected.

FOREST INVENTORY SURVEYS

Forest inventory surveys are basis for a proper and planned exploitation of this national asset. The data which need to be collected relate to the stocking of various species, gross increment, cuts, natural losses by fire, insects and diseases and climatic factors, potential increment, production of minor forest produce, etc. These surveys need not form part of regular, annual forest statistics. The proposals regarding forest inventory survey are fully dealt with in Chapter 46 on Forest Planning, Research and Education.

ORGANIZATIONAL SET-UP

Forest statistics, as already mentioned, are collected mainly as byproducts of forest administration and management and would continue to be so. However, with increased requirements of statistical data for policy formulation, planning and implementation of forest development programmes, the existing agencies at different levels for collection of these data are inadequate and need to be strengthened. Range is the lowest administrative unit for forest management and at this level the Range Forest Officer is responsible for the collection and reporting of data in addition to this other duties. In order to enable the collection of the various types of data suggested by us, we are of the view that a full time Forester (Statistics) should be provided in each range to attend to maintenance of registers, culling out data from the records and reporting them to higher level in the prescribed proformae. At the divisional level, the Divisional Forest Officer should be assisted by a Range Forest Officer (Statistics) on a whole-time basis for this work. In addition to consolidation of information at the divisional level, he should also visit the different ranges and verify the accuracy of the various types of data collected in the ranges. He may be assisted by a Junior Statistical Assistant in compiling and consolidating the returns. At the circle level, the statistical agency will consist of a Class II Statistical Officer, assisted by requisite complement of Statistical Assistants and Clerks. Their functions will be not only to consolidate the data received from the different divisions, but also to analyze and interpret the data so as to help in the planning and formulation of suitable programmes.

At the State headquarters the Chief Conservator of Forests should be assisted by a Director of Forest Statistics of the rank of Conservator of Forests. He should be assisted by requisite number of statisticians to deal with different aspects of forestry statistics. Corresponding strengthening is necessary at the level of the Ministry of Agriculture also. The existing statistical unit in the Central Forestry Commission should be developed into a full-fledged Statistical Division and put under the charge of a Statistician in an appropriate scale.

ITEMS OF INFORMATION AVAILABLE

The principal forest statistics relate to area under forests, volumes of standing timber and firewood, quantity and value of out-turn of timber, firewood and minor forest produce, employment in forestry and forest industries, foreign trade and data on revenue and expenditure. Miscellaneous information on the progress of working plans, breaches of forest rules and grazing of cattle in Government forests is also collected. The scope of forest statistics has been expanded since 1958-59 to include data on area afforested and deforested, area surveyed, classification of forests by management status, silvicultural system and density, out-turn of logs and sleepers, and wholesale prices of forest produce. The Central Forestry Commission which was set up in 1865 collects data on certain aspect of forestry such as area under forests by ownership, legal status, composition, out-turn of forest produce, etc.

Detailed data on the area under 'coniferous' or soft wood and 'non-coniferous' or broad leaved forests are reported by the State Forest Departments according to types of ownership. Data on area under forests according to legal status, i.e. 'reserved', 'protected' and 'unclassed' are being collected for coniferous and non-coniferous forests separately. Some of the data particularly out-turn are available according to species such as *deodar, chir, kail,* and *fir* among coniferous trees and *sal*, teak, *suso, simul* and others in non-coniferous species. The importance of various types of wood varies from State to State.

Statistics of out-turn of major forest produce are at present available for timber, fuel, logs, sleepers etc. both in terms of quantity and value. These are classified into 'coniferous' and 'non-coniferous' wood. Separate data are also available for sawn timber, round wood and fuel wood including charcoal wood and wood for distillation. In regard to minor forest produce, only statistics of value of production are available for bamboos and canes, drugs, fibres and flosses, fodder and grazing, grass other than fodder, lac, gums and resins, dye-stuffs, tanning materials, *bidi* leaces, vegetable oils and seeds, charcoal, ivory, honey and bee-wax. Data on annual average wholesale prices of various species of timber, sleepers, fuelwood, pulpwood and plywood are reported for important assembling and marketing centres in different States.

The State Forest Departments report at present the number of persons employed annually in management, extraction and primary and secondary industries under various categories. Data on permanent and temporary labour force are also reported by some States.

Data

The subject was one of the theme at the Annual Conference of India Society of Agricultural Economics, 2000. During discussion participants mentioned that the data from various sources on forestry related matters were not consistent with each other. The area, productivity, and rate of deforestation varied widely depending upon the source of data. The Group discussed three important sources of these data: (i) Forest Survey of India, (ii) Land Use Statistics, and (iii) the data available from National Remote Sensing Agency (NRSA). Apparently, researchers often used these data without fully understanding how these data were collected and what definitions and parameters were considered for collection of the data. It was also pointed out that in some states, the area under forest cover changed from one year to another because definition of 'forest' was changed and these states included social forestry plantations in the category of natural forests, thus ending to over-estimation of the area of natural forests. It was argued that the NRSA data were more reliable but often these data were not available in disaggregate form particularly for micro level analysis. It was recommended that researchers should use Geographical Information System (GIS) data for area and quality of forest cover. The data related to other aspects of forestry such as number of species available, the type and natue of Non-timber Forest Products (NTFPs), method of collection and distribution, etc., were generally not available. It was pointed out that some states have created a special cell within the Forest Department to collect information related to NTFPs and bio-diversity. However, these data were not made available to the public for research or other purposes. Some efforts were also being made by the NGOs and individuals but these were not sufficient. The Group felt that the Forest Department should make concerted efforts to generate a data bank on NTFPs and plant species in different forest ecology.

Valuation of Forest Resources and Products

The Group also debated the valuation of forest resources and products. It was pointed out that market prices often did not reflect the true value of resource or product for two reasons: (i) most forest products often did not enter the market, and (ii) markets for forest produce were often distorted for a variety of reasons including restrictions on trading. It was argued that the value of forest could only be determined by considerations of both direct and indirect use values as well as non-use (existence) value of forest and their products. To determine the real value of forest, social-cost benefits and contingent evaluation methods were suggested. However, the Group noted the limitations of these methods and it was argued that these methods often gave only crude estimates. The Group recommended that there was need for detailed discussion on forest valuation. It was also suggested that the valuation of forests and their product should form essential part of Agricultural Economics curriculum.

EXISTING SHORTCOMINGS AND IMPROVEMENTS DESIRED

(i) There is a large discrepancy between the area under forests as published in 'Forestry Statistics India' and the figures published in 'Indian Agricultural Statistics'. According to land use statistics the total area under forests is 68.75 million hectares during 1996-97. Area as reported in Forest Statistics India aggregate to 76.5 million ha. This difference should be reconciled. At the State level, the Chief Conservator of Forests and the crop reporting authority should get together and take steps to eliminate the differences.

(ii) Complete information is not available in respect of forests under civil authorities, cooperate bodies and private individuals.

(iii) With regard to classification, the importance of various types of wood varies from State to State. While the State Governments may adopt a more detailed classification for collection of information in their own State, it is desirable that they should collect the data on the uniform classification so that compilation at All-India level becomes possible.

(iv) There is considerable quantity of timber and fuelwood grown outside the forest lands. Suitable procedures have to be devised to frame estimates of unrecorded production through sample surveys or otherwise.

(v) Crops being cultivated in the forest areas are not being recorded in the total production estimates. This is a serious deficiency from the point of national accounting. This has to be removed.

(vi) In the case of minor forest produce, quantitative estimates of out-turn are not reported for several items. With greater emphasis on the exploitation of minor forest produce, there is need for collection of data on both quantity and value of all the minor forest products.

(vii) For ensuring inter-State uniformity and correct estimation of the contribution to the national income from the forest sector, the concept of value of out-turn, of both major and minor forest products, should be clearly defined and should relate to the value at the first point of sale by the forest departments.

(viii) Wholesale prices of various species of timber, sleepers, fuelwood, pulpwood and plywood should be collected by size-classes at different sites at intervals of a fortnight or a month. Wholesale prices of minor forest produce should be collected regularly. For a study of the trends in prices of forest produce, compilation of index numbers of wholesale prices of major and minor forest produce should be initiated.

(ix) A careful analysis of the costs of various operations from the stage of plantations to the actual marketing of timber is necessary. This will help in deciding the lines on which improvements in the efficiency of forest management can be achieved. Similarly, compilation of data on cost of collection of minor forest produce together with the data on prices received for them would be useful.

(x) Regular data on labour employed in activities such as forest plantations, silvicultural operations, communications, tree-feeling, transport, collection of forest produce and primary and secondary industries should be collected according to uniform concepts and definitions.

(xi) The forms in which the data are collected are not in conformity with the proformae issued by F.A.O. for collection and dissemination of forest statistics. At present every State has its own forms, its own methods of collection and presentation. The forms should be of uniform pattern and the collection of data and presentation of results need improvement.

(xii) Forest inventory surveys should be undertaken periodically and data that needs to be collected should include stocking of various species, gross increments, cuts, natural losses by fire, insects, diseases and climatic factors, etc.

Issues and Strategies Assam, one of the north-eastern states is situated between the latitude of 22 degree N and 28 degree N longitude 90 degree E and 96 degree E having boundaries common with Arunachal Pradesh, Nagaland, Mizoram, Meghalaya, Tripura and international boundaries with Bangladesh and Bhutan. Geographically, the State can be divided into Brahmaputra and Barak valleys, separated by the hilly tracts of North Cachar Hills and Karbi Anglong. The climate sub-tropical with mean annual rainfall varying from 1,500 mm. to 3,750 mm and mean annual temperature between 5 degree celsius in winter to about 39 degree celsius.

Annexure 5.1

Area Under Forests ('000 ha) in 1993-94

Name of the State/UT	As per land record System	As per forest surveyor India
Andhra Pradesh	6246	4290.7
Arunachal Pradesh	5154	6860.2
Assam	1984	2382.4
Bihar	2949	2652.4
Goa	125	124.7
Gujarat	1886	1158.7
Haryana	168	60.4
Himachal Pradesh	1043	1252.1
Jammu & Kashmir	2747	2044.0
Karnataka	3076	324.0
Kerala	1081	1033.4
Madhya Pradesh	14645	13119.5
Maharashtra	5282	4601.9
Manipur	602	1741.8
Meghalaya	938	1565.7
Mizoram	1303	1877.5
Nagaland	863	1422.1
Orissa	55534	4673.0
Punjab	290	138.7
Rajasthan	2426	1335.3
Sikkim	257	312.9
Tamil Nadu	2144	1704.3
Tripura	606	544.6
Uttar Pradesh	5165	3399.4
West Bengal	1194	622.6
A & N Islands	691	664.7
Chandigarh	1	0.7
D & N Haveli	20	20.4
Daman and Diu	-	0.3
Delhi	1	2.6
Lakshadeep	-	-
Pondicherry	-	-
All India	68421	62857.0

6

Area Statistics

METHODS OF COLLECTION OF AREA STATISTICS

From the standpoint of collection of area statistics, the country can be divided into three categories. In the first category are the former temporarily settled States where the village revenue agency collects the statistics as part of land records. The agency consists of village official[1]—one incharge of a village or a group of villages. The collection of primary data on the basis of field to field inspection of crops and land utilization at periodic intervals is part of their duty. After each crop inspection, the village official is required to submit to his superior officer a statement showing the land utilization statistics in each season, in standard forms prescribed for the purpose. The superior officer called 'Kanungo' or Revenue Inspector, who is in charge of a revenue circle varying in size from 30 to 100 villages, controls and supervises the work of the village officials. The second category consists of former permanently settled States of West Bengal, Orissa and Kerala where no such village revenue agencies exist. As such, the land utilization and crop area statistics in these States are based on sample surveys. The third category consists of areas which are neither cadastrally surveyed nor possess the requisite revenue agency and occurs in parts of both the first and second categories of States. In these areas the statistics reported are in the nature of estimates based on the personal knowledge of the revenue officers as in the absence of cadastral survey and village officials complete enumeration and sample surveys cannot be conducted. Thus, of the total reporting area of about 304.87 million hectares, estimates for 81.7 per cent of the area are based on complete-enumeration, 9.2 per cent on sample surveys and those for the remaining 9.1 per cent of the area are based on conventional methods or impressionistic estimates by Village Headman, Chowkidars and Superior Revenue Officials.

---

[1]The village official is called 'Patwari' in Punjab, Haryana, Jammu & Kashmir, Himachal Pradesh, Delhi, Rajasthan and Madhya Pradesh; 'ekhpal' in U.P.; 'Karnam' in Tamil Nadu and Andhra Pradesh; 'Shanbhog' in Karnataka; 'Talathi' in Maharashtra and Gujarat; 'Karamchari' in Bihar and 'Mandal' in Assam.

AGENCY FOR AREA STATISTICS

In the area where all fields have been cadastrally surveyed and mapped, the geographical area of each survey number and sub-number is accurately known and thus the area under the crop for a given region can be determined accurately. If, however, the whole field is not under the same crop or if there are patches included in the field for which only the total geographical area is known, the area under the crop is normally estimated approximately by the Patwari. Thus, as a system, the collection of data based on land records is the best, provided the basic records are maintained properly. Since the basic land records are maintained by the Patwari, he is the best person to do the crop inspection. He is the most knowledgeable man in the field and, as such, the most suitable man for getting reliable information if he has the will to do it and if he can be persuaded to do an honest job or enabled to do so. Further, land records being authoritative and legal documents, data based on them have certain statutory validity also. The association of Patwari with the land records and the agricultural statistics brings to bear upon the system of collection, the authority and prestige that is associated with revenue agency in the villages.

In actual practice, however, it has been found that due to a number of reasons the Patwari does not devote the time and attention that is needed to the collection of agricultural statistics, resulting in inaccuracies in recording and delays in submission of returns. Firstly, the geographical jurisdiction of each Patwari is large, particularly in North India. Secondly, his functions and responsibilities have considerably increased during the recent years. The Patwari is called upon to assist the local development agencies in various ways including the certification of loan applications with regard to the title to the land offered as a security. Further, whenever any major campaign or programme such as population census, drought and flood relief, preparation of electoral rolls, elections, etc. is launched, his services are indented for. It is these more pressing and immediate items of work which distrupt the normal schedule of duties of the Patwari with regard to the collection of agricultural statistics and timely submission of land records and other returns. Apart from this, the basic reason for the unreliability and time-lag in the collection of agricultural statistics is the indifference shown by the Patwari and his superior officers to statistical data collection in recent years. After varifying the position at his field level, it is necessary is find out ways and means to improves the situation.

As the collection of timely and reliable agricultural statistics is basic to agricultural planning, considerable thought to the question of improvements in the existing situation needs be given. The three possible ways to remedy the situation are: (a) to replace the Patwari by an alternative agency for the primary collection of statistics, (b) to see that the Patwari agency works better under proper supervision with appropriate training and adequate guidance, and (c) to discard complete enumeration and have the basic data through random sample surveys. However, the creation of an independent primary reporting agency responsible for collection of agricultural statistics working under the Agriculture Department in coordination with the Revenue Department, need not necessarily bring about the desired improvement in agricultural statistics. First, the number of such primary reporters needed will be so large as to be prohibitively expensive. Secondly, these primary workers too need the assistance of the Patwari with regard to the village map and the identification of survey numbers and even if the additional expenditure is incurred, it is doubtful whether this agency will have the authority and the prestige of the Patwari to deal with agricultural statistics at the base level.

The alternative method of having independent sample surveys for providing the various agricultural statistics replacing the complete enumeration, is not favoured because, firstly, the sample survey cannot give estimates at lower geographical levels unless the number of samples chosen is very large; secondly, such surveys will not give reliable estimates of the area under minor crops. For agricultural planning, particularly planning from below, detailed statistics at the block/taluk level and above are needed. As such, the method of sample surveys cannot be recommended as a substitute for complete enumeration. Sample surveys, however, have an important role to play, namely in providing a check on the reliability of complete enumeration and also to give supplementary information needed for agricultural planning.

Thus, the only way of improving the basic structure for agricultural statistics is to enable the Patwari to do his job better and also to ensure that the Patwari and the revenue inspectors at higher level devote adequate attention to the collection of agricultural statistics and give top priority to the work especially during the periods of crop inspection. Firstly, the Patwari agency should be enabled to work better by reducing the jurisdiction of each Patwari to manageable proportion. Secondly, intensive supervision both through normal revenue agencies and statistical staff, should be organized over the work of the Patwari. The primary and supervisory agencies should, therefore, be suitably strengthened. The measures necessary for improvement of area statistics through the Timely Reporting Scheme are discussed later in this chapter.

AGRICULTURAL STATISTICS OF INDIA

Coverage statistics of the distribution of gross cropped area by crops are published in the Agricultural Statistics of India, Vols. I and II. They are based on the information contained in the Season and Crop Reports issued annually by the State Governments. For quite a long time, area statistics by crops were available for a limited number of crops and were collected and reported for most of the British Provinces and a few of the Indian States. Before Independence, the coverage of crop forecasts was not only incomplete, but it also differed from crop to crop. The forecast covered only those States where the crop was grown to an appreciable extent and where facilities for reporting were available. Conventional estimates of acreage and production of these crops in respect of non-reporting areas were developed in the interest of complete coverage for the country. The coverage of food crops is complete from the year 1948-49; conventional estimates are still prepared for those areas where no regular returns exist. The geographical coverage of commercial crops is now much larger than before and is fairly complete in respect of important ones.

The classification earlier adopted for area under different types of crops was not detailed and accurate enough for the purpose of food and agricultural administration. On the recommendations of the Inter-Departmental Committe on Agricultural Statistics, the scope of the classification was extended. Detailed figures are now available in respect of kharif and rabi cereals and pulses separately. The category 'pulses' has been split up into gram, tur or arhar and other kharif and pulses.

Statistics of irrigated area under these crops are also available now. The scope of the group of crops known as condiments and species has also been enlarged. The general head 'oilseeds' has been split up into edible and non-edibles; sesamum, rape and mustard, coconut and groundnut being considered as edible and linseed as well as castor being treated as non-edible. The classification of crops is fairly detailed and separate figures are now published in respect of the following groups and subgroups (Table 6.1).

Forecasts

Acreage figures for a current year are periodically made available through crop forecasts. Normally two to three forecasts are issued for each crop, and in the case of certain crops like cotton, even five forecasts are issued. The first, which is released a month after sowing, gives a tentative idea of the area sown and of the germination conditions. The second estimate issued two months later supplies the estimate of area brought up to date, and also the condition of the crop. These preliminary estimates (both first and second) are based on eye-estimation reports only. The final estimate which gives an accurate picture of the area and production is based on field-to-field inspection made by the Patwari (village accountant). Some revisions are made in the final forecast figure later, on the basis of the 'Season and Crop Reports' issued by the States. Numbers of forecasts issued and their timings for each crop are shown in Table 6.2.

The available data are, however, not of uniform standard of accuracy and reliability as methods of their collection in the various States vary at present. This is mainly due to the differences in the administrative and land revenue systems prevalent in the country. Broadly speaking, the whole country can be divided into two barts based on the system of Land revenue settlement, namely, the temporarily settled areas and the

Table 6.1 Classification of Crops for Which Area Statistics are Released

I.	Food crops	
	(a) Foodgrains	
	(i) Cereals	Rice-autumn, winter, summer and total, cholum or jowar—kharif, rabi and total, cumbu or bajra, maize, ragi or marua, wheat, barley, other cereals and small millets—kharif, rabi and total, total cereals and millets.
	(ii)	Gram, tur of arhar, other pulses—kharif, rabi and total, total pulses. Total foodgrains.
	(b) Sugar, sugarcane, others, total.	
	(c) Condiments and species	Pepper (black), chilli, ginger, turmeric, cardamoms, moms, betelnuts, others, total.
	(d) Fruits and vegetables including	Fruits—dried—cashewnuts, others.
		fresh—mangoes, citrus fruits, bananas, grapes, others.
	root crops	Vegetables—potatoes, tapioca, sweet potatoes, onions.
		Others—kharif and rabi.
		Total fruits and vegetables.
	(e) Other food crops	
		Total food crops.
II.	Non-food crops	
	(a) Oilseeds	Groundnut, castor, sesamum (til or jinjili), rape and mustard, linseed, coconut, others, total.
	(b) Fibres	Cotton, Jute, mesta sannhemp, others, total.
	(c) Dyes and tanning materials	Indigo, others, total.
	(d) Drugs and narcotics	Opium, coffee, tea, tobacco, cinchona, Indian hemp, others, total.
	(e) Fodder crops	
	(f) Green manure crops	
	(g) Others non-food crops	
		Total non-food crops.

permanently settled areas. The position in respect of each of the above two parts, is discussed below.

Temporarily Settled Areas

In the case of temporarily settled areas the entire system of land revenue assessment is revised at fixed intervals. Land revenue is collected by Government directly from the land-holder or the cultivator. A vast organization of Patwaris (village accountants), Kanungoes (circle inspectors) and revenue officers exists for the purpose of land

Table 6.2 Due Dates of Receipt of State Returns and Issue of All-India Crop Estimates

Crop	Estimate	Due date of receipt of returns from States	Due date of issue of all-India estimate
		Foodgrains	
1. Rice	First	October 15	October 20
	Second	December 15	December 20
	Final	February 15	February 20
2. Jowar	First	October 31	November 21
	Second	January 31	February 21
	Final	March 31	April 21
3. Bajra	First	October 31	November 21
	Final	February 28	March 21
4. Maize	First	October 31	November 21
	Final	February	28 March 21
5. Ragi	First	October 31	November 15
	Final	February 28	March 15
6. Small millets	First	November 5	November 15
	Second	February 5	February 15
	Final	May 20	May 20
7. Wheat	First	January 15	January 30
	Second	March 15	March 20
	Final	May 25	May 30
8. Barley	First	January 15	January 30
	Second	March 15	March 30
	Final	May 15	May 30
9. Gram	First	January 15	January 30
	Second	March 15	March 30
	Final	May 15	May 30
10. Tur	First	September 15	September 25
	Second	January 15	January 25
	Final	May 15	May 25
11. Other kharif pulses	First	September, 15	September 25
	Final	January 15	January 25
12. Other rabi pulses	First	January 15	January 25
	Final	May 15	May 25
		Oil Seeds	
13. Groundnut	First	August 15	August 20
	Second	November 10	November 15
	Final	February 10	February 15
14. Castor	Final	April 30	May 10
15. Sesamum	First	August 15	September 1
	Second	October 15	October 20
	Third	January 1	January 15
	Final	April 15	April 20
16. Rapeseed and mustard	First	December 20	January 1
	Second	March 1	March 15
	Final	May 15	June 1

Table 6.2 Due Dates of Receipt of State Returns and Issue of All-India Crop Estimates (Contd.)

Crop	Estimate	Due date of receipt of returns from States	Due date of issue of all-India estimate
17. Linseed	First	December 20	January 1
	Second	March 1	March 15
	Final	May 15	June 1
18. Nigerseed	Final	February 28	March 15
19. Safflower	Final	May 15	May 30
20. Coconut	Final	September 5	September 15
		Fibres	
21. Cotton	First	August 10	August 15
	Second	October 10	October 15
	Third	December 10	December 15
	Fourth	February 10	February 15
	Final	May 5	May 10
22. Jute	First	July 31	August 15
	Final	October 20	November 7
23. Mesta	First	July 31	August 15
	Second	October 20	November 7
	Final	March 7	March 15
24. Sannhemp	First	August 15	August 20
	Final	January 15	January 20
		Miscellaneous Crops	
25. Sugarcane	First	June 21	July 1
	Second	October 21	October 31
	Final	May 15	May 25
26. Tobacco	First	January 15	January 24
	Second	March 20	April 1
	Third	May 20	May 31
	Final	August 10	August 20
27. Potato	First	January 31	February 5
	Final	June 15	June 20
28. Pepper (Black)	Final	March 26	April 5
29. Chillis (Dry)	Final	April 25	May 5
30. Ginger (Dry)	Final	March 5	March 15
31. Arecanut	Final	September 5	September 15
32. Turmeric	Final	June 15	June 30
33. Banana	Final	September 15	September 25
34. Guarseed	Final	January 15	February 1

administration, i.e. for the assessment and realization of land revenue and the maintenance of compulsory system of land registration in these areas. The assessment of land revenue is based on land use, the crops grown in each season, etc., and this necessitates a continuous detailed record of crops, etc. For every village or group of villages there is a Patwari, who collects the primary data on the basis of field to field inspection at periodic intervals. After each crop inspection, the Patwari is required to submit consolidated statements showing the areas under different crops, etc., in each season to the circle inspector on the prescribed forms. The circle inspector, in charge of each revenue circle consisting of about 100 villages, controls and supervises the work of Patwaris. The work of collection and compilation of agricultural statistics is supervised and controlled at successive stages by the tehsil and district officers of the Revenue Department. Estimates of area under crops are thus compiled on the basis of complete field to field enumeration by the primary reporting agencies in all the States except in West Bengal, Orissa and Kerala where such elaborate agencies do not exist.

Temporarily settled areas are mostly surveyed cadastrally except for some minor portions for which the maps do not indicate boundaries separating two fields. The absence of such demarcations renders exact reporting by the Patwaris difficult and, therefore, area statistics of such tracts are of an approximate character.

Permanently Settled Areas

In the permanently settled areas land revenue has been fixed permanently. These areas mainly consist of large estates of *jagirs*. Land revenue, which is fixed in perpetuity, is paid to Government by the estate holders, called jagirdars. As this system of land settlement and revenue collection did not require the maintenance of area and crop statistics for each farmer, there used to be no elaborate agency for the collection of these statistics and there were no revenue officers in the villages. In the absence of the Patwari agency, the work of primary collection of agricultural statistics in these areas is generally entrusted to the village chowkidars who belong to the Police Department, are not trained in crop reporting and are often illiterate. There is also no adequate supervision over the work of the primary agency for the collection of statistics. The estimates are framed by ascertaining the relation which the area under a crop in each season bears to the normal acreage under that crop during the settlement year. These estimates are generally based on the personal knowledge of the tehsildars and the reports of the village chowkidars. The estimates framed by the tehsildars are again modified by the district officers on the basis of their personal knowledge.

In the absence of an elaborate reporting agency in the permanently settled areas agricultural statistics are not perfect either in availability or reliability. During the past few years steps have been taken to improve the quality of these statistics through the adoption of the method of random sampling surveys and by extending the coverage under complete enumeration. In the States of Kerala, Orissa and West Bengal area statistics are based on sample surveys only. Efforts are being made to institute the system of complete area enumeration in these States also.

Area Statistics

From the point of view of collection of area statistis, the States in the country are divided into three broad categoris:-

(i) States and U.Ts. which have been cadastrally surveyed and where area and land use statistics are built up as a part of the land records maintained by the revenue agencies (referred to as "Land Record States"). The system of land record is being followed in 15 states namely Andhra Pradesh. Assam, Bihar, Gujarat, Haryana, Himachal Pradesh, J & K, Karnataka, M.P., Maharashtra, Punjab, Delhi, Rajasthan, Tamil Nadu and U.P. and also in 3 UTs of Chandigarh, Dadar and Nagar Haveli and Pondicherry. These stats/UTs accout for about 86% of reporting area.

(ii) The states where area statistics are collected on the basis of sample surveys (normally known as non-land record states or "Permanently Settled" States which are three in number viz. Kerala, Orissa and West Bengal). A scheme for Establishment of Agency for Reporting of Agricultural Statistics (EARAS) has been introduced in these three states which envisages, inter-alia, estimation of areas by sample surveys in a sufficiently large sample of 20% villages/investigators zones. These states account for about 9% of reporting area.

(iii) Assam (Hilly districts) and North-Eastern Region where no reporting agency had been functioning and the work of collection of Agricultural Statistics is entrusted with the village headmen (5%).

While the area statistics are collected on complete enumeration basis in respect of states in category (i) above, on ad-hoc methods based on impressionistic approach in case of states in category (iii) above, a scheme for Establishment of Agency for Reporting of Agricultural Statistics (EARAS) has been introduced in the three states in category (ii) above.

Reliability of Acreage Statistics Collected by the Primary Reporting Agency

In the temporarily settled areas where, as stated, above the statistics of acreage are collected as part of land records by the Patwaris, the method of collection is one of field to field enumeration of the entire area under the jurisdiction of the Patwari, twice or thrice a year. Though this method of complete enumeration was sound in principle, it could not always be claimed to be so in practice owing to defects in the primary reporting agencies. Serious doubts had in fact been entertained in certain quarters regarding the reliability of acreage statistics provided by Patwaris owing to the tendency on their part to neglect making a rigorous personal inspection of the fields and to rely for their information on the reports received from villagers. As the supervision exercised on Patwaris' records by superior officers was not sufficiently comprehensive, the data were considered all the more doubtful. The experience of the Indian Council of Agricultural Research, which had been conducting crop-cutting surveys on crops, however, showed that these statistics were not in any way substantially inaccurate.

A good deal of evidence has, in fact, been collected in recent years which shows that the picture of land utilization based on Patwaris' records, as at present maintained, is broadly correct and suggests that given adequate and effective supervision over their work, the Patwari system can be depended upon to give reliable statistics of acreage. However, improvements in acreage statistics by enforcing adequate and independent supervision over the work of the Patwari has been emphasized. Financial assistance, on matching basis, was given by the Centre to the States to induce them to take up the scheme for rationalized supervision during the Second Five Year Plan period.

In the permanently settled areas, in Bihar, the State Government has already switched over from the chowkidari system of reporting the acreage to that of complete enumeration, with the help of specially appointed field staff. In West Bengal and Orissa, the State Governments have changed over from the traditional method of reporting to random sample surveys. Table 6.3 indicates the crops along with the years when the method of estimation changed in these States.

Table 6.3 Crops and Method of Estimation

State	Crops	Year when the method of estimation changed
Bihar	Rice, maize, wheat, barely, gram, sugarcane, jute and tobacco	1948-49
	Jowar, bajra, ragi, sesamum, rape and mustard, linseed, and castor seed	1949-50
West Bengal	Rice	1947-48
	Gram	1948-49
	Wheat, barley, linseed, rape and mustard	1949-50
	Sugarcane	1950-51
	Jute	1951-52
Orissa	Rice and Jute	1959-60

In case of jute in West Bengal, the acreage was based on random sample surveys in 1949-50 and on eye-estimates in 1950-51. Since 1951-52, it has been based on random sample surveys except for Darjeeling District.

Estimates of Area and Production

Area and production statistics are also published in Estimates of Area and Production of Principal Crops issued by the Directorate of Economics and Statistics. The latest one, the seventy-ninth issue of the publication was released in May, 1999. It contains statistics of area, production and average yield of principal crops, All-India aggregates have been given for the period 1950-51, 1960-61 and 1970-71 and 1997-98 and state-wise statistics for 1980-81, 1990-91 and 1992-93 to 1997-98. Estimates of production of principal crops on calendar year basis have also been given in addition to the presentation of their estimates on agricultural year basis..

The first issue giving the estimates of area and production was published in the year 1899 under the name 'Area and Yield of Certain Crops' and gave data relating to rice, wheat, cotton, linseed, rape and mustard, sesamum, jute and indigo for the years 1891-92 to 1898-99. In 1900-1901, sugarcane and groundnut were added subsequently tea was also included. The 16th issue published in 1915 was titled 'Estimates of Area and Yield of Principal Crops in India, 1913-14' and gave besides the estimates for the crops mentioned earlier, a supplementary table giving area and yield of barley, jowar, bajra and gram. Coffee and rubber were added to the list of crops for which estimates were given in 1920-21, castor in 1925-21, castor in 1925-26 and tobacco in 1926-27. In view of the diminishing importance of indigo, estimates for the crop were dropped from 1932-33 onwards, but included again later.

The 'Estimates of Area and Yield of Principal Crops' was published more or less in this form by the Department of Commercial Intelligence and Statistics up to the year 1943-44. Soon after partition, the Directorate of Economics and Statistics issued an ad hoc publication entitled 'Estimates of Area and Yield of Principal Crops' for the years 1936-37 to 1945-46 which gave separate figures for Indian Provinces, Indian States and Pakistan Provinces and Pakistan States separately. Subsequently, ad hoc publications containing the estimates were issued from time to time. Estimates of Area and Production of Principal Crops in India, has now become a normal annual feature. This provides all-India figures for practically all the important crops from 1949-50 and State-wise data for the five years. From the 58th issue released in 1969, the scope of the publication was widened by including variety-wise figures for cotton and tobacco.

Minor Crops

As regards the minor crops, area and production of these crops in each State is relatively so small that periodical crop estimates are not issued. Yet, in view of their commercial importance, special efforts are made to collect figures of area and production. The information available in the State Season and Crop Reports, Agricultural Statistics returns and other ad hoc data received from the States are utilized in preparing these estimates. The data in respect of papaya, indigo, opium and stick lac are now issued by the Directorate of Economics and Statistics. The quality of these estimates, however, differs from that of the forecast crops.

While utilizing the estimates of area and production given in the publication mentioned above, the following points may be borne in mind.

The geographical coverage of the estimates for different crops is not complete. Till recently figures in respect of each crop related to areas where the crop was extensively grown or was commercially important and tracts where the crop was of minor importance were excluded. Moreover, the areas where no arrangements existed for reporting crop estimates also did not furnish the necessary returns. Recently, however, attempts are being made to extend gradually the coverage of the estimates, although it is not yet complete in respect of several crops especially the non-food crops. In the case of cereals and grams, estimates for non-reporting areas are also available from the triennium ending 1938-39. Up to 1942-43, the estimates are based on information published in the 'Food Statistics of India, 1946'. Estimates for the years 1943-44 to 1947-48 are based on the average figures for the seven years ending 1942-43 after making due allowances for transference of area from non-reporting to the reporting fold. From 1948-49 onwards, these estimates are based on special returns received from the States and on the information contained in the Season and Crop Reports and Agricultural Statistics and as such are not comparable with the corresponding estimates for earlier years.

NSS Series of Acreage Statistics

Up to the 26th round of NSS, data on land utilization showing area under seven cereals were collected on the random sampling basis. Estimates of area under crops are given in terms of 'gross area' and 'allocated area'. The 'gross area' under a crop is defined as the area under the crop grown singly (pure) together with the total area under all mixed having that crop as one of the components. The allocated area under a crop is defined as the area under the crop grown singly plus only the apportioned area under the crop from all the mixed crops having that particular crop as one of the components. For obtaining the apportioned area under the crop, gross area under a mixed crop is allocated to its different components at the plot level by an eye estimation on the basis of the relative intensity of plants. The estimates are presented for all-India and census zones.

A comparison between the NSS estimates of acreage under cereals and the official estimates shows close agreement at the all-India level. The agreement, however, is not sufficiently close in the case of zone-wise and crop-wise figures. The differences may be accounted for by (i) the differences in coverage of crops/seasons, (ii) non-comparability of the experience in the field work between the two agencies, (iii) mis-classification of area under the grain crop and the fodder crop, (iv) differences in the methods of allocation of area under mixed crops, and (v) possible sampling errors.

Pre-Harvest Surveys

Advance estimates of crop production have become extremely necessary in planned economy for policy and administration purpose; particularly for the preparation of National Food Budget. An experiment was first made by the National Sample Survey by launching large-scale sample surveys to obtain pre-harvest estimates of crop acreages of the principal crops. Field work was conducted by the Patwaris under the State authorities and processing was done by three agencies—the State authorities, the Directorate of National Sample Survey, Government of India and the Indian Statistical Institute. The scheme had, however, to be given up because of a number of administrative and technical problems.

Such advance estimates are now being prepared on the basis of qualitative information obtained from the States and also reports received from inspecting officers of the Market Intelligence Unit of the Food and Agriculture Ministry posted in the various States. These cannot in any way be considered as fully reliable and scientific.

Supervision of Crop Area Enumeration

According to the instructions laid down in the Land Records Manual, the Patwari is required to move from village to village and inspect each *khasra* (field) number and record its areas under different crops and other land-uses in a register called the *khasra* register.

The revenue inspector has to visit each village at least once in each field inspection season, and check the land-use and crop statistics recorded by the Patwari in respect of a few *khasra* numbers selected in rotation. Some *khasra* numbers are also revisited before they come in rotation of inspection as an extra check against possible neglect of work by the Patwari.

The superintendents and assistant superintendents of Land Records are required to tour for 130 to 150 days in the year and inspect each Patwari's work in villages selected by rotation. In the villages visited, they check 50 per cent of the entries in the *khasra* register already checked by the revenue inspector and a sufficiently large number of additional entries to ensure that the Patwari has done the field inspection properly and the revenue inspector has verified his work correctly. The villages for supervision in a particular year are selected by rotation in such a manner that all are covered in a course of 5 to 7 years.

Thus, the Land Records Manual makes elaborate provision for adequate supervision of Patwari's work. The prescribed supervision serves the twin purposes of improving the accuracy of basic agricultural data and imparting instructions to Patwaris through actual spot inspection. The Patwaris are also made familiar with the new concepts and definitions introduced in the field of agricultural statistics from time to time through personal contact and practical illustrations. This procedure, however, suffers from two defects. Firstly, the selection of villages and *khasra* numbers by rotation gives a prior knowledge to the Patwari as to which villages and fields are not likely to be inspected in a particular year and how he can afford to neglect the work in them. Secondly, the results of the supervision are not recorded in a suitable proforma so that they might be processed to give an idea of the extent of errors in the areas of different crops and land utilization recorded by Patwaris.

During recent years, this revenue staff has been called upon to undertake multifarious duties connected with the various departments of government. The village official has, therefore, not been able to devote due time and attention to the proper compilation of agricultural statistics.

The Technical Committee on Coordination of Agricultural Statistics, 1949, recommended *inter alia* that supervision over the work of the primary reporting agencies in the temporary settled areas might be rationalized by selecting the villages and fields to be inspected on a random basis. The advantages of this method would be two-fold. Firstly, it will put the primary reporter in the proper psychological frame of mind to report reliable data and secondly, it would be possible to develop correction factors for adjusting the figures as reported by the primary reporters for errors of omission and commission. The problem was further discussed at the State Agriculture and Cooperation Ministers Conference held in September 1953. It was observed that there was room for considerable improvement in the supervision of the work of the primary reporting agency and that steps should be taken to improve it on a rationalized basis.

Some of the cotton growing States initiated random checks in 1953-54 on a pilot basis. The result of the scheme were found to be encouraging and it was, therefore, decided that the scheme might be extended to cover all crops and land-use classes and taken up as a normal measure along with the existing crop inspection programme. A scheme was then prepared and circulated to the States. Under this scheme it was envisaged that the kanungos and tehsildars should do a part of their normal work of supervision in a rationalized way. For this purpose, 10 per cent of the villages are to be selected randomly. In the selected villages, 10 per cent of the fields selected on a random basis, are to be inspected. In respect of each selected survey number, the kanungo is required to note down the entry made in the *khasra* register on the basis of the crop inspection done by the Patwari and also the area under the crop grown according to his own spot inspection. On the basis of these two sets of figures, the States statisticians may work out correction factors at the district level, if considered necessary.

AREA UNDER MIXED CROPS

Sowing of two or more crops in mixture is practised more or less all over India. The problem of correct recording of area under mixed crops becomes difficult on account of the fact that even within a State or a district, cultivators practise quite a large number of mixtures. Further, there is considerable variation in the proportion of seeds of the component sown in the case of the same type of mixtures from area to area and even from field to field. Again, the method of sowing of mixtures also varies considerably. Mixtures may be sown either broadcast or in rows, the number of rows of the crop alternating with those of another crop may vary.

Methods of recording areas under mixed crops have to be considered in relation to: (i) estimation of total production of crops, and (ii) estimation of area under the components. In so far as the former is concerned, the difficulty of estimating accurately the area under each of the component crops does not affect the accuracy of the estimated out-turn if the gross area under the mixture is recorded separately and the average yield per acre in respect of mixed crops is also estimated on the basis of the gross area. In practice, however, this may not be easy as for the same crop there are numerous mixtures and it might be difficult to record the gross area under each of these mixtures. This would add considerably to the work at primary and subsequent levels. In regard to the estimation of the acreage under the component crops in the mixtures, apportioning has, however, to be done and the net areas under crops presented to give an account of the utilization of the area.

The question of the adoption of a scientific method for recording the area under mixed crops both for purposes of yield estimation and land utilization statistics was considered by the Technical Committee on Coordination of Agricultural Statistics and it was recommended that:

(i) In all cases, gross unadjusted acreage of the mixture should be recorded separately for each major crop mixture and published in the Season and Crop Reports and Crop Forecasts along with the net acreages of the components.

(ii) Where fixed rates are used for apportioning the areas under mixtures, they should be fixed for each district and their accuracy should be tested at periodical intervals during the crop-cutting surveys.

(iii) For minor crop mixtures, the areas should be allocated to the various components by eye judgement at the field level. In these cases only net acreages after apportionment need be recorded and there is no necessity for recording the gross unadjusted acreage under minor crop mixtures.

The main principle on which the above proposals were based is that estimates of total production would be based on gross area and that the net areas under crops need be presented only to give an account of the utilization of the area. These recommendations were subsequently considered by the State statisticians. The criteria for deciding whether a particular crop mixture is major or minor were laid down as follows:

(i) order of importance of the component crop;

(ii) extent of area under the mixture; and

(iii) actual percentage of the constituent crops in the mixture.

It was further laid down that the method of calculating the net acreage under the component crops of a major crop mixture should be to divide the gross acreage under the mixture in the proportion of corrected seed rates. i.e. the seed rates of the component crops should be reduced to a common scale. Thus if a kg and b kg are the seed rates of two component crops in a mixture and if m kg is their normal seed rates when shown pure, the proportion of the area under the two crops will be $a/m:b/m$.

Present Position

With due consideration to the recommendations discussed above, improvements have been made from time to time. The position as it exists today is that gross areas of some major crop-mixtures as widely practised, are published by some States in their annual tables of Agricultural Statistics and/or Season and Crop Reports. In respect of other crop-mixtures in these States and all crop-mixtures in other States, the proportionate net areas of each component crop from all crop-mixtures involving it are obtained and added to the area sown singly (pure) with it to give its net area which alone is published.

The allocation of gross area of a crop-mixture to its different component crops is done either at the source, i.e. at the field level, by the Patwari during the course of his crop-inspection (*girdawari* or *partal*) and the net area of each component crop is recorded separately in the crop statement (*jinswar*), or the Patwari is allowed to record the whole area of crop-mixture treating it as a single crop and the total area of the mixture is separated to the component crops at the district level. The assignment of net areas to different component crops at the field level is made in proportion to the number of their rows, if they are sown in separate lines. In case the crops in the mixture are sown after thoroughly mixing the seeds, this allocation is done in proportion to actual amount of seeds sown or seed-rates adjusted for mixed sowing or by eye-estimation of the relative stands of component crops. The components occupying negligible area or area below certain specified minimum are in some States, ignored and their areas allocated to the chief component alone or proportionately to all component crops of a mixture. The apportionment of net areas of component crops of a mixture at the district level is done on the basis of a fixed ratio which is supposed to represent the average conditions with regard to one or more of the aforesaid factors for all the fields of the mixture in the district.

The different States in India can be grouped under the following three category with regard to the procedure followed in the allocation of net areas of component crops of a mixture:
1. States in which allocation is done entirely at the field level.
2. States in which certain major crop-mixtures are recognized as single crop and allocation of net areas of their components is done not at the field level but at the district level, while in the case of unrecognized mixtures the allocation is done at the field level.

3. States in which the allocation is done entirely at the district level on the basis of fixed ratios.

Allocation at Field Level

Under the first category can be listed the States of Assam, West Bengal, Andhra Pradesh, Tamil Nadu, Karnataka, Orissa, Maharashtra, Gujarat and Kerala. In most of these States mixed cropping is not very important.

In Assam, mostly two crop-mixtures are reported to be sown. The practice of sowing three or more crops as substantial components of the mixture is rare. Therefore, the Land Records Manual prescribes a simple rule that the gross area should be allocated half-half between the two principal components, the subsidiary crops, if any, being ignored altogether.

The acreage under crop-mixtures is reported to be small in West Bengal also. No special procedure is, therefore, laid down for plots having mixed crops. The instructions to the field staff are that in such cases, an estimate of the extent of each individual crop in terms of number of plants covering the field should be made. Taking the entire plot as equivalent of 16 annas, the area should be allocated to each crop so as to total to 16 annas for all crops in the plot.

The Land Records Manual for the Telangana region of Andhra Pradesh prescribes that if the constituent crops are sown in separate rows, the area of the mixed field should be allocated to them in proportion to the number of their rows. But if the seeds of constituent crops are mixed together and then sown, the net areas of component crops should be apportioned in the ratio of adjusted seed rates. For example, if a kgs, b kgs and c kgs are the seeds employed for sowing a mixture of three crops in an acre of land and if l kgs, m kgs and n kgs are their normal seed-rates when sown pure, the proportion of the areas of the constituent crops is estimated as $a/l : b/m : c/n$. If one or two components of the mixed sowing are not important and their proportions are extremely small, say a few plants scattered here and there in the field, they are ignored, and the whole area is sown as pure provided the remaining constituent crop is one only, if the remaining constituent crop still happens to be a mixture, the net acreage under each of them is separated on the basis of adjusted seeds-rates as explained above.

In the remaining parts of Andhra Pradesh and the whole of Tamil Nadu, Karnataka, Orissa and Gujarat States and the whole Maharashtra State excepting Wardha, Bhandara, Nagpur and Chanda districts, the area occupied by components of a crop-mixture are apportioned on the spot by the primary reporting agency presumably in proportion to the number of their rows in the case of row-sowing and by eye-appraisal of the relative stands of their plants in the case of mixed-seed sowing.

In Kerala, the procedure adopted in the case of a mixture of a perennial crop and seasonal crop is to record the number of trees and plants of the perennial crop and the area actually under the seasonal crop. In the case of mixtures of two perennial crops, the number of trees or plants of each is recorded separately. In the case of the mixture of two seasonal crops, the procedure of the 'corrected seed-rates' is followed and the apportionment is done on the spot by the investigators.

Allocation Partly at Field and Partly at District Level

Under the second category can be grouped the States of Bihar, Punjab, Rajasthan and Jammu & Kashmir. In Bihar, the field level primary reporter (Karmachari) records the gross area in the case of wheat-gram, wheat-barley and barleygram mixtures without apportioning net areas of the components. In respect of other mixtures, he apportions the gross area to component crops by taking into consideration the quantities of seeds sown and the nature and extent of the crops grown, assessed on the basis of his own personal knowledge and judgement and information gathered from reliable and intelligent cultivators. The component which appear to occupy one per cent or less area of the whole field are treated as nominal crops and are ignored and their areas are distributed to the remaining components. If one or more additional components are sown mixed with a recognized two-crop mixture and each appears to occupy more than one per cent of the area of the mixed field, the area of each one of them is apportioned and recorded under it and the balance is recorded under the recognized mixture.

In Punjab, the Patwari records at the source both the gross unadjusted acreages and the net acreages of the components of the mixture of wheat and gram; wheat and barley; wheat; gram, barley and massar; wheat and sarshaf; wheat, gram and sarshaf; barley and gram; jowar and bajra; jowar and gowara; jowar and moth or mung or mash; bajra and moth or mung or mash; maize and mash; cotton, til and mash or moth or mung; barley and massar and gram and massar which constitute the major crop-mixtures in the State. In respect of the mixtures of wheat and gram, half the area under the mixtures is reckoned as under-wheat. In the case of other mixtures, the Patwari makes an eye-appraisement of the ratios in which the mixtures are grown and apportions the gross area to the component crops at the source itself.

In Rajasthan, crop-mixtures like gojara (wheat-barley), gochani (wheatgram), bejar (barley-gram), jowar-mung and bajra-moth are entered as mixed in the crop-statement and areas of the components are not apportioned by the Patwari. But in the case of other mixtures, the estimated area covered by each constituent is recorded.

In Jammu & Kashmir, allocation of area under mixed crops to its components is done at the primary stage except in the case of goji (wheatbarley). The Patwari makes the allocation according to eye-estimate taking seed-ratio also into consideration. In the case of goji, the acreage is recorded as such from the primary stage to the final stage.

Allocation at District Level

Under the third category can be placed the States of Uttar Pradesh and Madhya Pradesh. In Uttar Pradesh, some major crop mixtures like jowar-arhar, bajra-arhar, wheat-barley, wheat-gram and barley-gram are recognized and are each allotted a column in the crop statement (jinswar). In the case of recognized crop mixture, with or without some subsidiary crops also added, the whole area is recorded under the heading mentioned in the crop statement. Obviously, if a crop-mixture consists of three or more crops but the heading recognizes only two crops, the whole area is recorded under this heading, the subsidiary crops being ignored altogether. For example, the whole area of wheat-barley-linseed mixture is recorded under the heading 'wheat-barley' as there is no such heading as 'wheat-barley-linseed' in the crop-statement and thus the linseed crop is ignored totally at the field level. Other oilseeds crops like rape and mustard, sesamum, castor and groundnut are also ignored in a similar manner at the field level. However, in the case of mixed linseed, its net area is calculated at the district level by taking half the total acreage under gram plus one-sixth of the total acreage under wheat and barley and their mixtures. Some such procedure is followed in respect of rape and sesamum crops also. But no such calculation is made in the case of other oilseed crops sown mixed.

In all the constituent units, viz. Mahakoshal, Madhya Bharat, Vindhya Pradesh and Bhopal regions of the present Madhya Pradesh State, and Wardha, Nagpur, Chanda and Bhandara districts of the Maharashtra State, a few recognized mixtures like cotton-tur (arhar), jowar-tur, bajra-tur, wheat-gram, wheat-berley, barley-gram, wheat-linseed-gram, urad-linseed, lakh linseed, kodo-tur, koda-jowar, koda-jowar-arhar, etc., are allotted separate columns in the crop-statement (jinswar) and the areas of these mixtures are recorded as such under the respective columns. If a mixture to which no special heading is allotted in the crop-statement is shown, it is described by the name which it ordinarily bears and its mixed area is recorded. There is, however, one important difference between the Mahakoshal, Madhya Bharat and Bhopal regions on the one hand and Vindhya Pradesh region on the other, with regard to recording of areas of subsidiary crops which are added in the main recognized or widely practised mixtures. In the first three units, the subsidiary crops are ignored, but in last unit, the area covered by each subsidiary crop is estimated on the basis of quantities of seeds sown and relative stands of component crops and apportioned and recorded separately by the Patwari on the spot and the balance is shown under the recognized mixture.

The assignment of net areas to component crops at the district level in the case of recognized mixtures in the States listed under second and third categories above, is done on the basis of prescribed ratios. The ratios fixed is the different States are given in Table 6.4 for important crop-mixtures for illustration.

Table 6.4   Ratio Fixed for Apportionment of Net Areas of Component Crops of the Mixture

State	Wheat-gram	Wheat-linseed	Gram-linseed	Wheat-barley	Gram-barley
Uttar Pradesh	50:50			50:50	75:25 to 50:50*
Madhya Pradesh	90-10 to 50:50*	95:5 to 50-50*	95:5 to 20:80*		
Punjab	50:50			50:50	50:50
Bihar	50:50			50:50	50:50
Rajasthan	70:30 to 39:61*			66:34 to 34:66*	50:50 to 44-60*

*The range indicates that different ratios are prescribed for different tracts or districts.
Source: Report of the Technical Committee on Crop Estimates, Planning Commission, 1967, p. 112.

The above ratios were fixed mostly at the time of settlements and were based on scanty observations. The characters which were observed by the Settlement and Revenue Officers for fixing these ratios are not clearly specified in the circulars which prescribe them but the basis had been an admixture of all types of observations and subjective assessments made with regard to relative stands of crops, pure and mixed seed-rates, relative spread of the practices of line-sowing and broadcast sowing, etc.

Allocation When Components are Harvested in Different Seasons

Crops sown in mixture simultaneously or in the same season are generally treated as mixed crops, whether they are harvested in the same season or in different seasons. Thus in most States jowar-tur (arhar), cotton-tur, maize-tur, kodo-tur, the components of which are sown simultaneously in the kharif season, but the first component is harvested in kharif and the second in the rabi season, are treated as mixtures and the whole gross area is divided between the component crops at the field or district level, according to the prevalent practice. The whole area of such mixtures is treated as double-cropped and is recorded under the first component (maize or kodo, etc.) in the kharif season as well as under the second component (arhar) in the rabi season.

RECORDING AREAS UNDER BUNDS

In many States, the method of recording areas under bunds has not been mentioned in land records manuals. There are two types of bunds: (i) permanent, and (ii) temporary. Permanent bunds are generally wide.

In some States, the areas under permanent bunds are excluded from the area of the fields at the time of settlement. However, in most of the States, the area under temporary bunds are generally included in the areas under the fields.

It has been suggested that the area under permanent bunds should be excluded from the crop-area and the area under temporary bunds should be included in the crop-area of the fields, but due allowance should be made at the stage of tehsil or district on the basis of the experience of superior officers or on the basis of some other objective approach like sample survey. Generally allowance is given from 2 per cent to 5 per cent of the cropped area for the bunds. It would be desirable if the areas under the bunds are estimated along with the average yield of crops by the method of random sampling. In fact, in some States, this method is being adopted recently as a routine measure.

RECORDING AREA UNDER UNCULTIVATED PATCHES IN CROP FIELDS

In the temporarily settled States, uncultivated patches for which no assessment of revenue is made are usually shown separately in the Khasra register as 'pot kharab'. This area is not taken into account while working out the area under the crop at the time of crop inspection. In case the patches are temporarily uncultivated, the primary reporter is required to make an eye estimate of the area of the patch and to make due allowance for this in the area under the crop recorded. In the land records manual of certain States, it is prescribed that uncultivated patches should be measured, but this is not enforced strictly in the majority of cases. A reasonably accurate estimate of area of the patches is very desirable. If the area under uncultivated patches does not change from what it was at the time of settlement, then there is not much difficulty; but if the area under such patches is reduced or converted to cultivated area, the primary reporter should make entries accordingly at the time of crop inspection.

AREA UNDER IMPROVED VARIETIES OF CROPS

Very little information is available at present regarding the area under improved varieties of crops. Some States record areas under cotton separately for improved and local varieties. Even for wheat and paddy such data are hardly available. It is essential that for important improved and local varieties such data should be collected so that estimates of production can be worked out accurately and assessment of the additional production can be made.

SEEDS BEDS

If the area under seedbeds is resown with some crop in the season, it will be recorded as cropped area. In case it is not resown or transplanted, it should be treated as current fallow.

STEPS TAKEN TO IMPROVE QUALITY AND TIMELINESS OF AGRICULTURAL STATISTICS

From the foregoing discussions one should not conclude that no serious effort is being made for improving the quality and timeliness of statistics of agricultural production. In fact, the seventies may perhaps be considered as a decade in which concerted efforts were made to improve the timeliness and reliability of the agricultural statistical system. In the earlier decades since independence, the ascent was mainly on increasing the scope and coverage of the system, adoption of uniform concepts, definitions and procedures, and in the evolution of suitable methodologies for surveys on different aspects of agriculture. As a result, the percentage of area for which land use and crop area statistics were available on the basis of complete enumeration increased from 47 in 1948-49 to 82 by complete enumeration or sample surveys in 1969-70. Similarly, while in the early fifties, production estimates for almost all the principal crops were based on the method of eye estimation, over 150,000 crop-cutting experiments were being planned in the different States in 1969-70 under the Crop-Estimation Surveys (CES) to estimate objectively the yield rates of principal food and non-food crops employing the technique of random sampling. These efforts were continued in the seventies also, as would be seen from the fact that at present area statistics for 87.5 per cent of the geographical area is covered by complete enumeration and sample surveys and over 230,000 crop-cutting experiments are being planned annually. About 95 per cent of the production of cereals and 73 per cent of the production of pulses and between 75 per cent and 99 per cent of the production of important commercial crops are based on Crop Estimation Surveys.

With the strengthening of the foundation of the agricultural statistical system, the need for paying attention to the aspects of timeliness and reliability of the system was felt. The need arose from the practical difficulties experienced in the implementation of the improved techniques and procedures at the field level. In regard to area statistics, while the system based on land records is suited to many States in the country, it was found, in practice, that due to a number of reasons, the Patwari was unable to devote adequate time and attention needed for collection of agricultural statistics. This affected their quality. The multifarious duties assigned to the Patwari also affected his normal schedule of work and resulted in delay in the submission of crop statistics. Three new schemes have been introduced.

1. Timely Reporting Scheme (TRS), 2. Improvement in Crop Statistics (ICS), 3. Establishment of an Agency for Reporting of Agricultural Statistics (EARAS).

Timely Reporting Scheme (TRS)*

The timely reporting scheme was initiated during 1968-69 on the recommendation of Data Improvement Committee and after that it has

---

*For more details on the working of these schemes, and refer to chapter 7 (Crop Yields).

been reviewed by National Commission on Agriculture, Expert Committee on Advance Estimates of Production and Working Group on Demand and Supply Projection and Improvement of Agricultural Statistics.

Objective

To obtain reliable and timely estimates of area under principal crops in each season with break up of area under irrigated/un-irrigated, traditional and high yielding varieties of crops by conducting Girdwari on priority basis in 20% randomly selected villages during normal Girdwari period. The estimates of production of principal crops covered under crop cutting experiments are also worked out by using the estimated area prepared on the basis of Girdwari of 20% villages under TRS for immediate use.

The current methodology and procedure which is being adopted under TRS was worked out by IASRI by which scheme provides for priority enumeration in a sample of 20% of villages selected at random and build up estimates of area sown under principal crops.

Status

This scheme is currently in operation in 13 major States and 2 Union Territories namely Andhra Pradesh, Assam, Bihar, Gujrat, Haryana, Himachal Pradesh, Jammu and Kashmir, Karnataka, Madhya Pradesh, Maharashtra, Rajasthan, Tamilnadu, Uttar Pradesh, Pondicherry and Delhi.

Specific Issues

The main requirement of Timely Reporting Scheme (TRS) is timely availability of area statistics and land utilization statistics which is also useful for designing of crop estimation survey. But delay in the availability of statistics and quality defeats the prime objective of this scheme. Delay in availability of area statistics also results into
   (a) Delay in final estimate of crop area.
   (b) Missing actual crops, reporting fake crops and inconsistent crop area reporting by primary workers.
   (c) Lack of provision for non-reporting of seed variety and irrigation particulars.

The main reasons for non completion of Girdwari in time has been the involvement of primary worker in various other work such as providing assistance to irrigation department, Public Health Department, Veterinary Department, Election Officer, Cooperative Societies, etc. As the work primarily depends upon primary worker, in case of any dislocation of primary worker the whole work gets affected. This matter has been discussed with States several times in HLCC meetings but not much improvement has been observed. States may give their views in tackling this problem so that priority Girdawari is completed in specified time period like deployment of staff on payment of honorarium basis of contract basis, etc.

(i) Under the Scheme, States are required to submit area estimates within two months of sowing of crops. But it is observed that many states are not submitting the same in prescribed period. The status is given in Table 6.5.

(ii) It is also observed that some of the States do not submit audited expenditure/utilization certificates in time. It may be appreciated that without submission of audited expenditure reports/utilization certificates for the last financial year, release of funds becomes very difficult for the Department of Agriculture, Government of India. It may not be possible to release of 2nd installment without the receipt of audited report for 1999-2000. States of Assam, Bihar, Himachal Pradesh, Jammu and Kashmir, Karnataka, M.P., Maharashtra and U.Ts. of Delhi and Pondichery have so far not submitted utilisation certificates for the year 2000-2001.

(iii) It has been observed that period of Girdawari in States have remained the same over years where as cropping pattern in most of the states have changed during these years. Due to change in temperature, rainfall etc. in various Agro-climitic regions, research and seed varieties the period of sowing have shifted during the years. It is therefore felt that the Girdawari period should also be changed by States so that estimates of area become suitably available in time. States may offer their views on the issue.

Establishment of an Agency for Reporting of Agricultural Statistics (EARAS)

Due to non-availability of land record system in the States of Kerala, West Bengal and Orissa, the system of field to field crop inspection by revenue agency does not exist in these States. Until 1974-75 the estimates of area and production of crops where being built up on the basis of a small sample or even on eye assessment.

In 1975-76 as per recommendation of Working Group on Demand and Supply Projections and Improvement of Agricultural Statistics, a scheme of Establishment of an Agency for Reporting of Agricultural Statistics (EARAS) was initiated in these States to cover a large sample size. The scheme was later on extended to some N.E. States (Arunachal Pradesh, Nagaland, Sikkim and Tripura) also. Under the scheme a stipulated time schedule for submission of reports relating to area and production estimates have been provided.

Objective

The main objective of the scheme is to obtain timely estimates of area and production of principal crops in these States and also to obtain statistics relating to land use on the basis of complete enumeration in

Table 6.5 Due and Actual Dates for Submission of Estimates

States/UTs	Kharif 1999-2000			Rabi 1999-2000		2000-2001
	Due date	Receipt date	Receipt date	Due date	Receipt date	Receipt date
1. Andhra Pr.	10.10	15.11.99	22.11.2000			
Jowar				10.2	19.2.2000	5.2.2001
Other crops				20.2	30.3.2000	16.3.2001
Paddy				30.4	15.5.2000	30.4.2001
2. Assam				10.2	18.4.2000	
Early Kharif	10.6	23.8.99	29.9.2000			
Late Kharif	10.10	6.1.2000	20.2.2001			
3. Bihar				15.2	NR	
Bhadai	1.11	14.3.2000	NR			
Aghanai	1.11	27.5.2000	NR			
4. Gujrat	15.11	20.11.99	22.12.2000	28.2	27.3.2000	23.3.2001
5. Haryana	31.10	16.12.99	22.11.2000	31.3	17.5.2000	
6. Himachal Pr.	10.10	19.11.99	5..3.2001	16.4	26.5.2000	
7. J & K	30.11	12.1.2000	20.3.2001	28.2	23.1.2001	
8. Karnataka	25.11	27.12.99	25.01.2001	26.3	29.5.2000	
9. M.P.	30.11	29.11.99	28.11.2000	15.3	15.3.2000	29.3.2001
10. Maharashtra	30.10	3.1.2000	7.3.2001	28.2	10.4.2000	
11. Rajasthan	31.10	29.10.99	11.12.2000	8.3	4.4.2000	
12. Tamilnadu	20.11	17.11.99	20.11.2000	15.2	14.2.2000	13.3.2001
13. Uttar Pr.	30.11	2.12.99	22.11.2000	28.2	7.4.2000	
14. Pondichhery	30.10	4.11.99	10.11.2000	28.2	25.2.2000	27.2.2001

20% sample of villages each year. States are required to submit reports relating to estimates of area and production as per stipulated time schedule.

Specific Issues

   (i) It has been observed that all of the States have delayed submission of reports regarding estimates of area for Kharif season during 2000-2001. Kharif reports have not been received from any of EARAS State accept Orissa and Kerala in spite of repeated reminders. These reports were due as on 31st January.

  (ii) Submission of quarterly expendiure reports is taking considerable delay by the States. States take much more time in sending expenditure reports. Quarterly expenditure reports for the quarter ending March 2001 have still not been received from States of Arunachal Pradesh, Tripura and Sikkim.

(iii) It is also seen that some of the States do not submit utilization certificates in time. It may be appreciated that without submission of audited expenditure reports for the last financial year, release of funds becomes very difficult for the Department of Agriculture, Government of India. Utilization certificates for the year 2000-2001 are still not received from any of the States except Orissa.

Improvement of Crop Statistics (ICS)

This is Centrally Sponsored scheme on 50:50 sharing basis. The scheme is in operation since 1975. Under the Scheme area enumeration and crop cutting experiments are checked on sample basis in a sample of 10000 villages. This sample is equally covered between National Sample Survey Organization (NSSO) and State Agriculture Statistics Authority. This Scheme is very important because the methodology being followed by States for area enumeration work and conduct of crop cutting experiments is supervised by the trained staff of NSSO and SASAs to ensure correctness. This scheme is implemented in the States of Andhra Pradesh, Assam, Bihar, Gujrat, Haryana, Himachal Pradesh, Jammu and Kashmir, Karnataka, Madhya Pradesh, Maharashtra, Rajasthan, Tamilnadu, Uttar Pradesh and Pondicherry.

Objective

The main objectives of the scheme are:

(i) Bring improvement in crop statistics by conducting spot check of area enumeration carried out by the Patwaries of the revenue Department in a set of randomly selected villages. Checking of area aggregation of different crops is also done in the same set of villages.

(ii) Inspecting crop cutting experiments at harvest stage, in pre-assigned sample of villages on random basis with a view to ascertaining the quality of fieldwork as well as to estimate yield rates of major crops in the State.

Specific Issues

(i) While reviewing the progress under the ICS Scheme, it has been observed that of ICS is in operation since 1973-74 with the main objective of the scheme is to locate the deficiencies in the States system of crop Statistics through joint efforts of Central and State agencies and suggest remedial measures to effect lasting improvement in the system. However, it is observed that the problems (like non availability of proper equipment for conduct of crop cutting experiments, non availability of updated village maps etc.) in the proper implementation of the scheme have remained the same over number of years. This is therefore high time to discuss the steps to be taken by States and NSSO to quantify the improvement in the system of crop statistics.

(ii) It has been observed from the various reports received from States that the extent of loss and miss of crop cutting experiment is very high for various crops in different States. NSSO and SASAs are requested to look into the matter and make all efforts by way of pre harvest visit to avoid missing of crop-cutting experiments.

(iii) It has been noticed that there is non-availability of standard weights and measuring tape with the primary workers to conduct crop-cutting experiments. These effect correct marking of plot and getting correct weight of produce in the selected plot. SASAs are requested to pursue this point with their counterparts in the Revenue Department of State and make sure that necessary standard equipments are made available to primary level workers for conducting crop cutting experiments.

(iv) It has also been observed from the minutes of High Level Coordination Committee Meetings of the States that above mentioned points are repeatedly discussed at that forum over the years. However, no improvement has been shown in the status of the Scheme in following HLCCs. States may take up this point with utmost sincerity and bring out definite improvements in the crop statistics.

(v) Non-receipt of utilisation certificates from the States in time is an issue under this scheme also. These are pending from the States of Assam, Bihar, Himachal Pradesh, J & K, Madhya Pradesh and Pondicherry.

REVIEW OF CROP ESTIMATION SURVEY ON FRUITS AND VEGETABLES

The growth of fruit, vegetables and flowers has been increasing over the years. The share of these crops has also increased substantially in the agriculture sector during this period. Production of fruits, vegetables and flowers in India has also increased to a very high level as compared to many developing and even developed countries in the World. Although India has progressed very well in the field of fruits, vegetables and flowers production, we do not have official estimates on large number of fruits, vegetables and flowers. This is one of the major data gaps in the Agricultural Statistical System in India. For preparation of various development progammes and for policy formulations etc., the availability of adequate, reliable and timely statistics on area, yield and production estimates of these crops is essential.

At present a scheme "Crop Estimation Survey on Fruits and Vegetables" is being implemented on a pilot basis only, under the Directorate of Economics and Statistics in the Department of Agriculture. This scheme is being implemented in 11 states namely Andhra Pradesh, Gujrat, Haryana, Himachal Pradesh, Karnataka, Maharashtra, Orissa, Punjab, Rajasthan, Tamilnadu and Uttar Pradesh (as centrally sponsored scheme with 100% central assistance for payment of salary, TA etc. to staff employed under the scheme) and covers only 14 fruits and vegetables namely, Apple, Banana, Grapes, Guava, Citrus fruits, Pineapple, Mango, Cauliflower, Potato, Onion, Tomato, Cabbage, Ginger and Turmeric. For estimation of area and production of Fruits and Vegetable crops, special methodology developed by IASRI is being used in the field.

Experience of the existing pilot scheme "Crop Estimation Survey on Fruits and Vegetables" reveal that implementing agencies face many difficulties in implementation which results in to non-availability of adequate, correct and timely statistics on crops covered under the scheme. Some of the bottlenecks in collection of adequate, correct and timely statistics on Fruits and Vegetables are mentioned below:

(a) Total area under fruits crop is not recorded by the village level primary worker as fruits are also grown on canal banks, field bunds, road sides, backyard of houses and even stray trees.

(b) It is difficult for the staff who conduct crop cutting experiment to be present at time of every picking as harvesting of fruits and many vegetables is done in a number of pickings extending over several weeks.

(c) Short duration crops of vegetables which are sown and harvested betwen two Girdawari periods are missed and therefore their area and production goes unreported.

(d) Land record manual in many States does not provide for recording of all important crops of fruits and vegetables and recording is done for many of the crops taken together.

(e) Even in case of the crops of fruits and vegetables wherever Land Record manual provides for recording of certain crops, Girdawari is not done correctly by the primary workers and therefore it does not give correct picture of area under that crop.

(f) Crops grown on Government land/unauthorised land are not included in Girdawari.

(g) In most of the States primary workers engaged in Girdawari work are much more overburdened with other work and therefore are not able to attach due importace to the Girdawri work.

(h) The area under vegetable and fruit crops grown in backyard/forayed of houses remains unreported in the present systm.

Specific Issues

(i) As there is no fixed time (month and date) at present for submission of area and production data of Fruits and Vegetables crops by the State, a time frame need to be discussed and prepared for each crop in the State for submission of estimates of area and production of these crops. Time frame so prepared needs to be followed by all SASAs in future.

(ii) It is also seen that some of the States do not submit audited expenditue/utilization certificates in time. It may be appreciated that without submission of audited expenditure reports for the last financial year, release of funds becomes very difficult for the Department of Agriculture, Government of India. These certificates are still pending from States of Gujrat, Karnatka and Himachal Pradesh.

(iii) States have repeatedly been requested by DES to forward data regarding area, production and productivity of fruits and vegetables covered by respective States for the years 1999-2000 and 2000-2001. None of the States except Orissa has given data for all the crops covered by them. All other States are requested to send complete data for all the crops so that it could be published.

(iv) States may give suggestion regarding coverage of more crops under the scheme.

(v) The pilot scheme covers only 11 States and selected crops. It is therefore, not possible to generate all India Estimates of Fruits and Vegetables. It is now being felt that the scheme of collection of horticultural statistics should be introduced in all the States during the 10th Five Year Plan covering all such horticultural crops which gained importance over time both in terms of value of product and area coverage. However, as it may not be possible to create the requisite number of posts on regular basis, a minimum number of posts—core staff, could be created on a regular basis, while the remaining post may be filled on contract basis. Keeping in view the above objective, States were requested to work out proposal and sent to DES along with following information:

(a) Number and name of important horticulture crops proposed to be covered in 10th Five Year Plan,

(b) Number (with detail of workers) to be engaged on contract basis under the scheme,

(c) Proposed expenditure on staff already sanctioned under the scheme-during each financial year of 10th Five Year Plan with break up of expenditure on salary, travel and contingencies in each year,

(d) Proposed expenditure on workers engaged on contract basis during each financial year of 10th Five Year Plan,

(e) Proposed time frame (dates with month) for submission of area, yield and production estimates of horticulture crops during each season to Central Government,

(f) Name of the proposed agency in the State (with the name of the Nodal Officer along with his telephone number for correspondence purpose) for implementation of scheme.

So far, detailed proposals have been received from 9 States in complete form. In addition to that incomplete proposals from 8 States have also been received. These States have been asked to give the complete proposals. The status is as below:

Received complete proposals	*Received incomplete proposals*
Himachal Pradesh	Assam
Karnataka	Andhra Pradesh
Madhya Pradesh	Arunachal Pradesh
Maharashtra	Bihar
Mizoram	Haryana
Orissa	Meghalaya
Punjab	Sikkim
Rajasthan	West Bengal
Uttar Pradesh	

Problem Areas

As a result of improvements and expansions in statistical activities during the last three decades, a large mass of data are now available than before in agriculture and allied sectors. However, much still remains to be done with regard to improvement in the quality and timeliness of data in several areas. Some of the important areas in which efforts need to be concentrated are:

(i) There is an urgent need to cover some of the crops like small millets, other pulses, coconut, banana etc., under crop-cutting experiments and to increase the coverage of some of the crops presently covered but with low coverage rate, so that the overall reliability of crop output measurement is improved.

(ii) Estimation of production of individual fruits and vegetables should be done by adopting suitably designed sample surveys. At present, there is an urgent need to cover the important fruits and vegetables like apple, mango, citrus fruits and grapes, onion and tomato.

(iii) At present, there is a greater use of high yielding varieties of rice. To estimate the value of output of rice more correctly, there is an urgent need of variety-wise estimates of production and price data of rice.

(iv) Some studies relating to sugarcane crop are required towards the calculation of reliable utilization rates in respect of seed rates and percentage of production consumed in chewing and juice-making.

(v) Data on prices of certain crops like small millets and other pulses are not available. It is essential that efforts are made for collection of prices in such cases.

(vi) Continuous studies are required to work out: (a) utilization rates, yield rates, conversion ratios of milk and milk products, (b) yield rates of meat and meat products for different categories of animals, the proportion slaughtered and estimates of fallen animals, (c) yield rates of goat hair, camel hair and pig bristle, and (d) estimation of operation cost of livestock products (ghee, butter, milk, hides, skins, eggs, poultry, wool, hair, honey, silk worms, cocoons).

(vii) For several items of inputs in agriculture including seed rates, use of fertilizers and feed, cost of livestock used on farm, the current data are hardly available. It is essential that the system is developed to obtain such data on a regular basis.

(viii) In forestry, efforts need to be made to: (a) record production of industrial wood-variety-wise and fuel wood and also to collect relevant price data, (b) estimate the minor forest products and their prices, and (c) evolve methodology for estimating under reporting and illegal removals of products. Lack of information on inputs and depreciation of machinery used in exploitation of forests also need to be looked into.

(ix) Scientific techniques should be developed: (a) to estimate the production of inland and subsistence fish and other fish products, and (b) cost of production for fishing industry.

(x) For improving the quality of output data of certain by-products like sticks, straws and stems of many agricultural crops, there is a need to extend the coverage of the existing crop-cutting experiments to collect dependable data on yield rates, conversion ratios, etc., pertaining to such by-products in relation to output of the main crop on a sub-sample basis.

(xi) Greater emphasis should be laid on carrying out integrated surveys in agricultural and allied sectors in which besides data on output, information on related inputs, factor payment (viz., agricultural wages, interest and rent) as well as capital expenditure under different categories of machinery and equipments like tractors, transport equipment, other equipments, construction in the form of land improvements, minor irrigation, grain golas, and inventory accumulation, are also collected.

(xii) The present scheme of cost of cultivation studies of the Directorate of Economics and Statistics, Ministry of Agriculture provides very useful data in respect of principal crops only: there is an urgent need for extending the scope of this scheme to provide more reliable input data on minor crops as well.

(xiii) The quality of price data used in evaluation of both outputs and inputs leaves much to be desired. The prevalent system of collection of wholesale prices used as a proxy to harvest prices needs considerable strengthening on the lines recommended by technical working group on prices set up by the CSO in 1975.

This shows that statistics used in the preparation of national accounts suffer from substantial gaps under several categories and for removing existing data gaps and deficiencies, suitable steps are required to be taken by not one single agency but by all agencies dealing with the subject of agricultural statistics, both at the Centre and in the States. It is high time that all the State agricultural departments, State agricultural universities, research institutions under Indian Council of Agricultural Research, and NSSO orient their future studies keeping in view the present day need to fill the important data gaps. Regular collection of data annually on all the aspects listed may not be feasible due to constraints of resources; there is, therefore, an urgent need for having a critical look into their various gaps in data with a view to chalking out a systematic programme of data collection through field surveys to be conducted at regular intervals of say, 3 to 5 years. No Attempt has been made to make use of Remote Sensing Technology for the purpose or for the standing of changes in habitation pattern or land use. A modest beginning has no doubt been done by ICAR, but much more needs to be done.

NATIONAL CROP FORECASTING CENTRE

National Crop Forecasting Centre was set up in the Directorate of Economics and Statistics by the Government in order to obtain advance forecast of important crops to meet the requirement of immediate/ad-hoc policy planning. The Centre organizes weekly meeting of the Crop Weather Watch Group with the participation of Indian Meteorological Department. Central Water Commission, Department of Science and Technology, Directorate of Plant Protection, Quarantine and Storage, etc. This Group assesses the condition of the crops after taking into account availability of water supply and other inputs like seeds, fertilisers, pesticides, etc and the condition of crop viz. pest and diseases and other related aspects. Based on these informations, National Crop Forecasting Centre (NCFC) tracks the crop prospects and prepares advance estimates for the use of the Government for policy decision. This is an on-going Central Sector Plan Scheme and staff-oriented. Presently the crops being closely monitored are Rice. Wheat, Maize, Jowar, Bajra, Tur, Gram, other Pulses, Oilseeds, Sugarcane, Cotton, Jute, Potato and Onion. The National Crop Forecasting Centre was involved in implementing the project called Forecasting Agricultural Output Using Space, Agro-meteorology and Land-based Observations (FASAL). The FASAL project sought to provide advance reliable assessments of crop acreage and production using remote sensing techniques and other available data bases.

FUTURE AGRICULTURE AND REMOTE SENSING

Remote-sensing is the science and art of obtaining information about an object, area or phenomenon through the analysis of data acquired by a device that is not in contact with the object, area or phenomenon under investigation.

While the remote-sensing data can be applied to develop information on most natural resources, but renewable or non-renewable, its potential in the area of agricultural activities needs great emphasis as our economy as a whole depends upon our effective agricultural activities and increased productivity. With increasing population, finite land available and small land holdings, future agriculture is a challenging job for national security. Remote-sensing as a tool has been found to be highly powerful and it offers real time warnings on the success or failure of agriculture year after year. It cannot, however, be stated that the remote-sensing mechanism all by itself can open our eyes to every situation as it has its own limitations also.

The remote-sensing data may provide commercial intelligence well in time to locate suitable and economically viable agricultural markets outside for bargaining and procurement and ensure food security for our millions, with the minimum impact on our economic progress.

The use of aerial photographs and its interpretations to develop certain information on soils, land use and water resources are already at an operational level. Although data obtained through aerial photography have a high resolution capacity and could be used for mapping with great accuracy. However, considering the cost, the problem of cloud cover and also non-availability of users both in the government and private sectors, the aerial photography has served restricted use only. In areas of land use, agricultural crops, water resources, meteorological information and fisheries we have established traditional methods available, but to get more authentic and real time information, the remote-sensing data systems in combination with ground truth are required to be established.

Originally in mid-seventies Americans used remote-sensing to monitor production of the wheat crop in Russia and other large countries and one of the well-publicised experiment was LACIE (large area crop inventory experiment). In Europe agriculture has the largest remote-sensing application and one of the noteworthy projects in Europe is called MARS (monitoring agriculture by remote sensing). This programme aims at getting crop inventories on a regional scale, monitor vegetation and other factors affecting yield and to develop an advanced European agricultural information system. Crop acreage satellite data combined with other information is used to predict yield and production estimates.

It can, thus, be stated that remote-sensing satellites is a powerful tool for agriculture-related application and indirectly contribute in planning food security. India has launched several remote-sensing satellites in series of the IES, and several experimental projects have been undertaken and estimation of crop acreage in respect of well defined crops like wheat, have been near operational.

Progress of Remote Sensing

Evergreen Revolution kept India away from large scale import of food. Earlier, technology, basically digital in character, like Remote Sensing, Geographical Information Systems (GIS), Global Positioning System

(GPS) and Geo-informatics were not available. Yet, India attained self-sufficiency. Agricultural scientists believe that remote sensing can help solve many issues, but they do not seem to have understood its limitations. Remote sensing describes the situation on the ground as observed, be it satellite or aerial survey.

While remotely sensed data has come a long way in spatial resolution, geographical location is still questionable, particularly when involving micro level planning processes like micro watersheds. The concept of watersheds is to improve conservation of water through rainwater harvesting and reducing soil erosion. But all this needs a good geographically and cartographically accurate data base of the land, which is now restricted to the Survey of India topographical maps (on 1:50,000 scale and in some areas on 1:25,000 scale maps with contours depicted at 20 metres). This is not suitable to delineate micro watersheds in plain or flat regions. So, plans based on enlarged versions of the existing topographical maps may not be correct.

One school of thought advocates integration of small farmers can be an advantage, because of the large number of people who become stakeholders in modernising agricultural practices. So policies should be drafted to help small holders use such technology.

For example, soil characteristics are highly heterogeneous in a field or farm oriented approach. Its micronutrient content also varies within a field. So farmers should be told to regulate improved inputs as required. Major variations can be detected by remote sensing data.

This leads to the problem of inaccurate revenue records, prepared almost a century or half a century ago in most States. These do not match the framework of the survey of India topographical maps. Some States do not have proper land records. Some feel that computerising land records, in the form of cadastral maps, will solve this problem. But they forget that wrong inputs will only create more problems. These records should be corrected by modern digital techniques, either by aerial photographic measuring or methods using instruments such as GPS, digital total stations or laser instruments. A combination of the two may yield economic and speedy results.

The present cadastral maps do not contain relief or information about heights, although the scales of such maps may be large enough—around 1:8000 to 1:10000. This means that there are no clearly defined drainage characteristics to enable delineation of micro watersheds. If these are well defined and accurately located, any farmer will know the water run-off pattern during rainfall and work to retain as much as possible. Otherwise even the meagre rainfall in dry and semi arid regions will go waste.

The watershed approach, for which the Government has made budgetary allocations, is the principal method in transforming rainfed agriculture into a viable production system. It can be used to grow crops that need plenty of water and also those that may not need much water.

Some scientists feel they do not know how much water is needed for a unit quantity for different crop varieties. Taking into account the element of evaporation loss due to high temperatures in tropical regions, it may be possible to apply only the actual amount of water required. Remote sensing can assist along with topographical maps of, say 1:50:000 scale, with 20 metre contour intervals, in some cases.

But when micro level planning and operations are involved, large scale maps are required to complement existing data. A map scale of, say, 1:5000 to 1:10000 with contour intervals of one metre or even lower to identify and delineate watersheds in correct position may be required. The contours have to be identified by levelling based on mean sea level and not on ad hoc benchmarks. This may take time but a beginning can be made in areas where the terrain is flat and where there are semi-arid conditions.

The ultimate goal should be to develop a full fledged land information system. This may seem complicated but is not impossible. Large scale topographical maps of the order of 1:50000 to 1:10000 scale with contours of the order of one may be the starting point. Cadastral maps and revenue records should then be corrected or adjusted against this. Land Information System (LIS) is an online depository of information related to land, that enables the most efficient use of land, now becoming a scarce resource.

The land information system needs to be three-dimensional depicting horizontal and vertical measurements. Changes can thus be easily incorporated. The scale adopted to develop this database is important since it leads to unambiguous definition of individual land holdings and will form the numerical cadastre or digital cadastre.

Such information systems also help in adapting what is called precision farming to suit our needs and cultural background.

Precision farming is site specific and takes into account the heterogeneous characteristics of an agricultural field to economise on the use of fertilizers and improving efficiency in water usage Mr. N.R. Ronalt Cantrell, Director General of the International Rice Research Institute, said recently that the techniques to grow more rice with less water are: wet seeding, intermittent rice irrigation, land levelling, improved weed management and management of cracked soils.

If adapted by those who are stakeholders and by the community at large, it can cause another green revolution or an evergreen revolution. A beginning towards this should be made as soon as possible since this concept is still evolving in India.

Satellite Data for Crop Monitoring

Since the launch of the American Landsat—the first satellite to inaugurate the era of space-based remote sensing—in 1972 data sent down by earth observation satellites have been routinely and extensively used for crop forecasting and monitoring agricultural fields over a large part of the world. Today a string of remote sensing satellites belonging to the USA,

Japan, Russia, China, France and the 14-nations European Space Agency (ESA) as well as India continue to help in studying global resources—both renewable as well as non-renewable.

In recent years, the satellite resources data have been finding an increasing use in the study of cotton, one of the most important commercial crops in the world. In India too cotton has established itself as a lucrative cash crop. No wonder, India's area under cotton is estimated to be one-fourth of the world's total area under this cash crop. In order to study the cotton acreage and environmental conditions suitable for its healthy growth, a satellite data-based project was carried out with a focus on Punjab, a major cotton growing state in India.

The project was jointly carried out by the Punjab State Remote Sensing Applications Centre (PSRSAC) and the Ahmedabad-based Space Applications Centre (SAC) of the India Space Research Organisation (ISRO). The objective of this experiment was to estimate the pre-harvest acreage under the cotton crop, monitor the conditions under which the cotton thrives and initiate yield model development by creating database of vegetation index profiles and other yield affecting variables. One most significant conclusion of the project was that the cotton yield estimation in terms of the area was quite accurate as compared to the conventional techniques which takes a larger duration for the acreage estimation. Similar studies of cotton crops using data from the American Landsat and the Indian IRS series of satellites have been undertaken in other cotton-growing states of India.

In the USA, the American Centre for Earth and Environmental Studies at the University of Texas is helping cotton farmers in Texas to gain an edge in the global cotton market through the monitoring of the cotton crop through satellite data. Both teachers and students of the university Texas centre interacted closely, with the cotton farmers of the Rio Granade valley who have maintained detailed records of their crops. The Rio Granade valley on the US-Mexico border is one of the richest cotton-growing areas in the world and is famous for its high quality Pima cotton used in marking bedsheets and dress material.

Cotton fields in this region were studied using 30-metre resolution colour images from the US Landsat-5 remote sensing satellite. Because these Landsat images cover up details only about 30-metre across, the images have had to be combined with 5-metre resolution black and white scenes obtained from the Indian IRS. The data from the Indian IRS is being marketed by the US firm-Space Imaging EOSAT.

As envisaged now, researchers will accumulate scenes over several years and compare them with actual yields recorded by farmers at the harvest time. The objective will be to come up with a reliable statistical model to predict the cotton yield at the end of the growing season.

Brightness and colour of the images vary according to the health of the crop under observation. Researchers measure the differences and compare the results to a studied actual crop yields. The successful culmination of this project will give cotton farmers of Texas a certain level of flexibility to set the prices lower earlier in the season which should help gain an edge over competitors. Texas farmers have also evinced interest in getting the feedbacks from cotton farms of China, Pakistan, India and Australia as this could help them set prices lower enough to outsell the international competitors.

The Australia-based Agricultural Reconnaissance Technologies Pvt Ltd has over the five years of research developed a model to predict cotton yields. According to a spokesman of the company, "a comparison of satellite and ground based agronomic yield estimates with post cotton farm yield results found that the satellite-based modifications are significantly more accurate than conventional ground based agronomic techniques."

SOME LIMITATIONS

The remote-sensing technology currently in use is able to produce some useful mappings of broad land use. However, the estimation of acreages under individual crops, except under some very special conditions such as monocropping over large continuous areas, is not a practical proposition today. Most cereal crops, for instance, are grasses and their signatures in the early periods of their growth do look very similar. Even after reaching full expression close to maturity, it is not easy to distinguish wheat from barley. Small strips of simultaneous stands of many different crops pose serious difficulties for developing usable area estimates of individual crops through remote-sensing. Long periods of cloud cover, such as we commonly experience during the monsoon season, may almost completely black out the possibility of producing a usable green cover estimate for the entire season. Nonetheless, it is of the utmost importance for the future of crop acreage statistics in India to develop close collaboration between the classical statisticians and modern technologists working on remote-sensing. This cooperation can bear fruit in developing techniques for on-the ground verification and calibration of the results obtained through space satellites.

CONCLUSION

Area statistics are collected by States, following different methods. According to the system adopted for collection of area statistics, the States and Union Territories (UTs) can be classified into three broad groups:-

States where are statistics are collected through complete enumeration (normally known as Land Records States or temporarily settled States).

The States where area statistics are collected on the basis of sample surveys normally known as non-land records states or permanently settled states.

States where area statistics are collected using conventional methods and satisfactory system of collection of area statistics is yet to be developed.

In the land records States, there exists a primary reporting agency (commonly known as Patwari), in charge of a village or a group of villages, to carry out field to field crop inspection in each crop season of a year and to record crop and land utilisation. The agency belongs to the Revenue (or the land Records) Deptt. and attends to the work along with the collection of land revenue and other duties. The Patwari is required to note the details of crop enumeration and land utilisation in a register, commonly known as the Khasra Register. After completion of entries for a village in a season the Patwari prepares an abstract of area under various crops and sends statement of crop abstract (*jinswar* statement) to the next higher officer in the revenue hierarchy. Similarly at the end of the year he prepares a land utilisation statement showing the abstract of area under different utilisations. The crop-wise and utilisation-wise area figures so compiled for villages are successively aggregated at the circle, tehsil and district levels. The district-wise figures are then reported to the State Agricultural Statistics Authority (SASA). The State level figures compiled by SASA are transmitted to the Directorate of Economics and Statistics in the Ministry of Agriculture, Govt. of India who are responsible for issuing the All India estimates.

The system of land records is being followed in 14 States viz. Andhra Pradesh, Assam, Gujarat, Haryana, Himachal Pradesh, Jammu & Kashmir, Karnataka, Madhya Pradesh, Maharashtra, Punjab, Rajasthan, Tamil Nadu and Uttar Pradesh, NCT Delhi, and in Union Territories of Chandigarh, Dadra and Nagar Haveli and Pondicherry. These States and Union Territories account for 86% of All-India reporting area. Three states, viz. Kerala, Orissa and West Bengal, where the estimation of area is through sample surveys, comprises 9% of the reporting area of the country. For the remaining 5% area, comprising of mainly hill district of Assam and North-Eastern states, a satisfactory system of collection of area statistics is yet to be developed. Agricultural Statistics are compiled in these areas mainly by conventional methods. There have been sporadic attempts to improve the situation in some of these States, but a regular system is required to be developed.

7

Estimation of Crop Yields

The total production of a crop is calculated as the product of the acreage under the crop and average yield per hectare. The average yield of a crop is obtained largely by the method of random sample crop-cutting surveys.

The technique of random sampling consists, in principle, of choosing a sample of elements out of a given totality of elements comprising the population in a manner as to offer each element of the totality an equal chance of inclusion in the sample. The technique not only ensures that the sample is representative of the population but also provides the means of knowing how far one is likely to be in error in estimating any characteristic of the population on the basis of the sample. The advantages of such a method in yield estimation are that we are able to obtain an unbiased estimate of the average yield per hectare and can determine, in addition, the margin of error by which the estimated average yield is likely to depart from the true unknown value of the yield for the tract surveyed.

It was seen that the principal defect of the traditional system of yield estimation was the absence of an objective procedure and a criterion for judging the magnitude of error inherent in it. In other words, in the traditional method not only the validity of the estimates obtained was seriously held in question but the margin of uncertainty associated with the estimate was also unknown. The present method of random sampling is an objective procedure, free from personal bias and provides means of knowing how far the results based on such a sample are likely to differ from the true value for the entire aggregate from which the sample is drawn.

EARLY SURVEYS

The need and importance of objective estimation of crop yield was felt in India as early as 1919, when the Board of Agriculture had recommended that crop-cutting experiments should be conducted in randomly selected fields.

Attempts to introduce the method were made in 1925 by Hubback on paddy in Bihar and Orissa. Although Hubback's surveys were a pioneering piece of work, randomization in the modern sense was completely lacking. Centres were not selected randomly, but were distributed evenly over the tract surveyed. Secondly, sampling at a given centre was limited to those fields where harvesting was in progress on the day of the sampler's visit. The sample unit was also cut at a short fixed distance from the boundary of the field. The estimate of yield obtained by this method was thus subject to bias from various sources and this bias could not be smoothed out simply by taking a large number of samples evenly spread over the tract and the harvesting season. Extremely small plot size (91/3200 acre or 13.6 sq ft in a triangular wooden frame) employed by Hubback was also an important source of bias, as plots of such small size have been found to lead to an appreciable over-estimation of yield. Hubback's method was employed for experiments on paddy by C.D. Deshmukh in Madhya Pradesh during 1928-30 and a little later by P.S. Rao in the same State. This technique did not provide a practicable solution of the problem, acceptable to State administrations as an annual routine.

The next advance in the problem of estimation of crop yield by random sampling survey came from the work of Mahalanobis who started experiments on jute in Bengal in 1939. Similar experiments were undertaken on wheat and sugarcane in one or two districts of Uttar Pradesh in 1941-42; on wheat and gram in two districts of Bihar in 1943-44 and paddy in Bihar in 1944-45. State wide yield surveys on jute and paddy were carried out in Bengal from 1942-43. The field work was entrusted to ad hoc parties of investigators who were required to move rapidly from place to place during the harvesting season to cut sample plots. The sampling was confined to those fields which were ready for harvest on the date of the investigator's visit to a place. It was experienced that a considerable portion of the crop had already been harvested or was not ready for harvest when the investigators visited the sample plots. A serious consequence of that method was that the principle of randomization was violated. There was no guarantee in the method that the fields maturing at different time would be sampled for harvest in the proportion in which they occur in the population. The principle of randomization requires that every field bearing a particular crop shall get due chance of being included in the sample. To achieve this objective, it is not only sufficient to select fields with the help of random numbers; but it is usually important to ensure that there are no subsequent omissions of fields with certain characters correlated with yield, such as fields in which the crop was already harvested before the experimenter could reach the spot or those where the crop was not ready for harvest at the time of his visit. Such deviation from strict randomization will introduce bias and result in an under or over-estimation of the average yield according to whether the rejected fields were lower or better yielders than the rest. Rejection of fields for reasons given above was allowed in the surveys discussed. Sample plots of very small size marked by portable frames or other similar apparatus were the essential feature of these surveys. Plots of various sizes and shapes and involving different methods of making them were experimented. In the Bihar survey of 1943-44, a triangular frame which was a modified form of Hubback's apparatus was used. The triangle was right angled isosceles one and enclosed an area of 12.5 sq ft. Two cuts totalling 25 sq ft were made on either side of the hypotenuse. In the Bengal survey of 1944-45, two sample cuts of sizes 5.2' × 5.2' and 10' × 10' were harvested. Ultimately three or four concentric circular plots with radii 2', 4',5'7$\frac{1}{2}$' and 8' were used for crop-harvest.

A different approach to the problem of objective method of crop estimation was followed by Panse and Kalamkar in 1942-43 when they carried out a survey in Akola district of Maharashtra for estimation of the yield of cotton, using the existing administrative machinery. Next year, i.e. in 1943-44 the survey was repeated in two districts, viz. Akola and Buldhana for estimation of cotton yield. In 1944-45 a State-wide survey on cotton was taken up in Madhya Pradesh. The yield survey on cotton was extended to former Bombay State in 1946-47. The design of sampling followed was one of three stage stratified samplings. The sub-divisions of the district formed the strata. The villages formed the first stage and the fields and plots of 1/10th of an acre were taken as the second and third stage units respectively.

The impetus to development of appropriate methodology for estimation of crop yields came in 1943 when the Inter-Departmental Committee of the Government of India called upon the Indian Council of Agricultural Research (ICAR) to evolve a suitable technique of random sampling which could be used for conducting annual surveys for estimating the yield of major food crops of wheat and paddy on a country wide scale. The work on yield surveys on wheat in Punjab and Uttar Pradesh carried out by Sukhatme in 1943 paved the way for enlarging the scope and content of crop estimation surveys in India. The objectives before the I.C.A.R. in initiating the surveys were:

(i) to evolve a sampling technique which can be handled by the departmental staff normally entrusted with the work of crop estimation;

(ii) to train the staff in the technique so evolved;

(iii) to demonstrate to the State administration the feasibility by employing the recommended technique as a routine measure:

(iv) to estimate the yield per unit area for each State with high precision, and

(v) to revise the existing normal yields in due course.

The special feature of these surveys was that it was dovetailed into existing administrative structure and was not necessitated any heavy additional expenditure on the field staff. With these objectives in view, surveys were conducted annually on the wheat and paddy crops since 1943-44 gradually covering almost all the wheat and paddy growing

States. The method subsequently was extended to other food and cash crops for estimation of yield. The sampling procedure developed by the ICAR is now being used in all the States except West Bengal, Orissa and Kerala, where a different sampling plan is followed.

ALLOCATION OF EXPERIMENTS

Based on earlier survey, the plan of work was finalized particularly regarding optimum allocation of experiments between different strata and between different stages of sampling within strata. This was worked out keeping in view that the survey would be an annual feature and to be carried out by the local departmental staff in the course of their normal work. The distribution of experiments among the different strata within a district directly in proportion to the area under the crop in the strata was found to give a sufficiently good allocation without significantly increasing either the cost of the survey or the standard error of the estimated mean.

The distribution of experiments between villages, field and plots of a stratum makes effective use of available resources. Results based on one of the pilot surveys (wheat survey in Moradabad district, U.P., 1944-45 and plot size; triangle 33' each side) showing the number of villages required for a given number of fields per village and plots per field for estimating the average yield with 5 per cent standard error are given in Table 7.1

Table 7.1

No. of fields per village	No. of plots per field			
	1	*2*	*3*	*4*
	No. of villagers			
1	88	74	70	68
2	63	56	54	52
3	54	50	48	47
4	50	46	45	45
5	47	45	44	43
6	46	43	43	42

Source: P.V. Sukhatme and V.G. Panse. 'Crop Surveys in India', Jour. Ind. Soc. Agri. Stat. Vol. III, 2, 1951.

It is seen that while the number of villages decreases rather considerably as the number of fields per village is increased from 1 to 2 and from 2 to 3, there is no such appreciable decrease in the number of villages with further increase in the number of fields. The increase in the number of plots selected within a field has hardly any effect on a number of villages.

The results show that 2 to 3 fields per village with one plot per field is about the optimum distribution within strata.

Plot Size

During the earlier attempt in crop surveys greater attention was paid in deciding the size of plot in a field. Various plot sizes were tried varying from 1160 of an acre for paddy to 1/10 of an acre for cotton. The plot size adopted in the earlier attempts by Hubback and Mahalanobis was very small, being of the order of 1/2000 of an acre. Attempts were made since 1944 to study the relative efficiency of various plot sizes for yield estimation. Five different plot sizes viz. three equilateral triangles each of side 33', $16\frac{1}{2}$'; and $8\frac{1}{4}$'; two circular plots of radius 2' and 3' were studied on wheat crop in 1944-45. The results showed that plots of area less than 30 sq ft gave serious overestimates of yield. The bias towards overestimation diminished with the increase in the size of the plot. In the case of paddy, different plot sizes studied were: a rectangular plot of 50 links × 20 links (area 435.6 sq ft), two circular plots of radius 3' each, two circular plots of radium 2' each and in addition, the whole of the remaining field was harvested. Results showed that while the yield estimate from the plot size of 50 links × 20 links was in close agreement with that from harvesting the whole field, those from small plots were considerable overestimates. Another study on paddy was made taking plot sizes: one rectangular plot of size 50 links × 25 links (area 544.5 sq ft) two isosceles right-angled triangles with equal sides each equal to 5 ft (area 12.5 sq ft), two equilateral triangles of side 15 links each (area 43.5 sq ft). The results of the investigation confirmed the previous results that the smaller plot size overestimated the yield. In case of jute also, the plots of size 10 links × 10 links were found to give a significant overestimation of yield as compared to plots of 25 links × 25 links size.

Present Design Adopted

The design of sampling adopted in the crop surveys is technically known as the stratified multistage random sampling. The region to be surveyed is first divided into the sub-regions called strata and from each of these a certain number of experimental plots are selected at random by the procedure of successive stages of selection. The administrative units like taluka or revenue inspectors' circles have usually been the strata and the experimental plots are selected in three successive stages by selecting villages in the first stage, field from a selected village in the second stage and a plot of specified size from each selected field in the third stage of selection. The allocation of experiments between the strata is done in proportion to the acreage under the crop subject to the availability of the field staff. Generally 2 to 6 villages are selected per revenue inspector's circle; two fields are selected from each selected village and one plot of prescribed size is marked in each selected field. The size and shape of the experimental plots for different crops vary from State to

State. The selection at each stage of villages, fields and plots respectively is made in conformity with the principles of randomness. The selection of villages and fields is carried out by the statistical staff. Only the last stage of selection, viz. of plots within fields is left to the field staff, thus minimizing the scope of errors in the random selection procedure.

The field of enquiry for a survey comprises the total area under the crop for which estimate is required. Sometimes inaccessible regions are excluded which, however, constitute a small fraction of the total cropped area. Fields growing the crop in mixture with other crops are not excluded unless the portion of the crop in question is so small as to be considered non-existent for practical purposes and the field is accordingly not reported as sown with that crop in the annual crop register maintained by the primary reporter. For example, if fields sown with barley, contain wheat plants as trace crop and such fields are shown under barley in Khasra Register; these are not selected for experiments on wheat.

A crop-cutting experiment in surveys on cereals consists locating and making of plot of a given size in a field selected by the method of random sampling and harvesting, threshing, winnowing and weighing the produce within the plot. Since the grain on the day of harvest contains moisture, the harvested produce is stored and reweighed after driage so as to make it possible to allow for the moisture contained in the produce in estimating the average yield. The procedure adopted for harvesting and processing the produce conforms to that adopted by the cultivators themselves. The sample, therefore, provides an unbiased estimate of the produce on the day of harvest. However, for the purpose of driage the produce collected from the sample is stored in bags whereas a cultivator usually allows his harvested produce to lie in open fields. Any damage caused to the harvested produce as a consequence of adverse weather conditions and other factors subsequent to the date of harvesting is thus not reflected in the survey estimate.

The crop surveys are organized in different States by the State Bureau of Economics and Statistics or the Department of Agriculture or the Land Records. The field work is generally entrusted to the staff of the State Revenue/Land Records/Agriculture/Development Departments. The Patwaris of the selected villages are required to render assistance in the conduct of experiments, particularly in securing local cooperation. Generally, a member of the field staff is allotted not more than 12 experiments in each crop season and which can conduct efficiently without affecting his normal work.

Each member of the field staff is supplied with a uniform set of equipment for his experimental work. This consists of a measuring tape, pegs, cross-staff and a string for marking the plot, scales with a set standard weights for weighting the produce and a gunny bag for storing a part of the produce to ascertain the loss due to driage.

The field staff, after receiving the list of selected fields, contacts the cultivators concerned and prepares a schedule of work for the different fields in accordance with the probable dates of harvesting fixed by the cultivators. A copy of this programme is sent to the superior officers to facilitate inspection. The supervising officers are required to attest on the spot the experiments supervised by them and offer their remarks on the efficiency or otherwise of the field work. They are also required to send independently consolidated inspection reports. It has been suggested that the experiments to be supervised by the departmental officers should be a random sample of the total number of experiments conducted, thereby ensuring the representative character of the supervision and also making available an independent estimate of the yield on the basis of the subsample supervised.

The procedure of selecting a plot within a field consists in measuring the length and breadth of the field, deducting a length equal to that of the plot from the length of the field and breadth of the plot from the breadth of the field, selecting a pair of random numbers less than the remainders so obtained, and locating the corner of the plot at the point determined by the selected pair of random numbers and finally marking the plot of specified size. The method implies a division of the field of length L and breadth B into $(L\text{-}a) \times (B\text{-}b)$ plots of the size $a \times b$ which are not distinct but overlapping and selecting one of those plots. It can be seen that by this procedure the central areas get a relatively larger chance of selection than those near the border of the field. However, this inequality in chance is too slight to vitiate the results worked out on the principle of equal chance for all plots in the field.

Instructions for Crop-cutting Experiments

A crop-cutting experiment involves different operations of field work:
  (i) Selection of field;
  (ii) Location and marking of an experimental plot;
  (iii) Harvesting and other operations; and
  (iv) Allowance for driage.

Specific instructions are issued to field staff for carrying out each operation of field work involved in conducting crop-cutting experiment. The field staff are trained specifically for this purpose accompanied by spot demonstration. In each revenue inspector's circle, a certain number of villages are selected for crop-cutting experiments. In each selected village, two fields sown with the crop are to be selected at random. In each selected field one plot of prescribed size is to be located at random.

Selection of Field

A field for the purpose of the experiment is understood to be a distinct patch or portion of land which has no bunds within it other than small irrigation bunds and which is demarcated on all its sides either by means of a bund or a narrow strip of uncultivated land or by means of a crop or crops different from the one grown in the patch. A Khasra number may contain one or more fields defined as above. If a Khasra number contains more than one field, then a Khasra number is to be selected first, and a field within the Khasra number is to be selected next. All the fields growing the crop will be considered whether they are sown with pure crop or mixed with some other crop.

Against each selected village, two random numbers of four digits are supplied. These two random numbers are to correspond to the two survey numbers (or Khasra numbers) of fields in which crop cutting experiments are to be conducted. The highest survey number in the village is found out from the village Khasra Register. If the given random numbers are higher than the highest survey number in the village, the two random numbers will be divided by the highest Khasra number and then the remainders will correspond to the survey numbers in which the crop-cutting experiments will be conducted. Consider a specific case. Suppose the selected village is Narela and the highest Khasra number in this village is 430. If two random numbers allotted for the village are 1143 and 308, then the first random number when divided by the highest Khasra number (430 in the present case) gives the remainder 283 which is selected survey number of the field for the crop-cutting experiment. The random number 308 which is less than 430 is the second survey number of the field chosen for the experiment. Thus the two fields selected for the crop-cutting experiment are having survey number 283 and 308. If any of the two survey numbers does not grow the desired crop or is not big enough so as to accommodate a plot of desired size, the same is to be rejected and in its place the next survey number which is growing the crop and is big enough to accommodate the plot will be selected. Suppose in the plot bearing survey number 283 the desired crop is not grown, then 284 will be selected if it is growing the crop and if this number also does not grow the crop, the next one, i.e. 285 will be selected. The procedure will be followed till a suitable field for crop-cutting is found out.

A Khasra number in a village will be selected once only for the purpose of experiment. If a Khasra number gets selected twice in the same village by virtue of repetition of the same number, another will be selected in its place by the procedure indicated above. If in a finally selected Khasra number there are several fields growing the desired crop, only one field which is nearest to the South-West corner of the selected Khasra number will be chosen.

Location and Making of an Experimental Plot

In each selected field one plot of size 10×5 m^2 (say) is to be located at random. This is to be done only on the day fixed for harvesting. The procedure of locating random plot is as follows:

Stand facing North with the selected field in front of you and to your right. This corner (South-West) will be the starting point. From this starting point measure the length and breadth of the field in metres.

Deduct 10 from the length and 5 from the breadth and obtain respective remainders. Select a pair of random number less than the remainders so obtained by consulting the random number lists of appropriate digits. Using the pair of random numbers and measuring from the starting point, locate the South-West corner of the plot and fix a peg at this corner.

Suppose the length and breadth of selected field are 72 m and 45 m respectively. Choose two random numbers less than 62 (i.e. 72-10) and 40 (i.e. 45-5) for locating the plot. Suppose the pair of random numbers selected is (25, 12). From the starting point of the field, measure 25 m along its length, then walk into the field along the breadth and stop at a distance of 12 m. Fix a peg at this point which will be the starting point (South-West) corner of the plot.

Tie a string to the peg, stretch it along the length of the field away from the starting point, i.e. South-West corner. Measure 10 m along it and fix another peg and put the cross-staff. Turn the string round the peg, stretch it at right angles away from the South-West corner of the field and measure 5 m along it. This will be the third corner of the plot provided the diagonal distance between the first peg and this point is about 11.2 m. Fix the third peg, use cross-staff, turn the string round the peg and stretch is parallel to the direction of the length of the field but towards the starting point and measure 10 m and fix the fourth peg provided the diagonal distance between second and fourth peg is about 11.2 m. Fix fourth peg, turn the string round the peg, stretch it to the starting point (first peg) of the plot. Check that the distance fourth and first peg is 5 m. The pegs should be straight and firmly fixed into the ground. See that the string is fully stretched on all the four sides. Lower the string to the level of the ground.

If the whole of the plot does not fall within the field owing to irregular shape of the field, reject the pair of random number. Choose a fresh pair of random numbers reading further down the columns in the random number-table and proceed as before to mark the starting point of the plot and then m∼ ∼ the plot as explained above. After ensuring that the whole p! ∋t falls within the field, consider the demarcated plot as final not ∼ ithstanding whether the crop inside the plot is poor or otherwise.

Harvesting and Other Operations

Harvest the crop which is only within the boundary (demarcated by string) of the plot. Observe carefully the plants located on the boundary. A bunch of plants on the boundary of the plot is to be harvested if more than half of it is inside the plot, otherwise leave the entire bunch. It is advisable not to allow the surrounding crop of the field to be harvested until the crop within the plot is harvested and removed to the threshing floor. Try to complete the harvesting before noon. Collect all the harvested produce without leaving any ear-head in the plot and spread it on a piece of cloth for a few hours before threshing and winnowing it. Threshing should be done by tramping under feet or by beating with a wooden rod on hessian cloth and the produce be winnowed with soops. Care should be taken to see that every grain is separated from the ear-heads. Weigh the cleaned produce carefully. All these operations should be done carefully so that there is no loss in the produce at various stages, viz. harvesting, carrying from field to the threshing floor, threshing, winnowing cleaning and weighing the produce. In the case of mixed crop, the weight of component crops should be recorded separately. Complete all the operation for a field on the same day but where the produce is moist and it is difficult to separate the grains from the earheads, it should be allowed to dry up for a day or two under the care of the Patwari. Record the results in the schedule prescribed for the purpose.

Allowance for Driage

The produce of a sub-sample of plots harvested is kept for estimating the allowance for driage. Normally, each revenue inspector (or the person in charge of conducting crop-cutting experiment) is asked to carry out the operations for estimating driage for the first plot harvested in each of the first two villages allotted to him for conducting crop-cutting experiments. The instructions issued are as follows.

After weighing the produce of a plot, store the whole of it in a small bag. Seal the bag, label it and keep in your office. The bag should be exposed to sun every day unopened for about a fortnight till the inside grains are well dried. At the end of the period, weigh the contents of the bag carefully, record the results of reweighing and other particulars. It is desirable that the re-weighment is done with the same set of scales and weights as used at the time of initial weighment. Return the produce to the owner after the grain has been re-weighed.

CROP SURVEY IN WEST BENGAL

For the purpose of the survey the jurisdiction of each police station is taken as a stratum. Samples are selected separately for each stratum, out the density of samples is the same. One sample unit (i.e. grid + 2.25 acres and square in shape) is selected at random on each half-square mile of the area under survey. These samples are divided into two sub-samples taking the alternative samples in each group. In order to select the samples, the mouza (revenue village) maps of a police station are arranged serially and cumulative total of the areas of mouzas in half-square-miles are noted. The area of a mouza is about half a square mile on the average. Any map is, therefore, allotted as many grids as there are 0.5 mile and integral values contained in the spread of the cumulative total over a mouza. It may be mentioned here that before arranging the mouzas serially, the first mouza is selected at random from the mouza list of the police station which insures the randomness of the sample.

Besides, after determining the number of samples to be allotted to a mouza the points at which grids are to be thrown are also selected at random.

Crop-cutting experiments are conducted from samples selected uniformly throughout the entire area under survey. A sufficient number of grids is selected at random from the first set of sub-samples used for area survey work to ensure even distribution over the stratum. The list of samples for crop-cutting experiments is supplied to the investigators at the commencement of the area survey. This enables them to get acquainted with the fields and their owners. Contact with the owners also enable the Investigators to get an approximate idea about the time at which the crop will be harvested. In every police station 30 per cent of the grids are selected at random from the first sub-sample and lists are prepared at headquarters arranging the numbers in order of selection. The Field Investigators are directed to take only one cut for each of the selected crops from any of the selected grids, trying the fields *seriatum* from the list of fields for that grid. The maximum number of cuts fixed for any primary worker is thirty. The size of the cut in respect of all the crops except arhar, potato and sugarcane is the usual circular area of about 100 sq ft divided into three concentric circles of radii 2', 4' and 5.65' respectively. The size of the cut for arhar, potato and sugarcane is a square plot of side 15'. The sample within the field is located with the help of pair of random numbers supplied to the primary workers. The first random number of the pair gives the number of steps the worker is to measure along the length of the selected field from one corner and the second number gives the number of steps he is required to walk into the field at right angles to the length of the field. The point located in such a manner is to be the centre of the sample that is of the three concentric circles from which the crop is to be cut. The workers are required to take the actual weight of the crop immediately after harvesting, threshing and winnowing.

In almost all the States in the country, estimates of yield rate are being prepared through crop-cutting experiments by the principle of random sampling every year for major food and non-food crops. At present, about 1,41,000 experiments on 19 food crops and about 41,000 experiments on 12 non-food crops are being conducted to estimate the yield rates.

The Field Operations Divisions of the National Sample Survey Organization is responsible since 1953 to provide technical guidance to the State authorities engaged in the work of estimation of yield rates and coordinate and consolidate the results at All-India level. It has also been associated in the training of field staff and supervision of the conduct of crop-cutting experiments.

SCHEME FOR IMPROVEMENT OF CROP STATISTICS (ICS)

This scheme was initiated from Rabi 1973-74 with the main objective to locate, through the joint efforts of the Central and State authorities, lacuna if any, in the State system of collection of area and yield statistics and suggest measures to effect lasting improvements in the system.

The programme of work under the scheme, when implemented in full, envisages: (i) physical verification of crop inspection done by Patwaris in four clusters of five survey numbers each within each of a sample 5,000 villages; (ii) checking of crop abstract statements relating to sample of villages; and (iii) inspection of 15,000 crop-cutting experiments at harvest stage. The programme of work is to be undertaken by the supervisory staff of the NSSO. The supervisory staff of the State Government will also take up an equal and non-overlapping sample under the scheme. A modest beginning of the programme of work envisaged under the scheme was made during Rabi 1973-74 with special emphasis on wheat in the nine major wheat growing States. In 1974-75, the programme of work was carried out on an extended scale and also covered other States.

Domain of Study

As the purpose of the surveys has been to estimate the average per acre yield for each State and its chief divisions and the quinquennial average yields for each district, the domain of study, technically speaking, for each individual survey has thus been the State as a whole and its chief divisions, while for the quinquennial period it has been an individual district. However, the desirability of providing the annual yield estimates for the major districts for the production of a particular crop has always been kept in view.

The field of enquiry for a survey comprises the total area under the crop in question. Inaccessible regions are excluded, which, however, constitute a very minor fraction of the total cropped area.

Design of Survey

The design of sampling adopted in the present surveys is technically known as the stratified multi-stage sampling in which the region to be surveyed is first sub-divided into sub-regions called strata from each of which a certain number of sampling units, namely, experimental plots, are selected at random, the drawing of sampling units proceeding in successive stages of selection. Except in West Bengal and Orissa, tehsils/ revenue inspector circle/sub-divisions (containing 100 to 300 villagers), serve as strata, a village as the primary unit of sampling, of field growing the specified crop (pure or in mixture with other crops) as the secondary unit of sampling. As regards West Bengal, the whole of the State is divided into grids of size 2.25 acres.

A random sampling of grids at the rate of 1 for every half a sq mile is chosen from all the Thanas. Odd number grids of the 'A' sample are chosen for the crop-cutting survey and from each selected grid generally one cut is taken for a crop. In Orissa, the whole State has been divided into strata consisting of groups of contiguous Thanas; from each stratum two independent sub-samples are selected for area estimation and from each of these sub-samples, 5 villages are sampled for yield survey and 3 crop-cutting experiments are conducted in each selected village.

The allocation of experiments between the strata is done generally in proportion to the acreage under the crops. Two to six villages are selected per taluka, 2 fields (sometimes 3 as in Maharashtra or even 5 as the case of paddy in Kerala) are selected in each village for each crop. The selection at each stage, of village, fields and plots is made in accordance with the principles of random sampling.

The selection of villages and even of fields in some cases is carried out directly by the statistical staff; the selection and demarcation of plots within fields is left to the field staff. A statement giving the shape and size of plots in different States for various crops is given in Table 7.2.

Field Organization

The field organization in States is drawn from the Revenue and/or Agriculture Department depending upon the administrative convenience. The staff to actually conduct the experiment is the kanungo in Uttar Pradesh, the revenue inspector in Telangana are of Andhra Pradesh and the agricultural demonstrator and extension officer (Agriculture) in Andhra area, the circle inspector (Revenue) or amin, the field supervisory investigator and junior statistical supervisor in Bihar, the village level worker in development areas and the circle inspector in other areas of Maharashtra and Gujarat, the *girdawar* kanungo or revenue inspector in Madhya Pradesh and Jammu & Kashmir, the agricultural demonstrator/ inspector and revenue inspector in Tamil Nadu, Karnataka, Haryana and Punjab and the land records inspector in Rajasthan. There are, generally below tehsil level, supervisory officers in the States.

In Assam special staff has been appointed for this purpose. The Patwaris of the selected villages are required to render assistance in the conduct of the experiments, particularly in securing local cooperation. The results of experiment along with related information regarding selected fields are entered in given proformas by the field staff and sent directly to the State Statistician. The ancillary information collected covers items like irrigation, soil type, variety of crops grown, etc. and, apart from its intrinsic value, also serves to check the representative character of the sample. On an average, a member of the field staff is allotted about 8-10 experiments for each season which he can efficiently conduct without prejudice to his normal duties.

Training of Staff

The field staff engaged in experimental work and that entrusted with its, supervision are trained intensively in the method of work, the training being invariably accompanied by spot demonstrations. The need for

Table 7.2 Size and Shape of the Plot Employed in Crop Estimation Surveys

State	Dimensions and the shape of the plot (n)	Size (ha)	Exceptions unless otherwise specified* (dimensions of plots (in metres)
(1)	(2)	(3)	(4)
Andhra Pradesh	5 × 5	1/400	for tur, castor, sesamum and cotton plot size is 10 × 10 i.e. 1/100 hectare.
Assam	5 × 5	1/400	—
Bihar	10 × 5	1/200	for tur jute, mesta, sugarcane and rape and mustard plot size is 5 × 5 i.e. 1/400 hectare.
Gujarat	5 × 5	1/400	for castor and cotton plot size is 10 × 5 i.e. 1/200 hectare.
Haryana	10 × 5	1/200	—
Himachal Pradesh	10 × 2	1/500	—
Jammu & Kashmir	10 × 5	1/200	for potato 5 × 5 i.e. 1/400 hectare.
Kerala	5 × 5	1/400	—
Madhya Pradesh	5 × 5	1/400	for cotton 10 m × 11 rows of variable plot of size 1/200 hectare.
Maharashtra	10 × 10	1/100	for rice konkan and ragi the plot size is 10 × 5 i.e. 1/200 hectare and for cotton and tur the plot size is 20 × 10 i.e. 1/50 hectare.
Meghalaya	5 × 5	1/400	—
Karnataka	5 × 5	1/400	for tur, castor and cotton the plot size is 10 × 5 i.e. 1/200 hectare.
Orissa	circle of radius 4'	1/866 acres	for jute 16.5' × 16.5' i.e. 1/160 of an acre.
Punjab	10 × 5	1/200	—
Rajasthan	5 × 5	1/400	for cotton plot size is 10 × 5 i.e. 1/200 hectare.
Tamil Nadu	5 × 5	1/400	for cotton, sugarcane and groundnut plot size is 10 × 5 i.e. 1/200 hectare.
Uttar Pradesh	equilateral triangle of size 10	1/230.8	for sugarcane and jute plot size is 5 × 5 (1/400 hectare) and cotton 20 × 10 i.e. 1/50 hectare for sugarcane (factory area) the plot size is 10 × 10 i.e. 1/100 hectare.

Table 7.2 *Size and Shape of the Plot Employed in Crop Estimation Surveys* (Contd.)

State	Dimensions and the shape of the plot (n)	Size (ha)	Exceptions unless otherwise specified* (dimensions of plots (in metres)
(1)	(2)	(3)	(4)
West Bengal	circle of radius 5/7"	1/435.6 acre	for tur and potato, sugarcane the plot size is 15' 15' i.e. 1/193.6 acre.
Dadra & N. Haveli	5 ×5	1/400	—
Delhi	5 × 5	1/400	—
Goa	5 × 5	1/400	—
Pondicherry	50 links × 20 links	1/100 acre	—

*The size and shape of the plots given in columns (2) and (3) are generally applied for almost all crops and the exceptions are presented in column (4).

associating the senior district officers of the departments with the training is imperative since it helps them to keep a vigilant eye on the work of the staff and make fruitful suggestions in improving the efficiency of work.

Checks on Field Surveys

When the list of selected fields for a given season is intimated to the field staff, the cultivators concerned are contacted and the staff prepares a schedule of work for the different fields in accordance with the probable harvesting dates and in consultation with the cultivators. A copy of the scheduled programme is required to be sent to superior officers to facilitate inspection. The surveys in all the States, except West Bengal and Kerala, are conducted under the technical guidance and supervision of the National Sample Survey Organization which maintains units of supervisory staff in all the States. At the State level the supervision over field work is exercised by the departmental supervisors and by the statistical staff.

The supervision which normally covers at least 8-15 per cent of the experiments provides an invaluable check on the accuracy of the primary data collected. The State supervisory officers are required to attest on spot the results of experiments supervised by them and offer remarks on the efficiency of work. They are also required to send independently consolidated inspection reports embodying their comments on the field work, and their suggestions have often been found to contribute considerably simplifying the field work.

Under a scheme drawn up by the NSSO and Directorate of Economics and Statistics, it is proposed to carry out central supervision over the conduct of crop-cutting experiments in a random sample of 5,000 villages. There will be a matching sample of 5,000 villages to be supervised by State statistical staff. The supervised Central and State samples will provide independent estimates of yield of principal crops at the State level.

Some Suggestions

There is, however, yet scope for improvement in the system of inspection in several directions. For instance, the experiments to be supervised by the departmental officers could be a random sample of the total number of experiments conducted thereby increasing the representative character of the supervision and also making available an independent estimate of the yield on the basis of this sub-sample.

An investigation revealed that a relatively large number of field samples selected in the crop-cutting experiments were drawn from larger holdings, the smaller holdings, although much larger in number than the larger holdings, did not get proportional representation in this method of sampling. The sample of field is, therefore, unrepresentative in respect of frequency of distribution of holdings in various size groups. However, justification to this procedure of sampling fields may be that larger holdings contribute proportionately a larger volume to total production. But in the ancillary information, it would be worth while to include information on the size of holding to which the sample field belongs.

The data at present being compiled are regarding the hect, yield of different crops up to the district level. no information is available below the district level and besides this, even at the district or the State level, separate information about irrigated and unirrigated yield is not available for any crop, it is desirable to extend in crop cutting technique to obtain information on crop yields in relation to the size of the farm and major improvements such as irrigation *versus* non-irrigation, soil conservation, fertilizer programmes, etc.

At present the design for such surveys is generally a composite one without any stratification according to input such as irrigation and seed. The yield rates are, however, worked out on a post-stratification basis using the ancillary data regarding inputs collected during the course of crop cutting experiments. The National Commission on Agriculture have recommended that the sampling design for crop cutting experiments should be modified with a view to introducing stratification according to irrigated and rainfed areas and also high yielding and local varieties. Some of the schemes for improving timeliness and quality of data are as below.

Timely Reporting of Estimates of Area and Production of Principal Crops

This is an on-going Centrally Sponsored Scheme, the objective of which is to obtain estimates of area of different principal crops and their production, in each season, by a specific date. The States are required to furnish these estimates by 30th November for kharif crops and by 30th April for rabi crops. These estimates are used for generating advance estimates of production of principal crops. The scheme is being

Cereal Yield

There has been a general improvement in the yield of cereals (per hectare) over the years globally. The yields have improved by a fourth globally and the high income group countries witnessed an increase to 4051 kg per hectare in 1996-98 from 3170 kg in 1979-81 while the middle income countries had nearly twice the yield rates of low income nations (Chart I).

Regionwise, while East Asia and South Asia improved upon their yields, Europe and Central Asia reported a drop in their yield in 1996-98 as compared to 1979-81 (Chart II) reflecting the neglect of agriculture in this part of the world.

Countrywise, France had the best cereal yield at 7126 kg per hectare in 1996-98 followed by Egypt at 6595 kg. The yields were high in Germany, Japan and the U.S. at more than six tonnes per hectare. The yield in China was more than twice that of India. Likewise, the yield in South Korea was substantially higher than in Sri Lanka in the latest year. And even Vietnam bettered the latter. Cuba were an exception to the general trend where the yield dipped to 1973 kg in the latest year from 2453 kg per hectare in 1979-81. Brazil and Germany increased their yields by more than half in the eighteen year period (Chart III).

As for agricultural productivity (value added per worker in 1995 $) it was very high in France, Japan, Australia, Norway and the U.S. at more than $30,000 per worker in 1996-98. The Slovac Republic had the distinction of adding more than $42,000 per worker.

Chart III

How They Improved
(kg/hectare)

Country	1979-81	1996-98
France	4700	7126
Egypt	4053	6595
S. Korea	4986	6450
Germany	4166	6366
Japan	5252	6017
Austria	4131	5693
U.S.	4151	5380
China	3027	4821
Brazil	2047	4081
Indonesia	2837	3916
Vietnam	2049	3754
Argentina	2183	3284
Sri Lanka	2462	3103
Malaysia	2828	3065
Thailand	1911	2466
India	1324	2200
Australia	1321	1973
Cuba	2458	1973

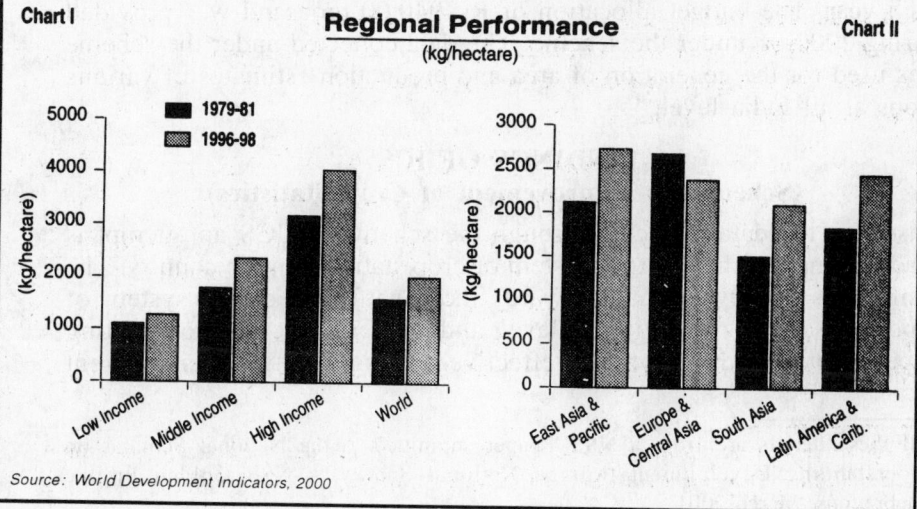

Chart I

Regional Performance
(kg/hectare)

Chart II

Source: World Development Indicators, 2000

implemented in 13 land record States and also UTs of Delhi and Pondicherry. The scheme is implemented on 50:50 basis between the Central Government and the State Governments. The budget allocation of Rs. 400,00 thousand was provided during 2000-01 as the share of the Central Government. The data generated under the scheme are being used for the generation of All India estimates of area and production of principal crops for kharif/rabi seasons.

Improvement of Crop Statistics

This scheme is also an on-going Centrally Sponsored Scheme and the objective is to improve the quality of statistics of area and production of crops through supervision and monitoring. Under this scheme, a sample check of area enumeration and crop cutting experiments of 10,000 villages and approximately 31,000 experiments at harvest stage are undertaken. It is being implemented in all those 13 States where Timely Reporting Scheme is in operation. The budget allocation of Rs. 258,00 thousands was provided under the scheme. The findings of such sample checks were published by National Sample Survey Organisation (NSSO) for each State and the same were discussed in the meeting of the State High Coordination Committee for improvement of agricultural statistics for taking appropriate remedial measure, whenever necessary. More details about the Scheme are given in Chapter 8.

Establishment of an Agency for Reporting of Agricultural Statistics

It is being implemented as a Centrally Sponsored Scheme in the permanently settled States of West Bengal, Kerala, Orissa, and North Eastern Region of Nagaland, Sikkim and Arunachal Pradesh. Under this scheme, an Agency has been established in these States for generating estimates of area and production of principal crops and land use statistics, on the basis of complete enumeration on the basis of 20 percent villages in each year. The budget allocation of Rs. 940,00 thousand was provided during 2000-01 under the scheme. The data collected under the scheme was used for the generation of area and production estimates of various crops at all India level.

FINDINGS OF ICS[1]
(Scheme for Improvement of Crop Statistics)

Based on the data collected through the scheme for ICS an attempt is made to analyse the existing system of crop statistics in the country. The analysis is mainly oriented towards the functioning of the system of reporting area at the village level and the conduct of crop cutting experiments. Findings of ICS effectively bring to the focus different

---

[1]All these details are from a NSSC paper submitted at the National Seminar on Understanding Development through National Surveys[6]—NSS Golden Jubilee Celebrations, March 2001.

aspects of deficiencies in the State system of crop statistics. Major areas of concern based on critical analysis of ICS data are given below:

Area Statistics

Work Load of the Primary Worker   The primary worker namely Patwari who is engaged in the collection of Agriculture Statistics is seen to be entrusted with multifarious activities and he is over burdened. Results of 1998-99 data of ICS shows that the number of villages per primary worker varies from 2 in Gujarat to 15 in Bihar. In terms of survey numbers the primary worker has to cover an area of 2700, survey numbers in Uttar Pradesh hills. Looking from the area to be covered by the Patwari it is seen that he has to cover an area of around 100 hects. in West Bengal to 1000 hects. in Rajasthan. Over the years it is observed through ICS that the position has not changed. State-wise status of workload is given in Annexure-I.

The perils of very heavy workload on the primary worker for collecting the data on agriculture coupled with his other responsibilities have obviously affected the timely completion of Girdawari as observed in the forthcoming paragraphs. The fact has been regularly highlighted in the State Status Reports over the years and have been put forward in various High Level Co-ordinating Committee (HLCC) meeting but not much has been done in this direction to reduce the workload per primary worker and to improve the quality of data.

Status of Implementation of TRS

The aim of TRS and EARAS is to make available the estimates of crop area in time. In other words timeliness is the essence of TRS/EARAS. ICS examines this aspect in terms of completion of Girdawari and submission of TRS statements. Analysis of All India figures (Table 7.3) for the four seasons—Autumn, Winter, Rabi and Summer, for the years from 1994-95 to 1998-99 reveals that around 55% of the TRS Girdawari is only completed in time except in Autumn season when it is still less at around 40%. State-wise status on this aspect for 1998-99 is given in Annexure-II. It is observed that the percentage of timely completion during different season was less than 5% in Assam, less than 10% in Bihar and around 30% in West Bengal during 1998-99.

Table 7.3 Completion of TRS girdawari in time (%)

Year	Autumn	Winter	Rabi	Summer
1	2	3	4	5
1998-99	39	58	57	53
1997-98	37	58	57	56
1996-97	35	57	52	53
1995-96	34	55	60	44
1994-95	43	55	53	51

TRS envisages submission of relevant statements to the higher authorities so as to consolidate the area figures without delay. ICS data from 1994-95 to 98-99 as mentioned does not show an encouraging trend (Table 7.4). In around 46% of cases only the TRS statement is submitted in time which totally defeats the objective of TRS. The percentage is abnormally low in autumn season, improves a little in subsequent seasons, and again falls in summer season. State-wise submission of TRS/EARAS statements during 1998-99 is given in Annexure-III. Timely submission of TRS statement is the essential requirement of the timely release of crop forecasts and any delay in this regard obviously affects the objectivity of the scheme.

Table 7.4 Submission of TRS statements in time (%)

Year	Autumn	Winter	Rabi	Summer
1	2	3	4	5
1998-99	27	43	45	32
1997-98	29	46	40	35
1996-97	29	44	36	34
1995-96	28	41	41	30
1994-95	25	42	40	32

Accuracy of Girdawari

In the process of locating the deficiencies in the system of crop statistics the scheme for ICS has observed three types of errors in area reporting (Table 7.5):
- Missing crops which are actually grown.
- Reporting crops which is not actually grown.
- Incorrect reporting of area under crop.

Table 7.5 Errors in Area Reporting (%)

Year	Autumn	Winter	Rabi	Summer
1	2	3	4	5
1998-99	30	34	30	18
1997-98	33	36	29	32
1996-97	32	37	32	38
1995-96	36	37	33	38
1994-95	43	36	31	42

The data reveal that in about 30 to 40% of the survey numbers while reporting the area by primary worker one or the other type of error occurs. This is a discouraging situation and indicates that the training given to the primary worker is not adequate. An in-depth study of the errors in different States reveals that Gujarat, Karnataka, M.P., Maharashtra, Tamil Nadu, UP & West Bengal have around 30% samples with one or the other type of error in area reporting. In Assam state, the data on Patwari records is not available.

Comparison of area Estimates

An attempt has been made to compare the areas as estimated from the figures reported by the primary worker and the supervisor under the scheme for ICS. The analysis enables to judge the deviation in estimates of area under crops. The Percentage difference of estimates of crop area at All India Level based on supervisor's entries and entries of State primary workers in the corresponding sampling unit of ICS are presented in (Table 7.6).

Table 7.6 Percentage Difference of Area Estimates

SL.NO.	CROP	1998-99	1997-98	1996-97	1995-96	1994-95
1	2	3	4	5	6	7
1	Rice (Kh)	13.38	15.05	28.76	18.24	22.52
2	Rice (S)	23.38	43.22	35.31	40.22	26.86
3	Jowar (Kh)	23.48	3.57	2.57	1.36	4.13
4	Jowar (R)	7.08	13.46	4.51	4.19	11.78
5	Bajra	11.64	5.32	4.23	4.42	3.74
6	Maize	8.13	9.23	12.89	8.23	32.04
7	Ragi	13.80	4.92	8.61	1.13	2.04
8	Wheat	32.69	21.03	11.35	9.34	13.18
9	Barley	2.07	9.82	.29	0	37.73
10	Gram	10.70	11.43	8.70	7.32	9.17

Note: Percentage is (Supervisor's-Patwari's) × 100/Patwari's

Table 7.6 brings to light revealing trend of under reporting of area, for all the ten major crops covered in the analysis. The trend has been persisting for long. The extent of deviations is noticed to be more than 10%. Rice and wheat account for nearly half of the total cropped area under food grains and about 3/4th of total food grains production in the country. Therefore, under estimation of area under these crops is a matter which requires serious consideration.

Yield Statistics

Precision of Estimates

The precision of the estimates of average yield is judged by the standard error of the estimate. NSSO has been impressing upon the states on the need for calculation of standard error. It is generally desired that yield rates should not have a standard error of more than 2% for major crops and 5% for other crops at state level to ensure that the reliability of estimates. It is observed that the standard errors are higher in a large number of cases, which calls for remedial action. The yield rate of few important crops for States and their % SE both for Crop Estimation Surveys (CES) and for ICS data are presented in the Table 7.7 for illustration for the year 1998-99.

Table 7.7 Comparison of Estimates of Yield under ICS (Pooled Sample) and CES

Sr. No.	State	I.C.S.				C.E.S.			
		No. of Expts.		Estimated Yield Rate Kg/Hect.	% SE	No. of Expts.		Estimated Yield Rate Kg/Hect.	% SE
		Planned	Analysed			Planned	Analysed		
1	2	3	4	5	6	7	8	9	10
				Crop: Rice (Kharif)					
1	Andhra Pradesh	500	406	2518	3.3	6708	6636	2541	0.4
2	Gujarat (Irr)	76	60	1943	7.0	818	816	3016	2.0
3	Gujarat (Un-Irr)	124	110	1008	6.0	976	966	1717	2.3
4	Haryana	240	237	2144	4.6	964	936	2239	1.8
5	Karnataka	320	298	2539	2.6	3170	3165	2535	1.2
6	Kerala (Wint)	320	298	1779	4.1	5015	3906	2000	1.0
7	Madhya Pradesh	600	484	1036	4.2	4560	3445	1097	—
8	Orissa (Wint)	640	638	1382	2.5	9778	9777	1318	0.5
9	Punjab	224	219	3257	2.0	1872	1855	3152	0.6
10	Tamil Nadu	400	386	3384	1.7	1260	1260	3483	1.0
				Crop: Jowar (Kharif)					
1	Andhra Pradesh	272	204	801	9.9	1370	1289	820	2.2
2	Gujarat	280	251	858	9.4	510	505	908	4.9
3	Karnataka	200	180	1398	7.4	2030	2006	1543	1.7
4	Madhya Pradesh	320	280	989	8.7	2598	2360	984	1.8
5	Rajasthan	220	173	284	14.2	750	676	287	4.5
6	Tamil Nadu	180	154	775	9.0	470	470	1011	3.8
				Crop: Bajra					
1	Andhra Pradesh	200	169	979	6.0	1050	981	760	2.8
2	Gujarat	324	268	898	6.4	1260	1184	1009	2.7
3	Haryana	280	268	898	6.4	1260	1184	1009	2.7
4	Karnataka	160	145	836	6.9	1280	1274	714	2.6
5	Madhya Pradesh	120	103	1175	6.5	404	371	1160	4.0
6	Punjab	36	34	897	10.4	36	34	1087	7.8
7	Rajasthan	320	239	426	7.3	800	729	431	4.5
8	Tamil Nadu	180	153	1280	8.7	360	360	1339	2.8

Table 7.7 Comparison of Estimates of Yield under ICS (Pooled Sample) and CES (Contd.)

Sr. No.	State	I.C.S.				C.E.S.			
		No. of Expts. Planned	Analysed	Estimated Yield Rate Kg/Hect.	% SE	No. of Expts. Planned	Analysed	Estimated Yield Rate Kg/Hect.	% SE
1	2	3	4	5	6	7	8	9	10
				Crop: Wheat					
1	Bihar	280	148	2027	5.8	10760	5441	2063	1.0
2	Gujarat (Irr)	188	159	2729	3.9	2026	2019	2712	1.0
3	Haryana	300	291	3953	1.7	2180	21.4	3916	0.6
4	Madhya Pradesh	600	552	1899	3.8	5234	4644	1854	1.1
5	Punjab	420	401	4231	1.2	2216	2207	4332	0.4
6	Rajasthan	420	384	2587	2.5	1000	887	2487	1.9

Comparison of Yield Estimates

Even though the sample size of ICS is quite less in comparison to that of CES, a broad dimensional check can be made in the comparison. Percentage difference of estimates of yield rates under ICS and CES at All India Level are given in Table 7.8 for 5 years since 1994-95 for major crops.

Table 7.8 Percentage Difference of Yield Estimates

SL.NO.	CROP	1998-99	1997-98	1996-97	1995-96	1994-95
1	2	3	4	5	6	7
1	Rice (Kh)	3.20	2.29	4.06	− 4.36	− 10.70
2	Rice (S)	1.83	1.05	7.04	− 2.79	− 4.55
3	Jowar (Kh)	4.32	− 17.17	0.64	− 8.42	− 13.27
4	Jowar (R)	1.22	− 31.55	− 2.41	− 3.53	1.82
5	Bajra	28.79	9.90	− 6.22	1.81	1.91
6	Maize	− 25.90	20.44	− 15.42	5.64	− 5.77
7	Ragi	− 9.09	− 12.96	− 0.69	− 3.58	− 0.27
8	Wheat	− 2.60	− 12.75	1.78	0.08	− 1.52
9	Barley	− 1.27	− 1.80	5.47	2.72	9.03
10	Gram	− 4.40	− 1.98	− 9.30	− 0.86	22.72

Note: Percentage is (Supervisor's-Patwari's) × 100/Patwari's

Errors in Crop Cutting Experiments

An analysis of the results of crop cutting experiment through the sample check under ICS during 1998-99 reveals that about 90% of experiments could only be conducted without error at All India level. However the position is quite different once State-wise analysis is made. Table 7.9 indicates the position of different types of errors observed during the conduct of crop cutting "experiments in Kharif season of 1998-99.

Table 7.9 Incidence of Errors in Crop Cutting Experiments—Kharif 1998-99

Sl. No.	States	% of expts. Where no error was noticed	% of expts. where error was noticed							
			E1	E2	E3	E4	E5	E6	E7	E8
1	2	3	4	5	6	7	8	9	10	11
1	Andhra Pradesh	80	0	0	2	1	0	7	4	9
2	Assam	92	0	0	1	0	1	0	0	6
3	Bihar	90	0	0	0	0	0	3	0	7
4	Gujarat	71	0	0	0	0	0	10	4	18
5	Haryana	80	0	0	3	2	0	16	1	5
6	Himachal Pradesh	76	0	0	0	0	0	14	7	5
7	Jammu & Kashmir	82	1	3	4	6	0	2	3	10
9	Kerala	100	0	0	0	0	0	0	0	0
10	Madhya Pradesh	92	0	0	0	0	0	2	0	5
11	Maharashtra	47	1	1	13	29	5	38	13	14
12	Orissa	96	0	0	0	0	0	1	0	1
13	Punjab	94	0	0	0	0	0	5	0	2
14	Rajasthan	67	4	3	5	7	0	25	5	0
15	Tamil Nadu	60	0	0	8	2	0	40	0	1
16	U.P.	71	1	0	11	8	2	14	1	3
17	West Bengal	98	0	0	0	0	0	2	0	1
18	Delhi	100	0	0	0	0	0	0	0	0
19	Pondicherry	100	0	0	0	0	0	0	0	0

Note: E1: Error in selection of Survey/Sub survey nos., E2: Error in selection of field with in Survey/Sub-survey No. E3: Error in the measurement of the field. E4: Error in selection of random nos, location and marking of plots, E5: Error in weighment of produce, E6: Error in recording ancillary information, E7: Inadequate arrangements for storing of produce for driage and incorrect reporting of constituents in mixture, E8: Others.

Occurrence of various types of errors, viz. selection of survey numbers, measurement of field, selection of field and random numbers etc, are observed in some of the samples. Mistakes that occur in the process of selection of survey numbers, selection of fields, measurement of plots and selection of random numbers for location of plots have a direct impact on the objectivity envisaged and results in upsetting the representative character of the experiments. Instances of errors in reporting ancillary information provides adequate evidence about the casual approach adopted by the primary worker even in eliciting the relevant data. It is necessary that the departure from prescribed procedure for conducting Crop Cutting Experiments needs to be taken with seriousness and strong administrative measures coupled with intensive training of field staff are resorted to.

Substitution of Experiments

Instructions for conduct of Crop Estimation Survey prohibit substitution of sampling units once selected. But instance of substitution of sampling units at village and field level is observed. During 1998-99, the incidence relating to substitution of villages was more than 5% in Assam, Haryana, Karnataka, Rajasthan, Tamil Nadu and Uttar Pradesh (Plains). The frequency of substitution of survey numbers/field was observed to be quite high in Karnataka (10%). Barring other reasons, in majority of these cases the fields were substituted either because the crop was harvested prior to selection of the field or crop harvested before the date fixed. Better liaison between the primary workers and the cultivators would go a long way to control such high incidence of substitution.

Delegation of Field Work of Crop Cutting Experiments

The field work of crop estimation surveys is entrusted to the officials who are normally one rank higher than the primary worker for area enumeration. Delegation of crop cutting work particularly to the junior rank has been observed in several states. For example, during 1998-99 year, the delegation of work was of the order of 4.2% in case of U.P. (Plains) in Kharif and 4.5% in Pondicherry in Rabi. Adequate arrangements are needed for ensuring proper training to the field workers entrusted with Crop Estimation Surveys to avoid the improper conduct of crop cutting experiments.

Use of Crop Cutting Equipments

While an untrained worker cannot conduct the experiment properly, supply of essential equipments and their proper use is also equally important to ensure accuracy in measurements. Annexure-V indicates the percentage of experiments without use and improper use of the crop cutting equipments in different States. The position is far from satisfactory particularly in the case of Bihar, Haryana, Himachal Pradesh, Jammu and Kashmir, Karnataka, Maharashtra, Punjab, Rajasthan and U.P. Even the supplied equipment was reported to have not been carried to the field for the conduct of crop cutting experiments in many cases in Karnataka, M.P., Maharashtra, Rajasthan and U.P. This calls for strong administrative measures for effecting further improvement. Table 7.10 gives the percentage of experiments without use and improper use of the crop cutting equipment during last 5 years as observed through ICS.

Table 7.10 Supply and Use of Equipments for Crop Cutting Experiments

Year	Percentage of experiments for which							
	concerned primary workers not supplied with				Concerned primary workers did not use the supplied items			
	Tape	*Pegs*	*Balance*	*Weight*	*Tape*	*Pegs*	*Balance*	*Weight*
1	2	3	4	5	6	7	8	9
1998-99	14	54	33	33	14	13	20	19
1997-98	15	16	36	39	20	18	26	24
1996-97	18	61	37	40	18	17	25	24
1995-96	17	60	37	39	18	16	24	23
1994-95	16	60	34	39	18	17	23	22

Institutional Arrangements for Improvement of the System Through Findings of ICS

State-wise and All India status reports on the system of Agricultural Statistics as observed through supervision under ICS Scheme are being prepared from the year 1973-74 onwards. The season-wise status reports for the state contains full account of the present position of estimation of crop production, the procedures followed for enumeration of area and yield, errors observed between the figures of primary workers and the supervisory staff and steps to be taken for improving the system of collection of crop statistics. The report for each state also gives the position of training of state staff entrusted with the crop cutting experiments, the equipments supplied to them, adequacy of experiments planned under CES, response rate, timeliness of crop enumeration, timeliness of submission of TRS statements with/without completing girdawari, transcription and recording errors by primary workers, aggregation errors, adherence to prescribed procedures by primary workers while conducting crop cutting experiments, delegation of work by the primary workers, estimates of yield rates from supervised experiments etc.

The reports are finalised in consultation with the Directorate of Economics and Statistics, Union Ministry of Agriculture and the concerned SASA. These reports are discussed by High Level Coordination Committee on Agricultural Statistics setup in the states. In the meetings of the Committee, various issues relating to area forecasts, estimates of yield rates and crop production, the working of TRS, EARAS and ICS schemes and other aspects of agricultural statistics are discussed. These meetings have proved useful in sorting out problems of co-ordination among different agencies, other operational problems and in taking steps for improving the working of the system.

Reorientation of ICS Scheme

Integration of Remote Sensing Technology

The ICS Scheme had been conceived with the aim of locating the shortcomings in the collection of crop Statistics as per prescribed methodology for area enumeration and yield estimation. However, in doing so, the scheme provides for collection of supervised data which has the potential of building an alternative set of area and yield estimates. National Advisory Board on Statistics considered the strength of ICS data and suggested for revamping the scheme with regard to methodology so as to provide statistically sound estimates of crop statistics in time bound manner. An Expert Group in the Ministry of Statistics constituted for this purpose under the Chairmanship of DG and CEO, NSSO with officials from CSO, NSSO, Ministry Agriculture, IASRI and states Statistical Bureaus considered various options of improvement in the methodology, and decided to take up a pilot study on the feasibility of integration of Remote Sensing Technology on crop area estimation with ICS field data collection in order to provide an upto date area frame for selection of primary stage units. In order to study the feasibility of the proposal and efficacy of the of the Remote Sensing Technology for area statistics, the pilot study was undertaken in 6 villages of three districts of Karnal, Kota, and Bhopal, during Rabi 1999-2000, wherein NSSO collected the data through field observation while-Space Application Centre (SAC), Ahmedabad took up the satellite data and estimated the area after NSSO completed the field work. The two agencies independently did the work.

Methodology

The pilot study was aimed to verify the crop and cropped area obtained from remote sensing technology through the ground verification by NSSO at village level only for important crops viz. Wheat, Mustard and Rape Seed. For the pilot study, the SAC acquired the IRS-LISS III, multi spectral data at spatial resolution of 23 meter for all study villages during the peak vegetation stage IRS PAN data of spatial resolution of 5.8 meter was also acquired. Further, the village boundaries available in the cadastral maps were digitized and over-layed on the village. Field data was collected during the peak vegetation stage of crop in and around the study villages. This involved the identification and collection of information related to crop phenology and its environment with the land cover classes.

Subsequently, spectral signature of crop including other land cover was generated by SAC based on the ground truth they had collected in the field. Image classification using maximum likelihood classifier was carried out to classify every pixel field with thematic crop. The crop area as proportion of the village geographical area was estimated.

NSSO collected the crop area statistics in the 6 experimental villages on complete enumeration basis through observation methods. Survey number-wise data so collected by field workers of NSSO was consolidated for arriving village level crop area statistics. The field work was also supervised by the field officers.

Findings

The findings of the two agencies using different methodologies for crop area under major crops in the 6 villages are tabulated in Table 7.11 in terms of percentage of crop area to geographical area.

Table 7.11

S. No	Village name	Village area as per		Main Crop name	Main Crop Area in % to geographical area.		Other Crop name	Other Crop Area in % to geographical area.	
		NSSO	SAC		NSSO	SAC		NSSO	SAC
1.	Baldi	236.97	265	Wheat	44.7	51.24	—	—	—
2.	Mainmati	316.98	321	Wheat	66.3	63.81	—	—	—
3.	Ranpur	386.23	4181	Wheat	4.4	5.36	Mustard	7.2	13.02
4.	Ghatoliya	151.23	158	Wheat	30.9	34.29	Mustard	32.2	18.86
5.	Aavala	1450.77	1162	Wheat	31.4	33.66	Gram	14.8	7.38
6.	Godakheri	280.00	347	Wheat	30.8	33.33	Gram	23.1	25.61

The Pilot Study has given encouraging results as the two sets of estimates of area under crop at village level is relatively close. It is, therefore, felt that it is possible to develop a suitable methodology for integrating Remote Sensing Technology with standard survey sampling method used in Agricultural surveys for estimation of area under crops. There may be scope for further improvement as well.

Further, an attempt was also made to compare the NSS and SAC sets of area figures with the area figures as reported by Patwari in the six villages after obtaining the data from Khasra register. The position of the 3 way comparison may be seen from the Table 7.12.

Modification in ICS Sampling Design

The present objective of ICS scheme do not strictly permit providing estimates of crop area and production as the scheme acts more as watch-dog on the State Agricultural Statistics System. This aspect has been receiving attention at various quarters for some time. It has also been recognised that present Sampling Design and the relatively small sample size has so far restricted its large scale use by user agencies although the ICS scheme has brought out the weaknesses in the agricultural Statistics system from time to time and several steps have been taken by State

Table 7.12 Comparison of Crop area Between NSSO and Patwari Agencies

(Area in hect.)

Sl. No.	Name of Village	Wheat NSSO	Patwari	R&M NSSO	Patwari	Gram NSSO	Patwari
1	2	3	4	5	6	7	8
1	Baldi	105.99	105.00	0.12	0.00	0.16	0.00
2	Mainmat:	210.10	207.00	0.63	1.00	0.05	0.00
3	Ranpur	169.07	169.00	277.68	290.00	0.87	10.00
4	Ghatoliya	46.77	42.00	48.68	54.00	0.28	0.00
5	Aavala	456.37	358.45	—	—	214.97	166.52
6	Godakheri	86.21	76.99	—	—	64.64	89.00

Note: The crop wise area by SAC has not been estimated in absolute terms.

Governments for improving the timeliness and reliability of Agricultural Statistics based on the findings from ICS, NSSO has been examining the need for reviewing the scheme after its implementation for about 25 years. The National Statistical Commission, taking note of the potential of the ICS Scheme, has proposed a review of the methodology by an Expert Group under Prof. Arijit Chaudhury of Indian Statistical Institute, Calcutta with a view to re-orient the ICS scheme to provide alternate estimate of crop production of at least principal crops and this Group has been deliberating this issue in detail. It will, therefore, be the endeavour of the NSSO to take all possible steps to effect further improvement with regard to timely availability and reliable crop production statistics.

Annexure 7.1

Workload of Patwari During 1998-99

Sl. No.	State	Average Work load per Patwari		
		Villages No.	Survey/ sub survey Nos. 000' per village	Geogaraphical Area (000,Hac) per village
1	2	3	4	5
1	Andhra Pradesh	3	1.3	1.1
2	Assam	10	1.0	0.2
3	Bihar	15	1.2	0.2
4	Gujarat	2	0.6	0.9
5	Haryana	3	3.2	0.9
6	Himachal Pradesh	11	0.9	0.2
7	Jammu and Kashmir	5	0.8	0.4
8	Karnataka	4	0.5	0.9
9	Kerala	#	#	#
10	Madhya Pradesh	6	0.7	0.5
11	Maharashtra	4	0.4	0.8
12	Orissa	9	1.0	0.3
13	Punjab	4	2.1	0.5
14	Rajasthan	6	0.7	1.0
15	Tamil Nadu	2	2.4	0.8
16	Uttar Pradesh (P)	5	0.6	0.3
	Hills	11	2.7	0.1
17	West Bengal	3	1.0	0.1
18	Delhi	2	1.6	0.5
19	Pondicherry	6	1.1	0.3

In Kerala, each primary worker is assigned with one zone.

Annexure 7.2

Timeliness in Completion of Girdawari During 1998-99

Sl. No.	State	Completion of Girdawari in time (Percentage)	
		Kharif	*Rabi/Sum.*
1	2	3	4
1	Andhra Pradesh	47	46
2	Assam	0	1
3	Bihar	8	5
4	Gujarat	52	38
5	Haryana	62	63
6	Himachal Pradesh	95	97
7	Jammu and Kashmir	45	54
8	Karnataka	84	77
9	Kerala	77	78
10	Madhya Pradesh	87	86
11	Maharashtra	40	47
12	Orissa	78	78
13	Punjab	65	35
14	Rajasthan	69	86
15	Tamil Nadu	78	88
16	Uttar Pradesh	58	62
17	West Bengal	29	31
18	Delhi	10	0
19	Pondicherry	67	89
	For States covered	58	57

Annexure 7.3

Timeliness in Submission of TRS Statement During 1998-99

Sl. No.	State	Submission of TRS Statement in time (Percentage)	
		Kharif	Rabi/Sum.
1	2	3	4
1	Andhra Pradesh	51	52
2	Assam	1	1
3	Bihar	0	1
4	Gujarat	37	33
5	Haryana	38	28
6	Himachal Pradesh	52	84
7	Jammu and Kashmir	23	14
8	Karnataka	72	67
9	Kerala	38	29
10	Madhya Pradesh	86	90
11	Maharashtra	34	40
12	Orissa	38	31
13	Punjab	36	17
14	Rajasthan	65	69
15	Tamil Nadu	79	88
16	Uttar Pradesh	36	28
17	West Bengal	13	23
18	Delhi	0	0
19	Pondicherry	100	100
	For States covered	45	43

8

Production

DEVELOPMENTS PRIOR TO INDEPENDENCE

Some data relating to crop production began to be reported for the provinces of British India from around the third quarter of the 19th century. Land tax was the main source of revenue for the British and the data on crop acreages and yields emerged as a byproduct of the land revenue settlement operations. As the land revenue settlement work was extended and permanent village level land records agency established, the coverage of the reporting area for land utilisation statistics (LUS) grew over time. By the time India emerged as an independent nation, the coverage of the reporting area for LUS had been extended to about 70% of the geographical area. However, the area covered by regular crop acreage reporting was far less.

Regular crop acreage statistics, based on field inspection by the permanent, village-level, land records agency, were available only from the cadastrally surveyed areas of the British Provinces under the temporary land revenue settlement system. Such areas constituted about 47 % of the geographical area of India in 1948-49. In remaining 53% of the geographical area, the data on crop acreages were either non-existent or, were derived from wild approximation and subjective impressions. The data situation was particularly weak in most of the Indian princely states, as even the cultivable land area under the jurisdiction was unknown in 1947. The crop acreage statistics in the unsurveyed portions of the British Provinces under temporary land revenue settlements as well as in three provinces of West Provinces under temporary land revenue settlements as well as in three provinces of West Bengal, Orissa and Kerala (covered under permanent land revenue settlements) were conjectural estimates based on purely subjective impressions of part-time local staff at the lowest rung of the administration.

The state of data on average crop yield per acre around the time of independence was even less satisfactory than acreage statistics. The average yields were usually estimated as a product of 'normal' or 'standard yields' and seasonal crop 'condition factor'. The standard yields were obtained through crop cutting experiments conducted in the fields which were considered (subjectively) by the officials to be bearing an average crop. These standard yields were revised once every few years, and often at times only as a part of the new land revenue settlement operations. The condition factor was a subjective index of the condition of crop in any particular season in relation to the 'normal condition' of the crop in a 'normal' year in the recent past. In other words, in the data on crop yields, at the dawn of Independence, subjective judgements played a far more dominant role than scientifically established facts. However, these judgements used to be exercised by well-trained permanent staff of the land revenue administrations whose familiarity with local conditions in their area of operations was carefully nurtured and encouraged.

MODERN METHODOLOGICAL DEVELOPMENTS AND THE SPREAD OF SCIENTIFIC CROP ESTIMATION SURVEYS

The 1930s and 1940s in India were a period of solid methodological developments in large scale survey technology. Prof. P.C. Mahalanobis at the Indian Statistical Institute (ISI), between 1937 and 1945, established the feasibilty of random sample surveys to estimate the acreage and production of jute and rice in Bengal and Bihar.

Dr. V.G. Panse of the Indian Central Cotton Committee (ICCC), between 1942 and 1948, concentrated his experimentation on the estimation of cotton yields in Madhya Pradesh and Bombay through the local revenue agency rather than the employment of a special field agency to conduct crop-cutting experiments. Dr. Panse did not favour the sampling approach to the estimation of crop acreages and accepted the field to field enumeration of crop areas produced by the local revenue agency. However, he insisted on the random selection of the sample plots for crop cuts conducted by the revenue agency.

Prof. P.V. Sukhatme of the Indian Council of Agricultural Research (ICAR) started experimental surveys on wheat in 1943-44. His approach was similar to that of Dr. Panse in case of cotton. This method of crop yield estimation through objective sampling was extended by the ICAR in the next few years to cover wheat and rice as well as the major portion of area under other foodgrains over almost the whole of India.

During the 1950s and the 1960s, two parallel systems of estimation of agricultural production, particularly the production of seven major cereal crops, were operating in India. The National Sample Survey Organisation (using Mahalanobis/ISI methodology) estimated crop acreages and yield rates through sample surveys for both, whereas the official estimates were obtained through complete enumeration of crop acreages through field-to-field inspection by the land revenue agency and sample surveys for yield rates. These two series (NSS and official) of production estimates differed from each other and often the differences were considerable (Tables 8.1 and 8.1A).

Table 8.1 Comparison of NSS and Official Series of Crop Estimates (million acres/million tonnes)

Year	NSS			Official		Difference			
	Area	Prodn	S.E	Area	Prodn	Area	%	Prodn	%
(1)	(2)	(3)	(4)	(5)	(6)	(7)	(8)	(9)	(10)
1957-58	189.7	68.06	2.3	202.8	52.18	(−)13.1	(−)6.4	15.88	30.4
1958-59	213.2	82.28	2.5	210.8	60.83	2.4	1.1	21.45	35.3
1959-60	227.9	83.86	2.8	212.1	61.86	15.8	7.4	22.00	35.6
1960-61	228.3	90.47	2.9	215.1	66.34	13.2	6.1	24.13	36.4
1961-62	225.9	82.85	1.8	217.8	67.81	8.1	3.7	15.04	22.2
1962-63	206.2	72.57	2.5	215.9	64.12	(−)9.7	(−)4.4	8.45	13.2
1963-64	203.1	72.24	2.3	216.5	67.09	(−)13.4	(−)6.1	5.15	7.7
1964-65	206.6	78.71	1.4	220.5	73.43	(−)13.9	(−)6.3	5.28	7.2
1965-66	203.3	67.61	NA	212.2	59.69	(−)8.9	(−)4.1	7.92	13.3

Note: (1) NSS estimates of area refer to "allocated area"
  (2) Difference in columns 7 to 10 NSS minus Official

Table 8.1A Sample Size of NSS series of Land Utilisation and Yield Survey

Year	Number of samples villages (Nos)		Clusters (thousands)	Fields (lakhs)	No. of c.c. experiments
	l.u.s	c.c.s			
(1)	(2)	(3)	(4)	(5)	(6)
1957-58	3,126	1,042	25.0	2.5	8,273
1958-59	2,616	872	15.7	1.6	9,051
1959-60	2,616	872	15.7	1.6	9,565
1960-61	2,532	844	15.2	1.5	12,843
1961-62	3,888	1,296	28.5	1.8	16,787
1962-63	4,236	1,412	19.8	1.4	21,959
1963-64	8,472	2,118	38.1	2.5	32,402
1964-65	8,472	2,118	38.1	2.5	34,741
1965-66	8,472	2,118	38.1	2.5	34,158

It was felt that one of the causes leading to divergences in the two sets of estimates might be due to differences in shapes and sizes of sample cuts used under the two schemes for estimating yield rates. In order to probe this issue, special field studies were conducted under the joint technical auspices of the Ministry of Agriculture, Central Statistical Organisation (CSO) and the Indian Statistical Institute. These studies were conducted on jowar (sorghum) in 1960 at Bundi in Rajasthan State and on wheat in 1961 at Barth in Bihar State. Both types of cuts (those used by NSS and ISI as well as those used in the official/ICAR methodology) were tried in same sets of fields. Also harvesting of whole fields was undertaken. All this work was done under close supervision of the participating organisations.

The lesson of the 1960 and 1961 joint studies was that the differences in yield rates based on different types of sample cuts were not statistically significant.

A deeper and more extensive probe to establish the comparative merits of the two methodologies was undertaken by the Technical Committee[1] set up by the Planning Commission, Govt. of India in 1963. Joint-crop cutting experiments on a much larger scale by both techniques (NSS/ICAR), under normal field conditions with normal degree of supervision, were planned. These experiments were done on maize (corn) in Bihar and rice in Andhra Pradesh in 1963-64, on wheat in Uttar Pradesh in 1964-65 and on jowar (sorghum) in Mysore in 1965-66.

The agreement on yield rates obtained from two of sample cuts was so close that either could be regarded as good as the other in the matter of bias in yield rates to differences in shape and size of cuts.

The area estimates in the two series, based on sample surveys (grid sampling) using gross concept of area in the NSS and the complete crop area enumeration by the land revenue agency in the official statistics exhibited wide differences. Although conclusive experimentation to assess the scientific validity of area (grid) sampling yet remains to be done, the inference drawn in India has been that complete enumeration of crop areas in sample villages is the right approach to estimation of area under different crops[2].

Among others, the two firm conclusions which emerged from the work of the, above Technical Committee, deserve to be repeated here:

(a) With proper training and supervision of the field staff, the shape of sample cuts does not matter and, beyond a certain minimum, the increase in the size of sample cuts adds to cost without significant improvements in the accuracy of yield rates.

(b) Field to field variation in yields is the major contributor to the variance in yield estimates. It is advisable, therefore, to have larger number of second stage sampling units (crop fields) rather than increase the size of third stage units (sample cuts).

---

[1]Planning Commission, Govt. of India (1968). Report of the Technical Committee on Crop Estimates.

[2]This particular inference was vehemently opposed by Professor Mahalanobis. He wanted to maintain a certain capability for sampling of crop areas with some technical organisation rather than become totally dependent on land revenue administrations of different states. In retrospect, his lack of confidence in the administrative agencies would appear to have been based on sound intuition. We shall revert to this issue later.

Based on the scientific work of Mahalanobis, Panse and Sukhatme, done in 1930s and 1940s, India began to introduce objective sampling methods for estimation of crop yields on a country-wide scale in the 1950s. This scientific activity gained more rigour and sense of purpose through the vigorous methodological debates of the 1950s and 1960s and the large scale crop-cutting experiments done between 1960 and 1966 to assess the comparative merits of different techniques. By 1971-72, under the national programme of Crop Estimation Surveys (CES), India had achieved an operational capability per year covering 30 major crops. By 1980-81 this capability had been expanded to about 275,000 experiments covering 63 crops. These indeed were fast developments.

By the early 1980s, in a period of about 35 years since independence, India also had pretty nearly completed its march towards establishing a system of LUS and area enumeration under different crops by season. The reporting area for LUS, which was about 47% of the geographical area of the Indian Union and area under different crops by seasons was being done for more than 80% of the country. The permanently settled states of West Bengal, Orissa and Kerala which had no regular official land revenue agency at the village level have now began reporting (with varying degree of success) LUS based on annual sample surveys.

A minor summing up might be in order at this juncture. Although the story of development of data relating to crop production is over 125 years old in India, comprehensive scientific estimation of crop output was achieved largely between 1950 and 1985. At the state level, the yield rates of cereals were being estimated with sampling errors ranging between 0.8% to 3.0%; at the district level errors ranged between 3.0% and 8.0%. Objective estimates of land utilisation began to be reported for about 90% of the geographical area of the country. In other words, the edifice of India's data system on crops statistics was almost complete. Also, by 1980s, it looked quite imposing and durable. It really appeared to be a shining achievement of independent India.

CROP FORECAST

Forecasts of crop production are of considerable importance for ensuring sufficiency of foodgrains and their equitable distribution in different areas in the country. Forecasts of commercial crops like cotton, jute and sugarcane are useful for trade and industry because the availability of raw material during the season is the basis of planning of manufacturing processes and trade operations. Where tax on agricultural land forms a principal source of Government revenue, the Government will be interested in forecasting the crop yields. The forecast of wheat was issued for the first time in 1884 and it was subsequently extended to commercially important crops. Crop forecasts were prepared only for 10 crops in 1943-44 and increased to 25 crops by 1951-52. At present crops forecast are issued for 42 field crops[3] besides the plantation crops of tea, coffee and rubber for which the relevant estimates are prepared by the respective boards. Adhoc estimates are also prepared in respect of a few minor crops like papaya, indigo and opium; and regular forecasts are proposed to be introduced in due course for these crops.

Forecasts of most probable production are made while the crop is standing in the field. The total out-turn of a crop is obtained as the product of the area under the crop and the average yield per hectare. In temporarily settled States the acreage under each crop is recorded in the village register which contains a list of all fields in the village and area of each field in which different crops are grown in each season. Crop acreage figures in permanently settled States are however obtained on the basis of sample surveys. Area figures for different crops in temporarily settled States are consequently known with a high degree of accuracy. Average yield, in the traditional method, is estimated by multiplying the 'normal yield' (or standard yield) and the 'condition factor'.

Forecasts

Generally two or three forecasts are issued during a year in respect of each crop with the exception of tobacco and cotton for which four and five forecasts respectively are issued. In respect of some minor crops such as castorseed, chillies, ginger, etc. only one forecast is issued. Information recorded in respect of crops for which three forecasts are made is discussed below.

First Forecast The object of the first forecast is to provide intelligence as early as possible regarding the area sown, germination of seed and the weather at sowing time. This forecast confines to the acreage and does not make any mention of the production. The figures are generally issued one month after the sowings have been completed in the major crop growing States.

Second Forecast The object of the second forecast is to report the entire area sown, including the late sown area and crop condition. Besides the acreage figures, this forecast brings out an advance information on production of crops also. These figures are based on impressions and no objective approach is involved.

Third and Final Forecast This forecast is based on complete inspection of all crop-fields. Area figures obtained are based on complete enumeration. Production figures generally relate to out-turn harvested or expected to be harvested. With the introduction of crop-cutting surveys,

---

[3]Rice, jowar, bajra, maize, ragi, small millets, wheat, barley, gram, tur, other kharif pulses, other rabi pulses, groundnut, castorseed, sesamum, rape-seed and mustard, linseed, nigerseed, safflower, sunflower, soyabean, coconut, cotton, jute mesta, sannhemp, sugarcane, tobacco, potato, pepper (black), chillies (dry), ginger (dry), arecanut, turmeric, banana, guarseed, tapioca, cardamom, coriander, garlic, sweet potato and onion.

the average yield of most of the important crops is estimated on the basis of crop-cutting results and therefore, the final forecast is supposed to give quite an accurate picture of the production of these crops. List of forecast crops and year of initiation is given Table 8.2.

Prescribed Forms

Standard forms have been prescribed for submitting crop-forecast returns by the primary reports as well as by the States. It gives the total area under the crop in the current year and the previous year and the corresponding increase or decrease in the same, *anna* valuation (or percentage estimate) of the crop, area irrigated in the current year. Space is provided to report whether sowings were early, normal or late in the case of earlier forecasts and whether harvesting commenced in time in the case of later forecasts. In the State forecast return, provision has been made in the form to report, in addition to area under the crop the yield both of current year as well as during previous year and also the condition factor.

Table 8.2 *List of Forecast Crops and Year of Initiation of Regular Estimates*

Crop	Year of initiation
Rice	1885
Jower	1945-46
Bajra	1945-46
Maize	1945-46
Ragi	1947-48
Small millets	1951-52
Wheat	1884
Barley	1947-48
Gram	1947-48
Tur	1951-52
Other kharif pulses	1951-52
Other rabi pulses	1951-52
Groundnut	1896
Castorseed	1926-27
Sesamum	1885
Rapeseed & mustard	1885
Linseed	1885
Nigerseed	1965-66
Safflower	1966-67
Coconuts	1965-66
Cotton	1885
Jute	1885
Mesta	1952-53
Sann-hemp	1958-59
Sugarcane	1900
Tobacco	1949-50

Table 8.2 List of Forecast Crops and Year of Initiation of Regular Estimates (Contd.)

Crop	Year of initiation
Potato	1949-50
Pepper (black)	1951-52
Chillies (dry)	1951-52
Ginger (dry)	1951-52
Arecanut	1966-67
Turmeric	1964-65
Banana	1966-67
Guarseed	1964-65
Tapioca	1967-68
Cardamom	1969-70
Coriander	1969-70

Estimates of Area and Production

Area and production statistics are also published in Estimates of Area and Production of Principal Crops issued by the Directorate of Economics and Statistics. They are issued in two volumes—'Summary Tables' and 'Detailed Tables'. While the Summary Tables are issued around the end of the calendar year and provide the data up to the previous agricultural year, there is a sufficient time-lag in the publication of the volume dealing with Detailed Tables.

The first issue giving the estimates of area and production was published in the year 1899 under the name 'Area and Yield of certain Crops' and gave data relating to rice, wheat, cotton, linseed, rape and mustard, sesamum, jute and indigo for the years 1891-92 to 1898-99. In 1900-1901, sugarcane and groundnut were added and subsequently tea was also included. The 16th issue published in 1915 was titled 'Estimates of Area and Yield of Principal Crops in India, 1913-14' and gave besides the estimates for the crops mentioned earlier, a supplementary table giving area and yield of barley, jowar, bajra and gram. Coffee and rubber were added to the list of crops for which estimates were given in 1920-21, castor seed in 1925-26 and tobacco in 1926-27. In view of the diminishing importance of indigo, estimates for the crops were dropped from 1932-33 onwards, but included again later.

The 'Estimates of Area and Yield of Principal Crops' was published more or less in this form by the Department of commercial Intelligence and Statistics up to the year 1943-44. Soon after partition, the Directorate of Economics and Statistics issued an ad hoc publication entitled 'Estimates of Area and Yield of Principal Crops' for the years 1936-37 to 1945-46 which gave separate figures for Indian Provinces; Indian States and Pakistan Provinces and Pakistan States separately. Subsequently, ad hoc publications containing the estimates were issued from time to time. Estimates of Area and Production of Principal Crops in India, has now become a normal annual feature. This provides all-India figures for practically all the important crops from 1949-50. From the 58th issue released in 1969, the scope of the publication was widened by including variety wise figures for cotton and tobacco. The present volume covers both forecast and non-forecast as well as plantation crops as detailed below.

Forecast Crops

Rice, jowar, bajra, maize, ragi, small, millets, total kharif cereals, wheat, barley, total rabi cereals, total cereals, gram, tur, other pulses, total pulses, total foodgrains, groundnut, castor, sesamum, rape and mustard, linseed, total five major oilseeds, safflower, nigerseed, sunflower, soyabean, cotton, cotton seed, jute, mesta, sann-hemp, potato, sugarcane (gur), sugarcane (cane), black pepper, dry chillies, dry ginger, turmeric, cardamom, garlic, tobacco, coconuts, guarseed, banana, arecanut, potato, onion, sweet potato and tapioca.

Non-forecast and Plantation Crops

Papaya, indigo, opium, stick lac, tea, coffee and rubber.

Estimates for plantation crops (except coconuts) are obtained from State Governments through special returns prescribed for the purpose. These estimates are also published in separate brochures dealing with tea, coffee and rubber.

As regards the minor crops and coconut, area and production of these crops in each State is relatively so small that periodical crop estimates are not issued. Yet, in view of their commercial importance, special efforts are made to collect the figures of area and production by the DES. The information available in the State Season and Crop Reports, Agricultural Statistics returns and other ad hoc data received from the States are utilized in preparing these estimates.

While utilizing the estimates of area and production given in the publication, the following points may be borne in mind:

(i) The geographical coverage of the estimates for different crops is not complete. Till recently figures in respect of each crop related to area where the crop was extensively grown or was commercially important and tracts where the crop was of minor importance were excluded. Moreover, the areas where no arrangements existed for reporting crop estimates also did not furnish the necessary returns. Recently, however, attempts are being made to extend gradually the coverage of the estimates, although it is not yet complete in respect of several crops especially the non-food crops. In the case of cereals and gram, estimates for non-reporting areas are also available from the triennium ending 1938-39. Up to 1942-43, the estimates are based on information published in the 'Food Statistics of India', 1946. Estimates for the years 1943-44 to 1947-

48 are based on the average figures for the seven years ending 1942-43 after making due allowances for transference of area from non-reporting to the reporting. From 1948-49 onwards, these estimates are based on special returns received from the States and on the information contained in the Season and Crop Reports and Agricultural Statistics and as such are not comparable with the corresponding estimates for earlier years.

(ii) Besides changes in coverage a number of improvements have also been introduced in the methods of estimation of area and production of crops in different States since independence. While these improvements have gradually improved the reliability of the absolute official estimates being issued by the Directorate of Economics and Statistics, they have also introduced an element a non-comparability in the data over time. To allow for these changes and to provide time series suitable for trend studies, index numbers of area under crops, agricultural production and productivity (yield) have been constructed by the chain-base method by linking the figures of each year with those of 1949-50 through pairs of comparable figures for each two successive years which are available under the present system of crop estimation. For details about the coverage, base period, weighting diagrams, method of construction, etc. a reference may be made to the publication 'Growth Rates in Agriculture' (December, 1964) issued by the Directorate of Economics and Statistics. These indices indicate correctly the trends in area, production and yield of various crops. The absolute figures of area, production and yield given in this issue are based on the best possible estimates in relation to the reporting year as prepared for the States/Union Territories. In any study of the trends of area under crops agricultural production and productivity, the correct procedure would be to compare the figures given in a particular Crop Estimate for the current and the previous years and to use the index numbers for making comparisons over a longer period. However, for a quantitative measurement of the increase in production over the years, a comparable series of 'Adjusted Estimates of Production of Principal Crops' taking into account the improvements effected up to the year 1965-66 has been prepared.

Crop-cutting Surveys

It was only in recent years that the method of obtaining average yields through the estimation of condition factor has been gradually abandoned in all the States. Yields are now based mostly on crop-cutting surveys. Position regarding the year from which the method of Random Sample Crop-cutting Surveys has been adopted for framing official estimates of production is shown in Table 8.3. Full particulars of this method have already been examined in Chapter 7.

Table 8.3 State-wise Position Regarding the Year from Which the Method of Random Sample Crop-cutting Surveys has been Adopted for Framing Official Estimates of Production

State	Region	Crops	Year from which the method of crop-cutting surveys was adopted
(1)	*(2)*	*(3)*	*(4)*
1. Andhra Pradesh	Telangana	Wheat[a]	1951-52
		Rice, jowar, bajra, maize	1952-53
		Ragi	1955-56
		Sugarcane	1956-57
		Groundnut, tur, sesamum	1959-60
		Cotton and tobacco	1962-63
	Andhra	Rice	1953-54
		Jowar, bajra, maize, ragi, sugarcane	1954-55
		Groundnut, tur, sesamum	1959-60
		Cotton and tobacco	1962-63
	Whole State	Castorseed	1966-67
2. Assam[b]		Rice (autumn and winter) and jute	1951-52
		Potato (winter)	1952-53
		Sugarcane	1957-58
		Rape and mustard	1958-59
		Matikalai (urad)	1963-64
		Potato (summer)	1963-64
3. Bihar		Rice (autumn and winter) and wheat	1948-49
		Barley and gram	1949-50
		Sugarcane and jute	1958-59
		Maize	1959-60
		Mesta potato (summer) and tur	1962-63
		Potato (winter)	1963-64
		Rice (summer), rape and mustard, Khsari, masur	1966-67
4. Gujarat	Former Bombay State portion	Rice (autumn), jowar, bajra, wheat	1949-50
		Maize, gram, cotton, groundnut, tobacco, Ragi (dangs district only)[c]	1951-52
		Kodra	1961-62
	Saurashtra and Kutch regions	Rice, wheat, jowar, bajra, gram	1956-57
		Groundnut, cotton	1957-58

*Table 8.3 State-wise Position Regarding the Year from Which the Method
of Random Sample Crop-cutting Surveys has been Adopted for
Framing Official Estimates of Production (Contd.)*

State	Region	Crops	Year from which the method of crop-cutting surveys was adopted
(1)	(2)	(3)	(4)
	Gujarat State	Kodra	1961-62
		Sesamum, ragi	1965-66
5. Kerala		Castor	1968-69
		Rice (autumn and winter)	1957-58
6. Jammu & Kashmir		Rice (summer)	1959-60
7. Madhya Pradesh	Mahakoshal Region	Rice and maize	1968-69
		Rice, jowar, wheat, gram, Kodon-kutki, tur	1951-52
		Bajra	1956-57
		Barley, groundnut, rape and mustard, Linseed, sesamum, cotton, lakh or khesari and potato (summer)	1957-58
		Maize	1958-59
		Chillis	1962-63
		Potato (winter)	1963-64
	Vindhya Pradesh Region	Rice, jowar, maize[d]	1952-53
		Wheat, barley, gram Bajra	1956-57
		Tur, groundnut, rape and mustard Linseed, potato (summer), kodon-kutki, sesamum, lakh or khesari, and cotton	1957-58
		Chillies	1962-63
		Potato (winter)	1963-64
	Bhopal Region	Rice, jowar, wheat	1951-52
		Gram	1952-53
		Bajra	1956-57
		Barley, tur, groundnut rape and mustard, linseed, potato (summer) kodon-kutki, sesamum, cotton, lakh or khesari	1957-58
		Maize	1958-59
		Chillies	1962-63
		Potato (winter)	1963-64

Table 8.3 State-wise Position Regarding the Year from Which the Method of Random Sample Crop-cutting Surveys has been Adopted for Framing Official Estimates of Production (Contd.)

State	Region	Crops	Year from which the method of crop-cutting surveys was adopted
(1)	*(2)*	*(3)*	*(4)*
	Madhya Bharat Region	Rice, jowar, gram	1955-56
		Bajra	1956-57
		Wheat, barley, tur, groundnut	
		Rape and mustard, linseed	
		Potato (summer), kodon-kutki, sesamum	1957-58
		Cotton, lakh or khesari	
		Maize	1958-59
		Chillies	1962-63
		Potato (winter)	1963-64
8. Tamil Nadu		Rice, jowar, bajra, ragi	1955-56
		Groundnut, sugarcane, cotton	1964-65
9. Maharashtra	Former Bombay State portion	Rice (autumn), jowar, bajra, wheat	1949-50
		Ragi—Ratnagiri district	1951-52
		—Kolaba, Nasik and Kolhapur districts	1962-63
		—Thana, Poona districts)	1964-65
		Cotton, groundnut, tobacco (Sangli and Kolhapur), gram	1951-52
		Tobacco (Satara)	1958-59
	Vidarbba Region	Rice (autumn), jowar, wheat, gram, kodon-kutki, tur (Nagpur division only)	1951-52
		Cotton	1954-55
		Groundnut	1957-58
		Bajra	1958-59
	Marathwada Region	Wheat	1951-52
		Rice (autumn), jowar, bajra, maize	1952-53
		Gram, groundnut, cotton	1957-58
	Maharashtra State	Sugarcane	1964-65
10. Mysore		Rice,ᶜ jowar, bajra, ragi	1951-52
		Wheat, gram, tur	1957-58

Table 8.3 State-wise Position Regarding the Year from Which the Method of Random Sample Crop-cutting Surveys has been Adopted for Framing Official Estimates of Production (Contd.)

State	Region	Crops	Year from which the method of crop-cutting surveys was adopted
(1)	(2)	(3)	(4)
		Sesamum, sugarcane, groundnut	1958-59
		Linseed	1961-62
		Cotton	1963-64
		Castorseed	1964-65
11. Orissa		Rice (autumn and winter) and jute	1959-60
12. Punjab (Prior to 1-11-66)	Including Pepsu Former Punjab State[f]	Bajra, maize, wheat, gram	1952-53
		Sugarcane	1861-62
		Rice, jowar and barley	1952-53
13. Rajasthan	Old State (i.e. excluding Ajmer)	Wheat, barley, gram	1951-52
		Jowar, bajra, maize	1952-53
		Cotton	1953-54
		Rape and mustard	1957-58
		Sesamum, linseed	1958-59
	Ajmer	Wheat,	1952-53
		Jowar, maize, barley	1953-54
		Gram, cotton	1956-57
		Rape and mustard	1957-58
		Sesamum, linseed	1958-59
14. Uttar Pradesh	State excluding hilly regions of Kumaon and Uttar Khand Divisions	Wheat, barley, gram	1949-50
		Rice, jowar, bajra, maize, tur	1950-51
		Jute	1955-56
		Groundnut and rapeseed and mustard (pure crop)	1957-58
		Peas, sesamum (pure crop), linseed (pure crop)	1959-60
		Sugarcane, cotton[g]	1960-61
		Masur	1964-65
	Hilly regions of Kumaon and Uttar Khand Divisions	Rice, ragi, wheat, barley	1961-62

Table 8.3 State-wise Position Regarding the Year from Which the Method of Random Sample Crop-cutting Surveys has been Adopted for Framing Official Estimates of Production (Contd.)

State	Region	Crops	Year from which the method of crop-cutting surveys was adopted
(1)	(2)	(3)	(4)
15. West Bengal		Rice (autumn and winter)	1947-48
		Wheat, barley, gram, rape and mustard	
		Linseed, jute[h]	1949-50
		Sugarcane	1950-51
		Potato (winter)	1951-52
		Tur, rabi pulses (except kulthi and others)	1952-53
		Mesta	1966-67
16. Delhi		Wheat[i]	1952-53
		Bajra	1964-65
		Gram	1958-59
		Rice and barley	1968-69
17. Himachal Pradesh (prior to 1.11.66)		Rice, wheat	1953-55
		Maize (excluding Chamba)	1958-59
		—Chamba	1961-62
		Barley	1964-65
18. Manipur		Rice and maize	1966-67

* Discontinued since reorganization.

b Plains only.

c Discontinued after the formation of Maharashtra and Gujarat States.

d. Experiments were not conducted during 1956-57 and 1957-58.

e. In Coorg from 1952-53.

f Includes Pepsu from 1955-56 in respect of Jowar and from 1956-57 in respect of Rice and Barley.

g Production was based on random sample surveys in 1953-54 and 1954-55 and on eye-estimates thereafter. Since 1960-61, the production estimates are a gain based on Random Sample Crop-Cutting Surveys.

h In the case of Jute, production was based on Random Sample Survey in 1949-50 and eye-estimates thereafter. Since 1951-52, it has been based on Random Sample Surveys except in the case of Darjeeling district.

i. Production estimates have been based on the traditional method since 1955-56 as the results of crop-cutting experiments have not been available on a regular basis since that year. Since 1958-59 the production estimates are again based on crop-cutting surveys.

Notes: 1. The years given in col. 4 indicate the years from which the production estimates based on traditional method have been replaced by production estimates based on the results of Random Sample Crop-cutting Surveys.

2. The districts of former Bombay State included under Gujarat an Maharashtra States respectively are given below:

   (i) *Former Bombay State Portion included under Gujarat*:
   Banaskantha, Mehsana, Sabarkantha, Ahmedabad, Kaira, Panchmahals, Amroli, Baroda, Broach, Surat and Dangs.

   (ii) *Former Bombay State Portion included under Maharashtra*:
   West Khandesh, East Khandesh, Nasik, Ahmednagar, Poona, Sholapur, North Satara, Thana, Bombay, Suburban, Kolaba, Ratnagiri, South Satara, Kolhapur.

Estimates for quite a few crops are still being obtained through less reliable methods due either to the unpracticability for applying statistical methods or the crop being of minor importance. Yield estimates are being published annually in the 'Estimates of Area and Production of Principal Crops.' They are available for the following crops (Table 8.4):

Cereals	— rice, jowar, bajra, maize, ragi, small millets, wheat and barley.
Pulses	— gram, tur, other kharif and rabi pulses.
Other crops	— sugarcane, potato, pepper, ginger, tobacco, cardamom, chillies, turmeric, guarseed, arecanut and tapioca.
Oilseeds	— groundnut, sesamum, rape and mustard, linseed, castor, nigerseed, safflower, soyabean cotton seed and coconuts.
Fibres	— cotton, jute, mesta and sunn-hemp.
Plantation crops	— tea, coffee, rubber.
Minor crops	— indigo, papaya, sweet potatoes, opium, lac, etc.

All these crops are broadly divided into three groups, viz. forecast crops, non-forecast crops and plantation crops.

Forecast Crops

Regular all-India estimates are issued for the forecast crops. The figures in respect of cereals and grams relate to both reporting and non-reporting areas while those for other crops refer to reporting areas only. Figures for 'non-reporting', areas for other crops are not available. Estimates of area and production of food grains for the 'non-reporting' areas for 1947-48 are based on the average for the seven years ending 1942-43, allowance having been made from year to year for the transference of a 'non-reporting' area to the 'reporting' basis. Estimates of these areas for 1948-49 onwards are based either on special returns received from the State Governments or information available in the Season and Crop Reports and the Returns of Agricultural Statistics. Figures for the 'non-reporting' areas for the two periods—(i) up to 1947-48, and (ii) 1948-49 onwards are thus not strictly comparable in coverage or method of estimation.

Table 8.4 Percentage of Area and Production of Principal Crops Covered by Crop-cutting Surveys, 1995-96, 1996-97 and 1997-98 (Final)—All-India

		1995-96		1996-97		1997-98	
Crop		% to total area	% to total produ-ction	% to total area	% to total prod-ction	% to total area	% to total produ-ction
(1)		(2)	(3)	(4)	(5)	(6)	(7)
Foodgains	Rice	98.0	98.2	98.0	98.2	98.0	98.2
	Jowar	99.6	99.7	99.7	99.8	99.7	99.8
	Bajra	99.7	99.7	99.8	99.8	99.8	99.8
	Maize	96.7	97.2	96.7	97.2	96.3	96.9
	Ragi	93.9	97.2	93.4	96.8	93.2	96.7
	Small Millets	74.4	64.5	77.2	66.5	76.1	64.7
	Wheat	99.9	99.9	99.9	99.9	99.9	99.9
	Barley	98.7	99.5	98.6	99.5	98.8	99.6
	Cereals	98.3	98.8	98.3	98.8	98.3	98.7
	Gram	97.6	97.8	97.8	97.8	97.8	98.0
	Tur	93.3	99.7	93.5	93.8	92.5	91.0
	Other Kharif Pulses	16.7	23.3	19.1	18.2	18.1	97.0
	Other Rabi Pulses	52.6	56.8	54.0	62.9	54.7	59.3
	Pulses	62.4	73.9	62.4	73.4	63.3	74.3
	Foodgrains	91.7	97.1	91.8	97.0	91.9	97.1
Oilseeds	Grcundnut	96.9	95.7	96.3	95.2	96.0	94.6
	Castorseed	85.5	90.4	85.7	91.9	83.2	91.4
	Sesamum	91.4	91.8	91.9	92.4	91.8	92.1
	Rapeseed and Mus-tard	93.7	93.3	93.1	93.5	92.5	93.1
	Linseed	84.2	72.4	76.8	82.0	68.8	80.3
	Safflower	94.9	97.0	95.6	97.2	96.2	93.7
	Nigreseed	12.8	8.0	14.0	11.9	12.7	9.6
	Sunflower	49.0	33.4	46.6	30.7	45.2	35.0
	Soyabean	77.3	77.1	77.3	74.0	74.7	76.1
Fibres	Cotton (Lint)	99.6	99.6	99.5	99.6	99.5	99.4
	Jute	99.8	99.8	99.8	99.8	99.8	99.8
	Mesta	56.6	72.4	58.1	77.9	57.8	72.2
Other Crops	Sugarcane	94.4	95.2	94.5	94.9	94.0	94.6
	Potato	85.6	88.3	86.0	89.0	84.4	85.8
	Black Pepper	96.4	97.3	95.8	96.7	95.8	96.9
	Chillies	36.4	51.0	41.7	58.3	34.3	43.6
	Tobacco	82.9	80.1	83.0	75.0	84.5	70.5
	Tapioca	86.0	95.0	87.5	95.5	89.4	95.9
	Onion	23.6	24.5	24.1	25.1	27.1	28.3

The number of crops included in this group is being increased and is now 42 in place of only 10, before the First Plan. Recently coconut, nigerseed, sunflower, turmeric, arecanut, guarseed, cardamom, tapioca and banana have been included in this category. District-wide data on area and production of various forecast crops are published in the different issues of 'Agricultural Situation in India' (*see* Table 8.2). (Average yield rates of irrigated and unirrigated crops, hamely rice, wheat, maize, bajra and jowar, are given in Appendix 3.)

Non-forecast Crops

These cover papaya, sweet potatoes, indigo, lac and opium. Estimates of area and production of these crops are ad hoc as distinct from the regular estimates of forecast crops and therefore, do not have the same degree of accuracy as the forecast crops.

Plantation Crops

The estimates of area and production of coffee and rubber are based on special returns received from the State Governments in connection with the all-India publications on these crops. Data regarding tea are as extracted from the publications of the Tea Board from 1960-61 onward, while for earlier years the data were based upon returns received from State-Governments. Coconut has since been included in Forecast Crops.

Some General Remarks

The following general remarks by way of explanation are of interest:
1. (a) Data for Assam exclude Arunachal Pradesh.
   (b) Data for Jammu & Kashmir exclude the Pakistan-held portion of the State.
   (c) Data in respect of foodgrains for Madhya Pradesh are inclusive of estimates for crops grown in forest areas also.
2. Figures of tea and rubber relate to calendar years, i.e. figures for 1947-48 relate to 1947 and so on.
3. Average yields per hectare are calculated by dividing the total production by the corresponding total area under each crop. In case of tea and coffee, they relate to 'plucked' area and in the case of rubber to 'tapped area'.
4. Data in respect of lac are as furnished by the Indian Central Lac Cess Committee and those of opium by the Narcotics Commissioner, Simla.
5. Production of sunn-hemp is estimated in terms of dry fibre.
6. Figures for sesamum, rape and mustard and linseed in the case of U.P. are inclusive of estimates for areas sown under 'mixed crops'.
7. Production of sugarcane is expressed both in terms of cane and raw sugar (gur or jaggery).
8. Production of groundnut is given in terms of 'nuts in shell'.

9. Production of cotton is given in terms of 'lint-cotton' and in bales of 170 kg each.
10. Production data of cotton seed are provisional as they are worked out on the basis of approximate lint to seed ratio.
11. Production of jute and mesta is given in terms of fibre and in bales of 180 kg each.

Preliminary, Final, Partially Revised and Revised Estimates (Official Series)

First or preliminary estimate for a crop is generally issued about a month after the completion of sowings and is intended to give an idea about the area sown under the crop and to afford intelligence regarding germination, weather conditions, and crop prospects. The second estimate generally follows about a couple of months later and indicates the area (including late sowings), the condition of the crop and the probable or expected yield in some cases. The final estimate contains estimates of the total area sown and yield harvested or expected to be harvested. An important distinction between the object and purpose of the final and pre-final estimates needs to be borne in mind. While prefinal estimates are intended to give an indication of what the production is likely to be, the final estimate mainly concerns itself with the actual quantity produced. Further, for the pre-final estimates, the primary reporting agency is required to give only rough quantitative estimates of area under the current crop compared with the previous year's crop. The final estimate, on the other hand, is generally based on field to field crop inspection.

Final estimates are, however, themselves subject to revision, if deemed necessary in the light of subsequent information. Such revision, if any, is generally done at the time of release of the estimate of the next year's crop. These revised estimates are called 'Partially Revised Estimates', as they might be incomplete for want of returns from some States. These partially revised estimates are subsequently revised when complete returns are obtained from the States, and these are known as the 'Revised Estimates'.

In preparing final estimates at the State level, in the absence of information in respect of certain areas, generally previous year's figures are used but the extent of these is quite negligible in comparison with the total area shown in final estimates. There are certain crops on which crop-cutting experiments are conducted but results are not utilized for framing estimates of food production. The reasons for not utilizing the results are mainly: (i) high non-response, (ii) late receipt of returns at the State headquarters, (iii) inadequate coverage, and (iv) high sampling errors. Generally the final forecast estimates include the results of all the crop-cutting experiments conducted 15-20 days before the issue of the final forecast. In the partially revised estimates, the results of crop-cutting experiments received from the field after the preparation of final forecast are also included. The number of experiments on which the estimates are based is practically the same for partially revised and revised estimates.

Pre-harvest Estimates

At present there is a considerable time-lag between the date of sowing and harvesting of the crops and the availability of crop estimates. Due dates for all-India forecasts have been fixed in relation to the date of completion of sowing and harvesting on an all-India basis. Where the same crop is sown for more than one season, the crop estimate is scheduled to be issued after the second crop is harvested. There is also considerable time-lag between the due date of the crop estimate and the date of its release. In some States, the sowing and harvesting operations take place much earlier than in others and it is important that the Central Government should get an idea of the estimates of area and production of each of the principal crops in each State as soon as the sowing and harvesting of the crops are completed. Pre-harvest estimates are needed by the trade and Government for policy and administration purpose. Such estimates will be based on the estimates of area reported as soon as the sowing of the crop season is completed. Yield estimates will, however, be based on biometrical measurements on the crop during the various stages of its growth and appropriate regressions used for predicting the yield on the basis of these biometrical measurements.

Some advanced countries have evolved suitable systems of physical measurements during the various stages of growth of crops for providing reliable pre-harvest estimates. It would, perhaps, be desirable to initiate pilot studies to evolve suitable techniques on the basis of the methods being followed in countries like Japan.[4]

We have already examined in the section dealing with area estimates the new scheme for timely reporting of estimates of area which is being implemented in the States of U.P. and Maharashtra. The scheme which is intended to provide valuable information regarding area and production of crops is intended to provide reliable data on crop estimates.

The main feature of the scheme is that a calendar of operation is drawn up on a monthly basis for each of the principal crops taking into account the sowing and the harvesting operations and on the basis of such a calendar, estimates of area will be reported as soon as the sowing of the crop of the season are completed and estimates of production as soon as the crops of the season are harvested.

It is also intended that the system of collection of agricultural statistics should be reorganized so as to provide independent and timely estimates at the all-India and State levels on acreage and production considerably in advance of the current estimates. Such an independent system has also to avoid duplication with the existing arrangements either at the Centre or in the State and has got to be dovetailed from time to time into existing system. The main features of the new scheme are as follows:

---

[4]Dr., R.S. Chada, Crop Forecasting in Japan, Agricultural Situation in India, March 1959.

  (i) For each State, a calendar of operations will be drawn up for each of the principal crops.

 (ii) On the basis of such a calendar, the State Governments will be asked to report estimates of area as soon as the crop is sown and estimates of production as soon as the crop is harvested. For this purpose, where the crop is grown in more than one season as in the case of autumn, winter and summer varieties of rice, or kharif and rabi jowar, the crop of each season will be treated as a separate one and separate estimates of acreage and production will be reported.

(iii) The estimates of acreage will be based on complete enumeration by the field agencies. In case this is not considered feasible, the preliminary estimates of area should be based on pre-harvest sample surveys, selecting one village from each Patwari circle and doing complete enumeration in that village immediately after sowing. The final estimates of area under the crops will, however, be based on complete enumeration of acreage in all the villages. Where this is not feasible, particularly in the case of crops of minor importance, they will be in the nature of rough estimates framed in relation to the actual acreage in the previous year and after making allowances for the increase or decrease during the current season.

 (iv) The estimates of production are to be based on crop-cutting experiments carried out during the harvesting time. For this purpose, steps have to be taken to ensure that the crop-cutting returns are dispatched by the primary agencies conducting the experiments to the State headquarters immediately upon conclusion of the experiment and that they are analyzed soon thereafter. Generally there will be one estimate of production based on crop-cutting experiments, for each crop in each season. In the case of cotton where the pickings are spread over time, two estimates of production may be reported one after two pickings are completed, and the other after all pickings are done. In the case of sugarcane, also, two estimates of production may be necessary.

  (v) Where irrigation is important and for crops for which irrigation plays an important role, the estimates of acreage will be given separately for irrigated and unirrigated areas. Similarly separate estimates of acreage will be given for high yielding and other varieties.

 (vi) The primary reporting agency in the case of area estimates will be the Patwari agency. But where the jurisdiction is large, the State Governments may employ the agencies of panchayat secretaries for complete enumeration in a part of the Patwari circle.

(vii) The village level figures will be consolidated by the State authorities. The returns will be compiled at the district or State level either directly from the village level or through successive levels of kanungo circle and tehsil. What is important is that the figures should be received at the Centre within ten days after the close of the month to which they relate.

(viii) The agency of progress assistants and district statistical officers may be utilized for compilation of data and for ensuring that the returns are sent in time to the State headquarters.

(ix) The agency for consolidation at the State level will be the crop-reporting agency as at present. But there will be close liaison between this agency and the Agriculture Department, i.e. with Agricultural Production Commissioner and the Director of Agriculture who are responsible for agricultural production programmes, in the States where such liaison does not at present exist.

NEED FOR IMPROVEMENT IN METHODS OF COLLECTION

To study the question in some detail, a Study Team was set up under the chairmanship of Dr. B. Ramamurti, ex-Regional Statistical Adviser to the United Nations and consisting of the representatives of the CSO, the ISI, DES and IARS for a deeper probe into the foodgrains production estimates for the years 1967-68 to 1969-70 and the evolving an objective approach for arriving at an agreed set of estimates.

After detailed examination of the methods of collection of statistics of area and yield followed by the States including the design of Crop-cutting surveys and supervision of field work and also special visits to a few States, the Study Team came to the conclusion that "the estimates furnished by the State Governments cannot unquestionably be taken as correct and there is the need for them to be critically examined". In regard to the upward revision of the estimates furnished by the State Governments which were considered unsatisfactory, the Study Team expressed its helplessness in providing any objective basis for such revision. It, therefore, opined that it was important to implement suitable measures for improvements in the design, methods of collection and scientific compilation and estimation so that, in future, better estimates were made available by the established agencies. The Study Team found that the State Governments' estimates of foodgrains production were unsatisfactory for the period 1967-68 to 1969-70 due mainly to the defects in the field implementation of methodology. Subsequently, the Ministry of Agriculture has taken a policy decision to adopt the figures furnished by the States after due scrutiny in consultation with them. Without going into the merits and demerits of this decision, the need for effecting improvements in the methods of collection of statistics cannot be minimized. It is important that not only the techniques employed should be scientific but due attention should also be paid to the implementation and supervision of the techniques as adopted in the field.

COMPARABILITY OF PRODUCTION DATA OVER TIME

The figures of area and production published from year to year are not strictly comparable due to changes in the coverage and method of estimation. Variations in the coverage since 1949-50 have, however, been small and, therefore, do not affect much the comparability of acreage data since that year. The improvements in the method of estimation of the rates of yield and total production were introduced mainly after 1949-50, especially in the case of foodgrains and have thus introduced an element of non-comparability in the estimates for the past and the present.

As early as 1953, the Ministry of Food and Agriculture took steps in consultation with the Central Statistical Organization to compile index numbers which would correctly indicate the relative change in the production of different crops over a period of years even though it was not practicable to maintain the comparability of absolute figures over such a period. These index numbers with the base year first as 1949-50 first were published in July 1954. Index numbers of area under crops, agricultural production and productivity (yield) are now being constructed by the chain base method by linking the figures of each year with those of 1949-50 through pairs of comparable figures for each two successive years.

In the construction of index numbers, the fact that for any two consecutive years comparable figures of production are always available under the existing system of crop estimate is made use of to get a reliable estimate of the relative changes in the volume of production of individual crops, important groups of crops like cereals, oilseeds, fibres, etc., and also for the total agricultural production taking all the commodities. For example, for the year 1999-2000, final estimates of production released would also give comparable revised figures for 1998-99. These two sets of figures have the same coverage and are based on the same method of estimation for any individual State (or sometimes region). Therefore, these figures give a correct estimate of the percentage change in two years in the production of individual crops or groups of crops. Similarly the relative position of previous years is already known on the same basis.

Working backwards, the relative production of each crop with 1949-50 taken to be 100 can, therefore, be correctly determined. Such an index is called the production relative of the crop. These production relatives for individual crops are utilized for the preparation of group indices like the index of production of cereals, index of production of foodgrains, and also the general index of agricultural production with the weights already assigned to individual commodities and groups. Such an index provides a fairly reliable idea of the increase in production.

On the recommendations of the Technical Committee on Index Numbers Relating to Agricultural Economy set up under the Chairmanship of late Dr. V.G. Panse, a revised series of index numbers of agricultural production with enlarged coverage and triennium ending 1961-62 as base was issued by the Directorate of Economics and Statistics. Presently, index numbers are being constructed with triennium ending 1981-82 as the base. These series were linked to the earlier ones and indices are available on comparable basis from 1949-50 onwards.

These two sets of figures (Index Numbers and Absolute Production figures) have two distinctive uses. The absolute figures of output are required for economic planning, for estimation of national income and for the analysis of agricultural production. These figures are an indication of the absolute quantity of output for purpose of determining the annual availability of various commodities. That way the figures are used for policy purposes. They are primarily, not exclusively, of topical interest, that is for the particular year they relate to. Index numbers, on the contrary, provide the indication of output trends over time.

In any study of the trends of agricultural production, the correct procedure according to the explanation given above would be to compare the figures given in a particular crop estimate for the current and the previous year and to use the index numbers for making comparisons over any longer period. In view of many changes in the coverage and methods of yield determination even the index numbers have limited comparability over long periods and cannot serve the purpose of historical series. Quantitative measurement of the increase in production of 'Principal Crops'—taking into account the improvements affected from year to year—are prepared by the Directorate of Economics and Statistics, Ministry of Agriculture.

Some of the new schemes to improve production estimates are discussed here.

Agro-Economic Research Studies

The Agro-Economic Research Scheme was initiated in 1954-55 for undertaking research studies on agro-economic problems of the country. The scheme is being implemented through 12 Agro-Economic Research Centres and 3 Regional Centres which are funded by the government through Central Sector Plan Scheme and by Non-Plans funds. These Centres were established to take up problem oriented studies on regional basis with a view to generating the requisite feedback from the grass-root level, the ways and means for improving the effective monitoring of various programmes/schemes implemented by the Ministry to cover the entire country, while the three Units undertake studies mainly on inter-regional or all India level. During 1999-2000, 39 number of such studies were completed and during 2000-2001 40 to 45 number of such studies are expected to be completed. At an average, about 40 research studies were completed annually by these 15 Centres. The budgetary allocation of Rs. 130,00 thousand as Central Sector Plan and Rs. 40800 thousand as Non-Plan was earmarked for 2000-01 for the implementation of the scheme. The report of these studies were being referred to for policy decision whenever required. A year book on Agro-Economic

Research was also brought out and sent to various ministries/institutions for reference/guidance, etc.

Crop Acreage and Production Estimation

This is an on-going Central Sector Plan Scheme. The main objective of the scheme is to develop improved methodologies for assessing area under different crops and their estimated production, based on sensor technology and integration of remote sensing, weather and field surveys. These estimates are to be generated at least a month before harvest of the crop. Major kharif crops covered under this programme for the ninth five year plan are rice, groundnut and cotton while for rabi crops are wheat, mustard and sorghum. For rice crop, the States of Orissa, Assam, West Bengal, Bihar, Punjab and Tamil Nadu are completely covered while the States of Madhya Pradesh, Uttar Pradesh, Andhra Pradesh, Haryana and Karnataka are partially covered. For wheat crop, the States of Haryana, Punjab and Uttar Pradesh are completely covered.

The scheme is funded by the Department of Agriculture and Cooperation and executed under the overall technical guidance of Space Application Centre who in turn coordinate with State Remote Sensing Application Centres, State Department of Agriculture, State's Bureau of Economics and Statistics and State's Agricultural Universities. The Budgetary allocation of Rs. 380,00 thousand was provided during 2000-01 under the scheme. The data collected under this scheme are being used for the generation of area and production estimates of principal crops at all India level.

Special Data Dissemination Standard

This is an on-going Central Sector Plan Scheme in the Directorate. Under this scheme, quarterly estimates of agricultural production pertaining to the Ministry of Agriculture are generated for use in the compilation of Quarterly National Accounts (QNA) by the Central Statistical Organisation. The scheme was undertaken in order to meet our obligations to the International Monetary Fund in this regard. The estimates of quarterly crop production generated are being furnished to Central Statistical Organisation. In the absence of direct data, quarterly production is estimated by using the estimates of kharif and rabi seasons in conjunction with crop calendar. During 2000-01, quarterly estimates of agricultural production are being generated as per prescribed time schedule and furnished to Central Statistical Organisation for their use in the compilation of QNAs.

In order to improve upon the quality of quarterly estimates by way of refining the estimation procedure and cross validation of results, available data from other sources such as National Sample Survey Organisation and Agriculture Marketing Division are also being used. This is a staff-oriented scheme and the budgetary allocation of Rs. 1600 thousand was provided during 2000-01.

Some Disturbing Administrative Developments

Certain minor blemishes notwithstanding, the progress of the data system for reporting crop production by the early 1980s had nearly reached its zenith. Despite a number of new schemes discussed above to improve data system. Unfortunately, certain administrative reforms at the state level appeared at about the same time and began to spell disaster for the old data flows, without putting anything new in their place. For reasons which might have been valid in regard to some objectives of reform, Chief Ministers (M.G. Ramachandran in Tamil Nadu, N.T. Rama Rao in Andhra Pradesh and R.K. Hegde in Karnataka) of the three southern states, dug out, root and branch, the old established village level revenue agencies from their respective states. These acts of reform in local administration at the district level, obliterated, probably unwillingly, a most useful adventitious function of data collection on crop acreages. In consequence, the crop acreage and production statistics of these states during the past 10-12 years have been reduced to bad fiction. The percentage of cropped area covered under field by field enumeration, which used to be nearly 100% in the southern states, has failed in recent years to touch even double digits. This, of course, is inclusive of coverage under TRS, which by itself was supposed to cover approximately 20% of the cropped area of each state in every season.

The State of Bihar (the existence of large staff of the permanent village level revenue agency, notwithstanding) virtually ceased reporting crop acreages in the 1980s. Of the three permanently settled states, Kerala has done a reasonably good job of developing a crop reporting system on a sampling basis. Orissa has done fair amount of work but has not yet made the sampling system for acreage reporting an operational success. Some confusion still exists in West Bengal between the Department of Agriculture and the State Directorate of Statistics.

On the basis of rough calculations, it would appear that about 35% of net sown area of India today does not have any observed data on crop acreage statistics by season. This situation has now been prevailing for nearly ten years. We have been sleeping over this because we have been extremely fortunate to have an exceptional run of good monsoons over the same long period.

Although the number of crop-cutting experiments has been expanded enormously[5] (around 275,000 in early 1980s), the sampling frame for these experiments have been vanishing over a large expanse of the country. TRS has totally failed in some states—Bihar, Tamil Nadu, Andhra Pradesh and Karnataka and worked unsatisfactorily in many other areas. In consequence, the sampling design sanctity of the estimates of average yield rates is being seriously violated.

---

[5] A major part of this expansion in the number of crop cuts, subjectively located, is being forced on the system for paying crop insurance compensation to the farmers from the public sector.

Over and beyond the large estimate (35%) of area which has virtually stopped reporting crop-acreage statistics from the field level, the quality of field level reporting by the revenue agency is also deteriorating at a fast rate in many other parts of the country. This fact, taken together with the growing element of subjectivity in the estimates of average yield rates, may lead us to conclude that the reported figures of production of individual crops, and also of aggregates like total foodgrains, are now based more on negotiations across the table than being the project of scientific procedures implemented on a country-wide basis between 1950 and the early 1980s.

The most disturbing political development in recent times has been the competitive race for the abolition of land revenue in state after state: It has already begun to affect the quality of field work of the revenue staff. Carried to its logical conclusion, this irrational political muscle-flexing may ultimately destroy the field by field crop-enumeration function of the village level land revenue agency all over India, but, more importantly, also the village level land records. If these avoidable events are allowed to happen, India would have become the victim of a far bigger disaster than the mere loss of data on crop acreages.

OUTLOOK FOR FUTURE

Our discussion must now face up to the question just raised. To gain a perspective on the future, we have reviewed the long Indian experience with the system of reporting crop acreages and yield rates. The system did record some brilliant successes during its evolution. However, some institutional changes of the recent past have begun to jeopardize the functional health and scientific validity of the system. Can we walk into some glorious arrangement of the past to secure a sustainable future for the system? I do not think we can.

In drawing contours of the future, it may seem wise to discard the options that have already failed the survival test. However, it should make good sense to mend the cracks in the elements of the system—those elements which somehow still work despite the cracks. Further we must anchor the repair work as well as new additions to the system on to the emerging developments in technology and institutions. A case in point, for instance, is to garner the rising popularity of the new arrangements for decentralised governance at the local level to secure sustained generation of reliable data at the village level[6&7].

---

[6]Minhas, B.S. (1998), "Decentralised Data Base for Local Level Development", paper read at the International Conference on Income and Wealth, 16-20 November, New Delhi.

[7]Minhas, B.S. (1989), "Decentralised Planning: Some Issues and Data Base for Local Level Development". Chapter 5 in Yugandha and Mukherjee (eds.) Readings in Decentralised Planning, Vol. I. Concept Publishing House, New Delhi (1991), pp 102-112.

Food Outlook

The Food and Agriculture Organisation in its September forecast has estimated global food production at 1881 million tones in 2000-01, some 15 million tonnes lower than its June forecast. The output will be nine million tonnes less than expected consumption of 1990 million tonnes.

Food production has been sliding marginally in absolute value since 1997-98 (Chart I). With steady rise in consumption cereal stocks had to be drawn down in the last two years. Wheat output is placed at 587 million tonnes and rice at 398 million tonnes (or paddy of 595 million tonnes), both lower than the actual output of last year. But production of coarse cereals will be up at 896 million tonnes as compared to last year.

The FAO's downward revision for overall cereal output is attributed to lower output in Asia especially China where there has been a persistent drought: The overall reduction in rice output has been ascribed to either a fail in area caused by low prices for paddy or policies designed to reduce output and, in some countries, to weather related damage, observes the FAO in its September outlook.

The ratio of global cereal stocks to consumption has been estimated at 16.5 per cent in 2000-01, lower than the 17-18 per cent that FAO considers as the minimum necessary to safeguard world food security.

At individual country level, China's cereal output is estimated to be lower in 2000-01 while India is likely to post a higher output (Chart II). These two countries account for 30 per cent of global cereal output.

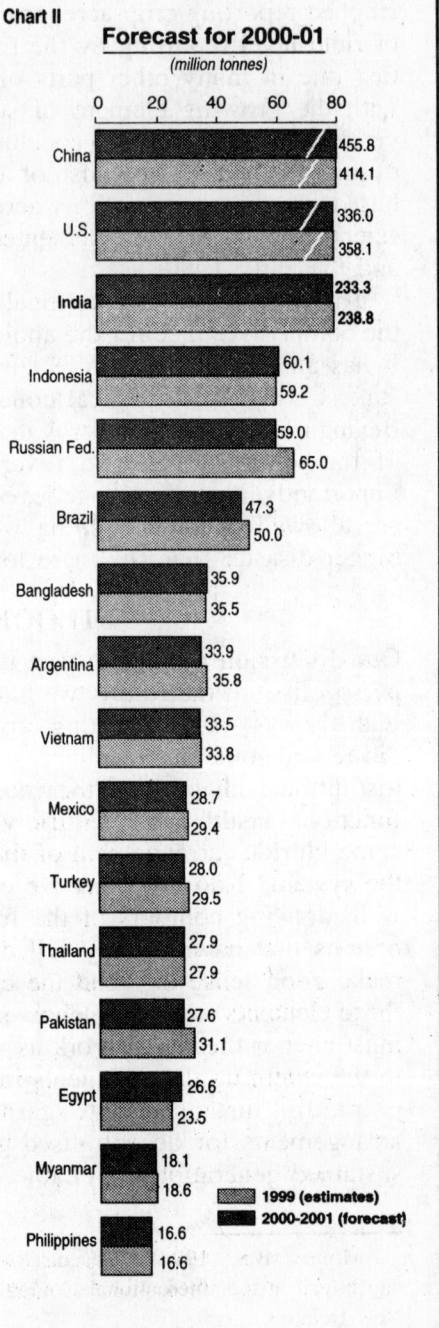

Chart II

Forecast for 2000-01
(million tonnes)

Country	1999 (estimates)	2000-2001 (forecast)
China	414.1	455.8
U.S.	358.1	336.0
India	238.8	233.3
Indonesia	59.2	60.1
Russian Fed.	65.0	59.0
Brazil	50.0	47.3
Bangladesh	35.5	35.9
Argentina	35.8	33.9
Vietnam	33.8	33.5
Mexico	29.4	28.7
Turkey	29.5	28.0
Thailand	27.9	27.9
Pakistan	31.1	27.6
Egypt	23.5	26.6
Myanmar	18.6	18.1
Philippines	16.6	16.6

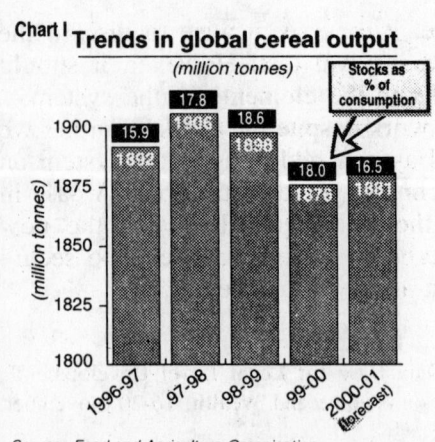

Chart I

Trends in global cereal output
(million tonnes)

Stocks as % of consumption

Year	Output	Stocks as % of consumption
1996-97	1892	15.9
97-98	1906	17.8
98-99	1898	18.6
99-00	1876	18.0
2000-01 (forecast)	1881	16.5

Source: Food and Agriculture Organisation

In a majority of the states, covering approximately two-thirds of the cropped area of the Indian Union, the regular reporting system for crop acreages by season as well as yields is still working in a reasonably satisfactory manner. The degenerate developments that have taken place since the mid 1980s are capable of being arrested and must be arrested. One such bad development has been the abolition of land revenue by many states. Among other things the high cost of collection of the land revenue from the landholders is often stated as the reason. For democratic decentralisation, which has been initiated through a couple of amendments to the Constitution recently, to be really effective, the Panchayats will need certain powers to borrow and tax. We propose that the levy of land revenue in all states should be assigned to Panchayats and its collection be made their responsibility. This one act also should go a long way in assuring continuity in the maintenance of land records for cross-referencing of sampling frames as well as motivate the Panchayats to play a critical role in the promotion of work on crop statistics.

To get back to the old system in Tamil Nadu, Andhra Pradesh and Karnataka may not be possible now. The old system of crop acreage and yield reporting has also broken down in Bihar. The new system (based on sampling of both areas and yields) has met with good success in Kerala but has problems in Orissa and West Bengal. Different options can be explored in different states. Over and beyond seeking all possible opportunities to anchor crop acreage and yield statistics at the village level on to the new arrangements for decentralised governance, certain critical inputs from remote-sensing technology can be exploited to impart a fresh impetus to area to sampling work in all states.

9

Fruits and Vegetables

NEED FOR ESTIMATES

The absence of production estimates in respect of a number of minor crops, for example, fruits and vegetables is a serious, lacuna in the existing production statistics. Recognizing their importance as the primary source of nutrition, the Planning Commission has already laid stress to increase their production. The ad hoc estimates of production available for some of the fruit and vegetable crops are not sufficient to meet the requirements of the situation. It is difficult to rely upon even the area figures under these crops.

The determination of their production involves some methodological investigations. The problem of recording the area under fruits and estimating their production is different from that of field crops. Fruit trees other than those grown in orchards, are scattered along the fields and as such an accurate determination of area under these scattered tree becomes difficult. Because of extensive mixed sowing, in the case of vegetables difficulty arises, in apportioning the area under various vegetable crops.

Statistics of area under different fruits are now available at all-India level from 1958 onwards for mangoes, citrus, banana, pome and other fruits among fresh fruit crops and cashewnut among dry fruits. In addition, estimates of area under papaya and banana and their production based on eye estimates are also published by the DES. Even though estimates of area under some of the fruit crops are available, reliable estimates of their production are lacking. The available data on production are mostly based on ad hoc surveys carried but by the Indian Agricultural Statistical Research Institute. (IASRI) and the Directorate of Marketing and Inspection (DMI). In the case of banana, crop-cutting surveys for estimation of yield and production are in vogue in important growing areas of Maharashtra, Madhya Pradesh and Karnataka. The available data on area and production of fruits are published with a considerable time-lag and in some cases the data do not cover all the principal States growing the crops.

So far as vegetables are concerned, separate figures of area are available for potato, tapioca, sweet, potato, onion and all other fresh vegetables taken together. Estimates of production are available only for potato, sweet potato and tapioca. In the case of some States, yield of a few crops like tapioca, and potato are based on crop-cutting experiments conducted every year.

The problems encountered in the estimation of area under fruits were first considered by the TCCAS in 1949 which observed that "It is not possible to include area under scattered trees in the estimates of cropped area given in Agricultural Statistics in India, as the land on which such trees stand is also covered by one or the other land use classification." Realizing the difficulties the collection of data relating to area and yield of different fruit crops, the IASRI conducted a series of pilot investigations in typical districts of selected States with a view to evolving suitable sampling methodology for estimating the extent of cultivation, yield rates and production of fruit crops as well as to collect reliable data on the cultivation practices adopted. As a result of these investigations, the IASRI evolved the requisite methodology but it is not being adopted in many States as high priority has not been given to the collection of these statistics necessary for planning horticulture. As a result adequate financial resources were not provided under the Plans.

RECORDING OF AREA UNDER FRUITS AND VEGETABLES

A careful consideration of the problems of collection of statistics of area and production of fruits and vegetables in the country would suggest that the agricultural statistics authority in each State should, in consultation with the Director of Agriculture or Director of Horticulture, prepare a list of important fruits and vegetables grown in the State. Arrangements should be made for collection of information regarding the area under each of the important crops in the normal agricultural statistics on the basis of complete enumeration done by the Patwaris. While recording the area under difficult fruit crops, only the area under regular orchards should be accounted for. In the case of orchards having two or more types of fruit trees grown mixed in such a way that each single fruit crop occupies roughly more than 10 per cent of the area of the orchard, area under different crops should be approximately allocated in proportion to the number of trees and distance between trees of the respective crops. In the orchards of bearing age growing inter or support crops, the entire area should be recorded both under the fruit crop as well as under the inter or support crop.

Census of Fruit Trees

In order to provide a sound basis for future planning, as well as supplying a reliable frame for conducting sample surveys for studying different aspects of fruit cultivation, a census of fruit trees which should include scattered trees also should be conducted once in every five years throughout the country. The census should provide data relating to number of trees of different commercially important local fruit crops according to bearing and young categories as well as according to important varieties. The planning of the census, which should be conducted through the State agencies, as well as the compilation and analysis of data should be done by a Central agency. Uniformity of concepts and definitions should be ensured in conducting the census. (Also *see* Appendix 2.)

Market Intelligence

Data on wholesale and retail prices of fruits and vegetables and their market arrivals are important for keeping a watch on the progress of their development. For the purpose whole time staff should be posted in all the important city fruit markets to collect and report data on prices and arrivals. Ancillary data on cold storages, stocks, marketing practices and movement of fruits and vegetables by different modes of transportation, i.e. by rail and road should also be collected at regular intervals.

Methodological Investigations

Many of the fruit trees are perennial crops and bear fruits after a period of a few years. In estimating the cost of production, the cost of cultivation up to the bearing stage has to be worked out and allocated to the crops during the subsequent years. Further in each orchard there will be mixture of young and fruit bearing trees. This presents problems of allocation of costs between the two. Methodological investigations should, therefore, be carried out to standardize the data collection techniques for estimating cost of production of fruits.

In the case of cashewnuts, a wide divergence is observed between the statistics published by the DES on the basis of data furnished by the States and those maintained by the Cashewnut Development Council. The discrepancy between the two sets of figures should be reconciled. It is possible that part of the difference is due to the inclusion or exclusion of data regarding cashewnuts grown in forests. Similarly with regard to some of the fruit crops, i.e. mango, the estimates given by the DMI are higher than those published by DES. One of the possible reasons for the divergence is that while the former includes estimated area covered by the scattered trees alongside canal banks, roads, etc., the latter figures relate to orchards only.

Organizational Arrangements

A separate Unit should be set up in the DES to coordinate data on fruits and vegetables collected by the State Departments and to bring about improvements in the data collection techniques from time to time. Research in the improvement of methodology should be conducted by the IASRI. A statistical unit should be set up in the Institute of Horticultural Research at Hessarghata which could maintain all the relevant data for use in the research work of the Institute. In the States where separate horticulture departments have been established, statistical units should be set up in the departments for looking after the work of statistics of fruits and vegetables. In other States, this work should be entrusted to a separate unit in the agricultural statistics sections.

Statistics of Processed Fruits and Vegetables

Statistics of processed fruits and vegetables are also required for planning the programmes for expansion of the industry and for keeping a watch on its progress. Data on the processed fruits and vegetables should be collected as part of the Annual Survey of Industries. Information is needed regarding the item wise capacity and actual production during different periods of the year, availability of processed fruits and vegetable products for internal consumption and exports and utilization of raw materials. Available information in this regard is being published by the Ministry of food Processing in their Annual Reports.

PROGRAMMES ENVISAGED

The NCA recommended that in order to arrive at objective estimates of production of important fruits, vegetables, and minor crops in various States, the IASRI should develop suitable methodology for the conduct of crop estimation surveys on these crops and that efforts should be made by the Directorate of Economics and Statistics to have the methodology adopted by the States on a large scale to provide for annual State level estimates of these crops.

In view of the fact that IASRI had already developed a suitable methodology for the conduct of crop estimation surveys on fruits and vegetable crops, it was decided to request the State governments to frame proposals for conduct of crop estimation surveys on important fruits, vegetables and minor crops in their respective States on the methodology developed by IASRI. To enable the State Governments to do so, a scheme for crop estimation surveys on fruits, vegetables and minor crops was included in the Fifth Five Year Plan with full Central assistance.

For further details regarding the present position in this regard please refer to chapter 6 on Area Statistics.

Present Position

Regular data series on area, production and yield of quite a number of fruits and vegetables at the All India and statewise is being published by the National Horticulture Board in their publication—Indian Horticulture Database—since 1991-92 (Tables 9.1 to 9.3). Data on Mushroom production (area not given) provides variety-wise and state-wise information (Table 9.4). This publication also provides data on the

Table 9.1 Area and Production of Fruits

Name of the crop	Area(ha.)		Production (mt.)		Percent change over			
					1996-97		1997-98	
	1996-97	1997-98	1996-97	1997-98	Area	Pro-duction	Area	Pro-duction
Apple	222702	227679	1308379	1320586	2.56	7.71	2.23	0.93
Banana	424664	441692	1243963	14141394	-1.93	-23.53	4.01	3.10
Citrus	474732	482720	4456165	4258514	4.55	17.32	1.68	-4.43
Grapes	42939	40842	1134667	969302	20.54	88.01	-4.88	-14.57
Guava	150895	151501	1601242	1631410	14.64	6.65	0.40	1.88
Litchi	51223	57844	377654	454742	5.46	3.57	12.92	20.41
Mango	1344870	1381177	9981250	10156963	4.82	-7.67	2.70	1.76
Papaya	63005	69204	1299296	1582130	3.42	-2.28	9.83	21.77
Pineapple	68738	69050	924589	946732	-3.56	-13.68	0.45	2.40
Sapota	45672	48224	588491	629312	-4.32	3.30	5.58	6.93
Others	690090	711771	6346780	7776854	20.16	-11.20	3.14	22.53
Total	3579530	3681704	40458152	42867919	6.62	-8.37	2.85	5.31

Source: *Indian Horticulture Database 1999*, National Horticulture Board, Ministry of Agriculture, Govt. of India.

Table 9.2 Area and Production of Vegetables

Name of the crop	Area (ha.)		Production (mt.)		Percent change over			
					1996-97		1997-98	
	1996-97	1997-98	1996-97	1997-98	Area	Pro-duction	Area	Pro-duction
Brinjal	464007	490725	6585605	7772364	6.86	2.21	5.76	18.02
Cabbage	210216	228130	3613436	4264727	-7.33	-6.42	8.52	47.04
Cauliflower	233881	248694	3419013	4462686	6.30	28.20	6.33	30.52
Okra	323171	324907	3040112	3238060	-24.93	-24.6	0.54	6.51
Onion	410000	340000	4180000	3140000	3.66	2.45	-17.07	-24.88
Peas	254439	272499	2339233	2421705	13.61	-0.09	7.10	3.52
Potato	1248800	1208900	24215900	17652300	12.60	28.51	-3.19	-27.1
Tomato	3911209	417815	5787858	6218470	9.98	6.35	6.80	7.44
Others	1979695	2097632	21893244	22613602	1.62	-9.07	5.96	3.30
Total	5515418	5629302	75074401	72831565	3.37	4.86	2.06	-3.01

Source : Indian Horticulture Database 1999, National Horticulture Board, Ministry of Agriculture, Govt. of India.

Table 9.3 State-wise Area and Production of Vegetables

State/UT's	Area(ha.)				Production (mt.)			
	1994-95	1995-96	1996-97	1997-98	1994-95	1995-96	1996-97	1997-98
Andhra Pradesh	16332	16948	194241	179830	234120	244429	1895011	2252172
Arunachal Pradesh	1722	1722	16732	16732	8012	8012	80508	80908
Assam	18838	24909	223203	223795	197001	248454	2074074	2180255
Bihar	80773	85685	602439	603470	1172632	1228470	8235720	8266184
Delhi	5126	5566	103047	83798	55123	61311	470716	329045
Goa	750	-	7500	7550	6500	-	68000	69460
Gujrat	12160	16788	171506	172006	172980	208909	2179350	2253850
Haryana	8500	9400	94500	96800	127500	142000	1385500	1290400
Himachal Pradesh	3837	3887	42850	42450	54400	56900	569000	574600
Jammu & Kashmir	3290	3290	26619	27998	35371	35371	328892	395075
Karnataka	29006	29314	312094	294800	566840	570514	4978686	4944930
Kerala #	24393	24393	243932	243932	278955	278955	2789555	2789555
Madhya Pradesh	18081	18979	199392	205956	224100	235300	2889500	2748700
Maharashtra	22085	21626	352364	275965	280902	295733	4275408	3317081
Manipur #	464	484	8039	8039	3500	3625	53150	53150
Meghalaya #	2540	2229	41792	43092	19984	21145	412152	411952
Mizoram	1189	1244	6764	7021	7665	7925	49581	47466
Nagaland	818	810	19278	20093	8710	8715	188397	204234
Orissa	80128	87710	868770	882650	789640	870565	8746050	9656520
Punjab	10250	10500	112935	120135	172138	177410	1612907	1634507
Rajasthan	6767	7595	82148	80232	28336	35691	388985	321891
Sikkim	869	870	12000	12620	2879	5064	54000	57600
Tamil Nadu	17482	17482	164415	176960	439793	439793	3990384	4085355

Table 9.3 State-wise Area and Production of Vegetables (Contd.)

State/UT's	Area(ha.)				Production (mt.)			
	1994-95	1995-96	1996-97	1997-98	1994-95	1995-96	1996-97	1997-98
Tripura #	3195	3200	32000	32000	32085	35848	358480	358480
Uttar Pradesh (Hill)	8650	8809	64185	65362	77441	79053	352839	362623
Uttar Pradesh (Plain)	74289	77637	673400	664102	1191166	1308254	12901812	9053410
West Bengal	49000	51000	831700	1034299	534000	539100	13670830	15015930
Andaman & Nicobar #	327	311	3115	3115	1638	1585	15850	15850
Chandigarh	-	-	408	460	-	-	10200	11500
Dadra & Nagar Haveli #	152	152	1522	1522	1356	1350	13565	13565
Daman & Diu #	006	006	56	56	103	103	1029	1029
Lakshadweep	025	025	260	250	013	014	697	715
Pondicherry #	251	221	2212	2212	3707	3357	33573	33573
Total	501295	532792	5515409	5629302	6728590	7159455	75074401	72831565

Note : # Data for the years are not available, last years data as such incorporated

Source : *Indian Horticulture Database 1999*, National Horticulture Board, Ministry of Agriculture, Govt. of India

Table 9.4: Production of Mushroom

State/UT's	Production	Type of Mushroom
Andhra Pradesh	2500	Agaricus/ Pleurotus
4000Goa	1000	Agaricus
Haryana	4000	Agaricus
Himachal Pradesh	500	Agaricus
Jammu & Kashmir	400	Agaricus
Karnataka	600	Agaricus/ Volvariella
Kerala	100	Pleurotus/ Volvariella
Madhya Pradesh	2000	Agaricus/ Pleurotus
Maharashtra	7000	Agaricus/ Pleurotus
Orissa	700	Pleurotus/ Volvariella
Punjab	4000	Agaricus
Rajasthan	50	Pleurotus
Tamil Nadu	10000	All
Uttar Pradesh	4000	Agaricus/ Pleurotus
West Bengal	250	Agaricus/ Pleurotus
North Eastern States (including Sikkim)	1000	Agaricus/ Lentinus
Others	1900	Agaricus/ Pleurotus
Total	40000	

Source : 1. Mushroom Compandium, 1997
2. *Indian Horticulture Database 1999*, National Horticulture Board, Ministry of Agriculture, Govt. of India

production of flowers (Table 9.5) and also World comparison (Tables 9.6 and 9.7). All these data can at best be used as rough indicators. While having an indepth study of horticulture in Himachal Pradesh and Jammu and Kashmir, it was found that leaving aside comparison with the State and Central data, there were wide variations between the horticulture data being released by the Departments of Agriculture and Horticulture respectively.

CROP ESTIMATION SURVEY OF FRUITS AND VEGETABLES

This scheme being implemented on a pilot basis since the Sixth Plan is operative in States namely Andhra Pradesh, Gujrat, Haryana, Himachal Pradesh, Karnataka, Maharashtra, Orissa, Punjab, Rajasthan, Tamil Nadu and Uttar Pradesh (as central scheme with 100% central assistance) and covers 14 fruits and vegetables namely apple, banana, grapes, guava, citrus fruits, pineapple, mango, cauliflower, potato, onion, tomato, cabbage, ginger and turmeric. None of the flower crops is, however, covered under this scheme. The area, production and productivity of crops covered under the scheme are estimated following Stratified

Table 9.5: State-wise Area and Production of Flowers

| State/UT's | Area(ha.) | | Production | | | |
| | | | 1996-97 | | 1997-98 | |
	1996-97	1997-98	Loose (mt.)	Cut (Lakh)	Loose (mt.)	Cut (Lakh)
Andhra Pradesh	7616	8420	22848	-	32900	-
Assam	442	442	79	-	79	-
Bihar	104	104	1710	3	1710	3
Delhi	1866	1866	10274	-	10274	-
Haryana	1850	1950	31120	471	33040	483
Himachal Pradesh	100	114	406	151	589	185
Jammu & Kashmir	133	167	1	54.5	1.6	78.51
Karnataka	19656	20780	115600	-	124290	-
Madhya Pradesh	1334	1334	13127	-	13127	-
Maharashtra	5439	4786	60012	-	33250	-
Manipur	78	78	29	-	29	-
Punjab	550	550	3355	-	3355	-
Rajasthan	2048	2048	2585	-	2585	-
Sikkim	50	60	1	0.023	1	0.023
Tamil Nadu	15856	16745	87208	-	92097	-
U.P Hills	160	161	183	-	195	-
U.P Plain	160	160	-	160	-	160
West Bengal	13720	13720	17685	5312	17685	5312
Daman & Diu	5	5	51	-	51	-
Pondicherry	46	46	427	-	427	-
Total	71213	73536	366701	6151.523	365685.6	6221.553

Source : 1. Concerned State Directorate of Agriculture/ Horticulture
2. *Indian Horticulture Database 1999*, National Horticulture Board, Ministry of Agriculture, Govt. of India

Multistage Random Sampling Technique. Indian Agriculture Statistics Research Institute, New Delhi, has provided the methodology. Main features of the sampling methodology are as below:

Sampling Design for Estimation of Extent of Cultivation and Production of Fruit Crops in a State

The important fruit crops are first identified. Since the cultivation of fruits is usually not so evenly spread and may in fact be concentrated in a few districts/ regions, the first steps in the planning of fruit survey is to identify the important growing areas for different fruits. A district is considered too large a unit of area for this purpose. However, taluks or sub divisions or equivalent areas in a district are considered appropriate. Thus, taluks that are important at least for one of the fruit crops, are identified as important fruit growing taluks. Importance of a taluk with

Table 9.6 *Major World Producers of Vegetables*

Country	Potato Production (000' Mt.)		Country	Tomato Production (000' Mt.)		Country	Onion Production (000' Mt.)		Country	Brinjal Production (000' Mt.)	
	1996	1997		1996	1997		1996	1997		1996	1997
World	311183	295407	World	91557	88222	World	35578	38146	World	16653	17415
India	24216	17652	India	5788	6218	India	4160	3140	India	6568	7772
China	52034	45534F	China	15532F	16382F	China	9630F	10030F	China	9325F	10025F
Russian fed	38700	40000F	U.S.A	11918	10762	Turkey	1900	2100	Indonesia	155F	155F
Ukraine	18410	19000F	Turkey	7800	6600	Pakistan	1098	1131	Turkey	850	850F
Poland	27217	20776	Egypt	6995	5950F	Brazil	963	883	Egypt	550	560F
Belraus	10881	11500F	Italy	6528	5539	U.S.A	2784	2898	Phillippines	140F	140F
U.S.A	22618	20861	Iran	2975	3500F	Iran	1200	1200F	Japan	484	491F
Germany	14264	12438	Brazil	2675	2602	Spain	1018	952	Italy	315	315F
Turkey	4950	5000	Spain	3367	2984	Japan	1262	1300F	Iraq	155	153F
Netherland	8081	8081F	Mexico	1994	1913	Russian fed	700	700	Syria	142	145F

Source: Indian Horticulture Database 1999, National Horticulture Board, Ministry of Agriculture, Govt. of India

Table 9.7 Major World Producers of Fruits

Country	Banana Production (000' Mt.)		Country	Grapes Production (000' Mt.)		Country	Orange (Mandarin) Production (000' Mt.)		Country	Mango Production (000' Mt.)	
	1996	1997		1996	1997		1996	1997		1996	1997
World	57998	58975	World	7619	7651	World	61142	63838	World	23036	23428
India	10014	10324	India	1135	969	India	1720	1472	India	9981	10156
Ecuador	5727	5727F	Spain	1300F	1300F	Brazil	21865	22999	China	2008F	2148F
Brazil	5619	5779	Italy	896F	894F	USA	10366	11636	Thailand	1400F	1350F
Indonesia	4768	4768F	France	887F	900F	Mexico	3985	4052	Mexico	1190	1444
Phillipines	3391	3500F	Turkey	560	567	China	2238	2308F	Indonesia	1128	1128F
China	2677	3141F	USA	309	315	Spain	2145	2602	Pakistan	908	914
Costarica	2400F	2400F	Argentina	206F	206F	Italy	1771	2079	Nigeria	500F	500F
Mexico	2210	2064	China	170	180F	Iran	1670	1600F	Phillipines	480F	480F
Coclombia	2150F	2200F	South Africa	165F	165F	Egypt	1613	1370	Brazil	456F	456F
Thailand	1750F	1700F	Thailand	1750F	1700F	Pakistan	1400	1410	Egypt	203	215

Source: Indian Horticulture Database 1999, National Horticulture Board, Ministry of Agriculture, Govt. of India

Note: F = F.A.O. estimates

respect to a fruit is determined on the basis of area under that fruit and thus a taluk important for a given fruit may not be important for other fruits.

All taluks/sub divisions as described above are taken as strata. The remaining area of taluks are further classified or grouped into 4 to 5 strata with respect to importance of individual fruit crops taking into account the geographical contiguity. Taluks may be considered as primary sampling units. Thus survey would then cover all important fruit growing taluks, ie. taluks in which fruit cultivation is concentrated as well as the selected taluks out of the rest.

In the selected taluks also, all the villages may not be growing all the fruits. A frame of villages growing different fruit in a stratum is, therefore, prepared. Accordingly, villages in a stratum may be classified into two categories (i) growing at least one fruit and (ii) growing no fruit at all. In category (i) on the basis of village wise area under fruits, villages may be identified as "reporting" or "non-reporting" for individual fruits. If the reported areas are considered as reliable, efforts may be concentrated only in the reporting villages for each fruit. However, experience shows that faulty reporting is not uncommon and, therefore, adequate representation may be given to non-reporting group. From the reporting group for a given fruit crop four villages are selected with replacement and with probability proportional to area reported under the fruit crop. From the non-reporting group of villages (in which other fruits are grown), a sample of two villages is selected in each stratum with Simple Random Sampling With Replacement (SRSWR).

For yield estimation, a sub sample of two villages out of four reporting villages is retained in all the major fruit growing taluks/strata and from each village 5 orchards and 3 clusters of 4 trees each of bearing age are selected for this purpose. The selected clusters of trees are observed for entire harvest. Exceptions to this procedure are made for certain crops like banana and grapes.

Sampling Methodology for Estimation of area and Production of Vegetable Crops

The sampling design is a stratified multistage random sampling. Taluks or equivalent areas are taken as main strata. Further, since area under vegetables varies considerably from one village to another in a taluk, sub stratification is done on the basis of village wise area under vegetables. For this purpose 3 to 4 sub strata with equal area under vegetables are formed. The area figures are available in revenue records. If not available, then a preliminary survey is conducted to obtain village wise area under vegetables. Within the strata, clusters of three villages are taken as primary sampling units. The allocation of clusters of villages to different strata is done in proportion to area under vegetables. The allocated number of clusters in different strata are selected with Simple Random Sampling Without Replacement (SRSWOR). For yield study, 50% of the clusters selected for area are retained and fields growing vegetables are selected in these clusters.

The selected clusters of villages are completely enumerated for area under vegetables. This provides a frame of vegetable fields for estimation of yield rates. For estimation of production, 6 to 8 fields of each important vegetable are selected in each of the clusters selected for yield study. In each of the selected fields, a randomly located plot 5m x 5m is demarcated and observed for all the pickings in the respective periods.

The scheme has so far not yielded the desired results as India is a vast country and cropping pattern differs from State to State. The States in many cases collect the data based on distribution of planting materials by Government and private sources. Moreover vegetable crops are also sown on a small area in patches and even in the backyard and front of houses and produce from this area is not covered in the available statistics.

Issues

The experience of the existing pilot scheme "Crop Estimation Survey on fruits and Vegetables" reveal that implementing agencies face many difficulties in implementation which results in non-availability of adequate, correct and timely statistics on crops covered under the scheme. Some of the issues in collection of adequate, correct and timely statistics on fruits and vegetables are mentioned below:

   (i) Total area under fruits crop is not recorded by the village level primary worker as fruits are also grown on canal banks, field bunds, roadsides, backyard of houses and even stray trees. The existing Land Record System does not provide recording of area under crops on canal banks, roadsides, etc.

   (ii) Present methodology for collection of production statistics provides for the presence of the staff who conduct crop cutting experiments at the time of every picking for recording quantity of produce. It is very difficult as harvesting of fruits and many vegetables is done in a number of pickings extending over several weeks.

   (iii) The area of short duration crops of vegetables which are sown after one Girdawari and harvested before second Girdawari is missed and therefore total area of that crop in a particular State remains under estimated. This has a bearing on production statistics also as in case of vegetable production is calculated by multiplying area with average yield.

   (iv) Land record manual in many States does not provide for recording of all important crops of fruits and vegetables and recording is done for many of the crops taken together. Therefore, area under individual fruit or vegetable crop is not available from revenue records.

   (v) Even in case of the crops of fruits and vegetables, wherever Land Record manual provides, for recording of certain crops,

Girdawari is not done correctly by the primary workers and therefore it does not give correct picture of area under that crop.

(vi) Crops grown on Government land/unauthorised land are not included in Girdawari. Therefore this part is uncovered in available statistics.

(vii) In most of the States primary workers engaged in Girdawari work are much more overburdened with the other work and therefore are not able to attach due importance to the Girdawari work.

Categorisation

According to the system of collection of area statistics presently in practise, the States and, Union Territories can be classified into three broad categories:

(i) States where area statistics are collected by complete enumeration (normally known as land record States). The system of land record is being followed in 14 States namely, Andhra Pradesh, Assam, Gujrat, Haryana, Himachal Pradesh, Jammu and Kashmir, Karnataka, Madhya Pradesh, Maharashtra, Rajasthan, Tamil Nadu, Uttar Pradesh and Pondicherry. These States account for 85 percent of all India area.

(ii) The States where area statistics are collected from the basis of sample surveys (normally known non-land record States or permanent settled States) such as Kerala, Orissa and West Bengal.

(iii) North East States and hilly districts of Assam where no agency exists.

The existing pilot scheme on collection of area production and productivity statistics on fruits and vegetables in selected 11 States and for selected crops (7 fruits and 7 vegetables) does not give much idea regarding statistics of the production of even crops covered in the scheme at National level. To obtain estimates of area and production of any crop we need related statistics from all the states in the country growing that crop whereas in present scheme only 11 States out of 32 States/ Union Territories are being covered. Moreover the area figures are taken from the Girdawari conducted by primary workers of Revenue Department posted at village level. These primary workers are overburdened with multifarious jobs assigned by different State Governments and therefore attach least priority to timely and accurate Girdawari. As production of vegetables is calculated by multiplying area under a particular crop by average yield of that crop, it gives incorrect figure of production if area figure is not correct.

Strategies

In order to build All India estimates of area and production of fruits and vegetables a proposal for covering all States/ Union Territories of the country is being formulated in the Directorate of Economics and Statistics will be in position to provide All India estimates of area, production and productivity of major Horticulture crops in the country.

Though there exists a system of working out advance estimates of crop production in case of cereals, pulses and oilseeds, none of the horticulture crops could be covered in the system due to several factors. Horticulture crops are not grown on a wider scale; rather they are grown in localized pockets and on smaller plots particularly vegetables. Moreover in case of these crops, some cropping activity, that of sowing, transplanting of harvesting takes place in some part or the other in the country hence crop monitoring is difficult. An attempt is being made to bring onion and potato under advance estimate crops to begin with.

A proposal for conduct of census for perennial crops and survey for non-perennial crops of fruits and vegetables has been submitted to Department of Statistics under proposed World Bank assisted project for modernization of statistical system. With the implementation of this project, it will be possible to obtain complete statistics on Horticulture crops for taking a number of policy decisions regarding production, pricing, processing, procurement, storage, transport, marketing, export/ import, public distribution and many other issues like investment planning in this field.

10

Irrigation

INTRODUCTION

The practice of irrigation in India can be traced back to 4000 B.C. Construction of minor irrigation works in the country dates back to the ancient times with evolution of agriculture. The farmers at that time practised irrigation with responsibility of the construction, maintenance and management of the village community. Historical records also confirm the existence of a number of old irrigation works in India. During pre-independence period, the main purpose of irrigation was to stabilize agricultural yields. The role of government was to provide water upto the outlets from the distributaries and minors. Water conveyance to the fields and application of water was left to the farmers. The technology of canals did not provide assured water supply. Prior to 1854 all the irrigation works were financed from general revenue only. After 1854, the categories of irrigation, viz. major and minor irrigation came into existence.

Indian Irrigation Commission (1903) recognized the importance of small irrigation and assessed that they were responsible for more than half of the irrigated area in the country. The importance of minor irrigation was later stressed by Royal Commission on Agriculture 1928. The campaign for minor irrigation started under 'Grow More Food' programme in 1943 for which government provided financial assistance. Although irrigation work in India can be traced back to the pre-historic period, substantial development took place only during the 20th century. Irrigated area in the country increased from about less than 1 million ha, in the year 1800 to about 5 million ha, in 1900, 16 million ha. in 1925 and 19 million ha. in 1947. Realising the importance of irrigation, Grow More Food Inquiry Committee (1952), Foodgrains Enquiry Committee (1957) and Agricultural Production team of the Ford Foundation (1959) have all emphasized the importance of minor irrigation to food production.

With the partition of India after independence, the country was left with total irrigated area of 19 million ha from all sources. The major irrigation source in India today are wells, canals and tanks which irrigate about 30% of net cropped area. Of this, wells account for 49%, canals

38% and tanks 7%. The traditional source of irrigation like tanks has a declining trend. The increase in groundwater exploitation is growing at a faster rate. There are 1359 large dams which provide irrigation with another 160 under construction. Dam technology for irrigation has led to serious ecological problems like loss of forest areas and migration of people. Planning in the country since beginning weighted more in favour of major and medium irrigation projects. With the result, that during 5 decades of planning. 58 million ha have actually been added to the gross irrigated area. However, the potential created is much higher.

IRRIGATED/UNIRRIGATED YIELDS

The gap between average yield and the normal rates of irrigated and unirrigated tracts, excluding the areas of assured rainfall is so wide that for a proper assessment of production potentialities, it is essential to have separate data for irrigated and unirrigated areas, according to different sources of irrigation and for different crops. In India, statistics of irrigation are collected along with those for land utilization. In using these data, it must be remembered that besides the area under irrigation, there are other areas which have assured and adequate rainfall and which are now classed as unirrigated land. Further, the mere fact that a certain area is irrigated does not necessarily imply that the irrigation water is adequate. It may be added, that in years of continued scanty rainfall, some of the irrigation sources are also not full with water and there is paucity of water for irrigation. Generally the irrigation sources, especially those described as minor, are most helpful in areas where rainfall is uncertain and unevenly distributed. All-India statistics are now available for the following:

1. Net area irrigated, source-wise.
2. Gross area irrigated (source-wise break up not available).
3. Distribution of gross irrigated area among various crops.

The States employ two agencies for the compilation and maintenance of irrigation statistics—(1) the Land Revenue/Land Records Department, and (2) Irrigation/Public Works Department. These statistics are collected at the village level and pass through more than one intermediate agency before being submitted to the State Government or the chief engineer. The statistics of the Revenue Department form part of the land utilization statistics, but those of the Irrigation Department are primarily for the collection of water rates. The Revenue Department's statistics include areas irrigated both by public and private works, but those of the irrigation department are limited only to public works. The Revenue and Land Records Department publish their statistics in the form of Season and Crop Reports. The statistics collected by the Irrigation Department are published in their Annual Report.

CONCEPTS AND DEFINITIONS

Statistics of irrigation comprise mainly data on area irrigated by different sources and the crops irrigated. Two types of irrigated area can be distinguished—net and gross. The net irrigated area is the area irrigated during an agricultural year (July-June) counting the area only once even if two or more crops are irrigated in different seasons on the same land. Gross irrigated area is the total irrigated area under various crops during a year, counting the area irrigated under more than one crop during the same year as many times as the number of crops grown, crops sown mixed being taken as one crop. From this it follows that the area irrigated more than once is obtained by deducting net area irrigated from gross area irrigated. Moreover, irrigated area is the cropped area to which water has been applied at least once in a season irrespective of whether the irrigation is adequate, inadequate or in excess of requirement. The irrigated area does not, thus, take into account the depth or the frequency of watering.

With regard to the concepts of irrigation, the gross command area is the total area covered by an irrigation project including unculturable area under habitation, roads, banks, barren and wasteland, etc. The culturable commanded area is the gross area commanded less the area of unculturable land included in the gross area. The irrigation potential of a project is expressed in terms of the gross area that is irrigable with the amount of water available and under the cropping pattern envisaged for the project. The utilization is the gross area actually irrigated each year. The ratio between the actual irrigation and the potential is termed as 'utilization ratio'.

For a meaningful analysis of the benefits of irrigation, certain other ratios are also important. These are crop irrigation ratio, net and gross irrigation ratio, intensity of irrigated cropping and that of irrigation. The crop *irrigation ratio* is the ratio of area irrigated under the crop to the total area under the same crop expressed as a percentage. The *net irrigation ratio* is the ratio of net area irrigated to net area sown in a year expressed as a percentage, while the *gross irrigated ratio* is the corresponding ratio between the gross area irrigated and gross cropped area in a year. The *intensity of irrigated cropping* is the ratio of gross area irrigated to net area irrigated expressed as a percentage, while *intensity of irrigation* is the sum total of the areas irrigated under different crops in a year expressed as a percentage of culturable command area of a project. These definitions should be adopted uniformly.

SOURCES OF IRRIGATION STATISTICS

The three main sources of irrigation statistics are: (i) Land Utilization Statistics (LUS) compiled as part of Indian Agricultural Statistics brought out by the DES and the State Season & Crop Reports (Annual), (ii) Annual Administration Reports, (ii) Annual Administration Reports of the State Irrigation Departments, and (iii) periodical progress reports compiled by the Planning Commission, Ministry of Water Resources and the State Departments concerned with irrigation schemes. Besides these main sources, data on irrigation are also available through the periodical reports prepared by the Central Water Commission on major and medium projects and various assessment and evaluation reports brought out by different organizations from time to time on the basis of sample surveys and other investigations.

Methods of Collection

The methods of collection of irrigation statistics are basically the same as those of other land use and crop area statistics of which they are a part. During the crop inspection, the Patwari records the area irrigated during the crop season and the source of irrigation in the relevant columns of the Khasra. When West Bengal, Orissa and Kerala also adopt complete enumeration, uniformity in the methods of collection all over the country can be ensured.

Primary and Intermediary Agencies in the Collection of Irrigation Statistics

The Revenue/Land Records Department uses the services of the village Patwari[1] for collecting the basic data. He collects statistics on various aspects of land-use including irrigation and inscribes them in what is known as the *khara* or 'Basic Village Form'. The form is prescribed by the Land Records Manual of the State. Information in this form is inscribed after a survey of each field, that is, on the basis of complete enumeration. Statistics relating to each item are added up in the Village Abstract and passed on to Tehsil/Revenue Circle Headquarters. The tehsil-wise returns are consolidated into a District Return at the District Headquarters and forwarded to the State Government. The collection of statistics by the Patwari is supervised by the supervisor (Kanungo) or circle revenue officers.

The system of collecting statistics described in the preceding paragraph obtains in all the States except Kerala, Orissa and West Bengal. In these States, land use and crop statistics are collected through sample surveys which give estimates for the whole State or for some districts. These statistics are highly inadequate. The Union Ministry of Agriculture has, for a long time, been pressing these States to make suitable arrangements for collecting statistics after the survey of each field as is being done in other States. Irrigation statistics of these States are thus only approximations. The Irrigation Commission has recommended that the system of surveying each field for reporting land-use statistics should be introduced in West Bengal, Orissa and Kerala and the primary agencies there should be adequately strengthened for the purpose.

---

[1]Also known as 'Lakhpal' in U.P., 'Karnam', in Tamil Nadu and parts of Andhra Pradesh, 'Talathi' in parts of Andhra Pradesh, 'Maharashtra and Gujarat, 'Karamchari' in Bihar and Mandal in Assam.

Contents of Statistics

Under the instructions of the Union Ministry of Agriculture the States are required to collect the following statistics which is to be entered in the Basic Village Form:

(i) Crop acreage, irrigated and unirrigated;

(ii) Sources of irrigation—canals, tanks, tubewells, wells and others; their classification according to ownership, i.e. whether owned by their Government or by private persons;

(iii) Classification of wells into masonry or non-masonry, in use or abandoned, whether used for irrigation or domestic purposes, etc.;

(iv) Method of water supply, lift or flow; lift by electric pump or oil-engine or traditional devices; and

(v) Capacity of irrigation and extent of the irrigated area—for a canal, mileage; for a tank, whether the ayacut exceeds 40 hectares or less; and for a well whether it is an independent ayacut or it supplements other sources of irrigation.

Irrigation statistics at the national level are compiled and published by the Directorate of Economics and Statistics, Union Ministry of Agriculture. The material for compilation is supplied by the State Governments and forms part of the land utilization statistics. Irrigation statistics include net area irrigated from different sources—public and private canals, tanks, tubewells, wells and other sources. They also include the gross irrigated area under different crops. For some crops such as rice, jowar, other millets and pulses grown in more than one crop season, the seasonwise break-up is also indicated.

Area of Crops Irrigated

Data on irrigated area under different crops are published in the Indian Agricultural Statistics. Its volume I provides State totals, while details at the district level are provided in volume II. From 1946-47, statistics are separately available in respect of irrigated area under autumn, winter and summer rice, kharif and rabi jowar, bajra, maize, ragi, wheat, barley, other kharif and rabi cereals, gram, tur or arhar, other kharif and rabi pulses, sugarcane, other food crops, cotton and other non-food crops. Groundnut, sesamum, rapeseed and mustard, linseed, other oilseeds, tobacco and fodder crops were added to the list in the 1956-57 issue which gives data from 1952-53 onwards. The total irrigated land under all crops represents the gross irrigated area and includes area irrigated under more than one crop during the same year; and areas irrigated more than once in a single harvest are counted only once.

In utilizing the data given in these publications, the following points may be kept in view:

(i) Classification of area irrigated by Government and private canals and other sources is not uniform throughout the country or in some cases even in the same state, over a period of time. In Madhya Pradesh, the figures for both Government canals and tanks are shown under private canals up to the year 1948-49. From 1949-50 the figures of tanks and Government canals are shown under respective heads.

(ii) The figures for Assam are estimated and relate to the plain districts only.

(iii) In the case of Tamil Nadu, Andhra Pradesh and Ganjam and Koraput districts of Orissa, the term 'tank' refers to a particular kind of reservoir which is formed by enclosing depressions or throwing dams across the valleys of rivulets and streams to intercept water during the rains.

(iv) The present classification of sources of irrigation does not afford their categorization into major, medium and minor which is so very necessary for realistic planning and watching of progress of irrigation development in the country through the different categories of works.

(v) In the case of Bihar, in the absence of any provision for compilation of net area irrigated by sources at the village level, the figures of areas irrigated by sources represent gross areas irrigated by these sources without taking into account the areas irrigated more than once.

Data for gross cropped area are broken down into gross irrigated and gross unirrigated areas. Gross irrigated area in turn is the sum of net irrigated area and area irrigated more than one crop during the year. There is also an attempt to distinguish between area irrigated by different categories of works such as canals, tanks and wells. But this information is available only in respect of net area irrigated. The criterion for classifying a piece of land as irrigated is simply whether it was supplied water from one or other categories of artificial sources at least once in a crop season. It does not distinguish between the intensities and qualities of water application. There is also some confusion about the treatment of land which has been served from more than one irrigation source.

The land use statistics also indicate the allocation of gross irrigated and unirrigated area by specific crops. In respect of the major cereal crops, the National Sample Survey until recently attempted an independent estimate on the basis of a multi-stage stratified random sample of the total area under different cereals. There are substantial differences between the two series. It has been suggested that one reason for this difference lies in the difference in the treatment of mixed crops between the two agencies. However, there seems to have been no comprehensive analysis on the basis of which these differences can be satisfactorily explained.

The conceptual difficulties in interpreting the statistics of irrigated area and of area sown more than once also deserve notice. The present method of recording irrigated area suffers from serious limitations because they do not distinguish between the intensity and quality of water supply which are known to vary substantially from area to area and sometimes even within the same area. Nor is it possible to get any idea about the extent to which different sources of irrigation are used in combination in the same piece of land. Ideally what one needs is information on the quantum of water-supply to crops in different seasons. This would straightaway provide basis for a more meaningful classification according to adequacy and quality of irrigation and also to assess the magnitude of waste in the use of water relative to crop requirement. But there seems to be no attempt to compile such information. At any rate even if this information is compiled, they are not published. Feasibility of collection of such data needs to be explored, at least on a pilot basis to begin with.

The statistics of irrigated area as reported by the Ministry of Agriculture, which, in turn, is derived from the primary reporting agencies as part of the overall land use statistics, need to be cross checked with the programme figures, i.e. estimates provided by the agencies responsible for irrigation development. The Working Group on Agricultural Statistics for the Fourth Plan drew attention to these discrepancies. The comparison is not quite valid because of different methods of estimation and also because the programme figures have to be adjusted for depreciation of existing works on which reliable data do not seem to be available. There is also the difficulty that the area irrigated is a function of the crop pattern and, to the extent actual crop pattern differs from those assumed in the investment programme, the two figures are bound to be divergent. Since the comparison of actual irrigated area with the planned growth is vital for evaluating current policy for regulating the use of irrigated water, a more systematic and continuous effort to nail down the divergence between two sets of data on irrigation is imperative. There should at least be a periodic study of a sample of projects to check the norms used by the project planning authority and to compare the expected outcome in terms of area with actual outcomes and the reasons for any discrepancy between the two.

The question of possible bias in the reporting of crop area, particularly in the irrigated area, is another question which has not received the attention it deserves. It is claimed that the statistics collected by some States under report the extent of area under summer crops. It has also been suggested that because of the relatively high rate of land revenue on irrigated land and the fact that in some States the high value crops carry cess, irrigated areas as well as total area under these crops may suffer from a downward bias. These are obviously important questions which can be and should be settled by conducting at least on a sample basis an actual field to field survey of the crops and comparing it with the information as recorded in the Patwari registers.

There is again a conceptual problem in interpreting the cropping intensity as calculated from the land use statistics. These statistics would appear to suggest that cropping intensity on irrigated area as measured by the ratio of gross irrigated to net irrigated area is not significantly

Freshwater

Freshwater resources are abundant in pockets of Latin America, Africa and Canada. These refer to total renewable resources, which include inflows of rivers and groundwater from rainfall in the country, and river flows of other countries. The low income countries had more than 6,000 cubic metres per capita availability in 1997 (Chart I). The middle and high income nations had more than one and half times the per capita availability of the former.

As much as 92 per cent of the population of the low income group utilised annual withdrawal of freshwater for agriculture and the balance went for industry and domestic purpose. But the high income countries consumed 45 per cent for industry, 40 per cent for agriculture and the balance for domestic use. The latter group has also better access to safe water (more than 90 per cent) than the low income countries.

Among individual countries, Congo Rep. has huge freshwater resources of the order of 300,000 cubic metres per capita (Chart II). Papua New Guinea had three times the per capita availability of Paraguay. Canada and Norway are also endowed with huge freshwater resources. The urban populations of these countries have very good access to safe water (right hand side of Chart II). In India the rural population had better access to safe water than the urban population.

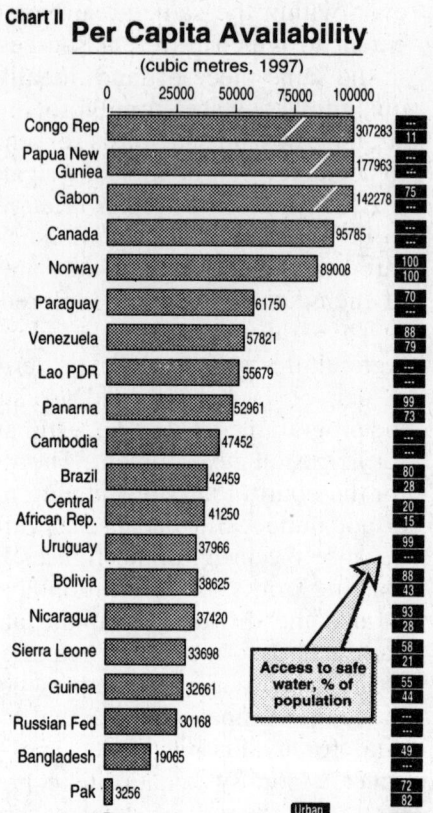

Chart II Per Capita Availability
(cubic metres, 1997)

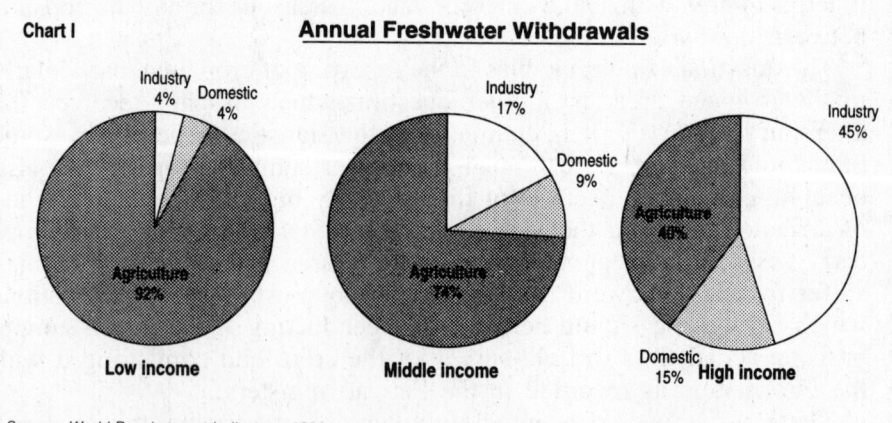

Chart I Annual Freshwater Withdrawals

Low income — Agriculture 92%, Industry 4%, Domestic 4%

Middle income — Agriculture 74%, Industry 17%, Domestic 9%

High income — Agriculture 40%, Industry 45%, Domestic 15%

Source: World Development Indicators, 1999

higher than on unirrigated land. However, this comparison is wholly misleading. For instance, if within an area commanded by an irrigation project, an unirrigated crop is followed by irrigated crop or vice versa, the cropping intensity is really two, but on the basis of the crop area statistics the intensity would appear to be one.[2] Moreover in a situation where different crops have different periods of maturity, the cropping intensity index which ignores these data is again somewhat misleading. This difficulty is likely to be greater in irrigated areas because long duration crops like sugarcane are more important in irrigated tracts. The recomputation of the cropping intensity index in terms of so many crop months per acre of net sown area would perhaps seem to be more appropriate.

SEASON AND CROP REPORT

All the State season and crop reports give statistics of area irrigated from different sources and the crops irrigated therefrom although the classification adopted varies from State to State. For example, in Tamil Nadu, total number of oil engines, tanks with ayacuts of less than 100 acres and of 100 acres and more, government and private tubewells and wells (masonry and non-masonry) are published. In Punjab data regarding the number of tubewells, masonry and non-masonry wells, classified into government and private and also wells used for domestic purposes only and wells not in use are given. In U.P. the number of tubewells (electric), other wells used for irrigation purposes classified into government and private and pucca and kacha wells and number of wells used for domestic purposes only and number of wells not in use are published. Information regarding number of tanks with ayacuts of less than 100 acres and 100 acres and more and oil engines is also published.

In the model season and crop report recommended to the States for adoption, provision has been made for the presentation of data on the number or size of the sources of irrigation and area irrigated by each source. Under the former come such data as number and mileage of government and private canals, number of tubewells, number of masonry and non-masonry wells, number of tanks and reservoirs with ayacuts of less than 100 acres and of 100 acres and more. When all the States collect this information at least periodically, it would be possible to improve irrigation statistics appreciably.

Other Sources

Formerly, irrigation data were also published in two reviews, namely, Annual Review of Irrigation in India and Triennial Review of Irrigation in India. Information in these Reviews pertained to total area irrigated

---

[2]This is true only if we use the ratio of gross to net irrigated area as a measure of cropping intensity. The ratio of gross to net sown area will of course be two.

by government works, the number of wells in actual use and the area irrigated therefrom and the number of wells not in use in respect of British Indian provinces only. These reviews have been discontinued. The former departments of works, mines and power issued statements showing final results of productive and unproductive irrigation, navigation and drainage works. No such statements have been published after 1945-46.

Some data regarding the results of operation of irrigation, embankment and drainage works are published in an abstract form in the Statistical Abstracts based on the returns received from State Governments and the 'Combined Finance and Revenue Accounts of Central and State Governments of India'.

The Central Water and Power Commission also collects, compiles and publishes statistics relating to major and medium irrigation works. It brings out two publications—(i) 'Annual Financial Statements of Irrigation Works in India' which contains statistics of the area irrigated, revenues collected and expenses incurred on major, medium works, and (ii) a 'quinquennial statement of irrigation statistics giving information on the engineering aspects of major and medium works and their final results along with physical performance'. The publication of irrigation statistics has, however, been intermittent.

It provides detailed information on all the major and medium irrigation works, about their operation as well as construction. Information is given for each project on cost, sources of water, year of commencement and, completion, mileage of canals and branches, catchment area, average annual run off, water spread area and of lake, full reservoir level, live storage length of dam, maximum height, discharge of canal at head, duty and annual rainfall. Information is also provided about the kind of soil in the irrigation boundary, gross commanded area, culturable commanded area, intensity of irrigation, cost of project per acre, crop patterns, per cent of gross area, cost of project per acre of gross area and rate of return on capital investment.

Section II deals with current water rates—State and crop-wise. Section III gives detailed information about the rates of betterment levy, State and project-wise. Section IV is a summary of the net and gross area irrigated from Agricultural Statistics. The other sections deals with:

  (i) Progressive expenditure on capital irrigation works.
 (ii) Gross income, working expenses, net revenue and direct receipts—
      all per acre of irrigated area.

Achievements Under Grow More Food Campaign

Information on number of irrigation works completed or repaired is given according to the following classifications for the last five years:

  (i) Sinking and repairs of wells.
 (ii) Construction and repairs of wells.
(iii) Installation of persian wheels, rahats and other water lifting
      appliances on wells.

(iv) Construction of irrigation tubewells.

(v) Pumping installation on rivers, channels, etc.

(vi) Other irrigation works including dams and channels (8,000 acres of area benefited).

Statistics of net and gross area irrigated and area irrigated more than once are also published in a summary form in the Economic Survey of Indian Agriculture, annually issued by the Directorate of Economics and Statistics.

Irrigation statistics are also published in the following publications:

Title	*Published by*
1. Report of the First Irrigation Commission, 1903.	Govt. of India,
2. Economic Effects of Irrigation, 1948.	Gokhale Institute of Politics and Economics, Poona
3. Irrigation Statistics in India, 1958.	Central Water and Power Commission
4. Report on Location and Utilization of Wastelands in India.	Wastelands Survey and Reclamation. Committee, Ministry of Agriculture.
5. Report of the Irrigation Commission, Vol. I, 1972.	Ministry of Irrigation and Power.

LACUNA IN EXISTING DATA

Like other area statistics, the statistics of irrigated area by source and crops flow as a by-product of the land records prepared primarily for land revenue purposes. Naturally, the reliability of these statistics depends on the extent to which the particulars of irrigation are systematically and distinctly recorded at the field level and correctly aggregated at the village and higher levels. Further, inter-State comparability of irrigation statistics is vitiated because of lack of uniform concepts and definitions and standard classification regarding irrigation particulars in the records.

Besides this, there are still gaps in the irrigation statistics. Distribution of gross irrigated area as between the sources of supply, length of irrigation canals—Government and private, number of wells, tanks, etc. are not known at present. Some of the State Governments publish some figures about the number of wells and tanks, etc. at periodical intervals in their Season and Crop Reports and the Administration Reports of the Departments of Irrigation and Public Works. Since there is no supervision over the collection of such data by the primary agency—the Patwari—it is very difficult to rely on the information given by some of the States.

The definitions and concepts either on all-India basis or in some cases even in the same State, have not been uniform over a period of time. In

Madhya Pradesh, for example, figures for both Government canals and tanks were shown under private canals up to 1948-49. In Uttar Pradesh, figures shown under Government canals include those under private canals, except for the districts of Basti, Budaum, Dehra Dun and Nainital for which separate figures in respect of areas irrigated by private canals are given.

In West Bengal, Bihar, Orissa and parts of Madras and Uttar Pradesh, the figures for areas irrigated by sources other than Government canals are only rough estimates. The figures for Assam and Coorg have been incomplete for a long time. Figures for wells in U.P. include those for tubewells. The definition of tanks is not uniform in different parts the country.

POTENTIAL AND ACTUAL IRRIGATION

Various Plan documents provide figures about the irrigation potential created and utilized during the previous Plan period based on data furnished in the Progress Reports of Irrigation Departments of the State Governments. Those calculations are not made from any field enquiry, but are invariably based on the amount spent, particularly in the case of minor irrigation. Then figures are generally additions and subtractions during the various Plan periods over the irrigation coverage before the First Plan. The land utilization statistics including irrigation are made available usually after a time-lag of three years. This adds further to the difficulty of finding out the exact position at any point of time.

Figures regarding the utilized potential as given in the Plan are invariably on the higher side. This may be attributed to:

(i) A long time gap between the completion of major irrigation works and the actual use of irrigation water.

(ii) Minor irrigation works going out of use are not taken into account.

It has often been pointed out that a large part of the irrigation potential created in the country has remained unutilized. According to available information, utilization of the irrigation potential created is estimated to be not more than 89 per cent. In absolute terms the gap between potential created and not utilized at the end of 8th plan was over 10 million hectares (Table 10.1). If irrigation facilities already created are to be fully utilized by the farmers, a staggering sum of Rs. 2 thousand crores will need to be invested for the construction of channels connecting the field with the distributory canals, land levelling and land shaping.

State-wise analysis of the data (Table 10.2a and 10.2b) shows that there are states like Punjab, Haryana, Madhya Pradesh and Gujarat, where present irrigated area according to Land Use Statistics (LUS) is more than irrigation potential created. If such states are not taken into consideration, unutilised irrigation potential will calculate to over 14.6 million hectares.

In the present irrigation parlance, '100 per cent utilization' means that water is either being actually supplied or has been made available for

**Table 10.1 Develpoment of Terrigation Potential (Culmulative)
Through Plan Periods**

(million ha.)

Plan	Major/Medium Irrgn.		Minor Irrigation		Total Irrigation		Gross Irrigated Area as Utl. Statistics
	Pot.	Utl.	Pot.	Utl.	Pot.	Utl.	
(1)	*(2)*	*(3)*	*(4)*	*(5)*	*(6)*	*(7)*	*(8)*
Pre-Plan	9.70	9.70	12.90	12.90	22.60	22.60	22.56
First (1951-56)	12.20	10.98	14.06	14.06	25.04	25.04	25.64
Second (1956-61)-GW	14.33	13.05	14.75 *(8.28)	14.75 (8.28)	29.08	27.80	27.98
Third (1961-66)	16.57	15.17	17.00	17.00	33.57	32.17	30.90
Annual (1966-69)	18.10	16.75	19.00 (12.50)	19.00 (12.50)	37.10	35.75	35.48
Fourth (1969-74)	20.70	18.69	23.50 (16.44)	23.50 (16.44)	44.20	42.19	40.28
Fifth (1974-78)	24.72	21.16	27.30 (19.80)	27.30 (19.80)	52.02	48.46	46.08
Annual (1978-80)	26.61	22.64	30.00 (22.00)	30.00 (22.(')	56.61	48.46	46.08
Sixth (1980-85)	27.70	23.57	37.52 (27.82)	35..5 (26.24)	65.22	58.82	54.53
Seventh (1985-90)	29.92	25.47	46.61 (35.62)	43.12 (33.15)	76.53	68.59	61.85
Annual (1990-92)	30.74	26.32	50.35 (38.89)	46.54 (36.25)	81.09	72.86	65.68
Eighth (1992-97)	32.96	28.44	56.60	52.31	89.56	80.75	70.64

*Component of Ground Water
Source: Ministry of Water Resources and Reports of Working Groups and Ninth Five
Year Plan Proposals of various states.

being supplied to all the lands which were planned to be irrigated in the
command areas concerned. The responsibility of the irrigation authorities
generally ends with the creation of distribution systems which do not go
beyond outlets meant to serve blocks of upwards of 100 acres each and
the way in which utilized beyond these outlets is not their concern. Also,
the frequency and the timing of irrigation are not related to 'utilization'
figures.

Agriculture Ministry officials believe that the causes of under-
utilization of the irrigation potential created by river valley projects stem

Table 10.2(a) **Statewise Irrigation Potential and Utilisation, 1994-95**

(' 000 ha.)

State	Irrigation	Potential Created			Utilisation			Gross Irrigated Area	Changes
	Major & Medium	Minor	Total	Major & Medium	Minor	Total		
(1)	(2)	(3)	(4)	(5)	(6)	(7)	(8)	(9)
1. Andhra Pradesh	3113	2948	6061	2894	2722	5616	5185	-431
2. Arunachal Pradesh	-	75	75	-	66	66	37	-29
3. Assam	204	611	815	134	502	636	572	-64
4. Bihar	2826	5389	8215	2397	4774	7171	4403	-2768
5. Goa	14	20	34	13	17	30	36	6
6. Gujarat	1321	1964	3285	1158	1835	2993	3655	662
7. Haryana	2065	1555	3620	1829	1512	3341	4592	1251
8. Himachal Pradesh	9	147	156	5	126	131	171	40
9. Jammu & Kashmir	173	374	547	146	359	505	430	-75
10. Karnataka	1557	1484	3041	1319	1444	2763	2923	160
11. Kerala	503	570	1073	454	533	987	506	-486
12. Madhya Pradesh	2157	2717	4874	1529	2447	3976	6071	2095
13. Maharashtra	2175	2552	4727	1150	2287	3437	3149	-288
14. Manipur	70	56	126	61	46	107	75	-32
15. Meghalaya	-	49	49	-	42	42	45	3
16. Mizoram	-	12	12	-	10	10	8	-2
17. Nagaland	-	67	67	-	57	57	65	8
18. Orissa	1458	1337	2795	1379	1165	2544	2510	-34
19. Punjab	2455	3382	5837	2395	3326	5721	7319	1598
20. Rajasthan	2170	2427	4597	1914	2345	4259	5815	1556
21. Sikkim	-	24	24	-	18	18	16	-2
22. Tamil Nadu	1552	2155	3707	1546	2152	3698	3588	-110
23. Tripura	2	97	99	2	89	91	60	-31
24. Uttar Pradesh	6976	21678	28664	5948	19760	25708	16823	-8885
25. West Bengal	1432	3015	4447	1341	2493	3834	2491	-1343
Total States	32232	54705	86937	27614	50127	77741	70545	-7196
Total U.Ts.	17	85	102	9	80	89	94	5
Grand Total	32249	54790	87039	27623	50207	77830	70639	-7191

from the basic fact that, by and large, these were conceived primarily as engineering works, and enough thought was not given during their planning and execution to the needs of agriculture. Three most important deficiencies have come to light during examination of the individual projects where utilization has been most unsatisfactory.

The first was the failure to construct water courses in time. A joint team of experts of the Food and Agriculture Organization, the United Nations Development Programme and Government of India, led by Sir

Table 10.2 (b) Statewise Irrigation Potential and Utilisation, 1994-95

(' 000 ha.)

State	Irrigation	Potential Created		Utilisation			Gross Irrigated Areas	Changes
	Major & Medium	Minor	Total	Major & Medium	Minor	Total		
(1)	(2)	(3)	(4)	(5)	(6)	(7)	(8)	(9)
Andhra Pradesh	3113	2948	6061	2894	2722	5616	5185	-431
Arunachal Pradesh	-	75	75	-	66	66	37	-29
Assam	204	611	815	134	502	636	572	-64
Bihar	2826	5389	8215	2397	4774	7171	4403	-2768
Jammu & Kashmir	173	374	547	146	359	505	430	-75
Kerala	503	570	1073	454	533	987	506	-481
Maharashtra	2175	2552	4727	1150	2287	3437	3149	-288
Manipur	70	56	126	61	46	107	75	-32
Mizoram	-	12	12	-	10	10	8	-2
Orissa	1458	1337	2795	1379	1165	2544	2510	-34
Sikkim	-	24	24	-	18	18	16	-2
Tamil Nadu	1552	2155	3707	1546	2152	3698	3588	-110
Tripura	2	97	99	2	89	91	60	-31
Uttar Pradesh	6976	21678	28654	5948	19760	25708	16823	-8885
West Bengal	1432	3015	4447	1341	2493	3834	2491	-1343
Total above	20484	40893	61377	17452	36976	54428	39853	-14575

Oseph Hutchinson inspected the Chambal project which was completeted about 40 years ago.

It reported that "when the canals were put in, construction was limited to main canals and major distributaries. No designs or layouts were prepared for the field network and this was left to the farmers. ... No investigations were carried out and no plans or instructions were provided for them".

Again, a World Bank team said about the Mahi-Kadana project in 1969 that "works completed to date include the Wanakbori Weir, a lined main canal and a distribution system capable of serving about 143,000 hectares in the right bank area". The area actually being irrigated, however, is only about 40,000 hectares primarily because of delay in construction of water courses and field channels.

The second failure, that of carrying out adequate soil surveys and providing drainage systems, is also illustrated by the experience of Chambal. Though soil surveys were carried out before the construction of the project, the dangers pointed out then were ignored by the authorities which constructed the project.

The third deficiency noticed was that "land was not properly developed for irrigation by levelling, grading and sub-division into compartments of optimum sizes'. Experience has shown that it is generally beyond the resources of the farmer to carry out such work on his own. Not only does he not possess the necessary financial resources, but there is also the absence of any agency which can carry out the work in an efficient and economical manner with the use of modern land levelling and earth moving equipment.

CENSUS OF MINOR IRRIGATION

Minor irrigation development in the States is dealt by different departments under different developmental sectors. The progress reports relating to minor irrigation programmes received from different departments at the Centre are used for compilation of minor irrigation data for the State. There has not been a single nodal department in the State to compile the minor irrigation statistics for the entire State. The structures installed by the farmers from their own efforts are generally not firmly recorded. The irrigation potential of ground water schemes are usually reported on the basis of certain assumed yardsticks. Usually no efforts have been made at the State level to provide a scientific basis for such yardsticks. In the case of State irrigation works the irrigation potential and utilisation are usually estimated on the basis of assumed water duties/water allowances. The reported figures of irrigation potential created by certain schemes during a particular period might have depreciated over a period of time but no depreciation is taken into account in reporting the figures of cumulative irrigation potential created. The figures in respect of private minor irrigation works installed totally by the efforts of the farmers are usually not based on any positive enumeration or sample survey.

In certain States there are no field agencies in the minor irrigation department to collect data relating to minor irrigation programme for administrative reports. Further, since minor irrigation programme is dealt by more than one department of the State, the administrative report of irrigation department gives the statistics pertaining to works maintained by the department.

During the discussions of annual plan proposals of the States hardly any State gives a clear picture of the development of minor irrigation in the State as a whole. A sub-committee on irrigation statistics set up by the Planning Commission in 1970, therefore, recommended a detailed census of minor irrigation works to strengthen the data base with regard to minor irrigation development in India. The National Commission on Agriculture endorsed this, adding that a census of irrigation sources be undertaken alongwith the Agricultural Census once in five years. Special irrigation surveys on the number of works and their utilisation might be undertaken by the States. The Technical Committee on Agricultural Census 1980-81 discussed the list of items in respect of data relating to minor irrigation proposed to be collected alongwith the agricultural census in 1980-81. It was felt that the agricultural census data were being compiled mainly from the existing land records. Since the required information on minor irrigation does not figure in the land records, it would not be possible to collect this information through the main agricultural census.

The Scheme for Improvement of Irrigation Statistics was launched in 1980-81 by the Department of Agriculture. Although a census of minor irrigation works was to be taken up under this scheme, it could not be conducted till 1985-86. While discussing various issues and problems in the irrigation sector in the Planning Commission in 1986, it was stressed that census of minor irrigation schemes be conducted within a period of one year. Thus commenced the first census of minor irrigation, with 1986-87 as the reference year. In Appendix Note the methodological details of this census are spelt out. Second Census of Minor Irrigation was also completed during 1992-93, but the Report is not yet available.

The census of minor irrigation data, though dated in time, adds to our information in two ways: (1) as a crosscheck on presently available estimates in this area and (2) as a source of information hitherto not known, or known vaguely, for the State or district as a whole. To illustrate, one example of type (1) is the number of minor irrigation works of various types that were in existence by the end of 1986-87, whereas the number of such works that have gone out of use-say, because of cumulative neglect of repairs and preventive maintenance (as in the case of tanks) and due to technological obsolescence (dugwells falling into disuse because of new tubewell technology)—would be an example of type (2).

COMMAND AREA DEVELOPMENT PROGRAMME

These are essentially water management issues in a broader sense to be addressed to, for optimum (if not maximum) utilization of the potential. The Centrally sponsored Command Area Development Programme (CADP) administered by the Ministry of Water Resources was launched in 1974-75 exactly with the objective of bridging the lag in utilization of the created potential and increasing agricultural production from the irrigated commands.

The Programme inter-alia envisaged the following main activities:
(1) Construction of field channels.
(2) Land levelling and shaping.
(3) Implementation of warabandi for rotational supply of water.
(4) Construction of field drains.
(5) Adoption of drip and sprinkler systems.
(6) Conjunctive use of surface and ground water.

In addition to these main objectives the programme also encompasses:

(1) Adaptive trials.
(2) Demonstration and training to farmers.
(3) Farmers' participation in irrigation.
(4) Introduction of suitable cropping patterns.
(5) Reclamation of water-logged areas (a new component included under the programme from 1996).

Despite operating the CADP, the gap between IPC and IPU has consistently increased as is evident from the evident from the position of the gap between IPC and IPU at the end of the First, Sixth, Seventh and Eighth Plan given below:

	Gap between IPC & IPU (Million hectares)		
	Major and Medium Irrigation	Minor Irrigation	Total
At the end of			
First Plan (1951-56)	1.2	0	1.2
Sixth Plan (1980-85)	4.1	2.3	6.4
Seventh Plan (1985-90)	4.4	3.5	7.9
Eighth Plan (1992-97)	5.2	5.2	10.4

The figures above reveal that the gap in the M&M sector (which is covered under CADP) remained almost stationary, while that in the MI sector (which is not covered under CADP) increased steadily. But this should not be the case with the MI sector, as the reasons for the lag in utilization stated earlier generally do not apply to the MI sector. This points to the question of veracity/reliability of IPC/IPU data in respect of MI sector in particular. On the other hand the relative stability of the gap figures in respect of the M&M sector also appears to be questionable as CAD Programme covers only a meagre percentage of M&M projects of the whole country and the rate of creation of potential is unlikely to match with the rate of utilisation-increase. For testing the reliability of the IPC/IPU data, it is appropriate to relate them with the Irrigated Area (Gross/Net) data generated by the Ministry of Agriculture.

The National Commission on Integrated Water Resources Development Plan, set up by the Government of India in 1996 has made the following recommendations in its report submitted in 1999.

"One of the major criticisms of irrigation schemes is about the large gap between potential created and its utilisation. The gap, which has persisted since long, should be reduced to the minimum. For this, it is essential to define a system for correctly reporting figures of potential and utilisation. Since there is no uniformity, in the norms and definitions adopted by different states and by different departments (Irrigation, Revenue and Agriculture) at present, it is necessary to lay down uniform guidelines for reporting the figures of potential and utilisation. Use of satellite imageries should also be made, for assessment of irrigated areas. It is suggested that definite guidelines may be laid down for reporting the figures of potential created and the utilisation achieved so that there is uniformity in the figures reported from all the states. The figures of the departments and land use statistics should be reconciled."

Conceptually, figures for Gross Irrigated Area (GIA) of MoA and IPU figures of MoWR should be close enough in so far as their difference is explainable and plausible.

The comparative position between GIA and IPU in 1996-97, is as follows:

  (i) GIA of Ministry of Agriculture = 73.275 m.ha
(ii) IPU of MoWR   = 80.759 m.ha
      Gap (ii)—(i)   = 7.484 m.ha

The issues therefore, to consider in respect of irrigation data required for water management endeavours at the instance of the Ministry of Agriculture and the Ministry of Water Resources are as follows:

1. A review should be undertaken of the village records/reports with the help of a senior level land records officer who should hold consultation with the concerned state officials and suggest changes with a view to bringing about, as far as possible, a common set of records, procedures of compilation and reporting.

2. State governments should ensure that computerization of land records is completed expeditiously.

3. In view of wide variation between the irrigated area generated by the Ministry of Agriculture and the Ministry of Water Resources, the State governments should make an attempt to explain and reduce the divergence to the extent possible through mutual consultation between the two agencies engaged in the data collection at the local level.

4. The State Statistical Bureaus (SSBs) should be made the nodal agencies in respect of irrigation statistics and they should establish direct links with the State and Central agencies concerned to secure speedy data flow.

5. Statistical monitoring and evaluating cells with trained statistical personnel should be created in the field offices of the Central Water Commission (CWC) in order to generate a variety of statistics relating to water use.

6. The Centrally Sponsored Scheme of the Ministry of Water Resources for rationalization of Minor irrigation statistics needs to be further strengthened in respect of the primary field work entrusted to the Patwari or the village level workers under the supervision of block level officials to ensure compulsory 5% sample check in randomly selected villages.

As a follow up the recommendations of the National Commission for Integrated Water Resources Development Plan, a Task Force has been constituted recently by the Ministry of Water Resources under the Chairmanship of Chief Engineer (IMO), Central Water Commission, to lay down guidelines and suitable standards for the collection and compilation of irrigation data. A senior officer of Ministry of Agriculture is also Member of the said Task Force.

DATA STORAGE AND RETRIEVAL

The Central Ground Water Board and the State Ground Water organisations are collecting data on various aspects of investigations, development and management of ground water. The task of developing programmes required for handling of data with the use of computers and micro-processors has been initiated in the Board. The data of ground water level from the Hydrograph Network Stations has been computerised. Storing of data of water quality and updating of personnel monitoring system have also been completed. Data on groundwater resources and reassessed irrigation potential are given in Tables 10.3 and 10.4.

EXTENT OF WATER RESOURCES

B.S. Nag and G.N. Kathpalia made an estimate of water resources of India for the National Commission on Agriculture for the year 1974 and also for the year 2025. Their estimate is summarised below.

Annual Water Resources of India, 1974 and 2025

(Million hectare metres)

	Year	
	1974	2025
Total precipitation	400	400
a. Immediate Evaporation	70	70
b. Run-off to surface water bodies	115	115
c. Percolation into the soil	215	215
Water utilisation	38	105
of which ground water contributes	13	35
surface flows	25	70

Source: The State of India's Environment, (1984-85), *The Second Citizen's Report*, Centre for Science and Environment.

The total rainfall is estimated at 400 million hectare metres and this is distributed in three important ways; 70 million hectare metres evaporate immediately; 215 million hectare metres percolate into the soil and help soil moisture and recharge ground water, and finally, 115 million hectare metres run-off into surface water bodies like rivers. Water utilised was 38 million hectare metres in 1974, which expected to rise to 105 million hectare metres by the year 2025. It has been estimated that irrigation accounts for 92 per cent of the water utilisation and domestic and industrial uses account for the balance of 8 per cent. With the growth of population and the increase in demand for products of agriculture and industries, the demand for water will also increase.

Scientists have attempted to estimate the maximum degree of exploitation of the annual precipitation. These estimates range from 86

Table 10.3 State-wise Reassessed Ultimate Irrigation Potential from Major, Medium and Minor Irrigation

(in thousand hectares)

Sl. No.	States	Ultimate Irrigation Potential				
		Major & Medium Irrigation	Minor Irrigation			Total
			Surface Water	Ground Water	Total	
1	Andhra Pradesh	5000	2300	3960	6260	11260
2	Arunachal Pradesh	0	150	18	168	168
3	Assam	970	1000	900	1900	2870
4	Bihar	6500	1900	4947	6847	13347
5	Goa	62	25	29	54	116
6	Gujarat	3000	347	2756	3103	6103
7	Haryana	3000	50	4462	1512	4512
8	Himachal Pradesh	50	235	68	303	353
9	Jammu & Kashmir	250	400	708	1108	1358
10	Karnataka	2500	900	2574	3474	5974
11	Kerala	1000	800	879	1679	2679
12	Madhya Pradesh	6000	2200	9732	11932	17932
13	Maharashtra	4100	1200	3652	4852	8952
14	Manipur	135	100	369	469	604
15	Meghalaya	20	85	63	148	168
16	Mizoram	0	70	-	70	70
17	Nagaland	10	75	-	75	85
18	Orissa	3600	1000	4203	5203	8803
19	Punjab	3000	50	2917	2967	5967
20	Rajasthan	2750	600	1778	2378	5128
21	Sikkim	20	50	-	50	70
22	Tamil Nadu	1500	1200	2832	4032	5532
23	Tripura	100	100	81	181	281
24	Uttar Pradesh	12500	1200	16799	17999	30499
25	West Bengal	2300	1300	3318	4618	6918
	Total States	58367	17337	64045	81382	139749
	Total Uts	98	41	5	46	144
	Grand Total	58465	17378	64050	81428	139893

Note: The ultimate Irrigation potential has been reassessed from 113.5 million hectares to 139.89 millionhectares. This has been done on the basis of there assessment of potential of surface minor irrigation from 15 million hectares to 17.38 million hectares. Thus, there has been an increase of 26.39 million hectares in the assessment of ultimate irrigation potential in the country.

Source: Annual Report 1999-2000, Ministry of Water Resources.

Table 10.4 Ground Water Resource and Irrigation Potential of India

Sl. No.	States/UTs	Total Replenishable Ground Water Resource (m.ha.m/Yr)	Provision for Domestic, Industrial & Other Uses (m.ha.m/Yr)	Available Ground Water Resource for Irrigation in Net Terms (m.ha.m/Yr)	Utilisable Ground Water on Resource for Irrigation in Net Terms (m.ha.m/Yr)	Gross Draft Estimated on Prorata Basis (m.ha.m/Yr)	Net Draft (m.ha.m/Yr)	Balance Ground Water Resource for future use in net terms (m.ha.m/Yr)	Level of Ground Water Development (%)	Weighted Average Delta (m)	Utilisable Irrigation Potential for Development (m.ha)
1	2	3	4	5	6	7	8	9	10	11	12
1	Andhra Pradesh	3.52916	0.52938	2.99978	2.69981	1.01318	0.70922	2.29056	23.64	0.047-1.472	3.96008
2	Arunachal Pradesh	0.14385	0.02158	0.12227	0.11005	-	-	0.12227	-		0.018
3	Assam	2.47192	0.37079	2.10113	1.89102	0.13455	0.09418	2.00695	4.48	1.283	0.9
4	Bihar	3.35213	0.50282	2.84931	2.56439	0.78108	0.54676	2.30255	19.19	0.40-0.65	4.94763
5	Goa	0.02182	0.00327	0.01855	0.0167	0.00219	0.00154	0.01701	8.3	0.87	0.02928
6	Gujarat	2.03767	0.30565	1.73202	1.55881	1.02431	0.71702	1.015	41.45	0.45-0.714	2.7559
7	Haryana	0.85276	0.12792	0.72484	0.65236	0.86853	0.60798	0.11686	83.88	0.385-0.6	1.4617
8	Himachal Pradesh	0.0366	0.00731	0.02929	0.02637	0.00757	0.0053	0.02399	18.1	0.385	0.0685
9	Jammu & Kashmir	0.44257	0.06639	0.37618	0.33858	0.00713	0.005	0.37118	1.33	0.385-0.6	0.70795
10	Karnataka	1.61857	0.24279	1.37578	1.23821	0.61443	0.4301	0.94568	31.26	0.18-0.74	2.57281
11	Kerala	0.79003	0.13135	0.65868	0.59281	0.14374	0.10062	0.55806	15.28	0.53-0.83	0.87925
12	Madhya Pradesh	5.08892	0.76332	4.3256	3.89298	1.01866	0.71312	3.61248	16.49	0.4	9.73249
13	Maharashtra	3.78673	1.23972	2.54701	2.29231	1.10576	0.77403	1.77298	30.39	0.43-1.28	3.65197
14	Manipur	0.3154	0.0473	0.2681	0.24129	Neg	Neg	0.2681	Neg	0.65	0.369
15	Meghalaya	0.05397	0.0081	0.04587	0.04128	0.0026	0.00182	0.04405	Neg	0.65	0.0351
16	Mizoram	Not Assessed									
17	Nagaland	-0.0724	0.0109	0.0615	0.05535	Neg	Neg	0.0615	Neg	-	
18	Orissa	2.00014	0.30002	1.70012	1.53009	0.20447	0.14313	1.55699	8.42	0.34-0.44	4.20258
19	Punjab	1.8655	0.18652	1.67898	1.51109	2.25109	1.57576	0.10322	93.85	0.518	2.91715
20	Rajasthan	1.27076	0.19945	1.07131	0.96418	0.77483	0.54238	0.52893	50-63	0.457-0.6	1.77783
21	Sikkim	Not Assessed									
22	Tamil Nadu	2.63912	0.39586	2.24326	2.01892	1.93683	1.35578	0.878748	60.44	0.37-0.93	2.83205
23	Tripura	0.06634	0.00995	0.05639	0.05076	0.02692	0.01885	0.03754	33.43	0.63	0.08056

Table 10.4 Ground Water Resource and Irrigation Potential of India (Contd.)

Sl. No.	States/UTs	Total Replenishable Ground Water Resource (m.ha.m/Yr)	Provision for Domestic, Industrial & Other Uses (m.ha.m/Yr)	Available Ground Water Resource for Irrigation in Net Terms (m.ha.m/Yr)	Utilisable Ground Water on Resource for Irrigation in Net Terms (m.ha.m/Yr)	Gross Draft Estimated on Prorata Basis (m.ha.m/Yr)	Net Draft (m.ha.m/Yr)	Balance Ground Water Resource for future use in net terms (m.ha.m/Yr)	Level of Ground Water Development (%)	Weighted Average Delta (m)	Utilisable Irrigation Potential for Development (m.ha)
1	2	3	4	5	6	7	8	9	10	11	12
24	Uttar Pradesh	8.3821	1.25743	7.12467	6.41233	3.83364	2.68354	4.44113	37.67	0.20-0.50	16.799
25	West Bengal	2.30923	0.34642	1.96281	1.76653	0.67794	0.47452	1.48829	24.18	0.33-0.75	3.31794
	Total States	43.14769	7.07414	36.07355	32.46621	16.42936	11.5006	24.573	31.88	-	-64.045
	Union Territories										
1	Andaman & Nicobar				Not Assessed						
2	Chandigarh	0.002966	-			0.00351	0.00245	0.000512			
3	Dadar & N. Haveli	0.00422	0.000633	0.003587	0.00323	0.00065	0.00046	0.00313	12.74	0.64	0.00504
4	Daman & Diu	0.0013	0.0002	0.0011	0.00099	0.00129	0.0009	0.0002	-	-	-
5	NCT Delhi	0.029154	0.017832	-	-	0.01684	0.0118		-	-	-
6	Lakshadweep	0.000243	-			0.00022	0.00016	0.000088	63.79	-	-
7	Pondicherry	0.002877	0.000432	0.002445	0.0022	0.00085	0.0006	0.00185	24.34	-	-
	Total Uts	0.04076	0.019197	0.007132	0.00642	0.02336	0.01636	0.00578			0.00504
	Grand Total	43.1885	7.093337	36.08068	32.47264	16.45272	11.5169	24.57878	31.92	-	64.0502

Source: Annual Report 1999-2000, Ministry of Water Resources.

million hectare metres to 105 million hectare metres. Even the maximum use of water supply of 105 million hectare metres by 2025 A.D. will be inadequate to meet the water demands of the country. Some scientists like Professor Chaturvedi of Indian Institute of Management, New Delhi, predicted a state of nationwide inadequacy of water even by the year 1995. Acute water shortages have already been experienced by most parts of Tamil Nadu including the city of Madras, Rajasthan, Gujarat, Orissa, etc.

DEFECTS IN STATISTICS

The main defects in irrigation statistics are: (a) time-lag in their availability, (b) lack of uniformity in concepts and definitions of terms like 'irrigation potential' and 'irrigation intensity', (c) discrepancy between the data based on LUS and those derived from the progress reports, and (d) their inadequacy to meet the requirements of planning and evaluation of progress.

The difference between the two figures is large. An attempt at the reconciliation of these two sets of figures was made, and since 1968-69, there has been an improvement and the discrepancy has become comparatively small. This can be seen from the fact that for the year 1968-69 while the LUS gives the gross irrigated areas of 35.4 Mha, the Planning Commission (Draft Fifth Plan) gives it as 36.0 Mha. Some of the steps taken, which have reduced this discrepancy are:

(i) In the figures of additional area benefited by minor irrigation, old irrigated area over which irrigation had been made more certain, the area benefited by water conservation-cum-ground water recharge schemes and the area protected by drainage, flood control etc. were included. Now these have been excluded since the beginning of the Fourth Plan.

(ii) In some of the southern States, major irrigation projects which improved the irrigation facilities in areas which were already being irrigated through minor irrigation tanks, etc. were also included in the new area irrigated. These have also been now excluded since the beginning of the Fourth Plan.

(iii) In the minor irrigation figures there was some over-estimation and account of the higher yardsticks for different categories of works, like wells, pumpsets, etc. adopted in the progress reports. These have now been rationalized on the basis of sample surveys.

(iv) Some of the minor irrigation works went out of use, but this area was not deducted when compiling total cumulative irrigated area in progress reports. This is now being done although there is need to further improve the estimates of depreciation of this account.

Some of the other steps which still need to be taken in order to reduce the difference between the figures of irrigated area according to LUS and the progress reports are:

(i) While in the case of the major and medium irrigation projects, cognizance is taken of the fact that there is a time-lag between the creation of irrigation potential and its utilization, in the case of the minor irrigation schemes, hundred per cent utilization is assumed as soon as the irrigation potential has been created. Surveys in Madhya Pradesh and some other States have indicated that this is not correct and as such utilization figures for minor irrigation works should also be separately estimated on the basis of actual recording or sample surveys, etc. It is also known that in the present circumstances, at the shallow tubewells and pumpsets installed for use of ground water are not being fully utilized since the number of hours run are comparatively small. Thus, although the potential for pumping out water is there, yet the utilization is rather low. The utilization could also be low due to lack of power or non-availability of diesel at certain times from year to year.

(ii) Quite a large number of tubewells and wells are now being constructed within the command areas of existing major and medium irrigation works to provide either supplementary irrigation or to provide irrigation additional cropped area within the command. The supplementary irrigation figures should not be added or, included in the normal irrigated areas as these areas have already been included in the benefits of major and medium irrigation works.

(iii) When major and medium works, replace certain areas of minor irrigation works, no deduction of areas under minor irrigation is made at present. It is suggested that this should be ascertained and correction made.

(iv) Because of intermixing of irrigation facilities in the area, through surface water from major and medium irrigation works and ground water through private minor irrigation works, it becomes difficult to apportion the area irrigated sourcewise, sometime resulting in duplication while reporting progress. A suggestion with regard to this is indicated later.

In view of the above, reconciliation of the two sets of figures should be done at the district level where the statistics reported in the LUS could be checked against the corresponding figures of additional irrigation benefits from the different schemes. This should be one of the functions of the Planning Unit proposed to be set up at the district level.

SUGGESTIONS FOR REVISED CLASSIFICATION

The sources of irrigation for which separate data on area irrigated are available are: (i) government canals, (ii) private canals, (iii) tanks, (iv) tubewells, (v) other wells, and (vi) other sources. This classification does not indicate separately irrigation from major, medium and minor sources and from surface and ground water sources. A more rational classification of the sources of irrigation will be as following:

I. Surface water
    Public surface water flow irrigation projects
        (i) tanks
            (a) large
            (b) small
        (ii) major and medium
        (iii) minor
    Private surface water irrigation works
        (i) flow irrigation
        (ii) lift irrigation
II. Groundwater
        (i) public tubewells
        (ii) private tubewells
        (iii) dugwells.

Definitions of the above classes are given in Appendix B.

Other Improvements in Statistics

For taking a forward view of the development of irrigation and also for drawing up programmes for its optimum utilization, it is not enough to obtain data regarding area irrigated from each source. What is necessary is to have the information whether or not water is available perennially throughout the year. As noted above the irrigated area relates to area on which water from any source is applied even once irrespective of whether it is adequate or not. Perennial water supply would enable two or more crops being grown on the same land but in most of the diversion schemes, water is available up to December or February. In the absence of information regarding the period of the availability of water, meaningful programmes for multiple cropping cannot be drawn up, nor can crop rotations and cropping patterns appropriate to different agro-climatic regions be determined. It is not necessary nor desirable to burden the normal agricultural statistics system with the collection of this information on an annual basis. But it should be possible to collect these data on a project basis, as part of Annual Administration Reports of the State Departments of irrigation.

Another inadequacy in the existing irrigation statistics is that sourcewise break-up of gross irrigated area is not available; so also the break-up of the total irrigated area classified according to major, medium and minor irrigation schemes is not available.

Although many State Governments publish some information on the number of irrigation sources, namely, wells, tubewells, tanks, etc. in their Season and Crop Reports (annual), no complete information on the number and type of irrigation sources, particularly minor sources, is available on an all-India basis. The basic data for compiling this information at the all-India level is available in the basic land records in some States. What is necessary is to undertake its compilation in other States and also to conduct special surveys to update the information once in five years. Therefore, a census of irrigation sources should be undertaken along with the agricultural census, and information on the number of public tubewells, private tubewells, dugwells, pumpsets and other irrigation sources, be compiled and published once in five years.

Some States like Karnataka and Madhya Pradesh have undertaken special surveys of irrigation sources and have compiled detailed information on the number of wells and their utilization. Other States also should consider the desirability of undertaking such special surveys periodically.

At the all-India level, area irrigated more than once is 18.14 million hectares or 32.9 per cent of net irrigated area, whereas the area sown more than once is 46.72 million hectares or 32.7 per cent of net area sown in 1996-97. There is a popular misconception that the difference between the two is all rainfed. This is not correct, for, this difference also includes area on which two crops are grown, one of which is irrigated and the other rainfed, the second crop being grown on the residual moisture or with the help of rainfall. This explains why in terms of percentages the two figures are close. If irrigation was not available on bulk of this area even in one season, perhaps it would not have been possible to raise more than one crop in such land. Of course, there are areas which receive adequate rainfall to enable raising of two or more crops in a year without the aid of irrigation.

At present, for reporting the statistics of sourcewise irrigated area under LUS, only the main or major source of irrigation is generally taken into account in cases where a particular area receives irrigation from two sources in a season. Because of this, the figures of area irrigated by the minor source are underestimated. Further, for the purpose of periodical progress reports on irrigation works, full benefits are reckoned even in case where only partial irrigation is provided by a source in any season. Part of the discrepancy between the two sets of irrigation data arises because of this. One way of handling the matter is to collect separate information relating to the area irrigated by more than one source—canal-tubewell, canal-well, etc. The figures would thus have to be collected for—

(i) total area irrigated by public and private surface water projects including area under (iii),

(ii) total groundwater irrigated area including area under (iii), and

(iii) portion of the total area irrigated by public and private surface water projects which has received supplemental irrigation from groundwater.

Item (iii) would give information regarding the area making conjunctive use of surface and groundwater, but it will not give a relative quantitative estimate of surface and ground water thus used. For making that assessment periodical sample surveys would be necessary. In working out the figures for total irrigated area those for item (iii) will have to be subtracted from the sum total of (i) and (ii). In the field, figures for (iii) should be recorded by the agency recording (ii).

There is scope for improving the statistical coverage of the Annual Administration Reports prepared by the Irrigation Departments. For example, information regarding the availability and status of water supply at the source of the irrigation systems, taking into account seasonal fluctuations, command areas and intensities of irrigation for which the projects are planned, the norms in regard to the duty of water or water allowances adopted in the design of the projects, and the cropping patterns for which the projects have been designed as well as the actual cropping patterns needs to be collected and published. Where it is not possible to collect some of the information through the prescribed returns (e.g. number of waterings and their intervals), periodical sample surveys should be conducted in the command areas of irrigation projects. These data should also be consolidated at the all-India level and published every year.

Drainage Statistics

Although absence of drainage is a major problem in several areas of the country, no accurate data are available regarding the extent of the problem, which is acute particularly in the case of rice in coastal areas, and in the delta areas of the larger rivers. Two types of data are relevant in this connection. The first is area benefited by the drainage schemes. This information can be collected from the progress reports on the schemes. The second and more important is the enumeration of area for which drainage facilities are inadequate. Even at present in the preliminary crop-cutting returns, information is called for on the level of land, specially in the case of paddy. The fields are categorized into high (or uplands), medium or low. This information can be tabulated once in five years.

Organizational Set-up

For handling the collection and analysis of irrigation statistics there should be appropriate statistical Units in the State Departments of Irrigation and there should be close coordination between this statistical unit and the Statistician in charge of agricultural statistics in the State. At the Centre, such coordination has been recently achieved in as much as that the Economic and Statistical Adviser to the Ministry of Agriculture would be in overall charge of the statistical matters of all the Departments in the Ministry. Water requirements of crops. are given in Table 10.5.

Table 10.5 Water Requirement of Crop

(millimeters)

Crop	Consumption	Humid	Semi Arid	Arid Tropical
CEREALS				
Rice	300-950	750	1200	2500
Jowar	350-650	600	950	1300
Maize	400-750	700	1220	1530
Wheat	300-450	400	650	900
Pulses				
Peas	370-475	600	920	1220
Soybeans	500-850	680	—	—
FRUITS				
Coconut	—	1200	1800	—
Banana	700-1700	1500	2800	—
Grapes	450-900	700	1220	1830
Mango	—	1200	1750	2500
Guava	—	600	800	1100
Citrus	600-950	—	1220	1800
Dates	900-1300	950	1340	1700
VEGETABLES				
Tomato	290-430	400	630	900
Brinjal	—	650	750	850
Ladyfinger	—	600	700	800
Beans	250-500	450	914	1220
Potatoes	350-625	450	900	1200
Beets	280-430	380	600	600
Cabbbage	290-460	400	650	700
Cauliflower	440-540	460	700	800
Melon	760-1040	900	1350	1750
Onion	229-640	360	500	700
OTHERS				
Sugarcane	1000-1500	1200	2700	—
Sugarbeat	450-850	—	1220	1830
Sisal	350-450	400	450	500
Cotton	550-950	760	1220	1830
Coffee	800-1200	1000	—	—
Tobacco	—	400	600	—
Pastures	—	680	910	1220

Source: Watershed Management in India, JVS Murthy, 1995.

Appendix 10.1

METHODOLOGY BEHIND MINOR IRRIGATION CENSUS

The Scheme for Improvement of Irrigation Statistics was launched in 1980-81 by the Department of Agriculture, Government of India. One of the objectives of the scheme was to conduct census of minor irrigation works on a quinquennial basis. Suitable number of staff were also proposed to be created in each State for compilation of minor irrigation statistics. Upto 1985-86, only 15 States implemented this scheme and appointed staff for the purpose.

At the beginning of the Seventh Five Year Plan, Planning Commission, insisted on preparing a sound data base for future planning of minor irrigation sector. Immediate action was initiated by the Ministry of Water Resources to conduct a census of all minor irrigation works. To avoid any delay, the entire funds for the purpose were provided by the Centre to the States and Union Territory administrations. A meeting of the officers incharge of minor irrigation programme in the major States was convened to discuss the various issues relating to census operation. The meeting discussed in detail the machinery to be involved, requirement of funds and information to be collected during the census. The details of the operation of Agricultural Census 1980-81 were also considered. Based on the norms and the mechanism devised after a number of meetings with the concerned Central Government Departments, the scheme of first census was finally formulated with the following objectives:-

(a) To enumerate completely the sources of minor irrigation in the States/Union Territories.

(b) To assess sources-wise area irrigated during Kharif, Rabi and summer seasons.

(c) To assess the contribution of these minor irrigation works by way of new irrigation or as supplementary irrigation source.

The census scheme was finally sanctioned on 13th March, 1987 for a total estimated cost of Rs. 3.5 crores. The reference year of the census was decided to be 1986-87. Each State and UT administration was requested to identify a nodal Department for conducting the census in its respective State/UT. The proposals for the nodal Deptt. of the State/UTs administration indicating the estimated cost in a specified format were received and scrutinised by the Minor Irrigation Division of the Ministry and placed before the sanctioning Committee for sanction of the amount required. 50 per cent of the estimated cost as sanctioned was released to the States/UTs in advance immediately after receiving the proposal. 25 per cent was released as soon as the primary enumeration work was completed and the balance 25 per cent after receiving the districtwise census abstract in the Minor Irrigation Division of the Ministry.

A small Advisory Committee under the chairmanship of Additional Secretary (MOWR) was constituted to oversee and monitor the implement-ation of the Census. The representatives of the Planning Commission,

Central Statistical Organisation, Department of Agriculture, and Department of Rural Development were the other members of the Committee.

Concepts and Definitions

Minor Irrigation Schemes were classified into 5 broad categories:-
  1. *Dugwells* (including dug-cum-bore wells).
  2. *Private shallow tubewells* In sedimentary formations depth of a shallow tubewell does not exceed 60-70 metres. These tubewells are either cavity tubewells or strainer tubewells. The tubewells give yeild of 100-300 cubic metres per day which is roughly 2 to 3 times that from a dugwell.
  3. *Deep tubewells* These usually extend to a depth of 100 metres and more and are designed to give a discharge of 100 to 200 cubic metre per hour. Their annual output of water is roughly 15 times of an average shallow tubewell.
  4. *Surface flow irrigation schemes* These schemes use the rain water for irrigation purposes either by storing it or by diverting it from a stream, nala or river. Sometimes, permanent diversions are constructed for utilising the flowing water of a stream or river. These schemes are of three kinds:

Storage Schemes

Storage schemes include tanks and reservoirs which impound water of streams and rivers for irrigation purposes. The essential features of these schemes are (a) a bund or a dam which is generally earthen but also sometimes partly or fully masonary, (b) anicuts and feeder channels to divert water from adjoining catchments, (c) a waste weir to dispose of surplus food water, (d) sluice or sluices to let out water for irrigation, and (e) conveyance and distribution system. The size of the storage is determined by the run-off expected on the basis of dependable monsoon rainfall in the catchment and by the fact whether the rainfall and cropping pattern would permit more than one filling of the tank.

Diversion Schemes Including Hilly Channels

The schemes aim at providing gravity flow irrigation by mere diversion of stream water supply without arranging any storage. Essentially, such a scheme consists of two parts: (a) an obstruction (weir) or bund constructed across the stream for raising and diverting water. The weir is called anicut in the South, bandhara in Maharashtra and Gujarat, and thingal in the Assam region, and (b) an artificial channel known as kuhl in the hilly areas, pyne in Chhota Nagpur and Bihar, dongs and ilhowkongs in the Assam region and so on.

Water Conservation-cum-Groundwater Recharging Schemes

Under this head are included schemes which serve primarily one or more of the following purposes: (a) submerging agricultural land during monsoons for sowing post-monsoon crops, (b) improving moisture regime of the adjoining fields downstream for raising of post-monsoon crops without irrigation, and (c) replenishing the groundwater.

Surface Lift Irrigation Schemes In regions, where the topography does not permit direct flow irrigation from rivers and streams, water has to be lifted into the irrigation channels.

These works are similar to those of diversion schemes, but in addition pumps are installed and pump houses constructed.

The statistics of irrigation mainly include data on area irrigated by different sources and under different crop seasons. Select definitions which are prevalent in respect of irrigated areas are as follows:

Gross Command Area The total gross area which can be physically irrigated from a scheme without considering the limitations of the quantity of water available.

Culturable Command Area It is the gross area, less the area of unculturable land including habitation area, ponds and land otherwise unfit for cultivation of the gross area.

Gross Irrigated Area The total irrigated area under various crops during a year, counting the area irrigated under more than one crop during the same year as many times as the number of crops grown.

Gross Irrigation Potential Created by a Scheme The total gross area proposed to be irrigated under different crops during a year by the scheme. The area proposed to be irrigated under more than one crop during the same year is counted as many times as the number of crops grown.

Irrigation Potential Utilised During a Year The gross irrigation potential created by the scheme as actually used during a particular year.

Supplementary Irrigation The gross cropped area is actually irrigated by two or more different sources of irrigation. All these different sources of irrigation are providing supplementary irrigation to the area.

The Census of minor irrigation works is to include all minor irrigation schemes situated in rural areas, urban areas and forest areas. The schemes which are used for drinking water purposes in addition to irrigation are to be covered under census. The minor irrigation schemes in the commands of major and medium irrigation schemes were also to be enumerated and come under the purview of the Census.

Procedure for Conducting Census Operation

The primary enumerators while filling in the schedules were to visit the owner of the minor irrigation scheme or its next neighbour and collect information on the basis of personal enquiry from him. The physical verifications of the schemes were also to be taken up by the enumerators.

Certain information relating to the schemes are to be collected by the enumerators by physical examination of the scheme.

Training-cum-workshops were to be organised by the Minor Irrigation Census Commissioner at the State headquarters in which the district level concerned officers were to participate. The details of the methodology to be adopted for the Census, its procedure, concepts and definitions etc. were to be discussed thoroughly and necessary clarifications given. The instructions for filling up the primary enumeration schedules alongwith the format for data consolidation at various stages were also to be discussed. In turn, the district level officers were to organise training-cum-workshops at the district headquarters where the primary schedules and the procedures for it were to be explained to enumerators.

Minor Irrigation Census Operation

A brief note giving the broad features of the scheme was circulated to the States/UTs in February, 1987. Stress was given on identifying a nodal department for undertaking the work with a view to completing it by 1987-88. The pre-testing of schedules were conducted in the States of Andhra Pradesh, Haryana, Himachal Pradesh, Maharashtra, Uttar Pradesh and West Bengal. In consultation with the Advisory committee the primary enumeration schedules and the formats for consolidation of data were prepared and circulated to the States in August, 1987. The following time schedule for census operation was intimated to the States in June, 1987.

The States/UTs were requested to submit their proposals alongwith the cost estimates in the prescribed format. During 1986-87 the proposals were received only from the State Governments of Andhra Pradesh, Haryana, Himachal Pradesh, Kerala, Sikkim, Tamil Nadu, West Bengal and Uttar Pradesh. These proposals were scrutinised and the administrative approval for conducting the census at the estimated cost were issued alongwith 50% Central assistance released in advance. Rest of the State Govts. and UT Administrations submitted their proposals in subsequent years.

Sl. No.	Operation	Date by which to be completed
1.	Pre-testing of schedules in selected states	14th August, 1987
2.	Communication of final schedules to the States/UTs	31st August, 1987
3.	Printing to format and training to personnel	15th November, 1987
4.	Primary enumeration	15 January, 1988
5.	Compilation of final figures at block level after completing the sample check	15th January, 1988
6.	Compilation of final figures at district level	31st January, 1988
7.	Compilation of final figures at State level and forwarding these to the Ministry of Water Resources	28th February, 1988

The districtwise abstracts of the census were to be supplied to the Minor Irrigation Division of the Ministry of Water Resources, Government of India. The States were also requested to bring out a minor irrigation census report in respect of their State, giving blockwise data relating to minor irrigation works. The tabulation plan for such a report was also sent to the Minor Irrigation Census Commissioners.

The National Informatics Centre (NIC), Department of Science and Technology, provided computerisation facilities at the district headquarters. A 2-day workshop was organised by the Ministry of Water Resources in association with the National Information Centre, Delhi in May, 1989. The Minor Irrigation Census Commissioners of the States participated in the workshop.

Limitations

The Census of Minor Irrigation Works has been conducted for the first time in the country and completed by the states on various dates in a span of about four years. A number of difficulties were encountered by the states. Depending on the gap between the reference year and the date of census, the reliability of data varies. Smaller the gap, more reliable the data collected. Despite best efforts by the minor irrigation census commissioners in the states, certain limitations remain.

1. Census of minor irrigation works could not be completed in Rajasthan. The work has been held up due to non-cooperation of patwaries, the primary enumerators.
2. West Bengal has conducted the Census of Minor Irrigation Works with reference to 1987-88 whereas other states have conducted it with reference to 1986-87.
3. Year-wise installation of minor irrigation works has not been collected during the census by some of the states such as U.P., Punjab and West Bengal.
4. The enumeration of groundwater structures in Kerala has not been taken up. Only the estimated number of dugwells in the state which are also used for irrigation has been estimated based on sample surveys. The details in respect of these dugwells are not available.
5. The State Government of Karnataka has not enumerated minor irrigation works which are installed in the commands of major and medium irrigation projects.
6. Distribution of dugwells and private shallow tubewells among the farmers of different holding size groups and the farmers of different social status has not been collected for Andhra Pradesh.
7. Distribution of groundwater structures by the farmers in different holding size groups and social status etc. is not available for all structures, specially in the case of Maharashtra.
8. The culturable command area (CCA) of a minor irrigation structure

has been higher than the gross irrigation potential created by it. Normally it should have been equal or less. Even if single irrigation crop is proposed to be grown during a year in the culturable command area of the scheme the gross irrigation potential created by it is equal to the culturable command area of the scheme. If more than one irrigated crop is proposed to be grown during a year the gross irrigation potential created would be higher than the CCA. Some of the states have intimated that due to less storage or less discharge the irrigation potential has been less but this may happen in a particular year and affect the utilisation of gross irrigation potential created by the scheme in that year. In case of a reduction in the capacity of the scheme, such as due to siltation in case of a tank, there is a shrinkage in the command itself and accordingly of the other parameters.

9. The actual utilisation of gross irrigation potential of a scheme in 1986-87 has been higher than the gross irrigation potential created by it. If the full capacity is being utilised in a particular year, the gross irrigation potential created is equal to the actual area irrigated by the scheme. In case of a reduction in the storage or less discharge, the actual area irrigated during that year would be less than gross irrigation potential created by the scheme.

10. The minor irrigation structures which are providing supplementary irrigation during 1986-87 have been showing higher area irrigated by other sources in the commands of the structures. Actually, it would have been at the most equal to the gross area irrigated by the scheme during the year. The scheme has provided supplementary irrigation only. Generally, a part of the gross area actually irrigated by a scheme is also being irrigated by some other source.

11

Agricultural Census

INTRODUCTION

The census of agriculture refers to the entire project of promoting a series of national agricultural censuses, with an operational agricultural holding as the normal unit of enumeration, taken all over the world in or around the same year within a world framework. There is a rapidly growing interest in economic planning on the part of the underdeveloped countries. Agricultural development is the most important component of this planning as it affects a vast majority of people in these countries, for whom it is a primary industry and also forms the base for other industries. Planning involves setting up national targets, the resources required for achieving them and a programme and a time-table for working towards these targets. The essential prerequisite of planning is knowledge which among other sources is provided by statistics of land, of farmers, of the present economic and agricultural situation and of potentialities for increasing production. This knowledge is equally essential for implementation of the plan. Agricultural census results contribute substantially to this knowledge. This census provides information on characteristics of holdings, the structure of agriculture and factors influencing production, which helps in assessing the type of development required and the optimum allocation and utilization of resources.

Agricultural census is a large-scale, periodic, government sponsored operation for the collection and derivation of quantitative information about the nation's agriculture, using the agricultural operational holding as the statistical unit. The operational holding is defined as all land, which is wholly or partly, used for agricultural production, and is operated as one technical unit by one person alone or with others, without regard to title, legal form, size or location. A technical unit is a unit under which the same management has the same means of production such as labour force machinery and animals.

OBJECTIVES

The main objectives of agricultural census are:
(i) To provide internationally comparable statistics;

268

(ii) To establish satisfactory bench marks for checking current national statistics, and for measuring future agricultural development;

(iii) To improve agricultural statistics systems in countries where they are lacking or unsatisfactory; and

(iv) To provide basis for regional planning.

The first action towards a world census of agriculture was taken in 1924 by the International Institute of Agriculture, Rome, by persuading member countries to carry out a general agricultural census on a uniform plan prepared by the Institute. The first census was conducted in 1930 and in which 63 countries and territories participated. The intention of the Institute was to repeat the census at intervals of 10 years, but the Second World War upset the programme for the 1940 census, which remained incomplete. The next world census of agriculture was carried out in 1950 under the guidance of the Food and Agriculture Organization of the United Nations which had replaced the International of Agriculture in 1945 and has taken over the responsibilities of the Institute. One hundred and six countries and territories participated in this census. The third world census for agriculture was conducted in 1960 and the fourth in 1970.

ITEMS ON WHICH DATA ARE COLLECTED

The census of agriculture aims at collection of data on the structure of agriculture by including in its programme the following items:

(i) The number of agricultural holdings and their principal characteristics, such as size, type, form of tenure, utilization of land, agricultural machinery, etc.;

(ii) The number and characteristics of the farm population;

(iii) Area under crops and number of livestock and poultry;

(iv) Number and characteristics of persons employed in agriculture;

(v) Volume of production of principal agricultural and of some livestock products;

(vi) Irrigation and drainage and the use of fertilizers and soil dressings;

(vii) Wood and fishery products obtained in agricultural holdings;

(viii) The extent to which agriculture is integrated with the processing industry.

Details about the holding as well as the holder are recorded. These include legal status of the holder, whether the holding is managed by the holder or operated jointly with others, location of holding, number of non-contiguous parcels and land which constitute the holding, produce from holding mainly for home consumption or sale, utilization, etc. Persons who are members of the holder's household and others living on the agricultural holding are enumerated. Further break up according to sex and age of individuals are recorded, along with their dependence on agriculture, non-agriculture or both. During the census week, information is recorded about the number of persons employed in agriculture separately for permanent, temporary and occasional workers. There has been a tendency in recent years for some industries to become interested in the operation of agricultural holdings and they enter into contracts with agricultural land holders. Recording of such data was introduced in the last census.

A uniform questionnaire for adoption by all countries is not proposed as this will vary according to local conditions. Before every census, a list of items is circulated on which internationally comparable statistics are expected from the censuses. To provide the necessary flexibility, this list is again divided into two parts; a short list for which data are desired from all countries and an expanded list which includes items of regional interest, on which some countries may wish and may be able to collect information.

The census, as the name implies, is conceived in principle as collection of data for all individual agricultural holdings by direct enumeration, but FAO recommends the use of complete enumeration, sample survey or both, depending upon the needs and circumstances of different countries. If data are needed for very small administrative units as a basis for regional planning, or in order to provide bench-mark information for current agricultural statistics, sampling methods may be uneconomic and complete enumeration unavoidable. In countries where such needs do not exist and specially in those taking agricultural census for the first time, sampling method may provide a convenient practicable alternative to complete census. In some countries detailed information may be needed for some items and only national totals for the others. In these cases the combination of complete enumeration and sample survey is indicated.

WORLD AGRICULTURAL CENSUS

The first world census of agriculture programme was launched by the International Institute of Agriculture (IIA) under the title programme of the 1930 World Census of Agriculture, in which 52 countries participated. It was intended to repeat the census at an interval of ten years, but due to second World War, the 1940 Census could not either be undertaken or completed where undertaken. Food and Agricultural Organization (FAO), being IIA's successor, undertook, as one its first major activities in food and agricultural statistics, the preparation and launching of the programme for the 1950 World Census of Agriculture.

Number of important changes in the methodology and operational aspects of the census were introduced for the first time by FAO, in the 1950 Agricultural Census, such as dividing the list of items into short and expanded list, and laying more emphasis on definition of various census items. The 1960 and 1970 World Agricultural Censuses further improved the methodology of Agricultural Census. The number of countries participating in the FAO Programme of Agricultural Census is continuously increasing. In 1970 Census, 102 countries participated as compared with 96 countries in 1960 and 78 in 1950.

AGRICULTURAL CENSUS IN INDIA

(1) *1950 Census* Data required by FAO was collected through sample survey carried out by National Sample Survey Organization in their 8th round (July 1954-April 1955).

(2) *1960 Census* National Sample Survey carried out Land Holdings Survey in its 16th 1960-August 1961) and 17th (September 1961-July 1962) rounds with agricultural year 1959-60 as the reference period. These sample surveys provided estimates for the country as a whole and for the States.

(3) *1970-71 Census* For the first time, the census was carried out on complete enumeration basis. It was one of the biggest ventures in agricultural statistics involving collection of data pertaining to nearly 70 million operational holdings in the country.

Methodology In 15 States and 5 Union Territories, which maintain comprehensive land records, the data on various items was collected by retabulation of the information available in the land records. In the remaining 6 States and 3 Union Territories, which do not have comprehensive land records, the data was collected by organizing special sample surveys.

Coverage Data on following items was collected with operational holding as the basic unit:

  (i) Number of Operational Holding by size class.
 (ii) Area under crops.
(iii) Land utilization.
 (iv) Irrigation—sourcewise and cropwise.
  (v) Tenure and tenancy.

In the non Land Records States, data on inputs like use of fertilizers, and pesticides, agricultural machinery and implements, livestock owned etc. was also collected by sample survey. The census was conducted with the agricultural year 1970-71 (July 1970 to June 1971) as the reference year. The field work was carried out by village Accountants (Patwaries) supervised and coordinated by the officers of Revenue and Land Records Departments. About 1.33 lakh primary workers were engaged in this operation. The field work and tabulation of census data was spread over a period of about two years.

1976-77 CENSUS

Scope Keeping in view the usefulness of the data thrown by the 1970-71 census, the Government of India decided to hold another Agricultural Census with agricultural year 1975-76 as the reference year, so as to make latest agricultural data available for the Sixth Plan. It was, however, subsequently decided to postpone the reference year from 1975-76 to 1976-77. This census comprised of two phases, viz. the Input Survey and the Main Census. In the Input Survey, data on application of inputs such as fertilizers, pesticides, etc. along with details of multiple cropping,

272 Agricultural Statistics in India

inventory of agricultural machinery and livestock was collected through a sample survey in about 2 per cent sample villages. The fieldwork of the input survey was taken up immediately after the close of each season to minimize the memory lapse. In few States, where there were no comprehensive land records, the field work was carried out along with the main census.

The second phase of the census, i.e. the main census consisted of collection of data relating to five principal characteristics, as in the last census, namely: (i) the number and area of operational holdings according to different size classes, (ii) land utilization, (iii) cropping pattern, (iv) cropwise and sourcewise irrigated area, and (v) tenancy particulars.

Reasons for Non-comparability of 1970-71 and 1976-77 Results

As mentioned earlier, the results of 1970-71 and 1976-77 Censuses are not comparable in respect of Himachal Pradesh, Tripura, Manipur, Nagaland due to differences in concepts, methodology, agency, etc. adopted for the two censuses. State-wise reasons are explained below.

(a) *Himachal Pradesh.* In Himachal Pradesh, the number of marginal holdings in 1976-77 went down against the general expectation that it would increase. It is explained that in 1970-71. Census, the individual, joint and copercency holdings of single right holders were treated as separate holdings whereas in 1976-77 Census, these were clubbed together. This resulted in the increase in the area of single holdings. Another reason extended for the reduction in the number of marginal holdings was that the definition of operational holdings was misinterpreted during 1970-71 census in four districts such as the holdings of married daughters were taken as separate holdings though these were actually operated by parent families. One more reason was that in 1970-71 Census, some Patwaries treated Patwari Circle as the cut out point for deciding the size of the operational holding whereas it should have been a tehsil.

As regards the unusual increase in the operated area in 1976-77, it has been clarified there was considerable allotment of Government land and also due to encroachment upon Government lands, Shamlat lands held by Panchayats were got partitioned and became private holdings adding to the operated area.

(b) *Tripura.* In Tripura also, there was considerable decrease in the number of holdings in the lowest size class (below 0.5 ha). It was explained that negligible kitchen gardens which were treated as operational holdings in 1970-71 Census were excluded in 1976-77 Census.

On the other hand, the operated area had gone up as per 1976-77 Census, partly on account of large scale allotment of surplus lands and Government khas lands and partly due to large scale encroachment of vacant Government khas and other lands.

(c) *Manipur.* The 1970-71 Census was conducted in Central Manipur district and 13 villages of South district only. The number and area operated as per 1070-71 Census, therefore, related to Central Manipur district and 13 selected villages of South district, whereas in 1976-77 Census all the six districts of the State were covered.

(d) *Nagaland.* Nagaland has not been cadastrally surveyed and there are no land records. About 80 per cent of the cultivated area is under jhooming which are difficult to approach. Jhooming cycle normally varies from 5 to 8 years.

The 1970-71 Census was conducted under severe limitations such as delay in starting the fieldwork, lack of trained staff, difficulties in proper supervision of the field work, non-cooperation or under reporting by the villagers and lack of time for proper scrutiny of the filled in schedules.

The operated area as per 1976-77 Census increased by 56 per cent over 1970-71. The 1976-77 Census results were considered more reliable due to various measures taken for proper conduct of the fieldwork, supervision, scrutiny and tabulation of the data. These estimates were also supported by the findings of Consultancy Report on Soil and Land Use Planning in Nagaland prepared by Indian Photo-Interpretation Institute, Dehra Dun in 1978. According to this report, total cultivated area was 235,077 ha whereas as per 1970-71 Census, it was only 99,358 ha.

Number of Statements.   State-wise 1970-71 and 1976-77 Agricultural Census results were presented in following six statements:

Statement   I— Distribution of number of holdings.

Statement   II— Distribution of operated area.

Statement   III— Percentage variation in number and area of operational holdings.

Statement   IV— Inter se percentage distribution of number of holdings.

Statement   V— Inter se percentage distribution of operated area.

Statement   VI— Average size of operational holdings.

Results.   As per all-India Report, there were 70.4 million holdings in 1970-71. Statement I, however, indicated this number as 71 million holdings. There were 517,640 holdings in Kerala with less than 0.04 ha areas. These were excluded in the 1970-71 census report as data on other characteristics were not collected for these holdings. These holdings were included in the number of holdings for Kerala and all-India estimates in Statement I. This accounted for the difference between the two sets of figures.

(a) *Number of Operational Holdings.* As per 1976-77 Census, the total number of operational holdings in the country was about 81.5 million whose break up by major size classes in given in Table 11.1.

Marginal farmers with less than one ha of land accounted for more than 54 per cent of the total holdings. This percentage varied from 9.5 in Nagaland to 87.7 in Kerala. It was higher than all-India average in Assam, Bihar, Tamil Nadu, Uttar Pradesh, Kerala, West Bengal, Tripura and Jammu & Kashmir. Small holdings between 1 to 2 ha formed 18 per cent of the total holdings. The inter-State variation for small farmers was

Table 11.1 Operational Holdings According to and 1970-71 1976-77 Census

Size class	No. in million		Percentage	
	1970-71	1976-77	1970-71	1976-77
Marginal (below 1 ha)	35.7	44.53	50.6	54.6
Small (between 1 and 2 ha)	13.4	14.70	19.0	18.0
Semi-medium (between 2 and 4 ha)	10.7	11.64	15.2	14.3
Medium (between 4 and 10 ha)	7.9	8.21	11.3	10.1
Large (10 ha and above)	2.8	2.44	3.9	— 3.0
Total	70.5	81.52	100	100.0

not as large as in case of marginal farmers. Large holdings with 10 ha and above accounted for only 3 per cent of holdings. In Nagaland, their percentage was as large as 24.5 followed by Rajasthan with 11.6 per cent. It was less than one per cent in Assam, Bihar, Tamil Nadu, Uttar Pradesh, Kerala, Meghalaya, West Bengal, Tripura, Manipur and Jammu & Kashmir.

When the number of holdings in 1976-77 is compared with the corresponding number for 1970-71 for the 15 States, where the results are comparable, it is observed that the number of holdings has gone up from 67.4 million to 77.7 million, indicating 15.3 per cent increase. The highest increase of 23.9 was recorded by marginal holdings and about 9 per cent each by small and semi-medium holdings. On the other hand, large holdings decreased by 12.5 per cent. The distribution varies largely from State to State, viz. the percentage increase in marginal holdings varied from 48 per cent in Bihar and 40 per cent in Rajasthan to 6.9 per cent in Meghalaya, 13.3 in Gujarat and 12.6 per cent in Uttar Pradesh. The percentage share of large holdings went up only in case of Assam (by 2.8 per cent) and in Meghalaya (where the number of large holdings was too small to indicate the correct position).

SUBSEQUENT CENSUSES

Methodology

The first Agricultural Census with reference year 1970-71 was conducted in the country by Department of Agriculture and Cooperation. So far five Agricultural Censuses have been completed at five yearly intervals and currently the sixth one with reference year 1995-96 is nearing completion.

The Agricultural Census is conducted following rigorous statistical procedure of sampling and survey methodology. The basic statistical unit for Agricultural Census is an operational holding[#] as against an ownership holding or a household. It is only through this approach that we can get data on individual, joint and institutional holdings as well as nature and degree of tenancy. As we are interested in studying the structure of agriculture and agricultural operations through the Census rather than the behaviour of a household, it is logical to take operational holding as a statistical unit. Further, an agricultural holding is the fundamental unit for making farm level decision regarding production and development of agriculture. As against this approach, if we take household as our technical unit, we may not be able to adequately capture the agricultural operations taking place on cooperative farmers, Government farms, farms owned or taken on lease by industrial firms for their captive cultivation.

The Census is carried out in three Phases. During Phase-I, a list of all the holdings with data on primary characteristics like area, gender and social group of the holder and its location code, etc., commonly known as, schedule L-1, is prepared. This list not only serves the purpose of a sampling frame for later phases of census operation but also yields basic results on number and area of holdings. During Phase-II, detailed data on irrigation status, tenancy particulars, cropping pattern, number of crops taken etc. are collected in Holding Schedule, also known as "Schedule-'H', Phase-III, popularly known as Input Survey, relates to collection of data on pattern of input use across various crops, states and size groups of holdings.

In the Land Record States, Phase-I of census operations is carried out for all the agricultural operational holdings. The data on number and area of holdings are collected in the specified schedules using the land records as benchmark. However, as per the concepts and definitions followed in the Census, an effort is made to obtain the *de facto* position rather than *de jure* position. For example, such holdings on which partitions had taken place in practice, though not legally, are counted as separate holdings. A number of parcels of land scattered within a tehsil but operated by an individual or a single household having common kitchen are clubbed together to make a single holding, in Schedule L-2; the tehsil being the boundary within which this clubbing of scattered parcels of land is done. Similarly, all lands, whether owned, leased in or otherwise operated, held and operated by a holder[#] is clubbed to make single operational holding, irrespective of the real owners. The village Patwari is expected to use his personal knowledge to update Schedule L-1 prepared on the basis of land record documents *(Khasra* and

---

[#]An Operational Holding is defined as "all land which is used wholly or partly for agricultural production and is operated as one technical unit by one person alone or with others without regard to the title, legal form, size or location"
[S]individual, joint or institutional

Khatauni) to get *de facto* position for *resident cultivators*. For non-resident cultivators Schedule L-2 is prepared which is exchanged with concerned Patwaris at tehsil level. Another Schedule L-3 is also prepared using L-1 and L-2 at village level to ensure that no part of land included in village geographical area is left out uncovered in census. The list of operational holdings formed after taking into account parcels located in other villages within the tehsil is manually sorted according to social groups, viz. SCs, STs and others, of the holder and size of the holding at village level to prepare basic tables on number and area. For the first time during 1995-96 Census, we have also collected data on gender of the holder and gender-wise classification of holdings is also being done. Various tables prepared at village level are then aggregated at Taluka, District and finally at State level. In Land Record States, during Phase-I, the data on all the holdings in 100% villages is collected using land records as benchmark. The list of items on which data are collected in Phase-I may be seen at Annexure-I.

In Non-Land Record States and UTs, viz., Kerala, Meghalaya, Manipur, Nagaland, Orissa, Tripura, Sikkim, West Bengal, Arunachal Pradesh, Goa, Daman and Diu, Lakshadweep and Mizoram, benchmark records are not available for preparing the frame for Agricultural Census. In these States, a list of land holding household is prepared in 20 percent villages which are same as those selected for the scheme Establishment of an Agency for Reporting of Agricultural Statistics (EARAS) for the reference year of the Census. The data for Phase-I is collected on all the holdings in these 20 percent sample villages.

For Phase-II, a detailed Schedule 'H' for collecting information on tenancy, land use, irrigation status, sources of irrigation, number of wells and cropping pattern is prepared in 20 per cent sample villages in Land Record States. Conventionally, these 20% villages are those selected for Timely Reporting Scheme (TRS) for reporting area from various States. Data in Schedule 'H' is filled by retabulation of revenue records, particularly those obtained through *Girdawari* or Crop enumeration. In non-Land Record States, varying procedures are adopted. Some States canvass Schedule 'H' to all the holdings in all the selected 20 per cent villages. In others like, viz., West Bengal, Kerala and Orissa, second stage sampling for holdings is resorted to in all the selected villages. Some other non-Land Record States, which conduct Phase-I only in 10 per cent villages, follow a complete enumeration procedure for Schedule 'H' also. The detailed list of items on which data are available from this phase may be seen at Annexure-I.

During Phase-III, popularly known as Input Survey, data are collected on input use pattern from 7 percent selected villages, which are out of 20 per cent villages selected for Phase-II. From each selected village 20 holdings (4 holdings from each of the 5 size categories, i.e. marginal, small, semi-medium medium and large) are selected for detailed personal inquiry on the items which are not available in land records. The reference period for this phase is the succeeding year of reference year for Agricultural Census. For example, in the next Agricultural Census operation, the Phase I and Phase II would relate to July, 2000 to June, 2001 and data for the same would be collected after June, 2001. The next input Survey would refer to the year 2001-02 and the data would be collected after completion of Rabi 2001-02. This system of reference period has perhaps been adopted to stagger the work at the Centre and State levels as also to ensure that a frame of operational holders become available for drawing of samples for canvassing schedules in Phase-III. The detailed list of items on which data are available from this phase may be seen at Annexure-I.

All India and State-wise estimates of characteristics focussed in Phase-II and Phase-II are built up using scientific statistical procedures. The data collected in last two phases is processed using computers. A comprehensive contract for the same, which includes development of computer programme, data entry and result generation at the cost of Rs. 9.4 crores has been given to NIC for 1995-96 Census.

Expenditure Pattern

Agriculture Census in India is conducted using the machinery of the State governments and is funded as a Central Sector Scheme (100% funded by Govt, of India). The salaries of the core manpower (one to six in each State) are paid from the scheme whereas their retirement benefits, office establishment costs are borne by the State government. The honorarium for the field staff is also paid from the scheme. The total outlay for the scheme during IX Plan was Rs. 48 crore. The break on this amount is as under.

• Printing of Schedules	— 15% of the outlay
• Establishments in States & UTs including salaries of staff	— 34% of the outlay
• Tabulation charges	— 26% of the outlay
• Honorarium	— 20% of the outlay
• Establishment at Central Headquarters including salary	— 5% of the outlay

As per the existing design of the Agricultural Census, it is one of the most economical ways of collecting primary data.

Time Schedule and Reference Period for Agricultural Census

The reference year for Agricultural Census is the Agricultural Year, e.g. the Agricultural Census, 1995-96 sought to record the agricultural operations undertaken during July, 95 to June, 96. As such, the major chunk of the data relating to agricultural Census had to be collected after completion of agricultural year. Under ideal conditions, the entire census operations in the country could be completed during a period of about three years reckoned from end of the reference year. The priority tables relating to number and area of operational holdings, which is based on Phase-I of the Census operations could, however, be generated within a year if the work of census operations was carried out in all the states as per schedule. Even if one or two States failed to complete their work, which was happening in all the Censuses, the publication of all-India results got delayed.

Reasons for Delays in Availability of Census Data

Even though the time lag in availability of detailed data from a large operation like Agricultural Census is considerably less as compared to that in population census or livestock census, there exists an scope for further reducing the time lag. A few factors, which have adversely affected the census operation, are enumerated in subsequent paras.

Design Related Factors

- With the overall objective of reducing the cost by making use of available information, the census is designed to be implemented through State governments. The State Revenue Secretary or some other officer is declared as Agricultural Census Commissioner for the State and funds are released to him through State Treasury for undertaking census operation. In this arrangement, the census related activities receive a low priority within the overall administrative affairs of the States as compared to activities, like elections, flood and drought.
- For nearly 87 per cent of the agricultural area is in the land record States, where the grass-root level statistical worker for census operations is the village Patwari who is vested with multifarious functions. Apart from priorities set by the state government, other functions such as land mutations etc are seen as more rewarding by the Patwaris, and consequently the census operations are relegated to the lowest priority. In many states like Maharashtra, the Patwari Association has occasionally refused to undertake the work of Agricultural Census. In the absence of an act to govern Census operations, the state government lack necessary teeth to deal with these type of situation.
- In many small non-land record States, like North-Eastern States, the technical manpower resources available for census operation are limited, keeping in view the size and scattered-ness of the holdings and the geographical features of the terrain.

Statistical Legislation

Unlike Population Census or Collection of Statistics Act for Industrial Statistics, there does not exist an act for Agricultural Census, which could provide statutory powers to the Agricultural Census Commissioner of India to command the state Agricultural Census Commissioners and the hierarchy down the line. Food and Agriculture Organization of the UN, has also made a recommendation in this regard.

Human Resources

Agricultural Census is a large-scale statistical activity involving statistical methodologies and tools as well as data management skills. Thus at apex level, the operation needs to be provided a professional leadership which incidentally have been found to be lacking in the part. The need for professional leadership has been echoed by the FAO of the United Nations in one of its recommendations, which is reproduced below.

"The head of census organization should be the National Census Coordinator (Agricultural Census Commissioner in our case) and the leader of the Census staff. This person has the overall responsibility of the census and should, therefore, be sufficiently qualified in statistics, have extensive experience in the management of large scale statistical operations including agricultural census and surveys, and be fully familiar with national agriculture."

As a result of overall reduction in manpower in the Census Division, the officers are not in a position to visit the States with desired frequency to guide and expedite the Census operations. Due to vacancies at lower level, we are not in a position to bring out a number of publications related to Census data. With a part-time Census Commissioner, much needed drive and direction to the Census operations becomes difficult.

CENSUSES-2001

The Department of Agriculture organises quinquennial Agricultural Census in the country keeping in view the data needs of the Department and the requirements of World Agricultural Census conducted by the FAO. The Census is followed by an Input Survey. So far, we have completed five Agricultural Census and are in the process of completing the sixth Census with reference year 1995-96. Seventh Agricultural Census with reference year 2000-2001 (Agricultural year), which will be followed by an Input Survey with reference year 2001-2002 are at planning stage.

Information is not yet available for 1995-96 Census. An analysis of the data (1990-91) throws interesting results (Tables 11.2 and 11.3). While average size of holdings has declined in all classes during 1970-71 and 1990-91, there is a slight increase in respect of large holdings during 1985-86 to 1990-91. Marginal and small holders constituting 78.2 per cent occupy only 32.5 per cent of the area. As against this, large farmers (only 1.6 per cent) have control on 17.3 per cent of the area.

The Census of operational holdings provides the key indicators of the structure of agricultural sector of the country which include data on number and area of operational holdings, dispersal of holdings, tenancy

Table 11.2 Average Size of Holdings by Different Size Classes

Major size classes	Average size of holdings (ha.)		
	1970-71	*1985-87*	*1990-91*
Marginal (below 1 ha)	0.40	0.39	0.39
Small (1 to 2 ha.)	1.44	1.43	1.43
Semi-Medium (2 to 4 ha.)	2.81	2.77	2.76
Medium (4 to 10 ha.)	6.08	5.96	5.90
Large (10 ha. and above)	18.10	17.21	17.33
All size classes	2.28	1.69	1.55

Source: Agricultural Statistics at a Glance, 2000, Directorate of Economics and Statistics, Ministry of Agriculture, Government of India.

Table 11.3 Number and Area of Operational Holdings by Type of Holding

Major Size Classes	Number ('000)			Area ('000 ha.)		
	1980-81	*1985-86*	*1990-91*	*1980-81*	*1985-86*	*1990-91*
Marginal (below 1 ha.)	50,122 (56.4)	56.147 (57.8)	63,389 (59.4)	19,735 (12.0)	22,042 (13.4)	24,894 (15.1)
Small (1 to 2 ha.)	16,072 (18.1)	17,922 (18.4)	20,092 (18.8)	23,169 (14.2)	25,708 (15.6)	28,827 (17.4)
Semi-Medium (2 to 4 ha)	12,455 (14.0)	13,252 (13.6)	13,923 (13.1)	34,645 (21.2)	36,666 (22.3)	38,375 (23.2)
Medium (4 to 10 ha.)	8,068 (9.1)	7,916 (8.2)	7,580 (7.1)	48,470 (29.6)	47,144 (28.6)	44,752 (27.0)
Large (10 ha. and above)	2,166 (2.4)	1,918 (2.0)	1,654 (1.6)	37,705 (23.0)	33,002 (20.1)	28,659 (17.3)
All size classes	88,883 (100)	97,155 (100)	1,06,637 (100)	1,63,724 (100)	1,64,562 (100)	1,65,507 (100)

Note : Figures within parentheses indicate percent contribution.
Source : Agricultural Statistics at a Glance, 2000, Directorate of Economics and Statistics, Ministry of Agriculture, Government of India.

particulars, land utilization, irrigation status, number of pumpsets, wells and tubewells and cropping pattern, etc. The Input Survey, which follows the Census operations, brings out detailed countrywide information like pattern of use of inputs like manures; pesticides, fertilizers, live stock, agricultural credit, etc. in the country.

Financing of the Scheme

Agricultural Census is conducted as a Central Sector Plan Scheme with 100 per cent assistance given to the States/UTs for payment of Salaries, office expenses, travel expenses, honorarium and tabulation cost, printing of schedules and instructions, etc. incurred under the scheme. The yearwise budget allocation is given in Table 11.3A.

Table 11.3A Yearwise Budget Allocation and Expenditure

(Rs. in thousand)

Year	Annual Allocation	Actual Expenditure (Booked by P.A.O.)
1995-96	18000	17441
1996-97	49800	48306
1997-98	23000	21656
1998-99	70000	68867
1999-2000	72800	72400
2000-2001	120000 (BE)	
	90000 (RE)	90000

The collection of primary data from the field is undertaken by a set of trained personnel, mostly revenue functionaries and village level workers, in land record States and in the non-land record states, the data are collected through interview method. The staff of the Statistical Department are usually engaged for the field work of Input Survey. The performance of the primary functionaries is supervised by nucleus staff provided at the respective State headquarters.

Targets-2000-2001

1. To complete the field work of Agricultural Census, 1995-96 in all States/UTs/.
2. To release All India report on Input Survey, 1991-92.
3. To complete the field work of Input Survey, 1996-97.
4. To complete the data entry work of Schedules of Agricultural Census, 1995-96.
5. To generate all prescribed Tables for Agricultural Census in all States/UTs.

Achievements-2000-2001

1. Field work of Agricultural Census, 1995-96 is nearing completion in all States/UTs.
2. All India report on Input Survey, 1991-92 has been released.
3. Field work of Input Survey, 1996-97 is nearing completion in all States/UTs.
4. Data entry work is nearly completed in all States/UTs.
5. Data processing for generation of tables is expected to be completed in major States/UTs.
6. Funds have been released as per the guidelines issued by Finance Division of the Department of Agricultural and Cooperation.

NSS LAND HOLDING SURVEYS

The NSSO has also been carrying out full-fledged surveys of land holdings (LHS) as part of its socioeconomic rounds. The first land holdings survey was conducted in 1954-55 (8th round) and the second in 1960-61 (16th round). It was repeated thereafter at intervals of approximately ten years with reference years 1970-71 (26th round), 1981-82 (37th round) and 1991-92 (48th round) (Table 11.4). The last three surveys also included a detailed enquiry on livestock holdings. The sample size of LHS was of the order of 4000 villages with 8 households per village in rural areas and around 2500 blocks with 9 households per block in urban areas. The LHS is not as detailed as the agricultural census in terms of item coverage for example, the LHS does not have details of crops grown in each holding). On the other hand, LHS provides useful additional information on household characteristics of the operational holdings such as the composition of the farm and livestock population attached to the holding. The Agricultural Census being essentially a re-tabulation of land records is not able to capture such details. Both, however, cover the major aggregates such as the structure of ownership and operational holdings, individual and joint holdings, area owned, leased in and leased out, number of fragments etc.

There are thus two sets of comparable estimates of the principal characteristics of land holdings produced by the agricultural censuses of 1970-71, 1980-81 and 1990-91, and the corresponding LHS with reference years 1970-71, 1981-82 and 1991-92 respectively.

A comparison of the two sets of the estimates brings out disturbingly wide divergence between them. Table 11.4 gives the estimate for the years 1980-81 and 1990-91 in respect of four major aggregates (1) total number of operational holdings, (2) area operated, (3) number of joint holdings and (4) number of holdings with "leased in" area.

It will be seen that the number of operational holdings was 88.7 and 106.6 million for the two years according to the Agricultural Census, while according to LHS, it was 76.9 and 103.6 million, the latter less than the corresponding AC estimates by 13.3 and 2.9 per cent respectively. The divergence in the estimates of the operated area is greater at 24.0 and 20.7 for the two years. The differences in the case of joint holdings do not even bear a comparison; the AC estimates are seen to be higher than the LHS estimates by as much as 95 and 99 per cent. By contrast, the estimated number of "leased in" holdings is higher according to LHS as compared to AC by about 11.7 and 11.4 per cent respectively. One can readily discern the impact of response errors and biases that give rise to under-reporting of joint holdings in the LHS and "leased in" holdings in the Agricultural Census. The households do not comprehend the concept of joint holdings and fail to enumerate them in full. On the other side, the village records are known to under-report the leasing operations. Large proportion of these are oral agreements between the owner and the tenant and do not enter the official record.

*Table 11.4 Comparison between Agricultural Census (AC) and NSS
Land Holding Survey (LHS)*

		1980-81/1981-82			1990-91/1991-92		
	Aggregate	AC	LHS	% diff	AC	LHS	% diff
1.	No. of operational holdings (million)	88.7	76.9	(–) 13.3	106.6	103.6	(–) 2.9
2.	Operated area (mha)	162.4	123.5	(–) 24.0	165.5	131.3	(–) 20.7
3.	No. of joint holdings million)	10.5	0.5	(–) 95.3	13.5	0.1	(–) 98.3
4.	No of operational with leased in area (million)	3.3	11.7	354.5	2.9	11.4	380.7
5.	No. of joint holdings as percentage of total no. of operational holdings	11.8	0.6		12.7	0.08	
6.	No. of operational with leased in area as a percentage of total no. of operational holdings	3.7	15.2			10.99	

In order to examine the reasons for the differences in the aggregates generated by the two sources, an expert committee set up recently (Feb, 2000) with Dr. Vaskar Saha as chairman, made in in-depth study and identified the assignable and plausible factors that could have contributed to the divergence. The assignable factors mainly relate to the discrepancy in coverage, concepts and definitions and methods of data collection, one by re-tabulation of land records and the other by household interview. Among the plausible reasons are ascertainment errors of unknown dimension both in the AC and the LHS relating to identification of operational holding, joint holding, operated area and leasing of land. The committee concluded that the observed differences were mainly due to ascertainment errors. The committee further observed that the procedure of retabulation of land records in the AC suffers from certain limitations which can be overcome only by the enumerators visiting the households to enquire the actual situation with respect to joint holdings and leased in area.

As mentioned before, the last three NSS land holdings surveys also included information on livestock holdings especially the livestock numbers. The main source of data on livestock numbers is, however, the quinquennial livestock census conducted by the state governments under the auspices of the Ministry of Agriculture. The census data are quite comprehensive and contain details of livestock classified according to various species of animals by breed, sex, age etc. A comparison of the livestock numbers available from LHS and the census (after appropriate adjustment for coverage, year of reference etc.) shows, once again, very wide divergence between the two estimates. For all major categories of livestock (cattle, buffalo, sheep/goat and pig), the NSS numbers are much less than the census numbers. The divergence in respect of cattle and buffaloes is more than 10 per cent in four out of six comparisons. In the case of the other two (sheep and pigs) the differences are even larger (Table 11.5). The Saha Committee examined this question and concluded that non-sampling errors particularly reporting lapses were the main reasons for such wide divergence.

Table 11.5 Comparison of number of Livestock estimated in Livestock Census (LSC) & NSS Land holdings/Livestock Survey

Number in million

Year (1)	Cattle (2)	Buffalo (3)	Sheep & Goat (4)	Pig (5)
1971-72				
LSC	178.0	57.0	108.0	7.0
NSS	175.0	51.0	80.0	4.0
% Diff	(–) 1.7	(–) 10.5	(–) 25.9	(–) 42.9
1982				
LSC	192.0	70.0	144.0	11.0
NSS	169.0	67.0	103.0	6.0
% Diff	(–) 12.0	(–) 4.3	(–) 28.5	(–) 45.5
1992				
LSC	205.0	84.0	166.0	13.0
NSS	172.0	73.0	104.0	6.0
% Diff	(–) 16.1	(–) 13.1	(–) 37.3	(–) 53.8

The National Statistical Commission (NSC) also reviewed the prevailing status of the agricultural and livestock censuses and was greatly concerned with their shortcomings. There is excessive delay in the availability of the final census results with time lag ranging between 4 to 6 years. The main reason for the delay in both the cases was the inability of the primary agency (patwaries for agricultural census and stock men of state animal husbandry departments for the livestock census) do not give the priority to the census work. The Commission also observed that the agricultural census being essentially a retabulation of land records does not enable collection of information on farm and livestock population associated with the operational holdings. On the other hand, the livestock census though based on household enquiry does not include data related to the household and its composition. The Commission has recommended that the agricultural and livestock censuses should be integrated and henceforth be taken together in a 20 per cent sample of villages in order to enable a better-controlled and more manageable programme. Moreover, merger of the two censuses has several advantages in terms of more information, reduction of operational costs on staff training, data processing etc. Overall decrease in the work of the field agency and early availability of the census results are other major factors in its favour.

The proposed quinquennial integrated agricultural and livestock census is a major operation as important as the population census. NSSO can certainly play an effective role in the conduct of the census. One of the essential requirements, however, is systematic training of the primary field and supervisory agency, which could be better handled by the NSSO jointly with the State Agricultural Statistical Authroity (SASA). While the regular supervision and control of the census rest with the administrative authorities, the NSSO and SASA should exercise a technical check on the operations in order to ensure the quality of the results. Synchronising the NSS land holdings survey with the census as recommended by the National Statistical Commission (NSC) will supploement as well as cross check the information from the census.

USES OF CENSUS DATA

Periodic Agricultural Censuses are important, as they are the main source of basic quantitative information on structure and other characteristics of agriculture that is needed in development planning, socio-economic policy formulation and establishment of national priorities. The census also provides the basis for development of a comprehensive integrated national system of food and agricultural statistics with major links between its various components of other national statistical system.

The census of agriculture provides data relating mainly to the organization and structure of agriculture and to the use of agricultural resources, such as manpower, land and water, livestock, machinery and other fixed assets and intermediate inputs.

In particular, the agricultural census is the principal statistical operation for obtaining the following essential data:

- (i) Comprehensive and up-to-date facts on agricultural land areas, crops, irrigation, and numbers and kinds of livestock.
- (ii) Bench-marks for improving current estimates of crop areas and production and of livestock resources and products.
- (iii) Measures of the State of and changes in the structural attributes of agriculture, such as size distribution of holdings, extent of various forms of tenancy and agricultural resources, production requisites, facilities and practices, as well as measures of the interrelationship among these attributes;
- (iv) Basic data regarding current use and changes in use of agricultural resources, such as people, land, livestock, and poultry, irrigation water and agricultural machinery and implement.

(v) Basic data for the formation of development and implementation of a comprehensive, integrated system of food and agricultural statistics.

The census provides essential information not only for the country as a whole, but also for major administrative sub-divisions and whenever possible, for agro-ecological zones and other small areas. This is one of the most important purposes of the agricultural census in the countries which have the means to undertake a complete or, at the least, large scale sampling of agricultural holdings. Information on agricultural holdings for small administrative and other divisions of the country will be particularly useful in development planning, especially for the efficient allocation of resources and the setting up of plan targets.

Deficiencies

There are, however, some inherant deficiencies which call for immediale attention. The agricultural census fails to produce data with cultivator as the unit of information, and so does the livestock census with household as the unit. Little thought is given to the immense amount of resources-perhaps because some of them come free-spent on the two censuses, the end products of which are numbers of livestock of different kinds. Worse, it is not realized that the separation of the subjects of land and livestock holdings is a totally unrealistic way of dealing with the most important sector of the economy where cultivation of land and animal husbandry are inseparable parts of an integrated single economic activity. The irony, again, is that the same GOI Ministry of Agriculture carries out the two independent censuses and has been knowingly blind to the simple task of integrating the two censuses. In fact, it took several years of sustained pursuit of the idea to bring home this simple truth. That resulted in the appointment of a Committee to implement the suggestion. But I do not know whether the two censuses have been integrated or continue to remain separate.

The agricultural census also illustrates serious case of missing something simple but vitally useful for the government in the mechanical thinking about a project. The only indicator available of inherent productivity of land is the rate of basic land revenue (at least in a large number of States). Although the census is no more than a census of land records, it did not include this simple item of recorded information. The Maharashtra census which included this item in 1985 also showed how the same census operation can be used to collect important items of information without extra cost. It collected data in 1985, from the records, on number of trees in the operational holding for "fuel" and "horticultural" purposes separately, and in the 1990 census, on classification of holders as males and females. Most importantly, it carried out my suggestion to tabulate the census results on a sample basis, to generate information for different classes of cultivators. Shows how the utility of a statistical project can be enhanced if its designers are sensitive to data needs of the government.

Availability of Data from Agricultural Census, 1995-96
and Input Survey, 1996-97

Major Classification	Sub-classification availability	Levels of
Phase-1		
1. Number and Area operated by Operational Holdings	• By size classes of 10 categories • By Gender • By Social Groups-S.C., S.T., and All Social Groups	State-wise and all-India
Phase-II		
2. Tenancy	• By Number and Area owned and Self operated • By leased-in area • By combination of owned and leased-in area • By Terms of leasing	State-wise and all-India
3. Land use	• By area sown • By fallow lands—current and other fallow separately • By cultivable (culturable) waste • By other uncultivated area, excluding fallow land	State-wise and all-India
4. Irrigation status	• By area irrigated—number of holding and area operated • By area unirrigated—no of holdings and area • By no. of holdings and area—partly irrigated and unirrigated area • By net area irrigated—no. of operational holdings and area irrigated	State-wise and all-India
5. Sources of irrigation	• By canal irrigation—no. of operational holdings and area • By Tanks irrigation—no. of operational holdings and area • By Wells irrigation—and area operational holdings and area • By other than above sources of irrigation—no. of operational holdings and area	State-wise and all-India

*Availability of Data from Agricultural Census, 1995-96
and Input Survey, 1996-97* (Contd.)

Major Classification	Sub-classification availability	Levels of
6. Number of Wells	• By well in use — With pumpsets — Without pumpsets • By tube wells — Electric — Diesel	State-wise and all-India
7. Cropping pattern	• By gross cropped area — Irrigated — Unirrigated • By crop-wise-details on — Number of operational holdings — Area irrigated — Area unirrigated	State-wise and all-India
Phase-III: Input Survey		
1. Distribution of	• By no of holdings of Major size-groups of Marginal, Small, Semi-medium. Medium and Large holdings • By area operated in each size-groups • By no. of parcels in each size groups	State-wise and all-India
2. Cropping intensity	• By area cropped once— Separately for Irrigated and Unirrigated • By area cropped Twice— under Irrigated conditions • By area cropped more than twice under Irrigated conditions • By area cropped more than once under Unirrigated conditions	State-wise and all-India
3. Usage of Chemical (inorganic) fertilizers	• By no. of operational holdings of Major size-groups — Growing one or more of crops — Growing and applying fertilizer for at least one of the crops grown	For Major crops All crops' Total; the data are presented separately for specific fertilizers like Urea, DAP, etc. State-wise and all-India

**Availability of Data from Agricultural Census, 1995-96
and Input Survey, 1996-97** *(Contd.)*

Major Classification	Sub-classification availability	Levels of
	— Area grown under High Yielding Variety	
	— Area grown under other variety	
	— Area treated with fertilizer out of area under HYV	
	— Area a treated with fertilizer out of area under Others	
	— Quantity of Fertilizers applied to the above K separately	
	— Quantity of Fertilizers applied to the above area under 'Other Variety'—N, P, K separately	
4. Usage of Biofertilizers	• Area treated by type of bio-fertilizer	
	• For major crops and all crops, total area, area treated with green manure, Rhizobium, Azetobactor, Blue green algae	
5. Usage of Organic	• By no of operational holdings of Major size-groups	For Major crops and All crops' Total; the data are presented separately for FYM, oilcakes, other organic manures
	— Growing one or more of crops	
	— Growing and applying fertilizer for at least one of the crops grown	State-wise and all-India
	— Area grown under High Yielding Variety	
	— Area grown under other variety	
	— Area treated with organic fertilizer out of area under HYV	
	— Area treated with	

Availability of Data from Agricultural Census, 1995-96
and Input Survey, 1996-97 (Contd.)

Major Classification	Sub-classification availability	Levels of
	organic fertilizer out of area under Others	
6. Usage of Pesticides	• Area treated with pesticides by crop	
7. Application of Certified Seeds	New items for 1996-97	State-wise and all-India
8. Area under Integrated Pest Management	New items for 1996-97	State-wise and all-India
9. Livestock	• Cattle—Male and Female separately	State-wise and all-India
	• Buffaloes—Male and Female separately	
	• Sheep	
	• Goats	
	• Horses and Ponies	
	• Donkeys	
	• Pigs	
	• Camels	
	• Others	
10. Agricultural Machinery and Implements	• By hand operated (14 items	State wise and all-India
	• Animal operated (16 items)	
	• Power operated (17 items)	
	• Miscellaneous (5 items)	
11. Agricultural Credit	• Number of holdings who took credit from	State-wise and all-India
	— Primary Agri. Credit Society	
	— Primary Land Development Bank	
	— Commercial Bank	
	— Rural Bank	
	• Amount of loan availed from above sources	
	• Loans taken by various categories of farmers for different agricultural purpose (fertilizers and other inputs)	
	• Break up of loan by long-term, medium-term and short-term	

12

Major Inputs

Three important types of input statistics are required for planning and policy purposes. The first relates to production and distribution of inputs like fertilizers, seeds, pesticides, insecticides and agricultural machinery (Table 12.1). It should be possible to compile most of these data with the cooperation of the concerned manufacturing companies and distribution agencies. Consumption of input crop-wise and according to holding size and other characteristics of the holding like irrigation, etc. are the second type of data required. These data are lacking at present. A standing committee set up under the chairmanship of a Member of the Planning Commission to evolve coordinated and integrated approach for improving the data base is seized of this problem and it is hoped some feasible solution would emerge in the near future. The last category of input data deal with the yardstick of production in relation to fertilizers, seed rates, irrigation, pesticides, and insecticides, etc. This information can be obtained by undertaking appropriate statistical analysis of the data collected under the experiments conducted on cultivators' fields following well-planned sampling procedures as also the controlled experiments conducted at agriculture research stations.

This chapter is concerned primarily with the first category dealing with fertilizers, seeds, etc. In addition to the work already done, IASRI has to play an important role in this respect. Data on the use of inputs for recent years is as in Table 12.1.

FERTILIZERS

With regard to fertilizers, necessary data relate to production, imports, quantities distributed by the different agencies, namely, Government, cooperatives and private traders, consumption of fertilizers, stocks held at different levels and prices. The available data are incomplete and suffer from several inadequacies. First, information on cropwise consumption of fertilizers is not available. Secondly, the data on consumption do not tally with those worked out on the basis of production, imports and changes in stocks. In addition, more reliable information is also required with regard to consumption by different size classes of

Table 12.1: Use of Agricultural Inputs

Programme	Unit	1980-81	1990-91	1992-93	1993-94	1994-95	1995-96	1996-97	1997-98	1998-99	1999-2k
I. Seeds											
I. Production of Breeder Seeds	'000' Qt	5.27	33.89	36.00	3~.00	40.11	43.36	46.03	46.13	38.99	47.76
II. Production of Foundation Seeds	L.Qt.	-	3.35	3.93	4.06	4.73	4.76	5.76	6.84	6.75	7.10
III. Distribution of Certified/ Quality Seeds	L.Qt.	25.01	57.10	60.33	62.20	65.86	69.90	73.27	78.79	83.00	91.00
2. Consumption of Chemical Fertilizers											
I. Nitrogenous (N)	L.T	36.78	79.97	84.27	87.89	95.07	98.23	103.02	109.02	113.54	N.A
II. Phosphatic (P)	L.T	12.14	32.21	28.44	26.69	29.32	28.98	29.77	39.14	41.12	N.A
III. Potassic (K)	L.T	6.24	13.28	8.84	9.08	11.25	11.56	10.29	13.72	13.32	N.A
Total (I.+II.+III.)	L.T	55.16	125.4	121.55	123.66	135.64	138.77	143.08	161.88	167.98	N.A
3. Consumption of Pesticides (Technical Grade Material)	'000' T.	45.00	75.00	70.79	63.65	61.36	61.26	56.11	52.24	49.16	N.A
4. Consumption of Plant Nutrients per unit of gross cropped area											
I. Nitrogenous (N)	Kg.	21.31	43.02	45.40	47.10	50.56	52.65	55.22	58.44	60.86	N.A
II. Phosphatic (P)	Kg.	7.03	17.33	15.32	14.31	15.59	15.53	15.96	20.98	22.04	N.A
III. Potassic (K)	Kg.	3.61	7.14	4.76	4.87	5.98	6.20	5.52	7.36	7.14	N.A
Total (I.+II.+III.)	Kg.	31.95	67.49	65.48	66.27	72.13	74.38	76.69	86.77	90.04	N.A
Gross Cropped Area (000 ha.)	'000' ha	172,630	185,740	185,700	186,595	188,053	187,470	189,540	-	-	-

Table 12.1: Use of Agricultural Inputs (Contd.)

Programme	Unit	1980-81	1990-91	1992-93	1993-94	1994-95	1995-96	1996-97	1997-98	1998-99	1999-2k
5. Area Covered under Soil Conservation (Cumulative)	M.ha	24.37	34.90	36.51	37.30	38.20	39.30	N.A.	N.A -	N.A	N.A
6. Irrigated Area	M. ha	54.1	70.8	74.5	75.7	77.5	79.3	80.7	81.8	83.6	-
Major and Medium	M. ha	22.7	26.0	26.6	27.2	27.5	27.9	28.4	28.9	30.1	-
Minor @	M. ha	31.4	44.8	47.9	49.1	50.2	51.4	52.3	52.9	53.5	-

Note : 1. * Provisional, E : Estimated

2. @ : The figures for minor irrigation indicate the net benefit after allowing for seepage.

Source : Agriculture Staistics at a Glance, 2000, Department of Agriculture & Cooperation Ministry of Agriculture holdings, dosages of fertilizers, the time of their responses, etc. Wherever necessary, special surveys should be carried out to obtain this information. Data on inputs were also collected through the Agricultural Holdings Survey conducted by the NSS in its Twenty-sixth Round. It is also possible to collect these data through the Comprehensive Scheme for Cost of Cultivation of Crops.

Data on the consumption of various kinds of fertilizers is obtained by periodic reports from the State Governments (Table 12.2). These reports provide information on the initial stocks of fertilizers, the receipts and sales during the period and closing stocks. Though these data are expected to cover the entire wholesale distribution system, private and public, in practice reliable data relate only to the public wholesale distribution. Based on this formula, annual publication—Fertilizer Statistics—issued by the Fertilizer Association of India, gives All-India and State-wise distribution of various types of fertilizers. The latest issue (in the series) relates to the year 1999-2000 and the first publication was issued in August, 1956. Along with distribution, the publication provides valuable information practically on all aspects of fertilizers including production and related statistics.

While this information over a period of time may give a reasonably accurate picture of actual consumption by farmers, it is not a reliable indicator as to the year to year changes in actual consumption. This would require information and inventory levels at the retailing points and with the farmers themselves. The published data cover transactions only up to the wholesale point. Sometime back a comprehensive reporting system extending right up to the farmers is reported to have been designed by the Indian Institute of Management, Ahmedabad. However, judging from the latest publication of Fertilizer Statistics, this scheme does not appear to have made much progress.

A major limitation of the fertilizer statistics and one which is derived from its coverage, is that it does not give accurate idea of actual consumption in a particular area. The statistics give only an idea of distribution at the wholesale level in that area. Apart from the fact that this may differ from the actual purchases by the farmers, there is also the possibility that what is recorded as having been distributed in a particular area may not all be used in the same area.

A third and more serious lacuna in the data relates to the distribution of total fertilizer consumption by crops. Some information on the proportion of area under different crops receiving fertilizers is available from the analysis of ancillary data collected at the time of crop cutting by National Sample Survey. But information as to fertilizer use on different crop varieties under different irrigation conditions, is not available on a regular basis. Recent surveys by the Programme Evaluation Organization give data on both the proportion of area fertilized and the quantum of fertilizers applied on high yielding and local varieties of major cereal crops. Some information in this aspect is provided by the survey conducted by the

Table 12.2: State-wise Consumption of Fertilizer

('000 tonnes)

Zone/State	1997-98				1998-99			
	N	P205	K20	Total	N	P205	K20	Total
NORTH	4112.65	1065.25	121.45	5299.35	4286.07	1028.78	115.49	5430.34
Haryana	649.93	181.80	3.79	835.52	662.67	171.77	3.95	838.39
Himachal Pradesh	27.00	4.38	3.47	34.85	29.13	5.22	4.20	38.55
Jammu & Kashmir	46.09	12.88	0.93	59.90	51.30	17.40	2.14	70.84
Punjab	1004.80	287.39	22.25	1314.44	1081.06	275.47	18.74	1375.27
Uttar Pradesh	2365.04	574.59	90.83	3030.46	2447.87	557.57	86.09	3091.53
Chandigarh	0.42	-	0.01	0.43	0.29	-	0.01	0.30
Delhi	19.37	4.21	0.18	23.76	13.75	1.35	0.36	15.46
SOUTH	2286.54	1050.21	651.12	3987.86	2540.05	1146.28	625.04	4311.36
Andhra Pradesh	1074.70	490.10	129.79	1694.59	1284.26	560.47	163.19	2007.92
Karnataka	605.06	314.93	189.24	1109.23	638.63	335.95	174.21	1148.79
Kerala	86.96	45.23	87.30	219.49	86.04	42.53	52.92	181.49
Tamil Nadu	507.58	194.95	239.98	942.51	518.61	202.07	230.21	950.89
Pondicherry	12.00	4.90	4.66	21.56	12.26	5.11	4.43	21.80
A & N Islands	0.20	0.10	0.05	0.35	0.25	0.15	0.08	0.48
Lakshadweep	0.04	-	0.10	0.14	-	-	-	-
EAST	1477.58	504.27	285.67	2267.52	1536.96	572.57	304.31	2413.84
Arunachal Pradesh	0.33	0.13	0.10	0.56	0.36	0.14	0.10	0.60
Assam	38.42	15.07	17.76	71.25	47.68	20.56	9.86	78.10
Bihar	645.19	159.41	55.87	860.47	666.48	172.66	55.85	894.99
Manipur	11.36	1.32	0.51	13.19	15.39	1.50	0.20	17.09

Table 12.2: State-wise Consumption of Fertilizer (Contd.)

('000 tonnes)

Zone/State	1997-98				1998-99			
	N	P205	K20	Total	N	P205	K20	Total
Meghalaya	2.21	1.01	0.08	3.30	2.81	1.38	0.15	4.34
Mizoram	0.20	0.44	0.33	0.97	0.25	0.53	0.37	1.15
Nagaland	0.28	0.23	0.06	0.57	0.39	0.35	0.06	0.80
Orissa	195.84	55.51	39.48	290.83	194.58	60.38	44.21	299.17
Sikkim	0.48	0.28	0.07	0.83	0.57	0.30	0.05	0.92
Tripura	6.34	2.32	1.77	10.43	6.97	1.81	0.98	9.76
West Bengal	546.62	259.85	169.64	976.11	579.69	305.77	192.48	1077.94
Tea Board (N.E)	30.31	8.70	-	39.01	21.79	7.19	-	28.98
WEST	3025.03	1293.82	314.22	4633.07	2990.70	1364.52	286.69	4641.91
Gujarat	702.77	264.83	60.29	1027.89	690.73	267.57	61.36	1019.66
Madhya Pradesh	747.48	403.01	55.63	1206.12	738.16	448.37	39.21	1225.74
Maharashtra	979.00	434.00	191.00	1604.00	1025.00	458.00	178.00	1661.00
Rajasthan	591.85	190.06	5.52	787.43	532.51	188.48	6.13	727.12
Goa	3.11	1.51	1.70	6.32	3.39	1.61	1.93	6.93
Daman and Diu	0.22	0.10	0.05	0.37	0.24	0.10	0.05	0.39
Dadra and Nagar Haveli	0.60	0.31	0.03	0.94	0.67	0.39	0.01	1.07
All India	10901.80	3913.55	1372.46	16187.81	11353.78	4112.15	1331.53	16797.46

Source: Fertilizer Statistics, 1998-99. The Fertilizer Association of India, Ministry of Agriculture, New Delhi.

National Council of Applied Economic Research. While these are useful additions to our knowledge about fertilizer use, a great deal more of data is required to be collected on a periodic basis and in much greater detail if we are to get reasonably accurate picture by major agroclimatic regions and by irrigated and unirrigated areas, of the trends in fertilizer use by crops. Similarly, more detailed data on the timing and quantum of fertilizer use for different crops and for different regions is necessary to plan the optimal distribution and stocking of fertilizers.

A scheme was started during the First and Second Five Year Plans by the Indian Council of Agricultural Research to carry out sample surveys on fertilizer and other manuring practices in selected districts in different States. The broad objective of these surveys was to estimate crop-wise consumption of different fertilizers and manures, areas benefited therefrom, rates of application, types of farmers using fertilizers, associated cultural practices, etc. In these districts about 800 cultivators were randomly selected to obtain information of crops grown, fertilizers and manures applied, source of procurement of fertilizers, time and method of their application, irrigation and its source, seed rate, variety of seed, preparatory and inter-cultural operations, etc.

Organic Manures

There is no accurate, estimate of either the quantity of organic manures used or acreage benefited from it. Some data were collected by the NSS about the cost of cultivation and published in their Report No. 32. The data pertain to the census regions of the country. Similar information was also collected by the Rural Credit Survey and the Farm Management Survey Reports.

The information already collected by the surveys gives a rough idea, but it has little utility for micro or even macro type of planning. The Directorate of Economics and Statistics is collecting some information regarding the compost pits dug and compost prepared by big panchayats as well as municipalities as a part of 'Grow More Food Campaign Statistics'. The documents which use these data publish the achievements in respect of urban and rural compost State-wise.

The 'Indian Agricultural Statistics' provide information about the area green manured for each District in the country. These figures, however differ widely from those released by the Plans.

If such data are to be of any practical utility, one should know not only the absolute quantity, but also the type and quality of the organic manure being applied to various crops in different parts of the country. The need is to have a cropwise data about the application of various organic manures. There is also the need to express the quantity of manure applied in some uniform unit, which is properly defined.[1]

---

[1]Data quite often given in cart loads vary in the size and weight of the cart load from area to area.

Fertilizer Consumption

Agricultural activities provide the much needed food and revenue for the developing countries but excessive use of the plant nutrients can degrade the natural resources. Poor farming practices can cause soil erosion and loss of fertility. Efforts to increase productivity through the use of chemical fertilizer, pesticides and intensive irrigation have environmental costs and health impacts, cautions the World Development Indicators.

Fertilizer consumption has been increasing recently the world over mainly because of increased use of nutrients by the developing countries. The high income countries have been able to reduce their consumption per hectare of arable land. On the other hand, low income countries more than doubled their fertilizer use in the past one and half decades. The upper middle income nations just maintained levels of nutrient consumption while the lower middle income group could effect a steep reduction (Chart I).

Among individual nations, the European countries with the exception of the U.K. were successful in bringing down the use of fertilizers. Bulgaria for example could reduce fertilizer consumption by one fifth in the one and half decades (1979-97). Japan too was successful in cutting down the fertilizer use, India increased nutient use more than two-and half times during the period under reference (Chart II).

Chart II shows that the use of tractors by advanced nations is prominent while the developing nations use them sparingly and instead apply conventional methods to plough the fields.

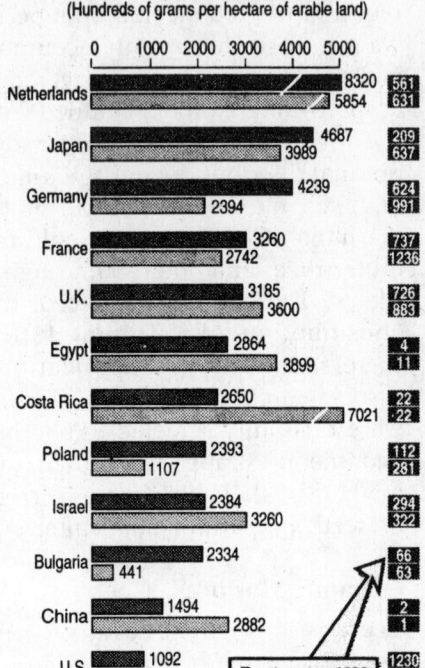

Chart III How Much They Used

(Hundreds of grams per hectare of arable land)

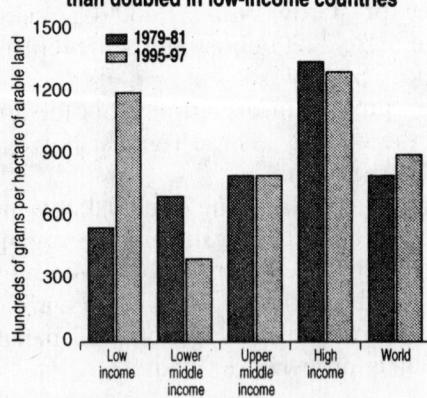

Chart I Fertilizer consumption has more than doubled in low-income countries

Legend: 1979-81, 1995-97

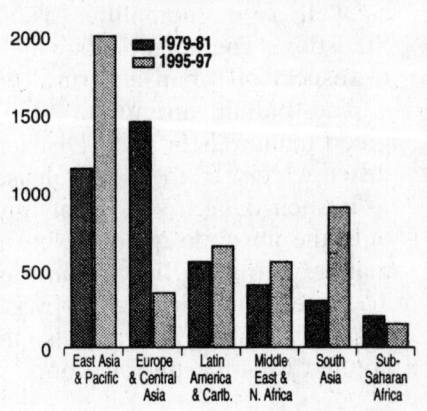

... and in East Asia and the Pacific

Legend: 1979-81, 1995-97

Source: World Development Indicators, 2000

Sample Surveys for a Study of Manuring

The ICAR has been carrying out sample surveys on fertilizers and other manuring practices in selected districts in various states during the previous Five Year Plans. The broad objective of the surveys is to estimate crop-wise consumption of different fertilizers and manures, area benefited therefrom, rates of application, associated agricultural practices, etc. Such information is useful in studying how the practices adopted by the farmers differ from those recommended by the agriculture departments for increasing agricultural production. It also enables the authorities responsible for developmental activities to observe what changes are taking place in the cultivation practices over the years and what steps may be taken for further progress. It is also useful in formulating realistic targets for fertilizer consumption.

In the light of the changes taking place in agricultural technology, it is necessary to widen the scope of the surveys. The objective of surveys during the various Plans has, thus, been to collect representative data on farming practices adopted by the progressive cultivators and other cultivators in areas where the spread of high yielding varieties has made a considerable headway. The districts to be selected will be those where high yielding varieties of rice, wheat or millets have been appreciably patronized.

IMPROVED SEEDS

Data on seed production is available in respect of seeds produced and distributed by the National Seeds Corporation (Tables 12.3 and 12.4). Additional information (Table 12.4) is also available regarding production and distribution of certified seeds. In addition, information on seeds distributed through Government agencies in the States is also available with the State Governments; but this information is not compiled at present at the Centre. Arrangements are also necessary for collecting the information from the private seeds companies. Data on seed rates of different crops/varieties should be collected to assess the requirement of seeds in different seasons and regions.

There seems to be considerable scope in regard to the improvement of the system of collection of data for acreage under improved varieties of crops. At present, the assessment is made by the Department of Agriculture through their subordinate officers. The Director of Agriculture collects this information from the Divisional Deputy Directors of Agriculture who in turn compile the information received from the various District Agriculture Officers. The District Agriculture Officer bases the figures on the information supplied by the Agriculture Officers in the Blocks and Agriculture assistants in the non-Block area. Acreage figures are calculated on the basis of improved seed distributed in different areas. The total area of distribution is calculated on the basis of average seed rate per hectare. Natural spread of the improved varieties is also taken into account, the assumption being:[2]

---

[2]Report of the Committee on Plan Projects, Survey of Coverage by Improved Varieties, Madhya Pradesh, Planning Commission.

Table 12.3: Production and Distribution of Breeder Seeds of Different Crops

(quintals)

Crop	1992-93		1993-94		1994-95		1995-96		1996-97		1997-98		1998-99		1999-2000	
	D	P	D	P	D	P	D	P	D	P	D	P	D	P	D	P
Wheat	5634.80	9626.12	5861.95	7968.40	5404.80	10033.27	7330.10	12715.52	8094.45	14305.91	9382.60	9926.16	7915.30	9595.20	7255.20	6375.50
Paddy	744.55	1239.47	511.40	835.90	602.78	1039.40	728.16	1186.60	874.77	2263.54	736.75	1181.18	974.19	1121.87	1111.65	1656.38
Sorghum	98.98	99.14	92.91	145.63	63.85	157.81	42.42	314.05	125.00	240.71	134.46	200.62	56.00	153.49	64.54	55.50
Maize	109.62	26.79	28.59	28.59	30.36	49.12	30.84	127.19	29.76	39.64	48.32	32.64	30.00	72.14	33.84	79.26
Barley	28.40	70.96	38.00	161.66	25.60	95.35	77.87	144.78	120.85	200.30	149.90	142.90	163.55	158.40	94.20	123.20
Pearl Millet	29.49	33.74	15.56	27.32	17.26	76.80	17.02	34.32	18.96	18.44	26.58	5.86	12.38	8.19	14.58	5.32
Small Millet	5.83	18.39	8.92	10.07	13.82	39.62	10.32	44.70	12.42	15.25	15.17	15.73	6.05	9.05	8.84	9.80
Pulse Crops	2650.34	2694.45	1483.79	2186.64	1814.56	1989.79	2836.40	2168.27	3054.39	3169.64	3334.98	3806.30	4190.01	3981.53	4103.82	5120.05
Jute/M&S	16.88	10.42	10.45	9.88	9.72	4.93	18.69	10.60	11.68	11.77	15.02	8.83	8.54	7.70	9.45	6.08
Cotton	180.86	1109.61	105.94	838.52	135.37	353.92	145.73	447.30	235.46	356.27	90.83	207.54	152.35	149.13	139.31	271.57
Forage Crops	341.75	300.10	353.95	410.93	283.58	381.95	360.34	413.72	366.57	467.97	343.41	447.42	329.59	214.01	420.47	427.16
Nine Oilseeds	7893.15	7689.19	6715.51	8103.46	11908.31	7708.33	15817.47	8183.80	10845.21	8398.17	10737.61	10654.34	12615.95	7554.18	10031.55	9448.15
Total	17671.94	23001.21	15225.17	20227.00	20310.03	21930.29	27415.36	25790.85	23789.52	29487.61	25015.63	29489.91	23024.89	—	23287.45	23577.97

Note: P — Production
D — Distribution

Source: Assistant Director General (Seeds), Indian Council of Agriculture Research, New Delhi.

Table 12.4 Distribution of Certified / Quality Seeds

(lakh quintals)

Year	Cereals	Pulses	Nine Oilseeds	Fibers	Potato	Others	Total
1986-87	35.27	3.39	6.29	-	-	-	-
1987-88	35.44	3.46	6.54	-	-	-	-
1988-89	33.94	3.48	11.12	-	-	-	-
1989-90	34.82	3.52	8.76	-	-	-	-
1990-91	34.70	3.41	8.59	2.16	7.97	0.27	57.10
1991-92	35.35	3.29	9.66	2.03	6.90	0.27	57.50
1992-93	36.72	3.40	10.75	2.09	7.10	0.27	60.33
1993-94	38.74	3.62	11.38	2.01	6.17	0.28	62.20
1994-95	41.35	3.60	12.01	2.20	6.62	0.08	65.86
1995-96	44.03	3.56	12.64	2.58	6.85	0.24	69.90
1996-97	46.43	4.19	12.53	3.18	6.69	0.25	73.27
1997-98	51.78	3.89	12.87	3.21	6.83	0.21	78.79
1998-99*	53.40	5.00	12.50	3.40	8.48	0.12	82.90

Note : 1 lakh = 0.1 million, * Target
Source : 1. Agricultural Statistics at a Glance, 2000, Directorate of Economics and Statistics, Ministry of Agriculture, Govt. of India
2. Indian Agriculture in Brief, 27th edition, 2000. Directorate of Economics and Statistics, Ministry of Agriculture, Govt. of India.

1. Paddy and jowar   Five times the area covered by direct distribution.
2. Wheat and gram   Three times the area covered by direct distribution.
3. Other crops   Four times the area covered by direct distribution.

No information is collected for the area under different varieties.

There are also a number of field surveys which have tried to get a measure of area under high yielding varieties by direct enquiry from the farmers. Most of the surveys, however, were confined to relatively small areas. The significant exceptions are the surveys of the Programme Evaluation Organization and of the NCAER which are nation-wide in their scope and also provide valuable information on the use of other inputs as well as costs and returns both for high yielding and traditional varieties. Besides, information supplied by the Annual Administration Reports of the Department of Agriculture about the coverage under these high yielding varieties, there is no systematic method of making them available to the research workers. Annual Reports of the Agricultural Prices Commission on Rabi and Kharif Foodgrains, however, publish some of the available data regarding the area under high yielding varieties under various foodgrains State-wise. Although no information is available about the average yields from high yielding varieties separately on a regular basis, the publication of the United States Department of Agriculture—New H.Y.V. in India's Agriculture and Outlook for Grain Production, June 1972, issued by the Economic Research Survey provides a comparative picture of the area as well as yield under high yielding and traditional varieties under irrigated as well as unirrigated crops. Since yield data separately from high yielding varieties are not being collected by any institution/organization on a continuing basis, the reliability of the data is a little doubtful.

Even with regard to the area coverage, the basis for the estimated provides by the administrative departments is not very clear. They are obviously not estimated from systematic surveys. It is believed that in general, the assessment is derived on the norms based on the quantity of improved seeds released and the average seed rate per hectare. This might be a reasonably reliable procedure in the case of hybrids and other improved seeds that are produced and marketed by organized agencies and where specific names of the varieties are clearly laid down. But in the case of crops like wheat and paddy, where the improved seeds can be produced by the farmer himself, such estimates can be quite unreliable. Though even here defining and identifying of what constitutes an improved variety will continue to present problems.

It is apparent that the procedure adopted for the determination of the area under improved varieties of crops cannot be considered as satisfactory. In the first place, it cannot be taken that all the seed which has been distributed, was used for sowing. Secondly, the assumption in respect of natural spread is hypothetical. Unless, therefore, the information is collected on the basis of adequate random sampling, much reliance cannot be placed on the figures. To start with, the Team[3] recommends that a pilot survey for the assessment of coverage of improved seed by random sampling in Raipur and Bilaspur Divisions for rice and Bhopal and Indore for wheat may be taken up. Besides the collection of information from the cultivators, samples of seed should also be taken from the standing crops, threshing floors, stores, etc. for conducting check tests for germination, purity weed seeds, other crop contents and disease or pest infection, etc. With the introduction of high yielding varieties of seeds, the importance of data on seeds has become all the more great.

PLANT PROTECTION

The existing data about Plant Protection measures are those released by the Plan Documents and Bulletins issued by the important Development Departments of different commodities. Basic information in this respect

---

[3]Report of the Committee on Plan Projects, Survey of Coverage by Improved Varieties, Madhya Pradesh, Planning Commission.

about the gross area covered is released in the Annual Administration Reports of the Central Ministry of Agriculture, Department of Agriculture. The figures released give a composite picture of seed treatment, ground operations, aerial spraying, weed control and rodent control measures. These publications also provide information about the various policy measures adopted during the year and the progress made in various projects in respect of plant protection.

A Bulletin—Pesticides Production, Consumption and Usage—issued by the Pesticides Association of India provides valuable information at one place regarding production and consumption of pesticides class-crop and region-wise as well as area covered.

There are no regular surveys or any other statistical method by which estimates of area covered by plant protection measures are made. This, however, depends on possibly the total quantity of various types of chemicals used for the purpose, multiplied by the unit yard stick. The reliability of these data may thus be considered a little better than that of the area covered by the improved seeds. Besides improving the data on plant protection measures, there is also the need to have regular information about the areas affected by pests and diseases. No such information is being collected at present on an all-India level.

The available information with all defects is being published by the ad hoc reports of the various Departments of Agriculture in the different States. At the Centre, information is provided by the Directorate of Economics and Statistics in their annual publication—Indian Agriculture in Brief. The latest issue provides these data for 1999-2000 (Tables 12.5 and 12.5A).

Table 12.5 Consumption of Different Pesticides

(M.T (technical grade))

Pesticides	1994-95	1995-96	1996-97
DDT	-	-	-
BHC	9154	8033	4167
Aldrin	-	-	-
Other Chlorohydro-Carbons	4298	4239	3904
Methyl Parathion	2237	2170	2236
Malathion	2622	2618	2695
Fenitrothion	448	334	490
Other organophosphate	17837	18058	17927
Synthetic Pyrethroids	1293	1584	1347
Carbomate Insecticides	2768	1744	1867
Sulphur	3315	2961	2364
Lime sulphur	33	50	15
Copper Compound	2536	2542	2416
Dithiocarbomate	3797	3620	3529
Other Fungicides	1447	1294	1546

Table 12.5 Consumption of Different Pesticides (Contd.)

(M.T (technical grade)

Pesticides	1994-95	1995-96	1996-97
Seeds dressing/organomercurials and others	141	96	99
2, 4-D	612	467	621
Triazine	472	207	353
Other herbicides	3158	2956	3429
Urea derivatives	2568	2410	2657
Plant growth regulators	51	53	53
Bromide	62	64	57
Aluminium phosphide	396	348	220
Other Fumigants	34	26	27
Anti Co-gulants	4	4	3
Other rodenticides	248	206	229
Misc. Pesticides	1826	5176	3863
Total	61357	61260	56114

Source : 1. Directorate of PP and Q & S, Faridabad
2. Indian Agriculture in brief, 27th edition, 2000. Directorate of Economics and Statistics, Ministry of Agriculture, Government of India.

Table 12.5 : Consumption of Technical grade Pesticides

(tonnes)

Name	1971	1994-95*
Insecticides	22013	51755
Fungicides	2067	22895
Herbicides	30	7620
Rodenticides	195	1860
Others	NA	900
Total	24305	85030

Note : * Projected
Source : *Compendium of Environment Statistics, 1999,* Central Statistical Organisation, Department of Statistics, Ministry of Planning and Programming Implementation, Govt. of India.

IMPROVED CULTIVATION PRACTICES

Apart from improved seeds, fertilizers and agricultural implements, improved cultivation practices which relate to methodological changes for field operations like line sowing, transplanting and other agricultural operations like dry farming techniques and multiple cropping practices, etc., contribute equally towards better agriculture. Here again, the basic source of information on the diffusion of these practices appears to be the reports of the administrative agencies. These reports suffer from all the limitations outlined in the case of high yielding seed varieties and the only way to get reliable data would be through periodic sample surveys. Such surveys have in fact been attempted by the National Sample Survey but these surveys generally provide estimates of only the proportion of area covered by these practices but not the intensity of their use. Partly the problem is of certain vagueness as to what constitutes an improved practice, as for example, in the case of dry farming techniques. Also if surveys are to be a reliable basis for formulating programmes and assessing their actual performance, they have to be conducted in areas where specific schemes to propagate the practice have been taken up. The designing of a proper sample survey which takes these dimensions into account would seem to present much more difficult problems than say, designing a survey to estimate the area under and the impact of fertilizers or improved seeds. The nature of these problems and the possible ways in which they could be overcome at reasonable costs do not appear to have received attention they deserve.

AGRICULTURAL MACHINERY AND POWER

The quinquennial livestock census is the only source of regular information about agricultural machinery and implements. Some changes have been introduced from census to census as discussed earlier. Information about ghanies (indigenous oil presses) was included for the first time in 1951. It was further divided according to capacity in 1956 into the following categories:

(a) Five kg and more.

(b) Less than 5 kg.

The Indian Central Oilseeds Committee published a leaflet, 'Power Oil Milling Industry—1954-56'. It supplies State-wise information about the number the oil mills, number of crushing machinery installed in the different oil mills, seed-wise break-up of the quantities of oilseeds crushed, oils and oilcakes produced in the mills.

Statistics of number of agricultural machinery and implements are collected through the quinquennial livestock censuses organized by the Directorate of Economics and Statistics. Separate data are available in respect of ploughs—wooden and iron, improved harrows or cultivators, improved seed drills, improved threshers, rotary chaff cutters, sprayers and dusters, carts, sugarcane crushers worked with power and bullocks, oil engines with pumps for irrigation purposes, electric pumps for irrigation purposes, persian wheels, tractors—government and private, power tillers and ghanis—five kilograms and over and less than five kilograms.

The coverage of implements in the Livestock Census is not quite comprehensive. There are about 22-25 types of agricultural implements in use in the country for different types of operations, but the census covers only a few of them.

The Indian Council of Agricultural Research also conducts surveys on the agricultural implements. The first all-India survey of indigenous agricultural implement was carried out in all the States except Himachal Pradesh. The survey covered important implements (viz. ploughs cultivators, harrow hoes, rollers, seed drills, harvesting implement and ridges), their descriptions and uses. The report also indicates the lines on which future research on agricultural implements should proceed. The other surveys under the Third Five Year Plan covered other implements like water lift, chaff cutter, groundnut decorticator, rice processing equipment, threshing devices, other common cart equipment bullock carts, etc.

COOPERATION

The 'Statistical Statements relating to the Cooperative Movement in India' issued by the Reserve Bank of India, give some of the main features of the progress of the Cooperative Movement during the year under review. These also furnish State-wise figures of the number of societies and their membership. Separate figures are available for the different types of societies.

The societies are classified as agricultural if the members are mostly agriculturists or if the main activity is agriculture. It may be mentioned that most of the primary societies are agricultural and their main business is to provide credit to the agriculturists. The abstract statement also furnish State-wise figures of the amount of working capital and loan transactions of primary societies. Information is also given for each State regarding the number of societies, number of members of primary societies and number of villages or towns covered by the primary societies. The statements also contain information on credit, marketing, distribution, cost of management, profit and loss, etc. of the primary credit societies. Besides, interest rates on advances are also given.

The detailed statements give data regarding operations of State and Central Banks, State Non-credit Societies and Central Non-credit Societies. These statements also give details of operations of Agricultural Credit Societies, Agricultural Non-credit Societies, Central Land Mortgage Banks, Primary Land Mortgage Banks, Agricultural Marketing Societies and other Agricultural Processing Societies, as follows:

Agricultural Credit Societies

The statistics are given separately for large-sized societies and small-sized societies. State-wise figures of number of societies are given separately for limited and unlimited societies. Data regarding number of villages served by societies, their population, and number of members are given according to States. Figures of working capital, paid-up capital, reserves, deposits and other borrowings are given under liabilities, whereas figures of cash on hand, balances with banks, investments, loans, etc. are given under assets. Items of operations cover figures on credit, marketing, distribution, cost of management, profit and loss, etc. State-wise figures for grain banks are also given separately on such items.

Agricultural Non-credit Societies. The statements contain State-wise figures of number of societies, number of members, total liabilities, working capital, paid-up capital, reserves, borrowings, total assets, investments, loans, profit and loss, etc.

Central and Primary Land Mortgage Banks

For the Central Land Mortgage Banks, State-wise figures are available on the number of members, total liabilities, working capital, paid-up capital, reserves, deposits, other borrowings, other liabilities, total assets, cash-investments, loans, interest and other assets, etc. For these Banks State-wise figures are also given for debentures issued, borrowings, deposits, advances made and cost of management, etc. Similar information is given separately in respect of primary land mortgage banks.

Agricultural Marketing Societies and Other Agricultural Processing Societies

Details of operations are also given for State and Regional Marketing Societies, Primary Marketing Societies, Sugarcane Supply Societies, Milk Supply Unions and Societies, Cotton Ginning and Pressing Societies, etc.

Tables regarding number, membership and financial position of various cooperative societies are also published in the 'Statistical Abstract of the Indian Union' issued by the Central Statistical Organization of the Cabinet Secretariat. Statistics on loans advanced to different cooperative societies, etc. were given by the Reserve Bank in its 'Technical Report on All-India Rural Credit Survey, Volume III.'

CREDIT

The Reserve Bank of India has been conducting periodical comprehensive surveys of the rural credit situation. These surveys provide a good basis for estimating the total gross and net investment, the sources through which they are financed as well as the problems at a point of time and of the change in these relevant dimensions over time. In so far as the institutional credit channel such as the cooperative system, nationalized commercial banks and the term lending institutions are concerned, comprehensive data are available on a yearly basis. Two major problems of analysis and interpreting this data relate to the extent to which the purpose for which credit taken ostensibly corresponds to the use to which it is actually put and the accuracy of data regarding overdues especially in the case of cooperatives. The latter is particularly a serious problem, although the published data do give estimates of overdues at the end of each year, there seems to be a general feeling that the extent of overdues tends to be underestimated. There would also appear to be room for some intensive studies of the overall financial position of the relatively small farmers and to assess the success of various programmes designed to provide them access to short and medium term credit at reasonable terms.

13

Agricultural Labour— Employment and Wages

PRESENT POSITION OF AGRICULTURAL LABOUR IN INDIA

Agricultural labour is provided mostly by economically and socially backward sections; poor sections from the tribes also swell their ranks. It may be divided into four types:
  (a) Landless labourers who are attached to the landlords;
  (b) Landless labourers who are personally independent but who work exclusively for others;
  (c) Petty farmers with tiny bits of land who devote most of their time working for others; and
  (d) Farmers who have economic holdings but who have one or more of their sons and dependants working for other prosperous farmers.

The first group of agricultural workers has been more or less in the position of serfs or slaves; they are also known as bonded labour. They do not normally receive wages in cash but are generally paid in kind. They have to work for their masters and cannot shift from one to another. They have to provide begar or forced labour. In some cases, they have to offer cash and also supply fowls and goats to their masters. Among the other groups mentioned above the second and the third are quite important. The problem of landless labourers is the most serious problem in the rural sector.

FIRST AGRICULTURAL LABOUR ENQUIRY

Magnitude of Agricultural Labour

Accurate figures about the number, income, standard of living, etc., of rural labour are not available. But some information is available in the form of the reports of committees and commissions.

A comprehensive first All-India Agricultural Labour Enquiry was conducted by the Ministry of Labour in 1950-51 in about 800 villages covering a sample of 11,000 agricultural labour families. Valuable data on employment and unemployment, wages and earnings of individual

308

earners and size and composition, earning strength, income, etc. of agricultural labour families had been thrown up by this Enquiry. The Reports of this Enquiry was published in 1954-55. The Second Agricultural Labour Enquiry was undertaken in 1956-57 by the Ministry of Labour. This Enquiry was conducted in 3,600 villages covering in all about 28,560 agricultural labour households. The report of this Enquiry was published in 1960.

The First Agricultural Labour Enquiry[1] was conducted in 1950-51 in three stages through three different schedules—the General Village, the General Family and the Intensive Family Schedules and covered a sample of 800 villages selected on the basis of stratified sampling. In the General Village Schedule broad information on the economy of the village available either from the village records or from local enquiries was collected and the results published in the Report under review in two volumes. Volume I of this Report contains all-India and State-wise information on quantitative analysis of agricultural labour families, wages and conditions of employment of attached and casual workers, fixation of minimum wages in agriculture, and 'begar' or involuntary labour. There are different modes of payments of wages to agricultural labour, viz. in cash, in kind and partly in cash and partly in kind. For purposes of this Enquiry, the payment in kind and perquisites were evaluated at ruling retail prices to arrive at the all inclusive average wage rates. Data regarding the existence of 'begar' or involuntary labour are also given in the Report. 'Forced labour or compulsory labour' was defined to mean "all work or service extracted from a person against his will either free or on payment of wages which were not a sufficient inducement to perform the work willingly". Names of Unions of Agricultural Workers in the various States along with their headquarters and membership are also given as an annexure. A separate chapter deals with wages paid to agricultural workers on Government farms.

Volume II of the Report contains statistical tables giving the following information: (a) distribution of both agricultural and other families according to different occupations, average size of the family and the relative importance of different occupations followed by the agricultural and non-agricultural population in the sample villages; (b) land utilization including information on extent of cultivable, uncultivable and cultivated land with a further break-up of cultivated area into irrigated and unirrigated and single crop area; (c) area under principal crops showing the suitability of land in each village for different kinds of crops; and (d) average time and piece rates of wages for each operation according to different methods of payment, i.e. in cash and/or kind, perquisites with quantitative details and their evaluation in terms of cash together with the average number of hours worked in 1949-50 for men, women and children separately. Frequency distribution of daily wage operations

---

[1]Issued by the Ministry of Labour.

in respect of men, women and children are also given. Average retail prices per maund of important cereals and pulses with and without perquisites for various agricultural operations are also published for 1938-39 and 1949-50.

A summary report of the First Agricultural Labour Enquiry was published in a publication—Agricultural Labour, how they work and live. This study presents in a nutshell the main facts relating to the working and living of agricultural labour and the essential statistics emerging out of the first enquiry. The statistics presented in this brochure may be broadly classified into: (a) background data, and (b) data relating to agricultural labour.

The statistics under group (a) cover area, land utilization, population, occupational structure of rural families and size and distribution of cultivated holdings. Those under group (b) relate to wages, employment, mode of wage payment, wage rates, income, cost and standard of living and indebtedness of the agricultural labour families. They cover the entire country and relate to each of the six census zones and also separately to each State in each zone. The size of the sample in some of the small States was so small that it could not be regarded as adequate.

Intensive Survey of Agricultural Labour

This series of Reports based on the Intensive Family Survey of the First Agricultural Labour Enquiry consists of 7 volumes.[2] Volume I deals with all-India and the other volumes are devoted to the States in each of the six zones into which the country was divided for the purpose of the 1951 population Census. The all-India Report contains background information on the growth of population in relation to land utilization and distribution of cultivators' holdings. Information on the occupational structure of families and that of labour force, employment on wages, self-employment and unemployment is also given. The data on unemployment relate only to adult male workers. Data on the wage structure of agricultural labourers are also included. The wage rates given are duly weighted according to man-days worked. The structure of agricultural wages as seen in different modes of wages payment, system of supplying perquisites and the regional and operational variations in the rates of wages are also presented and analyzed.

The income of agricultural labour families has also been analyzed according to sources. The Report also includes data on cost and level of living, indebtedness and child labour in agriculture. The Zonal Volumes also give similar information in respect of the States in each zone. The precision of the estimates in respect of some of the varieties is also indicated in the All-India Report, Second Agricultural Labour Enquiry, 1956-57.[3]

---

[2] Issued by the Ministry of Labour based on the First Agricultural Labour Enquiry.
[3] Issued by the Labour Bureau, Ministry of Labour and Employment in 1960.

RURAL MANPOWER AND OCCUPATIONAL STRUCTURE

This monograph relates to the second stage of the First All-India Agricultural Labour Enquiry namely, the General Family Survey which was conducted in 812 villages selected on the principle of stratified random sampling.[4] The families surveyed numbered in all 103,548. Important information regarding occupational distribution of families, age and sex classification of rural population, size of families classification according to economic status, working strength of families, structure of rural occupations, subsidiary occupations of earners, cultivators' holdings, livestock and implements and housing conditions in rural areas is given for all-India and States. Fifteen important all-India tables have been presented in appendices. In these tables, besides the figure for each State, the unweighted totals of all the sample villages are given and no estimation for all-India has been made. In the chapter giving all-India Summary, however, weighted figures for all-India and for each census zone have been given in the case of important statistics. Separate chapters dealing with 'child labour in agriculture' and 'women in agriculture' are also included. This Report thus gives valuable information for estimation of the total labour force, its composition and its relation to the size of the holdings, the work animals and implements.

Second Agricultural Labour Enquiry

The Second Agricultural Labour Enquiry (1960) was conducted in about 3,600 villages selected on the principle of stratified random sampling by the Ministry of Labour and Employment. The field work of the Enquiry was entrusted to the Directorate of National Sample Survey. This Enquiry was conducted with the primary purpose of obtaining comparative picture of the conditions of agricultural labourers in the country as between 1950-51 and 1956-57. As compared with the First Enquiry, certain improvements in concepts, definitions and procedures were introduced. The first volume of the Report on the Second Enquiry issued by the Labour Bureau, Ministry of Labour and Employment contains all-India and State-wise information on employment, wages, income, consumption, cost of living, women and child labour in agriculture, etc. Essential statistics for all-India, Zonal Council areas and States on area and population, agricultural labour households, employment and unemployment, range of agricultural wage rates, mode of wage payment, annual income and expenditure of agricultural labour households, economic levels of living, etc. are also included. The results given in this Report are estimates based on simple data and are, therefore, subject to sampling errors, An idea of the reliability of the estimates has been given in an Appendix for some of the characteristics, viz. State-wise, all-India, C.P.A. and other than C.P.A. data on: (i) average number of days spent by agricultural labourers per year in (a) agricultural

---

[4]Issued by the Ministry of Labour based on the First Agricultural Labour Enquiries.

wage employment, (b) self-employment and (c) unemployment, and (ii) average daily wage of casual male agricultural labourers in (a) ploughing, (b) harvesting, and (c) all agricultural operations.

The data collected during the First and the Second Enquiry are not strictly comparable with each other on account of changes in concepts and definitions introduced in the latter Enquiry. The more important changes in concepts, definitions and methodology are mentioned below.

(i) *Agricultural Labour* In the First Enquiry, the definition of agricultural labourer was confined to those employed for wages in the process of crop production, while in the Second, hired employment in other agricultural occupations like dairy farming, horticulture, raising of livestock, bees and poultry etc. were also covered besides cultivation on land for farming purposes. Further, in the First Enquiry, an agricultural labour family was defined as the one in which either the head of the family or majority of the earners were employed as agricultural labourers for 50 per cent or more of the total number of days worked by them during the previous year. In the Second Enquiry, the criterion was changed to income and not employment. An agricultural labour household was defined as one for which the major source of income during the previous year was from agricultural wages.

(ii) *Employment* In the First Enquiry, work for less than half a day was ignored and that for half a day or more was considered as full day's occupation. In the Second Enquiry, however, four intensity classes were laid down, viz. full, half, nominal and nil. A full day's work meant 3/4th or more of the normal working day of ten hours. More than 1/4th and less than 3/4th of the normal hours was considered as work with half intensity; less than 1/4th was deemed as 'nominal' work with 1/8th intensity and nil intensity signified no work done during the reference period. This refinement in the method of calculating the intensity of employment has resulted in bringing out a smaller quantum of employment. The comparative picture of the employment position at two points of time, viz. 1950-51 and 1956-57 given in this Report has, therefore, to be viewed with due caution.

(iii) *Income Estimation* In the Second Enquiry, perquisites and other such incomes received in kind were evaluated in cash at ruling wholesale prices as against ruling retail prices in the First Enquiry.

Due to reorganization of States after the First Enquiry, it was necessary to recompile the data of the First Enquiry for purposes of comparison with those of the Second Enquiry. This was done by adopting a suitable weighting process. The recompiled data of the First Enquiry have been published in a pamphlet entitled 'Agricultural Labour Statistics 1950-51 for Reorganized States'.

According to the Second Agricultural Labour Enquiry published in 1960, agricultural labour families constituted nearly 25 per cent of all rural families. According to this, more than 85 per cent of the rural workers are casual, serving any farmer who is willing to engage them and only 15 per cent of agricultural labourers are attached to specific landlords. More than half of the workers do not possess any land, and even the rest of them own only very little of land. Agricultural labourers predominantly belong to the scheduled castes, scheduled tribes and other backward classes. According to one estimate, between 75 and 80 per cent of all agricultural labourers belong to the scheduled castes.

Other Sources

According to the National Commission on Rural Labour (1991), during 1987-88, out of a total of 108.4 million rural households, 43 million households belonged to rural labour households and among them, agricultural labour households were of the order of 33.3 million. In relative terms, rural labour households accounted for 39.7 per cent of total labour households and agricultural labour households were of the order of 30.7 per cent. This implies that agricultural labour households constituted about 77 per cent of all rural labour households in 1987-88.

Analysis of 1981 census data reveals that agricultural labourers were 64.4 million. As a percentage of total workers (main plus marginal) which were 224.6 million, agricultural labourers constituted 26.3 per cent of the total labour force. In 1961, agricultural labourers numbered only 31 million. This indicates that there has been a sharp increase in the number of agricultural labourers. The National Commission on Rural labour states: "During the seventies and the eighties, the rural population registered an annual growth rate of 2 per cent and 1.5 per cent respectively. However, for the corresponding decades, the growth in the number of agricultural labourers has been at higher levels of 4.1 per cent and 3.0 per cent per annum respectively."

This implies that marginal farmers have been swelling the ranks of landless labourers. On account of the increasing economic compulsions in terms of past debts, they have been forced to sell their lands. This supports the popularly held view that the benefits of millions of rupees invested in irrigation, tubewells, fertilizers or roads have gone to the big farmers. It also implies that cooperatives and rural banks have also helped the rich farmers.

Another finding of the National Commission on Rural Labour (NCRL) is that whereas during 1977-78, the average days worked per year by men and women of agricultural labour households in agricultural wage employ-ment were 230 days and 184 days respectively, the corresponding figures for the year 1983 (4th Rural Labour Enquiry) were 159 days and 136 days respectively. This decline in the days of employment did produce an adverse effect on the earnings and debt conditions of agricultural labour households.

It has also been found that the proportion of wage labour to total work force increased at the all-India level from 34.1% in 1972-73 to 41.4% in 1987-88. During the same period, the proportion of casual wage labour to total wage labour increased from 64.8% in 1972-73 to 75.8% in 1987-88. Explaining the growing trend towards casualisation of agricultural labour, NCRL states unequivocally: The technological change in agriculture, marginalisation of small farmers, eviction of tenants, destruction of traditional cottage industries, inflation etc., are some of the important factors that are operating differently in different regions of India leading to the swelling of the number of agricultural labourers."[5]

AGRICULTURAL WAGES IN INDIA

Statistics of wages in India have not been collected at regular intervals either by official or non-official committees or commissions or by any government department under statutory sanction as has been done in other countries of the world. This state of affairs was emphatically criticized by the Royal Commission on Labour which pleaded for better and more comprehensive data about wage level in various industries in different centres. Agricultural wages present another problem and the data available about them are extremely scanty and defective. It is supposed that the condition of agricultural labourers is worse than that of the industrial labourers and it is necessary to solve the problems of the agricultural labour and to study the various aspects of the agricultural economy from the statistical point of view.

Agricultural labour forms the largest single sector of India's labour force. In recent years, especially after independence, the question of formulating ameliorative measures for agricultural labour has been receiving increasing attention, but the main difficulty was lack of comprehensive data on the economic conditions of agricultural labour. Till 1950, regular statistics of wages of agricultural labour were not being collected. The only data available were those collected during the quinquennial wages census carried out in some of the States. In former Bombay and Madhya Pradesh States, some wages data were being collected and published in the Annual Administration Report.[6] Since 1950, however, regular statistics of wages are being collected from selected villages in almost all the States on the basis of a scheme prepared in the Directorate of Economics and Statistics, Ministry of Agriculture. These are published in Agricultural Situation in India (Monthly) and Agricultural Wages in India (Annual) since the year 1951-52, issued by the Directorate of Economics and Statistics.

Agricultural Wages in India gives detailed statistics of wages of agricultural labourers separately for: (a) skilled labour, (b) field labour, (c) other agricultural labour, and (d) herdsmen. The first groups, i.e. skilled labour has been sub-divided into carpenters, blacksmiths and cobblers.

---

[5]Ministry of Labour, Report of National Commission on Rural Labour (1991), Vol. I p. 59.

[6]For brief historical comments on collection and compilation of agricultural wage data prior to 1951-52, see "Relative movements of agricultural wage-rates and cereal prices: some Indian evidence", Nilakantha Rath and R.V. Joshi, Artha Vijnana, Vol. 8 No. 2, June 1966, pp. 115-131.

Separate data regarding wages of men, women and children are available in respect of the other three groups of labourers. Field labour includes, ploughmen, sowers, reapers, harvesters, weeders, transplanters, etc. Other agricultural labour includes coolies employed for watering the fields, load carriers, well diggers, labourers cleaning the silt from waterways, embankments, etc. Herdsmen include persons whose main work is to collect livestock from different owners' houses and feed them in the jungle during the day and again take them back to the owners' places. Wage data relate to calendar months and represent the most common rates current during the month. The normal number of working hours which constitute a day are also reported in each Centre. Agricultural wage rates at different jute centres, viz. Barasat, Monoharpur, Samsi, Belakoba (West Bengal), Chakia, Purnea (Bihar), Bhadrak, Kendrapara (Orissa), Barpeta and Nowgong (Assam) are also published in an appendix to this publication— 'Indian Labour Statistics'.[7] The first issue of the publication came in 1951-52 and is being continued with a time lag of 3-4 years.

Wages and Earnings of Agricultural Labourers

Data about the wages paid to agricultural labourers reveals that the agricultural labourers do not receive notified minimum wages except in certain parts of the country like Kerala, Haryana and Western U.P. Even in these states, females do not get remuneration as per the notified minimum wages. Growing awareness and organisations of agricultural labour, wherever active, have pushed up wages closer to the minimum wages. Wherever agricultural labourers are unorganised and thus have weak bargaining power, the gap between actual wage paid and the minimum wage fixed by the state is large. Despite this, real wages have increased in all the states without exception during 1970-71 and 1988-89. In most of the states, real wage rates registered larger increase during the decade of the 1980s as compared to 1970s.

Two more tendencies have also become evident. Firstly, there has been a decline in regional disparities in real wages. Secondly, the disparity between the wages paid to male and female agricultural labourers has also shown a distinct decline over the years. NCRL explaining the decline in the disparity of male-female wages of agricultural labour mentions: "Factors like implementation of rural employment and afforestation programmes (which stipulated minimum wages and catered to the employment needs of poor rural women), periodical revision in minimum wages and notification of equal wages for equal work, productivity gains brought about by new technology and growth of general awareness seem to have contributed significantly to the higher increases in real wages for rural females in agricultural sector."[8]

---

[7]Issued by the Labour Bureau, Ministry of Labour and Employment, in 1960.

[8]Ministry of Labour, Report of the National Commission on Rural Labour (1991), Vol. I, p. 62.

NATIONAL SAMPLE SURVEYS

In India, the National Statistical Survey Organisation (NSSO) collects data on employment and unemployment using alternative reference periods corresponding to three approaches. These are—the usual status (US) approach, based on a reference period of one year; the current weekly status (CWS) approach, based on a reference period of one week; and the current daily status (CDS), based on the activity pursued on each day of the reference week.

While all three approaches are used for collection of data on employment and unemployment in quinquennial (after every five years) surveys the first two approaches are only used for the intervening annual surveys. Every fifth year, the sample size is of the order of 120,000 households. In the intervening years, the sample size is of the order of 40,000 households. Each survey is divided into four subrounds, with each sub-round of three months duration. The survey covers the whole of the rural and urban areas of India, except for a few inaccessible and difficult pockets. The activity status of each person in the households is collected with reference to the previous 365 days, the previous 7 days and daily for 7 days.

A person is considered to be working or employed on US basis if he or she was engaged for a relatively longer time during the past year in any one or more work-related economic activities. A person is considered unemployed on this basis, if he or she was not working, but was either seeking or was available for work for the major part of the reference year.

A person is considered to be working or employed on CWS basis if the he/she was engaged for at least one hour on any one day of the previous week on any work related economic activity. A person is considered unemployed under this concept if he or she had not worked even for one hour during the week, but was seeking or was available for work.

The CDS approach attempts to classify employment by persondays, rather than by persons. A person is considered to be "working" (employed) for the entire day if he/she has worked four hours or more during the day. If a person has worked one hour or more, but less than four hours, he/she is considered to be employed for half the day, and seeking/available for work (unemployed) or "not available for work" (that is, not in the labour force) for the other half of the day depending on whether he/she is seeking or available for work.

The US unemployment rates is generally regarded as the measure of chronic open unemployment during the reference year. The CWS unemployment rates also measure chronic unemployment, but with the reduced reference period of a week. The CDS is considered to be the most comprehensive measure of unemployment, including both chronic and invisible unemployment.

Of the three concepts, the US covers 'principal' and 'subsidiary' workers and is the closest to the concept used in the Census to enumerate workers. By including even those who are not principal workers but work in a subsidiary capacity, like students and pensioners, the usual status concept comprehensively covers all those engaged in or seeking economic activities. Moreover, the US concept is seen to yield more stable estimates of employment in contrast to the other two concepts which have shorter reference periods of a week or an average day of the week respectively. Projections of labour force and employment have therefore been made on the US concept, and qualified, where necessary, on the basis of the other two concepts.

The National Sample Survey Report No. 33—Wages, Employment, Income and Indebtedness on Agricultural Labour Households in rural areas—was based on the 11th and 12th rounds covering the period September, 1956 to August, 1957. The data show average daily wage (in Rs.) of casual adult male agricultural labourer by type of operation over the year September, 1956 to August, 1957; the operations distinguished for this purpose being ploughing, sowing, transplanting, weeding, harvesting, other agricultural operations, and non-agricultural operations. The Report contains information about roughly a quarter of all rural households and has been shown to the extent possible in a form comparable with the results of the First Agricultural Labour Enquiry 1950-51, conducted by the Ministry of Labour. A very fruitful analysis of the available wage data from the Agricultural Wages in India, National Sample Survey, Agricultural Labour Enquiry etc. is given by Dr. V.M. Rao in one of his papers.[9]

In the 25th round of N.S.S. conducted during 1970-71, a study was made of the economic conditions of the weaker sections of the population in rural areas. In such selected villages, all households were divided into three sub-strata—(i) households having no cultivated land, (ii) the lowest 10 per cent of the households having cultivated land, and (iii) remaining households. Non-agricultural households were excluded from the first two sub-strata. Information was collected regarding time disposition during the reference week for all the members along with their demographic particulars as well as earnings of the wage earners, consumer expenditure, particulars of household holding, etc. State-wise reports on employment and the employment situation among the weaker sections of population in rural areas have been mimeographed. These tabulations give very useful information on the following items separately for 'small cultivators' and 'non-cultivators':

  (i) Percentage of man days worked on non-farm and exchange labour; worked on other farms and non-farm occupations; and available and/or seeking work.
 (ii) Percentage of households reporting willingness to take up regular full time employment either in the village or outside village.
(iii) Average rate of earnings.

---

[9] V.M. Rao, Agricultural wages in India—a reliability analysis, Indian Journal of Agricultural Economics, July-September, 1972.

This publication contains statistics relating to average daily employment in different coffee, tea and rubber plantations and index numbers with 1951 as base for the last 12 years based on the information collected by the Directorate of Economics and Statistics from the State Governments through official agencies. It also contains data on earnings of different plantation workers in Assam for over a decade. Separate data on men, women and children are available in respect of Assam valley and Cachar regarding average monthly cash earnings of settled labour. The statistics are based on the annual Reports on the working of Tea Districts Emigrant Labour Act, 1932 published by the Controller of Emigrant Labour. For the purpose of these statistics, a labourer has been defined as a person working on wages not exceeding 50 rupees per month (excluding a clerk, domestic servant, motor mechanic, carpenter, mason, brick-layer or other artisans). The figures are based on tea estates submitting returns. The coverage is, therefore, incomplete and varies from year to year. The figures in respect of the years prior to 1953-54 are based on 2 months' average (March and September), whereas those for 1953-54 and later years are for all the 12 months of the respective years. NSSO has been undertaking surveys on employment and unemployment as well as Rural Labour. List of these published in Sarvekshana is as in Table 13.1.

OTHER SOURCES

Data on agricultural wages which are published later in the volume Agricultural Wages in India as already discussed are also published in respect of some centres in the monthly journal of the Directorate of Economics and Statistics, Agricultural Situation in India. This also provides some information regarding daily agricultural wages in some States. Although utility of the data is limited, it is worthwhile to have some basic intelligence on agricultural wages. A few States which were not reporting earlier on a regular basis have started collecting such data. There are, however, still some States like Jammu and Kashmir and Manipur which have not been collecting such data.

Some information about plantation labour employed under tea, coffee and rubber used to be provided in the annual publications of the Directorate of Economics and Statistics under Tea in India, Coffee in India and Rubber in India. In the case of tea, the daily average number of persons employed in the different plantations in different districts is given. Separate figures are also available in respect of permanent garden labour, permanent outside labour and temporary outside labour. Average monthly wages of labourers employed in the different gardens of Assam are published separately for 'settled labourers' and 'faltu and basti labourers' based on the information collected and furnished by the Controller of Emigrant Labour, Shillong. These are calculated on the average daily working strength of typical months (March and September) and refer to all cash earnings, but exclude non-cash payments. The minimum rates of daily wages for tea plantation labour in force during

Table 13.1: NSS Reports Published in Sarvekshna

	Topic covered	Round	Survey	Volume period	No.	Month/ year	Issue no.	Notes/ survey	Pages
1	2	3	4	5	6	7	8	9	10
	Employment and Unemployment								
	First quinquennial Survey								
1	Employment-Unemployed situation at a glance	27	Oct. 72-Sep. 73	I	2	Oct. 1977	2	N	81 to 102
2	All India and State-wise results	27	Oct. 72-Sep. 73	III	3	Jan. 1980	11	N	75 to 85 S-7 to S-104
	Second quinquennial survey								
1	Some key results	32	July 77-June 78	II	2	Oct. 1978	6	N	35 to 55
2	Preliminary results for persons aged 15 to 59	32	July 77-June 78	II	4	April 1979	8	N	149 to 158
2.3	Activity situation pertaining to Women usually engaged in domestic duties	32	July 77-June 78	IV	3 & 4	Jan-Apr. 81	14	N SR	1 to 71 S-1 to S-249
2.4	Final results All India	32	July 77-June 78	V	1 & 2	Jul-Oct 81	15	N SR	1 to 49 S-1 to S-190
2.5	Selected important results for 8 States: A.P. Maharashtra, Bihar, Gujarat, Haryana, Punjab, Tamil Nadu and West Bengal	32	July. 77-June 78	VI	1 & 2	Jul.-Oct. 82	17	N SR	18 to 23 S-1 to S-192

Table 13.1: NSS Reports Published in Sarvekshna (Contd.)

	Topic covered	Round	Survey	Volume period	No.	Month/year	Issue no.	Notes/survey	Pages
1	2	3	4	5.	6	7	8	9	10
2.6	Selected important results for 4 States: Kerala, M.P., Rajasthan and U.P.	32	July 77-June 78	VI	3 & 4	Jan.-Apr. 83	18	SR	S-89 to S-198
2.7	Selected important results for 5 States/Uts: Assam, Delhi, H.P. Karnataka and J & K	32	July 77-June 78	VII	3	Jan. 1984	20	SR	S-79 to S-188
2.8	Selected important results for 9 States/Uts: Arunachal Pradesh, Goa, Daman and Diu, Manipur, Meghalya, Orissa, Pondicherry, Tripura, Chandigarh and Nagaland	32	July-June 78	VII	4	April 1984	21	N / SR	7 to 11 / S-1 to S-160
2.9	Employment/Unemployment situation in cities and towns during late seventies.	32	July-June 78	X	2	Oct. 1986	29	N / SR	33 to 50 / S-1 to S-115
	Third quinquennial survey								
3.1	Preliminary results based on first two sub-rounds data	38	Jan.-Dec. 1983	IX	4	April 1986	27	N / SR	S-103 to S-134 / S-125 to S-213

Table 13.1: NSS Reports Published in Sarvekshna (Contd.)

	Topic covered	Round	Survey	Volume period	No.	Month/year	Issue no.	Notes/survey	Pages
1	2	3	4	5	6	7	8	9	10
3.2	Employment and un-employment (All India)	38	Jan.-Dec. 1983	XI	4	April 1988	35	N / SR	1 to 73 / S-1 to S-222
3.3	Additional 10 tables on employment and Unemployment	38	Jan.-Dec. 1983	XII	3	Jan.-Mar. 1989	38	SR	S-189 to S-245
3.4	Employment-Unemployment (9 State results)	38	Jan.-Dec. 1983	XIV	1	Jul.-Sept. 90	44	N / SR	5 to 9 / S-1 to S-306
3.6	Employment and Unemployment (8 State results)	38	Jan.-Dec. 1983	XIV	2	Oct.-Dec. 90	45	N / SR	1 to 6 / S-1 to S-263
	Fourth quinquennial survey								
4.1	Results of fourth quinquennial survey on employment and unemployment (All India)	43	July-87-June 88	Special No.		Sep. 1990		N / SR	1 to 148 / S-1 to S-424
4.2	Employment and Un-employment situation of scheduled tribe and scheduled caste population during late eighties	43	July 87-Jun. 88	XV	2	Oct.-Dec. 91	49	N / SR	1 to 102 / S-1 to S-80

Table 13.1: NSS Reports Published in Sarvekshna (Contd.)

1	2 Topic covered	3 Round	4 Survey	5 Volume period	6 No. period	7 Month/year	8 Issue no.	9 Notes/survey	10 Pages
4.3	Results of fourth quinquennial survey on unemployment (18 states in 18 booklets)	43	Jul.-87-June 88	Special issue		January 1992			
4.4	Results of fourth quinquennial survey on employment and unemployment for 9 major States	43	July 87-Jun 88	XVI	2	Oct.-Dec. 92	53	N SR	1 to 11 1 to 486
4.5	Do remaining 9 States	"	"	"	3	Jan.-Mar. 93	54	N SR	1 to 11 1 to 486
4.6	A note on employment and unemployment situation in cities and towns during late eighties	43	July 87-June 88	XVII	2	Oct.-Dec. 93	57	N SR	1 to 18 S-3 to S-63
	Fifth Quinquennial Surveys								
5.1	Employment and unemployment in India 1993-94	50	1993-94	XX	1	Jul.-Sept. 96	68	N SR	1 to 150 S-1 to S-423
5.2	Participation of Indian Women in household work and other specified activities, 1993-94	50	1993-94	XXI	2	Oct.-Dec. 97	73	N. SR	65 to 89 S-266 to S-284

Table 13.1: NSS Reports Published in Sarvekshna (Contd.)

Topic covered	Round	Survey	Volume period	No.	Month/ year	Issue no.	Notes/ survey	Pages
2	3	4	5	6	7	8	9	10
5.3 Economic activities and school attendance by children in India, 1993-94	50	1993-94	XXI	2	Oct.-Dec. 97	73	N SR	90 to 104 S-285 to S-345
5.4 Employment and Unemployment situation among Social Groups in India 1993-94	50	1993-94	XXII	4	April-June 1999	79	N SR	1 to 99 S-1 to S-314
5.5 Employment and Unemployment situation in Cities and Towns in India 1993-94	50	1993-94	XXIII	1	July-September 1999	80	N SR	1 to 18 S-1 to S-108
5.6 Unemployed in India 1993-94 Salient Features	50	1993-94	XXIII	1	July-September 1999	80	N SR	19 to 38 S-109 to S174
Rural Labour								
1.1 Indebtedness of rural labour households	32	July 77-June 78	VIII	3 & 4	Jan.-Apr. 85	24	N SR	1 to 32 S-1 to S-129
1.2 Wages and earnings of rural labour household	32	Jul. 77-Jun. 78	X	4	Apr. 87	31	N SR	20 to 27 S-1 to S-109

the year in various States are given in tea statistics issued by the Tea Board of India. As for coffee, the Coffee in India contains district-wise statistics on daily average number of persons employed in coffee plantations. The data are given under separate heads of permanent garden labour, permanent outside labour and temporary outside labour. Detailed labour statistics in respect of coffee estate are also published by the Coffee Board in their annual report, Coffee Statistics Relating to India. These publications are no longer being published.

Statistics under Minimum Wages Act

This Act which was passed in the year 1948 lays down the fixation of minimum wages for employees in a number of employments both agricultural as well as non-agricultural. This is a protective measure to improve the income of agricultural labourers. Under this legislation minimum wages for agricultural workers have been fixed throughout the States of Kerala, Orissa, Punjab, Rajasthan, Delhi and Tripura and for specified area in the States of Assam, Andhra Pradesh, Bihar, Bombay, Himachal Pradesh, Madhya Pradesh, Mysore, Uttar Pradesh and West Bengal. Minimum wages have also been fixed by the Central Government in certain agricultural demonstration farms and military farms under the Central Ministries of Food and Agriculture and Defence respectively. All these statistics are published by the Labour Bureau, Government of India.

Census Data

In the population censuses of 1961, 1971, 1981, 1991 and 2001 as has been mentioned earlier, statistics were collected about the number of agricultural labour households. Though no wage statistics were collected during the census, the data collected would provide a sound basis for all agricultural labour wage studies which may be conducted in future. An agricultural labourer was defined in the last census as a person who worked on somebody else's land in lieu of payment (in cash or kind) and who had no responsibility connected with supervision or direction of the work, who had no ownership or tenancy right on land on which he worked and who was not responsible for profit or loss of cultivation.

Labour Bureau Consumers Price Index Numbers for Agricultural Labour (Interim Series)

The Minimum Wages Act of 1948 (which is applicable *inter alia* to employment in agriculture) requires fixation as well as revision of minimum wages in accordance with changes in cost of living. As such this work was given to the Ministry of Labour and Employment. Now the Labour Bureau under this Ministry compiles indices of consumer prices for agricultural labourers.

AGRICULTURAL LABOUR AND MINIMUM WAGES

After the Minimum Wages Act, 1948 was passed, pressure was brought upon the Government to extend the Act to cover agricultural labour. The Act was subsequently extended but there are still some States which have not brought large sections of agricultural labour within the ambit of the Act. Even where the Act is implemented, the machinery for the fixation and enforcement of minimum wages is not uniform. In some states, it is the Revenue Department which implements the Act and in some others this is done by the Labour Department. But generally speaking:

(i) The Act has been a dead letter in every state; (ii) minimum wages in agriculture have not been revised over long periods; (iii) almost everywhere, the actual wages rule higher than the minimum wages during the peak season and tend to fall in slack seasons; (iv) the machinery for enforcement is hopelessly inadequate to cope with the task of effective implementation, the institution of proceedings under the Act is almost negligible and successful prosecution even more disappointing; and (v) other difficulties in the implementation of the Act arise mainly from poverty and illiteracy of agricultural labour, absence of knowledge of the existence of legislation, scattered nature of agricultural farms, casual nature of employment, unorganised character of agricultural labour, etc.

There is strong opinion in favour of suspending the operation of the Minimum Wages Act in rural areas. The basic argument is that at the peak of the agricultural season, can dictate its own terms and naturally actual wages will tend to be much higher than the minimum wages, under these conditions the enforcement of minimum wages has no meaning. On the other hand, during the slack season, the supply of agricultural labour is much in excess of demand and, therefore, the enforcement of the minimum wages may be difficult. The National Commission on Labour gave due weight to this view, yet it strongly recommended the continuance of the Act on the ground that in the long run, with greater awareness of their rights on the part of agricultural labourers, the fixing minimum wages would be useful. As regards enforcement, the Commission suggested that the Panchayats might be asked to enforce minimum wages, even though this has obvious defects. The Commission also suggested wide publicity to the fixing of minimum wages and the notification of wages at a public place which would make the employers cautious in denying to their workers the notified wage.

There are considerable disparities in wages between regions, between different crops as well as between wages paid to men, women and children. The National Commission on Labour had sufficient evidence before it to conclude that between 1956 and 1963 the incomes of agricultural labour increased faster than the wages of industrial workers. This was mainly due to the fact that the average wage in rural areas was increasing significantly. This was especially true in the case of Punjab and in some selected areas of Tamil Nadu.

The Labour Ministers's Conference held in August 1981 on the question of minimum wages under the Minimum Wages Act decided that (i) minimum wages should not fall below the poverty line, (ii) mechanism should be devised to link minimum wages with the consumer price index numbers as has been done by some States, to the extent possible, and (iii) to introduce a comprehensive legislation to amend the Minimum Wages Act to remove the defects and to make it more effective.

In pursuance of these recommendations, a new concept of General Minimum Wages was devised which would provide for the necessities like food, fuel and shelter in respect of workers in general who may not be covered under the Minimum Wages Act. It may be noted that the abolition of rural poverty largely depends upon the guarantee of minimum wages. According to the Annual Report of the Ministry of Labour (2000-2001), there was considerable variation in the Minimum Wages prescribed for agricultural workers (Table 13.2).

Bonded Labour

One item of the 20 point economic programme was the abolition of bonded labour. It came as a great surprise to most urban dwellers that millions of landless labourers were still being treated as bonded labour or contract labour and that they have been living like serfs or slaves. Bonded labour has existed in India for centuries. It is a peculiar phenomenon of our agricultural economy. The system grew out of extreme poverty and helplessness of scheduled castes, Adivasis and semi-tribal communities, who have always depended on wage-income which too they received only for a part of the year. When they needed foodgrains during the lean agricultural season or when they needed money for special occasions such as marriage or festival or for medical treatment, they had to borrow but they had no security of offer in the form of land, jewellery or any other property except their own labour. Accordingly, they 'pledged' themselves. The moneylenders and the high caste landlords took advantage of their helplessness and ignorance, and entered into repressive contracts. The wages were so low and the rate of interest so high—often 25 to 50 per cent—that the total loan got accumulated with the passage of time. In fact, the total burden of the loan became so huge that it could not be repaid even with the labour of many generations of the debtor's family. Once a landless labourer borrowed money, he and his descendants were doomed to perpetual slavery. Even in modern times, the scheduled caste agricultural labourers who could secure employment for hardly five or six months a year had to subsist for the rest of time on money and foodgrains borrowed from their landlords. Bonded labour is known by various names in the country, as for example, 'Paniyas' in Tamil Nadu, 'halia' and 'mulia' in Orissa, 'baramasia' in North Bihar and 'Kamia' in South Bihar, 'harwaha' in Madhya Pradesh, 'sewak' and 'haris' in Uttar Pradesh, etc.

Table 13.2 State-wise Details of Minimum Wages

As on 1.10.2000

Sl. No.	Centre/States/UTs	No. of Scheduled Employments	Range of Minimum Wages per day (Rs.)	
			Minimum	Maximum
(1)	(2)	(3)	(4)	(5)
1.	Central Sphere	44	80.74	90.19
2.	Andhra Pradesh	61	27.00	63.19
3.	Arunachal Pradesh	25	35.60	37.60
4.	Assam	64	32.08	50.70
5.	Bihar	74	49.19	61.59
6.	Goa	18	21.00	125.00
7.	Gujarat	53	34.00	92.40
8.	Haryana	50	70.30	74.30
9.	Himachal Pradesh	24	26.00	51.00
10.	Jammu & Kashmir	18	30.00	-
11.	Karnataka	64	26.00	74.03
12.	Kerala	36	30.00	164.77
13.	Madhya Pradesh	36	50.46	56.46
14.	Maharashtra	65	42.46	108.95
15.	Manipur	5	44.65	55.60
16.	Meghalaya	24	50.00	-
17.	Mizoram	3	70.00	-
18.	Nagaland	36	40.00	-
19.	Orissa	83	42.50	-
20.	Punjab	60	69.25	151.32
21.	Rajasthan	38	47.05	60.00
22.	Sikkim (Minimum Wages Act, 1948 has not yet been extended and enforced)			
23.	Tamil Nadu	60	35.00	115.80
24.	Tripura	11	20.63	45.00
25.	Uttar Pradesh	62	42.02	70.62
26.	West Bengal	45	48.21	87.28
27.	Andaman & Nicobar Islands	5	50.00	86.76
28.	Chandigarh	44	81.65	-
29.	Dadar & Nagar Haveli	43	60.00	71.00
30.	Daman & Diu	71	50.00	60.00
31.	Delhi	29	93.00	-
32.	Lakshadweep	9	46.80	-
33.	Pondicherry	4	19.25	65.00

Source: Annual Report (2000-01), Ministry of Labour.

What is worse, many states even deny the existence of bonded labour. But in many parts of the country, lands and houses belonging to the poorer farmers have been progressively passing into the hands of the usurious moneylenders and thus swelling the ranks of the bonded and contract labourers. During the period 1961 and 1971 alone, the number of landholders declined from 93 million to 78 million but the number of landless labourers shot up from 27 million to 47 million. This shows the clear trend of growing concentration of property with a few and the growing pauperisation of the rural community.

Bonded labour generally borrowed foodgrains during the lean agricultural season from the rich landlords. The repayment of these loans is generally in kind and the extent was 1.25 to 1.5 times the original amount. As a result of this type of loans, the rich cultivators remained almost assured of regular supply of labour for their agricultural operations. The bonded labour incurred double burden in the form of paying high interest rate and selling their labour cheaply to their masters. Most bonded labourers worked as hereditary serfs in the houses, gardens and farms of the upper classes. Their work ranged from tilling the land to menial domestic chores. In Maharashtra, Andhra, Bihar and other States, the Adivasis have suffered severe humiliation at the hands of the high caste cultivators and money lenders.

Efforts were made in the past to abolish bonded labour. The earlier effort was the law passed in 1933 by the British Parliament to abolish slavery throughout the British empire. Unfortunately it did not have any impact in India as the different states felt that there was no slavery in India. After Independence, the Constitution prohibited slavery, *begar* and other forms of forced labour. Soon after some states passed laws to abolish bonded labour. But the system persisted since the laws were not enforced and the urban people were either not aware of the evil or did not take notice of the evil. A series of agitations by the bonded Adivasi labourers against their exploiters were organised by the communists. They focused attention of the Government and of the general public to their terrible exploitation by the high caste land-owners and rapacious money-lenders. Often these movements were condemned as communists uprisings and were cruelly suppressed. At the same time, the Government was influenced by the regular reports of the Commissioner for Scheduled Castes and Scheduled Tribes highlighting the exploitation and the humiliation of the backwards communities. The bonded labour system was abolished throughout the country with effect from 25th October 1975 under the Bonded Labour System (Abolition) Act, 1976. For the first time, the Government took swift action against money-lenders, building contractors, quarry-owners and others who have been found practising some form of bonded and contract labour.

COSTS OF LIVING FARM LABOURERS

A serious lacuna in the body of the economic statistics in India has recently been filled by a 'new series' of consumer price index numbers (general) for agricultural labourers, worked out by the Labour Bureau, Simla. The data used for this series are based on price quotations collected from a fixed set of 422 villages distributed into 39 agricultural zones on a fixed day during the first week of every month. Time lag between the release of data is hardly a few months. The index released is for the major states-general and food separately. The base for this index has now been changed to 1986-84 = 100.

INDIAN LABOUR JOURNAL

A regular monthly publication of the Labour Bureau, Ministry of Labour, Govt. of India, publishes valuable data on prices and price indices of Industrial Workers, Agricultural Labourers' Consumer Price Index, Employment and Absenteeism, etc. List of various items is as in (Table 13.3 and 13.3A).

Table 13.3 Data on Prices and Price Indices of Industrial Workers

MONTHLY STATISTICS

1. PRICES AND PRICE INDICES
Industrial Workers' Consumer Price Index

Labour Bureau's Series of All-India Average Consumer Price Index Number for Industrial Workers (Base: 1960 = 100)

Labour Bureau's Series of Consumer Price Index Numbers for Industrial Workers (Base: 1960 = 100)

Average Monthly Consumer Prices of Selected Articles

Labour Bureau's Series of Consumer Price Index Numbers for Working Class (Base shifted to 1949 = 100)

Labour Bureau's Series of Consumer Price Index Numbers for Industrial Workers in (a) Tripura (Base: 1961 = 100), (b) Himachal Pradesh (Base: 1965 = 100), (c) Goa (Base: 1966 = 100), (d) Bhilai (Base: 1966 = 100), (e) Bhilwara (Base: 1966 = 100), (f) Chhindwara (Base: 1966 = 100), (g) Kothagudem (Base: 1966 = 100), and (h) Rourkela (Base: 1966 = 100).

Agricultural Labourers' Consumer Price Index

Labour Bureau's Series of All-India Average Consumer Price Index Numbers for Agricultural Labourers (Base: 1960-61 = 100)

Labour Bureau's Series of Consumer Price Index Numbers for Agricultural Labourers (Base: 1960-61 = 100)

Average Monthly Prices of Selected Items for Agricultural Labourers at Rural Centres

Urban Non-Manual Employees' Consumer Price Index

Consumer Price Index Numbers for Urban Non-Manual Employees (Base: 1960 = 100)

2. EMPLOYMENT

Number of Cotton Mills (Spinning Departments of all Mills) by Shifts Worked

3. EMPLOYMENT EXCHANGE STATISTICS

Employment Service Statistics

4. ABSENTEEISM

Labour Bureau's Series of Absenteeism in Certain Industries in India.

Table 13.3 Data on Prices and Price Indices of Industrial Workers (Contd.)

SERIAL STATISTICS

1. PRICES AND PRICE INDICES

All-India Average Consumer Price Index Numbers for Industrial Workers (Base: 1949 = 100 and on Base: 1949 = 100 and on Base: 1960 = 100)

Labour Bureau's Series of Consumer Price Index Numbers for Industrial Workers (Base: 1960 = 100)

Labour Bureau's Other Series of Consumer Price Index Numbers

All-India Average Consumer Price Index Numbers for Agricultural Labourers (Base: 1960-61 = 100)

Labour Bureau's Series of Consumer Price Index Numbers for Agricultural Labourers (Base: 1960-61 = 100)

Consumer Price Index Numbers for Urban Non-Manual Employees (Base: 1960 = 100)

All-India Index Numbers of Wholesale Prices (New Series) (Base: 1970-71 = 100)

2. EMPLOYMENT

Number of Cotton Mills (Spinning Departments of all Mills) by Shifts worked
Employment in Cotton Mills
Employment and Total Number of Manshifts Worked in Coal Mines

3. EMPLOYMENT EXCHANGE STATISTICS

Employment Service Statistics

4. WAGES AND EARNINGS

Average Weekly Earnings of 'Below Ground' Miners and Loaders in Coal Mines Earnings of the Lowest-paid Workers/Operatives in Cotton Textiles Mills

5. PRODUCTIVITY

'Productivity of Workers Employed in Coal Mines

6. ABSENTEEISM

Absenteeism in Certain Manufacturing, Mining and Plantation Industries in India.

Table 13.3 (a) Comprative Statement of Variations in Consumer Price Indices (CPI) for Industrial Workers (IW) and Agricultural Labourers (AL)

Year	CPI (IW)	Percentage Variation (annual)	CPI (AL)	Percentage Variation (annual)
1	2	3	4	5
1984-85	582	6.4	521	0.19
1985-86	620	6.53	546	4.8
1986-87	674	8.71	572	4.76
1987-88	736	9.2	629	9.97
1988-89	802	8.97	708	12.56
1989-90	853	6.36	746	5.37
1990-91	951	11.49	803	7.64

Table 13.3(a)   Comprative Statement of Variations in Consumer Price Indices (CPI) for Industrial Workers (IW) and Agricultural Labourers (AL) (Contd.)

Year	CPI (IW)	Percentage Variation (annual)	CPI (AL)	Percentage Variation (annual)
1	2	3	4	5
1991-92	1080	13.56	958	19.30
1992-93	1183	9.54	1076	12.32
1993-94	1272	7.52	1114	3.53
1994-95	1400	10.06	1247	11.94
1995-96	1543	10.21	1381	10.75
1996-97	1686	9.27	1508	9.20
1997-98	1804	7.00	1555	3.12
1998-99	2041	13.14	1726	11.00
1999-2000	2110	3.38	1802	4.40

Note :   1. Index values are annual average of the respective financial year.
2. Base: CPI (Agricultural Labourers) 1960-61 = 100 CPI (IW) 1960 = 100. Values of CPI-IW for the year 1988-89 onwards (w.e.f. October, 1988 index) have been derived from the figures of CPI (IW) base 1982 = 100 by conversion factors (4.93). Similarly in case of CPI (AL) values for the year 1995-96 w.e.f. Nov., 1995 index have been derived from the figures of CPI (AL) on base 1986 = 87 = 100 by using the relevent linking factor (5.59).

Source: Annual Report (2000-01), Ministry of Labour.

Labour Force Structure

The labour force in an economy consists of the supply of labour available for the production of goods and services. Worldwide the labour force grew by 1.78 per cent annually on an average between 1990 and 1998 (Chart I). The right hand side of Chart I shows that 40 per cent of the labour force are women. Twelve to 15 per cent of children in the age group 10-14 were active in the Nineties.

China has the largest labour force at 743 million (Chart II). Nearly 90 per cent of its economically active population in the age group of 15-64 form the labour force. India ranks second with 72 per cent of its economically active population in the labour force. In the developed economies, the U.S. is at the top and Switzerland at the bottom.

The Russian Federation, China, the U.S., Thailand and Canada are the countries where women constitute more than 45 per cent of the labour force (right hand side of Chart II). Most child workers are in Asia. The share of working children is high in Brazil. Thailand and India are the other two countries with significant proportion of children engaged in some form of economic activity.

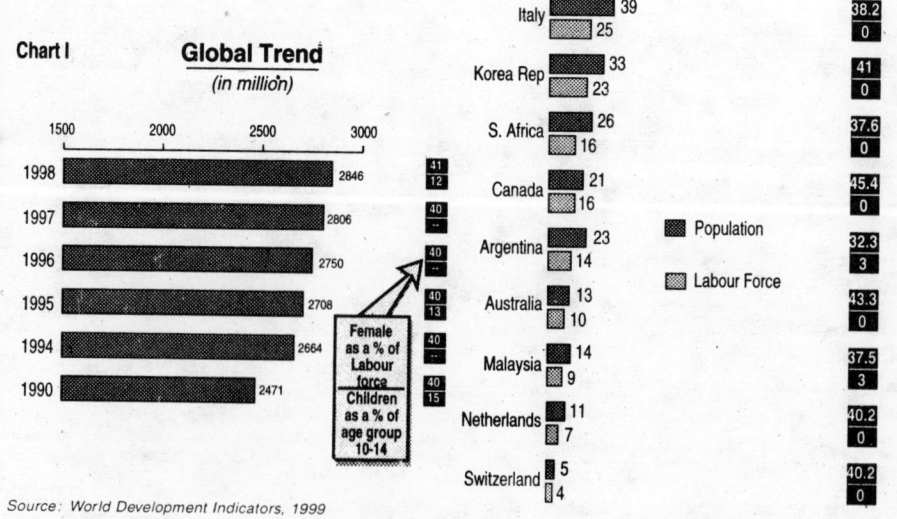

Chart I

Global Trend
(in million)

Year	Labour Force	Female as a % of Labour force	Children as a % of age group 10-14
1998	2846	41	12
1997	2806	40	--
1996	2750	40	--
1995	2708	40	13
1994	2664	40	--
1990	2471	40	15

Chart II

Labour Force v Population
(in million, 1998)

Country	Population	Labour Force	Female as a % of Labour force	Children as % of age group 10-14
China	837	743	45.2	9
India	595	431	32.1	13
U.S.	178	138	45.7	0
Indonesia	130	98	40.4	9
Russian Fed	101	78	48.9	0
Brazil	108	76	35.4	15
Japan	87	68	41.2	0
Germany	56	41	42.1	0
Mexico	59	38	32.6	6
Thailand	42	37	46.3	14
Philippines	44	32	37.6	6
U.K.	38	30	43.7	0
France	39	26	44.8	0
Italy	39	25	38.2	0
Korea Rep	33	23	41	0
S. Africa	26	16	37.6	0
Canada	21	16	45.4	0
Argentina	23	14	32.3	3
Australia	13	10	43.3	0
Malaysia	14	9	37.5	3
Netherlands	11	7	40.2	0
Switzerland	5	4	40.2	0

Source: World Development Indicators, 1999

14

Commodity Statistics

Besides the general publications relating to area, production, prices and foreign trade, etc. some specialized data dealing with principal agricultural commodities have been presented in important publications in an integrated manner. The first attempt in this direction was made by the Directorate of Economics and Statistics which brought out a series of commodity brochures. The important ones were as follows:

1. Cotton in India
2. Jute in India
3. Sugar in India
4. Oilseeds in India
5. Tobacco in India
6. Lac in India
7. Tea in India
8. Coffee in India
9. Rubber in India

The publication of the first six brochures was started from 1950-51. The brochures on tea, coffee and rubber were being issued by the Department of Commercial Intelligence and Statistics; the last issues brought out by that Department related to the years 1940, 1940-41 and 1942 respectively. The publication of these was then taken over by the Directorate of Economics and Statistics. Besides the above annual brochures, two ad hoc publications entitled Food Situation in India and Rice Economy of India were also brought out by the Directorate of Economics and Statistics. All these bulletins have since been discontinued from the year 1962-63 or 1963-64. It is, however, desirable that these publications be resumed.

Generally, each of the brochures contains an introductory note reviewing the principal features concerning the crop in Part I and the relevant statistical information is presented in the form of tables in Part II. Originally a main volume dealing with each commodity was published once in four years followed by a supplement every year. With effect from 1960-61 the main volume was issued once in five years, synchronizing with the last year of the five-year plans. While the main volume contained data for five years, the supplement gives data generally for the last two or three years only. The review given in the main volume covered the entire position regarding production, utilization, trade, prices, etc. during the preceding five years period and that given in the annual supplement dealt with the latest years covered by each. Selected tables giving the principal data regarding the crop in the world were also given in most of brochures.

A New Publication — *Bulletin of Commercial Crop Statistics*, 1963-64 to 1968-69—was issued for the first time in March 1971 by the Directorate of Economics and Statistics. This issue presented within a brief compass an integrated picture of area, production, yield, market arrivals, imports, exports, distribution, prices and availability etc. of major commercial crops, i.e. cotton, jute (including mesta and sannhemp) oilseeds (including castor, cotton seed, coconut, safflower, niger seed and soyabean), sugarcane, spices (pepper, chillies, ginger, turmeric and cardamom), fruits bananas, cashewnuts, papaya), root crops (potato, sweet potato and tapioca), tobacco, opium, arecanut, guarseed and lac. The data contained in this publication which were drawn from a large variety of sources did not possess the same degree of accuracy. A detailed discussion with regard to some of the important commodities like cotton and sugarcane for which varied number of publications are available is discussed here.

COTTON

Besides the normal source of supply of data regarding area, production, yield, prices, etc. of various commodities as discussed elsewhere, there are a few specialized publications dealing with agricultural statistics pertaining to cotton in a comprehensive way. The most important of them are:

1. *Indian Cotton Annual* and 2. *Cotton Situation* (monthly)— unpublished.

Indian Cotton Annual

The Indian Cotton Annual, formerly styled as Bombay Cotton Annual is issued by the East-India Cotton Association Limited, Bombay. It is an authoritative compendium of all information relating to every branch of the Indian Cotton containing statistical tables on crops, exports, imports, prices, stocks, consumption, Government notifications, etc. designed to meet the requirements of all those who are interested in the cotton and cotton textile situation in India. The statistical tables are divided into the following 13 broad heads.

1. Cotton grown in India
2. Rainfall
3. Crop forecasts
4. Pressing returns
5. Consumption
6. Receipts into and exports of cotton from Bombay

7. Imports of cotton into Bombay
8. Imports of cotton into India.
9. Exports of cotton from India
10. Stocks of cotton at Bombay and all-India level
11. Statistics of Indian Textile Industry including handloom and power-loom
12. Statistics of foreign cotton particularly U.S.A., North America, South America, Sudan, Tanzania, U.A.R., Uganda and Japan.
13. World cotton statistics.

While area, production and yield data both at the State level and according to trade descriptions are given for the previous 5 years, such information by staple lengths, variety-wise for each State and districtwise is given only for one year with a time-lag of one or two years. All-India Summary Forecasts of India cotton crop, fully revised estimates, trade estimates, average yield (final forecasts), area, production, consumption and exports of Indian cotton along with mill consumption, imports, exports and mill stocks are given from the year 1947-48. Data are also provided for cotton seed production from 1959-60, kapas production from 1963-64 and index numbers of area and production under agricultural crops in India from 1952-53.

Weekly statement of cotton pressed by States for the latest year, similar monthly statements for the last two years and annual statement from 1959-60 are provided State-wise. Under consumption, information is provided regarding consumption of cotton by mills by States and monthly consumption of Indian and foreign cotton are provided for two years; a similar all-India summary is provided from 1963-64, mill consumption of cotton in India by staple lengths from 1951-52. Indian mills cotton consumption from 1941-42, distribution of Indian cotton crop from 1958, State-wise consumption of cotton for production of khadi cloth from 1963-64, distribution of cotton received at mills from 1962-63 and receipts at the mills in Indian Union of cotton classified by varieties for one year.

Data on weekly receipts into and exports of cotton from Bombay are provided for one year. Such monthly data for two years and yearly data from 1959-60 are also provided. Monthly receipts and exports of cotton into Bombay by road are available from 1965-66 and such yearly data are given from 1960-61. Similarly monthly exports and imports of Indian cotton from Bombay are provided for two years while yearly data in this respect are from 1944-45.

Monthly imports of foreign cotton showing quantity and value by variety in staple lengths are given for two years. Foreign cotton allocation for imports and foreign cotton licensed for imports are available from 1964-65. Similar import data are provided from 1963-64 and total imports and exports of raw cotton with their value from the year 1948-49. Similar information with regard to exports of cotton from India from chief ports Shipper-wise, variety-wise, country-wise in terms of quantity and value are also given over a long period.

Half-yearly and yearly stocks of cotton with trade in Bombay are given for two years, such monthly stocks with mills from 1964-65. Half yearly and yearly stocks with mills and trade are provided from 1954. At the all-India level, monthly stocks of cotton with mills, State-wise, are provided for two years. Summary of all-India mills, carry-over of Indian and foreign cotton by varieties is given from 1964-65. Stocks of Indian and foreign cotton with mills and trade as on 31st August is provided for two years.

Progress of the Indian cotton mills is given from 1866, number of cotton mills and their capacity from 1951, cotton consumption and cotton textile production from 1951 and cotton textile mills in India (State-wise) for two years. Similarly, yearly yarn production by Counts is given from 1951 and total imports and exports (both quantity and value) of cotton mill waste, yarn and cotton textiles in India is given from 1957.

The foreign section contains information with regard to area, production, yield, imports and exports, consumption and stocks, etc. for the individual countries mentioned earlier and the world as a whole.

Cotton Situation

This is a monthly unpublished bulletin issued by the Economics and Statistics Adviser to the Government of India, Ministry of Food and Agriculture with a time-lag of about two months. The introductory note gives a review of the cotton policy and other developments for cotton. The Statistical Section provides the latest available data with regard to area and production under cotton both official and trade estimates, arrival of cotton (kapas) from 35 selected markets in major cotton producing States, imports and exports of raw cotton, movement of raw cotton within the country by rail and river, consumption, month-end stocks and statistical position of raw cotton with mills, balance sheet of raw cotton on the basis of trade estimates and wholesale prices of kapas and cotton lint and cotton seed, along with the index numbers of wholesale prices of cotton, groundnut, jowar, bajra and sugarcane, cotton policy including export and import quotas, export and import duties, price policy giving floor and ceiling prices over the last 10 years, instructions regarding stock limits for a period of about 5 years, main exemptions giving margins and ceilings from time to time. An idea is also given about cotton textile policy with regard to prices and production control for different textile varieties.

In the world section, information is given regarding estimates of world production and consumption of cotton, world balance sheet of raw cotton and cotton prices for important countries like U.S.A., Mexico, Brazil, Pakistan, Uganda, U.S.S.R., Peru, Sudan, and Egypt.

Monthly Cotton Market Report

This report is issued by Patel Volkart Limited, Bombay and provides day-to-day data on cotton supply and distribution estimates, crop estimates, foreign trade, cotton consumption and stocks by local mills, import quotas, Indian cotton price movement, local cotton mills, production and stocks of textiles and a report from abroad with some useful information.

Indian Textile Bulletin

This is a monthly publication issued by the Economics and Statistics Branch of the Textile Commissioner, Bombay. The first issue of the journal appeared in June, 1955. Since its inception significant changes have taken place in the textile industry of India in regard to such aspects as structure, pattern of production and the nature of consumer demand. The growth of spinning mills, the expanding role of the decentralized sector in the production of cotton cloth, the increasing volume of production and availability of man-made fibre textiles and the district trend of preference towards blends are some of the areas, where the changes have been felt. It has been their endeavour, in keeping with the objective of presenting a factual and integrated picture of the textile industry in the country in its different sectors, to keep track of these changes and effect modifications in the presentation of data in the Bulletin accordingly. The Indian Textile Bulletin makes an attempt to reflect the developing trends in the field of textiles and maintain its utility as a reference volume to industry and labour, planners and policy-makers, administrators and traders as also to researchers.

The alternation in the get-up of the Bulletin in the metric system has necessitated a rearrangement of the contents. While every effort has been made to maintain the earlier system of presentation of statistics, it is to be noted that certain new items have also been added. Statistics relating to blended yarn and mixed fabrics have been introduced since September, 1968. The overview of the Bulletin is that while in Part I historical summary data have been presented, each of the subsequent parts is devoted to individual sectors of the industry. It is hoped that these revisions will enhance the utility of the publication, and facilitate easier reference.

The Statistical information is based on the monthly statistical returns submitted by the units of the various sectors of the Textile Industry under the Essential Commodities Act, 1955. The tables have been arranged accordingly to the different sectors of the Textile Industry. The primary data which form the basis of the tables presented have been drawn from various sources which have been indicated wherever necessary under the relevant tables.

Each of the issue provides information regarding cotton mills separately for spinning and composite mills, number of mills and spindles installed, raw cotton consumption both Indian and foreign separately and the productions of yarn as well as cloth both for the mill and the decentralized sector from the year 1951. Similarly non-cotton textile production separately for staple fibre, filament yarn, staple fibre spun yarn, man-made fibre fabrics and woollen textiles are also published from 1951. Foreign trade data regarding exports and imports of cotton textiles, handloom fabrics, handloom manufacturers, etc. as well as raw-cotton and cotton yarn are given from the year 1957. Similar information regarding imports and exports and man-fibres and woollen textile is provided from the year 1960-61.

Data on the production of textile machinery are provided from the year 1957 and exports and imports from 1960-61. Per capita availability of cloth is given from 1951 and index number of prices for important crops from 1963.

Besides the information provided on an all-India level as detailed above, State-wise information is given for the current year with regard to installed capacity of mills, shift-wise working of mills, labour employment machine activity, raw cotton consumption and stocks, cotton wastes soft and hard production, utilization and deliveries of cotton yarn, mill production, packings, deliveries, processing, exports of cotton fabrics, production of miscellaneous fabrics, production and deliveries of blended textiles, blended yarn, woollen yarn and woollen fabrics. Similar data for the current year are provided in the foreign trade sector for the current year, as discussed earlier. All-India information for 5 to 7 years is also provided with regard to various items discussed in this para along with the position regarding labour and employment by sex and States.

International Cotton Advisory Committee

This Committee which is located at Ashington is bringing out a quarterly bulletin—Cotton World Statistics—for the last 35 years. It is world-wise Association of Governments for the purpose of keeping in close touch with developments affecting the world cotton situation, compiling and publishing authentic information on this subject and promoting cooperation in the maintaining and developing of a sound world cotton economy. The information supplied in the journal is invariably obtained directly from the member countries.

The information contained in the journal pertains to area and yield, production, supply and distribution, consumption, exports, imports and stocks of cotton for the individual countries as well as the world as a whole. Such information which is available both in terms of bales of cotton as well as metric units is available for a period of 9-10 years. Similar data pertaining to production, imports and exports of cotton yarn, cotton cloth and rayon cloth for each of the member countries is also available for a period of about 5 years. Cotton prices for important varieties (CIF Liver Pool) available in the world are published for a period of 3-4 years. This is followed by country tables and each of the bulletin has 2 special tables at the end. The July 1972 issue for example provides information regarding world consumption of fibres and per capita consumption of all fibres, cotton, wool, rayon and synthetic fibres.

JUTE

The important sources of information on jute and jute manufacturers are at present the following specialized publications:

1. Jute Situation—a monthly Bulletin issued by the Directorate of Economics and Statistics, Ministry of Agriculture.
2. Monthly Summary of Jute and Gunny Statistics issued by the Statistics Department of Indian Jute Mills Association, Calcutta.

The two bulletins provide only statistical information. The Jute Situation is similar to other Bulletins of the same type for different commodities and is no longer being published. Information contained in this Bulletin relates to estimates of area, production and yield for jute as well as mesta, wholesale prices of raw jute at Calcutta and up-country markets as well as mesta at Calcutta and index numbers of wholesale prices of raw jute and mesta. It has a national balance sheet of raw jute for a period of about 10 years and monthly data pertaining to foreign trade of raw jute, production and stocks of jute goods, inland trade, rate of hedge contracts in jute goods, market arrivals of jute from villages, minimum/maximum purchase quotas for jute and purchases of raw jute by mills and State Trading Corporation as well as Jute Corporation. In addition to all this, it provides the current minimum support price of raw jute at Calcutta and derivative minimum support prices at secondary markets in Assam, Tripura, Bihar, Orissa as well as Andhra Pradesh, Madhya Pradesh and U.P. Detailed information is also available in respect of raw jute price policy, export policy duty, import duty, cess and excise duty leviable, bank advances against raw jute and jute goods and the commodities to which Forward Contracts Act is applied. In section 2 of the bulletin, international data are available pertaining to production, exports, imports and wholesale prices of raw jute for the important countries of the world.

The Monthly Summary of Jute and Gunny Statistics is the most authoritative source for various types of data on jute and jute goods. It provides 11 comprehensive tables in each of its monthly issues. The figures, in general, are shown in metric units but in respect of items for which old British and Indian measures are still very much in practical use, old units are also given either side by side or in a separate table.

Official forecasts pertaining to area and production of jute as well as mesta are reproduced immediately they are available. The supply and distribution table is, however, based on trade estimates of the crop which, as discussed elsewhere, is always different from the official data relating to production. The overall raw jute position for the industry is provided in a comparative statement of stocks, deliveries, consumption and exports of raw jute. The information in respect of mills is compiled from returns received from the members of the Association and some non-member mills and cover more than 90 per cent of the industry.

The data for Jute and Jute Goods Buffer Stock Association (J & JGBSA) represent all its members some of which are not covered by mill returns. Both receipts and purchase figures shown here include transfers from J & JGBSA. Purchases indicate actual purchases (including cuttings) irrespective of deliveries. Actual figures are revised when annual returns are compiled. Imports of raw jute into Calcutta and mill stations shows the arrival of Indian Jute into Indian Jute Mill Association (IJMA) mills from different States by various modes of transportation. Stocks, production and despatches of gunnies are compiled from returns submitted by mills in the membership of the Association and certain non-member mills. They represent more than 90 per cent of the jute mills in India on a loomage basis. Despatch figures indicate the amount of goods sent out from India.

Data pertaining to export of gunnies from India by countries are compiled from the monthly statistics of the foreign trade of India issued by the Director General of Commercial Intelligence and Statistics, Government of India. The current data are, however, compiled by the Association and are subject to revision when the regular publication is issued. The information supplied here is with regard to the quantity and value of such experts.

The stock and consumption figures for U.S.A. are obtained from the Association's New York office and are estimates for the whole U.S. jute industry. Based on the returns received by the Textile Bag Manufacturers Association, similar data are collected for imports of burlap as well as carpet backing into U.S.A. Figures regarding inventories and deliveries of carpet backing in U.S.A. are those held by members of the Jute Carpet Backing Council in U.S.A. and the deliveries effected during the month. The inventories cover only 'spot goods' and not 'afloat' goods including those on board on steamers docking on the last day of the month. JCBC figures account for about 85 per cent of the total U.S.A. carpet backing. Weekly prices of jute and gunnies for India at Calcutta are those obtained through Calcutta brokers.

SUGARCANE

Besides the normal sources (discussed elsewhere) which provide the usual data, there are two specialized monthly journals which are useful from the point of view of most up-do-date data on practically all aspects of the sugar economy. 'Indian Sugar' being published by the Indian Sugar Mills Association is one of the oldest journals in this field. The journal was started 30 years back in 1950 and in addition to the specialized articles on current topics relating to the sugar economy, the statistical tables supply the data on the following items:

1. Production, despatches and stocks of sugar State-wise. The October issue for example giving the position as on Ist September.
2. Area under sugarcane, yield of sugar, cane production, number of factories, working capacity, cane crushed, recovery, sugar production, duration and the production of molasses at the all-India level for the period 1932-33 up-to-date.

3. State-wise sugarcane acreage, production, cane crushed by central sugar production factories, sugar production directly from cane, average recovery of sugar, average duration of crushing season and number of factories in operation for the period 1950-51 onward State-wise.

4. Monthly releases of sugar (both levy and free) since partial decontrol.

5. Existing levy price for different zones with and without excise duty for the latest 3 years. State-wise consumption of sugar for a period of 13 years.

6. Opening stocks, production, available supply, consumption and exports of sugar at the all-India level for 10 years.

7. Grade-wise production of sugar for the last 10 years.

This very Association brings out its annual publication entitled 'Indian Sugar Year Book' which has a time-lag of about two years. The first issue for the year 1964-65 was brought out in November 1966. This gives a comprehensive review of the Indian as well as international sugar situation for the current year with reference to a much longer period of 10 to 15 years.

Cooperatives are today playing a very important role in the total production of sugar in the country, accounting for over 40 per cent of the production. Once the sanctioned licensed capacity is also installed, they are expected to increase their share to over 50 per cent. A monthly journal—Cooperative Sugar—of the National Federation of Cooperative Sugar Factories Limited is being issued since 1969. The statistical tables provide useful information on the following items:

1. State-wise sugar production, despatches and stocks of sugar for the current year, in the cooperative sector.

2. Opening stocks, production, imports, consumption and exports of sugar since 1950-51.

3. Utilization of sugarcane for different purposes from 1960-61.

4. State-wise number of sugar factories in operation, crushing seasons, cane crushed, sugar produced and average recovery for the period 1961-62 onward. This information is supplied separately for all-India as well as share of the cooperative sector.

5. Latest available monthly data on average wholesale prices of sugar, ruling in principal markets.

MISCELLANEOUS SOURCES

There are a few other sources where other useful information is also available. Area, production and yield in respect of the Development Schemes under sugarcane is compiled by the Directorate of Sugarcane Development, Ministry of Agriculture. They, however, do not publish this information themselves but the Season and Crop Reports of some of the State Governments provide this data with a time-lag of 3-4 years. Similarly, prices of sugarcane paid by the sugar mills are available with the Directorate of Sugar and Vanaspati but here again this is not published by them, Some of the annual reports of the Agricultural Prices Commission pertaining to Price Policy for Sugarcane supply this data. Information is also available from this very source in respect of minimum statutory prices recommended by the Commission and those accepted by the Government. Data on ex-factory sugar prices are also compiled by the Sugar Policy Section of the Department of Food, Ministry of Agriculture as well as the Directorate of Sugar and Vanaspati. The Reports of the Agricultural Prices Commission also provide valuable data on different aspects of the sugar economy including some other unpublished data.

The Directorate of Economics and Statistics, Ministry of Agriculture brings out a monthly bulletin—Sugar Situation (of course for official use only). Besides the usual information on different aspects of sugar, as already discussed, some of the additional information available in this Bulletin is as follows:

1. Month-end (Friday) wholesale prices of sugar, gur and khandsari.
2. Production of sugar in some important countries of world.
3. Prices of sugar in foreign markets—latest available.
4. Arrivals from villages of gur in certain selected markets in major gur producing States.
5. Policy in respect of production, distribution, prices and trade of sugarcane, sugar, gur and khandsari.

OILSEEDS AND OILS

The last issue of the annual publication of the Directorate of Economics and Statistics, Oilseeds in India, was for the year 1963-64. Thereafter it was only the first issue of the Bulletin on Commercial Crop Statistics (1963-64 to 1968-69) which presented at one place data pertaining to area, production, yield, market arrivals, inland movement, foreign trade, utilization, prices and world information in respect of groundnut, rape, mustard, linseed, castor, cotton seed, coconut, safflower, niger seed and soyabean. The latest issue of the Bulletin relates to the year 1978. There is also the monthly brochure, Oilseeds Situation issued by the Directorate of E & S, Ministry of Agriculture. Just like similar brochures for other commodities, this is also intended for restricted circulation and besides usual information regarding area, production, yield, etc. it also provides estimated production of solvent extracted oils and deoiled cakes in India as well as consumption of raw oils by the vanaspati industry. Current information on policy problems like exports of oilseeds, vegetable oils and oil cakes, export/import duties on oilseeds and oils, forward trading in this commodity, provisions regarding directives regulating bank advances against oilseeds and vegetable oils as well as fiscal incentives for the increased production of various oils, etc. is also provided.

A good deal of information regarding the vanaspati industry with regard to the number of factories, production of vanaspati ghee, capacity of the various factories and consumption of oil by the industry, etc. are available with the Sugar and Vanaspati Directorate of the Department of Food, Ministry of Agriculture. This is not, however, being published on a regular basis. The Vanaspati Manufacturers Association is now bringing out a regular Bulletin providing useful data on oils and oilseeds which is available with the various government and private sector institutions but not being published.

The annual reports of the Agricultural Prices Commission on Price Policy or Groundnut, Soyabean and Sunflower seed also provide valuable information concerning price analysis and basic price data along with other ancillary information on different aspects of various oilseeds and oils for the country. A special publication on vegetable oilseeds, oils and allied industries was issued by the East India Oil Millers Association in July 1970. This contains informative papers by authoritative sources on different aspects of oils and oilseeds followed by valuable statistics like those of State-wise list of oil mills in the country and estimated pattern of consumption of various oilseeds and oils by end-uses in India. A useful table on relative importance of ghanies and power mills in vegetable oil production and oil recovery rates of each is also provided. A Report on Minor Oilseeds published by the Ministry of Agriculture during 1970 has brought at one place all the information pertaining to minor oilseeds in the country. The State Trading Corporation of India which is responsible for the import/export of oilseeds and oils collects information on international prices for various oils and oilseeds as well as world demand and supply situation for its internal use. The Soyabean Council of America located at New Delhi has readily available with it all the data pertaining to world prices as well as demand and supply situation of soybean and soybean oil.

15

Livestock and Poultry

INCREASING ROLE OF LIVESTOCK IN THE NATIONAL ECONOMY

India possesses the largest livestock population in the world. According to the 1992 census data, the country had the highest number of cattle (212 m) and buffaloes (90 m), second highest number of goats (121 m), third highest number of sheep (57 m) and sixth highest number of chickens (375 m) in the world. Livestock forms one of the important sub-sectors of Indian agriculture. Although the share of GDP from agriculture as a whole has been declining over the years, the contribution of livestock to the GDP increased from less than 5% in 1980-81 to over 7% in 1997-98, according to the provisional estimates of the CSO, gross value of output from the livestock sector at current prices was about Rs. 1113 billion during 1997-98, which was about 30 per cent of agricultural output. In fact, animal husbandry and fisheries sectors play an important role in the national economy and socio-economic development of the country.

This sector plays in important and vital role in providing nutritive food, rich in animal protein to the general public and in supplementing family incomes and generating gainful employment in the rural sector, particularly among the landless, small and marginal farmers and women. As many as 72% of the families who own milch animals are landless, marginal and small Major part of the livestock population is concentrated in the marginal/small size of holdings. But the quality of animals held by them is poor. Cross breed cattle and quality buffaloes with this class is rather small. Milk production is thus very low in these area. BIMARU states where poverty is the highest fall in this category.

The development of animal husbandry has been envisaged as an integral part of sound system of diversified agriculture. With its large livestock population, India has vast potential for meeting the growing needs of its teeming millions, particularly in respect of livestock products such as milk, eggs, meat and wool. This sector provides animal protein and various types of raw materials for industrial use.

Livestock is also the principal source of draft power in rural areas contributing about 40 million horsepower or 30,000 megawatt of energy.

344

Draft power from animal sources is estimated at Rs. 10,000 crores—around 10% of the contribution. However, a declining trend of animal draft power is evident following mechanization of agriculture. The share of draft animals in farm power was almost 72 per cent in 1961. It came down to 23 per cent by 1991 and many of the farm operations have been switched over to electrical and mechanical sources of power. Likewise, rising expectations and migration has reduced the scope of draft animal power, which is labour intensive.

Bullock power still continues to be the main source of draught power in agricultural operations and transport of agricultural products to the nearby markets and is likely to remain so for a long period to come. Besides, cattle, camels and donkeys are other important effective draught animals and it is estimated that draught animal power from livestock caters to about 86% of the total mofussil motive requirement of our country. Agricultural production programmes get valuable organic manure provided by the livestock. Biogas production based on dung is a very efficient source of non-conventional energy used for domestic cooking and lighting.

Gender equity is more pronounced in livestock sector with women constituting 71% of the labour force as against only 33% in crop farming. About 10 million families in India are engaged in sheep, goat, rabbit and pack animal, fur/skin processing, fibre/wool handling and meat production. Livestock indeed is considered as an important economic activity that can help to alleviate poverty. Livestock production systems are based on low cost agro by-products as nutritional inputs, using traditional technologies. The spectacular growth of livestock products especially milk, meat, eggs and poultry meat is, however, attributed to the initiatives taken by the organized sector and the rising demand for these products in response to rising incomes in urban and rural areas. It has been observed that with increasing income, demand for cereals is decreasing. While Green Revolution was supply driven, Livestock Revolution is demand driven. With ever increasing demand for livestock products, its impact on agricultural economy becomes immensely important.

ALL-INDIA LIVESTOCK CENSUS

Historical Review

Attempts are said to have been made in the Moghul period to take a cattle census but it was only from the end of the last century that any regular census system was initiated. The work was first taken up in certain districts of the Punjab and later in Bengal and other British provinces. In most parts, the statistics were collected annually. They were collected neither at the same time nor were the methods of enumeration uniform throughout the country. With a view to standardizing the methods of collection and making the data comparable and more useful, the then Government of India decided in 1916 that a census should be taken throughout British India during the cold weather of 1919-20 and that this census should be repeated quinquennially thereafter.

The first census in British India was held from December 1919 to April 1920. Forty-eight Princely States representing about 29 per cent of the total area of these States took part in the census. The second census was taken in British India during the winter of 1924-25 when twelve more Indian States participated, bringing the total area covered by the States to about 38 per cent. It was subsequently felt that the period of enumeration of the previous two livestock censuses, viz. December to April, was too long and that the results obtained were, to some extent, vitiated by the inter-provincial and inter-State movement of cattle. The Royal Commission on Agriculture also drew attention to this shortcoming and recommended that the livestock census should be held simultaneously throughout India in as short a period as possible, so that the results were more accurate and reliable. Accordingly, the third, fourth, fifth and sixth censuses were held generally in January in the years, 1930, 1935, 1940 and 1945, respectively. The third census (1930) was taken in all the provinces and India's 83 princely States, covering about 50 per cent of the total area of the Indian States. In the fourth census (1935), Bengal, Bihar and Orissa did not participate mainly due to financial reasons. A large number of Indian States, however, participated in it accounting for about 66 per cent of the total area. In the fifth census (1940), Uttar Pradesh and Orissa did not join owing to the need for economy during World War II but a larger number of Indian States took part increasing the coverage to 70 per cent of their total area. The sixth census (1945) was conducted in all the Provinces and Administrations in British India and Indian States (92 per cent); Uttar Pradesh, however, conducted the census in 1944 and Bengal in 1946.

The seventh livestock census (the first livestock census of the Indian Union after Independence in 1947) was due to be conducted in January, 1950 but was postponed to May, 1951. This was done with a view to combining it with the F.A.O. Census of Agriculture. However, when it was decided to postpone the F.A.O. Census, it was felt that the livestock census should not be postponed any further. Instructions were accordingly issued by the Government of India to the States in April, 1950 to hold the livestock census in May, 1951. For ensuring uniformity in concepts and obtained comparable data, the Government of India prescribed uniform proforma and also issued detailed instructions for carrying out the census. Some of the States could not carry out the census according to the stipulated programme because of some administrative and local difficulties. In Ajmer and PEPSU, it was carried out during June, 1951, in West Bengal in September, 1951, in Rajasthan in February 1952 and in Travancore-Cochin in August, 1952. These States were, however, asked by the Central Government to take account of the inter-State movement of cattle since May, 1951. In Orissa, financial difficulties and in Manipur lack of proper primary agencies for collecting the required data, stood in the way of carrying out the census in 1951.

With the initiation of the First Five-Year Plan for economic development of the country, need was felt for rationalizing the conduct of livestock census and for effective improvements in the content and reliability of data. It was felt that it would be a distinct advantage if the alternate livestock censuses were held in the same years as those fixed for the population censuses. The list of households prepared for the population census could be utilized for the livestock census at least during the alternate censuses. This would reduce the work-load of the livestock census. As the census of population was conducted in the month of February, it was decided that the livestock census be held as early as practicable thereafter. It was also desirable to avoid monsoons as well as the hot summer months when the livestock often migrated on account of lack of local grazing facilities. From these points of view, the first fortnight of April was considered suitable for carrying out the enumeration. It was also decided to carry out the enumeration with reference to a fixed date as in the case of census of population so as to avoid double counting as a result of movement of livestock. Accordingly, the eighth livestock census was conducted in 1956 with April 15, 1956 as the reference date. Due to administrative and other difficulties, West Bengal, Orissa and Manipur conducted the census only in 1957. The reference date was April 15, 1957 in the case of Orissa and December 15, 1957 in the case of Manipur. West Bengal carried out the enumeration in 1957 with the original reference date, i.e. April 15, 1956.

Some procedural improvements were made in the conduct of the livestock census of 1956. The proformae and instructions for the census were finalized at a conference of the State Livestock Census Officers convened by the Directorate of Economics and Statistics in August, 1955 at New Delhi. These were uniformly adopted by all the States. In this census, data were separately collected for rural and urban areas. Arrangements were also made to publish the provisional estimates of the census immediately after the conduct of the census. A central post enumeration check was also introduced by National Sample Survey Organization on the results of livestock census obtained by the States.

The ninth all-India Livestock Census was held with April, 15, 1961 as the reference date. Due to administrative and other difficulties, Jammu & Kashmir and Manipur could not adhere to the all-India programme, Jammu & Kashmir carried out the census with November 1, 1961 and Manipur with October 15, 1962 as the reference date. The proformae and instructions of the ninth census were generally the same as for the eighth census except that a new classification of Yaks, was added under bovine. Separate information was collected for desi and improved fowls. The list of implements was also modified so as to collect data on pumps for irrigation purposes and persian wheels or rahats.

The tenth all-India Livestock Census was held with **April 15, 1966** as the reference date. Due to administrative and other difficulties, **Jammu & Kashmir** could not adhere to the all-India programme, **Jammu &**

Kashmir carried out the census with November 15, 1966 as the reference date. The proformae and instructions of the tenth census were generally the same as for the ninth census except for the inclusion of information on fishing craft and tackle for the first time and addition of a few more columns by way of an amplification of certain items of data. Such as sheep up to one year, camels four year old and under and pigs were further classified into male and female. The female goats one year old and over were further classified into milk, dry and others. Separate information was collected for desi and improved chicken. Six new items, viz. improved harrows and cultivators, improved seed drills, improved threshers, rotary chaff cutters, sprayers and dusters and 2-wheel-walking tractors or power tillers were added under the head 'Agricultural Machinery and Implements'.

During this census, several improvements were made in the organization and in the collection of data, i.e.

   (i) The work connected with the conduct of the census was distributed among a larger number of officers for ensuring greater accuracy;

  (ii) The experienced staff utilized earlier for the 1961 population census was employed as far as possible;

 (iii) Departmental supervision was strengthened and rationalized supervision on random sampling basis was introduced in all the States;

 (iv) A post-enumeration check was also undertaken by the National Sample Survey Organization;

  (v) The enumerators and supervisory staff were given some practical training;

 (vi) In addition to the departmental scrutiny, Block Development Officers and District Statistical Officers also exercized scrutiny of the data.

1982 Censuses

At the time of the 1982 census, the central government authorities, in their wisdom, changed the reference date to 15th of October. They also changed the age-old functional classification of the adult cattle and buffalo males. Instead of the earlier threefold classification of the adult males as between animals (1) 'used for breeding', (2) 'used for breeding and work' and (3) 'used for work only', they also introduced a twofold classification as between (1) 'castrated' and (2) 'uncastrated'. It seems that they did so because they were overtaken by the euphoria of the time about the so-called white 'revolution' led by crossbred cows. They, perhaps thought that *work* as a functional category, in other words draught power contribution of the cattle and buffalo males was no longer important for Indian agriculture. It is notable in this context that enumeration of crossbred cattle was introduced for the first time in 1982, even though crossbreeding, as a matter of policy, had been started as early as 1966.

Both these changes, that is the change in the reference date of the census and the change regarding functional classification of the adult cattle and buffalo males, had their deleterious consequences. The change in the reference date was made in such a messy way that out of 32 states and union territories none carried out the census on the new reference date. In fact half of them had already carried out the 1982 census on the old reference date of 15th April before the change was made. Things improved gradually with subsequent censuses. Yet as many as 19 enumerating units in 1987 and 14 in 1992 did not take the census on the reference date. They took the census one to two years later. As a result we have an anomalous situation of an Indian Livestock Census enumeration which takes two years to complete.

The change in the functional classification of the adult male animals marred the comparability of the number of working animals across various censuses. In response to criticism previous classification was restored in 1987. But the 1982 figures of the castrated and uncastrated males hang out separately.

Subsequent Censuses

These followed quinquennially thereafter with expanded coverage and scope. Until the 13th Census, the scheme used to be a non-plan activity and funds for conducting it were provided from the State Budget. This used to result in delays in organizing field work, tabulation and publication of final results by the states. Hence, a Centrally Sponsored Scheme for providing assistance to states for conducting Livestock Census was initiated in the 7th Five Year Plan for conducting 14th Livestock Census in 1987-88. The scheme aimed at assisting the states to the extent of 50 per cent and UTs upto 100 per cent in respect of the principal components of the census i.e. primary enumeration, supervision, contingencies and support for tabulation of results of the census. Inspite of this, a number of states/UTs did not conduct the census. The number of defaulting states increased from 2 (1982) to 7 (1992). What is most distressing is the fact that a progressive state like Punjab is among the defaulting states since 1982.

Some of the States/UTs had not adhered to reference dates in the past, leading to problems of non-comparability of the data at all India level. The scheduled date of reference for conducting the livestock census in 1977, 1982, 1987 and 1992 were not followed by a number of States/UTs. Hence many states could not conduct the census on the reference date (i.e. 15-10-87) on account of shifting of cattle for various reasons. The conduct of the Census was postponed to 1988 and for some States/UTs even to 1990. This affected the conduct of the 15th Census with 15-10-1992 as reference date as the States/UTs which conducted the census in 1990, did not think it proper to conduct the same again in 1992.

In view of the difficulties encountered during the earlier livestock, the sub-Group on Animal Husbandry Statistics and Information for Ninth

Plan had recommended that the 16th Livestock Census, with reference date 15-10-1997, should be taken up as a Central Sector Scheme. This was also agreed by the Technical Committee constituted by the Government for advising it on conducting the 16th Census. The EFC in its meeting held on 14-12-98 not only approved the cost on the basis of 100 per cent Central assistance but also approved to enhance the rate of honorarium of Rs. 2/- per household. However, 100 per cent assistance was released by the IFD of the Ministry of Agriculture with effect from 1999-2000 onward.

For the first time it was decided to provide financial assistance for computerization of the work of livestock census both at the district and the State Headquarters level by providing one personal computer (PC), a printer and a constant voltage stabiliser (CVT) each at a cost not exceeding Rs. 5,500/- per unit.

Despite all this the progress of work of the Sixteenth Livestock Census is not up to the mark. Reports from a number of States/UTs have not been received as yet, while some of the States/UTs have submitted only incomplete reports. There are still others like Bihar, which have not as yet started the enumeration work.

LIVESTOCK PRODUCTS

As regards livestock output statistics, it may be noted that there are two sets of products—products from live animals and products from the fallen and slaughtered animals. In making the estimates of outputs of the livestock products, one will agree, reliable statistics on yield parameters are critical to estimation. Let us first consider output from the fallen and slaughtered animals. It may be a surprise to know that for estimation of output of products like bones, horns, hoof, edible offals, fats etc. the CSO still uses enquiry-based yield rates given in the DMI (Directorate of Marketing and Inspection) Reports of the 1950s and early 1960s. One may ask whether those yield-rates have not at all changed over this long period of about half a century? Certainly they must have changed, indeed for the better, in view of the fact that the average body-weight of the slaughtered as well as the fallen animals must have increased due to growth in per animal feed availability, arising out the agricultural growth during this period. Is the central government so helpless that it can not organise even DMI-like enquiries to update the yield rate figures periodically?

Beside the quality of the output estimates minor products, hides and skins from the fallen and slaughtered animals and meat from the slaughtered animals are major products of the livestock sector. The situation in regard to the yield and output statistics on these products are hardly better. The only reliable up-to-date estimate regarding meat is from the registered slaughter houses across the country. The same can be said about the number of hides and skins from the slaughter houses. For the rest, i.e. output figures of meat from slaughtering in the vast countryside, and the number of hides and skins from the fallen animals are indeed conjured up figures in the offices of the Animal Husbandry Departments of the state governments. For estimation of the hides and skins from fallen animals one ought to know their number. How one knows that number in the absence of any organised system of reporting?

What the CSO does for it's own purposes is to apply the mortality rates as given in the old DMI Report of 1961 to the estimated numbers of various categories of the livestock population in the relevant year, in order to get the outputs of hides and skins from the fallen animals. Here again, one should ask, whether mortality rates have stayed where they were 40 years ago?

Come to the most important product, namely milk, whose value of output, on CSO's reckoning, accounts for about two-third of the total value of output from the livestock sector. In order to appreciate the present position and the problems of milk production estimation, a bit of history is necessary as a background.

In the early 1950s the Directorate of Marketing and Inspection in the Ministry of Agriculture used to prepare all India milk production estimates. It was generally agreed that their estimates were not quite reliable. Major defect from which the estimates suffered was the use of milk-yield data supplied by the State Departments of Animal Husbandry and Veterinary services, which were obtained on 'subjective enquiry basis'. In order to get better milk-yield figures the Nation Sample Survey Organisation, collected yield data from sample survey enquiries, in their 12th and 15th Rounds (Reports No. 72 and 90) carried out during March-August, 1957 and July-June 1959-60 respectively. It turned that in a short span of two years between the two NSS Surveys, estimated milk production showed a fall of over 30 percent, even though the 15th Round, covering the whole year was an improvement over the 12th Round. Apparently, the milk-yield figures obtained from the NSS Surveys were also unreliable. As V.N. Amble remarked later, attempts to obtain reliable milk-yield estimates from any type of enquiry were indeed 'futile'.

In the meanwhile IASRI had begun conducting milk production surveys in typical tracts of the country during the Second Five Year Plan, and continued them during the Third Plan. The hallmark of these surveys was that data on milk-yield were obtained by actual weighment of daily milk yield of cows and buffaloes at the sample households during the three seasons of the year. Based on the survey results, all India milk production estimates were made at the IASRI first by Amble, then by Goel and others, and again by Raut and others respectively for the livestock census years, 1961, 1966 and 1977.[1]

That much about history. It was against this background that the methodology developed by the IASRI for estimation of milk production

---

[1]Mishra S.N. the Status of Livestock Statistics in India, *Journal of the Indian Society of Agricultural Statistics*, December 1999.

was officially accepted by the Ministry of Agriculture and the CSO in 1965 as the one which should be relied upon for getting reliable estimates. The design of an Integrated Sample Survey (ISS) covering all types of animals of a livestock-holding, and all types of outputs and inputs—not just milk-yield, but meat-yield from slaughtering, dung, eggs produced and birds disposed, particulars of animals, their feed consumption etc.— was prepared and was supposed to be annually carried out from the Fourth Plan onward by the States and Union Territories all over the country.

However, it took ten years before some states carried out the Integrated Sample Survey in 1977-78. Few of them carry out the Survey regularly and not all of them carry it out in any given year. So, how in a situation like this annual milk production estimates are made? States, which do carry out the Survey supply their 'Survey estimate' to the Ministry of Agriculture at the centre. States, which do not carry out the Survey, supply to the centre what is called 'official estimate.' In 1979-80 a committee called Technical Committee of Direction for Improvement of Animal Husbandry and Dairy Statistics was appointed by the central government for purposes of scrutinising, reconciling two sets of the estimates supplied by the states and finally approving state wise and all India milk production estimates for official release. The task of the Technical committee is onerous and continuing. The so called 'official estimates' of milk production supplied by the unsurveyed States are no better than those prepared by the DMI in the early 1950s. There are problems with the 'Survey estimates' as well. A sub-committee set up to make an in-depth examination of the estimates found that the survey design is not strictly followed in operation, actual weighment of milk yield is not done as often as required and non-response rate is quite high (Technical Committee Report, [1988]). In view of the doubtful reliability of the official estimates' and infirmity associated with the 'Survey estimates' it is not surprising that the Technical Committee takes about two years to finalise and put the official seal on the state wise and all-India milk production estimates. Finally if the estimates supplied by the states were reliable and timely, there would be no need for a Technical committee of Direction to sit over them.

As referred earlier to the FAO's estimates of India's milk production, in the context a study we did an appraisal of livestock development in the country, we examined FAO's estimates in some detail (Mishra and Sharma[2]). Our interest arose from the fact that FAO was the only agency which had been publishing an annual series of estimates since 1951. Whereas our own 'approved official estimates' were available only for the census year up to 1966.

---

[2]Mishra S.N. and Sharma R.K. 1990, Livestock Development in India—An appraisal, Indian Institute of Economic Green Vikas, New Delhi.

We found that the FAO figures for the Indian Livestock Census Year, 1951 to 1966 were identical with the official estimates. This feature apparently operated as a constraint on their figures for inter-census years. Even if independently estimated these figures had to be so adjusted as to fall in with the census year figures. So was the case indeed. This is reflected in the very wide variation of the annual growth rates of cow and buffalo milk production at short intervals in the series. The adjustment also required them to change the ratio of buffalo to cow milk production each year in favour of buffaloes—a very unlikely case in real life. Their estimates for the inter-census years for the period 1951 to 1966 were, thus, rendered unreliable.

Realising this, perhaps, the FAO changed track from 1967. They decided to free themselves from the constraint of having to accept official Indian estimates, and to make independent annual estimates. But in doing so they produced a more strange spectacle. Our analysis of their series from 1967 to 1982 showed this time, quite in contrast to the period before 1966, they kept the ratio of buffalo to cow milk production constant at 1.31:1.00. This they did by letting the cow and buffalo milk production grow exactly at the same rate from one to the next year through the whole sequence. As one can see, both assumptions are arbitrary, having no connection with reality. And both of these, embedded as they are in the FAO series from 1967 to 1982, the series becomes completely unreliable.

The FAO changed track again in 1983. They seemed to have woken-up to the story that crossbred cows had become carriers of white revolution in India. Accordingly, they began to slide down the ratio of buffalo to cow milk production in order to give higher weightage to cow milk production in the total. This change of course necessitated showing different annual growth rates for cow and buffalo milk production. Our examination of the FAO series covered the period up to 1986 only.

Before ending the story, however, we must mention one more feature of the FAO estimates. Since 1967 their figures never coincided with the official Indian estimates of total milk production. They were generally higher, and in some year higher by close to a million ton or more. They had, thus, a pleasing ring for us. The recent media hype about India having become largest milk producer in the world, perhaps, was inspired by the same pleasing but unreliable statistics.

VALUE OF LIVESTOCK OUTPUT

Problems relating to data regarding livestock products are further reflected in the value estimates released by the C.S.O. every year in the publication—Economic Survey.[3]

---

[3]A detailed not about the procedure adopted by the C.S.O. for various livestock products is given in Annex 1.

There is at present a good deal of arbitrariness about data in livestocks as well as prices, leading to a good deal of confusion. CSO, for example, provides annual data regarding the value of output from livestock sector under the heads—(1) Milk Group, (2) Meat Group—meat, beef, mutton, pork, poultry meat, meat products, by-products, hides, skins, other by products (3) Eggs (4) Wool-Hair—wool, hair and bristles (5) Dung—dung fuel, dung manure, (6) Silk worm cocoons and honey.

All calculations about the contribution of a particular sector in the national economy and its growth from year to year is to be calculated only from this source. Obviously the numbers given here are assumed to be based on the unit value of each of the items listed above. Since no reliable information is available either about the quantities produced or the unit prices of the same, final results are bound to suffer from non representative nature of the real ground situation. Table below provides value of livestock products as given by the C.S.O. in their annual National Accounts Statistics for the years 1990-91 and 1997-98. Available information on output for items like milk, various types of meat and eggs is also given for these two years. Unit value is then derived for each one. There is no information about the production of other items which constitute only 16 per cent of the total value. Serious discrepancies are observed in these data relating to livestock. For instance the unit value of beef and veal for the year 1990-91 comes to Rs. 3.1 per kg., while for poultry the calculated unit value is Rs. 66.5 per kg. Similarly for 1997-98, the year for which the latest data are available, the unit value of mutton is reckoned at Rs. 117.5 per kg., and for poultry this comes to Rs. 102.3 per kg (Table 15.1). There seems to be an error either at the level of production of these products or in their total value (or in both of these factors) included in the National Accounts for the Livestock sector. It is essential to reconcile these discrepancies. This type of a situation further strengthens our earlier recommendation about the need for a very reliable data base of this sector.

INTEGRATED SAMPLE SURVEY FOR ESTIMATION OF PRODUCTION OF MAJOR LIVESTOCK PRODUCTS

The scheme on 'Sample Survey for Estimation of Production of Major Livestock Products' which was initiated in 1975-76, has been continuing since then in the States either as a Centrally Sponsored Scheme, or as a State Sector Scheme. Since the Seventh Five Year Plan, the scheme is being implemented as a Centrally Sponsored Scheme, titled "Integrated Sample Survey for the Estimation of Production of Major livestock Products' and the same has been continued during the Eighth and Ninth Five Year Plans.

The broad objectives of the scheme are as under:
  (i) Estimation of livestock numbers,
 (ii) Average yield per animal (in respect of milk, eggs, wool and meat) at State and National level.

Table 15.1 Value of output from livestock and unit value

Commodity	1990/91			1997/98		
	Output (000 tonnes)	Value Rs. Million	Unit Value Rs./Kg.	Output (000 tonnes)	Value Rs. Million	Unit Value Rs./Kg
Milk	58,400	292,690	5.0	71,000	719,580	10.1
Meat	3,710	60,470	16.3	4,200	197,375	47.0
Beef and Veal	2,361	7,300	3.1	1,295	27,050	20.9
Buffalo meat	@	@		1210	17,125	14.2
Mutton	623	24,240	38.9	675	79,340	117.5
Pork	361	4,870	13.5	420	9,480	22.6
Poultry meat	362	24,060	66.5	600	61,380	102.3
Eggs (million pcs.)	22,913	13,430	0.6	30,000	36,160	1.2
Sub-Total		366,590			953,115 (126.6%)	
Meat Products		2,380				
By Products (I)		6,970				
Wool and Hair (mil.kgs)	40.6	1,450				
Dung		43,470				
Others	15,820					
Sub-total	70,090					
% share in total value		16.0				
Grand Total		436,680				

Note : I) Includes hides, skins, others; Output at factor costs included under beef and veal.
Source : Central Statistical Organization: National Account Statistics 1993 and 1994.

(iii) District level estimates of production of milk and eggs including average yield per animal.
(iv) Product utilization.
(v) Feeds provided to animals of different species, and
(vi) Cost of production per unit of milk and eggs in the selected districts.

There are three components of the scheme:

(a) Central Sector Scheme on "Strengthening of the Animal Husbandry Statistics Cell at Headquarters" in the Department of Animal Husbandry and Dairying.

(b) Centrally sponsored Scheme on "Integrated Sample Survey for Estimation of Production of Major Livestock Products viz., milk, eggs, wool and meat" in States.

(c) Central Sector Scheme on "Strengthening of Animal Husbandry Statistics" in Union Territories.

At present, the scheme is being implemented in all the States and Union Territories for estimation of production at State/UT level. The surveys for preparation of the district level estimates of production of milk and eggs are being conducted in all States, while cost of production surveys for milk and eggs have been undertaken in a few selected districts of States. The Animal Husbandry Statistics unit in the Department of Animal Husbandry and Dairying, Ministry of Agriculture, provides technical guidance and training and undertakes occasional supervision of the surveys at field level, examines/analyses the reports and coordinates the information/statistics regarding production of major livestock products and other related aspects as All India level. Estimates of production of milk, eggs, wool and meat and other related statistics are compiled and published by the Department of Animal Husbandry and Dairying.

These surveys have a comprehensive coverage with 15 per cent of the total villages and for complete enumeration of livestock population (5 per cent villages for each of the 3 seasons). Scientific methods are then applied for the production of milk, egg and wool. The results are presented to the Technical Committee which releases these estimates every year.

CROP-CUTTING EXPERIMENTS

The greatest handicap in collecting statistics of livestock products has been the absence of suitable techniques for the purpose. With a view to bridging this serious gap, the random sampling techniques developed for the purpose of estimation of yield of major crops through crop-cutting experiments were extended to the estimation of livestock products in the beginning of the Second Five Year Plan period. The estimation of livestock products, however, is formidable as compared to estimation of crop production in the sense that: (1) the number of producing units is much larger in the case of livestock products as compared with the number of fields which produce crop yields. (2) The production of livestock products takes place all the year round whereas in the case of crop production, the production is purely seasonal. (3) In the case of livestock, the population is extremely dynamic while the population of fields is subject to only minor variations and that too occasionally. All these features make it a somewhat difficult task to estimate livestock production.

The only means for ensuring objectivity is the use of random sampling techniques. For estimating the annual production of milk in an area, for example, a sample of animals representative of the entire population of animals in the entire year was selected. The sample was sufficiently large to take care of differences that exist in milk due to breed, climate conditions, order and stage of lactation, supply of feed and a variety of other management practices. The milk yield of a large sample of animals was recorded on the spot with fairly accurate balances both in the morning and in the evening and in some cases in the noon also. Changes in the size of the population of milch animals and animals in milk were estimated in each season or in each month for building up the estimates of production. It is well known that the number of animals in milk in an area varies widely from season to season. The same thing is also true in the case of other practices relating to cattle and buffaloes.

Similarly, for estimating the sheep population or wool production in an area, it is necessary that the sample has adequate representation of all breeds, age groups and sex not only for stationary but migratory flocks, which make a substantial contribution to the total wool production, also. Wool yield of the selected sheep for both the shearings in the year was recorded by actual weighment at the time of shearing. Again for estimating egg production, it is most essential that large fluctuations in the number of birds not only from season to season but also from month to month are adequately taken into account. Similarly, in the case of estimates of meat production, one will have to cover in the sample not only registered slaughter houses and households but also unregistered slaughter houses which account for a sizeable proportion of meat production. The two requirements of (i) objectivity and (ii) physical observations have been the basis of all the surveys on livestock products conducted by the Institute of Agricultural Research Statistics. The sampling design used for these surveys was broadly, as follows:

For estimating the production in an area, districts were adopted as the strata, a cluster of two contiguous villages was the primary unit of sampling. A cluster of 2 to 10 households was the unit of sampling at the second stage of sampling. An animal was the unit at the ultimate stage of sampling. The data were collected with the help of ad hoc field staff. The techniques developed by the Institute provide estimates of annual production of livestock production with a fairly high precision. These techniques have been successfully demonstrated to the State Governments by conducting sample surveys using these techniques in a number of States. However, the Institute of Agricultural Research Statistics, being a research institute, is not in a position to undertake extension of these techniques to all the States of the country and, therefore, the States themselves should come forward and conduct sample surveys on the lines suggested by the Institute. Methods thus evolved have been fully elaborated in the reports and monographs brought on these investigations. A few States have already included these surveys in their plan programmes for collecting statistics of livestock products. The remaining States are also likely to take up the surveys in course of time.

SUGGESTIONS FOR FURTHER WORK BY IARSI

It may be recalled that the two pilot investigations in northern region comprising the States of Punjab, Haryana and Himachal Pradesh during 1969-70 to 1971-72 and in Andhra Pradesh of Southern region during 1971-72 to 1973-74 was conducted with the object of developing an integrated sampling methodology for estimation of annual output of principal livestock products, viz. milk, wool, eggs and meat simultaneously every year through one survey conducted each year. The programme envisaged conducting a full scale survey on one product in a given year for obtaining estimate of output of that product with sufficiently high precision while at the same time covering other products on a smaller scale in the same area in order to build up indices of changes in their output. These pilot investigations were undertaken in continuation of the pilot and large scale sample surveys undertaken earlier for estimating the production of these livestock products on individual product basis. The investigations undertaken in the past included studies on the choice of the method of stratification, sampling units at the various stages, determination and allocation of the sample size among stages, the method of estimation, etc. Studies on these aspects were undertaken not only from the point of view of statistical efficiency but also taking into account the feasibility and other practical aspects. The details of such investigations have been published in the reports and monographs already brought out and study on these aspects were, therefore, not repeated. The aspects being covered under the present investigations are: (i) studying the feasibility of obtaining data on all the four products simultaneously, (ii) study of the correlation pattern between occasions for various characters, (iii) studying the efficiency of alternative estimations of number/production of a particular species product on an occasion making use of the data collected on other occasion also, and (iv) the determination of optimum replacement fraction from one occasion to another, etc. The sub-sampling fraction for collecting data on products other than the major one has to be determined on the basis of practical considerations rather than statistical ones.

SAMPLE SURVEY FOR THE ESTIMATION OF INTER-CENSAL LIVESTOCK NUMBERS

Livestock Number Surveys

Sample survey technique offers a direct approach as an alternative to the mathematical method based on census data. If properly adopted it not only reflects appropriately the conditions of season, feed, diseases, etc. which characterized the year of survey but provides estimates within limits of precision at a reasonable cost.

With a view to determining the feasibility and usefulness of sampling methods in rationalizing the methods of supervision on the work of primary enumeration during census years in order to ensure reliability of the census results and for estimating the numbers of major categories of livestock during inter-census years, the Indian Agricultural Research Statistics Institute conducted a pilot survey in 1951 in district Etawah in U.P., and another survey in 1953 under different conditions in the district of Wardha in the former State of Madhya Pradesh. The results of these surveys were utilized for extending the survey on a State-wise scale in the former Bombay State during 1954. These investigations suggest that random sampling can be utilized usefully and successfully for estimating livestock numbers (ICAR Research Series No. 25).

A study of the data collected in these surveys also indicated that the stratification by size of villages (size being defined by the total number of households in the villages) is most effective in reducing the sampling variance. In a study made in Etawah district for a suitable auxiliary variable which could improve the efficiency of the estimate by following the ratio method of estimation, it was found that the total number of households as auxiliary information is most useful. Next to that was the agricultural area.

From the analysis of the Bombay survey it was concluded that selection of about 70 taluks and 12 villages per taluk and 6 clusters of 5 households each per selected village, which accounts for less than 1 per cent of the total number of households in the State would be the most appropriate design to be adopted in any State-wise survey for estimating bovine numbers and would provide estimates with sampling errors of the order of 2 per cent. The sampling fraction had to be increased if estimates were to be obtained for important categories of livestock separately.

It is amply clear from the foregoing findings of the IARSI that the sampling plan devised is not only suitable for providing rationalized supervision over the work of primary enumerating staff during census operations so that independent estimates of livestock numbers can be obtained much more quickly than the census data but also for estimation of livestock numbers in inter-census years.

Integrated Surveys

The IARSI has been engaged in evolving a suitable design for undertaking integrated surveys for obtaining estimates of output of livestock products and numbers of various categories of livestock spread over a period of five years. Every year one main livestock product was selected and studied sufficiently intensively so that reliable information on the number of animals and the output of that product together with related information on feeding and other animal husbandry practices associated with that species is collected. In the other years, only indices of change in the numbers and output in relation to the base year were worked out. The concept of integrated survey is sound in principle and that the methodology has now been developed. With the setting up of statistical units in the Animal Husbandry Departments of all the States, it should be possible to extend these surveys to all the States and all the livestock products. The system of periodical release of all-India and State estimates of livestock products should be introduced, as soon as practicable. The details of the timing of these estimates and their scope and coverage should be worked out.

Integrated Surveys for Livestock Products   More recently the IARSI has initiated pilot surveys for developing an integrated plan for estimation of all the principal livestock products. The plan envisages conducting in each State a major survey in any given year for obtaining estimate for the production of a specified product (say milk) for the State as a whole with sufficient precision, while at the same time samples on a smaller scale would be canvassed in the same State to secure indices of changes in output of other products (say eggs, meat, etc.) from year to year.

Once such data become available regularly it would also be possible to look into any modifications needed in the design to ensure rotational sampling in an optimal manner and the corresponding estimation procedures which would take into account not only the data for the given year but also those for previous years to provide estimate with greater precision.

Once the integrated plan is adopted, the State Animal Husbandry Departments should also ensure that the District Seasonal and Animal Condition Reports discussed earlier not only flow in regularly but that the information reported there in respect of various factors is quantified to the maximum extent possible. Where measurements or counts cannot be had, resort will have to be taken to scoring and grading. Once this is done it should be possible to attempt a study of the influence of various factors on livestock numbers. It is only through such studies that a stage may perhaps be reached when it would be possible to attempt objective adjustments for annual fluctuations to trend estimates in case in any year survey estimate is either not available or is late in forthcoming.

IMPROVEMENTS IN OTHER DATA

Data on improved breeds of livestock and poultry should also be collected through sample surveys on a systematic basis. Various types of other statistics related to the livestock economy are needed to meet the present day requirements of planning for livestock development. The periodicity of their collection and the methodology to be adopted depend on the nature and magnitude of the variation in the items. For example, while data on livestock numbers should continue to be collected on a complete-enumeration basis once in five years, data on variations in numbers should be collected through annual sample surveys. Data on wholesale and retail prices of livestock, livestock products and livestock feed and fodder should be collected at selected centres on a weekly basis. These would be useful in more objective evaluation of the value of output from the animal husbandry sector. Information regarding market arrivals of major livestock products should be collected at weekly intervals. Data on production of livestock feed including cattle, poultry and other feeds should be collected from the major units producing these feeds on a monthly basis. Data on fodder should be collected on a seasonal or annual basis. With the rapid development of processing of livestock products, the methods of marketing and the proportions of livestock products converted into various indigenous products such as butter, ghee, cheese, etc. are also changing. The DMI should carry out fresh market surveys to collect up-to-date information in respect of these items.

Monitoring and Evaluation of Development Programmes A number of development programmes are being implemented for increasing the production and availability of livestock products. For assessing the progress of programmes at various stages of implementation as well as measuring the impact of these programmes, data on indicators of various activities should be systematically collected, processed and analyzed. For instance, in the field of cattle development programmes, the items of information should relate to the number of artificial inseminations carried out, number followed up, number found successful, number of cross-bred calves born, number of cross-bred cows in production, number of bulls castrated, number of vaccinations against rinderpest and foot and mouth disease, etc. These data should be reported regularly by the development staff provided under the programmes and appropriately compiled and analyzed. In addition, statistical staff should undertake surveys for assessment and evaluation of different programmes.

Collection of Data from Dairy and Other Plants   With the organization of dairy plants and improved arrangements for collection and processing of data, a lot of useful information could be collected in respect of these plants. For example, information regarding the quantity of fresh milk procured and processed by the plants and prices paid can be collected on the basis of prescribed returns by each dairy plant. Similarly the amount of milk processed into different livestock products and their production can also be collected through prescribed returns. The livestock statistics unit in the Animal Husbandry Division of the Ministry of Agriculture should study the nature of data at present being maintained in the dairy plants for their own normal administrative purposes and prescribe standard proformas through which this information could be collected, compiled, tabulated and analyzed at the State and all-India levels. As in the case of dairy plants, information should also be collected, compiled and processed in respect of plants handling other livestock products such as slaughter houses, bacon factories, poultry dressing plants, feed manufacturing plants, bone digesters, etc.

Collection of Data through Development Staff One of the reasons for the limited availability of data on animal husbandry hitherto was the non-availability of technical staff in the field. With the expansion of the animal husbandry and dairy development programmes, a large number of field staff with qualifications and experience in animal husbandry development are available in the field at different levels. It is necessary that information regarding the developmental aspects of animal husbandry programmes should be collected through this field staff. While it is not intended that the field staff should be burdened with a lot of paper work involved in the submission of progress reports, yet it would be possible to collect valuable data on the implementation of these programmes. There is a feeling that the data reported by developmental agencies are likely to increase work. But this problem could be overcome by suitable deplayment of staff.

Quarterly District Report on Livestock Situation   There is need for developing a proper system of reporting detailed data on the livestock situation from the districts. In the context of planning, it will be useful to develop a system of reporting, on quarterly basis, the prevailing conditions relating to season, climate, incidence of disease, availability of animal feed and fodder, price situation of livestock and livestock products, etc. to the State headquarters. The types of data to be collected, the level at which they are required, the periodicity and the mode of collection are given in Table 15.2.

Table 15.2 Periodicity and Mode of Collection of Livestock Statistics

Type of statistics	Level at which required	Periodicity	Mode of collection
1. (a) Livestock			
(i) Selected items	Village and upwards	Quinquennial	Complete census
(ii) Other items	District/State	"	Sample survey
(b) Variations in numbers	State	Annual	"
2. Average yield and output of livestock products	District and State	Season and annual	"
3. Mortality among animals	"	Monthly	Prescribed return
4. Consumption and utilization of livestock products	"	Season and annual	Sample survey
5. Wholesale and retail prices of	Selected centres	Weekly	Prescribed return
(a) Livestock			
(b) Livestock products			
(c) Components of livestock, feed and fodder			
6. Market arrivals of major livestock products	Selected centres	Weekly	"
7. Trade in livestock and produces	State	Monthly	"
8. Dairy plants			
(a) Capacity and average throughput	Unit-wise	Annual/monthly	"
(b) Procurement/sale price	"	"	"
(c) Utilization of milk	"	"	"
9. Slaughter houses	"	"	"
10. Production of livestock feed for cattle, poultry and other	"	Monthly	"
11. Production of fodder	District and State	Season and annual	Sample survey
12. Cost of production of livestock products and indices	Region	Annual	"

Table 15.2 Periodicity and Mode of Collection of Livestock Statistics *(Contd.)*

	Type of statistics	Level at which required	Periodicity	Mode of collection
13.	Assessment and evaluation of development programmes	Project-wise	,,	,,
14.	Report on condition of livestock situation	District	Quarterly	Prescribed return
15.	Economic and technical data on livestock economy	—	Ad-hoc	Sample survey
16.	Data needed for cattle insurance	District	Periodical	Special studies

ORGANIZATIONAL SET-UP

The collection of comprehensive data is possible only when a proper organizational set-up is established from the district to the State and all-India levels. At the district level, the District Animal Husbandry Officer should have the help of requisite computational and other staff in the collection, compilation and submission of various types of animal husbandry, dairying and animal health statistics. At the State level, the Director of Animal Husbandry should have a full-fledged statistical division to serve the requirements of data on various facets of livestock economy for proper planning, execution of plans and appraisal of development programmes. This division should also be responsible for collection, compilation, analysis and dissemination of all animal husbandry statistics. During the last decade or so, statistical cells have been set-up in many of the State Animal Husbandry and Dairy Departments. However, due to lack of appreciation of the importance of these data, these units could not be developed fully as adequate financial support was not made available for their development in the successive five year plans. It is important that each State should have a fairly senior statistician not below the rank of a Joint Director of Animal Husbandry attached to the Directorate of Animal Husbandry. The division should consist of the three units, viz. assessment unit, analytical unit and livestock census unit, for undertaking large scale sample benchmark and assessment surveys of development projects, surveys on cost of production of livestock products, analysis of breeding data, progeny testing, sire evaluation, operational research, planning of livestock census, publication and dissemination of livestock data etc. Each of these units should be under the charge of a professional statistician of a suitable rank. The statisticians in the Directorate of Animal Husbandry should be in the general line of promotion in the field of statistics in the State. For economic analysis of the various projects and for undertaking evaluation studies in the State, an economist of a suitable rank should also be provided in the division. The major dairy plants should also have economists on their staff to render advice on the pattern of rational conversion of milk into various products.

At the Central level, the statistical work should continue to be coordinated by the Statistical Unit in the Animal Husbandry Division in the Ministry of Agriculture and Irrigation which should be considerably strengthened. For undertaking evaluation and cost-benefit studies and for economic analysis of various projects, an economist of Joint Director level should be provided in this Unit. The officer in charge of this Unit should be of the rank of Additional Economic and Statistical Adviser.

The units at the Central and State levels should continue to be under the administrative control of the Animal Husbandry Commissioner or the Director of Animal Husbandry as the case may be, but in technical matters their work should be supervised by the Economic and Statistical Adviser in the Ministry of Agriculture at the Centre and the State Agricultural Statistician in the States.

When the integrated and other sample surveys for providing intercensus estimates of livestock numbers, estimation of production of various livestock products including by products, cost of production studies, etc. are conducted, new problems both methodological and others, will arise from time to time. There should be provision for undertaking methodological research and pilot investigations. This work should continue to be done at the Centre by the IARSI. Similar methodological studies should also be taken up by agricultural universities with financial assistance from the Centre.

CONCLUSIONS

In dynamic times of today one cannot take comfort in the past. The role of knowledge or intellectual capital in Policy making and Research is well appreciated. Right answers to any issue will depend on reliable database; hence the importance of statistics. With the livestock sector assuming an important role in the national economy, one needs to improve the present state of livestock statistics. Although considerable resources have been directed toward collecting and disseminating information on basic crops, little attention has been given to collecting, disseminating, and analyzing livestock and livestock product data. Timely information on volumes produced, quantities traded, locational availability, prices and stocks is largely unavailable. They have to meet the challenges of New Economy, the Global Economy or what we would call the 'Knowledge Economy'.

Reliable and timely data is not only a key input for informed planning and decision-making by various participants, but also for effective government policymaking and administrative decision-making. There is an urgent need to collect a comprehensive data of the livestock sector through the modern Information Technology. In view of the growing importance of livestock sector in India, it is essential to have reliable statistics on the various facets of this sector for various policy formulation purposes. Major heads on which data need to be collected and analyzed are given in Table 15.3.

Table 15.3 Major Heads on Which Data Need to be Collected

1. Number: Cattle, Poultry, Piggery, Small ruminent, sheep, goats etc.	10. Processing of livestock products
2. Production: Livestock Products	11. Drought Power
3. Consumption of livestock products	12. Foreign Trade
4. Breeding	13. Economics of Livestock
5. Feed and fodder	14. Fisheries
6. Diseases	15. Demand/Supply of major livestock products
7. Livestock Health Care	16. Apiculture
8. Marketing	17. Employment
9. Prices	18. Livestock Credit Programme

It is important to note that there obviously is a need for further comprehensive data base for proper planning and policy formulation for the development of livestock sector. The basic requirement of data relates to number and productivity of livestock and the economics of the production from livestock enterprises of different sizes. Besides, different types of related statistics/information are also needed for scientific livestock development programmes. This includes information on rearing animal husbandry practices, feed and fodder, impact of individual inputs on the productivity of animals; inputs and output relationship in milk production, substitution possibilities as means of lowering costs and increasing the returns; balanced nutritional feed for different animals; prices of animals (breedwise); requirement and consumption of various livestock products; cost of production of milk, eggs etc.

Similarly, for any scheme for livestock insurance, basic data on the productivity of animals, their life span, mortality rate and general animal health services available are needed. For the development of a good system of marketing of livestock products, the need for basic data are the price to be paid to the producers and the price to be received from the consumers etc. The data on prices of livestock sold in major markets/ fairs need to be collected. Thus, there is an urgent need to develop a proper system of collection of information and creation of data base for livestock sector during the Tenth Plan.

From what has been discussed in the preceding sections, the following conclusions emerge:

(i) Inter-census estimates are essential both for assessing the contribution of livestock sector to national income and for purposes of planning for livestock development.

(ii) In the absence of direct information on inter-census livestock numbers through sample surveys (as for example for the past period when surveys were not carried out in many States during many years) the census data can be utilized, with appropriate precautions and adjustments, for securing inter-census estimates: (a) through the method of fitting trend curves, or (b) through the use of appropriate interpolation formulae. The former method should be preferred to the latter as the trend curve approach can also provide an idea of a measure of reliability reflected by the goodness of fit of the curve and as the choice of the appropriate interpolation formula may be difficult in situations in which the trends are not polynomial.

(iii) The sample survey technique has been demonstrated to be a practicable approach to securing inter-census estimates with required degree of precision at a reasonable cost. The survey technique provides estimates which may suffer much less from non-sampling errors than the trend estimates based on census data and what is extremely important, would also reflect directly the effects of environmental changes occurring due to disturbances in weather, grazing condition, availability of feeds, incidence of diseases, etc. whereas the estimates based on census data would only lead to expected values from which in a particular year the actual value may deviate considerably. This is borne out by the few comparisons which could be made between the trend estimates and the corresponding survey estimates as obtained in IARSI surveys. The survey technique also offers a convenient procedure for rationalized supervision over the census, capable of providing independent estimates.

(iv) It is not necessary to undertake surveys exclusively for estimating livestock numbers. The sample surveys for estimation of livestock products require complete enumeration of households for livestock in the selected villages to secure a sampling farm. The data collected in the process can be utilized for obtaining inter-census estimates. The precision on such estimates in the surveys carried out by the IARSI so far has ranged generally from 2 to 6 per cent. In case it is desired to secure in any year and in any State estimates with greater precision this can be very well done by augmenting the sample size with a supplementary sample of villages which would only be enumerated and not studied for livestock products.

(v) The plan for integrated surveys on principal livestock products being developed by the IARSI provides for the enumeration of all the households in the selected villages for all principal livestock and poultry. The integrated survey can thus lead to providing estimates of livestock numbers in successive years for any State in which the integrated plan is adopted.

Steps should be taken to ensure that the relevant data are processed quickly and the inter-census estimates of livestock numbers made available to the integrated agencies such as, CSO, Planning Commission, etc., without undue loss of time.

(vi) It is desirable to ensure that the district animal husbandry officers in different States prepare and transmit quarterly reports on the conditions of season, grazing, availability of feeds and fodder for livestock, diseases, etc. An attempt should be made to quantify the items on which information is provided in these reports. Such information in conjunction with estimates of livestock numbers from annual surveys would throw light on the influence of various environmental factors on livestock numbers and may lead to adjustment factors for annual variations for trend estimates in case surveys are not carried out in a particular year. The trend estimates themselves would then be based on available annual survey estimate.

Annexure 15.1

PROCEDURE FOR ESTIMATING VARIOUS LIVESTOCK PRODUCTS

Position in respect of various livestock products and the procedure adopted by the National Income Unit of the Central Statistical Organization. The livestock products are divided into the following categories:

1. Milk and its products.
2. Meat, edible offals and other by-products.
3. Hides and skins.
4. Wool, hair and bristles.
5. Eggs and poultry meat.
6. Bones, horns, hoof, etc.
7. Dung used for purposes of fuel, manure and other domestic uses.

Milk and its Products

The total production of milk is obtained by multiplying the average milk yield rate per breeding animal with the total estimated number of breeding animals. The formula adopted for the purpose is as follows:

(a) average lactation yield = (average daily yield) × (average lactation period)

(b) average annual yield (per animal kept for breeding or milk production)

$$= \frac{(\text{average lactation yield}) \times (\text{percentage of animals in milk})}{100}$$

(c) total milk production = (average annual yield) × (number of animals kept for breeding or milk production)

Till recently official estimates of milk production available in the country were those based on the information collected by the Directorate of Marketing and Inspection at the time of conducting market surveys.

Annual production estimates were worked out according to the following formula:

Total annual milk production = (Average daily milk yield per animal in milk) × (average lactation period) × (total number of breeding animals) × (percentage of animals in milk)

The livestock census provided the factor 'percentage of animals in milk.' The number of animals in milk as reported in the livestock census, however, was that on the reference date on which enumeration took place.

These estimates suffer from the following deficiencies:

1. Estimate of average daily milk yield and lactation period are based on personal and not on scientific inquiry.
2. The estimate of milk production refers to the lactation period of animals in milk on the reference date of the census and not to the whole year for all the animals that give milk during the year.
3. The effect of seasonal variations in the number of animals in milk such as those connected with the calving season, etc. are not taken into account in this estimate.
4. Since the livestock figures are available on quinquennial basis and the surveys for finding out the average yield of milk of each category of milch animals are conducted occasionally, year-to-year changes in milk production have become difficult to assess.

Choudhury and Narang of the Central Statistical Organization suggested the following improved formula to get over this lacuna:

$$\text{Annual milk production} = \frac{Y \times L \times B}{P} \times 365$$

where:

Y is the average daily milk yield per animal in milk

L is the average lactation period

B is the number of animals kept for breeding or milk production, and

P is the average calving interval (in days).

Although this formula eliminated the drawback in the earlier formula of the Directorate of Marketing & Inspection, this too had a defect in that 'factor B' not only included breeding animals in milk and dry but also animals over three years which had not calved. The estimates of milk output based on this formula could not, therefore, be considered as accurate since the average milk production for animals which had not calved was taken to be the same as for animals which had calved. Moreover, reliable information on some factors used in the formula, like the average calving interval and the average lactation period, were not available. Consequently this formula was also considered as of limited significance. The Central Statistical Organization, therefore, convened a meeting in 1965 of the representatives of the Directorate of Marketing and Inspection (DMI), Institute of Agricultural Research Statistics, Central

Statistical Organization and the Animal Husbandry Commissioner to discuss the question of estimating milk production with accuracy. It was then decided that the Central Statistical Organization would estimate milk production in future. The following simple formula was then evolved for estimating milk production.

Annual production of milk $= M \times B \times Y \times 365$
where:
M is the number of milch animals (breeding animals in milk and dry),
B is the average annual percentage of animals in milk, and
Y is the average daily yield per animal in milk.

The Central Statistical Organization thereafter estimated annual production of milk this formula for the years 1951, 1956 and 1961.

This simple formula also suffers from a limitation. It gives an underestimate of the output of milk inasmuch as animals kept for breeding which had not calved by the reference date might have calved later in the year and started giving milk. It is, therefore, necessary to resolve this problem of underestimation by suggesting a suitable correction factor for estimates arrived at by employing the above formula. It will also be necessary to work out a correction factor for adjusting seasonal variations in the number of animals in milk during the census year, since the number given in the livestock census refers to the number on the reference date on which enumeration had taken place.

The information on the yield rate of milk and percentage of animals in milk to total milch animals is available for 12 States separately for cows and buffaloes from the results of the IARS Survey. For Himachal Pradesh and Jammu & Kashmir the rates applicable to Punjab Hills are used. For the remaining States/Union Territories the data supplied by the DMI/State Government have been used.

The salient features of the IARS survey results are:
(a) The estimates are based on objective enquiries and pertain to recent years.
(b) Samples, spread over one full year covering all important seasons, were selected in each survey.
(c) Surveys covered both rural and urban areas of the tract.
(d) Sample of animals, out of those in milk, was selected on each working day and the milk yield was recorded by physical weighment on the spot.
(e) The field work was carried out by whole time and trained staff and their work was intensively supervised by ad hoc staff who were trained in Animal Husbandry and Veterinary Science.

The IARS surveys for the States of Tamil Nadu, Karnataka, Bihar, Andhra Pradesh and Madhya Pradesh were conducted in the years 1965-1966/1966-67 which were affected by drought conductions. Since milk production is affected by drought conditions, it would be desirable for the IARS to repeat similar surveys in these States so as to get the average yield in a normal year.

No objective surveys have been carried out by any agency to estimate the production of goat milk. DMI has, however, collected information on the average daily yield of goat milk, average lactation period, average calving interval and percentage of milch goats to total goats from the State Governments which are rough in nature, SSB Andhra Pradesh and collected information on goat milk at the time of the rationalized supervision of the 1961 livestock census. SSB West Bengal had also prepared estimates of production of goat milk on the basis of livestock survey conducted by them in 1953-54 in two districts. The data collected by SSB Andhra Pradesh are also used for Tamil Nadu and Karnataka and the results thrown up by the livestock survey of West Bengal are used for that State. For the remaining States/Union Territories the DMI figures are used.

No information is available on the production of camel milk from any source and thus the milk production estimates are underestimated to this extent.

Estimates of the Production of Milk Products   Ghee, butter, yoghurt and cream etc. are worked out by the Directorate of Marketing and Inspection by applying the appropriate conversion ratios to the figures of milk production applied by the Central Statistical Organization. The data on the quantity of milk utilized in different States for conversion into various milk products and the average yield of each of the products per quintal of milk are collected by the Directorate of Marketing and Inspection from the State Departments of Animal Husbandry/Veterinary Services/Marketing, etc. from time to time. Statistics of milk products will improve with the improvements in the statistics of milk production. For enhancing the reliability of data on milk products conducting of scientific surveys on regional basis for arriving at reliable estimates of conversion ratios is very essential.

Meat Production

Official estimates of meat production in India used to be prepared by the Directorate of Marketing and Inspection. The estimates are based on: (1) the number of animals slaughtered in recognized slaughter houses, (2) the number of animals slaughtered privately, and (3) the average production of meat per animal.

Of the above three components (2) and (3) were collected through the market surveys, but these surveys were not based on any scientific sampling design. They were in the nature of more or less subjective inquiries. Information for arriving at these estimates is at present provided by the State Departments of Animal Husbandry/Veterinary Services, Bureaus of Economics and Statistics of local boards, etc. Regularity is not observed in estimating production of meat as this is done only as part of marketing surveys on any type of meat or meat products.

Estimation of Meat Production

The estimation of meat production is based on the information regarding.
(a) The total number of animals slaughtered;
(b) the average meat production per animal; and
(c) the total meat production;

The information on the number of animals slaughtered is obtained from two sources namely, (i) from the sample of households reporting slaughter of animals and from all the butchers and other agencies in the villages selected in the sample, and (ii) from records maintained at all the slaughter houses in the State.

Despite the fact that such a detailed information is collected with regard to meat production, this is not being published. Similarly data being annually collected regarding various types of animals, feed and utilization of various products in the annual Sample Survey is also not analyzed.

To secure more reliable estimates of annual meat production, it is necessary to conduct sample enquiries adopting modern sampling techniques on an adequate scale to provide with a reasonable margin of error, estimates of (i) the number of animals slaughtered privately, and (ii) the average meat production per animal. The estimate of annual meat production will then be obtained as a product of the two factors, viz. (i) number of animals slaughtered in recognized slaughter houses and the estimates of the number slaughtered privately during the year, and (ii) estimates of average meat production per animal. The Institute of Agricultural Research Statistics conducted pilot surveys in Tamil Nadu during 1966-67 and Haryana during 1968-69 for developing a suitable sampling methodology for estimates of meat production. The data collected during the surveys have helped in building up estimates of number of animals slaughtered privately and the average meat production per animal and the total animal meat production in the tract. The surveys for estimation of meat production are still in the exploratory stage and till the sampling technique is finalized and the surveys are carried out in all the States, we have to be content with ad hoc estimates only.

The Directorate of Marketing and Inspection also used to estimate annual wool production in the country as part of their marketing surveys. The estimates were arrived at after making enquiries from the State Departments concerned and taking into consideration the total population of sheep, the percentage of animals clipped, the yield of wool per animal per clip, the number of clips in the year; the total production of pulled wool and tannery wool is estimated separately. Since these surveys were not based on scientific sampling techniques, there was scope for improvement in the estimates of wool production worked out by the Marketing Directorate. The Institute of Agricultural Research Statistics took initiative and formulated a scheme for evolving a suitable sampling technique for estimates of wood production and collected information on sheep keeping practices. The surveys were conducted in five typical tracts of the country.

On the basis of these sample surveys in different regions of the country, IARS has attempted to build up all-India Estimates of Wool Production. The methodology does not Cow Sheep shearing and wool extension centres as well as sheep breeding farms located in different states. Even otherwise these surveys are still in exploratory stage and after sampling techniques are finalized the surveys need to be carried out in all the States so that a reliable estimate of wood production in the country can be obtained.

Animal Fats and Other By-products

The estimates of production of animal fats and certain important by-products are worked out by the Directorate of Marketing and Inspection by multiplying the average yield of each by-product obtained from different species of animal slaughtered in the different States by the number slaughtered. The data on average yield are collected through the State Departments and by the ad hoc enquiries. In certain cases actual weighment is done in slaughter houses to assess the yield. In regard to by-products from fallen animals, these estimates are made during enquiries from the State Departments on factors like average life span of animals, mortality due to causes other than natural death, etc. In this case, an allowance is also made for the percentage of animals which are not claimed after death.

Hides and Skins

The estimation of annual production of hides and skins is being done by the Directorate of Marketing and Inspection. As in the case of meat and products thereof the production of hides and skins is estimated with the help of the State Departments of Animal Husbandry/Veterinary Services, Local Boards, etc. The following are the factors that determine the production of hides and skins:

  (a) The population of cattle, buffaloes, sheep, and goats.
  (b) The rate of mortality.
  (c) The number of animals slaughtered.

The estimation of production of bones in the country is being done by the Directorate of Marketing and Inspection as part of its marketing surveys. The factors taken into consideration for estimating production of bones are:

  (i) Livestock numbers.
  (ii) The rate of mortality.
  (iii) The slaughtered every year.
  (iv) Yield of bones per animal on dry basis which depends on the breed, size, age and body condition of the animals.

Goat Hair

Estimation of production of goat hair is also done by the Directorate of Marketing and Inspection on lines similar to those for wool.

Bristles

The Directorate of Marketing and Inspection estimates annual bristle production in the country after taking into consideration the pig population, the proportion of pigs from which the bristles are plucked and the yield of bristles per pig (which widely) in the country.

16

Fisheries Statistics

INTRODUCTION

The fishery resource of a country like India having a long sea coast as well as considerable inland water areas, naturally falls into two categories, viz. marine and inland. It has a vast coast line extending over 6000 km and inland fisheries resources covering both fresh and brackish waters (i.e. saltish water) extend over 9.6 million hectares (Tables 16.1 and 16.2). India is one of the nine major fish producing countries in the world employing over a million persons in fishing and its allied industries. The leading fishing nations of the world are Japan, U.S.A., U.S.S.R., China, U.K., Peru, Norway and Canada. Fish production in the world is about 70 million tonnes. In spite of vast resources, fish production in India is estimated to be only about 2.4 million tonnes. Of the marine fish-catch, about two-thirds of the production is from West-coast and one-third from East-coast. The production estimates cannot be said as reliable as the task of obtaining reliable statistics is not easy in view of large coast line, multitude of inland fisheries sources, the diversity of fishing practices and scattered distribution of the exploiting units.

Little attention was paid to fisheries statistics up to World War II. The attention of the Government to the need for such statistics was, however, drawn by a number of Committees after the War. The whole issue was examined in detail by the All-India Fisheries Conference held at New Delhi in September 1948. From the time of the publication of the Report of the Technical Committee on Coordination of Fisheries Statistics set up by the Ministry of Food and Agriculture in 1950, some attempts have been made towards collection and coordination of fisheries statistics in the country. But the progress seems to be very poor.

The matter came up again for consideration by the Government of India at the Madras Conference which recommended that the Directorate of Economics and Statistics in the Ministry of Food and Agriculture should organize collection of regular data on economic and commercial intelligence pertaining to fisheries and potential resources in the States. The F.A.O declared 1957-58 as the fisheries year and recommended collection of fisheries data by member countries. Under the Five Year

Table 16.1 Length of Coastline and Population of Coastal States and Islands

S.No	States/Union Territories	Length of Coastline (Km.)	Area (Thousand Sq. Km)	Population 1991 (lakh)
1.	Gujarat	1,600	196.00	41.20
2.	Maharashtra	840	307.70	78.70
3.	Goa	300	3.70	1.20
4.	Karnataka	400	191.80	44.80
5.	West Bengal	950	88.70	68.00
6.	Tamil Nadu	720	130.10	55.60
7.	Orissa	560	155.70	31.50
8.	Kerala	1,014	39.00	29.00
9.	Andhra Pradesh	960	275.00	66.30
10.	Andaman and Nicobar Islands	-	8.50	0.30
11.	Lakshadweep	-	0.03	0.05

Source : *Compendium of Environment Statistics, 1999, Central Statistical Organisation*, Department of Statistics, Ministry of Planning and Programming Implementation, Govt. of India.

Table 16.2 State-wise details in Brakishwater Area available under Culture and Production for the Year 1995-96

States	Total B\W area (ha.)	Area covered (ha.)	Production live weight (tonnes)
Andhra Pradesh	1,50,000	50,000	27,140
Goa	18,500	650	550
Gujarat	37,600	884	546
Karnataka	8,000	3500	2,050
Kerala	65,000	14,657	9,000
Maharashtra	80,000	716	740
Orissa	31,600	11,000	6,000
Pondicherry	800	37	10
Tamil Nadu	56,000	2,879	1,092
West Bengal	405,000	34,660	23,445
Total	11,90,900	1,18,983	70,573

Source : *Hand Book on Fisheries Statistics, 1996.* Ministry of Agriculture (Department of Agriculture and Cooperation), Fisheries Division, Govt. of India.

Plans much emphasis has been laid on the development of fisheries and sufficient financial allocations made for the purpose, but reliable data are not available even today for an overall assessment of the fisheries schemes.

In order to fill the gaps in the basic fisheries statistics required for purposes of national income estimation and planning, the Technical

Committee on Coordination of Fisheries Statistics, 1950, recommended the following programme of work:

1. Data to be obtained by complete enumeration:
   (a) Once in five years—
       Water resources—nature, number, area and exploitation;
       Families and population engaged wholly or partially in any branch of fish industry;
       Fishing crafts and tackles, and fish transport vessels;
       Numbers of curing yards, fish farms, warehouses, iceplants, refrigeration and transport equipment; and
       source of supply of spawn, fry and fingerlings.
   (b) At shorter intervals—
       Arrivals at selected markets (daily);
       Internal trade;
       Output of processed fish and fish products, such as fish liver oil, fish oil, fish meal and fish manure (annual); Data on spawn, fry, fingerling and fish collected, reared, and dispersed off by inland fish farms under government or quasi-government management and large commercial farms (annual); and
       Landings, wholesale and retail prices of fish at selected centres of production and consumption (weekly).

2. Data to be obtained through periodical sample surveys:
   (a) Once in 5 or 10 years, conducted on an intensive basis—
       Extent of exploitation of different classes of fisheries;
       Sources of supply of gear, yarn, nets and crafts and other materials required for fishing;
       Efficiency of different fishing practices;
       Efficiency of different types of craft and gear;
       The marketing, storage, transport and refrigeration facilities;
       The economics of fish industries, manufactured fish products and by-products;
       Sources of supply of finance and indebtedness of fishermen;
       Consumption of fish by fishermen and non-fishermen;
       Economic and sociological conditions of population engaged in fishing and allied industries

3. Data to be obtained through continuous sample surveys—
   Catches of inland and marine fish.

4. Data requiring controlled experiments and observations over a long period—
   Data on biological factor.

EARLIER METHODS

The earliest records of estimates of fish catch were provided by the 'Report on the Marketing of fish in the Indian Union', 1948. The estimates were being prepared on the basis of figures supplied by various States which used to collect such data through their Departments of Fisheries.

Different procedures followed by State departments to obtain the production estimates are: (i) figures supplied by the fish curing yards on catches of fish at landing centres; (ii) number of fishing boats and average daily fish-catch per boat; (iii) number of adults engaged in fishing operation and amount of catch per head as reported; (iv) figures worked out on the basis of salt distribution for curing at the fish curing yards, and (v) data collected on export, import, market arrivals; consumption, etc. These methods were obviously neither objective nor the data provided were complete or accurate.

Developments The question of collection, coordination and improvement of fishery statistics has been receiving attention of both the Central and State Governments as well as other organizations for a long time. As early as 1945 the Fish Commodity Committee of the Indian Council of Agricultural Research pointed out the need of accurate fisheries statistics. In 1949, the Ministry of Agriculture. Government of India, in pursuance of the recommendations of the All-India Fisheries Conference held in 1948 constituted a Technical Committee for the coordination of fisheries statistics. An attempt for developing suitable sampling technique for the estimation of the catch of the marine fish was first made by the Statistical Wing of the ICAR in 1949-50 by initiating a pilot survey in the Malabar coast and later on extended to various parts of the Indian coast, in the light of the encouraging results obtained. In all, 11 pilot and extension surveys (8 in West-coast and 3 in the East-coast) were carried out during the period 1950-56 utilizing various sampling designs for the estimation of the marine fish-catch. These surveys successfully demonstrated the feasibility of employing suitable sampling technique for the estimation of marine fish production.

PRESENT POSITION

A number of organizations are at present engaged in the collection, compilation and publication of fisheries statistics. In the Ministry of Agriculture, the Directorate of Economics and Statistics is collecting data on fish prices and progress of various fisheries development schemes; the Directorate of Marketing and Inspection publishes comprehensive data on various aspects of fisheries in their Report on the Marketing of Fish in India; the Central Marine Fisheries Research Institute, Cochin is in charge of collection of data on marine fish catches, catch of individual species, the number of different types of fishing units and other biological data and the Central Inland Fisheries Research Institute, Calcutta collects data on inland fisheries. The Directorate of National Sample Survey is in charge of data on inland fisheries, fish catches and consumption. The State Governments also collect some data on inland and marine fisheries (Table 16.3).

Fisheries of India may broadly be divided into the following two main categories:

Table 16.3 Fish Production and Per Annum Growth Rate

Year	Fish Production			Percentage Annual Growth Rate		
	Marine	Inland	Total	Marine	Inland	Total
1980-81	15.55	8.87	24.42	-	-	-
1981-82	14.45	9.99	24.44	-7.07	12.63	0.08
1982-83	14.27	9.40	23.67	-1.25	-5.91	-3.15
1983-84	15.19	9.87	25.06	6.45	5	5.87
1984-85	16.98	11.03	28.01	11.78	11.75	11.77
1985-86	17.16	11.60	28.76	1.06	5.17	2.68
1986-87	17.13	12.29	29.42	-0.17	5.95	2.29
1987-88	16.58	13.01	29.59	-3.21	5.86	0.58
1988-89	18.17	13.35	31.52	9.59	2.61	6.52
1989-90	22.75	14.02	36.77	25.21	5.02	16.66
1990-91	23.00	15.36	38.36	1.1	9.56	4.32
1991-92	24.47	17.10	41.57	6.39	11.33	8.37
1992-93	25.76	17.89	43.65	5.27	4.62	5
1993-94	26.49	19.95	46.44	2.83	11.51	6.39
1994-95	26.92	20.97	47.89	1.62	4.96	3.06
1995-96	27.07	22.42	49.49	0.56	6.91	3.34
1996-97	29.67	23.81	53.48	9.6	6.19	8.06
1997-98	29.5	24.38	53.88	-0.63	2.39	0.74
1998-99	26.97	25.65	52.62	-8.57	1.1	-2.59

Note : *Provisional
Source : *Agricultural Statistics at a Glance*, 2000. Directorate of Economics and Statistics, Ministry of Agriculture, Govt. of India.

1. *Marine Fisheries* These includes fishing in ocean, coastal and off shore waters, river estuaries and back waters.
2. *Inland Fisheries* This covers catching, taking and gathering of fresh water fish from rivers, irrigation and other canals, lakes, tanks, inundated tracts, *jhils* or even rice fields.

Marine Fish Production

The Central Marine Fisheries Research Institute (CMFRI), immediately, after it was set up in 1947, started periodical collection of data on fish production. In the initial stages, due to lack of resources, estimates of production were obtained from selective sampling. The scale of this work was gradually increased and improvements were made in the methodology from time to time. As more field staff was made available to the Institute full scale random survey was introduced from 1959 for the entire coast line of India for the purpose of estimation of marine fish production. At present the CMFRI collects data on marine fisheries following sampling designs similar to those tried and developed by the

Statistical Wing of the ICAR. The estimates on marine fish production furnished by the CMFRI are regarded as official figures for all purposes.

ICAR Surveys The Statistical Wing of the ICAR embarked upon the programme of sample surveys in different regions of the Indian Coast with two objectives, namely:

(a) To evolve sampling techniques for estimation of fish-catch regionwise in accordance with the fishing practices therein, and

(b) To dovetail-sampling procedures into routine duties of departmental staff who, finally are to take over the charge of collection of data.

Considering the fishing practices, the Indian coastal-length was divided into five broad regions, viz. (i) Kathiawar and North Bombay, (ii) Kanara, (iii) Malabar (including Travancore-Cochin), (iv) Catamaran (comprising former Madras and Andhra coasts), and (v) Deltaic area (North of Chilka lake). Sample surveys covering each of the regions separately were progressively conducted since 1950. Though the various designs adopted varied in details, space and time stratification was followed in all surveys. The stratification followed in all the surveys was with a group of contiguous landing centres. Different types of primary sampling units were also tried. In some surveys, the centre-day was taken as the primary unit, in others it was centre-group of days. Regarding the size of the ultimate sampling units, several sizes were tried out from small time intervals to a whole day. In case of time intervals, two-hour interval was more efficient. Further, systematic selection of intervals was more efficient. Further, systematic selection of intervals was more efficient then a random selection of these intervals. These surveys helped to arrive at some broad conclusions regarding the type of stratification to be followed and the size of the sampling units at various stages and their relative intensity of sampling. The Directorate of National Sample Survey has given an account in its mimeographed publication (1958) entitled 'Sample Surveys for Estimation of Catch of Marine Fish, 1950-56' regarding the details of these surveys.

CMFRI Survey The design adopted by the CMFRI is based on stratified multi-stage sampling. The stratification is made by dividing each maritime State into several zones on the basis of fishing intensity and geographical considerations. The total number of landing centres included in each zone range from 11 to 30.

One zone and a group of 10 days are taken as the sizes of space-time stratum. A landing centre-day is selected as the first stage unit. For instance, if there are 20 landing centres in a zone, there will be $20 \times 30 (= 600)$ landing centre-days in that zone for that month. In certain States on the East-coast, a centre-two days unit form the first stage unit. For the purpose of observation, a month is divided into three groups of 10 days each. From each group, a cluster of 6 consecutive days are selected as follows:

From the first 5 days of the first month in a year, a day is selected at random, which together with the next 5 consecutive days from the first cluster of 6 days.

The next clusters of 6 days from the other groups are selected systematically. This means that there will be a ten-days gap between the starting days of two consecutive clusters. Three centres in a zone are randomly selected for observation over 6 days and each selected centre is observed for two days (on the first day in the afternoon and the next day in the forenoon), for a 6-hour duration each day and from these the landings for a day (12-hours) are estimated. The night landings obtained by enquiry on the second day covering the period 18.00 hr of the first day to 06.00 hr of the next day are added to the previous figure obtained so as to arrive at the landings for one centre-day (24-hours). Thus in a 10-day period, landings for 3 days at 3 centres (i.e. 3 centre-days) are determined and in a month 9 landing-centre-days are sampled.

As it is difficult to observe the catches of all the boats landing during the observation period, sampling of boats is resorted to. When the total number of boats operating in a centre is 10 or less, the total landings from all the boats are enumerated for catch composition and other particulars. When the total number of boats exceeds 10 the percentages of boats sampled are different. 50 per cent boats are sampled when the number of boats operating in a centre is 11 to 2-; 20 per cent when the number is 21 to 50 and 10 per cent when the number is 51 and above. The weight of fish in each sampled boat is recorded. On a sub-sample basis, the length of some commercially important fishes like oil sardine, mackerel and prawns is recorded at the landing centres.

The programme of work which includes the names of landing centres to be visited and details such as date and time of observations at each landing centre is prepared by the statistical staff at the headquarters. At the end of every month, the field staff receives by post the programme of work for the following month. Surprise checks are carried out at frequent intervals by the supervisory staff of the Institute.

ROLE OF NSS AND ICAR

The work relating to the evolution of suitable techniques for estimation of fish catches, entrusted to the Indian Council of Agricultural Research consisted mainly of pilot investigations in typical coastal regions with a view to evolving suitable sampling techniques for estimating the marine fish catches which could be adopted by the State Fisheries Department as an annual routine measure. These investigations covered Malabar Coast in 1950-51, Madras State in 1953-54 and Travancore Cochin Coast in 1954-55 and Canara and North Bombay Coasts.

On the basis of the experience gained during the pilot and extension surveys, the ICAR prepared an All-India Marine Fisheries Survey Scheme for estimating the total catch of marine fish, for implementation during 1956-57. In the meantime, work relating to fisheries surveys was transferred to the Directorate of National Sample Survey. Except for compilation and analysis of some pending data, the Directorate of NSS did not proceed with the plans prepared by the ICAR. The Directorate of NSS, however, formulated a scheme for estimation of marine fish catches on an all-India basis for implementation during the Third Plan period.

This scheme was considered by an Inter-Departmental meeting held in April 1962, in the Central Statistical Organization. It was felt that since the Mandapam Institute had built up an expertise in marine fish catch surveys, the Institute should continue its work. States' participation in the sample survey work of the Institute should be encouraged to enlarge the sample size with a view to providing State-wise estimates of marine fish catches.

LIVESTOCK CENSUSES

A Technical Committee on Fisheries Statistics has been set up in the Department of Statistics to look into various aspects of collection of fisheries statistics. Data on number of fishing crafts and gears were collected on complete enumeration basis during the livestock census, 1966 for the first time. This has been continued in the subsequent censuses also. The list of items for which information has been collected is as under:

1. Fishing Crafts—
    (a) Catamarans.
    (b) Dugout canoes.
    (c) Big, size 32 ft and above.
    (d) Small, size less than 32 ft.
2. Power Vessels—
    (a) Fishing boats worked by power,
    (b) Carrier boats worked by power.
3. Fishing Nets—
    (a) Fixed or stationary.
    (b) Bag and purse.
    (c) Boat seine.
    (d) Shore seine.
    (e) Drift and gill.
    (f) Scoop.
    (g) Trawl type.
    (h) Cast.
    (i) Others.

INLAND FISHERIES

Earlier Information

The only statistics available in this regard earlier were those given in the Report on the Marketing of Fish in the Indian Union published in 1951 by the Directorate of Marketing and Inspection.

This Report contained the following data:

1. Estimated production of sea fish in India according to varieties and by regions.

2. Estimated marketable surplus of fresh water fish according to varieties and by regions.
3. Approximate number of vessels used for sea-fishing.
4. Number of persons engaged in fishing.
5. Seasonal variations and annual trends in production.
6. Imports and exports of fish and fish products.
7. Prices prevailing in some important centres in producing as well as consuming areas by varieties of fish and by States.
8. Gross distributive margins.
9. Purpose-wise distribution of fish, e.g. fish, consumed in fresh form, fish used for salting and sun drying and fish used as manure, etc.

The year of reference though not explicitly stated anywhere in the Report is 1948 as stated by the Central Statistical Organization in its 'National Income Statistics'. These data are not based on any scientifically planned surveys but mostly on trade enquiries and similar other evidence. The freshwater fish estimates depend on the information supplied by local officers, trade and municipalities as no other exact data of any other kind are available.

Inland fisheries can now be divided into two broad groups, viz. freshwater and brackishwater fisheries. Freshwater fisheries exist in the rivers, canals and irrigational channels, large freshwater lakes, numerous small lakes, jheels, reservoirs, ponds and tanks. The brackish water fisheries comprise the fisheries in typical estuarines of river-mouths, brackishwater lakes, lagoons and swamps lying along the coast line. There is, however, another important way of sub-dividing the inland fisheries into two classes, viz. capture and culture fisheries. In capture fisheries the role of the human agency is limited only to capturing fish or utmost to regulating the mode of capture. In culture fisheries which are provided by impounded waters of tanks, ponds and embanked brackishwaters, the human beings undertake various positive measures for culture effecting definite increase in production. In other words, in capture fisheries human beings only reap the aquatic harvest without having to sow, culture, tend and nurse before reaping.

The collection of inland fisheries statistics is far from satisfactory. A step for developing suitable sampling techniques for estimation of inland fish-catch was taken up during 1955-56 when pilot investigation was launched by the ICAR in two districts of the erstwhile Hyderabad State. In pursuance of the Government decision the work relating to the estimation of catch of fish was transferred from the ICAR to the Directorate of National Sample Surveys (NSS) in April, 1956.

In 1962-63 the Directorate of NSS conducted pilot surveys in three districts of Orissa, viz. Cuttack, Mayurbhunj and Sambalpur for estimation of: (i) number and areas of ponds, tanks and swamps, and (ii) total catch of fish from these sources. Based on the experience gained in that survey, the NSSO initiated integrated pilot surveys in Murshidabad district in West Bengal, Karimnagar in Andhra Pradesh and Madurai in Tamil

Nadu. The Central Inland Fisheries Research Institute, Calcutta (CIFRI) also conduct surveys for the estimation of inland fish covering mainly selected rivers, estuarines, lagoons such as the estuarine area of the river Ganges, Chilka lake etc. Attempts are being made by IASRI to develop a satisfactory technique for the estimation of inland fish catch.

State Departments of Fisheries are furnishing estimates of inland fish production largely based on factors like lease amount, issue of licences, departmental exploitation, market arrivals and transaction by cooperative societies, etc.

In the pilot survey undertaken in Orissa, the design adopted was stratified two-stage sampling in which strata were sub-divisions in each district. Gram panchayats formed the first stage units and villages in second stage units. The information on off-season catches was obtained by enquiry and that on bulk catches by actual verification. Data on bulk catches were collected through only one visit. On the whole, the procedure adopted was not very satisfactory.

There are various items which are covered under fisheries statistics. Data on the basic statistics required are: (i) fishermen population; (ii) fishing crafts, tackle, nets, (iii) inland water resources; and (iv) marine and inland fish-catch (species-wise and gear-wise). Other ancillary statistics are: (i) prices; (ii) market arrivals and sources of supply; (iii) utilization of fish-catch; (iv) household consumption; (v) trade; and (vi) mechanization of boats. Data on fishing crafts, tackle and nets are being collected at the time of quinquennial livestock census. Similarly, data on number of fishermen is being collected through the population census once in ten years. Although estimation of marine fish-catch is somewhat satisfactory, much is desired as far as inland fishery is concerned. Unless satisfactory technique for estimation of inland fish-catch is evolved, the fishery statistics cannot be obtained accurately. Information should be collected on the quantities of fish stored in cold storage. Data on utilization of fish and also processing should be collected at periodic intervals.

State Organizations

Some of the State Governments have also taken steps during recent years to collect various types of fishery statistics with the help of existing agencies. But there does not appear to exist any uniformity in the items of information being collected, method of collection agency employed, etc. It will not, therefore, be far wrong to say that we have still no reliable fishery statistics on an all-India level.

From among the various States, Tamil Nadu has a large number of government curing yards. They are maintaining regular data on species-wise daily catches of fish at landing centres lying within the jurisdiction of their yards. Some stray efforts have also been made to collect statistics about inland fisheries since 1945. All the available information on fisheries has been published in an ad hoc publication of the Department of Statistics, Madras—'Statistics for the Reorganized State of Madras', 1950. This contains fisheries statistics pertaining to intensive (fish) seed collection and distribution, fishing vessels (under Deep Sea Fishing Scheme), fish canning transactions and shark liver oil production in the reorganized State for 1956-57. Data collected in some of the exploratory studies are being published in the Annual Reports of the Fisheries Department.

The State Department of Fisheries, Maharashtra also publishes in its annual report some of the scattered data available with them on the subject. The Statistical Abstract of Orissa, published by the State Bureau of Economics and Statistics, gives figures of export of fish from Chilka Lake for the years 1955-57. The Quarterly Bulletin of Statistics, Orissa, gives data on quantity of fish sold in the Municipal markets of Orissa and the average price per unit sold. Similarly, the Directorate of Economics and Statistics, Himachal Pradesh, has also built up estimates of fish caught for the years 1950-51 to 1956. States like Uttar Pradesh and Madhya Pradesh have also formulated their ad hoc estimates of out-turn of fish, etc. Table 16.4 provides information in inland water resources statewise.

Table 16.4 State-wise details of Inland Water Resources of Various Types, 1993

(lakh ha.)

States / UTs	Rivers and Canals (Length in Kms.)	Reservoir	Tanks, Lakes and Ponds	Beels, Oxbow, Lakes and Derelict water	Brackish water	Total water bodies
Andhra Pradesh	11,514	2.34	5.17	-	0.64	8.15
Arunachal	2,000	-	0.01	0.03	-	0.04
Assam	1,820	0.55	0.21	1.10	-	1.86
Bihar	3,200	0.60	0.95	0.05	-	1.6
Goa	250	0.03	0.03	-	-	0.06
Gujarat	3,865	2.43	0.71	-	0.95	4.09
Haryana	5,000	Neg.	0.10	0.10	-	0.2
Himachal Pradesh	3,000	0.40	0.01	-	-	0.41
Jammu & Kashmir	27,781	0.07	0.17	0.06	-	0.3
Karnataka	9,000	2.11	3.52	-	0.08	5.71
Kerala	3,092	0.30	0.03	2.43	2.43	5.19
Madhya Pradesh	20,661	2.91	1.17	-	-	4.08
Maharashtra	3,200	2.79	0.32	-	0.10	3.21
Manipur	3,360	0.01	0.05	0.40	-	0.46
Meghalaya	5,600	0.08	0.02	Neg.	-	0.1
Mizoram	1,743	-	0.02	-	-	0.02
Nagaland	1,600	0.17	0.5	Neg.	-	0.67
Orissa	4,500	2.56	0.64	1.80	4.33	9.33
Punjab	15,270	Neg.	0.07	-	-	0.07

Table 16.4 State-wise details of Inland Water Resources of Various Types, 1993 (Contd.)

(lakh ha.)

States / UTs	Rivers and Canals (Length in Kms.)	Reservoir	Tanks, Lakes and Ponds	Beels, Oxbow, Lakes and Derelict water	Brackish water	Total water bodies
Rajasthan	N.A	1.20	1.80	-	-	3.00
Sikkim	900	-	-	0.03	-	0.03
Tamil Nadu	7,420	0.53	2.24	5.24	0.56	8.57
Tripura	1,200	0.05	0.12	-	-	0.17
Uttar Pradesh	31,200	1.50	1.62	1.33	-	4.45
West Bengal*	2,526	0.17	2.76	0.42	2.10	5.45
Andaman and Nicobar	115	0.01	0.30	-	1.15	1.46
Chandigarh	2	-	Neg.	Neg.	-	0
Dadra and Nagar Haveli	54	0.05	-	-	-	0.05
Daman and Diu	12	-	-	-	-	0
Delhi	150	0.04	-	-	-	0.04
Lakhadweep	-	-	-	-	-	0
Pondicherry	247	-	Neg.	0.01	0.01	0.02
Total	1,70,282	20.90	22.54	13.00	12.35	68.79

Note : 1. N.A : Not Available
2. * : Provisional
3. Neg. : Negligible

Source : 1. *Hand Book on Fisheries Statistics*, 1996. Ministry of Agriculture (Department of Agriculture and Cooperation), Fisheries Division, Govt. of India.
2. *Compendium of Environment Statistics, 1999*, Central Statistical Organisation,

Estuarine Surveys

The estuarine surveys being conducted in West Bengal for the Hooghly-Matla estuarine system by the Central Inland Fisheries Research Institute is a multi-purpose survey which gives information on fish production, salinity, plankton, fish eggs and larvae and fish biology. The sampling design consists of a total enumeration in some areas in the lower estuary at the lending centres and a multi-stage stratified cluster sampling in the upper stretches. All the gears in the upper estuary were first recorded at village level. The upper estuary is stratified into 4 strata. Three to four villages are taken per stratum at random with the restriction of keeping the average distance between villages to about 15 miles. For each village, 2 clusters of 2 days at a distance of a fortnight are then selected and for each day the effort by different gears and their catch are observed. Production is then estimated using a ratio method by taking the number of gears possessed per village as the auxillary variate. During the fortnightly visits the data collected each day relate to the number of different types of gears used, catch by type of gear, time spent in fishing, number of hauls made, species-wise catch, etc. In addition, water samples are collected for salinity and temperature. At the landing centres data collected consist of type of unit employed, fishing ground, species-wise catch, number of men, boats and gears employed and tidal condition.

The second estuarine survey being conducted by the Central Inland Fisheries Research Station is on the Mahanadi estuary. It is a combination of two surveys, a market survey to get estimates of total dry fish marketed and the other surveys, to get other fishery information. For the market surveys all the major markets are covered on days selected at random every month. For minor markets a simple random sample of a few markets is selected and then sampled on random days. The data are collected on quantity of dry fish marketed and other allied information. For the second surveys, the entire catch is stratified into 8 water zones and each water zone is covered for 2 days every fortnight with the help of motorized water transport. This survey aims at collecting data on fish biology, salinity, plankton, fish eggs and larvae, etc. There is another survey for collecting data in respect of hilsa fish. The survey is conducted in Krishna and Godavari Estuaries. It is a parallel of the Hooghly-Matla survey.[1]

An appraisal of the progress achieved indicates that the methodology developed for estimation of resources and fish catch has attained a more-or-less standardized form as far as ponds and tanks are concerned. However, there is a need to cover all types of water bodies by the programme so as to enable the States to have a reliable assessment of resources and production of uniform lines. During the Tenth Five Year Plan, it is proposed to extend the scope of the scheme to the remaining categories of water bodies with a view to standardizing the methodology for resource and catch assessment on scientific lines.

The Scheme is in operation in 17 States at present. This has to be extended to other states and Union Territories so that the estimation of fishery resources and production in all states/UTs are done on a scientific basis leading to reliable estimates. Remote sensing techniques have been found to be quick, reliable and cost effective in identification, classification and assessment of inland water spread area which is a prerequisite for realistic assessment of inland fishery resources. This methodology has been extensively tested for its effectiveness in the field of fishery surveys. It is proper to use this technique in future to assess the inland fishery resources.

Riverine Surveys

The Central Inland Fisheries Institute has been conducting survey on Ganga and Jamuna rivers to collect data on species-wise catch, fishing

---

[1] R.S. Chadha, Fisheries Statistics in India, Agriculture Situation in India, Jan. 1963.

grounds, gears, etc. The coverage is incomplete at present as the stretches of Ganga and Jamuna covered are only 800 and 400 miles respectively and the tributaries are not surveyed as yet. The design of the survey consists of dividing the entire stretch of Ganga and Jamuna from Fatehgarh to Rajmahal and Agra to Allahabad respectively into 8 zones, each having about 3-4 assembling centres. 2-3 days catch are selected at random for sampling each assembling centre. Preliminary work has also been started on Krishna-Godavari and Narbada Tapti riverine systems.

INTEGRATED PROGRAMME

The Technical Committee on Coordination of Fisheries Statistics (1950) recommended an integrated programme of statistical work for organizing the collection of statistics both for administrative purposes as well for planning the future development of Indian fisheries. Very little action was, however, taken on the recommendations of this Committee which are valid even today after a lapse of fifty years. There are still a large number of gaps in the coverage of fisheries statistics and no headway has been made in effecting improvements therein. Collection of the following types of statistics at intervals noted against each, is necessary.

(i) Basic statistics ..... Periodicity
    (a) fishermen population ..... decennial
    (b) fishing crafts, tackle nets (gears) ..... quinquennial
    (c) inland water resources (marine inland) ..... quinquennial
    (d) biological and research statistics ..... periodical
    (e) fish production marine and inland ..... monthly
        species-wise and gear-wise)

(ii) Ancillary statistics ..... Periodicity
    (a) prices (producer's price at first trans- ..... weekly
        action, whole sale and retail prices)
    (b) market arrivals and sources of supply ..... weekly
    (c) utilization of fish catch ..... monthly
    (d) household consumption ..... periodical
    (e) trade (external as well as internal) ..... monthly
    (f) mechanization of boats ..... annual
    (g) ice and cold storage and preservation ..... annual
        plants (capacity etc.)

FISHERIES RESOURCES

For planning the development of inland fisheries, it is necessary to have a critical assessment of the total inland fisheries resources available for development as well as those being exploited at present. The inland fisheries resources being biological in nature, are continuously changing due to complex interrelationship of various biotic and abiotic factors. It is, therefore, necessary to survey these resources periodically, specially with reference to geographical, physical, chemical and biological factors.

The inland fish resources should be classified according to size of water area, depth, salinity, soil type, production potential, degree of utilization, culture/capture practices, yield rates, etc.

With regard to marine fisheries resources, a continuous resources survey is necessary to collect information on various biological characteristics such as growth, recruitment, mortality, measurement of lengths, age determinants, etc. Information on these basic parameters is important for the evaluation of yield from fishery under varying biological and environmental factors and for working out suitable population models for studying the dynamics of exploitation. It is also necessary to prepare an up-to-date inventory of all marine resources such as length of coastline, area of continental shelf, number of marine villages, number of active fishermen, etc. Such a survey should be conducted at least once in five years by the CMFRI with the help of the State Governments. Data on number of fishermen are already being collected through the population census once in ten years.

Mechanization of Boats

Every year a number of mechanized boats are introduced for marine fishing. While new boats are introduced, some of the existing boats go out of use each year. A mere periodical census as on a day might not bring to light the exact number of boats, etc. available even in the census year. It would be desirable to have a registration of small mechanized boats of size below 25 gross registered tonnage (GRT). This would be useful not only from the point of maintaining statistics but also for keeping a watch on the growth of mechanization.

With regard to larger vessels above 25 GRT, even now, in the course of their operation lot of information relating to operational details and performance of the vessels, specially in the context of commercial fishing becomes available; but it is necessary to collect and analyze these data systematically for working out the economics of deep-sea fishing and for demonstrating its potentialities.

Seed Fish Statistics

Statistics of seed fish were till recently not collected in an organized manner by most of the States. The Fish Seed Committee (1963) gave some idea of production of spawn, fry and fingerlings for 1964-65. For subsequent years, the States have been collecting the required data, though their coverage has been found to be incomplete. As the State Departments of Fisheries broadly know the centres for production of spawn, fry and fingerlings, both private and departmental, they should collect reliable estimates of seed fish available for further development. It is also necessary to develop appropriate technical coefficients such as mortality at various stages of fish growth, etc.

Prices, Market Arrivals and Other Statistics

Adequate arrangements are also necessary for collecting data on producers', wholesale and retail prices of different categories of fish. Difficulties of specification of price quotation are likely to arise, particularly as the price of fish depends upon the variety, the size, the consumer preference and the state of freshness of the fish. It becomes sometimes difficult to apply the concept of modal price to transactions in fish. What is, however, important is to see that reliable data on prices of fish are collected for standard varieties and pre-determined specifications. With regard to market arrivals, it is suggested that, as a first step, arrangements should be made with the municipalities and municipal corporations for collection of data on market arrivals of fish on a periodical basis. Similar information should also be collected on the quantities of fish stored in cold storage, etc. Data on utilization of fish and also processing need to be collected at periodical intervals.

There is also scope and need for compiling derived statistics such as index numbers of production of fish and of prices. Once reliable data on production, prices and inputs are available, it should be possible to work out the contribution of fisheries sector to the national income more accurately.

TRADE STATISTICS

Statistics of foreign trade in fish and fishery products are published as part of the general import/export trade by the Ministry of Commerce. But one important gap in the available data is the absence of information regarding unit value realization of marine products exported from India. Marine Products Export Development Authority should undertake an analysis of the unit value realized by the various items from India in important foreign markets along with the corresponding unit values realized for similar products by other countries. This analysis will be helpful in exploring the possibilities of diversification of exports of marine products.

Efforts should be made to collect statistics of internal trade and movements covering rail, river and road-borne traffic. As proper arrangements for refrigerated transport are essential for a perishable commodity like fish, data on internal trade and movements are important.

OTHER DATA

Periodical evaluation of the various fisheries projects at the Central and State levels is necessary to provide guidance on the formulation and implementation of the development programmes. Another important data requirement is in respect of cost of production of fish. Appropriate methodology has to be developed for this purpose.

ORGANIZATIONAL SET-UP

For proper development of fisheries statistics on the lines indicated in the foregoing paragraphs, it is necessary to set up suitable organizations or strengthen the existing ones for the collection, compilation and analysis of data at different levels. Very few States have full-fledged statistical units in the Fisheries Departments to look after the collection and compilation of fisheries statistics. It is, however, necessary that every State should have a strong Statistical Unit in the Fisheries Department manned by properly qualified statisticians and other statistical personnel, to deal with all aspects of fisheries statistics. At the Central level, the Fisheries Statistics Unit, located in the Fisheries Division should be strengthened and placed under a Joint Director, who should work in close collaboration with the DES. For economic analysis of the various projects and undertaking evaluation studies an economist should be added to the Fisheries Statistics Unit at the Central and State levels.

The Central fisheries institutes like the CMFRI, CIFRI and CIFT have regular statistical units for the collection and interpretation of statistical data. With increasing emphasis on research data for proper evaluation and assessment of potential of inland and marine resources and progress of their exploitation, these units will have to undertake larger responsibilities. They should, therefore, be suitably strengthened with qualified staff at various levels. For the work of economic evaluation in the field of fish culture, fishing practices, as also the economic suitability of various types of engines, crafts and gears, the assistance of economists should be provided to the statistical units in these institutes.

SUGGESTIONS FOR IMPROVEMENT

For a real improvement, the sampling design of the Mandapam survey should be made truly random to enable an objective estimation of marine fish catches. In order that State-wise estimates with reasonable accuracy become available, the sample size should be suitably increased by associating the State fisheries development staff with the Scheme. At present sampling errors of the estimates are not available. To enable an assessment of the accuracy of the estimates thrown up by the CMFRI Cochin, sampling errors of the estimates should also be worked out and published along with the estimates of production, etc.

In view of the paucity of data in the field of inland fisheries, it has been recommended that the Directorate of NSS should take up the work of evaluation of techniques for estimation of inland fish catches on a priority basis. After the necessary techniques have been evolved for different types of inland fisheries, their extension on an all-India basis with the help of the State Fisheries Development staff needs to be taken up.

While steps are being taken by various organizations to collect a variety of fisheries statistics, much leeway still remains to be made up to place the fisheries statistics of the country on a firm footing. For this purpose concerted effort will have to be made by the Ministry of Agriculture for coordinating the work of different agencies and organizing the collection of different types of data on uniform lines throughout the country.[2]

---

[2] R.S. Chadha, *op. cit.*

Various other types of data required to be collected in the sphere of fisheries may be classified into the following four broad categories, viz.

  (i) *Potentialities*: The potentialities of development of fisheries will depend on the availability of water resources for exploitation, the number of persons engaged in fishing and allied industries and the equipment required for fishing.

 (ii) *Production*: The statistics of production should include both marine and inland fish and also of the manufactured products like shark liver oil and fish meal, which are necessary for estimating the contribution of fisheries to food supply and also trends therein.

(iii) *Utilization, Demand and Supply*: These statistics relate to market arrivals, internal movement, prices received by fishermen and prices paid by the consumers.

(iv) *Indicators of Fisheries Development*: These refer to the fixation of targets and assessment of progress of the different schemes for fisheries development.

Some of the gaps in data availability for inland fisheries which need to be addressed to for the coming plans are:—

  (a) National inventorying and mapping of inland fisheries resources.

  (b) Census of fishers engaged in the inland fisheries sector with their socio-economic status, inventory of craft and gear, marketing and distribution.

  (c) Catch assessment through sampling techniques.

  (d) Compilation of data and estimation of results by computerization of the whole process and creating information networking using district level NIC setup.

  (e) Transferring the methodology for ponds and tanks to the States and enhancing their data handling capabilities.

  (f) Continuing the programme in freshwater ponds and tanks in respect of those states where the scheme has not yet been tried out sufficiently to lead to formulation of standardized methodology.

  (g) Providing assistance to the States to extend the coverage of the scheme to all the districts.

  (h) Developing suitable methodology for resource and catch assessment in respect of reservoirs, floodplain lakes, rivers and canals, estuaries, etc.

  (i) Use of Remote Sensing to assess inland fishery resources by developing a suitable methodology.

17

National Sample Surveys

FORMATION

With the independence of the country, the full impact of large gaps in the statistical information available in India was soon felt and an urgent need arose to tone up its quality and quantity. At the instance of the then Prime Minister, Jawaharlal Nehru, P.C. Mahalanobis prepared a scheme of organizing a National Sample (NSS) which was approved in principle by the Government of India is January 1950.

The National Sample Survey (NSS) was created in 1950 with the object of obtaining comprehensive and continuing information relating to social, economic, demographic, industrial and agricultural statistics, through sample surveys on a country-wide basis. By then, the Indian Statistical Institute (ISI) had established itself as a premier body in the field of statistics with specialization in sample survey techniques. It had done considerable spade work in the form of pilot and research studies and was well equipped for guiding large scale sample surveys. It was, therefore, natural that while instituting the NSS, the Government should have turned to the ISI for providing technical direction to its surveys. Accordingly, the work relating to sampling design and schedules of enquiries, writing of instructions, training of field staff, processing and tabulation of data and writing of reports was all entrusted to the ISI. Only the field work was assigned to the Directorate of National Sample Survey, created for the purpose by the Government of India. In West Bengal and Bombay city, however, the field work was also given to ISI.

The general approach in the planning of NSS was entrusted to Indian Statistical Institute together with the Gokhale Institute of Politics and Economics, Poona, running under the direction of late Prof. D.R. Gadgil. As the experience and field of activity of the Calcutta and Poona Institutes had been very different, it was not unnatural that certain differences of opinion emerged at the early stages. However, as a result of joint discussion, a plan for the sample design (in its more restricted sense of allocation and the methods of selection of the sample units, etc.) was evolved.

392

The objective of the NSS is to carry out nation-wide annual sample surveys to cover the gaps in data required for estimation of national income and for preparation of development plans. Initially for nearly two decades, the ISI was responsible for survey design, data processing and report writing. A field organisation was set up under the Central government for collection of data. Later, an organisation (NSSO) was created in the DoS to take up complete responsibility for the NSS under the technical control of an autonomous Governing Council to which ISI nominates two members. The autonomous Governing Council is meant to ensure that the data collected are free of administrative bias.

Since its inception, the NSS has made significant additions to the national database, particularly in the following areas: (i) household consumption—leading to many studies about the extent of poverty in the country, (ii) employment and unemployment—sorting out conceptual difficulties in the definition of employment in the Indian context, (iii) manufacturing and trade-in the unorganised sector, (iv) land holding, (v) crop area and yield, (vi) literacy and education, (vii) morbidity, disability, maternity and child care, (viii) utilisation of public distribution system, (ix) housing condition, (x) prices, and (xi) household debt and investment.

A departmental Computer Centre (CC) was set up in 1967 to serve the data processing needs of the Central government. When the Department of Electronics (DoE) established the National Informatics Centre (NIC) with its own network of computers (NICNET), much of the work was transferred to it. The major responsibility of the CC has since then been to process data collected through the NSS and surveys conducted by the CSO. In the past, processing of NSS data at the ISI on Unit Record Machines and later at the CC on computers used to take a much longer time than anticipated, primarily because of the difficulty in removing internal inconsistencies from the falliole data collected from the field—a process metaphorically but aptly called *cleaning*. Data cleaning is essentially a statistical procedure. Only competent statisticians, experienced in the field of application, are capable of developing an efficient data-cleaning procedure. The procedure can there be computerised. If this essential pre-requisite is not fulfilled, even the largest electronic computers with the most brilliant computer software engineers would fail to produce results in time. This elementary lesson was learnt at a great cost when the NIC was entrusted with the processing of an entire round of NSS data with disastrous consequences. The summarised data never saw the light of the day. The NIC has been transferred from the DoE to the Planning Commission.

The importance of data cleaning and the *role* of concerned statisticians in developing appropriate procedures are better understood now. Statisticians in the NSSO are now themselves engaged in processing of NSS data on in-house computers at the NSSO. Though these computers are only of moderate power, there has been noticeable improvement in cutting down delays in processing of data. This is indeed very heartening.

ORGANIZATION

Significance. The idea of using sampling method for collecting economic data was not new. It can be said to be a projection of the 'Scheme for an Economic Census of India' prepared by Professors. A.E. Bowley and D.H. Robertson in 1934. Sampling is, of course, the only possible approach if it is desired to collect data about various facts relating to agriculture, industry, trade and services, etc. The only possible method is to send round investigators to collect information from a comparatively small number of individual households, that is, from a sample of households, selected in such a way that it would be possible to estimate on the basis of the sample, the required information for the country as a whole. Where the scope of the survey is wide and the territory to be covered is large, the sample survey is the only practical means for obtaining infomation at short intervals. This is especially true of a rural economy of the size of India covering a vast area of 12.6 lakhs of square miles.

Method. For administrative purposes India is till recently divided into 29 States (some of which are very small), about 300 districts, about 2,500 tehsils (or equivalent units), 3,000 towns, and about 586,000 villages in round figures. The total area of India is 3,280 million square kilometres broken up into some hundreds of millions of 'plots' of land, and as per the 2001 Census, population of India was 1027 millions. Turning now to the livelihood pattern we find that less than one-third of the people are self-supporting and of these again, less than a third derive their income principally from non-agricultural sources.

As regards the sampling design, it can be stated very briefly that the rural area of the country was divided into about 250 geographical strata from which about a thousand sample villages were selected. In the first three rounds the villages were directly selected within a stratum but in subsequent rounds two tehsils were selected in each stratum and two villages were selected within each sample tehsil (an administrative unit of about 500 square miles on an average). Finally a sample of households was taken up for the household enquiry and a sample of clusters of plots for the land utilization survey. From the third round, the survey was extended to urban areas with a stratification of towns by size.

A general idea of the nature of information collected is given below:

(a) *Sample Villages*. General economic information, and weekly prices of selected commodities; rates of daily wages of skilled and unskilled workers, etc.

(b) *Households*

(i) *General particulars*: Age, sex, marital status, economic, and employment status; births, deaths, etc. details regarding holdings, use of land under various categories, livestock, real assets, loans, savings, housing conditions, etc.

(ii) *Consumer expenditure*: On a very large number of items.

(iii) *Household enterprises*: Agriculture and animal husbandry; acreage and production of different crops; particulars of industry, crafts and trade, including fixed capital machinery and tools, fuel power, raw materials, quantity and value of production, source of finance, etc.

(c) *Utilization of Land*. Survey of sample of revenue plots.

(d) *Crop Survey*. Crop acreage and estimates of the yield of crop per acre by direct crop-cutting experiments.

(e) *Manufacturing Establishments*. Sample survey of manufacturing establishments (with 10 operatives or more with power, or 20 operatives or more without power) covering practically all groups of industry over the whole of India. With increasing demand for reliable estimates at State and regional levels, the need for larger samples has been increasingly felt, and efforts made to enlarge the sample size over the years. At present the NSS covers, in each round, a sample of about 12,000 to 14,000 villages and blocks at the all-India level in the "Central sample" (covered by the NSSO) and an independent sample of about 14,000 to 16,000 villages and blocks at the all-India level through "State samples" (covered by various States/ Union Territories). The field work for the Central sample is undertaken by a team of highly trained investigators of the Field Operations Division of the NSSO. NSS data on socio-economic surveys are regularly released through the quarterly publication *Sarvekshana* issued by the Department of Statistics.

The statistical work of NSS (including the preparation of the sample design and schedules, the processing and tabulation of the data and the preparation of the reports) is being done in the ISI. The first report was published in December 1952 and since then a chain of reports and technical papers have been continuously coming out. In addition special surveys have been conducted and reports and data in tabular form have been supplied from time to time to different agencies, for example, Fact Finding Committee of the Ministry of Rehabilitation (survey of economic conditions of refugees of West Bengal), the Press Commission (habits of newspaper reading), the Taxation Enquiry Commission (household consumption by expenditure levels), the Ministry of Rehabilitation (survey of refugees in Bombay), Ministry of Works, Housing and Supply (survey of housing), and some good work in connection with Mysore Population Study conducted by the United Nations and the Ministry of Health and so on.

The information is collected in the NSS mainly by the 'interview method' in which the investigators visit each household included in the sample and make direct enquiries from the householder. In case of crops and certain other items, the investigators collect the data by their own direct observations. The investigators are employed on a whole-time basis and work throughout the year; in addition, there is a whole-time inspecting and auxiliary staff. The total strength of the field branch of the NSS is about 600 who work under the direct control of the Department of Economic Affairs, Ministry of Finance.

Assessment of Results

It would be instructive to note here some of the criteria for the assessment of the results of the NSS. The main difficulty arises out of the fact that the information on many aspects of economic conditions in the rural areas of India has been obtained for the first time. In most cases similar data are not available for the purpose of direct comparison. There can be three broad approaches which, of course, are complementary and must be used jointly and simultaneously. First, the scientific merit of sampling method is that in a properly designed sample survey, it is possible to calculate the margin of error of the results from the sample data themselves. Such calculations supply a powerful tool to judge the significance of comparison based on the NSS estimates. Secondly, in a properly designed sample survey it is also possible to study, for example, by using an interpenetrating network of sub-samples, and sometimes to eliminate the effect of non-sampling errors which arise from bias, recording mistakes and other disturbing factors operating at the stage of collection of the primary information. NSS has used this method with considerable success. Thirdly, special 'quality' checks may be carried out by highly trained and experienced workers (including senior statisticians) who would themselves go out to the field and directly collect some of the critical primary data. The results thus obtained can be used to determine the reliability of the data collected by the regular investigators. All these methods are internal, in the sense that information would be collected by the NSS itself in many different ways with a view to improving the reliability of the results. A second broad approach is to use external checks by comparing the NSS results with data obtained from entirely independent sources. External checks are of great value, and it is intended to include test items in the NSS schedules from time to time with the deliberate intention of using such information for purposes of comparison with data obtained from independent sources.

In the case of all scientific investigations, there exists a final criterion, namely, the reliability of forecasts made on the basis of present knowledge. In the case of the NSS also inferences drawn in a valid manner on available evidence will have to be judged by future events. The validity of the NSS results, will thus have to be assessed by piecing together a large mass of evidence based partly on internal consistency, partly on external checks, and ultimately on the accuracy and social usefulness of the estimates and forecasts. The different stands of evidence cannot be expected to be all concordant. Some of the results may be contradictory. It may easily happen, especially in the initial stages, that certain items of information are reliable while data on certain other items are still untrustworthy. Even in abstract principle all the results cannot be always accurate. The theory must sometimes prove wrong. All that can be said at present is that the results of the NSS are definitely encouraging and provocative of thought.

So far as the present endeavours go it is hoped that it would be possible in the future to conduct three or four regular rounds of surveys every year with a standard programme of work covering important sectors of information. These regular surveys would be designed with a view to supplying, from year to year, repeated or seasonal estimates of important economic factors to indicate economic trends. It is also proposed to conduct from time to time, may be once in each year, special surveys relating to particular subjects such as education, transport, health, etc. in connection with the Ministries concerned. It is intended in addition to keep a certain amount of work-load free for ad hoc enquiries at short notice. In this way it is hoped that the NSS would supply in future a continuous stream of essential information relating to the economic progress of the country for purposes of planning.

REORGANIZATION OF THE NSS

The organization of the work of the NSS was reviewed by the Government from time to time. In July 1969, a three-man committee consisting of B. Sivaraman, the then Cabinet Secretary, V.M. Dandekar, and Raghuraj Bahadur was set up to advise the Government on the lines of its reorganization. The Committee recommended, in main, entrusting of all aspects of NSS work to a single government organization located in the Cabinet Secretariat and governed by a Governing Council, the Council being given sufficient independence and autonomy of decision so as to ensure that the collection, processing and publication of NSS data were free from undue influence.

The NSS is a continuing, multi-subject organization. Integrated survey, being conducted by it are in the form of successive rounds; a round covering several subjects but with emphasis on one or two of these during a specific period, generally coinciding with the agricultural year. The subjects covered, more or less regularly in the past few rounds, are household income and consumer expenditure, rural retail prices of selected commodities, employment and unemployment particulars, labour force statistics, demographic characteristics and crop surveys. Data on subjects like small scale enterprises (manufacture, transport and trade), professions and services, village statistics, landholdings, savings and indebtedness, etc. are collected periodically. Subjects such as vital statistics, disposal of cereals by producer households, capital formation, building construction, farming practices, economic condition of agricultural or rural labourers, animal husbandry, livestock products, family planning, migration, etc. have also been taken up in some rounds. Besides, a few ad hoc survey, such as income and expenditure surveys of middle class and working class, post-census surveys of population and livestock, etc. are also undertaken from time to time. With a view to obtaining comprehensive data at the State level most of the State Statistical Bureaus have also been participating in the socio-economic enquiries with a matching sample. Information as number of strata, sample size, etc. is in Table 17.1.

RECENT DEVELOPMENT

By the time the Council was constituted in March 1970, the 24th round of the NSS was in progress. The Council, therefore, started functioning

Table 17.1 List of Subjects Covered and Reports Brought out for the NSS Rounds 36 to 50.

Report No.	Title of the Report
(1)	*(2)*

<table>
<tr><td colspan="2" align="center">Round No. 36 (July' 81 to Dec.' 81)
Survey of Disabled Persons (Sch. 26)</td></tr>
<tr><td>305</td><td>Report on Survey of Disabled Persons</td></tr>
<tr><td>337</td><td>Characteristics of Disabled Persons</td></tr>
<tr><td colspan="2" align="center">Round No. 37 (Jan. '37 (Jan. '82 to Dec.' 82)
Land Holding and Livestock Holdings (Sch. 18.1)</td></tr>
<tr><td>318</td><td>Assets and Liabilities of Rural and Urban Households (States and all-India)</td></tr>
<tr><td>322</td><td>Some Aspects of Indebtedness of Rural and Urban Households (States and all-India)</td></tr>
<tr><td>328</td><td>Some Aspects of Indebtedness of Rural and Urban Households (Pt-II, States and all-India)</td></tr>
<tr><td>330</td><td>Some Aspects of Household Ownership Holdings (States and all-India)</td></tr>
<tr><td>331</td><td>Some Aspects of Operational Holdings</td></tr>
<tr><td>334</td><td>Broad Features of Capital Expenditure Incurred by Rural and Urban Households during '81-'82 (States and all-India)</td></tr>
<tr><td>338</td><td>Estimates of Live-stock and Agricultural Implements Classified by Household Operational Holdings</td></tr>
<tr><td>340</td><td>Extent and Nature of Borrowings and Repayments of Rural and Urban Households during July '81-June '82 (States and all-India)</td></tr>
<tr><td>344</td><td>Features of Operational Holdings during Kharif and Rabi Seasons of the Agricultural Year 1981-82 (States and all-India, Rural sector)</td></tr>
<tr><td>349</td><td>Assets, Liabilities and Capital Expenditure of Urban Households by Population Size Class of Towns (all-India)</td></tr>
<tr><td colspan="2" align="center">Round No. 38 (Jan. '83 to Dec. '83)
Consumer Expenditure (Sch. 1.0)
Employment and Unemployment (Sch. 10)</td></tr>
<tr><td>315</td><td>Key Results of Last Three Quinquennial NSS Enquiries on Employment and Unemployment.</td></tr>
<tr><td>319</td><td>Report on the Third Quinquennial Survey on Consumer Expenditure</td></tr>
<tr><td>332</td><td>Pattern of Consumer Expenditure of S.C. and S.T. Households.</td></tr>
<tr><td>333</td><td>Pattern of Consumer Expenditure of Households Self-employed in Agriculture and of Agricultural and Rural Labour Households</td></tr>
<tr><td>336</td><td>Report on Sources of Drinking Water and Energy Used for Lighting and Cooking</td></tr>
<tr><td>339</td><td>Tables with Notes on Particulars of Dwelling Units</td></tr>
</table>

Table 17.1 List of Subjects Covered and Reports Brought out for the
NSS Rounds 36 to 50 (Contd.)

Report No.	Title of the Report
(1)	*(2)*
341	Report on the Third Quinquennial Survey on Employment and Unemployment: all-India
341/1	Report on the Third Quinquennial Survey on Employment and Unemployment: Andhra Pradesh
341/2	Report on the Third Quinquennial Survey on Employment and Unemployment: Bihar
341/3	Report on the Third Quinquennial Survey on Employment and Unemployment: Kerala
341/4	Report on the Third Quinquennial Survey on Employment and Unemployment: Maharashtra
341/5	Report on the Third Quinquennial Survey on Employment and Unemployment: Karnataka
341/6	Report on the Third Quinquennial Survey on Employment and Unemployment: Madhya Pradesh
341/7	Report on the Third Quinquennial Survey on Employment and Unemployment: Orissa
341/8	Report on the Third Quinquennial Survey on Employment and Unemployment: Rajasthan
349/9	Report on the Third Quinquennial Survey on Employment and Unemployment: Tamil Nadu
341/10	Report on the Third Quinquennial Survey on Employment and Unemployment: Uttar Pradesh
341/11	Report on the Third Quinquennial Survey on Employment and Unemployment: West Bengal
341/12	Report on the Third Quinquennial Survey on Employment and Unemployment: Gujarat
341/13	Report on the Third Quinquennial Survey on Employment and Unemployment: Haryana
341/14	Report on the Third Quinquennial Survey on Employment and Unemployment: Punjab
341/15	Report on the Third Quinquennial Survey on Employment and Unemployment: Assam
341/16	Report on the Third Quinquennial Survey on Employment and Unemployment: Himachal Pradesh
341/17	Report on the Third Quinquennial Survey on Employment and Unemployment: Jammu and Kashmir
341A	Employment and Unemployment Situation of S.C. and S.T. Population during Early Eighties
341B	Employment and Unemployment Situation in Cities and Towns during Early Eighties
348	Per Capita and Per Consumer Unit per Diem Intake of Calorie, Protein and Fat and Perception of the People on Adequacy of Food

Table 17.1 List of Subjects Covered and Reports Brought out for the NSS Rounds 36 to 50 *(Contd.)*

Report No.	Title of the Report
(1)	*(2)*
352	Monthly per Capita Consumption of Cereals for Various Sections of Population
353	Level of Nutritional Intake of Population Distributed over Different Expenditure Classes
356	Tables with Notes on the Effect of Adjustment of Energy Intake for Meals Consumed Free and Meals served to Others
357	Tables with Notes on Distribution of Households by Monthly Per Capita Expenditure Class after Adjustment (Considering Annual Expenditure)
387	Distribution of Households and Persons by Household Monthly Per Capita Expenditure for Different Calorie Intake Levels

Round No. 39 (Jan. '84 to Jun. '84)
Population, Births and Deaths Enumeration (Sch. 12)
Population, Births and Deaths Enumeration and
Re-enumeration (Sch. 12.1)
Village Particulars (Sch. 3.1)

350	Effect of Drought on the Pattern of Employment and Unemployment: a Comparative Study of the Survey Results of NSS 38th and 39th Rounds
351	Population, Birth and Death Rates
354	Fertility Rates in India

Round No. 40 (July '84 to Jun. '85)
Unorganised Manufacture: Non-directory Establishments and
Own Account Enterprises (Sch. 2.2B)

363/1	Tables with Notes on Survey of Unorganised Manufacture: Non-directory Establishments and Own Account Enterprises—all-India
363/2	Tables with Notes on Survey of Unorganised Manufacture: Non-directory Establishments and Own Account Enterprises—States (Vol. I and II)

Round No. 41 (July '85 to Jun. '86)
Trade: Non-directory Establishments and
Own Account Enterprises (Sch. 2.41B)

3661/1	Tables with Notes on Own Account Trading Enterprises and Non-directory Establishments: all-India
366/2	Tables with Notes on Own Account Trading Enterprises and Non-directory Establishments: States (Vol. I and II)

Table 17.1 List of Subjects Covered and Reports Brought out for the
NSS Rounds 36 to 50 (Contd.)

Report No.	Title of the Report
(1)	(2)

Round No. 42 (July '86 to Jun. '87)
Maternity, Child Care, Family Planning and Utilisation of
Public Distribution System (Sch. 25.1)
Participation in Education (Sch. 25.2)
Survey on Persons Aged 60 Years and above (Sch. 27)
Survey on Ex-armed Force Personnel (Sch. 28)
Consumer Expenditure (Sch. 10)

355/1	Tables with Notes on Consumer Expenditure for Assam, Bihar, Manipur, Meghalaya, Mizoram, Nagaland, Orissa, Rajasthan, Sikkim, Tamil Nadu, Tripura, U.P., West Bengal and Pondicherry
355/2	Tables with Notes on Consumer Expenditure for all-India, Andhra Pradesh, Gujarat, Haryana, H.P., J & K, Karnataka, Kerala, M.P., Maharashtra, Punjab, A & N Islands, Chandigarh, D & N Haveli, Delhi, Goa, Daman and Diu, Lakshadweep
361	A profile of Households and Population by Economic Class and Social Group and Availability of Drinking Water, Electricity and Disinfection of Dwellings
362	Utilisation of Public Distribution System
364	Morbidity and Utilisation of Medical Services
365/1	Participation in Education: all-India
365/2	Participation in Education: Major States (Vol. I)
365/2	Participation in Education: Major States (Vol. II)
367	Socio Economic Profile of the Aged Persons
368	Child and Maternity Care
369	Utilisation of Family Planning Services

Round No. 43 (July '87 to Jun. '88)
Consumer Expenditure (Sch. 1.0)
Employment and Unemployment (Sch. 10)
Travel Habits of Households (Sch. 21)

371A	Employment and Unemployment Situation of Scheduled Tribe and Scheduled Caste Population during Late Eighties
371B	Employment and Unemployment Situation in Cities and Towns during Late Eighties
372	Pattern of Consumer Expenditure
373	Particulars of Dwelling Units (SS-I)
374	Pattern of Consumption of Cereals, Pulses, Tobacco and Some Other Selected Items

Table 17.1 List of Subjects Covered and Reports Brought out for the NSS Rounds 36 to 50 *(Contd.)*

Report No.	Title of the Report
(1)	*(2)*
	Round No. 44 (July '88 to Jun. '89)
	Village Characteristics (Sch. 3.1)
	Level of Living of Tribals (Sch. 29.1)
	Economic Activities of Tribals (Sch. 29.2)
	Particulars of Migration and Ownership of Land by
	Non-tribals in Tribal Areas (Sch. 29.3)
	Housing Condition (Sch 1.2)
	Particulars of Construction (Sch. 1.4)
370/1	Tables with Notes on Consumer Expenditure (all-India), Semi Rounds 1
370/2	Tables with Notes on Consumer Expenditure (all-India), Semi Rounds 1 and 2
375	A Report on Some Important Characteristics of Villages in Tribal Areas
376	Report on Housing Condition
377	Report on Building Construction
378	A Report on Living Conditions of Some Major Tribes of India
379	An. Economic Profile of Some Major Tribes of India
380	A Report on Living Conditions of Tribals and Non-tribals of Tribal Areas
389	A Report on an Exploratory Survey of Living Conditions of Tribals of Nagaland
	Round No. 45 (July '89 to Jun. '90)
	Unorganised Manufacture: Non-directory
	Establishments and Own Account Enterprises (Sch. 2.2)
	Consumer Expenditure (Sch. 10)
381	Tables with Notes on the Third Annual Survey on Consumer Expenditure
396/1	Tables with Notes on Survey of Unorganised Manufacture: Non-directory Establishments and Own Account Enterprises, Part-I: all-India
396/2	Tables with Notes on Survey of Unorganized Manufacture: Non-directory Establishments and Own Account Enterprises, Part-II: States
	Round No. 46 (July '90 to Jun. '91)
	Trade: Non-directory Establishments and
	Own Account Enterprises (Sch. 2.41.2)
	Consumer Expenditure (Sch. 1.0)

Table 17.1 List of Subjects Covered and Reports Brought out for the
NSS Rounds 36 to 50 *(Contd.)*

Report No.	Title of the Report
(1)	*(2)*
386	Tables with Notes on Fourth Annual Survey on Consumer Expenditure and Employment—Unemployment
403	Small Trading Units in India
403/1 Vol.-I	State Level Results on Small Trading Units in India
403/1 Vol.-II	State Level Results on Small Trading Units in India

Round No. 47 (July '91 to Dec. '91)
Village Facilities (Sch. 3.1)
Survey of Disabled Persons (Sch. 26)
Developmental Milestones of Children (Sch. 26.1)
Literacy and Culture (Sch. 30)
Consumer Expenditure (Sch. 1.0)

388	Tables with Notes on Fifth Annual Survey on Consumer Expenditure and Employment-Unemployment
392	Availability of Some Education and Culture Related Facilities in Indian Villages
393	A Report on Disabled Persons
394	Literacy in India
395	Participation in Cultural Activities

Round No. 48 (Jan. '92 to Dec. '92)
Land and Livestock Holdings (Sch. 18.1)
Debt and Investment (Sch. 18.2)
Consumer Expenditure (Sch. 1.0)

397	Household Consumer Expenditure and Employment Situation in India
399	Some Aspects of Household Ownership Holdings
407	Operational Land Holdings in India, 1991-92, Salient Features
408	Livestock and Agricultural Implements in Household Operational Holdings, 1991-92
414	Seasonal Variation in the Operation of Land Holdings in India, 1991-92
419	Household Assets and Liabilities as on 30.6.91

Round No. 49 (Jan. '93 to Jun. '93)
Particulars of Slums (Sch. 0.21)
Housing Condition and Migration (Sch. 1.2)
Consumer Expenditure (Sch. 1.0)

400	Household Consumer Expenditure and Employment Situation in India
417	Slums in India
429	Housing Conditions in India

Table 17.1 List of Subjects Covered and Reports Brought out for the NSS Rounds 36 to 50 (Contd.)

Report No.	Title of the Report
(1)	*(2)*

Round No. 50 (July '93 to Jun. '94)
Household Consumer Expenditure (Sch. 1.0)
Employment and Unemployment (Sch. 10)

401	Key Results on Household Consumer Expenditure, 1993-94
402	Level and Pattern of Consumer Expenditure
404	Consumption of Some Important Commodities in India
405	Nutritional Intake in India
406	Key Results on Employment and Unemployment
409	Employment and Unemployment in India, 1993-94
410/1	Dwellings in India
410/2	Energy Used by Indian Households
411	Employment and Unemployment Situation in Cities and Towns, 1993-94
412	Economic Activities and School Attendance by Children of India, 1993-94
413	Sources of Household Income in India, 1993-94
415	Reported Adequacy of Food Intake in India, 1993-94
416	Participation of Indian Women in Household Work and Other Specified Activities, 1993-94
418	Unemployed in India, 1993-94, Salient Features
422	Differences in Level of Consumption among Socio-Economic Groups
423	IRDP Assistance and Participation in Public Works, 1993-94
424	Ownership of Livestock, Cultivation of Selected Crops and Consumption Levels
425	Employment and Unemployment Situation Among Social Groups in India, 1993-94
426	Use of Durable Goods by Indian Households, 1993-94
427	Consumption of Tobacco in India, 1993-94
428	Wages in Kind, Exchange of Gifts and Expenditure on Ceremonies and Insurance in India, 1993-94

*For Earlier Reports, Please Refer to the Previous Edition of this Book.

with the formulation of the subject programme of the 25th round. Since its inception the Council has been of the view that the collection of primary data and building up of estimates in the field of agriculture should be the responsibility of the State Governments and that the NSS Organization should devote its attention to assisting the States in the improvement of these statistics. It was in pursuance of this view that the Council decided at its second meeting, held on 16-18 April 1970, to reorientate, from the 25th round (1970-71), the NSS Land Utilization

Survey (NSS-LUS) and Crop-Cutting Experiments (CCE) so as to integrate them with the State system of crop estimation. Accordingly, the NSS-LUS was to be taken up mainly as a statistical check on the primary enumeration of crop areas by the State Revenue Agencies; the CCE as such was to be dropped. The NSS-LUS was further linked up with the scheme of the Ministry of Agriculture for timely reporting of crop areas (TRS) by keeping the NSS sample villages as part of the TRS sample.

The progress of the NSS-LUS in its modified form did not, however, come up to expectations. There was found to be a lack of synchronization between the crop inspection work of the Patwaris and the NSS-LUS work of the socio-economic (SE) investigators of the NSS. The new work actually caused an additional burden on the Patwaris, as they had also to carry out similar early inspection of the State crop surveys. The SE investigators too were required to pay repeated visits to sample villages to collect the results of advance crop inspection from the Patwaris. Study of State Land Records by the SE investigators, an essential prerequisite for the sample check, added further to their work load. All these caused considerable interference with the normal work of the SE investigators resulting in a sizeable fall in their output of socio-economic enquiries. The Technical Working Group on Agricultural Statistics, set up by the Governing Council to examine critically all these problems, recommended that from the agricultural year 1972-73 the NSS-LUS should be entrusted to the Agricultural Statistics Wing (AS Wing) of the Field Operations Division (FOD) of the NSS Organization, the scale of sampling envisaged was the same as was adopted for the NSS-LUS in the 26th round. The scope of the NSS-LUS was recommended to be enlarged to cover all food crops, all non-food crops and all land uses.

While accepting the recommendations of the Technical Working Group, the Council, at its ninth meeting, January 1972, emphasized that the resources released on account of the transfer of NSS-LUS to AS Wing should be utilized for enhancing the coverage of the socio-economic enquiries for which the need was recognized. The Council also agreed with the Technical Working Group on the lines along which the agricultural statistics work should be improved and desired the CEO to take steps to augment suitably the strength of the AS Wing to meet the objective.

A Scheme on Improvement of Crop Statistics was accordingly drawn up. With a moderate beginning in 1972-73, the scheme aims at filling the gaps still existing in agricultural statistics and evolving methodology in the fields unexplored so far but considered important from the viewpoint of agricultural production. An important feature of the scheme is to integrate the work of supervision of area and crop-cutting experiments with the TRS of the Ministry of Agriculture in that sample villages for statistical check of the crop areas and for crop-cutting experiments will not only be common but also form part of TRS villages selected from year to year. The scheme also lays emphasis on collection of ancillary data such as those on irrigation, fertilizers, high yielding varieties, multiple-cropping pattern, reasons for cultivator's crop preferences, areas under bunds, etc. through the supervision of crop-cutting experiments. In addition to its normal studies, the AS Wing will also undertake new studies relating to allied fields of agriculture, like estimation of output of fish, livestock numbers, livestock products, etc. through intensive investigations as well as large scale sample surveys.[1]

Socio-economic Surveys

At its first meeting held in March 1970, the Council laid stress on the need for undertaking a study of the economic conditions of the weaker sections of the rural population. Accordingly, it directed that the socio-economic programme of the 25th round (1970-71) be concentrated on the problems of the 'Small cultivator households' and the 'rural non-cultivating wage earner households'.

For the 26th round (1971-72), the Reserve Bank of India approached the NSS Organization to organize an all-India debt and investment survey to enable it to study the changes, if any, in the debt and investment position since the last survey carried out by the Reserve Bank in 1961-62. Also the Ministry of Agriculture, having decided to participate in the world agricultural census, 1970 sponsored by the Food and Agriculture Organization of the United Nations, desired the NSS Organization to organize, as in the past, a sample survey of landholdings. The Council accepted these proposals and dovetailed the two surveys so as to canvass a common set of households in the selected villages. In order to meet the requirements both of the Ministry of Agriculture and the Reserve Bank of India, the survey period of this round had to be extended to 15 months (from July 1971 to September 1972) divided into 3 visits to the selected households.

In view of the importance attached by the Planning Commission to the study of employment and unemployment situation in the country and following the recommendations of the Expert Committee on Unemployment Estimates (Dantwala Committee) set-up by the Planning Commission, the Council decided at its sixth meeting held on 16-17 April 1971 to undertake an employment and unemployment survey in the 27th round from October 1972 to September 1973.

The size of the Central sample for the rural survey was about 8,400 villages and 50,000 households during the 25th round and about 4,500 villages and 55,000 households during the 26th round. For the urban survey, it was about 4,600 blocks and 9,000 households in the 25th round and 4,800 blocks and 19,000 households in the 26th round. The size of the Central sample approved by the Governing Council for the 27th round is of the order of 10,000 villages and 5,000 urban blocks

---

[1]For further details about the Scheme refer to Chapter 26.

with a sample of about 1,20,000 rural and 60,000 urban households. The larger sample was necessary in order to give estimates of employment by seasons and by subseasons of States as recommended by the Dantwala Committee.

Tabulation of NSS Data

The council has been laying stress on the need for expeditious tabulation of NSS data so that the results, at least, on the major characteristics are made available within a reasonably short time after the completion of the field work of each survey. Even if only a few important results, however provisional, could be brought out quickly, it would be possible to arouse active interest in the NSS data. While examining the overall work load involved in machine tabulation, it was noticed that a large proportion of the punched card had effectively one single round to the tabulator. Hence, it seemrd that a considerable part of the tabulation could with advantage be done manually. Apart from reducing the heavy burden on the machine, this would be cheaper and, with appropriate decentralization would facilitate pooling of the State and Central sample results.

Recent Developments in the NSSO

The 1990's have been marked by modernization of the work of the NSSO on a number of fronts. A significant step taken in the recent past is the use of palm-top computers for collection of data in the field. These were introduced in the 52nd round (1995-96) on an experimental basis with the objective of reducing the existing time lag in release of survey results significantly.

Computerisation of the sample selection process, use of modern software packages in design of schedules and instruction manuals and in-house development of generalised software packages for data entry and data validation have eliminated several sources of error and improved the work environment in the NSSO. Attractive and lucid presentation of results is now achieved by the use of computers. The NSS reports are now offered for sale to the public as soon as they are released. Reports are sold both in the form of hard copy and on magnetic media. Also on sale are raw (household-level) data, containing a wealth of information that scholars in various disciplines need for research. These are available on magnetic media at a reasonable cost price. Tables 17.1 and 17.2 give details of all the Reports brought out by NSS rounds 36 to 50 and subjects covered under these rounds.[2]

The increased use of computers has led to great advances in the work of data processing in the last few years. The entire job of data processing, from data entry to table generation, is now done at the Data Processing

---

[2]For information on earlier rounds please refer to previous issues of this publication.

Table 17.2 Index of Subjects Covered in NSS Rounds

Sl. No.	Subject	Round/year
(1)	(2)	(3)
1.	Consumer Expenditure	1 to 9, 15 to 18, 26 to 28, 32, 38, 42 to 55
1a.	Income and Expenditure	10 to 14, 29
1b.	Consumer expenditure and income of rural household	18, 29
2.	Employment and Unemployment	9 to 12, 14 to 17, 19, 27, 32, 38, 43, 45 to 55
2a.	Urban labour force	13, 16 to 22(U)
3.	Rural labour enquiry	11, 12, 19, 20, 29
3a.	Economic condition of small cultivators' households	25
3b.	Economic condition of the rural non-cultivating wage-earner households	25
4.	Unorganised manufacture	1, 3 to 10, 14, 19 to 25, 29, 33, 40, 45, 51
5.	Trade	3 to 10, 15, 19 to 25, 29, 34, 41, 46, 53
6.	Debt and investment	26, 37, 48
6a.	Household indebtedness	8, 16
6b.	Capital formation in household sector	15(R), 17(U), 19, 21 to 24
6c.	Current building activities in rural areas/construction activities	25, 27(R), 44, 49
7.	Land and livestock holding	26, 37, 48
7a.	Land holding	8, 16, 17
7b.	Livestock and livestock products	1 to 7, 13, 15, 19 to 24, 30
7c.	Farming practices	8, 22
7d.	Survey on irrigation	31
7e.	Production of milk and utilisation of cattle dung	12, 30
8.	Participation in Primary Education and drop-outs for children 5-14 years	35, 42, 52
8a.	Education and Activity particulars of youths of 15-24 years	35, 52
8b.	Participation in post primary and higher education	35, 52
8c.	Education particulars of non-resident students	35, 52
8d.	Activity particulars of educated persons	35
8e.	Survey on literacy and culture	47
9.	Housing condition	7, 10, 11, 12, 14 to 19, 20, 22, 23, 28, 44, 49
9a.	Economic condition of slum dwellers	31, 49
10.	Morbidity	7 to 13, 17, 28, 35, 42, 52

Table 17.2 Index of Subjects Covered in NSS Rounds (Contd.)

Sl. No.	Subject	Round/year
(1)	(2)	(3)
10a.	Availability and utilisation of Public Health Services	35, 42, 52
10b.	Maternity and Child Care	28, 35, 42, 52
10c.	Survey on persons aged 60 years and above	42, 52
11.	Survey on disabled persons	16, 24, 28, 36, 47
11a.	Survey on development milestone of children	36, 47
12.	Population, births and death	2 to 23, 28, 39
12a.	Family planning	16, 22, 23, 28, 35, 42
12b.	Couple fertility/historical fertility	2 to 6, 9, 17 to 19, 28
12c.	Marriage	7 to 13, 28
12d.	Migration	9, 11 to 15, 18 to 23, 38, 43, 49
13.	Village statistics	2 to 4, 6, 7, 9 to 14, 18, 42, 44, 47, 49
14.	Land utilisation	1, 4 to 26
14a	Crop cutting experiments	10 to 26
14b.	Driage experiments	17 to 25
15.	Transport	3 to 10, 15, 19 to 25, 29, 34
15a.	Hotel and Restaurant	29, 34
15b.	Profession, services, financial operation	1, 3 to 8, 18 to 25, 29, 34
15c.	Mining and quarrying	29
16.	Travel habits of households	43, 54
16a.	Survey on railway travel	30
17.	Level of living of tribal and economic activity and enterprise account of tribals	44
18.	Weekly wholesale and retail prices of selected commodities/collection of rural retail price	5 to 10, 21 to 50

*From NSS 33rd round it includes own a/c enterprises and non-directory establishments.

Division of the NSSO. Intensive study of sources and incidence of error has led to the development of appropriate software packages for identification of errors, particularly "howlers', and cleaning of data.

With these improvements, the NSSO was able to draft all the reports based on the surveys conducted up to the 5th round (January—June 1998) by the end of 1999.

NATIONAL SAMPLE SURVEY ORGANISATION (NSSO)— A CRITIQUE

This is an organisation which has gained world-wide recognition for the innovative approach to generating a comprehensive database within a short period for the entire country with the help of well-trained field investigators and supervisors. However, a few major shortcomings of data obtained through the National Sample Surveys which are being conducted at present on a matching basis by the NSSO at the Centre and State Statistical Bureaus (SSBs) at the State level are yet to be overcome. Pooling of the sub-sample estimates based on both the Central and the matching State sub-samples for the same socio-economic characteristic would normally provide a more dependable estimate and also give an idea of the "margin of uncertainty" of these estimates. Although sub-samplewise estimates are now provided in the NSSO documents for the Central sample only for important socio-economic parameters, the State sub-sample estimates are not available on time for a majority of the States. This results in getting less precise estimates, although the State sub-samples are being canvassed on a regular basis for a long period at enormous cost to the public exchequer. If the States are not in a position to provide State sub-samplewise estimates on time so as to promote pooling of Central and State sample estimates, effective steps should be taken urgently by the DoS to remove the bottlenecks. Alternatively, financial and manpower resources should be saved by curtailing drastically the canvassing of the State Sample schedules till the concerned States show their adequate capability for timely processing of the collected statistics.

States should normally not depend upon the NSSO for their data needs, for they can use data from their own matching sample. But the matching sample arrangement dictates that the States should produce tables according to the NSSO tabulation programme (TP), and that massive TP takes up most of their resources preventing them from producing information on demand, unless they make special efforts.[5]

The NSS should review the very concept of a catch-all TP and the associated idea that once its tables are produced, the use of NSS data and the responsibility of the NSSO are over. A vicious circle seems to operate here. The fear that unless a table considered useful (by one or more "users" on the GC) is put in the TP, it might not ever get prepared on demand, tends to pack as much as is conceivable in the TP, in turn, ties down processing resources for this single objective, making it impossible for the NSS to produce any "on-demand" tabulations, and thus reinforcing the tendency of users to "put it in the TP if you will ever want it'.

There is no denying that one should have a basic TP. The question is about its orientation. In line with what I perceive to be the information needs of the government, the basic TP should contain Statewise—and where sampling errors permit, regionwise—tables showing the estimates of the subject parameters, and where relevant, their distributions according to SE classes of households. The household classification based on monthly per capita expenditure (MPCE) or fractiles is relevant for macro-level analysis and policies but not for policies of which different groups of people are the foci. People do not carry MPCE or fractile identification as they carry identification by their SE classes. Further, I do not see much point in the same type of macro-level analysis by MPCE or fractile classes for each round. Analysis by SE classes will bring out changes in the conditions of different SE groups over the years. Further, if the basic TP contains only such simple tabulations, its bulk will be reduced considerably. I had once demonstrated, by actual tabulation of consumer expenditure data for Maharashtra, how these simple tables—which go a long way in being useful—can be speedily produced, cutting down the gigantic size of the TP by a factor of 10!

The other major shortcoming is lack of longitudinal/panel data in respect of many complex socio-economic characteristics which would have provided more dependable estimates for planning and policy-making. The NSSO generates only cross-sectional data which are not adequate for studying the direction of change over time of several complex socio-economic characteristics, like (i) gender-specific time use data on economic activities especially of female members of the households, (ii) income, expenditure and indebtedness, (iii) chronic unemployment and under-employment, (iv) households having members visibly deprived of "basic human needs", etc. The potentiality of Sample Registration Areas (SRA) (introduced by the office of the Registrar General of India under the Sample Registration System) in generating meaningful longitudinal/panel data as advocated in a recent article [9] needs to be considered carefully to strengthen the current national data system. For instance, longitudinal data generated from SRAs even if collected at regular intervals of 3-5 years would bring out more precisely the direction of change in the percentage of "visibly poor" (who are deprived of several basic human needs) over a period of years. A comprehensive analysis of estimates of poverty derived from cross-sectional data collected by the NSSO and longitudinal data that could be generated from SRAs would provide a better insight to the policy-makers into the real change in the incidence of poverty in different parts of the country.

Again the Department of Statistics (DoS) has failed to incorporate into practice much of the methodological developments in statistics that took place during the last 40 years. Except for minor adjustments, the basic design of the NSS is still the same as it was when the NSS was started. It is not every well known that the original sampling design for the NSS—*two-stage stratified sampling in an interpenetrating network of sub-samples, with probability of inclusion of a unit proportional to size at the first-stage and uniform at the second, the actual selection being done in a circular systematic manner*—was actually a plan worked out by the renowned statistician Debabrata Lahiri at the ISI to meet a contingency. Until then, all large-scale surveys conducted by ISI used the technique of *areal sampling* for this. In the short time available for selecting the first-stage units to be surveyed in the very first round, it was just not possible to collect all the maps from all over India. It was necessary to devise a sampling plan using lists of first stage-units instead of maps. That the design adopted turned out to be quite an effective design is another matter. The efficiency of any two-stage sampling design depends on the number of first-stage units to be selected from a stratum, and the number of second-stage units to be chosen from each selected first-stage unit. The statistical theory is well known, but no serious attempt has been made to use the theory in the context of the NSS. It is a matter of shame that, even after fifty years of operation, we have not even an approximate idea about how the sampling error depends on the number of sampling units at the various stages of sampling.

Though powerful techniques exist by which auxiliary information can be exploited to improve the accuracy of estimates obtained from current surveys, no use has ever been made of such techniques. For example, in the case of repetitive surveys like the NSS, information from previous rounds, or from neighbouring areas, or from external sources can be used to improve the accuracy of estimates for the current round, through time series analysis or regression techniques. But this has never been tried. There is a great demand for information at the grass-roots level. No attempt has, however, been made for applying *small-area estimation techniques* that enable one to get fairly reliable estimates for small areas from nationwide sample surveys without unduly increasing the size of the sample.

The National Sample Survey, set up as an independent professional organisation to generate data on aspects not covered by government agencies, has made no doubt made valuable contributions in improving data. It has demonstrated the effectiveness of sample survey techniques as a cost-effective and reliable way of getting information. In some areas—consumption, employment and assets—it is the only source of detailed and comparable data over time. The fact that its programmes, survey design and field procedures are reviewed and decided in close interaction with users and academics, is its strong point.

However as the organisation has become huge and depends on a permanent cadre of field staff, ensuring reliability of field work has become more difficult. The efficacy of existing procedures for this purpose—supervision, inter-penetrating sub-samples, separate surveys by the Central and the State organisations using common designs, concepts and procedures—need to be reviewed. Reducing sample size through stratified selection procedures; simplification of schedules; research on techniques of field investigation to reduce the time and strain on informants—these are some of the areas which need attention. Of course, this will call for more resources. But resources will not be enough, unless there is a sustained effort, with constant interaction and feedback from field staff and backed by continuing research, in a more intensive way than at present (in NSSO as well as academic and research/institutions) on survey design and methodology.

OTHER SIMILAR CASES

While poverty data is great news for the pro-reform lobby in the country, it's certain to result in ferocious debate in the country. Apart from the fact that the results are at complete variance to the results from the NSS 'thin' sample of previous years, another discomforting fact is in a very large number of cases, no two sets of data give even broadly similar results—thus, commerce ministry figures on trade will be different from those of the RBI, and so on. In fact, in February 2000, the government actually got a report from an Expert Committee that was set up to examine the wide variations in data sets on the same subjects!

In the case of landholdings, for instance, while the NSSO's Land and Livestock Survey shows that the number of operational land holdings in the country as 77 million, the Department of Agriculture's survey put it at 89 million just a year earlier! The percentage difference between the two estimates are as high as 26 per cent for states like Andhra Pradesh, Maharashtra and Tamil Nadu. In terms of the total area, the NSSO puts it at 123 million hectares while the Department of Agriculture puts it at 164 million. Again, the difference between the two estimates is huge for all states, except for Uttar Pradesh where the difference is just 3 per cent. A similar difference between NSSO and Department of Agriculture data exists for 1991-92.

And while part of this difference can be explained in difference in categorisation of land as 'operational' and non-operational, similar differences in data-sets are seen in the case of cattle—here, surely, sheep can never be categorised as poultry, no matter how much you stretch the definitions! So, while the NSS says India had 172 million head of cattle in 1992, the livestock census done by state governments put the number at 205 million. For poultry, the difference is even more stark—over 25 per cent—with the NSS putting the poultry number at 226 million against the Livestock Census' 307 million.

What's even more of a statistician's nightmare, is the sharp differences that come up within the same data set when different parameters are used. If, for instance, people are asked to define what non-durables they bought in the last one week, you get one set of poverty figures. If, however, you ask them what they bought in the last one month, you get a totally different set of numbers! Between 1994 and 1998, if you went by the 'one-month' set of questions, rural poverty ranged between 36 and 43 per cent, says Pravin Visaria who heads the governing council of the NSSO. If, however, you use the 'one week' recall method, you get rural poverty estimates of a significantly lower 19 to 24 per cent. Similar changes are seen for urban India as well.

While the poverty reduction figures between 1993-94 and 1990-00 are both based on the 'one-month' recall method and are therefore compatible, the current debate in the Planning Commission on the latest 'large sample' is quite hilarious. The debate is on whether households should have been asked about their weekly consumption patterns before they were asked about their monthly consumption, or whether these questions should have been asked the other way around, as this could distort the replies! The debate rages on. As an old Chinese saying puts it: It's difficult to prophesy, especially about the future!

CENSUS VERSUS NSSO

Students of the Indian economy, especially those who have a crush with statistics, may find it interesting to note certain recent developments in the reporting of official statistics that have far-reaching implications. First, the population statistics, which was earlier updated only through the decadal census operations and through interpolation for the intercensal periods has been discarded. Instead the population estimates based on the National Sample Survey Organisation's (NSSO) quinquennial estimates are used.

The revised GDP and NDP estimates of the CSO (Central Statistical Organisation) with the new base of 1993-94 was based on population estimates provided by the NSSO's 50th round survey of 1993-94. Whether the State level income figures can also be estimated using State-level population estimates for 1993-94 as base year, however, is not yet known.

The second noteworthy shift has been noticed in the official acceptance of the literacy rate estimates provided by the NSSO's quinquennial/ annual surveys. The Human Resources Ministry, for example, has released the literacy figures for all India to be 62 per cent for 1997. The apparent advantage of this shift is updating the observed literacy rates every year or at least every five-years as opposed to every ten years previously.

Census Versus Survey Estimates

It is useful to ponder over the effect of this shift away from census based statistics to one based on the NSSO's quinquennial/annual surveys. First, let us compare the relative merits and demerits of 'census' and 'survey' estimates. The census is a complete enumeration of the population every ten years as on March 1 of the census year that normally is the first year of the decade. The NSSO quinquennial surveys are nationally representative sample surveys conducted all over the country. About 1.15 lakh households are selected using a multi-stage stratified sampling technique. It is expected that in 1999 there are about 175.5 million households in India. Thus, one single NSSO quinquennial survey household actually represents 1,526 households at the national level. Any error in selecting a sample household is surely going to affect the final estimate of any parameter, be it literacy or consumer expenditure. The sample size for the NSSO annual series surveys is much smaller. For example, the sample size for the 52nd round was only 48,568.

While the census is a complete enumeration and reasonable adjustments are made after post-enumeration checks, it is expected that the estimates are free from sampling biases. Certain types of non-sampling errors, however, can be inherent in the estimates.

On the other hand, the NSSO estimates can never be free from sampling as well as non-sampling errors. Besides, variations in both these types of biases between the two different surveys are also likely to be substantial.

The statistical interpretations especially of the rate of change are best done when the estimates from the same source are compared over time. For example, with adequate caution, it is fair to compare the literacy rates estimated from various Indian censuses.

Similarly it is perfectly legitimate to compare the literacy rates from two different NSSO quinquennial surveys provided the definitions are held constant. Strictly speaking, statistical theory makes us believe that averaging estimates from many sample surveys conducted in the same universe can give robust and conclusive estimates. Thus, in practice, there is no estimate which is conclusive at least in the social sciences.'

18

Consumption and Stocks of Foodgrain

ORGANIZATIONAL SET UP

Collection of statistics of consumption and stocks of agricultural commodities on a country-wide scale is rendered difficult in view of the diffused character of trade and the channels through which the commodity passes from the producer to the consumer. For commodities entering as raw materials for industries such as, cotton, jute, etc. and foodgrains, however, statistics relating to consumption and stock in certain sectors are available.

There are two types of estimates available in so far as they relate to food consumption in the country. One is based on what is called the food balance sheet. These data are being published by the Directorate of Economics and Statistics in their annual publication—Food Statistics. This bulletin is published annually since 1951 and provides data for the previous year. The consumption of foodgrains according to this method is equated with net availability which is calculated by taking into consideration the requirements of feed, seed and wastage at $12\frac{1}{2}$ per cent, net imports of foodgrains and changes in government stocks (Table 18.1). Since no information is available about the private stocks, they are for all practical purposes assumed to be constant which, of course, is one of the major drawbacks in all such calculations.

This Bulletin also provides information about the per capita availability of rice, wheat, other cereals, gram, pulses and total foodgrains, along with that of fish, sugar as well as vanaspati ghee in the country. There is a time lag of 3-4 years in the publication of this Bulletin, but all this information is being published annually in the Economic Survey which is regularly published on March 1 of every year. This publication also provides data on per capita availability of other consumption items (Table 18.2). Calculation are also being made with regard to per capita consumption of total calories and their distribution among various constituents, but this is not being published. This information is also being supplied to the Food and Agriculture Organization of the United

416

18.1 Net Availability of Cereals and Pulses

Year	Cereals					Pulses	Per Capita net availability per day (grams)		
	Population (million)	Net production (million tonnes)	Net imports (million tonnes)	Change in Government stocks (million tonnes)	Net availability (Col. 3+4+5) (million tonnes)	Net availability (million tonnes)	Cereals	Pulses	Total
1	2	3	4	5	6	7	8	9	10
1951	363.2	40.1	4.1	(+)0.6	44.3	8.0	334.2	60.7	394.9
1952	369.2	40.7	3.9	(+)0.6	44.0	8.0	325.4	59.1	384.5
1953	375.6	45.5	2.0	(-)0.5	48.0	8.6	349.9	62.7	412.6
1954	382.4	53.6	0.8	(+)0.2	54.2	9.7	388.1	69.7	457.8
1955	389.7	51.7	0.6	(-)0.8	53.1	10.1	372.9	71.1	444
1956	397.3	50.4	1.4	(-)0.6	52.4	10.2	360.4	70.3	430.7
1957	405.5	52.8	3.6	(+)0.9	55.5	10.6	375.3	71.8	447.1
1958	414.0	49.5	3.2	(-)0.3	52.9	8.8	350.3	58.5	408.8
1959	423.1	57.4	3.9	(+)0.5	60.8	11.6	393.4	74.9	468.3
1960	432.5	57.1	5.1	(+)1.4	60.8	10.4	384.1	65.5	449.6
1961	442.4	60.9	3.5	(-)0.2	64.6	11.1	399.7	69.0	468.7
1962	452.2	61.8	3.6	(-)0.4	65.8	10.2	398.9	62.0	460.9
1963	462.0	60.2	4.6	Neg.	64.8	10.1	384.0	59.8	443.8
1964	472.1	61.8	6.3	(-)1.2	69.3	8.8	401.0	51.0	452.0
1965	482.5	67.3	7.4	(+)1.1	73.7	10.8	418.5	61.6	480.1

18.1 Net Availability of Cereals and Pulses *(Contd.)*

Year	Population (million)	Cereals			Pulses		Per Capita net availablity per day (grams)		
		Net production (million tonnes)	Net imports (million tonnes)	Change in Government stocks (million tonnes)	Net availability (Col. 3+4+5) (million tonnes)	Net availability (million tonnes)	Cereals	Pulses	Total
1	2	3	4	5	6	7	8	9	10
1966	493.2	54.6	10.3	(+)0.1	64.8	8.7	359.9	48.2	408.1
1967	504.2	57.6	8.7	(-)0.3	66.6	7.3	361.8	39.6	401.4
1968	515.4	72.6	5.7	(+)2	76.2	10.6	404.1	56.1	460.2
1969	527.0	73.1	3.8	(+)0.5	76.5	9.1	397.8	47.3	445.1
1970	538.9	76.8	3.6	(+)1.1	79.3	10.2	403.1	51.9	455.0
1971	551.3	84.5	2.0	(+)2.6	84.0	10.3	417.6	51.2	468.8
1972	563.9	82.3	(-)0.5	(-)4.7	86.5	9.7	419.1	47.0	466.1
1973	576.8	76.2	3.6	(-)0.3	80.1	8.7	380.5	41.1	421.6
1974	590.0	82.8	5.2	(-)0.4	88.4	8.8	410.4	40.8	451.2
1975	603.5	78.6	7.5	(+)5.6	80.6	8.8	365.8	39.7	405.5
1976	617.2	94.5	0.7	(+)10.7	84.4	11.4	373.8	50.5	424.3
1977	631.3	87.3	0.1	(-)1.6	89.0	10.0	386.3	43.3	429.6
1978	645.7	100.1	(-)0.8	(-)0.3	99.6	10.7	422.5	45.5	468.0
1979	660.3	104.8	(-)0.3	(+)0.4	104.1	10.8	431.8	44.7	476.5
1980	675.2	88.5	(-)0.5	(-)5.8	93.8	7.6	379.5	30.9	410.4

18.1 Net Availability of Cereals and Pulses *(Contd.)*

Year	Population (million)	Cereals				Pulses	Per Capita net availability per day (grams)		
		Net production (million tonnes)	Net imports (million tonnes)	Change in Government stocks (million tonnes)	Net availability (Col. 3+4+5) (million tonnes)	Net availability (million tonnes)	Cereals	Pulses	Total
1	2	3	4	5	6	7	8	9	10
1981	688.5	104.1	0.5	(-)0.2	104.8	9.4	417.3	37.5	454.8
1982	703.8	106.6	1.6	(+)1.3	106.8	10.1	415.6	39.2	454.8
1983	718.9	103.0	4.1	(+)2.7	104.4	10.4	397.8	39.5	437.3
1984	734.5	122.0	2.4	(+)7.1	117.4	11.3	437.8	41.9	479.7
1985	750.4	116.9	(-)0.3	(+)2.7	113.9	10.5	415.6	38.4	454.0
1986	766.5	119.9	(-)0.1	(-)1.6	121.5	12.3	434.2	43.9	478.1
1987	782.7	115.2	(-)0.4	(-)9.5	124.4	10.4	435.4	36.4	471.8
1988	799.2	113.2	2.3	(-)4.6	120.1	10.7	411.8	36.7	448.5
1989	815.8	136.6	0.8	(+)2.6	134.7	12.5	452.6	41.9	494.5
1990	832.6	138.4	Neg.	(+)6.2	132.3	12.5	435.3	41.1	476.4
1991	851.7	141.9	(-)0.6	(-)4.4	145.7	12.9	468.5	41.6	510.1
1992	867.8	136.8	(-)0.7	(-)1.6	137.7	10.9	434.5	34.3	468.8
1993	883.9	145.8	2.6	(+)10.3	138.1	11.7	427.9	36.2	464.1
1994	899.9	149.6	0.5	(+)7.5	142.6	12.2	434.0	37.2	471.2
1995	922.0	155.3	(-)3	(-)1.7	154.0	12.7	457.5	37.8	495.3

18.1 Net Availability of Cereals and Pulses *(Contd.)*

Year	Population (million)	Cereals				Pulses	Per Capita net availability per day (grams)		
		Net production (million tonnes)	Net imports (million tonnes)	Change in Government stocks (million tonnes)	Net availability (Col. 3+4+5) (million tonnes)	Net availability (million tonnes)	Cereals	Pulses	Total
1	2	3	4	5	6	7	8	9	10
1996	939.5	147.1	(-)3.6	(-)8.5	152.1	11.3	443.6	32.6	476.2
1997	955.2	162.0	(-)0.6	(-)1.8	163.2	13.0	468.2	37.3	505.5
1998	970.9	156.9	(-)2.8	(+)6.1	147.9	11.7	417.3	33.1	450.4
1999(P)	986.6	164.7	(-)1.5	(+)7.0	156.2	13.2	433.7	36.7	470.4
2000(P)	1002.1	168.7	(-)1.0	(+)8.7	159.1	11.4	434.8	31.2	466.0

(P) Provisional
Neg. Negligible
Notes : 1. Mid-year population figures from 1971 to 1980 are based on projections made by the office of the Registrar General of India. Estimates from 1981 onwards are provisional and are worked out by taking 1991 Census provisional population figures.
2. Production figures relate to the agricultural year July-June 1991 figures correspond to the production of 1950-51 and so on fro subsequent years.
3. Net production has been taken as 87.5% of the gross production, 12.5% being provided for seeds, feed requirement and waste.
4. Figures in respect of change in stocks with traders and producers are not known. The estimates of net availability above should not, therefore, be taken to be strictly equivalent to consumption."
5. Net Imports from 1981 to 1994 are only on Government account and from 1995 onwards the Net Imports and Export of the Country.

Source : Directorate of Economics and Statistics, Department of Agriculture and Cooperation.
Economic Surgery 2000-01

Table 18.2 Per Capita Availability of Certain Important Articles of Consumption

Year	Edible oil ©# (Kg.)	Vanaspati # (Kg.)	Sugar (Nov. - Oct.) (Kg.) +	Cotton ©© (metres)	Man-made (metres)	Total (metres)	Tea* (Gm.) ##	Coffee* (Gm.)	Electricity (Domestic) (KWH)
1	2	3	4	5	6	7	8	9	10
1955-56	2.5	0.7	5.0	14.4	NA	NA	362	67	2.4***
1960-61	3.2	0.8	4.8	13.8	1.2	15.0	296	80	3.4
1961-62	3.2	0.7	5.8	14.8	1.2	16.0	337	79	3.8
1962-63	3.1	0.8	5.5	14.4	1.2	15.6	296	77	4.2
1963-64	2.7	0.8	5.0	14.7	1.2	15.9	266	81	4.4
1964-65	3.6	0.8	5.1	15.2	1.6	16.8	343	76	4.7
1965-66	2.7	0.8	5.7	14.7	1.7	16.4	346	72	4.8
1966-67	2.7	0.7	5.2	14.0	1.7	15.7	399	72	5.2
1967-68	3.4	0.8	4.3**	13.6	1.7	15.3	339	69	5.7
1968-69	2.6	0.9	5.0	14.4	1.9	16.3	376	73	6.0
1969-70	3.0	0.9	6.1	13.6	2.0	15.6	430	62	6.5
1970-71	3.5	1.0	7.4	13.6	2.0	15.6	401	68	7.0
1971-72	3.0	1.1	6.8	12.4	2.2	14.6	426	65	7.3
1972-73	2.4	1.0	6.2	13.2	2.0	15.2	458	69	7.3
1973-74	3.4	0.8	6.1	12.0	1.9	13.9	492	64	8.1
1974-75	3.3	0.6	5.8	12.9	1.7	14.6	471	62	8.8
1975-76	3.5	0.8	6.1	12.6	2.0	14.6	446	62	9.7

Table 18.2 Per Capita Availability of Certain Important Articles of Consumption (Contd.)

Year	Edible # oil © (Kg.)	Vanaspati # (Kg.)	Sugar (Nov. - Oct.) + (Kg.)	Cotton ©© (metres)	Man-made (metres)	Total (metres)	Tea* (Gm.) ##	Coffee* (Gm.)	Electricity (Domestic) (KWH)
1976-77	3.2	0.9	6.0	11.4	2.4	13.8	450	71	10.4
1977-78	3.8	0.9	7.2	9.5	4.0	13.5	516	73	10.9
1978-79	3.8	1.0	9.6	10.2	4.8	15.0	599	77	11.9
1979-80	3.7	1.0	7.8	10.1	4.6	14.7	521	73	12.1
1980-81	3.8	1.2	7.3	12.9	4.4	17.3	511	74	13.5
1981-82	5.1	1.3	8.2	12.2	4.9	17.1	466	79	15.1
1982-83	4.5	1.3	9.0	11.8	4.3	16.1	525	82	17.0
1983-84	5.8	1.2	10.5	12.6	4.7	17.3	519	78	18.3
1984-85	5.5	1.3	10.7	12.6	4.6	17.2	576	72	21.0
1985-86	5.0	1.3	11.1	15.4	6.1	21.5	589	71	22.9
1986-87	5.0	1.2	11.4	15.2	6.6	21.8	545	76	25.1
1987-88	5.8	1.2	11.7	14.0	7.0	21.0	592	72	28.2
1988-89	5.3	1.2	12.1	15.0	8.0	23.0	612	79	30.9
1989-90	5.3	1.1	12.3	14.6	8.1	22.7	571	65	36.1
1990-91	5.5	1.0	12.7	15.1	9.0	24.1	612	59	38.2
1991-92	5.4	1.0	13.0	13.7	9.2	22.9	655	64	41.9
1992-93	5.8	1.0	13.7	15.6	8.9	24.5	649	60	45.6
1993-94	6.1	1.0	12.5	15.9	10.3	26.2	667	56	48.8
1994-95	6.3	1.0	13.2	15.2	10.8	26.0	664	55	53.0
1995-96	7.0	1.0	14.1	16.3	11.7	28.0	646	55	56.2

Table 18.2 *Per Capita Availability of Certain Important Articles of Consumption* (Contd.)

Year	Edible oil @ (Kg.) #	Vanaspati (Kg.) #	Sugar (Nov. - Oct.) (Kg.) +	Cotton @@ (metres)	Man-made (metres)	Total (metres)	Tea* (Gm.) ##	Coffee* (Gm.)	Electricity (Domestic) (KWH)
1	2	3	4	5	6	7	8	9	10
1996-97	8.2	1.0	14.6	16.2	13.1	29.3	657.0	58.0	58.6
1997-98	7.5	1.1	14.5	15.9	15.0	30.9	636.0	58.0	64.3
1998-99	10.3	1.4	14.9	13.1	15.1	28.2	676.0	65.0	67.9
1999-2000(P)	9.2	1.4	15.6	14.2	16.4	30.6	NA	53.0	NA

P   Provisional

Na   Not Available

@   Includes groundnut oil, rapeseed and mustard oil, sesamum oil, nigerseed oil, soyabeen oil and sunflower oil but excludes oil from manufacture of vanaspati.

@   Data relate to calender year: figures for 1955 are shown against 1955-56 and so on. Figures for blended/mixed fabrics were not separately available prior to 1969. These have been included under man-made fibre fabrics after 1969.

*   Figures upto 1971-72 relate to coffee season and are thereafter on calender year basis. The figures for 1972-73 correspond to 1973 and so on.

**   From 1967-68 onwards sugar season from October to September.

***   Relates to 1956.

+   Relates to actual releases for domestic consumption.

Relates to financial year.

Relates to calender year.

Sources: 1. Directorate of Vanaspati, Vegetable Oils and Fats, Ministry of Food, Consumer Affairs and Public Distribution. 2. Department of Sugar and Edible Oils. 3. Ministry of Textiles. 4. Tea Board. 5. Coffee Board. 6. Central Electricity Authority, Ministry of Power.

Note: The date of cloth; prior to 1980-81 is calender year-wise; in meters upto 1984-85; in square meter from 1985-86 onwards.

Nations which brings out an annual publication—Food Balance Sheet—providing such data for the member countries. Useful data on Public Distribution and Buffer Stocks are given in Tables 18.2a and 18.2b.

Table 18.2a Total Distribution of Food Grains through Public Distribution System

('000 tonnes)

Year	Rice	Wheat
1994-95	8013.0	5114.0
1995-96	9750.0	5808.0
1996-97	11143.7	8520.4
1997-98	9901.0	7080.4
1998-99	10743.2	7949.1
Total	49550.9	34471.9

Source: "Directorate of Economics and Statistics, Ministry of Agriculture, Govt. of India."

Table 18.2b Buffer Stock of Foodgrains (Central and State Governments)

(Mt.)

As on	Rice	Wheat	Coarse Grains	Total
1.7.1982	5.1	10.2	0.2	15.5
1.7.1983	3.8	13	0.2	17
1.7.1984	4.6	17.8	0.1	22.5
1.7.1985	7.8	20.7	0.2	28.7
1.7.1986	9.3	18.9	0.1	28.3
1.7.1987	8.4	14.8	0.1	23.3
1.7.1988	4.2	7.5	0.2	11.9
1.7.1989	3.9	9.5	Neg.	13.4
1.7.1990	7.5	13.2	0.2	20.8
1.7.1991	9.7	11.0	0.2	20.9
1.7.1992	8.3	6.7	Neg.	15.0
1.7.1993	10.4	15.2	0.7	26.3
1.7.1994	14.4	17.8	0.2	32.4
1.7.1995*	17.1	19.3	Neg.	36.4
@1.7.1996*	12.9	14.1	-	27.0
@1.7.1997*	10.9	11.4	-	22.3
@1.7.1998*	12.0	16.5	Neg.	28.5
@1.7.1999*	10.7	21.6	Neg.	32.3

Note :   1.   Neg.   :   Negligible
2.   *   :   Provisional
3.   @   :   Stocks of food grains (central pool) only.
Source :   *Agricultural Statistics at a Glance.* 2000, Directorate of Economics and Statistics, Ministry of Agriculture, Government of India.

A good deal of information with regard to the consumption of foodgrains is being collected by the National Sample Survey through multipurpose sample surveys on socio-economic subjects since 1950 on a national scale in their continuing rounds. But for few rounds which also provide quantitative data, the information being generally provided by these surveys is mostly in monetary terms. Quantitative data were being released only at intervals of 5 years. From 1991 onward it is available annually (Table 18.3). Annual data are based on a smaller sample and 5th years (say 1983, 1987-88, 1993-94) are based on a larger sample and more reliable. Since most of the consumption items even within the same commodity have different qualities and hence different prices which also vary from place to place, the data collected are of little utility for any kind of perspective planning in the country. Another difficulty in the NSS method is that this information is being collected by the enquiry method and at a particular point of time in the year. It is thus very difficult to get the correct answer and accurate information about the quality of a particular commodity consumed by a person. More so, when the person answering these enquiries does not maintain any type of personal accounts. Consumption habits of the people vary from season to season. Unless the surveys are spread out according to these observed variations in the consumption habits which might be different in different parts of the country, the results are not likely to be of much practical utility.

Table 18.3 Consumption Pattern of Cereals by Period in Rural and Urban India (Monthly per Capita in Kg.)

NSS round	Year	Rice	(%)	Wheat	(%)	Coarse cereals	(%)	Total cereals	(%)
				Rural					
17	1961-62	8.77	50	2.63	15	6.15	35	17.55	100
	1970-71							15.35	100
27	1972-73	8.56	56	3.83	25	4.84	32	15.26	100
28	1973-74	6.9	46	3.52	23	4.67	31	15.09	100
32	1977-78	7.12	45	4.05	26	4.51	29	15.68	100
38	1983	6.63	45	4.46	30	3.71	25	14.8	100
42	1986-87	7.11	49	4.77	33	2.49	17	14.37	100
43	1987-88	7.04	49	4.94	34	2.49	17	14.47	100
44	1988-89	7.07	49	4.73	32	2.76	19	14.56	100
47	1991	7.1	49	4.6	32	1.7	12	13.8	100
48	1992	7.2	49	4.5	31	1.7	12	13.8	100
49	1993	7.2	49	4.5	31	1.6	11	13.6	100
50	1993-94	7	52.2	4.4	32.8	2	15	13.4	100
51	1994-95	7.1	49	4.3	30	1.4	10	13.2	100
52	1995-96	7	48	4.2	29	1.5	10	12.9	100
53	1997	6.7	46	4.5	31	1.4	10	12.8	100
54	1998	6.8	47	4.3	30	1.2	8	12.5	100

Table 18.3 Consumption Pattern of Cereals by Period in Rural and Urban India (Monthly per Capita in Kg.)

NSS round	Year	Rice	(%)	Wheat	(%)	Coarse cereals	(%)	Total cereals	(%)
				Urban					
17	1961-62	6.16	50	4.1	33	2.09	17	12.35	100
	1970-71							11.36	100
27	1972-73	4.94	43	4.82	42	1.61	14	11.37	100
28	1973-74	5.38	48	4.32	38	1.62	14	11.32	100
32	1977-78	5.48	47	4.87	42	1.27	11	11.62	100
38	1983	5.32	47	4.82	43	1.16	10	11.3	100
42	1986-87	5.33	49	4.82	44	0.83	8	10.98	100
43	1987-88	5.35	48	4.98	45	0.86	8	11.19	100
44	1988-89	5.35	48	4.81	43	0.9	8	11.06	100
47	1991	5.2	47	4.9	44	0.4	4	10.7	100
48	1992	5.2	47	4.9	44	0.4	4	10.7	100
49	1993	5.3	48	4.5	41	0.6	5	10.5	100
50	1993-94	5.28	49.7	4.72	44.4	0.63	5.9	10.63	100
51	1994-95	5.1	46	4.9	44	0.6	5	10.7	100
52	1995-96	5.3	48	4.7	42	0.4	4	10.6	100
53	1997	52	47	4.6	42	0.4	4	10.3	100
54	1998	5.3	48	4.7	42	0.4	4	10.4	100

43rd Round : July 1987 - June 1988	49th Round : January 1993 - June 1993
47th Round : July 1991 - December 1991	50th Round : July 1993 - June 1994
48th Round : January 1992 - December 1992	51st Round : July 1994 - June 1995
52nd Round : July 1995 - June 1996	54th Round : January - June 1998.
53rd Round : January 1997 - December 1997	

Note: Percentage of total cereal consumption.
Source: NSSO, Survey on Consumer Expenditure, Various Rounds.

NATIONAL SAMPLE SURVEY

NSS Report No. 1

This Report gives data on the average consumer expenditure per household and per person in rural areas on various items of consumption during the year July 1949 to June 1950. The figures are given for all-India and for each of the six population zones. The items of consumption include foodgrains, pulses, milk and milk products, meat, eggs and fish, fruits, spices, sugar and tobacco. The expenditure figures include not only the value of purchases (cash and barter), but also the imputed value of articles produced and then consumed at home. The Report also contains quantitative estimates of consumption of foodgrains and milk during July 1949 to June 1950 for all-India and six population zones. The foodgrains include rice and rice products, wheat and wheat products, barley, maize, jowar, bajra, ragi and that part of gram and small millets which was consumed as cereal. In the erstwhile State of Travancore-Cochin, a certain amount of tapioca was consumed as cereal and this was also included in these figures. The figures of consumption of foodgrains per person per day based on a number of other surveys such as, 'Calcutta Middle Class Survey, 1939', 'Bengal Urban Middle Class Survey, 1942', 'Calcutta Middle Class Survey, 1950-51', 'Jagaddal Working Class Surveys, 1941, 1942 and 1945', 'Bengal Waving Surveys, 1936', 'ICMR Diet Studies in States, 1944-48' and 'Uttar Pradesh Survey in 16 villages, 1948-49' have been also published.

National Sample Survey Report No. 2

This Report is based on the data collected during the second round of NSS covering the period April 1951 to June 1951 and gives data on average consumer expenditure per household and per person in rural areas by different items of consumption for a period of 90 days, for all-India and the six population zones separately. Weekly value of consumption of different foodgrains, edible oil, vegetable, milk and milk products, meat, egg and fish, fruit, spices, sugar and tobacco during April to June 1951 are given by population zones. In the case of foodgrains, separate figures are given for rice, wheat, jowar, bajra, maize, barley, small millets, ragi, gram, other foodgrains and pulses. Percentage distribution of households in rural areas by level of monthly expenditure is given by population zones. Information by level of monthly expenditure is given by population zone. Information on the degree of monetization in consumer expenditure is also included.

During the second round of NSS, the reference period for a number of items was a week, for another group of items a month and for a small number of items a year, depending on the nature of the items. All the data were reduced to a common period of three months (or rather 3 standard months of 30 days each), i.e. 90 days. As the reference periods related to periods preceding the data of interviews, there was a lag between the period of reference and the period of collection of data.

National Sample Survey Report No. 3

This report contains data on consumer expenditure collected in the third round of NSS during the period August 1951 to November 1951. As compared with the first two rounds of the NSS which were confined to rural areas only, the third round was extended to urban areas, and made it possible; for the first time, to obtain information for the country as a whole and also of the comparative position of the rural and urban areas. As in the case of the second round, the reference period was different for different items. All the data have, however, been reduced to a common period of three months (90 days), to make them comparable with the estimates for the earlier rounds although the data were collected over roughly a period of four months.

Summary tables giving in one place the comparative figures of consumer expenditure per household and per person by items of consumption for cities, towns, urban and rural areas for all-India and the six population zones have been included. Estimates for the urban areas are weighted averages of the estimates for cities and towns. Value of consumption of foodgrains, rice, wheat, jowar, bajra, maize, barley, small millets, ragi and gram, per household and person is given separately for rural and urban areas. The figures for the rural areas have been arranged by the population zones, and those for the urban areas by towns of different sizes and cities. A separate table gives a comparative picture of the pattern of consumer expenditure on basis of data collected in the first, second and third rounds. Figures of imputed value of the part of consumption obtained in kind per household per week have also been presented for some of the items to show the degree of monetization in consumer expenditure (Tables 18.4 and 18.5)

National Sample Survey Report No. 18

The data on consumer expenditure given in this Report are based on the fourth round of NSS (April-September 1952). In this report information

Table 18.4 Per Capita Per Year Consumption of Rice, Wheat and Cereals (kg), in the Years 1970-71 and 1973-74 for Rural Areas of States

State	Consumption of rice per capita per year (kg)		Consumption of wheat per capita per year (kg)		Consumption of cereals per capita per year (kg)	
	1970-71	1973-74	1970-71	1973-74	1970-71	1971-74
(1)	*(2)*	*(3)*	*(4)*	*(5)*	*(6)*	*(7)*
1. Andhra Pradesh	117	127	1	2	193	190
2. Assam[a]	182	127	7	6	188	184
3. Bihar	115	106	33	39	197	180
4. Gujarat	21	16	24	44	180	166
5. Haryana	19	9	117	131	218	199
6. Jammu & Kashmir	144	131	30	36	242	229
7. Karnataka	55	57	4	4	189	187
8. Kerala	94	88	2	3	96	92
9. Madhya Pradesh	80	79	50	66	198	205
10. Maharashtra	31	29	16	16	154	161
11. Orissa	175	176	5	4	193	191
12. Punjab	13	12	114	130	186	179
13. Rajasthan	3	4	45	60	215	225
14. Tamil Nadu	114	126	1	1	167	177
15. Uttar Pradesh	52	54	69	98	196	195
16. West Bengal	131	127	27	24	160	156
17. All-India[b]	82	83	32	42	184	191

Table 18.5 Per Capita per Year Consumption of Rice, Wheat and Cereals (kg), in the Years 1970-71 and 1973-74 For Urban Areas of States

(1)	(2)	(3)	(4)	(5)	(6)	(7)
1. Andhra Pradesh	133	134	9	9	160	157
2. Assam	139	132	16	15	155	148
3. Bihar	83	91	72	57	164	159
4. Gujarat	23	19	59	69	124	129
5. Haryana	8	9	123	131	140	147
6. Jammu & Kashmir	128	132	43	37	175	172
7. Karnataka	76	70	15	10	143	135
8. Kerala	84	87	6	8	91	95
9. Madhya Pradesh	39	40	98	94	155	150
10. Maharashtra	27	19	54	41	117	111
11. Orissa	142	135	26	24	171	161
12. Punjab	10	8	111	117	135	132
13. Rajasthan	6	5	93	99	157	156
14. Tamil Nadu	116	127	3	2	128	137
15. Uttar Pradesh	29	33	97	107	141	150
16. West Bengal	76	78	54	51	131	131
17. All-India[b]	66	63	49	52	136	136

Source: Cols. (2), (4) and (6) National Sample Survey Report No. 250 (mimeo). Cols. (3), (5) (7) derived from tables of NSS 28th Round contained in *Sarvakshana* Journal of the National Sample Survey Organization, Vol. I, No. 1, July 1977.
[a], Results for 1970-71 are for the State of Assam including Meghalaya.
[b], Including Chandigarh, Delhi, Goa, Daman & Diu, Himachal Pradesh, Manipur, Pondicherry and Tripura for which the results are not shown.

on the pattern of consumption at various levels of living is given for the first time for both rural and urban areas. The sample households were classified by the total monthly expenditure which gave only a rough idea of the level of living for the first time for both rural and urban areas. The sample households were classified by the total monthly expenditure which gave only a rough idea of the level of living because no allowance was made for the size of the household. Another important feature of the fourth round was the use of two sets of questionnaires with two different reference periods, a week and a month for a number of items, which were otherwise identical. This was done to study the effects on estimates when the same questions were asked with different reference periods. The estimates prepared from questionnaires with a particular reference period (say a week) are found to differ from those prepared from a different reference period. This might be due to several factors, e.g. lapses of memory on the part of the informant, the system of purchase (daily, weekly, monthly or otherwise) of the household, over or understatement by the respondent etc. The sample house-holds in each selected village were divided into two equal groups, and questionnaires with a week as the reference period were completed from one group and those with a month as the reference period, from the other groups. The figures in this Report are based on particulars collected from the sample households belonging to the latter group i.e. those with a month as the reference period. The scope of the data contained in this Report is discussed below.

Figures of consumer expenditure per household and per person by items of consumption for a period of 30 days are given in summary tables by classes of expenditure level for rural and urban areas separately. For rural areas the figures are given by population zones. For urban areas the break-downs by size of town are published. The items of consumption have been classified into 12 groups of items. These 12 groups have also been merged into two major groups of items, viz. food and non-food. The food group includes: (1) foodgrains; (2) milk and milk products; (3) edible oil; (4) meat, egg and fish; (5) sugar; (6) salt; and (7) other food. The foodgrains group includes husked grains of rice, wheat, jowar, bajra, maize, barley, small millets, ragi, gram and other foodgrains. Milk and milk products include milk, ghee, butter, dahee, ghol (lassi), khowa and other milk products. State-wise figures of consumer expenditure per household and per person by items of consumption have also been given in separate tables for the rural sector only. A separate table gives the pattern of consumer expenditure for the first, second, third and fourth rounds. Information regarding the proportion of consumer expenditure which did not enter into the monetized sector is given separately for the rural and urban areas for the third and fourth rounds. The figures of consumer expenditure include imputed values of supplies obtained in kind, the imputation being based on the prevailing local prices.

National Sample Survey Report No. 20

This Report gives information on household consumption in India from round to round, from region to region and at various economic levels of living based on the data collected from the second to the seventh rounds covering a period of three years beginning from April 1951 to March 1954. The economic level of living is indicated by the level of expenditure per person for a period of 30 days. In Report No. 18 the sample households were classified by their total expenditure per month without making any allowance for the size of the household. In this Report, the classification of sample households has been done one the basis of expenditure per person per 30 days. Another important feature of this Report is the study of the effects of changes in the reference period on the results of the survey.

The data have been given separately for the rural and urban sectors. In the case of rural areas, the figures have been arranged by population zones and for urban areas by towns and cities of three sizes and by four big cities. The values for the items of consumption have been arranged by 13 groups of expenditure levels.

National Sample Survey Report No. 39

This Report contains data on consumer expenditure collected in the eighth round of NSS during the period July 1954 to March 1955. The reference period adopted for collection of data on consumer expenditure was a period of 30 days ending on the day preceding the day of enquiry. Consumer expenditure comprised only that part of expenditure of the house-hold which related to domestic consumption of the household. Expenditure on household enterprises was not included. Loans, monetary as well as in kind, like grain loans, were also excluded. Total consumption included consumption out of home-grown stock as well. Such consumption and consumptions out of gift and charities as well as of articles through barter exchanges were evaluated at the prevailing retail rates of the items concerned.

Tables on consumer expenditure in rupees per person per 30 days and pattern of consumer expenditure by expenditure class and item-wise breakdowns, presented in this Report, give estimates for the Indian Union with rural and urban break downs (Table 18.5).

National Sample Survey Report No. 40

This Report, contains data on consumer expenditure collected in the ninth round of NSS during the period May to November 1955. This survey covered rural as well as urban areas, including the State of Jammu & Kashmir but excluding Andaman and Nicobar Islands and Part B Tribal Areas of Assam. The type of data contained in this Report are generally similar to those contained in the Report on the previous round, except that the periods of the two surveys are different. In this Report more stress has been laid on the statistics relating to the four big cities of Bombay, Calcutta, Delhi and Madras. The information on the other two breakdowns of rural and urban areas is generally of the same type. Some information for the earlier rounds is as in Table 18.6.

SUBSEQUENT REPORTS

Details of subsequent Rounds have been given in Chapter 17. Published data are available in Report No 448 (June 1999) for the 54th Round, Latest survey completed is that of the 55th Round (1999-2000), which is based on a larger sample. It is for the first time that the survey was based both on a monthly and weekly recall period. Details about the sampling design etc. for 54th round are as follows.

Sample Design and Estimation Procedure For 54th Round—January/ June 1998

General

Subject Coverage   The fifty-fourth round of NSS had as its main subject a household enquiry on common property resources in rural areas,

Table 18.6 National Sample Surveys—

Round	Report number	Year of publication	Period covered	Geographical coverage
(1)	*(2)*	*(3)*	*(4)*	*(5)*
10th	47	1961	December 1955 to May 1956	Rural and Urban areas of Indian Union excluding Andaman and Nicobar Islands, and Part B Tribal Areas of Assam.
11th	77	1963	August 1956 to February 1957	"
12th	78	1963	March 1957 to August 1957	"
14th	102	1965	July 1958 to June 1959	Entire Indian Union excluding the Andaman and Nicobar Islands, the islands of Amindivi, Laccadive and Minicoy, the North East Frontier Agency and the rural areas of Ladakh district in Jammu & Kashmir
15th	120	1963	July 1959 to June 1960	"
16th	138	1969	July 1960 to June 1961	Entire Indian Union excluding the Andaman and Nicobar Islands, the islands of Amindivi, Laccadive and Minicoy, the North East Frontier Agency and the rural areas of Ladakh district in Jammu & Kashmir.
17th Part 1	200	1969	September 1961 to July 1962	Entire Indian Union excluding the Andaman and Nicobar Islands, the islands of Amindivi, Laccadive and Minicoy, the North East Frontier Agency and certain disturbed areas of Manipur and Ladakh district of Jammu & Kashmir.
18th	190	1968	June 1963 to May 1964	Entire rural part of the Union Territories of Manipur and Tripura, excluding the disturbed areas of Manipur State.

(Contd.)

Remarks

---

(6)

Complete information of sample households receipts and disbursements, and tables presented give information about consumer expenditure only.

”
”

As compared with the reports of the earlier rounds, the scope of information of the present report has been enlarged to a considerable extent. This was mainly because of the requirements of some of the principal users of the consumer expenditure data such as the National Income Division (CSO), the Ministry of Food and Agriculture, etc. The additional information furnished in the report relates to the State-wise distribution of vegetarian and non-vegetarian population, consumption of individual items (rice, wheat, etc.) of the cereal group in terms of quantity and value, cash and barter purchases and consumption out of home grown stock for a large number of items.

Appendix I contains outline of the sampling design and the method of estimation Appendix II contains two Summary Tables, viz. (i) pattern of consumer expenditure by items and by rounds for all India and (ii) distribution of per capita total consumer expenditure by States for rural and urban sectors separately.

Appendix I contains outline of the sampling design and the method of estimation, Appendix II contains a summary of the pattern of consumer consumer expenditure in rural and urban areas of the Indian Union for the last five rounds (including the current round).

Altogether 3762 sample households from 3738 sample villages in the rural areas and 2568 sample households from 2236 sample blocks in the urban areas (including 306 sample households from 309 sample blocks in the four big cities of Bombay, Calcutta, Delhi and Madras) were surveyed in this round. The estimates in all tables are given by a pair of independent and interpenetrating sub-samples and also by the combined sample. The usual technique of interpenetrating network of samples (IPNS) had been employed to both at the collection and tabulation stages. Quantitative consumption data for rural and urban India was supplied separately for the first time.

The report was brought out in two parts—Part I includes the test and the tables of series A only and Part II, the tables of series B only. Whereas the preliminary report, viz. NSS 135 furnishes estimates of value of consumption for 11 broad groups of items as provided in the summary block only, this present report supplies estimates of value of consumption for 100 items (that is, 15 broad groups items, 45 sub-groups of items and no individual item) selected from primary blocks (blocks 10-15) of the schedule. In addition, the present report gives estimates of quantity of consumption for 52 different items (including 4 broad groups, 13 sub-groups and 35 individual items). The estimates in both the reports have, however, been given by levels of monthly household expenditure as well as by levels of monthly per capita expenditures. In this Report tables showing consumer expenditure in rupees per person for a period of 30 days by items of consumption and by monthly per capita expenditure classes are presented. The items of consumption have been merged into 10 major groups.

The ten major groups are: (1) cereals, (2) cereals and cereal substitutes, (3) pulses, (4) milk and milk products, (5) other food items, (6) clothings, (7) fuel and light, (8) rent,

Table 18.6

Round	Report number	Year of publication	Period covered	Geographical coverage
(1)	*(2)*	*(3)*	*(4)*	*(5)*
19th	213	1970	July 1964	Rural and urban areas of the Indian Union excepting Andaman and Nicobar Islands, Laccadive, Minicoy and Amindivi Islands, the Union Territories of Goa, Daman and Diu and Pondicherry, North East Frontier Agency, Nagaland, Ladakh district of Jammu & Kashmir, Lungleh sub-division of Mizo Hills (Lushai) in Assam and Mao, Ukhrul and Tammlong- sub-division of Manipur.

Table 18.7 Details of Data on Consumer Expenditure—28th Round (1972-73)

Table (1): In-migration and out-migration rates per 10000 persons: State-wise and all-India.

Tables Rural Series-1 State-wise and all-India: Distribution of sample households, percentage distribution of estimated number of households and estimated number of adult males, adult females and children per household by monthly per capita expenditure classes.

Tables Rural Series-2 State-wise and all-India: Consumer expenditure per person for a period of 30 days by broad groups of items and by monthly per capita expenditure classes.

Tables Rural Series-3 State-wise and all-India: Quantity and value of consumption per person for a period of 30 days of cereals, gram and cereal substitutes by monthly per capita expenditure classes.

Tables Urban Series-1 State-wise and all-India: Distribution of sample households, percentage distribution of estimated number of households and estimated number of adult males, adult females and children per household by monthly per capita expenditure classes.

(Contd.)

Remarks

---

(6)

---

(9) taxes, and (10) other non-food items. The tables also show estimates relating to: (i) all food items, (ii) all non-food items, and (iii) all items.

For the first time in NSS a number of socio-economic enquiries like demography, employment, consumer expenditure, enterprise and capital formation which had so far been conducted independently, have been integrated together and the data relating to these enquiries have been collected in a common schedule from a common set of sample households in this round. Besides the usual information on consumption, the Report gives quantitative data regarding the consumption of rice, wheat and cereals for rural and urban areas for the 15th to 19th rounds. Details of data availability for the 28th round is as in Table 18.7.

Table 18.7 Details of Data on Consumer Expenditure—28th Round (1972-73) (Contd.)

Tables Urban Series-2 State-wise and all-India: Consumer expenditure per person for a period of 30 days by broad groups of items and by monthly per capita expenditure classes.

Tables Urban Series-3 State-wise and all-India: Quantity and value of consumption per person for a period of 30 days of cereals, gram and cereal substitutes by monthly per capita expenditure classes.

Tables Big Cities Series-1: Distribution of sample households percentage distribution of estimated number of households and estimated number of adult males, adult females and children per household by monthly per capita expenditure classes.

Tables Big Cities Series-2: Consumer expenditure per person for a period of 30 days by broad groups of items and by monthly per capita expenditure classes.

Tables Big Cities Series-3: Quantity and value of consumption per person for a period of 30 days of cereal, gram and cereal substitutes by monthly per capita expenditure classes.

sanitation, hygiene and services. The usual household consumer expenditure enquiry was also thrown in. Information on availability and use of common property resources and use of common property resources and infrastructure facilities at village level was collected through a separate schedule. It may be mentioned that while some information on hygiene, sanitation and services were collected in the earlier NSS round, viz. 44th, 47th and 49th rounds, this is the first NSS study of common property resources and also the first nationwide survey on the subject in India.

Schedule 1.0, as usual, was used to collect data on household consumer expenditure and some important characteristics on employment-unemployment based on a small sample of 4 households per first-stage unit (FSU) surveyed.

Geographical Coverage   The survey covered the whole of the Indian Union excepting (a) Ladakh and Kargil districts of Jammu and Kashmir. (b) 768 interior villages of Nagaland situated beyond 5 km of the bus route and (c) 195 villages of Andaman and Nicobar Islands which remained inaccessible throughout the year.

Period of Survey and Work Programme   The 54th round survey was of 6 months' duration from January 1998 to June 1998. The survey period of this round was divided into two sub-rounds, each with a duration of three months. The first subround period was from January to March 1998 and the second sub-round period was from April to June 1998. Equal numbers of sample villages and urban blocks were allotted for survey in the two sub-rounds. Each village/block was generally surveyed during the sub-round period to which it was allotted. This restriction was not strictly enforced in Andaman and Nicobar Islands, Lakshadweep and rural areas of Arunachal Pradesh and Nagaland because of difficult field conditions.

Sample Design

General: As usual, a stratified sampling design was adopted. The first-stage units were census villages (*panchayat* wards in case of Kerala) in the rural sector and the NSSO Urban Frame Survey (UFS) blocks in the urban sector. The ultimate-stage units were households in both sectors.

Sampling Frame for First Stage Units

Rural   The lists of census villages of the 1991 population census (1981 census list for Jammu and Kashmir) constituted the sampling frame for the rural sector. For Kerala, however, the list of *panchayat* wards was used as the sampling frame in the rural sector. For Nagaland, the sampling frame was formed by the villages located within 5 km of a bus route, and for Andaman and Nicobar Islands, by the list of accessible villages.

Urban   The lists of latest UFS blocks for all cities and towns were used to draw up the sampling frames.

Stratification

Rural The following three strata were first formed at the State/UT level.

    Stratum 1:   List of uninhabited villages (as per 1991 census).

    Stratum 2:   Villages with population 1 to 50 (including both the boundaries) as per 1991 census.

    Stratum 3:   Villages with population more than 15,000 as per 1991 census.

Stratum type 1 (or 2 or 3) was formed in a State/UT provided there were at least 10 villages in the State/UT qualifying for inclusion as per 1991 population census. If the number of such villages was less than 10, they were included in the general strata as described below.

    General strata: After formation of the stratum types 1, 2 and 3 (wherever applicable), the remaining villages of the State/UT were considered for formation of general strata. Each district with population less than 2 million as per 1991 census formed a separate stratum (however, districts having a population of 2 million or more were divided into a number of strata as per usual procedure followed in NSS). For Gujarat, some districts cut across NSS regions. In such cases, the part of a district falling in an NSS region formed a separate stratum.

    Urban Strata were formed within each NSS region by grouping towns as indicated below.

Stratum No.	Composition of strata (considering population as per 1981 census for Jammu and Kashmir and as per 1991 census elsewhere)
1.	all towns with population less than 50,000
2.	all towns with population 50,000 or more but less than 2 lakhs
3.	all towns with population 2 lakhs or more but less than 10 lakhs
4.5	each city with population 10 lakhs or more

Sub-stratification

Rural There was no sub-stratification at the stratum level.

    Urban Each stratum was divided into two 2 sub-strata as follows:

Sub-stratum 1: UFS blocks identified as 'slum area'

Sub-stratum 2: remaining UFS blocks of the stratum.

    Sample Size The all-India sample size of FSU's (rural and urban combined) was 7030 in the Central sample and 7988 in the State sample.

Allocation of First-stage Units (FSU's)

The all-India sample size of FSU's was allocated to the States/UTs in proportion to their investigator strength in the Central sample. State/UT level sample size was allocated between rural and urban sectors in proportion to their population. State/UT-level rural/urban allocations along with number of surveyed FSUs, households and persons are given in Table 18.8.

A suitable sample size (minimum = 2 and maximum = 6 villages; exact number depending on the total number of villages in the frame) was allocated to stratum type 1 (in all 68 sample villages were allocated to stratum type 1 in the rural sector). From stratum type 2, a sample of maximum size = 6 villages was selected. Number of sample villages selected from stratum type 3 was 2 or 4 according as the number of villages in the frame for stratum type 3 was less than 20 or more. The remaining sample size (i.e. total allocation for the rural sector less the allocations for stratum type 1, 2 and 3) at the State/UT level for the rural sector was allocated to the general strata (i.e. strata other than stratum types 1, 2 and 3) in proportion to their population. Similarly, the allocation of sample at State/UT level to the urban strata was in proportion to their

Table 18.8 Number of villages/blocks allotted and surveyed and number of sample households and persons surveyed

State/ U.Ts	Number of					Number of surveyed		
	Villages		Blocks			Households		Persons
	Allotted	Surveyed	Allotted	Surveyed	Rural	Urban	Rural	Urban
(1)	(2)	(3)	(4)	(5)	(6)	(7)	(8)	(9)
Andhra Pradesh	364	360	132	132	1440	523	6286	2383
Assam	214	205	28	28	819	112	4324	457
Bihar	478	471	72	72	1875	288	10318	1529
Gujarat	190	188	96	96	748	382	3722	1849
Haryana	82	80	24	24	308	96	1794	463
Karnataka	204	202	88	88	801	348	4082	1666
Kerala	*204	*204	72	72	728	288	3423	1413
Madhya Pradesh	372	370	112	112	1464	448	7521	2277
Maharashtra	344	340	212	212	1345	848	6475	4070
Orissa	220	216	36	36	860	144	4127	602
Punjab	166	165	72	72	640	288	3404	1401
Rajasthan	228	226	64	64	888	250	4929	1259
Tamil Nadu	338	336	176	176	1334	700	5423	2842
Uttar Pradesh	638	632	156	156	2513	623	14593	3507
West Bengal	340	336	124	124	1333	495	6648	2206
North-Eastern	448	408	124	121	1602	484	7809	2300
North-Western	338	251	152	122	976	475	5149	2050
Southern	74	68	48	48	262	191	1222	82
All-India	5242	5058	1788	1755	19936	6983	101249	33086

*Figures denote number of Panchayat wards

population. Stratum-level allocations were made in multiples of 4, wherever possible. The sample allocation for an urban stratum was further allocated between the two sub-strata in proportion to the number of UFS blocks in the respective sub-strata with double weightage to sub-stratum 1 subject to a minimum sample size of 2 or 4 blocks to sub-stratum 1 depending upon whether stratum level allocation was 4 or greater than 4. All sub-stratum level allocations were made in multiples of 2.

Selection of First-stage Units Sample FSU's were selected in the form of two independent sub-samples as shown in Table 18.9.

Table 18.9

Sector	Stratum type	Sub-stratum	Selection Procedure
Rural	1	—	CSS with equal probability @
	2	—	-do-*
	3	—	-do-*
	others	—	CSS with pps
Urban	Each	Each	CSS with equal probability**

(CSS: circular systematic sampling. pps: probability proportional to size. size = population)

@ arrangement of villages in the frame is same as that of census

• after arranging the FSUs in ascending order of population

** after arranging the towns by districts and further arranging the towns in each district in ascending order of their population.

Formation of hamlet-groups in large villages and number of hamlet-groups selected for survey Large villages were divided into a number of hamlet-groups (hgs) having equal population content and geographical contiguity. The frame for selection of households in such villages was constituted not by all households in the village but by households belonging to a number of randomly selected hamlet-groups of the village. The D of hamletgroups formed and the number d of hamlet-groups selected for formation of the frame for selection of households was determined as per Table 18.10.

However, for rural areas of Himachal Pradesh, Sikkim, and Punch, Rajouri, Udhampur and Doda districts of Jammu and Kashmir, the procedure was: $D = 1$ for population less than 600. $D = 4$ for population 600–1199, $D = 5$ for population 1200–1499, $D = 6$ for population 1500–1799, and so on. Number of h.g.s. selected for survey was $d = 2$ for $D = 4$ to 10, $d = 3$ for $D = 11$ to 20, $d = 4$ for $D = 21$ to 30 and $d = 5$ for $D > 30$.

Selection of Households A sample of 4 households for schedule 1.0 from each sample FSU (both rural and urban) were selected for survey

Table 18.10

Approx present popu-lation of the village	Number of h.g.s formed (D)	Number of h.g.s selected for survey (d)
less–1200	No h.g. formation	entire village selected for survey
1200–1999	5	3
2500–2999	6	3
3000–3499	7	3
3500–3999	8	3
4000–4499	9	3
4500–4999	10	3
5000–5499	11	4
14500–14999	30	4
15000–15499	31	5 @
and so on		

@ s.h.g.s. were selected for survey from each selected village having approx. present population of 15,000 or more

after arranging all the households by means of livelihood code. The sample households were selected circular-systematically with independent random starts from the respective frames of households.

Estimation Procedure

The following notation is used:

s = subscript for stratum

t = subscript for sub-stratum

i = subscript for sample village/block

k = subscript for sample household

b = subscript for sub-sample ($b = 1,2$)

z = size of the sample village/block used for selection ($z = 1$ for each block)

Z = total size for a stratum or substratum as per the frame

n = number of sample villages/blocks (i.e. number used for tabulation) surveyed including uninhabited for zero cases and excluding casualty and other not-received cases

D = number of hamlet-groups formed in the sample village

d = number of hamlet-groups selected for survey

H = total number of households listed in the frame

h = number of sample households available for tabulation

y = value of any characteristic observable in a sample village/block household

Y = estimate of population total of the characteristic y

Formulae for Estimation
For the rural sector.

$$Y_{sh} = \frac{Z_s}{n_{sh}} \sum_{i=1}^{n+h} \frac{D_{shi}}{d_{shi}} \frac{1}{Z_{shi}} \frac{H_{shi}}{k} \Sigma y_{shik}$$

For the urban sector,

$$Y_{sh} = \sum_{i=1}^{2} \frac{Z_{st}}{n_{sth}} \sum_{i=1}^{n_{sth}} \frac{H_{sthi}}{h_{sthi}} \Sigma_k y_{shik}$$

Note:
1. For stratum type 1, 2 and 3 in the rural sector, $z = 1$ and $Z =$ total number of villages in the frame of the respective strata whereas for other strata in the rural sector, $z =$ population of the sample village as per the frame used for selection and $Z =$ total population of the stratum.
2. For estimating the number of villages possessing a character, $y = 1$ for sample villages possessing the character and $y = 0$ otherwise.
3. When $D = 1$, the value of $d = 1$. When $D \geq 4$, $2 \leq d \leq 5$.
4. When $H > 0$ but $h = 0$ for any second stage stratum, that second-stage stratum was treated as merged with any of the other two second-stage strata. In particular, if $h = 0$ for $H > 0$ in second-stage stratum 1, it was merged with second-stage stratum 3. If second-stage stratum 2 became a casualty, it was merged with second-stage stratum 3. Lastly, if second-stage stratum 3 became a casualty, it was merged with second-stage stratum 1.

Estimate of Aggregates
The pooled estimate Y, based on two subsamples was obtained as

$$Y_s = \frac{1}{2} \sum_{h=1}^{2} Y_{sh}$$

The pooled estimate Y at the region/State/UT/all-India was obtained by summing the stratum estimates Y, over all the strata of the region/State/UT/all-India.

Ratio Estimates
The estimate of the ratio $R = Y/X$ (X is the population total of an auxiliary variable) was given by

$$R = \frac{Y}{X}$$

19

Cost of Production

INTRODUCTION

With sustained efforts at planned development of agriculture involving introduction of improved technology, the need for data on cost of production of principal crops is being increasingly felt both for policy formulation and for organizing extension work. Adequate knowledge of the cost structure of principal crops is essential for working out schemes for providing adequate incentives to the farmers. To implement the policy of guaranteed minimum prices of agricultural commodities, it is necessary to have an idea of the cost of production of different crops.

A number of surveys as discussed below have been carried out in different parts of the country to collect information on the cost of production of various crops. These surveys and studies carried out at different times with diverse objectives by different agencies have not followed uniform concepts and do not provide information for all the major crops on a comparable basis. Most of them were not specifically designed to collect data on cost with a view to formulating price policy at the national and State levels.

The first study which was of a continuing nature and is still in progress was that of Farm Accounts[1] initiated by the Punjab Board of Economic Inquiry, 1923 with the major objective of studying the costs and returns as well as farm resource use pattern in different regions of the State to serve as a basis for agricultural policy-making by the Government. Whereas these and most of the later cost of production studies served at least some, though limited purpose for price policy purposeful, the other major objective of these studies to introduce farm efficiencies could not be fulfilled because they lacked data on specific resource restrictions and production potential of the individual farm organizations. Also, the inputs used could not be classified into fixed resources inputs and variable resources inputs for budgeting better resource use and production potential

---

[1]'Farm Accounts in the Punjab' published annually by the Board of Economic Inquiry, Punjab (India).

of the individual holding. From this angle these studies were not very useful for the purpose of reorganization of the farm business.[2]

In 1926, an investigation into farm costs was conducted by Patil[3] (1926) to provide 'modus operandi' for cost accounting and support income measures most suitable to Indian farming. The income measures used were 'farm business income' and 'family labour income'. An attempt was made for the first time, in this study to calculate opportunity costs and allocate them in accordance with cost accounting principles.

The cost studies conducted under the auspices of the ICAR during 1933-34 to 1936-37 in the principal sugarcane and cotton growing tracts of India constituted perhaps the first systematic effort in the direction of studying the economics of crop production. The main objective of this survey was to collect data relating to cost of production of sugarcane in the country and to decide the areas in which the sugar industry had the best chance of development. The surveys also covered other principal crops grown in the selected regions and were spread over a period of three years.

During 1952-53, the ICAR, in collaboration with the Indian Central Cotton and Oilseeds Committee carried out a pilot study into the cost of production of cotton and its rotation crops in the district of Akola. The objective of the pilot study was to provide guidance on such methodological problems at the sampling design, sampling units and method of recording data.

The scope of the cost studies organized under the auspices of the ICAR had been gradually widened. The Indian Central Sugarcane committee of the ICAR sponsored studies on the cost of production of sugarcane in four major sugarcane growing States, viz. U.P. Bihar, Andhra Pradesh and Punjab during 1955-56 to 1957-58, covering 23 districts in U.P., 7 in Bihar, 5 in Andhra Pradesh and 3 in Punjab. The Studies were further extended to Maharashtra and Mysore in 1956-57 and 1960-61 respectively, covering 5 districts in each State. On the basis of the results of the Akola Pilot Study, the ICAR and the Cotton and Oilseed Committees jointly organized a study of the cost of cultivation and cotton and its rotation crops (jowar, wheat and groundnut) in the principal cotton tracts, viz. Punjab, Maharashtra, Gujarat and Mysore, covering the period 1960-61 to 1962-63. The study covered four districts in Punjab, six in Maharashtra, seven in Gujarat and three in Mysore.

A three-year study on the cost of production of jute and its competing crops, namely, paddy, in West Bengal, Bihar and Assam, sponsored by the erstwhile Indian Central Jute Committee in 1963-64, was completed in 1970. The Indian Central Coconut Committee and the Indian Central Arecanut Committees also were interested in working out the cost of

---

[2]A.S. Kahlon, Farm Management, ICAR, 1972.

[3]P.C. Patil, Principles and Practices of Farm Costing in the Farm Management Studies.

production of their respective commodities and had financed surveys for the purpose in Kerala and Mysore.

FARM MANAGEMENT STUDIES

A comprehensive programme of Farm Management Studies was launched by the Directorate of Economics and Statistics, Ministry of Food and Agriculture, in collaboration with the Research Programme Committee of the Planning Commission in 1954-55. These studies were initiated in 1954-55 in five regions in Punjab, U.P., Madras, West Bengal and Maharashtra. The objective of the study was two-fold: to obtain guideline data for formulating agricultural policy and for extension work, and to determine the relative merits of the cost accounting and survey methods for collection of data on cost. The studies provided data on cost for major crops grown in the concerned regions, viz. paddy, maize, wheat, jowar, bajra, sugarcane, cotton, groundnut, etc. as well as on other aspects of the farm economy such as cropping pattern, the relative profitability of different crops grown on the farm, farm investment, and return to the farm business, human and bullock labour employment, etc.

The Studies were later extended by the Directorate of Economics and Statistics to more regions in the country, covering selected areas in different States. Some of these recent studies are in the nature of repeat surveys. These recent studies while retaining the objective of collecting farm management data on the pattern of the past studies, also aim at providing information on the economics of improved agricultural practices. Details about crops taken up for studies during different periods are as Table 19.1 and various agencies involved in Table 19.2.

With a view to studying the improvements affected towards better utilization of available irrigation water and related inputs together with changes in cropping pattern through the Command Area Development Programme as well as other related problems like optimum utilization of irrigation potential, the Directorate of Economics and Statistics initiated two problem-oriented Farm Management Studies in the command areas of Jayakwadi (Maharashtra) and Tawa (M.P.) during 1980. Another study in the command area of Nagarjunasagar Project (Andhra Pradesh) would be taken up shortly. Besides, two other studies on the problems of increasing the production (i) pulses (gram) in Sriganganagar district of Rajasthan, and (ii) oilseeds (groundnut) in North and South Arcot district of Tamil Nadu are proposed to be taken up.

The scheme for studies in the economics of farm management is being continued as a Central Plan Scheme in the Ministry of Agriculture from the beginning of the Second Five Year Plan. Under the scheme, investigations into the economics of farm management have been carried out in 27 selected regions/districts of the country.

Programme for 1980/85 Besides these two studies mentioned above, three more studies were taken up during the year 1980-81. These studies related to: (1) extension of the command area study to Nagarjuna **Sagar** irrigation project area (Andhra Pradesh), (2) problem-oriented farm management study relating to the problems of increasing oilseeds (groundnut) production in South and North Arcot districts of Tamil Nadu, and (3) problem-oriented farm management study relating to the problems of increasing the production of gram in Sri Ganganagar district of Rajasthan. These three studies which were completed in the eighties, were proposed by the concerned Divisions in the Department of Agriculture and Cooperation and the Ministry of Irrigation. In view of the orientation of the farm management studies towards programmes of specific areas/crops, it was then proposed to merge the old scheme of Intensive Agriculture District Programme into Farm Management Intensive Agricultural Programme Scheme.

NATIONAL SAMPLE SURVEYS

An enquiry on some aspects of cost of cultivation was undertaken by the NSS during its fifth Round (December 1952 to March 1953) and information was collected on all the important crops for items such as seed, manure, water, human and animal labour. The enquiry was repeated in the two subsequent rounds—sixth and seventh. The number of households covered in these rounds was 4,287, 4,385 and 3,144 respectively. The entire country except Jammu & Kashmir and Andaman and Nicobar Islands was covered by the survey. Estimates were given for the total cost in terms of money by adding to the cash outlay the imputed value of material and labour inputs.

Subsequently, the NSS undertook another survey on some aspects of the cost of cultivation of important crops in its eleventh round of investigation (August 1956 to February 1957), covering the same crops as in the earlier investigations. The survey covered the entire country except Andaman and Nicobar islands, the North-East Frontier Agency and the Naga Hills. A full discussion of the reports published on the subject follows.

National Sample Survey Report No. 32

The report deals with some aspects of cost of cultivation. This Report is divided into three parts. The first part deals with 4 major crops, viz. paddy, wheat, jowar and bajra. The second part covers barley, maize, ragi, gram, small millets, cotton and jute, while the third part deals with such crops as minor cereals, pulses, sugarcane, oilseeds, potato, spices and tobacco. The total area covered by the three Reports is about 98 per cent of the total cropped area. The first Part contains a good deal of explanatory text along with the relevant tables, but the second and third parts contain mainly tables with short introductory notes.

A three-stage stratified sampling design was adopted for rural areas (urban areas not considered) in all the three rounds of the survey from fifth to seventh. The first, second and third stage units were tehsils,

Table 19.1 Crops Taken up for Study During Different Years under the Comprehensive Scheme for Studying the Cost of Cultivation of Principal Crops

State	Total Clusters	1984-85 to 1986-87	Total Clusters	1987-88 to 1989-90
(1)	*(2)*	*(3)*	*(4)*	*(5)*
1. Andhra Pradesh	60	Paddy, jowar (sorghum) ragi, urad (black gram) moong (green gram) groundnut and sugarcane.	60	Paddy, jowar (sorghum), ragi, urad (black gram), moong (green gram), groundnut, cotton and sugarcane.
2. Assam	45	Paddy, rapeseed and mustard and jute.	45	Paddy, rapeseed and mustard and jute.
3. Bihar	60	Paddy, wheat, maize, moong (green gram), jute, potato and sugarcane.	60	Paddy, wheat, maize, moong (green gram), jute, barley and sugarcane.
4. Gujarat	60	Bajra, arhar (red gram), groundnut, onion and cotton.	60	Bajra, arhar (red gram), groundnut, cotton and Tobacco.
5. Haryana	30	Paddy, wheat bajra, bengal gram, rapeseed and mustard and sugarcane.	30	Paddy, wheat, bajra, bengal gram, rapeseed and mustard and cotton.
6. Himachal Pradesh	30	Maize, wheat and potato.	30	Maize, wheat, potato and ginger.
7. Karnataka	45	Paddy, jowar (sorghum), ragi, red gram (tur) groundnut, safflower, sunflower, cotton and sugarcane.	45	Paddy, jowar (sorghum), ragi, red gram (tur) groundnut, safflower, sunflower, cotton and sugarcane.
8. Kerala	30	Paddy and tapioca.	30	Paddy and tapioca.
9. Madhya	60	Paddy, wheat, jowar (sorghum), maize, urad (black gram), moong (green gram), Bengal gram, arhar (red gram), soyabean and cotton.	60	Paddy, wheat, jowar (sorghum), maize, urad (black gram), moong (green gram), Bengal gram, arhar (red gram), Soyabean, linseed and cotton.

*Table 19.1 Crops Taken up for Study During Different Years Under the Comprehensive
Scheme for Studying the Cost of Cultivation of Principal Crops* (Contd.)

State	Total Clusters	1990-91 to 1992-93	Total Clusters	1993-94 to 1995-96
(1)	*(6)*	*(7)*	*(8)*	*(9)*
1. Andhra Pradesh	60	Paddy, jowar (sorghum) ragi, arhar (red gram), urad (black gram), moong (green gram), groundnut, cotton and sugarcane.	60	Paddy, jowar (sorghum), bajra, maize, ragi, urad (black gram), moong (green gram), cotton groundnut and sugarcane.
2. Assam	45	Paddy, rapeseed and mustard and jute.	45	Paddy, rapeseed and mustard and jute.
3. Bihar	60	Paddy, wheat, maize, jute, potato and sugarcane.	60	Paddy, wheat, maize, bengal gram, jute, potato and sugarcane.
4. Gujarat	60	Wheat, jowar (sorghum) bajra, arhar (red gram), groundnut and cotton.	60	Wheat, jowar (sorghum) bajra, arhar (red gram), groundnut, rapeseed and mustard, cotton and sugarcane.
5. Haryana	30	Paddy, wheat, bajra, bengal gram, rapeseed and mustard, cotton and sugarcane.	30	Paddy, wheat, bajra, bengal gram, rapeseed and mustard, cotton and sugarcane.
6. Himachal Pradesh	30	Maize, wheat, potato and Ginger.	30	Paddy, wheat, potato.
7. Karnataka	45	Paddy, jowar (sorghum) bajra, ragi, arhar (red gram) groundnut, safflower, sunflower, oion, cotton and sugarcane.	45	Paddy, jowar (sorghum), bajra, maize, ragi, groundnut, safflower, sunflower, onion, cotton and sugarcane.
8. Kerala	30	Paddy and tapioca.	30	Paddy and tapioca.
9. Madhya Pradesh	60	Paddy, wheat, jowar (Sorghum), maize, urad (black gram), moong (green gram), bengal gram, arhar (red gram), soyabean, linseed and cotton.	60	Paddy, wheat, jowar (sorghum), maize, urad (black gram), moong (green gram), bengal gram, arhar (red gram), rapeseed and mustard

Table 19.1 Crops Taken up for Study During Different Years under the Comprehensive Scheme for Studying the Cost of Cultivation of Principal Crops *(Contd.)*

State	Total Clusters	1984-85 to 1986-87	Total Clusters	1987-88 to 1989-90
(1)	(2)	(3)	(4)	(5)
10. Maharashtra	60	Jowar (sorghum), bajra, ragi, arhar (red gram), moong (green gram), urad (black gram), groundnut, safflower, sunflower, sugarcane, cotton and onion.	60	Jowar (sorghum), Bajra ragi, arhar (red gram), moong (green gram), urad (black gram), groundnut, safflower, sunflower, sugarcane, cotton and onion.
11. Orissa	45	Paddy, moong (green gram), urad (black gram), groundnut, jute and onion.	45	Paddy, moong (green gram), ragi, urad (black gram), groundnut, jute and onion.
12. Punjab	30	Paddy, wheat, maize and cotton.	30	Paddy, wheat, rapeseed and mustard and cotton.
13. Rajasthan	60	Wheat, bajra, maize, barley, bengal gram, moong (green gram) and rape and mustard.	60	Wheat, bajra, maize, barley, bengal gram, moong (green gram), rape and mustard and sesamum.
14. Tamil Nadu	60	Paddy, jowar (sorghum), ragi, urad (black gram), groundnut, sugarcane, onion and cotton.	60	Paddy, jowar (sorghum), ragi, urad (black gram), groundnut, sugarcane, onion and cotton.
15. Uttar Pradesh	75	Paddy, wheat, bajra, maize, barley, bengal gram, urad (black gram), arhar (red gram), rapeseed and mustard, sesamum, linseed, soyabean, sugarcane and potato.	75	Paddy, wheat, bajra maize, barley, bengal gram, urad (black gram), rapeseed and mustard, sesamum, linseed, soyabean, sugarcane and potato.
16. West Bengal	60	Paddy, urad (black gram), jute and potato.	60	Paddy, wheat, jute and potato.
17. Andhra Pradesh	30	V.F.C. Tobacco (special study)	30	V.F.C. tobacco (special study)

Table 19.1 Crops Taken up for Study During Different Years Under the Comprehensive Scheme for Studying the Cost of Cultivation of Principal Crops (Contd.)

State	Total Clusters	1990-91 to 1992-93	Total Clusters	1993-94 to 1995-96
(1)	(6)	(7)	(8)	(9)
10. Maharashtra	60	Jowar (sorghum), bajra, ragi, arhar (red gram), moong (green gram), urad (black gram), groundnut, safflower, sunflower, onion, cotton and sugarcane.	60	Jowar (sorghum), bajra, ragi, moong (green gram), urad (black gram), groundnut, safflower, sunflower, onion, cotton and sugarcane.
11. Orissa	45	Paddy, ragi, moong (green gram), urad (black gram), groundnut, jute and onion.	45	Paddy, ragi, arhar (red gram), moong (green gram), urad (black gram), groundnut, jute and onion.
12. Punjab	30	Paddy, wheat, rapeseed and mustard, cotton and sugarcane.	30	Paddy, wheat, rapeseed and mustard, cotton and sugarcane.
13. Rajasthan	60	Wheat, jowar (sorghum) bajra, maize, barley, bengal gram, moth, rapeseed and mustard and sesamum.	60	Wheat, jowar (sorghum) bajra, maize, barley, bengal gram, rapeseed and mustard sesamum, soyabean and cotton
14. Tamil Nadu	60	Paddy, jowar (sorghum), bajra, ragi, urad (black gram), groundnut, sesamum, sugarcane and cotton.	60	Paddy, jowar (sorghum), bajra, ragi, arhar (red gram), urad (black gram), groundnut, Sesamum, sugarcane and cotton.
15. Uttar Pradesh	75	Paddy, wheat, bajra, maize, barley, bengal gram, urad (black gram), arhar, (red gram), rapessed and mustard, sesamum, linseed, soyabean, sugarcane and potato.	75	Paddy, wheat, bajra, maize, barley, bengal gram, urad (black gram), arhar (red gram), rapeseed and mustard, sesamum, soyabean, sugarcane and potato.
16. West	60	Paddy, wheat, jute and Potato.	60	Paddy, wheat, jute and Potato.
17. Andhra Pradesh	30	V.F.C. Tobacco (special study)	30	V.F.C. tobacco (special study)

Table 9.1 Crops Taken up for Study During Different Years Under the Comprehensive Scheme for Studying the Cost of Cultivation of Principal Crops (Concld.)

State	Total clusters	1996-97 to 1998-99
(1)	*(10)*	*(11)*
1. Andhra Pradesh	60	Paddy, jowar (sorghum), bajra, maize, ragi, urad (black gram), moong (green gram), sunflower, cotton groundnut and sugarcane.
2. Assam	45	Paddy, rapeseed and mustard and jute.
3. Bihar	60	Paddy, wheat, maize, bengal gram, jute, potato and sugarcane.
4. Gujarat	60	Wheat, bajra, arhar (red gram), groundnut, rapessed and mustard and cotton.
5. Haryana	30	Paddy, wheat, bajra, bengal gram, rapeseed and mustard, cotton and sugarcane.
6. Himachal Pradesh	30	Maize, wheat, potato and ginger.
7. Karnataka	45	Paddy, jowar (sorghum), bajra, maize, ragi, groundnut, safflower, sunflower, onion, cotton and sugarcane.
8. Kerala	30	Paddy and tapioca.
9. Madhya Pradesh	60	Paddy, wheat, jowar (sorghum), maize, urad (black gram), moong (greengram), bengal gram, arhar (red gram), rapeseed and mustard, soyabean, nigerseed, sesamum and cotton.
10. Maharashtra	60	Jowar (sorghum) bajra, ragi, moong (green gram) urad (Black gram), arhar (red gram), groundnut, soyabean, safflower, sunflower, onion, cotton and sugarcane.
11. Orissa	45	Paddy, ragi, arhar (red gram), moong (green gram), urad (black gram), groundnut, jute, nigerseed, sesamum and onion.

Table 19.1 Crops Taken up for Study During Different Years Under the Comprehensive Scheme for Studying the Cost of Cultivation of Principal Crops (Contd.)

State	Total clusters	1996-97 to 1998-99
(1)	(10)	(11)
12. Punjab	30	Paddy, wheat, rapeseed and mustard, cotton and sunflower.
13. Rajasthan	60	Wheat, jowar (sorghum) bajra, maize, barley, bengal gram, rapeseed and mustard, sesamum, soyabean and cotton.
14. Tamil Nadu	60	Paddy, jowar (sorghum), bajra, ragi, arhar (red gram), urad (black gram), groundnut, sesamum, sugarcane and cotton.
15. Uttar Pradesh	75	Paddy, wheat, bajra, maize, barley, bengal gram, urad (black gram), arhar (red gram), rapeseed and mustard, sesamum, sugarcane and potato.
16. West bengal	60	Paddy, rapeseed and mustard, jute and Potato.
17. Andhra Pradesh	30	V.F.C. tobacco (special study)

Note: 1. For crops selected between 1970-71 to 1983-84, please refer to previous volumes.
2. Crop selection from 1981-82 onwards is based on crop-complex approach. Earlier it was based on single-crop approach.

villages and households respectively. The total sample size of 480 tehsils was first of all allocated to natural divisions on the basis of total consumer expenditure estimated from the first round of the NSS. Each national division was then sub-divided into strata by grouping tehsils in such a way that: (1) the tehsil-wise density of population was more or less the same in a stratum, (ii) the number of strata in a natural division was half the number of tehsils allocated to it, and (iii) populations of strata within a natural division were roughly equal. The first stage units, viz. tehsils were selected from each stratum with probability proportional to area of population and with replacement and at the second stage, two villages were selected from each selected placement. At the third stage, a systematic sample of fixed proportion of households was selected from

Table 19.2 Agencies Implementing the Comprehensive Scheme of Cost of Cultivation and Cost of Production in Different States and the Crops Selected for the Block year 1999-2002

State	Number of Holdings	Implementing Agency	Crops Selected
(1)	*(2)*	*(3)*	*(4)*
1. Andhra Pradesh	600	College of Agriculture Rajendra Nagar, Hyderabad	Paddy, sorghum (jowar), maize, ragi, Block gram, green gram, red gram (tur), groundnut, sunflower, cotton and sugarcane.
2. Assam	450	Assam Agricultural University, Jorhat	Paddy, rapeseed and mustard and jute.
3. Bihar	600	Rajendra Agriculture University, Pusa, Samastipur	Paddy, wheat, maize, bengal gram, lentil (Masur), jute, potato and sugarcane.
4. Gujarat	600	Sardar Patel University Vallabh Vidya Nagar	Bajra, wheat, red gram, groundnut, rapeseed and mustard, sesamum and cotton.
5. Haryana	300	Haryana Agriculture University, Hissar	Paddy, wheat, bajra, bengal gram, rapeseed and mustard, cotton and sugarcane.
6. Himachal Pradesh	300	Himachal Pradesh University, Shimla	maize, wheat and potato.
7. Karnataka	450	University of Agricultural Sciences, Hebbal, Bangalore.	Paddy, sorghum, ragi, maize, red gram (tur) groundnut, safflower, sunflower, cotton, onion, sugarcane and arecanut (special study).
8. Kerala	300	University of Kerala, Thiruvanantha-puram.	Paddy and tapioca. coconut and black pepper (special study).
9. Madhya Pradesh	600	Jawahar Lal Nehru Krishi Viswavidhyalaya, Jabalpur.	Paddy, wheat, sorghum, maize, black gram, bengal gram, red gram, lentil (masur), soyabean, rapeseed and mustard, nigerseed, sesamum cotton.

Table 19.2 Agencies Implementing the Comprehensive Scheme of Cost of Cultivation and Cost of Production in Different States and the Crops Selected for the Block year 1999-2002 (Contd.)

State	Number of Holdings	Implementing Agency	Crops Selected
(1)	(2)	(3)	(4)
10. Maharashtra	600	Mahatma Phule Agriculture University, Rahuri	Sorghum, bajra, ragi, red gram, green gram, black gram, groundnut, safflower, sunflower, soyabean, sugarcane, cotton and onion.
11. Orissa	450	Orissa University of Agriculture and Technology, Bhubaneshwar.	Paddy, green gram, black gram, red gram, nigerseed, sesamum, jute and onion.
12. Punjab	300	Punjab Agricultural University, Ludhiana.	Paddy, wheat, rapeseed and sunflower and cotton.
13. Rajasthan	600	Rajasthan Agriculture University, Udaipur	Wheat, sorghum, bajra, maize, barley, bengal gram, black gram, green gram, rapeseed and mustard, soyabean, sesamum and cotton.
14. Tamil Nadu	600	Tamil Nadu Agriculture, University	Paddy, sorghum, ragi, red gram, black gram, groundnut, sesamum, sugarcane and cotton.
15. Uttar Pradesh	750	R.B.S. College Bichpuri, Agra	Paddy, wheat bajra, maize, barley, bengal gram, black gram, lentil (masur), rapeseed and mustard, sesamum, sugarcane and potato.
16. West Bengal	600	Bidhan Chandra Krishi, Visvidyalaya, Kalyani, Nadia.	Paddy, rapeseed and mustard, jute and Potato.
17. Andhra Pradesh	300	Directorate of Tobacco Development, M/o Agriculture, Chennai.	V.F.C. Tobacco (Special Study)

each sample village. In the fifth and sixth rounds, this selection of households was made from the frame constituted by all the households in the village. In the seventh round, however, a separate frame of households with activities in agriculture and animal husbandry classes was prepared in each sample village for selection of households for detailed enquiry in this respect and consequently, the effective sample size and the total size were the same in this round.

The information collected during these investigations related to land possessed and cultivated, area under crops, crops sown and harvested, crop-wise production, cost of materials and labour, other agricultural production such as fruits and nuts, wood, timber, fodder etc. with costs and details of livestock produce and related costs. As regards production, both quantity and value were ascertained in respect of principal and subsidiary products, the valuation of total quantity of production was made at farm prices that existed at the time of harvest. This was done in respect of each sample unit separately by the investigator at the time of enquiry. Information regarding quantity of seed and manure used in cultivation was collected from the agriculturists both in respect of household and purchased quantities. Value of the quantities consumed by the household was calculated at the current market price to get the total cost in money terms. Cost in respect of water included only the actual payments for water and excluded the labour charges of irrigation incurred by the sample house-holds. Data on human and animal labour were collected separately for households and hired labour. Feed and service charges for the maintenance of livestock were not considered and instead the total charges were estimated on the basis of current local marked rates.

This Report is divided into five chapters dealing with cost of material, cost of labour, gross production and estimates of balance of value of production, i.e. value of production minus the share of major items and inputs. A critical examination of the reliability of estimates presented in the Report is given in an appendix to it. Under material costs, all-India and zone-wise data on: (i) quantity and value of seed used per acre of area harvested, (ii) quantity of seed purchased as percentage to total quantity used, (iii) quantity and value of manure used per acre of area harvested, (iv) quantity of manure purchased as percentage to total quantity used, and (v) water charges per acre of area harvested have been given. Under labour costs, all-India and zonal estimates of labour utilization in terms of human and animal labour days per acre of area harvested, percentage of hired human and animal labour days utilized by different agricultural operations per acre of area harvested, human and animal labour charges for various agricultural operations, etc. are published. Under gross value of production are given all-India and zonal estimates of quantity of production of both crop and straw per acre of area harvested. These estimates are based on data collected from households by the interview method with reference to a season or seasons prior to the time of investigation of sometimes even a little remote.

According to the Report, "production and income data based on interview method often have a tendency to be under-reported giving a downward bias to the estimates". This limitation may be kept in view while utilizing these data. Under the balance of value of production, different constituents of costs are examined in relation to the gross value of production and the balance of value of production has been calculated. Input has been considered under four heads, viz.: (i) seed, (ii) manure, (iii) water, and (iv) animal labour. These four groups of items do not, however, exhaust all the costs to arrive at the net estimates.

The National Sample Survey Report No. 81

(Tables with notes on some aspects of cost of cultivation of paddy, wheat, barley, millets, pulses, oilseeds and vegetables, Fifth to Seventh Rounds, 1951-52 and 1952-53.)

The Report[4] is similar to the one discussed above, but for the fact that while the earlier report pertains to the rural areas, this report relates to the urban sector of the economy. The data for the present report too were collected during the same rounds and the method of collection of data, evaluation procedure, computation of cost, etc. were also the same as for the report discussed in the previous section.

A three-stage stratified sampling design had been adopted for the survey. The first, second, and third stage units are town, blocks and household, respectively. In all, 171 households were surveyed in the fifth round, 163 in the sixth round and 242 in the seventh round.

The coverage of the survey was the total of urban areas in the country and the crops selected for presentation in the Report are paddy, wheat, barley, maize, millets, pulses, oilseeds and vegetables. However, the Report accounts for a very small proportion of the total cropped area in the country (2 per cent).

The most important objective of the Report was to see how fairly the results of rural and urban surveys compare with each other. But mainly because of the inadequacy of the effective sample size, results of the urban sector had not been presented in a similar way as in case of rural results. A large number of crops were omitted and figures for some of the crops were combined. The Report also combines the results of the different rounds and the different seasons.

The Report was divided into four chapters. The first chapter gave the scope of the survey, the second discussed cost of material, the third dealt with the cost of labour and the fourth was devoted to production and balance of value of production.

Composite Demonstration Data

Some data on cost of production of 'progressive', farmers are available from the records of Composite Demonstration organized in the districts

---

[4]Issued by the Cabinet Secretariat.

covered under the Intensive Agricultural District Programme. The data give estimates for two categories, viz. control costs and income and 'demonstration' costs and income, together with the yields in the two categories of plots. The costs relate to operational expenses only and do not include fixed costs. In West Godavari (Andhra Pradesh) and Thanjavur (Tamil Nadu), the Farm Management Specialists, appointed under the IADP, have been maintaining, for some years, farm records of the various farmers in the district. The records contain data on the input-output structure for the farm as a whole. Data on the various 'enterprises' are not separately recorded.

Farm Record Products

With a view to obtaining cost of production data under the improved levels of farm technology, the Agricultural Prices Commission in collaboration with the Directorate of Extension initiated a Farm Record Project in all the 15 IADP districts during 1966-67. A Farm Record Book was designed in consultation with the Directorate of Extension and the Farm Management Specialists of the IADP districts. The Record Book provided for collection of such data as would enable the Commission to get an estimate of the average cost of important crops in each of the IADP districts. Data were collected only from the progressive farmers. A 'progressive' farmer was defined as one for whom farm plans were prepared and actually implemented for the past three years. Equal representation was given to the small, medium and large farmers in the sample in each district.

After completing the preliminary work relating to the demarcation of zones, selection of tehsils, villages and holdings, the selected agencies in most of the States started field work under the scheme. In the States of Haryana, Madhya Pradesh, Punjab and Rajasthan, the collection of field data started from rabi 1970-71 and, in the remaining States, the field work under the scheme started subsequently at different points of time after February 1971. In some of these States, viz. Andhra Pradesh, Bihar, Kerala, Tamil Nadu and Uttar Pradesh, the field work started only in late 1971 and in West Bengal in early 1992; in some of the States, viz. Mysore, Tamil Nadu, Uttar Pradesh and West Bengal the collection of data was confined only to a part of the sample clusters selected for study.

COMPREHENSIVE SCHEME FOR STUDYING THE COST OF CULTIVATION OF PRINCIPAL CROPS

The need for collecting data on costs of cultivation/production of agricultural commodities on a comprehensive and continuing basis has been felt for a long time in the context of formulation of appropriate price policies for these commodities. No doubt, a number of studies providing, *inter alia*, data on cost of production were carried out in the past in different parts of the country. However, they did not quite meet the requirements of price policy as they were carried out at different times with diverse objectives by different agencies, did not follow uniform concepts, and as such, did not provide information for all the major crops on a comparable and comprehensive basis. The Government of India, therefore, set up, in 1967, a Standing Technical Committee on Indices of Input Costs to examine, among other things, the available data on cost of production of agricultural commodities collected through Farm Management Studies and other surveys, to make suggestions for bringing the available data-up-to-date and to advise on the scope and design of future surveys on cost of production proposed to be organized on a coordinated basis in different parts of the country.

The Standing Technical Committee examined the adequacy of the available data on cost of production of principal crops, the question of bringing them up-to-date and the manner of collecting fresh data in future so as to meet the requirements of price policy. It recommended, *inter-alia*, that a Comprehensive Scheme be introduced for studying the cost of cultivation of principal crops on an all-India basis. The Government of India accepted the recommendation and decided, in 1968, to launch the Comprehensive Scheme. After completion of preliminaries relating to the selection of agencies to be entrusted with the data collection work, finalization of samples to be studied, etc. the field work started in four States in 1970-71 and 12 other States subsequently, at different points of time.

The technical details of the Comprehensive Scheme were worked out by the Indian Institute of Agricultural Research Statistics in accordance with the recommendations of the Standing Technical Committee and were incorporated in the First Report of the Committee. These and the related matters such as the procedure for estimating the cost of cultivation/ production of the principal crops taken up for study, cost concepts followed and the programme of work under the Scheme are discussed below.

The Comprehensive Scheme envisages, collection of representative data on inputs and outputs and estimation of cost of cultivation per hectare and cost of production per quintal (different concepts) of the principal crops grown in the country. The study of different crops is taken up by rotation; a detailed survey is carried out in respect of principal crops, which may differ from State to State, for a period of one year followed by sub-sample surveys for the crops concerned in the subsequent few years. It may be added that, although for a particular year the samples for study are selected with reference to the specified principal crops, data are collected for all the crops grown on the sample holdings.

Cost accounting method has been adopted for purposes of collection of field data, which means that the data on inputs and outputs (both in physical as well as monetary terms) are collected by whole time fieldmen residing in the villages selected for study on the basis of day-to-day observations and contact with selected cultivators as various agricultural operations take place. The work of the fieldmen is supervised by Field Supervisors and a Field Officer in each State, who undertake frequent tours of the selected villages for this purpose as well as for providing on-the-spot guidance to the fieldmen, under the overall guidance of the Officer-in-Charge who is a senior officer of the Institution implementing the Scheme in the State concerned.

The responsibility relating to the field work under the Scheme has been entrusted, as recommended by the Standing Technical Committee, to the agricultural universities except in: (a) Gujarat, Himachal Pradesh, and Kerala, where the implementation has been entrusted to the Sardar Patel University, Vallabh Vidyanagar, Himachal Pradesh University, Simla and Kerala University, Trivandrum, respectively, and (b) the State of Jammu & Kashmir where the Scheme is to be implemented by the Directorate of Evaluation & Statistics, Government of Jammu & Kashmir. A special study on Cost of Cultivation of V.F.C. Tobacco, which is being taken up shortly, has been entrusted to the Directorate of Tobacco Development, Chennai. A Central Analytical Unit, headed by an officer-on-special duty (Cost of Production Studies), has also been set up in the Directorate of Economics and Statistics for undertaking the necessary coordination and supervision of the field work, the processing and analysis of the data collected under the Scheme and the preparation of reports thereon.

The design of the study is stratified three stage random sampling with tehsil as the primary sampling unit, a cluster of three villages as the secondary unit and an operational holding within the cluster as the third and ultimate stage sampling unit. For the purpose of the study, a State is demarcated into a number of homogenous zones having regard to the cropping pattern, irrigation, rainfall, soil types, etc. The total number of first stage units (i.e. Tehsils) to be selected for study in a State is also decided, taking into account the need for getting cost estimates with reasonable precision and the size of the State concerned. The first stage units are then allocated to the different zones in proportions of the area under the principal crop in the zones concerned to the total area under the crop in the State. From each zone, the allotted number of tehsils are selected with replacement and probability proportional to the area under the principal crop taken up for study. In each selected tehsil again, after selecting one nucleus village with varying probability as in the selection tehsils, a cluster of three villages is formed around the nucleus village as second stage unit. Finally, in each cluster, list of operational holdings[5] is prepared in an ascending order of their size and, after stratifying the holdings into five size-classes in such a manner that the total operated areas falling in the different size-classes are about equal, two holdings are randomly selected from each size-class. In addition, two progressive

---

[5]To be identified first as cultivators or potential cultivators of the crop concerned, in case of those crops which may be expected to be grown in much less than the total number of operational holdings in the cluster concerned.

farmers are also selected at random, if possible, otherwise purposively, for collection of data on newly developing technologies.

As already observed, a detailed survey in respect of a principal crop is to be followed by a sub-sample survey for it for a few years. The size of the sub-sample is generally one-fourth of the main sample. Thus if the main sample consists of 20 clusters of villages, the sub-sample would have five such clusters. For purposes of selection of the clusters for the subsample, they are first allocated to the different zones formed in the State in proportions, as far as possible, of the area under the principal crop in the zones concerned to the total area under the crop in the State. This done, the sub-sample clusters so allotted to the different zones are selected randomly without replacement from the clusters originally selected for the main sample in the zones concerned. In the clusters so selected, the same sample holdings continue to be studied as before when they were a part of the main sample.

One of the objectives of the Comprehensive Scheme is to ensure collection of cost data according to certain uniform concepts. It may be mentioned here that Cost A1 pertains to the paid-out costs or expenses incurred in cash and kind on material inputs, hired human labour, bullock and machine labour (both hired and owned), etc. When rent for leased-in land is added to Cost A1, one gets Cost A2, i.e. paid-out cost of a tenant cultivator. Cost B is obtained with the addition, to Cost A2, of the imputed rental value of owned land and interest on owned fixed capital, and total cost, i.e. Cost C with a further addition of the imputed value of the cultivator's family labour. Total cost (Cost C) can also be broken up into operational cost and fixed cost by regrouping its constituents. The operational cost includes, among other things, all the material and labour inputs; fixed cost is made up of these cost items which generally do not vary with the output. These cost concepts may be used both for cost of cultivation per hectare and cost of production per quintal in respect of individual holdings or group thereof (i.e. at cluster, zonal and State levels).

For purposes of cost estimation it becomes necessary to impute the value of owned inputs, allocate joint costs of different crop enterprises and so on; procedures generally adopted in this regard are also set out on the procedure for cost estimation is as follows. First, the estimates of cost of cultivation per hectare (different concepts) are made for individual size-classes within the clusters by dividing the total cost of cultivation (different concepts) of the two holdings selected in each of the size-classes in a cluster by the total area under the crop of the holdings concerned. These estimates for the size-classes in a cluster are then weighted in proportions of the areas[6] under the crop of all the holdings

---

[6]These areas are presently estimated by multiplying the averages of the areas under the crop of the two holdings selected in each of the different size-classes by the total number of the holdings in the size-classes concerned.

(selected as well as others) in the respective size-classes to the total area under the crop in the cluster as a whole so as to obtain the estimates of cost of cultivation per hectare at the cluster level. This done, simple averages of these cluster level estimates are taken to generate estimates at the zonal and State levels, the sample design being a self-weighted one.

The estimates of yield of the grain per hectare, its value per hectare, the value of the by-product per hectare, as well as the estimates per hectare of all the individual cost items, are also computed following the same procedure as that outlined above for estimation of the cost of cultivation per hectare.

The estimates of cost of production per quintal (different concepts) at the different groups levels are then derived by dividing the relevant estimates of cost of cultivation per hectare (net of the value of by-product) at these levels by the corresponding estimates of the yield per hectare.

If the data for all the clusters/zones are not available, due to non-response or for any other reason, computation of cost estimates ceases to be as simple as indicated in the preceding paragraphs, as this disturbs the self-weighting nature of the design. So, for getting representative estimates of different characteristics, recourse has to be taken to combining the estimates for different zones in proportion to the area under the principal crop selected for study. The estimates at the zonal level continue to be obtained, as when complete data available, as sample averages of the estimates in respect of the different clusters for which data are available. But as the numbers of clusters finally analyzed at the zonal levels may, in a few cases, be less than those planned, the cost estimates generated in the process may be subject to a greater margin of sampling error.

The procedure for estimation of cost at the State level on the basis of the data collected for the sub-sample is as follows. First, estimates of cost per hectare of the different cost items are made for individual size classes within the sub-sample clusters by dividing the total cost of the concerned items to the two holdings selected in each of the size-classes in a cluster by the total area under the crop of the holdings concerned. These estimates of the cost (per hectare) of individual items computed for the size-classes in a cluster are then weighted in proportions of the areas[7] under the respective holdings (selected as well as others) in the respective size-classes to the total area under the crop in the cluster as a whole and averaged so as to obtain the estimates of the cost per hectare of the different cost items at the cluster level. This done, simple averages of these cluster level estimates are taken to generate estimates at the zonal level. Zone-wise averages of the cost per hectare of the

---

[7]These areas are presently estimated by multiplying the averages of areas under the crop of the two holdings selected in each of the different size-classes by the total number of holdings in the size-classes concerned.

individual cost items are computed in this manner for both the base year (i.e. the year of the detailed survey) and the year under study. Relating the zone-wise estimates for the year under study to those in respect of the base year, both being based on the same clusters as are included in the sub-sample, the percentage variations between the two years in the costs per hectare of the individual cost items are worked out. The percentage variations thus obtained at the zonal level are then applied to the zone-wise estimates of the cost per hectare of the individual cost items generated for the base year on the basis of the complete sample studies then in order to compute similar zone-wise estimates for the year under study (i.e. the year of the sub-sample). These latter estimates are then weighted in proportion to the area under the crop in the different zones so as to arrive at the estimates of the cost per hectare of the individual cost items in the year under study, at the State level. The sum total of the State level estimates of cost per hectare of the individual cost item is taken to be the total cost of cultivation per hectare of the crop concerned during the year under study.

The State level estimates, for the year under study, of the yield per hectares as also the value thereof, and the value of by-product produced per hectare, are computed following the same procedure as adopted in respect of the individual cost items. This being done, the estimates of the cost of production per quintal of the crop concerned during the year under study is, obtained by dividing the State level estimate, for the year under study, of the total cost (Cost C) of cultivation per hectare (net of the estimated value of by-product per hectare) by the corresponding estimate of the yield per hectare.

In case it is desired to have a combined estimate of cost of production per quintal for two or three adjoining States with similar conditions of cultivation, the State-wise estimates of the cost of cultivation per hectare (net of the value of the by-product) and those of the yield per hectare would have to be put together using weights based on the State-wise areas under the crop concerned and then the combined estimate of cost of cultivation per hectare (net of the value of the by-product) divided by the combined estimate of the yield per hectare.

Along with the overall estimates of cost of production at the State level estimates of cost of production can be and are often made for specific sub-categories of operational holdings such as those growing high yielding varieties and others cultivating the local ones, those using bullock power and others using tractor power, and irrigated and unirrigated holdings. Also, estimates of the cost of production for crop other than the principal crop may be derived in respect of such of the selected holding as may have grown these crops. Since, however, the selection of the sample holdings is done with reference to the principal crop taken as a whole and not its sub-categories or crops other than the principal crop the cost estimates that may be generated for the sub-categories/ other crops may not be taken to be representative at the State level, but only suggestive or indicative of the cost conditions obtaining for them in areas to which they belong.

In addition to computation of estimates of cost of production of principal crops and specific categories thereof, other crops grown by the selected holdings, etc. it is proposed to study farm business income from crop production, yield response to fertilizer use in different size-classes of holdings, pattern of employment of family labour, marketed surplus and market dependence of the different size-classes of holdings, payments made to the factors of production in relation to their marginal productivities and so on. This naturally involves voluminous work. An idea of the volume of work involved in undertaking these studies can be had from the fact that the transfer of compiled data to flow in from the sixteen States where the field work is currently going on would mean punching and verification of 5 million cards; this would increase further as and when the Scheme is introduced in more States.

Naturally, safeguarding the quality of data is of crucial importance if the studies mentioned above are to yield reliable and worthwhile results. A number of steps are being taken towards this end. Supervision and on-the-spot guidance of the fieldmen working in the villages by the whole-time Field Supervisors and the Field Officers of the implementing agencies has already been referred to. The Officers of the Directorate of Economics & Statistics also visit the selected villages as and when necessary for an on-the-spot study of the field work being done there. In addition, both the implementing agencies and the Central Analytical Unit of the Directorate undertake detailed scrutiny of the data collected/compiled so as to iron out weak reporting cases before the final processing and analysis is undertaken. It may be added that Technical Workshops of the Officers-in-Charge and Field Officers of the implementing agencies as also the officials of this Directorate and Department of Agriculture are organized from time to time so as to exchange views and experience of the different implementing agencies in the matter of collection of data and maintenance of their quality apart from deciding on the programme of work to be undertaken in the different States.

Finally, it may be mentioned that the holding-wise data on cost of cultivation of the principal crops, together with the main results of analysis, are made available to the State Governments and the implementing agencies in the concerned States and also discussed with them so as to take into account their views on the subject before finalizing the reports on cost of production and forwarding them to the Commission far Agricultural Costs and Prices (CACP) for their reference.

As already observed, the field work under the Comprehensive Scheme is currently going on a sixteen States. In Jammu and Kashmir it is likely to be taken up in the near future. The field work for the special study of the Cost of Cultivation of VFC Tobacco is being collected in Andhra Pradesh.

The comprehensive scheme for studying the cost of cultivation of principal crops in India continued to be organized and coordinated by the

Department of Agriculture and Cooperation through the Directorate of Economics and Statistics during 1980. The cost estimates of principal crops selected in each State generated under the scheme were submitted to the Agricultural Prices Commission to assist in the formulation of price policy. During 1980-81, the scheme was in progress in 16 States and the State-level cost estimates were computed for paddy, wheat, jowar, bajra, maize, gram, barley, cotton, jute, groundnut, mustard and VFC tobacco. The field work had been entrusted to the Agricultural Universities which are the implementing agencies for the scheme. The Special Study on VFC Tobacco was, however, under the charge of the Directorate of Tobacco Development, Chennai. The implementing agencies had full responsibility for organizing the field work and for undertaking scrutiny and compilation of data. The compiled data received from the implementing agencies were processed and analyzed in the Directorate of Economics and Statistics in consultation with the concerned implementing agencies. The State Governments' views were ascertained on State-level estimates of cost of cultivation/production in finalizing them.

The working of the cost of cultivation scheme on aspects such as scope, methodology, organization and related matters was reviewed during 1980 by a Special Expert Committee on Cost of Production Estimates under the Chairmanship of Dr. S.R. Sen. The report of the Committee was accepted by the Government and the recommendations were implemented.

Design of Study and Method of Estimation

The design of the study is stratified three stage random sampling with tehsil as the primary sampling unit, a cluster of three villages as the second stage unit and operational holding within the cluster as the third and ultimate stage sampling unit. For the purpose of the study, a State is demarcated into a number of homogenous zones having regard to the cropping pattern, irrigation, rainfall, soil types, etc. The total number of first stage units (i.e. tehsil) to be selected for study in a State is also decided taking into account the need for getting cost estimates with reasonable precision and the size of the State concerned. The first stage units are then allocated to the different zones in proportions of the areas under the principal crop in the zones concerned to the total area under the crop in the State. From each zone, the allotted number of tehsils are selected with replacement and probability proportional to the area under the principal crop taken up for study. In each selected tehsil again, after selecting one nucleus village with varying probability as in the selection of Tehsils a cluster of three villages is formed around the nucleus village as second stage unit. Finally, in each cluster, a list of operational holdings is prepared in an ascending order of their size and after stratifying the holdings into five size-classes in such a manner that the total operated areas falling in the different size-classes are about equal, two holdings are randomly selected from each size-class.

Under the Comprehensive Scheme, a detailed survey in respect of a principal crop is to be followed by a sub-sample survey for it for a few years. The size of the sub-sample is generally one-fourth of the main sample, Thus, it the main sample consists of 20 clusters of villages, the sub-sample would have five such clusters. For purposes of selection of the clusters for the sub-sample, they are first allocated to the different zones formed in the State in proportions, as far as possible, of the areas under the principal crop in the zones concerned to the total area under the crop in the State. This done, the sub-sample clusters so allotted to the different zones are selected randomly without replacement from the clusters originally selected for the main sample in the zones concerned. In the clusters to selected, the same sample holdings continue to be studied as before when they were a part of the main sample.

Method of estimation of various items of cost of cultivation per hectare for the principal crop in cases where the cost analysis is based on the main sample, is as follows:

Let Y_{ijkl}, A_{ijkl} be the cost of cultivation and area under the principal crop respectively of the lth holding in the kth size-class of the jth cluster in the ith zone. The estimate of cost per hectare for the kth size-class is given by

$$Y_{ujk} = \sum_{l=1}^{2} Y_{ijkl} \Big/ \sum_{l=1}^{2} A_{ijkl} \tag{1}$$

The estimate of cost per hectare in the jth cluster (i.e. jth tehsil as *there is only* one cluster in each tehsil) is given by,

$$Y_{ij} = \sum_{k=1}^{5} Y_{ijk} \times W_{ijk} \tag{2}$$

where $W_{ijk} = \dfrac{X_{ijk} \sum\limits_{l=1}^{2} a_{ykl}}{\sum\limits_{k=1}^{5} X_{ijk} \sum\limits_{l=1}^{2} a_{ijkl}}$

X_{ijk} is the total area under the principal crop in the kth size-class in the jth cluster of the ith zone. As the tehsils are selected with probability proportional to area under the crop, the estimate for the ith zone is given by

$$\bar{y}_i = \frac{1}{n_i} \sum_{j=1}^{n_i} \bar{y}_{ij} \tag{3}$$

where n_i is the number of cluster selected from the ith zone.

As the number of tehsils in different zones is in proportion of the areas under the principal crop in the zones to the total area under the crop in the State as a whole, the estimate for the State as a whole is given by

$$\bar{y} = \frac{\sum\limits_{i=1}^{m} n_i Y_i}{\sum\limits_{i=1}^{m} n_i} \qquad (4)$$

where m is the number of zones.

If the number of cluster and zones analyzed are less than those originally planned, due to non-response the self weighting nature of the sample design is disturbed. Equations (3) and (4) above have, therefore, to be modified as follows in order to derive the estimates of cost of cultivation.

The estimates for the ith zone is given by

$$Y'_i = \frac{1}{n'_i} \sum\limits_{j=1}^{n'_i} Y^1_{ij} \qquad (5)$$

where n'_i is the number of respondent clusters in the ith zone $(n_i \, L_{ni}')$.

The estimates for the State as a whole/group of zone in the State is given by

$$\overline{}^1 Y = \sum\limits_{i=1}^{m'} A_i \, \bar{Y}^1_i / \sum\limits_{i=1}^{m'} A_i \qquad (6)$$

where A_i is the area under the principal crop in the ith zone and m' is the number of respondent zones $(m' \, Lm)$.

Thee method of estimation of yield per hectare for the principal crop is the same as that given above in respect of cost of cultivation per hectare.

The estimates of cost of production per quintal at different levels are derived by dividing the estimates at the corresponding levels of the cost of cultivation per hectare (net of the value of the by-product) by those of the yield per hectare.

The method of cost estimation in cases where the analysis is based on the sub-sample is as under:

Estimates of cost per hectare of the different cost items at the cluster level were obtained for the crop season under study in the same manner as indicated for the main sample in paragraph four.

Let S_{ij} be the estimate of cost per hectare in the jth cluster of the ith zone.

The cost per hectare for the ith zone during the season under study is obtained by

$$S_i = \frac{\sum\limits_{j=1}^{L_i} S_j}{\sum\limits_{j=1}^{L} S'_{ij}} \times S'_i \tag{7}$$

where L is the number of clusters selected from the ith zone s'_{ij} is the cost per hectare for the jth cluster of ith zone in the base year and s'_i is the cost per hectare in the ith zone in the base year. The estimate of cost per hectare at the State level are obtained by combining the estimates for different zones in proportion to the area under the crop.

$$S = \frac{\sum\limits_{i=1}^{M} A_i S_j}{\sum\limits_{i=1}^{M} A_i} \times S'_i \tag{8}$$

where A_i is the area under the crop in the ith zone and S_i the total number of zones.

The same procedure as above is followed for obtaining the yield per hectare and the value of the by-product per hectare at the zonal and State levels.

The cost of production per quintal is obtained by dividing the cost per hectare (net of the value of by-product) by the yield per hectare at the State levels.

Concepts of the Costs and Procedure for Evaluation and Allocation of Joint Costs

I. *Components of Costs.* A number of cost concepts such as Cost A_1, Cost A_2, Cost B, and Cost C have been followed in the analysis. The input items included under each category of cost are indicated below:

Cost A_1 = (i) Value of hired human labour,
(ii) Value of hired bullock labour.
(iii) Value of owned bullock labour,
(iv) Hired machinery charges.
(v) Value of owned machine labour.
(vi) Value of seed (both farm produced and purchased)

(vii) Value of insecticides and pesticides.
(viii) Value of manure (owned and purchased)
 (ix) Value of fertilizers.
  (x) Depreciation on implements and farm buildings.
 (xi) Irrigation charges.
(xii) Land revenue, cesses and other taxes.
(xiii) Interest on working capital.
(xiv) Miscellaneous expenses (Artisans, etc.),

B_1 = Cost A_1 + Imputed interest on owned fixed capital (excluding land). Interest on value of owned fixed capital assets (excluding land)

Cost A_2 = Cost A_1 + Rent paid for leased-in-land.

Cost B = Cost A_2 + Imputed rental value of owned land (less revenue paid thereon)

Cost C = Cost B + Imputed value of family labour.

The individual cost items included in total cost, that is Cost C, can also be grouped into operational and fixed costs as under:

Operational = Value of family labour.
Costs + Value of hired human labour.
+ Value of hired and owned bullock labour.
+ Value of hired and owned machine labour.
+ Value of seeds (farms grown and purchased).
+ Value of manure and fertilizers.
+ Value of insecticides and pesticides.
+ Irrigation charges.
+ Interest on working capital.
+ Miscellaneous expenses (Artisans, etc.).

Fixed costs = Cost C—Operational costs.

II. Procedure for Imputation of Values of Owned Inputs. Some of the inputs used in the production process come from family resources. In computing the cost of cultivation, it is necessary to impute value of these owned inputs. The procedures used for the imputation of values for such inputs are indicated below:

Item	*Procedure*
1. Family labour	On the basis of wages of attached farm servants. Since not all the farmers have attached servants, average per day rate has been estimated for the cluster as a whole by relating the total wages of the attached servants to their employment and then used for evaluation of family labour.
2. Owned bullock labour.	On the basis of cost of maintenance of bullocks which includes the following items:— (i) Cost of green and dry fodder. (ii) Cost of concentrates.

(iii) Depreciation on animals and cattle sheds.

(iv) Upkeep labour charges.

(v) Other expenses, if any.

From the total of the above, the value of dung produced, and receipts, if any, against hiring out of the bullocks are deducted to get the net maintenance cost. In the case of labour charges on upkeep and depreciation on cattle sheds, details of which are available for all the livestock together, apportionment as between the draught animals and other categories has been done on the basis of numbers of standard units in the different categories, which are:

(i) Bullock, cow, buffalo, horse above 2 years	One animal unit.
(ii) Camel above 2 years	Two animal units
(iii) Sheep or goat	1/5 animal unit.
(iv) Young stock between one and two years	1/2 animal unit.
(v) Young stock below one year.	1/4 animal unit.

In the even of death of a draught animal, the inventory value (less the value of hide and skin) is charged to the maintenance account. The net maintenance cost has been related to the hours of employment of draught animals and wage rate per work hour so estimated used in evaluating the bullock labour cost for individual crops.

3. Owned machinery charges — The rate of expenditure per hour of machinery utilization has been estimated by relating total maintenance expenditure (including depreciation) to the number of hours of use. This rate has been applied to the hours of utilization of the concerned machinery on the individual crops.

4. Implements — Depreciation and charges on account of minor repairs.

5. Owned seed — Farm produced seed has been evaluated at the village prices prevalent at the time of sowing.

6. Farm produced manure — Evaluated at rates prevalent in the villages.

7. Rent on owned land.	Estimated on the basis of : (a) prevalent rents in the villages for identical types of land, or (b) the total value of output (main product and the by-product) taken together, (c) the capital value of land.
· 8. Interest on owned fixed capital	Interest on the present value of fixed assets (excluding land) such as farm buildings,, implements and machinery, irrigation, structures and equipment, livestock (only draught animals) has been charged at the rate of six per cent per annum.
9. Interest on working capital	Interest has been charged at the rate of ten per cent per annum for a period of three months on the working capital, i.e. cash or kind expenses (excluding items in respect of which payments are generally made after harvest, i.e. , rent, land revenue etc.) incurred during the period of cultivation.
10. Kind payments and perquisites	The kind payments have been evaluated at prices prevalent in the villages at the time of payments. Perquisites have been included in kind payments and evaluated at market prices.

III. *Procedure for Imputation of Value of the Main Product and the By-product.* The value of the main product and the by-product and the by-product are imputed at the post-harvest prices prevailing in the selected clusters of villages.

IV. *Allocation of Joint Costs to Different Crop Enterprises.* The expenditure incurred or imputed for some of the input items relate to the whole or a part of the farm. For the purpose of computing the cost of cultivation of individual crops, it is necessary to allocate the joint costs among individual crops, main and by-product and among different categories of livestock, as the case may be, on the basis of certain principals. The procedures followed are indicated below:

A. *Allocation of Cost to Individual Crops*

(a) Depreciation on farm buildings	In proportion to the acreage under the crops. In case buildings are used only for a particular crop, the whole amount has been charged to that crop.
(b) Depreciation on Implements.	Normally, the depreciation is allocated in proportion to the human/bullock labour inputs in each crop. However since necessary data in

this regard were not available for the entire year, allocation has been done in proportion to the area under the crop.

(c) Rent of leased-in land and rental value of owned land. •
: In proportion to the area under the crop.

(d) Land revenue, cesses and taxes
: Same as in (c)

(e) Interest on owned fixed capital.
: Same as in (c)

B. *Allocation of Cost between Main Product (Grain) and By-product (Bhusa).*

The value of by-product (bhusa) has been deducted from the gross cost of cultivation to get the cost of cultivation of the main product.

V. *Procedure for the Evaluation of Farm Assets.*

1. Owned and self cultivated land
: Self cultivated land evaluated at rates prevalent in the village taking into account the differences in type of soil, distance from village, source of irrigation, etc.

2. Farm buildings (cattle sheds, storage sheds, etc.)
: Evaluated at prices prevailing in the villages

3. Implements and other farm machinery.
: Evaluated at prevailing market prices.

4. Livestock (draught animals)
: Evaluated at market prices. Even if the age of animal exceeds the age at which the value of animal is supposed to have depreciated fully, the prevailing market value is taken.

In addition to the demand for cost estimates of principal crops required by the Agricultural Prices there has been a growing demand in recent years for supply of cost estimates of other crops like urad, moong, tur, rapeseed and mustard, soybean, sunflowerseed, potato, onion, etc. Other agencies like the Planning Commission, Central Statistical Organization. State Governments, Universities, Research Bodies, Members of Parliament have also shown keen interest in the cost estimates of various crops. The scheme has gained greater importance with the Government decision to fix support prices of various agricultural commodities. Recently, the Government have revised the terms of reference of the Agricultural Prices which enjoins upon that organization to make price support recommendations for a wide range of crops. APC has accordingly requested the Directorate of Economics and Statistics to extend the coverage under this scheme to meet their revised terms of reference. The name of the commission has been changed to 'Commission for Agricultural costs and Prices' (CACP).

The Government of India again appointed in 1990 an Expert Committee for Review of Methodology of Cost of Production of Crops. Partially modifying the recommendation of this Committee relating to valuation of labour, the Government decided that the basis of valuation of labour should be statutory wage rate or the actual market rate whichever is higher. The Government also accepted the Committee's recommendation relating to computation of a separate Cost (Cost C3) in order to account for managerial input of the farmers.

Sampling Design of the Scheme

The design of the Scheme continues to be a three-stage stratified random sampling design with tehsils as the first stage unit, village/cluster of villages into homogeneous agro-climatic zones based on cropping pattern, soil type, rainfall, etc. The primary sampling units (tehsils) are allocated to different zones in proportion to the total area of all crops covered in the study. The primary sampling units are selected in each zone (stratum) with probability proportional to the area under the selected crops, and with replacement. Within each tehsil, the village/cluster is also selected following the same procedure. In each selected village/cluster, all the operational holdings are enumerated and classified according to size into 5 size classes, the class limits being fixed uniformly for all villages/clusters. In each size class, two holdings are selected by simple random sampling without replacement. However, if in any village/cluster, a particular size class does not contain even two holdings, more holdings are selected from the adjacent size classes to make up the deficit.

In view of the growing demands for the cost data and the observation on the existing scheme by Parliamentary Committee on Public Undertaking and by others, the Government of India appointed a High-Power Special Expert Committee in 1979 to go into the working of the existing scheme and make necessary recommendations. One of the major recommendations of the Committee relates to change in the approach towards sampling design of the scheme. The Committee also recommended switch-over from the existing single-crop approach to crop-complex approach under which cost estimates will be available for a number of crops. These recommendations have been accepted and implemented, for 1981-82.

REGIONAL OR CENTRAL SERIES OF INDEX NUMBERS

On the basis of data collected during the studies in the economics of farm management, the following 12 indices are constructed under the 'Scheme for Compilation of Indicators in the sphere of Agricultural Economy'.

1. Index Numbers of Wages of Field Labourers   Unpublished
2. Index Numbers of Farm Prices   "
3. Index Numbers of Prices Received   "
4. Index Numbers of Farm Cost   "
5. Index Numbers of Cost of Cultivation—
   Major Crops   "
6. Index Numbers of Cost of Production—
   Major Crops   "
7. Index Numbers of Gross Value of Farm
   Production   "
8. Index Numbers of Quantities Marketed—
   Major Crops   "
9. Index Numbers of Stocks   "
10. Index Numbers of Farm Employment   "
11. Index Numbers of Non-Farm Employment   "
12. Index Numbers of Total Employment   "

The scheme is in operation in 9 centres at present. The base period for each centre is the same as the period of farm management enquiry in that centre, viz. 1954-55 to 1956-57 for Amritsar and Ferozepur (Punjab), Meerut and Muzaffarpur (Uttar Pradesh), Salem and Coimbatore (Madras), Hooghly and 24-Parganas (West Bengal) and Ahmedabad and Nasik (Maharashtra) and 1955-56 to 1956-57 for Akola and Amravati (Maharashtra) and 1957-58 to 1959-60 for West Godavari (Andhra Pradesh), Sambalpur (Orissa) and Monghyr (Bihar). These indicators are constructed with a view to measuring changes in certain important aspects of rural economy with the help of additional information collected on key items in the subsequent years in comparison with the base line data thrown up by the farm management studies.

An attempt has also been made to test the efficiency of the various index numbers constructed under this scheme by comparison with such comparable estimates as are available. The results of this test have shown that the trend in wages and prices as revealed by the indices constructed under the Indicators Scheme shows consistency over time except in the case of Punjab and U.P. centres. Even in these centres, the trends of prices and wages appear to be better revealed by these indices than the trends revealed by agricultural wages and harvest prices data collected through the staff of State Governments. With regard to seasonal variations in wages, the Indicators Scheme data show more or less consistent rising trend of wages during the harvest period, while the agricultural wages data do not reveal any such consistent tendency. The weighting diagram of the Indicators Scheme compared with the structure of costs obtained from the ICAR studies reveals that the input structure has not undergone any significant change over the period.

DEFICIENCIES IN THE EXISTING DATA

As discussed earlier, a number of surveys have been carried out in the different regions in the country to collect information on cost of production of various crops. The Farm Management Studies too *inter alia* give information about cost of production of various crops. These surveys and studies carried out at different times with diverse objectives by different agencies have not followed uniform concepts and do not provide information for all the major crops on a comparable basis. Most of them were not specifically designed to collect data on cost with a view to formulating price policy at the national and State level.

The coverage of the Farm Management Studies, sponsored by the Directorate of Economics and Statistics, is confined to one or two selected districts, representing a typical soil-crop complex in each State covered by these studies. Thus, although these studies give detailed data in respect of the inputs and outputs for the different crops cultivated and for other enterprises carried out on sample farms, the data cannot be regarded as representative of the States covered. The sampling design followed for these studies until 1966-67 was such that small farms received weightage, despite their relatively limited importance insofar as marketable surplus is concerned. This deficiency sets a boundary to the usefulness of the cost data collected under these studies. The sample design has been modified in the case of studies taken up under the Fourth Five Year Plan so that a part of this defect could be removed.

The studies carried out by the ICAR are aimed at studying the cost of cultivation of particular crops. They generally cover crop tracts extending over several States. As such, these studies are more comprehensive from the point of view of area coverage than the Farm Management Studies. However, their results are also subject to many limitations. In the earlier studies relating to cost of cultivation of sugarcane, attention was concentrated only on sugarcane. In the more recent studies relating to cost of cultivation of cotton, an attempt has, however, been made to collect information about cotton as well as its rotation crops. Although the ICAR studies are designed to provide an estimate of cost for a State as a whole, holding-wise information about the output of crops has not been recorded for all the holdings under each study and for all the years. In the case of cotton and its rotation crops, cost estimates have been presented separately for small, medium and large farms. However, the classification adopted for categorizing the farm into small, medium and large is such that the upper limit for the small farms is itself very high, being around 15 acres. There is also considerable disagreement about certain imputation procedures adopted for these studies.

The NSS studies have covered different regions without any particular reference to the crop complex or crop tracts having predominance of particular crops. The data collected under these studies would be of limited use for price policy, as these studies cover only certain aspects of cost of cultivation. The household has been used as the sampling unit in these studies, where the holding is a more appropriate sampling unit for getting reliable data on cost of cultivation. Moreover, the NSS studies have relied primarily on the 'survey' method for the collection of data, which has considerable memory bias and is not generally regarded as a reliable method for the collection of data on cost of cultivation of particular crops.

The Cost of Production Surveys conducted by the State Government and local organizations, have limited coverage and scope and are meant to provide answers to specific local problems.

In order that the estimates of cost of production may be useful for price policy, it is necessary to decide about the components of cost that will be relevant from this point of view. Among the concepts of cost used in the various studies are the following four concepts been used in the Farm Management Studies:

Cost A_1 = Cash and kind expenses (or paid out costs) actually incurred by owner operator. These include cash and kind expenditure on items like hired human labour, owned and hired bullock labour, seed, manure, fertilizers, land revenue and cess, irrigation charges, depreciation charges of implements, machinery and buildings and interest on crop loans.

Cost A_2 = Cost A_1 + rent paid for leased-in land.

Cost B = Cost A_2 + rental value of owned land and interest on owned fixed capital excluding land.

Cost C = Cost B + imputed value of family labour.

In the Studies of Cost of Production of Sugarcane and Cotton sponsored by the erstwhile Commodity Committee of the ICAR too, varying concepts have been used, which differ from those used in the Farm Management Studies. These divergencies are still wider for the Studies sponsored by the State Governments.

In addition, there is lack of uniformity between the various studies also in regard to procedures for evaluation. For example, differences in procedures for evaluating family labour are observed between the Farm Management Studies and the Cost of Cultivation Studies carried out by the ICAR and the erstwhile Commodity Committees. The cost of family labour constitutes a considerable part of the total cost of an average Indian farm. In the Farm Management Studies, the family labour has generally been evaluated according to the wages paid to permanent farm servants; under the ICAR studies, going casual labour rates in the respective regions have been adopted for the purpose. The NSS studies do not seem to have included family labour as an element of cost.

Similarly, different procedures have been adopted insofar as imputation of managerial allowance is concerned. While the Farm Management Studies do not make any allowance for managerial responsibilities, in the studies carried out by the Sugarcane Committee, allowance of managerial responsibilities has been provided on the following basis:

(i) The imputed value of labour put in per acre of sugarcane per adult male family member. (This is intended to compensate the farmer for different kinds of work off the field.)

(ii) Plus 10 per cent of gross income from produce. (This is to remunerate the former for the managerial responsibilities undertaken by him.)

In the Study of Farm Management and Cost of Production conducted by the Government of West Bengal, allowance for management has been imputed at the rate of 7 per cent of the costs incurred.

The Agricultural Prices Commission has commented that while multistage stratified random sampling design has been adopted for the Farm Management Studies, the estimates of cost are not properly weighted. Analysis of the data as collected is not geared to provide answers to the specific issues relevant to the task of taking decisions about prices either. For instance, not all the Farm Management Reports present data on the frequency distribution of farms by categories of cost. The estimates of expenses actually incurred in cash are not available in all the studies. The studies carried out by the ICAR suffer from similar limitations. They do not give information on frequency distribution of cost classes, nor on relationships between different costs and sizes of farms. The estimates of crop yields are based on crop-cutting experiments wherever such data were considered adequate and on unofficial estimates of production in other cases. Holding-wise production data are generally not available.

A general limitation of all the cost studies carried out so far is that they do not give estimates of cost of production according to varieties of crops and according to the type of technology used.

The other serious difficulty arises from the fact that the data were collected at different points of time and in several cases may have become out of date. The first series of Farm Management Studies were carried out, as far back as 1954-55 to 1956-57, and further studies have been undertaken at varying periods in different regions in the country, with the result that their results are neither strictly comparable nor can they be aggregated. The studies carried out by the NSS mostly relate to the period 1951-53, the data obtained are likely to have become obsolete by now. The same difficulty is met with in the case of studies carried out by the other agencies and the State Government.

In order that comparable data on cost for various regions and crops in the country would be made available, certain basic issues must first be resolved. The data should be such as would fulfil the requirements for the formulation of price policy. Some of the issues needing consideration in this connection are the objectives of the price policy, the recognized components of costs, the agency whose cost should be taken into account and the level to which the estimates should pertain, i.e. State, Region, etc.

The objectives of agricultural price support policy can be and have in fact been diverse in different countries. In the main, the price support policy can be either income-oriented or production-oriented. While in our present conditions the requirements of production have to be given a high priority, it would still be necessary to keep in view the interest of small farmers. Another issue posed sometimes is whether in formulating price policy, we are concerned with: (i) the relative profitability of agriculture as a whole vis-a-vis other sectors, or with (ii) the allocation of resources between the various crops at a given time. These alternatives, in a way, represent long-term and short-term objectives. While in the long run resource shifts might take place between agriculture and the other sectors of the economy, in the short term resource shifts might take place only between crops.

Another important issue is: (i) while costs, and (ii) whose costs are relevant for determining price policy. As indicated above, different concepts of costs have been used in the Cost of Cultivation and Farm Management Studies carried out so far. A view has been expressed that only the 'paidout costs' should be taken into consideration while determining minimum support prices; on the other hand some other interests have strongly argued that the total cost (Cost 'C' of the Farm Management Study) should form the basis of minimum support prices. It has also to be recognized that 'purchasable physical inputs', viz. interest on capital—working or fixed—employed and other essential tariffs like irrigation rates and land revenue, are important elements of cost. Whereas the concept of the marginal variable cost would be relevant for price policy in the short term, fixed capital is an important factor in the long run; it might be necessary to determine how much of the national capital is of the fixed type. While working out the cost estimates for the individual crops, it would also be necessary to keep in view the elements of joint cost, since the fixed cost incurred on different items such as land shaping, bunding and irrigation channels would be distributed over the different crops.

Allowances for family labour and managerial skill, as mentioned above, have been treated differently under the different studies conducted in the past. While economists in general maintain that it is essential to make allowance for family labour in the estimation of cost, there is a view that it would be unrealistic to do so, since the particular cost of family labour is in most cases likely to be marginal or nil. The controversy boils down to specifying the opportunity cost of family labour. A further problem is the rate at which the family labour should be evaluated. The inclusion of family labour also gives rise to the peculiar dilemma that the higher the cost the higher is the income since part of the cost is income. It is not, however, considered necessary to make a separate provision for managerial allowance. Any profits earned by the farmer over and above the normal cost would represent the compensation for his managerial responsibilities.

The other problems relate to yet other components of cost and the procedures for their imputation. Very few of the inputs used in agriculture are standardized. Extreme variations in the quality of inputs such as land, bullock labour, seeds, etc. can be noticed; yet these inputs are generally treated as homogeneous in quality.

A basic issue involved in the computation of cost for the fixation of prices is the determination of the parties whose cost of production should be taken as the basis for price fixation. These types of cost estimates have been suggested as relevant:

(a) The average cost of all farmers;
(b) The average cost of the efficient farmers; and
(c) The bulk-line cost.

Of the above approaches the first has some merits as well as limitations. The concept of average cost of all farmers, has relevance for price determination only if the variance in costs is not too wide. In case the inter-farm variance is very large, a majority of the farmers may have costs higher than the average. The argument advanced for linking price to the average cost of the efficient farmers is that it should be the objective of price policy to reward efficiency. However, in order to translate this approach into practice, the question of defining the efficient farmers has to be satisfactorily resolved. Efficiency is by definition a relative concept. Various measures of efficiency have been employed in the Farm Management Studies. Efficiency can be viewed from the point of view of the efficient use of land resources, or that of labour or capital. Efficiency can also be measured by the degree of correspondence between marginal productivities of these inputs and their respective prices. Again, the question of efficiency of resources used in relation to a particular activity on the farm can be differentiated from the efficiency of the resources used for all types of activities on the farm. Further, it may also be necessary to distinguish between economic efficiency and technological efficiency.

Another approach suggested is that bulk-line cost should be taken into account for price fixation. The bulk-line cost has been defined as that cost which would cover, say, the cost of producing 85 per cent of the total output. Assuming that the farms are arranged in an ascending order by reference to the unit costs of production, the bulk-line cost is the marginal cost of producing the 85th unit of total output. The main difficulty in this case is that of the divergence in the cost estimates when the 85 per cent coverage concept is applied exclusively to production, ignoring the coverage of the area under the crop or the number of holdings. It is likely that the bulk-line cost as related to output may not cover the cost of production for a significant proportion of the holdings. It would not, therefore, be appropriate to use bulk-line cost relating to a specified percentage of production, area or number of farmers as the basis for estimation of cost. Since the notion of marginal cost implied in this case is related to demand, which is likely to vary over time, it is felt that a more suitable approach would be to forecast the demand and then to determine the marginal cost of the supply, which would meet the demand.

The basic question involved is to determine the likely level of marginal cost involved for achieving the production targets of particular crops in the different States and regions in the country.

It may be that in deciding upon the elements of price policy, different approaches may have to be followed under different situations over a period of time. This would indicate the need for collecting the maximum possible information about cost of production. It would be necessary to cover all types of farms and study the relationship between farm-size and the cost of production. It may be left to the agency responsible for formulating price policy to decide as to what type of data it would use.

Another basic question in formulating estimates of cost is the level to which these estimates should pertain, i.e. whether they should be on district, State or regional basis. As the major policy decisions are taken at the State levels, it may be necessary in due course to have State-wise estimates. In case, conditions differ significantly within a State, separate estimates may be required also for different regions or districts in the State. All-India estimates would still be needed to obtain a broad picture of the variations occurring in the costs of particular crops in the country as a whole. These data compiled by the Directorate of Economics and Statistics (Ministry of Agriculture) are published by them and the latest one is 'cost of cultivation of Principal Crops, 1997-98. The Commission on Agricultural Costs and Prices also publishes the latest available data in their different reports.

20

Agricultural Prices

OBJECTIVES

Regular collection of data on prices of agricultural commodities is needed by the Government for its policy decisions and by the trade organizations for sale and purchase business. Price-data is required not only for the formulation of current policy and for planning of future programmes but also for assessment of progress in the implementation of these policies and plans. For this purpose the trends in price levels are relatively more important than the absolute prices. The trading organizations on the other hand, are interested more in actual prices than in price-trends. In order to meet the demands of various sections the reporting of prices according to uniform definitions and concept is very important. This involves specification of stage of marketing, variety of a commodity and its quality, unit of quotation etc. Following the broad frame-work laid down by the Agricultural Prices Enquiry Committee, 1954 fairly detailed, comprehensive and reliable data on prices of agricultural commodities are available in India.

TYPES OF PRICES

Agricultural commodities are often exchanged several times at different prices between the stage at which these leave the producer and that at which they reach the ultimate consumer. The price which the farmer gets for his commodity at the village site is known as the 'farm (harvest) price'. The price which the ultimate consumer pays specially for relatively small transactions is the 'retail price'. The prices in between these two are known as 'wholesale prices'. There are three types of wholesale prices accordingly as the commodity passes through the primary, the secondary and the terminal markets. Generally the primary wholesale price is closer to the farm price. The margin between these two prices is accounted for by the incidental charges such as *'Aratdars'* commission charges for bagging, weighing, storage, transport, etc. The terminal wholesale price is generally nearer to the retail price. The difference between the terminal wholesale price and the retail price is composed of retailer's profit, transport, storage, packing and other incidental charges. The term agricultural prices covers wholesale, retail and harvest prices of agricultural commodities as well as those of livestock and livestock products. For a proper understanding of the subject, each of these has been discussed separately.

Wholesale Price

Connotation The wholesale price is generally taken as the rate at which relatively large transactions of purchase are effected for further sale. The quotation should relate to the actual price at which transaction takes place irrespective of the terms of contract and without excluding the incidental charges, if these are normally included in the price quoted.

Frequency The wholesale prices are collected on Friday every week. Where the markets are held on specified days of the week the prices reported relate to the market day preceding Friday. If the day fixed for the price reporting happens to be a holiday, the price quoted relates to the previous working day.

Crop and Variety Specification The variety and the quality of the commodity to which the price relates is specified for each market. If only a single variety is commonly transacted and its arrivals are continuous throughout the year, then this variety is selected for quoting the price. Sometimes two or three varieties which are commonly transacted are selected for price-reporting.

Sometimes when the old stock of a commodity is marketed, new crop also comes to the market. Generally, there is price differences between the old and the new crops. In such cases, the prices of both old and new crops are quoted for 4 to 6 weeks since the arrival of the new crops and thereafter the quotation for old crop is dropped.

Time for Reporting There are variations in the quotations through time due to genuine factors of demand and supply. Generally, 4 possible types of quotations are observed, viz. opening, closing, maximum and minimum. The opening quotation represents the anticipation of the current day's supply and demand position and is not influenced directly by the day's supply and demand factors. The closing quotation is the resultant of the supply and demand position of the current day. The maximum and minimum levels attained during the day represent the range between the extreme points of equilibrium and at different times of the day depending again on the factors of demand and supply operating at the respective points of equilibrium. One should not compare the maximum of one day with the minimum or even average of another. Earlier, the wholesale prices reported referred to the closing quotation of the day in most of the cases. On the recommendation of the Agricultural Prices Enquiry Committee, the quotations now relate to the modal price, i.e. the price at which most of the transactions take place during the peak period of marketing. Where even during this period there does not exist a single quotation but a range of quotations, the one at which most of the transactions take place is quoted. The peak period need not be the same hour of the day throughout the season or the year.

Centres The Agricultural Prices Enquiry Committee suggested in consultation with the State Governments a list of Centres from which the prices data should be collected. The prices regarding cereals and pulses are being obtained regularly by the Directorate of Economics and Statistics, Ministry of Agriculture and also by States. The Directorate obtains tele-graphically daily wholesale prices of foodgrains in respect of 140 markets covering primary, secondary and terminal markets. Weekly wholesale prices are collected from about 530 markets in respect of 130 agricultural commodities. The price data of cereals are also obtained from different centres spread throughout the country for the purpose of building price index.

In India there are about 4,145 regular wholesale markets besides over 22,000 periodical markets or in *mandis* held bi-weekly or fortnightly all rural areas. Of the total number of wholesale markets, 2,936 have already been regulated and the scope of regulation is being gradually extended to others.

Historical Development

The earliest series of wholesale prices data available in the country related to 1897 and were published in 'Prices and Wages', a publication issued by the Department of Commercial Intelligence and Statistics. Government of India, up to 1922. The series of index numbers of wholesale prices with 1873 as the base were published continuously by the same Department in their 'Index Numbers of Indian Prices' (1861-1931) with annual addenda.

The data were mainly based on the reports received from the selected commercial bodies at the important market centres. The compilation of these index numbers was discontinued from 1940. The Report on the Enquiry into the Rise of Prices in India, 1914, by K.L. Datta also published a good deal of data on prices for the period 1890-1912.

Another price series, viz. 'Wholesale Prices of Certain Selected Articles at Various Centres in India' was published in the *Indian Trade Journal* from January 1931 to September 1939 and subsequently continued as a separate publication till 1950, when it was discontinued.

Before World War II, the price data collected and published by the Department of Commercial Intelligence and Statistics related only to a few important markets. When controls and restrictions were imposed on movement, etc. of foodgrains during the War, the data being collected were found inadequate to meet the requirements. The then Department of Food started collecting prices from a large number of centres in the country. All this work was later on centralized in the Directorate of Economics and Statistics, Ministry of Agriculture. Arrangements were made to obtain regularly the requisite data relating to wholesale prices of cereals and gram from about 600 centres distributed all over the country, every week by telegram.

Wholesale prices prevailing during the harvesting season were also being collected previously by the Imperial (State) Bank of India through its branches and Pay Offices. These data which were unutilized before, were also made use of by the Directorate.

Wholesale prices are now collected mostly under the Market Intelligence Scheme of the Directorate of Economics and Statistics. The centres selected for the collection of prices are distributed all over the country and are so chosen as to represent all the important *mandies*, rural and urban in the producing and consuming and surplus, deficit as well as self-sufficient regions.

Retail Prices

While fairly reliable wholesale prices are available over a long period, the same is not the position with regard to retail prices. The Labour Bureau, Ministry of Labour, has been the principal organization at the Centre interested and responsible for the collection of retail prices. It has been compiling index numbers of working class cost of living and or retail prices at selected industrial, rural and urban centres. Eighteen series of working class cost of living index numbers for various industrial centres are compiled and published by it. These centres are intended to supplement those for which reliable cost of living index numbers are being compiled and published by the State Governments. These index numbers purport to measure the trends in the overall changes from the level in the year 1944 (which is the base period for most of the centres) of retail prices of goods and services that enter into the working class expenditure as revealed by the Family Budget enquiries carried out at these centres during the years 1944 and 1945. The retail prices are generally obtained through part-time staff belonging to the Departments of Labour, Industries and Supplies, Revenue, etc. Apart from the cost of living index numbers, the Labour Bureau also compiles and publishes in the Indian Labour Gazette simple retail price relatives of certain selected articles, including food items at 18 urban and 12 rural centres. Daily retail prices of foodgrains are collected from over 90 centres and weekly retail prices of agricultural commodities from 215 centres.

Retail prices for a few commodities like vegetables, fresh and dry fruits, fish and livestock products are also being collected by the Directorate of Economics and Statistics, Ministry of Agriculture and published in its weekly Bulletin of Agricultural Prices. Retail prices for some of the other important agricultural commodities like the various foodgrains, etc. are also being collected at some selected centres and published by the Directorate in its annual publication, 'Agricultural Prices in India'.

Retail and wholesale prices are collected by the various State Governments since a long time mostly through Revenue and Agriculture Departments, Economics and Statistics Departments. Marketing Departments, etc. For building up consumer price index numbers of agriculture labourers, retail prices of agricultural commodities are collected through the NSS from a fixed set of 422 villages.

In spite of all this, the existing data on rural retail prices are not sufficient to enable one to determine the spread between producer and consumer prices. Detailed information on agricultural retail prices on a more comprehensive basis is extremely necessary in a developing economy. It is useful to determine the relationship between quantities demanded with changes in relative prices. The Market Intelligence Service in the Directorate of Economics and Statistics should come quite handy for the purpose.

Present Position

The scheme was taken up in 1966 with the main objective of keeping a close watch on the price position of essential commodities. At present price data on essential commodities are collected from 113 selected Centres in different States which include: (i) urban centres having a population of 50,000 and above; (ii) industrial towns irrespective of size; (iii) smaller centres (thinly populated); and (iv) drought affected areas.

The data on prices are collected in respect of 49 groups of commodities which include both agricultural and non-agricultural commodities such as soft coke, cement, spices, tea, etc. On the basis of the price reports, weekly bulletins on retail prices of essential commodities and weekly notes on price position of food articles are brought out. In addition, information on daily prices of edible oils is prepared and sent to the Directorate of Vanaspati, Oils and Fats every fortnight. A weekly note on retail prices of atta, suji and maida is also sent regularly to the Department of Food.

Farm (Harvest) Price

Connotation Farm price of a commodity is defined as the average wholesale price at which the commodity is disposed of by the producer to the trader at the village site during the specified harvest period. If village site transactions do not take place, the prices relate to what the farmer receives for his produce and can be calculated by subtracting transport and other market charges from the wholesale prices quoted at the *mandi* where the produce is disposed of.

Crops Farm prices are collected in respect of important crops grown in the State. These are to cover all the crops for which forecasts are issued.

Centres A certain number of representative villages are selected for district at the rate of 1, 2 or 3 villages from each Tehsil/Taluka depending upon the extent to which the crop is grown in the Tehsil. Generally, at least 10 villages are selected in a district for collection of price data.

Variety Specification In each district, a particular variety of the crop which is grown to a larger extent is specified for quoting the farm price. In some cases, however, the prices for more than one variety are collected when the price differences between the varieties are large, as for instance the price of American and *Desi* cotton.

Period and Frequency   The harvest period of a crop differs depending upon the variety of the crop and the nature of cultivation. For most of the commodities, 6 to 8 weeks after the commencement of the harvest, the farmers are generally expected to dispose of their produce. The harvest period of each crop is generally fixed by the State Governments to facilitate proper reporting by the primary reporters. During the harvest period, the price data are filled in specified forms on every Friday. If no sales take place on the day the price at which the commodity was sold last during the week is to be recorded instead.

Agency   In some States the primary revenue agency collects the data on farm prices. In other States, this work is entrusted to superior officers like Kanungo, Supervisor and Revenue Inspector of the revenue department. In some cases, primary teachers are also utilized for this purpose. In Important markets whole-time price reporters have been appointed under the scheme for Improvement of Market Intelligence. There are about 500 such reporters working in different markets of the country which report regular price and other market data to the centre as well as to the States.

Average Price

The average price of a commodity for the State as a whole is worked out by the method of weighted average with the district production figures for the current year as weights. The average prices for the district for each week are obtained as the simple arithmetic average of the Tehsil prices, which are in turn the simple arithmetic averages of village prices. The average price for the season is the simple arithmetic average of the district prices for each week. The average prices for district are computed at the District Headquarters, while the average prices for the State as a whole are worked out at the State Headquarters.

Data on harvest prices of principal crops are available in the country for a fairly long time. These were formerly published in the 'Agricultural Statistics of India'. These Farm (Harvest) Prices are generally collected by the State Governments in accordance with a scheme drawn up by the Union Ministry of Agriculture.

Under this scheme, prices at which producers dispose of their produce at the village site during the specified harvest period, are collected from the selected villages in each district. Generally ten villages are selected in each district. The average harvest price for the State as a whole is worked out for each crop as a weighted average, with the district production figures for the current year as weights.

At present, 8 States and 2 Union Territories are collecting the data. The data in the other States are collected only from a few selected centres and are not thus fully representative of prices obtaining in rural areas. In order that harvest prices are available on a uniform basis for the whole of the country, it is necessary that those States which have not adopted the scheme, should also make a beginning.

The harvest prices are at present received from the State Governments with a considerable time-lag which varies from State to State and ranges from 1 to 6 years. One of the reasons for this big time-lag seems to be that the harvest prices are sent in the State Returns. It is, therefore, necessary that the returns on harvest prices should be sent separately.

Most of the State Governments have also not yet specified the varieties and qualities of all the commodities for which harvest prices are collected. To ensure that the variety and quality of a commodity selected for a district does not vary from year to year, it is necessary that the most commonly produced variety and quality of the commodities in each district may be fixed and harvest prices be reported for the selected variety and quality.

VARIOUS AGENCIES AND PUBLICATIONS

Price data at present are being collected by a number of agencies. The important ones are:

1. Directorate of Economics and Statistics, Ministry of Agriculture.
2. National Horticultive Board, Ministry of Agriculture.
3. Directorate of Marketing and Inspection.
4. Indian Labour Bureau, Ministry of Labour.
5. National Sample Survey.
6. Commodity Committees concerned with the commodity concerned.
7. State Revenue; Agriculture and Marketing Departments and Statistical Bureaus.

Director of Economics and Statistics It collects the price data mainly through the primary agencies nominated by the State Governments. These primary reporters usually belong to the Revenue, Marketing, Civil Supplies, and Economic and Statistics Departments of the States. Commercial agencies and Banks also supply price data to it in certain cases. Its publications on prices are:

1. Bulletin of Agricultural Prices (weekly).
2. Wholesale Prices of Foodgrains (weekly).
3. Agricultural Prices in India (annual). There is a time-lag of about 5 years in this.
5. Agricultural Situation in India (monthly journal).

National Horticultural Board brings out a monthly Bulletin—*Horticulture Information Service*. It provides market information service for fruits and vegetables of commercial importance, wholesale price and arrival trends for fruits apple, aonla, banana, ber, lime, mandarin, mosambi, pomegranate, papaya, sapota and vegetables—potato, onion, tomato, okra, brinjal, bitter gourd, ginger, green chillies, garlic, cabbage, cauliflower, peas on weekly basis for important centres in the country. Additional information supplied relates to wholesale and retail rates— A comparison, flower and floriculture products, crop situation, price fluctuations and forecast and market profile or major markets.

Directorate of Marketing and Inspection   Prices collected by it relate only to such commodities as are not normally covered by any other agency. These prices are also not published regularly. Instead, they are given in marketing reports in the form of appendices with the result that the time-lags in the availability of these data are great.

Indian Labour Bureau   The Indian Labour (Monthly) Gazette publishes all the data collected by the Bureau.

NATIONAL SAMPLE SURVEY

Wholesale and retail prices were also being collected by the NSS up to the 13th round as a part of their socio-economic surveys. The investigators employed in the survey collected these prices on weekly basis for randomly selected centres located in rural and urban areas. Of these, only weekly retail prices were published by the Indian Statistical Institute in their 'Weekly Price Bulletin.' The published data pertained to rice, wheat, jowar, bajra, ragi, gram, barley, arhar dal, gram dal, masur dal, moong dal, urad dal, kheshari dal, gur, potato, onion, dry chillies, turmeric, fire wood, arecanuts, tobacco, betel-leaf and straw.

Besides the prices collected in the schedule, the NSS has also collected ex-farm prices, in respect of a large number of agricultural commodities as part of their cost of cultivation studies. The rural retail data are being collected by the NSS since the early 50's-from the 5th round (Dec. '52-Mar. '53) onwards. In addition, the NSS collects data on retail prices from a number of urban centres. The rural retail prices are used by the Labour Bureau to construct consumer price index (CPI) numbers for agricultural labourers, and the urban retail prices are used by the CSO to conduct CPI numbers for non-manual workers.

Commodity Committees

Data on wholesale price of various agricultural commodities are collected by the respective Central Commodity Committees (now called Regional Development Centres) as part of their normal statistical work, for providing market intelligence to growers, traders, consumers and the Government. The data are collected through a variety of agencies like market reporters, market committees, non-official organizations, such as commercial firms of repute, chambers of commerce, etc. depending upon the agencies available at the market centres.

The Indian Sugar Trade Information Service of the Indian Institute of Sugar Technology was started in March 1934 to meet a very keen demand for information regarding statistics of sugar in the country. Daily wholesale prices of sugar, gur and khandsari are collected from important sugar and *gur* markets and published in the 'Sugar Market Daily' and weekly bulletins.

The Indian Central Cotton Committee collects daily prices of cotton, kapas, and lint, and cottonseed from important upcountry centres through the cotton market committees at these centres. Weekly (Wednesday) FOB prices of varieties of cotton permitted for export are also collected from the ports of shipment, viz. Mumbai, Kolkata and Chennai through an important cotton firm. The weekly average prices of cotton, kapas, etc. are published in the *Indian Cotton Growing Review*, a Quarterly Journal issued by the Committee.

The Indian Central Jute Committee collects detailed data on jute prices at Kolkata and upcountry markets through its own technical staff as well as private agencies. The data collected are disseminated to the public mainly through radio and the monthly Bulletin of the Committee. Although the prices obtained for the varieties and grades are fairly representative of the areas from which they are received, the number of such centres is not large enough to give a comprehensive picture of the price movements in the entire jute growing area.

The Indian Central Oilseeds Committee does not collect any price data of its own but maintains a record of the prices of important oilseeds, oils and oilcakes published by various official and no-official organizations. The Indian Central Tobacco Committee collects weekly, monthly and quarterly wholesale and retail prices of tobacco from important tobacco markets in the country. Prices are published in the Committee's Tobacco Bulletin every month. There is, however, a large diversity in the published data. In some cases, for example, the lowest and highest prices are quoted, in others the average price is given while for a majority of cases, only a single price is quoted.

The Indian Central Coconut Committee collects daily and weekly wholesale prices of copra, coconut oil and coconut oilcake from important assembling, importing and exporting centres, through local leaders, market, committees, etc. Prices of coconut and coconut products in respect of Cochin, Alleppey, Calicut, Badagara, Mangalore, Arsikre and Tiptur markets are published in the Committee's monthly Bulletin.

These committees have since been abolished, but the work done by them has been taken over the Regional Development Officer for each commodity under the overall control of the ICAR.

State Governments

One of the important sources of the price data in the States has been the revenue departments. The State Revenue Departments need information on prices for purposes of periodical land revenue assessment operations. In some of the States, the district collectors are required to indicate the current price position for the 'Season and Crop Reports'.

In Northern India, particularly in the Punjab, price data are also being collected by the revenue agency at Cantonment Stations, mainly for the use of military authorities. While a part of this information is not published, a large number of States have been publishing the data in their respective State Gazettes.

The quality and the quantity of the price data collected by the Revenue or Agriculture Departments or other agencies like the State Statistical Bureaus in the country varies from State to State. They cover both wholesale and retail prices. Previously, there was wide duplication in respect of the collection of prices by various agencies. As a result of the recommendations of Agricultural Prices Enquiry Committee, 1954, however, the work of price collection has been rationalized and prices collected by one agency are now usually not collected by another agency. The data collected by the State Revenue or Agriculture Departments are supplemented by prices of more important commodities collected by the State Statistical Bureaus through the district statistical officers. These prices are published in the quarterly/monthly State Statistical Bulletin and Annual Statistical Abstracts of the Bureaus. Table 20.1 lists various types of data being collected by various State Governments.

LIVESTOCK AND LIVESTOCK PRODUCTS

Practically no information was available about the prices of livestock, livestock products and cattle feed before 1948. As already mentioned, some scattered data were published in the State Gazettes. Besides the information now available in the Marketing Reports, State Statistical Bulletins of the Statistical Bureaus and the NSS, the Directorate of Economics and Statistics, Ministry of Agriculture is now publishing price data in the mid-month issue of the Weekly Bulletin of Prices, on different categories of livestock and poultry. Wholesale and retail prices of major livestock products along with those of fish and oilcakes are also published in the Bulletin. In addition to this, average month-end and annual wholesale prices of important categories of livestock, livestock products and cattle feed in respect of important selected markets are published in the Directorate's annual publications 'Indian Livestock Statistics' and 'Agricultural Prices in India' in respect of selected centres. There is also a good deal of unpublished data available with the Directorate of Economics and Statistics. The National Income Unit of the Central Statistical Organization has given a comprehensive summary of all the available data on livestock as well as farm products.

SUPPORT PRICES

The agricultural price policy in India remained consumer-oriented until the need was recognized in the Third Five Year Plan (1961-66) for extending it to subserve the interests of the producer too. Consumer protection was often sought through resort to such regulatory measures as statutory control over prices, public distribution of commodities in short supply, restrictions on their inter-State movements, regulation of bank credit and forward trading and adjustments in export and import quotas. Even though Government of India started fixing procurement prices of foodgrains and statutory minimum and maximum prices for

Table 20.1 Details of Price-Data Collected by States and Union Territories

State/UT	Price-Data	Periodicity
1. Andhra Pradesh	1. Retail prices of 64 essential commodities	Weekly
	2. Prices of 48 non-food items	Monthly
	3. Wholesale prices of 125 items of livestock, livestock products and feeds	Monthly
	4. Wholesale prices of 30 agricultural commodities	Monthly
	5. Prices of building material	Quarterly
	6. Farm harvest prices of agricultural commodities	Kharif, rabi
	7. Daily agricultural labour wages from 66 centres	Monthly
2. Arunachal Pradesh	1. Retail prices of 85 essential food items	Fortnightly
	2. Retail prices of 82 non-food items	Monthly
	3. Prices of 12 essential commodities sold at Fair Price shops	Monthly
	4. Rates of service charges of 10 items from 12 markets	Quarterly
3. Assam	1. Urban and rural retail prices	Weekly/ Monthly
	2. Wholesale prices of food and non-food items	Weekly/ Monthly
	3. Prices of building materials	Quarterly
4. Bihar	1. Farm prices of all crops	Seasonal
	2. Retail prices of consumer items agricultural commodities	Weekly
5. NCT of Delhi	1. Retail prices of 74 food and other items	Weekly
	2. Retail prices of 42 items	Monthly
	3. Wholesale prices of agricultural and other commodities	Weekly
	4. Building material rates and wage rates	Quarterly
6. Goa	1. Retail prices of essential items of food, fuel and light	Weekly
	2. Retail prices of items pertaining to middle class non-manual employees	Monthly
7. Gujarat	1. Wholesale and retail prices of selected agricultural items	Fortnightly
	2. Retail prices of six types of iodised and non-iodised salt	Monthly

Table 20.1 Details of Price-Data Collected by States and Union Territories (Contd.)

State/UT	Price-Data	Periodicity
8. Haryana	1. Retail consumer prices	Weekly/ Monthly
	2. Rural retail prices	Fortnightly
	3. Retail prices of essential commodities	Weekly
	4. Wholesale prices of agricultural commodities	Weekly
9. Himachal Pradesh	1. Retail prices of sixteen essential commodities	Weekly
	2. Wholesale and retail prices of selected commodities	Fortnightly
	3. Prices of livestock and poultry	Half-yearly
10. Jammu and Kashmir	1. Retail prices of essential commodities	Weekly
	2. Wholesale prices of agricultural commodities	Weekly
11. Karnataka	1. Prices of 20 selected commodities	Weekly
	2. Wholesale and retail prices of 110 agricultural commodities	Fortnightly
	3. Harvest prices of agricultural commodities	Kharif, rabi and summer
	4. Prices of building materials	Quarterly
12. Kerala	1. Wholesale prices of 38 agricultural commodities	Daily
	2. Retail price of essential commodities	Daily and Monthly
	3. Retail prices of food items	Weekly and Quarterly
	4. Retail prices of agricultural commodities	Weekly
	5. Wholesale prices of coir and husk	Weekly
	6. Wholesale prices of agricultural commodities	Fortnightly
	7. Retail prices of farm products	Monthly
	8. Wholesale and retail prices of salt	Monthly
	9. Retail prices of essential non-food items	Monthly
	10. Retail prices of forest products	Quarterly
	11. Prices of building materials	Quarterly
	12. Retail prices of 1059 ayurvedic items	Annual
13. Madhya Pradesh	Wholesale prices of 290 agricultural commodities	Monthly

Table 20.1 Details of Price-Data Collected by States and Union Territories (Contd.)

State/UT	Price-Data	Periodicity
14. Maharashtra	1. Urban retail prices of 84 essential commodities from 31 centres	Weekly
	2. Rural retail prices of 59 essential commodities from 75 centres	Weekly
	3. Wholesale prices of essential commodities from 28 district HQs., and 10 chemical fertilisers from 30 centres	Fortnightly/ Monthly
	4. Retail prices of 30 important commodities from 59 centres	Monthly
15. Manipur	1. Retail prices of essential commodities and services from District HQs.	Monthly
	2. Retail prices of livestock and livestock products from district HQs.	Monthly
16. Meghalaya	Retail prices	Weekly/ Monthly
17. Mizoram	1. Retail prices of essential commodities, and prices of food and non-food items from urban towns	Weekly/ Monthly
	2. Retail prices of food and non-food items from Aizwal centre	Weekly
	3. Wholesale prices of 23 items from six urban centres	Monthly
18. Nagaland	1. Wholesale and retail prices of essential commodities	Weekly
	2. Rates of service charges from 9 centres	Weekly
19. Orissa	1. Rural retail prices	Fortnightly
	2. Farm harvest and wholesale prices of agricultural commodities	Weekly
	3. Prices of livestock and poultry	Monthly
	4. Prices of meat, egg and milk products	Fortnightly
	5. Prices of animal by-products	Quarterly
20. Punjab	1. Retail prices from all district HQs.	Weekly
	2. Retail price of 70 items for working class population	Weekly
	3. Retail prices of 82 items from six centres	Monthly
	4. Rural retail prices of 44 items from one village in each district	Monthly
	5. Wholesale prices of 49 commodities from 4 centres	Weekly

Table 20.1 Details of Price-Data Collected by States and Union Territories (*Contd.*)

State/UT	Price-Data	Periodicity
21. Rajasthan	1. Retail prices of 49 essential commodities	Weekly
	2. Prices of building materials and wage rates of construction labourers	Quarterly
	3. Prices of livestock and livestock products of 61 items from 31 Dist. Hqs.	Weekly
22. Sikkim	NA	NA
23. Tamil Nadu	1. Wholesale and retail prices from 96 centres	Daily
	2. Wholesale prices from Chennai city	Monthly
	3. Wholesale and retail prices for Chennai city	Weekly
24. Tripura	1. Retail prices from Batala and Maharajganj	Weekly
	2. Retail and wholesale prices at sub-divisional HQs.	Fortnightly
	3. Rural retail prices from 168 markets	Monthly
25. Uttar Pradesh	1. Urban retail prices	Monthly
	2. Rural retail prices	Monthly
	3. Prices of building materials	Quarterly
26. West Bengal	1. Prices from Calcutta	Weekly
	2. Prices from 20 urban centres	Fortnightly
27. Lakshadweep	Prices of essential goods and services	Monthly
28. Dadar and Nagar Haveli	Farm harvest prices of agricultural commodities	Weekly
29. Daman and Diu	Retail prices of 97 commodities	Weekly
30. Andaman and Nicobar Islands	Retail prices for food and non-food items	Weekly
31. Chandigarh	None	None
32. Pondichery	Wholesale and retail prices of important essential commodities	Weekly

cotton during the World War II and the principle was later stretched to sugarcane and jute, consumer protection continued, by and large, to be the guiding principle. Situations did arise when prices of some commodities, such as foodgrains in 1954-55, tended to decline to uneconomic levels and Government lent support to the market to provide some relief to the producer, but such intervention was undertaken more for improving the emergent situation rather than as an instrument of a long-term policy to support agricultural development programmes.

The Third Five Year Plan emphasized that the producer of foodgrains must get a reasonable return, that the farmer should be assured that the prices of foodgrains and other commodities that he produced would not be allowed to fall below a reasonable minimum and that a policy designed to prevent sharp fluctuations in prices and to guarantee a certain minimum level was essential in the interest of expanded production. It was thus recognized, for the first time as it were, that the fixation of minimum prices for important agricultural commodities was essential for an effective programme of augmenting agricultural production, which was in the interest of both producer and the consumer. Price fixation, such as was being done by the Government then, was weighted more by administrative requirements of the Ministry concerned with the individual commodity than by economic considerations that underlie an integrated multi-commodity approach. Again, foodgrain markets could be manipulated by the trader, particularly under conditions of scarcity which could lead to some distortions in the market structure. These situations led to the need for setting up an organization to give continuous thought to evolving a balanced and integrated agricultural price policy that would be fair both to the producer and the consumer and achieve for the country an optimum land use and production pattern broadly in the light of national requirements. The Agricultural Prices Commission was accordingly set up in January 1965 to fill this role.

The Commission announces support/minimum statutory prices for different commodities each year and collects a good deal of related data which, of course remain unpublished. The support prices for different commodities as recommended by the Commission from time to time is given in Table 20.2.

Table 20.2 Minimum Support Price/Procurment Price for Crops (Crop Year Basis)

(Rs/quintal)

Commodities	1980-81	1990-91	1994-95	1995-96	1996-97	1997-98	1998-99	1999-2000	2000-2001
Paddy (Procurement price)									
Common	105	205	340	360	380	415	440	490	510
Fine	-	215	360	375	395	-	-	-	-
Super fine	-	225	380	395	415	-	-	-	-
Grade 'A'	-	-	-	-	-	445	470	520	540
Wheat (Procurement price)	117	225	350	360	380	475	510	550	580
Coarse cereals (Jowar, Bajra & Ragi)	105	180	280	300	310	360	390	415	445
Maize	-	180	290	310	320	360	390	415	445
Barley	-	200	275	285	295	305	350	385	430
Gram	145	450	670	700	740	815	895	1000	1015
Arhar	190	480	760	800	840	900	960	1105	1200
Moong	200	480	760	800	840	900	960	1105	1200
Urad	200	480	760	800	840	900	960	1105	1200
Sugarcane (Statutory minimum price) @	13.00	23.00	39.10[3]	42.5	45.90	48.45	52.70	56.10	-
Cotton									
F-414/H-777	304	620	1000	1150	1180	1330	1440[7]	1575	1625
H-4	-	750	1200	1350	1380	1530	1650	1775	1825
Groundnut	206	580	860	900	920	980	1040	1155	1220
Jute (TD-5)	160	320	470	490	510	570	650	750	785
Rapeseed/mustard	-	600	810	830	860	890	940	1000	1100

Table 20.2 Minimum Support Price/Procurment Price for Crops (Crop Year Basis) (Contd.)

(Rs/quintal)

Commodities	1980-81	1990-91	1994-95	1995-96	1996-97	1997-98	1998-99	1999-2000	2000-2001
Sunflower	183	600	900	950	.960	1000	1060	1155	1170
Soyabean									
Black	183	350	570	600	620	670	705	755	775
Yellow	-	400	650	680	700	750	795	845	865
Safflower	-	575	760	780	800	830	910	990	1100
Toria	-	570	780	800	825	855	905	965	1065
Tobacco (per kg)									
VFC F-2 (Black soil)	-	13.25	18.50	19.00	19.00	20.50	22.50	25.00	-
L-2 (Light soil)	-	14.25	21.00	21.50	22.00	23.50	25.50	27.00	-
Copra (milling)2	-	1600	2350	2500	2500	2700	2900	3100	3250
Copra balls2	-	-	2575	2725	2725	2925	3125	3325	3500
Sesamum	-	-	-	850	870	950	1060	1205	1300
Niger seed	-	-	-	720	720	800	850	915	1025

1. Includes a central bonus of Rs. 25.00 per quintal.
2. For calender years 1981, 1991, 1992, 1993, 1994, 1995, 1996, 1997 and 1998.
3. Linked to a basic recovery of 8.5 per cent, subject to a premium of Rs. 0.46 for every 0.1 percentage point increase in the recovery above that level upto 10 per cent and Rs. 0.60 for every 0.1 percent point increase in the recovery about 10 per cent.
4. Paddy is now classified into two categories for the MSP purposes instead of three varieties earlier from season of 1997-98.
5. Includes a central bonus of Rs. 60.00 per quintal payable on the Wheat sold to the procurement agencies upto 30th June 1997.
6. Includes central bonus of Rs. 55 on top of MSP of Rs. 455 for procurement beginning April 1998 upto 30th June, 1998.
7. For J-34 Variety also.
@ Statutory Minimum Price linked to a basic recovery of 8.5% with proportionate premium for 0.1% increase in recovery above that level.
Source: Economic Survey, 2000-2001.

21

Index Numbers of Prices

Index numbers are devices for measuring differences in the magnitude of a group of related variables over a period of time, between places or between like categories. These variables may be in terms of price of commodities or the physical quantity of goods produced or marketed. Generally, the object of index numbers is to combine prices of a large number of different commodities into one meaningful summary, reflecting the average change from time to time.

PURPOSE

Index numbers of prices may be studied in order to enforce price controls to maintain stability in purchasing power. Many a time wages may be adjusted so that real wages remain constant. Index numbers are also useful for comparison between the cost of living at different places, for measuring changes in physical volume over a period of time in trade, agricultural, industrial and factory production, sales and stocks, profits, etc. They are important for devising forecast indices.

In India, index numbers are fairly old. Index numbers of prices of exported and imported articles, retail prices of foodgrains and wholesale prices were compiled earlier with 1873 as the base year. A quinquennial publication named *Index Numbers of Indian Prices* and its annual supplements published all the above indices.

The nature, scope and method of construction of index number series relating to agriculture are discussed below. The series relates to:

1. Commodity prices.
2. Agricultural production.
3. Working class cost of living.
4. Foreign trade.

INDEX NUMBERS OF COMMODITY PRICES

By far the most important index numbers relate to prices. At present in India, separate indices are being compiled for harvest prices, wholesale prices, retail prices in rural areas, retail prices in urban areas, etc.

The following series have been described in detail:
1. Index number of harvest prices compiled by the Ministry of Agriculture.
2. Index number of wholesale prices compiled by the office of the Economic Adviser, Ministry of Commerce and Industry.
3. Index number of wholesale prices in Calcutta, compiled by the DGCIS, Ministry of Commerce and Industry.
4. Index number of retail prices (urban centres) compiled by the Labour Bureau, Ministry of Labour.
5. Index number of retail prices (rural centres) compiled by the Labour Bureau.

HARVEST PRICES INDEX

In pursuance of the recommendations of the Inter-Departmental Committee on Official Statistics, 1946, the Directorate of Economics and Statistics, Ministry of Agriculture undertook the compilation of Index Numbers of Harvest Prices of Principal Crops in India. A brief description of the scope and method of construction of these index numbers is given below.

Base Period The base period of the series is the agricultural year 1938-39, i.e. July 1938 to June 1939.

Weights A system of double weighting is being adopted in working out this series. In the first instance to work out a commodity index, moving weights are used for combining the price relatives for different States into the commodity price relative taking their weighted geometric mean, figures of the current year's production in the different States covered being used as weights. Subsequently, to work out the all-commodity index, weights are assigned to the different crops in proportion to the average value of production of each crop in the States covered by the series during the three years ending 1938-39. Production is then evaluated at harvest prices prevailing in the different States during the period under reference.

Crops Covered The index covers the following 15 crops divided into three groups:
(a) *Foodgrains*—
   Rice, jowar, bajra, maize, wheat, barley and gram.
(b) *Oilseeds*—
   Groundnut, seasmum, rape and mustard and linseed.
(c) *Miscellaneous*
   Sugar (raw), tobacco, cotton and jute.

Other important crops such as pulses other than gram, plantation crops, spices, etc. could not be included in the index numbers because of the non-availability of the prices and other relevant data for these commodities in the base year.

States Covered The States covered by the index are the former part 'A' States of Andhra, Assam, Bihar, Maharashtra, Madhya Pradesh, Tamil

Nadu, Orissa, Punjab, Uttar Pradesh and West Bengal and Delhi. The total geographical area of these States formed about 60 per cent of the total geographical area of the country.

Nature of Prices Data The prices data forming the basis of the index numbers are 'Harvest Season Prices' reported by the branches of the State Bank of India. For each crop, important marketing centres have been selected in the States covered by the index and for each of these centres, weekly wholesale prices during the prescribed harvest period of 6-8 weeks are reported by the concerned branches of the State Bank of India. A simple average of the weekly quotations is taken representing the 'Harvest Season Price' for that commodity at that centre. It is these prices that are utilized in the construction of the index.

These 'Harvest Season Prices', it may be pointed out, are different from the 'Farm (Harvest) Prices' published by the Directorate of Economics and Statistics in 'Agricultural Prices in India'. The Farm (Harvest) Price is defined as the average wholesale price at which the commodity is disposed of by the producer at the village site, during the specified harvesting period. The Farm (Harvest) Price data are collected every week from a number of villages, selected on a purposive basis, during the specified harvest period of six to eight weeks in respect of the important crops; the weekly prices are averaged into tehsil and district averages by taking their simple mean; and the State average is worked out as a weighted average of the district prices with the production of the crop in the districts as weights. The Farm (Harvest) Prices are not being reported by all the States at present, and, as such, the question of their utilization in the construction of the index is yet to wait.

Method of Construction

Chain base method has been used in the construction of the index in view of the fact that price quotations are not uniformly available throughout the period. The current year's price relatives are computed in relation to the previous year and are linked with the base year through the intermediate years.

The detailed method of computing the price relatives and averaging is as under:

Computation of State Price Relative for Each Crop The price relative for each crop is worked out for each State as follows:

(i) For each year, the price relative for each variety of crop at each centre is computed in relation to the corresponding price for the previous year.

(ii) A simple geometric average for such price relatives for the different varieties of the crop at each centre gives the price relative of the crop at that centre.

(iii) A simple geometric average of the price relatives at the different centres gives the single price relative for the State for the crop.

Computation of All-India Price Relative for Each Crop The price relatives for the different States are combined into the commodity price relative taking their weighted geometric mean figures of the current year's production in the different States covered being used as weights. As the price relative in each year is computed with the previous year as the base, the system of moving weights has been adopted.

Linking with Base Year After compiling the price indices for each year relative to the previous year, these are linked through the successive intermediate years with the base year i.e. Agricultural year 1938-39 to get the index numbers for each of the crop.

Group and All-crop Indices The weighted arithmetic mean of the index numbers for the individual crops with the average value of their production during the three years ending 1938-39 as weights, give the All-India Index Numbers of Harvest Prices for 'Groups' and 'All-Crops'. 'Group' and 'All-Commodities' indices was weighted geometric mean. This has now been changed to 'weighted arithmetic mean' to fall in line with other current series of index numbers such as agricultural production, wholesale prices, etc. The 'Group' and 'All-Commodities' index numbers, published earlier, have been revised according to the revised method of averaging.

ECONOMIC ADVISER'S INDEX NUMBER OF WHOLESALE PRICES

Background of the Earlier Indices of Wholesale Prices

The office of the Economic Adviser to the Government of India undertook to publish for the first time Index Numbers of Wholesale Prices from the week commencing from 10th January 1942 with base week ended 19th August 1939 = 100. The index was calculated as the price relatives of 23 commodities which were assigned equal weights and was known as the sensitive number of prices. The index was classified into four groups, viz. Food and Tobacco, Agricultural Commodities, Raw Materials and Manufactured Articles.

An index for Food Articles was prepared in 1945 with a wider coverage, with the last week of August 1939 as base. The index was a weighted geometric mean, the weights being proportional to the values of marketable surplus of the various commodities during the year 1938-39. The base period of the index was afterwards changed to the year ending August 1939. Subsequently, this series was expanded to cover other groups besides weighted index numbers of the wholesale prices with base year ended August 1939 = 100.

Compared with the earlier series containing 23 commodities, this series included as many as 78 commodities to give a more comprehensive picture of price movements in all important commodities, whether domestically produced or imported. The data published each week included both price relatives and absolute prices of the various representative specifications of articles at representative markets.

The commodities were arranged into sub-groups, groups and the individual index numbers were combined each week to give index value for these sub-groups and groups. In order to combine the indices for individual articles into groups or sub-groups in the series, each commodity was weighted by the importance which it represented in the total market ing during 1939. The combination of 215 individual quotations for 78 commodities into group indices was worked out by the weighted geometric mean method.

The partition of the country and the major changes in the economic structure made the index out-of-date. Many new commodities, specially in the field of manufactures, became significant and the relative importance of commodities other than manufactures also changed. Moreover, the year ending August 1939 had ceased to be appropriate as the base year. In accordance with the recommendation of the Standing Committee of Departmental Statisticians, the Economic Adviser's Office issued a revised series of index with 1952-53 as base. This consisted of 112 commodities comprising 555 individual quotations. The arithmetic average was adopted in preference to the geometric mean adopted in the series. Cereals were covered comprehensively on the basis of 99 markets specified by the Agricultural Price Enquiry Committee (also known as Thapar Committee). As regards the non-agricultural commodities; these were selected on the basis of availability of price data at producing and consuming centres and markets were selected on the basis of suggestions given by State Governments and various organizations like Chambers of Commerce and Trade Associations. The existing Revised series of index numbers with 1952-53 as base was being issued regularly every week from April 1956. The old series with 1939 as base was also continued for some years in order to provide comparability in watching the trends of the two series over a period of time. It was discontinued with effect from March 1960.

The weighting pattern of this index was based on the year 1948-49, although the price-base was 1952-53. The weights assigned to various commodities were derived from the estimates of marketed values of domestic produce and the values of imports inclusive of duty. For manufactures the figures were taken from the Third Census of Indian Manufactures 1948 and imports were also taken into account. With regard to intermediate products, only the portion produced for sale was taken note of. For the Food Group, only marketed surplus and imports were taken into account; the estimates of percentages of marketable surpluses to total production were based on pre-1939 estimates in the absence of more up-to-date data, although the total production referred to 1948-49.

New Series (1961-62 as Base)

The earlier series as stated above covered comprehensively agricultural commodities as recommended by the Thapar Committee but it did not include the non-agricultural commodities as extensively as it should have been done. It was, therefore, decided that while the earlier index should be published, there should be an enquiry into the choice of quotations, etc. for the non-agricultural portion of the Index of Wholesale Prices and arrangement made for placing them on a satisfactory basis as was done for the agricultural commodities by the Thapar Committee. With a view to remedying this drawback in the Index, the Government of India in the then Ministry of Commerce and Industry constituted a Committee for improving the coverage and mode of collection of price quotations of non-agricultural commodities utilized in the compilation of Index Number of Wholesale Prices in India.

The terms of reference of the Committee were as follows:

(1) to examine the collection and processing of prices of non-agricultural items for the compilation of Index Number of Wholesale Prices; and

(2) to suggest improvements.

The Committee sent communications to various Chambers of Commerce. Trade Associations, State Governments and Central Government Ministries and other interested bodies inviting suggestions for incorporation of new commodities in the wholesale prices index along with specifications and markets. After the replies were received, they were scrutinized and a list of additional non-agricultural commodities, for which price quotations were available on a regular basis, was prepared.

The Committee went into other technical aspects of the Index, e.g. weighting diagram, base period, content of prices, method of compilation and commodity classifications, etc.

The new series was largely based on the recommendations made by the Committee and covered a number of additional items particularly in the manufactured category which had assumed greater importance in the national economy and their incorporation went a long way in improving the coverage. Besides, the base was also shifted to a more recent year (1961-62).

REVISED INDEX NUMBERS OF WHOLESALE PRICES
(Base 1970 = 100)

While introducing the series based on 1961-62 = 100, it was also decided to constitute a Working Group to look into the methodology of the construction of wholesale price indices and work out a new series with a more recent year as the base. The revised series (1970-71 = 100) being introduced in the first week of Jan. 1977 was based on the recommendations of this Working Group. The revised series covered 142 additional items, particularly in the manufactured category, which over years assumed greater importance in the national economy. Incorporation of such items was considered to go a long way in improving the coverage of the wholesale price index. The price comparison base of the revised series had also been shifted to a more recent year, i.e. 1970-71. A new weighting pattern had been adopted. The following paragraphs bring out in detail the important changes introduced in the commodity coverage, system of classification, weighting diagram, etc. in the revised series in comparison to those adopted in the existing series.

Coverage of the Revised Series

The revised series contained 360 commodities as against 218 (as redefined) in the existing series. Owing to increasing sophistication of industrial production, some of the specifications of the existing series were treated as items in the revised series with the result that the number of commodities included in the existing series were shown as 218 instead of the present number of 139 for comparing it with the revised series. The criteria adopted for the selection of non-agricultural commodities were that: (a) a large number of new industrial items should be included to reflect the strides made by the country in the industrial field, (b) items with a total value of production of more than Rs. 1 crore as per 1965 ASI data should be included, and (c) items of which indigenous output was small but had substantial imports should be included. Actual selection of industrial items had, however, been based on the response of the principal manufactures and associations in the matter of furnishing relevant price data.

The number of quotations included in the new series stand at 1.275 as compared to 767 in the existing series. Thus 508 additional quotations were included in the revised series. Most of the additional quotations pertained to new industrial items added in the index. The number of quotations under 'manufactured products' had increased from 404 in the existing series to 842 in the revised series. Table 21.1 gives a comparative picture of the distribution of commodities and quotations of the two series.

As far as possible, specifications and markets for the existing quotations had not been changed unless the specification was longer representative of the commodity.

Price data were collected through official as well as non-official sources. The official sources were: Agricultural Marketing Departments of the Government of India, State Bureau of Economics and Statistics, District and Sub-Divisional Offices. Forest Officers, Registrars of Cooperative Societies and other primary agencies belonging to the State Governments, Directorate of Economics and Statistics of the Central Government, Collectors of Customs, Central Government Commodity Boards and Committees, State Bank of India, etc. The non-official sources were Chambers of Commerce, Trade Associations and leading manufacturers and business house.

System of Classification

In the existing series (base 1961-62 = 100) commodity classification was based on the Standard International Trade Classification with slight

Table 21.1 Commodity Distribution of Two Series

Maker groups	No. of commodities		No. of quotations	
	Existing index	Revised index	Existing index	Revised index
I. Primary articles	61	80	340	405
1. Food articles	31	39	234	261
2. Non food articles	22	26	92	114
3. Minerals	8	15	14	30
II. Fuel, power, light and lubricants	8	10	23	28
III. Manufactured products	149	270	404	842
	218	360	767[a]	1275

[a]Seven quotations of the existing series have been dropped in the revised series.

adjustments to suit Indian conditions. In the revised series the Standard Industrial Classification was adopted to bring about greater uniformity with the classification adopted in some other important indices like the Agricultural Production Index and the Industrial Production Index and also to facilitate comparison of trends in the wholesale price index with trends of comparable groups and subgroups of other indices.

In the new classification, commodities were distributed under three major groups, viz.

   I. Primary articles;

  II. Fuel, power, light and lubricants;

 III. Manufactured products.

The major group 'primary articles' comprised three groups: (i) food articles, (ii) non-food articles, and (iii) minerals. In other words, the major group 'primary articles' was broadly comparable with two groups of the existing classification, viz. 'food articles' and 'industrial raw materials' with certain minor adjustments. Sub-groups as: (a) edible oils, (b) sugar, gur and allied products, and (c) processed food and salt which were being included in the 'food articles' under the existing classification are now being shown in the group 'food products' of the major group 'manufactured products' as per the Standard Industrial Classification. Likewise, raw tobacco which featured in the 'liquor and tobacco' group under the existing classification was shown under 'non food articles'. The non-food articles, consisted of commercial crops and other primary products which were for further processing.

The major group 'fuel, power, light and lubricants' in the revised series consisting of coal coke, lignite, mineral oils and electricity was broadly comparable with the group 'fuel, power, light and lubricants' of the existing series except that the revised series excludes castor oil and rectified spirit which were included, under the major group 'manufactured products' in the revised series.

The major group 'manufactured products' contained 11 groups under which semi-manufactured and manufactured products had been classified. In the existing classification, the group 'manufactures' was divided into two sub-groups: (i) intermediate products, and (ii) finished products.

Weighting System

In the (base 1961-62 = 100) series weights were allotted to 139 commodities on the basis of transactions of only those commodities of which the prices featured in the index. The weights of individual commodities were added up to arrive at the sub-group and group weights. The weights assigned to agricultural commodities were generally on the basis of marketable surplus of domestic produce and the value of imports inclusive of import duty and excise duty if any. In the case of manufactured articles, gross value of products for the year 1961-62 were taken into account. Imports, import duties and excise duties were of course also added to the values wherever applicable.

Strictly speaking, the series, aimed at reflecting the price changes of the commodity-items included in the index and did not represent the price movements of all the wholesale transactions in the economy. In the revised series, an attempt had been made to improve upon the system of allocation of weights to groups, sub-groups and commodity-items so that these might as far as possible carry their own weight for groups and sub-groups as a whole, and reflected their respective price movements. The sub-groups and groups have, no doubt, to be the aggregated of commodities produced and processed in the country or imported into it, which flow into primary for sale. Another basic change adopted in the system of allocation of weights was that the value of transactions of non-selected commodity items were assigned or imputed to those selected commodity-items whose nature and price trends were likely to be more or less similar to the former. The transaction values of non-selected items had been proportionately distributed to items under the sub-groups to which such non-selected items belong, where it had not been possible to locate selected items of a similar nature.

Another improvement introduced was in the system of allocation of weights to the commodities. In the existing series, 'condiments and spices' 'other ores', 'electrical machinery', 'tools and implements', 'machinery other than electrical', 'vehicles', 'iron and steel manufactures', 'cutlery and hardware', 'glass manufactures', 'fertilizers', 'paints and varnishes', 'paper and paper products', 'rubber tyres and tubes', 'other rubber products' and 'oilcakes' were treated as single commodities (although within these commodities there were a number of easily identifiable items which were treated as specifications because separate weights could not be given), and weights were allotted accordingly. However, in · the revised series, all identifiable items which were treated as quotations in the existing series such as chillies, turmeric, gypsum, bauxite, electric motors, electric fans, transformers, cables and wires, machine tools, boilers, textile machinery, diesel engines, trucks, cars, steel plates, pipes, bars and rods, tip plates, etc. were treated as separate commodities, and weights were allotted to each of them.

The weights in the revised series were allotted on the basis of values of transactions which consisted of: (a) value of marketabe surplus in the case of agricultural commodities and value of products for sale in the case of manufactured products, (b) total value of imports, (c) total value of import duties, if any, and (d) total value of excise duties, if applicable. In the case of manufactured products, gross value of production of the sample sector of Annual Survey of Industries (that is all factories employing 10 or more workers if using power, and employing 20 or more works if not using power on any day in the reference year but employing less than 50 workers if using power and less than 100 workers if not using power) upto three digit level of classification had also been assigned or imputed to the selected commodities depending upon the sub-group/group to which this three digit level of industry belongs. The value of imports and import duties of the non-selected commodities had also been assigned or imputed to the selected commodities. The method adopted was more or less identical with the one adopted for assigning the value of production.

In the index (base 1961-62 = 100), the weights, both for agricultural and non-agricultural commodities were determined on the production data of one year, i.e. 1961-62. Since agricultural production is subject to the vagaries of weather and fluctuates widely from year to year, and that a single year would also not be sufficiently representative of different crops or of different sectors of the agricultural economy, in the revised series weights between agricultural and non-agricultural sectors, had been apportioned on the basis of the average value of aggregate transaction for three years ending 1969-70 to avoid any distortion in the weights. The allocation of weights among different commodities within the agricultural sector had been done on the basis of the average value of marketable surplus during the three years ending 1969-70 in respect of each commodity. Imports, import duty and excise duty, if any, had also been added. However, as production data of coir fibre, soyabeans, mahua seeds and tanning materials were not available, the weights of these items were allocated on the basis of their production during 1968-69.

As regards 'minerals', three years' average value of production (including, imports, import duty, and excise duty, if any) had been taken up to the level of sub-group 'metallic and non-metallic minerals'. The allocation of weights to the individual minerals within each sub-group had been done in proportion to the value estimated for 1968-69. For 'crude petroleum', the weight had been based on the average production of three years. The average value of production of three years ending 1969-70 had also been estimated for the major group 'fuel, power, light and lubricants'.

The allocation of weights among different commodities, sub-groups, and groups within the major group 'manufactured products' had however, been done on the basis of value of production (inclusive of excise duty and value of imports) during a single year 1968-69. Value of products as given in the ASI-68 census and sample sectors had been generally utilized for assigning weights. While assigning the value of production to groups, sub-groups and commodities, necessary adjustments had been made by excluding the value of by-products from the main products and including them under the appropriate industry.

The main sources of basic data for calculation of weights in the revised series were:

1. National Accounts Statistics 1960-61.
   1972-73 Disaggregated Tables.
2. Estimates of Area and Production of Principal Crops.
3. Farm (harvest) Prices of Principal Crops.
4. Mineral Statistics of India.
5. Indian Petroleum and Chemicals Statistics.
6. Annual Survey of Industries—1968 Census Sector Detailed Results and Sample Sector Summary Results.
7. Customs and Central Excise Statement of the Indian Union.
8. Indian Customs and Central Excise Tariff Volume II.
9. Monthly Statistics of Foreign Trade in India Volume II.
10. Marketing Reports brought out by the Office of the Agricultural Marketing Adviser to the Govt. of India.

In the case of agricultural commodities the values were arrived at on the basis of State-wise/all India average harvest prices or average wholesale prices. In the case of minerals, value referad to the sale value of minerals at mine site. For petroleum products, quantity was valued at net delivered rate exclusive of sales tax and dealers' commission. Value of manufactured products represented exfactory value for sale. Products consumed for further manufacture in the factory were excluded.

The weights for major groups, sub-groups and individual items of the revised series as compared with those of the existing series are given in Table 21.2. This also provides weights of the main groups of articles in the two series, the revised and the existing one (after regrouping the existing series from SITC to SIC).

It will be seen that the new system of weights reflects some important changes. The weight of the major group 'primary articles' decreased in the revised series from 42.6 per cent to 41.6 per cent, while the weight of the group 'food articles' increased from 29.2 per cent to 29.8 per cent in contrast with non-food articles which decreased from 13.0 per cent to 10.6 per cent. The weights of the group 'minerals' and the major group 'fuel, power, light and lubricants' moved up owing to increased production

Table 21.2 Weights of the Main Groups

		Revised series	Existing series
A.	Primary articles	416	426
	i) food articles	(298)	(292)
	ii) non-food articles	(106)	(130)
	iii) minerals	(12)	(4)
B.	Fuel, power light and lubricants	85	60
C.	Manufactured products	499	514
	All commodities	1000	1000

and the inclusion of a large number of items than in the existing series. The weight of the major group 'manufactured products' showed a minor downward shift from 51.4 per cent to 49.9 per cent. However, the weights of two series were not strictly comparable owing to a different methodology adopted in the calculation of the weight of the revised series. Due caution, therefore, needs to be exercised in drawing any conclusion that the weight for 'manufactured products' declined in those years. Although the growth of industrial production in physical terms had been higher than that of agricultural production the relative weight had not changed in favour of industry owing to a greater rise in the prices of agricultural commodities in relation to industrial items. It may, however, be noted that major groups 'B' and 'C' (namely; 'fuel, power, light and lubricants' and 'manufactured products') taken together had a higher combined weight in the new series, whereas excluding mineral from the primary articles' group, the combined weight of food and non-food articles was less for the revised series.

Choice of Base Year

Then existing wholesale price index had 1961-62 as the base year both for weights and prices. The year was chosen as it was considered a 'normal' year from the point of view of price trends. In the light of recommendation made by the Technical Advisory Committee on Statistics of Prices and Costs of Living that common year should be adopted for all indices constructed by the Central Government and since the indices of industrial production and consumer price had already been revised with the calendar years 1970 and 1971 respectively as base year, for the revised series of wholesale price index, 1970-71 had been adopted as the prices base and the triennium ending 1969-70 as the weight base. Although ideally, it would have been desirable to have the same base year for both price comparison as well as weights, this was not possible in practice as production data at the ultimate digit (product) level were available only up to 1968-69, at the time of the initial preparation of the weighting diagram. The shifting of the price base to a more recent year, i.e. 1970-71, had the additional advantage that it enabled the collection of price data for a large number of new items, which might otherwise not have been available (from 1968-69). Before the finalization of the revised index, it was possible to add the year 1969-70 to the weight base. The adoption of a three year average for the weight base was calculated to avoid distortions arising from fluctuations in annual output of agricultural commodities.

Collection of Prices

The object of index numbers of wholesale prices being to measure the changes in the general level of prices of commodities in the primary markets, the index has therefore, been based on producer's prices, i.e. ex-mine/ex-factory prices and selling agents prices for imported commodities. In the case of foodgrains, since ex-farm transaction are not considered important the commodities have been priced at the first important stage of transaction after leaving the farmer. However, it may be mentioned that sometimes sales are held ex-warehouse and in such cases price quotations include an element of cost of transportation from the farm, mine or factory to the warehouse. In some others, the terms, of delivery may include transportation up to the point of consumption.

There is no change in the system of price collection between the existing and the revised index. In the existing series, weekly quotations for the prescribed varieties on or about each friday are collected.

Method of Calculation

The 1970-71 series was calculated on the principle of weighted arithmetic mean as in the 1961-62 series. The price relatives are calculated as the percentage ratios which current price quotations bear to those prevailing in the base period. In other words the price relative for each variety in a market was calculated by dividing the current price quotation by the corresponding base price (1960-71) and multiplying it by 100. The commodity index was arrived at as the simple arithmetic average of price relatives of varieties or quotations in different markets. The subgroup and the index for the major group was derived as the weighted arithmetic mean of commodity indices. Likewise, the all-commodities index was computed as the weighted arithmetic mean of major group indices.

Linking Factor

The revised series of wholesale prices with base 1970-71 = 100 was introduced from the first week of January, 1977. In order to maintain continuity in the index numbers of wholesale prices, it is usual to produce linking factors for the base period in respect of individual commodities, sub-groups, groups and the general index so that the revised series may be compared with the outgoing one. The office of the Economic Adviser had in the past used simple arithmetic conversion method. In this method, index figures in the old series corresponding to the base period of the new series provide the linking factor. If the index in the old series corresponding to the base period 1970-71 was say, 181.1 then 181.1/ 100 = 1.811 would be the linking factor. An index figure in the new index when multiplied by 1.811 would give the estimate of the index the earlier series which was linked to the new.

Since there are different methods available for linking any two series, the choice of the method of linking the revised series of wholesale prices with the old series is being given to the users.

Subsequent Changes

The 1970-71 index was changed to 1981-82 and again with base 1993-94 = 100, with effect from 1994-95. (Table 21.3).

Index Number of Wholesale Prices in Calcutta

The Department of Commercial Intelligence and Statistics, Ministry of Commerce and Industry, compiles this index. It is monthly and is published in the *Indian Trade Journal*. The index is compiled from 69 items although formerly it contained 72 items. The 69 items are grouped in the following 16 groups (Table 21.4).

Table 21.4 Groups Constituting the Index Number of Wholesale Prices in Calcutta

Group	Number of items
1. Cereals	8
2. Pulses	6
3. Sugar	3
4. Tea	3
5. Other food articles	9
6. Oilseeds	3
7. Oil mustard	2
8. Jute, raw	3
9. Jute manufactures	4
10. Cotton	2
11. Cotton manufactures	6
12. Other textiles (wool and silk)	2
13. Hides and skins	3
14. Metals	6
15. Other raw and manufactured articles	8
16. Building materials (teakwood)	1
Total	69

Table 21.3 Index Numbers of Wholesale Prices Base : 1993-94 = 100

1	Primary articles					Fuel, power, light & lubricants	Manufactured products						All commodities
	Total	Food articles Total	Food-grains	Non-food articles	Minerals		Total	Food products	Textiles	Chemicals & chemical products	Basic metals, alloys & metal products	Machinery & machine tools	
	2	3	4	5	6	7	8	9	10	11	12	13	14
Weight-Base(1981-82)=100	32.3	17.39	7.92	10.08	4.83	10.66	57.04	10.14	11.56	7.36	7.63	6.27	100
Weight-Base(1993-94)=100	22.03	15.4	5.01	6.14	0.49	14.23	63.75	11.54	9.8	11.93	8.34	8.36	100
Last week of (1981-82 = 100)													
1986-87	136	144	130	138	101	140	132	130	120	128	144	129	134.2
1987-88	157	168	151	167	98	148	144	142	135	133	161	139	148.5
1988-89	157	174	166	156	99	155	157	149	144	137	192	158	156.9
1989-90	167	177	160	176	110	165	175	169	169	144	210	171	171.1
1990-91	196	211	196	211	109	189	190	191	178	154	228	189	191.8
1991-92	225	255	243	228	115	214	214	210	198	178	242	223	217.8
1992-93	232	269	239	224	118	246	231	244	209	201	265	233	233.1
1993-94	259	280	280	280	138	278	254	252	244	216	287	244	258.3
Last week of (1993-94 = 100)													
1994-95	121	115	119	137	104	109	118	113	128	122	116	109	117.1
1995-96	125	124	127	129	93	115	123	118	126	130	123	113	122.2
1996-97	136	138	144	133	109	130	126	130	115	136	128	117	128.8
1997-98	142	144	139	142	100	148	129	137	117	137	132	115	134.6
1998-99	153	157	167	146	118	153	135	150	114	152	133	116	141.7
1999-00	159	168	176	141	104	193	139	150	116	160	137	116	150.9

Table 21.3 Index Numbers of Wholesale Prices Base : 1993-94 = 100 (Contd.)

	Primary articles					Fuel, power, light & lubricants	Manufactured products						All commodities
	Total	Food articles Total	Food-grains	Non-food articles	Minerals		Total	Food products	Textiles	Chemicals & chemical products	Basic metals, alloys & metal products	Machinery & machine tools	
1	2	3	4	5	6	7	8	9	10	11	12	13	14
Average of weeks (1981-82 = 100)													
1986-87	137	148	129	134	104	139	129	129	116	125	141	127	132.7
1987-88	153	161	141	163	101	143	139	141	127	132	150	132	143.6
1988-89	160	177	162	160	99	151	152	148	140	136	176	151	154.3
1989-90	164	179	165	166	102	157	169	165	158	140	206	166	165.7
1990-91	185	201	179	194	109	176	183	182	171	148	220	180	182.7
1991-92	218	241	216	229	114	199	203	206	188	168	235	208	207.8
1992-93	235	271	242	229	116	227	226	224	201	193	257	231	228.7
1993-94	251	284	261	249	134	262	243	247	220	208	277	238	247.8
Average of weeks (1993-94 = 100)													
1994-95	116	113	115	124	105	109	112	114	118	117	108	106	112.6
1995-96	125	122	122	135	95	115	122	118	129	127	120	112	121.6
1996-97	136	137	138	134	107	126	124	125	119	131	126	116	127.2
1997-98	139	141	139	138	100	144	128	135	115	137	131	115	132.8
1998-99	156	159	152	152	111	148	134	150	114	146	133	116	140.7
1999-00	158	165	176	143	110	162	137	151	115	155	135	116	145.3

Table 21.3 Index Numbers of Wholesale Prices Base : 1993-94 = 100 (Contd.)

	Primary articles					Fuel, power, light & lubricants	Manufactured products						All commodities
	Total	Food articles Total	Food-grains	Non-food articles	Minerals		Total	Food products	Textiles	Chemicals & chemical products	Basic metals, alloys & metal products	Machinery & machine tools	
1	2	3	4	5	6	7	8	9	10	11	12	13	14
1999 - 00													
Apr	156.7	162.8	168.2	144.7	117.6	152.6	135.2	149.4	113.7	151.8	133.1	116.1	142.4
May	155.3	160.8	169.7	144.3	117.4	152.7	136.3	152.6	113.6	152.4	133.2	115.9	142.8
June	156.5	162.9	172.8	143.6	117.4	153.3	136.6	150.3	114.2	154.8	133.5	116.0	143.3
Jul	157.9	165.3	175.8	142.5	117.4	153.5	136.6	149.8	114.0	155.0	134.0	116.1	143.7
Aug	160.6	168.8	180.5	143.6	117.4	154.3	136.8	150.7	113.5	155.2	134.3	116.3	144.6
Sep	160.7	167.7	183.2	146.5	117.4	157.5	137.3	152.8	113.4	155.1	134.9	116.3	145.3
Oct	161.1	169.2	182.9	145.4	103.0	164.9	137.9	154.1	114.7	155.3	135.3	116.4	146.9
Nov	160.2	169.1	180.9	142.2	102.8	167.2	137.9	153.2	115.4	155.5	135.6	116.3	147.0
Dec	156.2	163.8	177.1	141.4	103.2	167.2	137.9	152.1	116.6	155.6	135.8	116.4	146.1
Jan	155.3	162.7	175.4	140.8	103.6	167.7	137.8	151.2	116.7	155.5	136.4	116.0	145.9
Feb	155.9	163.8	174.8	140.2	103.6	170.5	137.8	149.6	117.5	155.8	137.1	115.6	146.4
Mar	159.5	168.8	175.3	140.7	103.8	182.8	138.6	149.7	116.7	160.2	137.3	115.6	149.5
2000 - 01													
Apr	161.6	171.4	177.6	141.5	104.0	193.8	139.0	149.8	116.9	160.5	137.3	116.7	151.7
May	162.5	172.1	178.0	142.9	104.3	193.6	138.9	146.4	117.0	161.4	138.1	118.2	151.8
June	164.6	174.1	178.4	145.1	110.5	194.3	139.2	144.8	117.9	162.6	138.3	119.1	152.6
Jul	163.9	171.8	179.0	147.9	115.8	194.5	140.1	146.3	118.5	162.1	139.0	120.3	153.1

Table 21.3 Index Numbers of Wholesale Prices Base : 1993-94 = 100 (Contd.)

	Primary articles						Total	Manufactured products					All commodities
	Total	Food articles Total	Food-grains	Non-food articles	Minerals	Fuel, power, light & lubricants		Food products	Textiles	Chemicals & chemical products	Basic metals, alloys & metal products	Machinery & machine tools	
1	2	3	4	5	6	7	8	9	10	11	12	13	14
Aug	162.8	170.3	176.2	147.7	115.6	195.6	140.7	146.5	119.8	161.9	139.9	121.0	153.4
Sep	161.9	170.2	172.7	144.8	114.7	202.8	141.6	146.3	120.6	163.2	141.4	122.6	154.7
Oct	164.1	172.8	170.5	146.2	115.3	219.0	142.2	145.6	121.4	165.2	141.1	125.0	157.9
Nov(P)	163.0	172.3	172.1	143.5	114.7	220.0	142.3	145.5	121.9	164.9	141.2	124.3	157.9
Dec(P)	163.1	171.5	174.1	146.0	115.2	206.4	141.4	146.0	120.5	163.5	140.5	122.6	155.4

(P) :   Provisional

Source : Office of the Economic Advisor, Ministry of Industry.

For each group a separate index is worked out along with one for all the groups. The base year is 1914. The prices refer to the wholesale prices prevailing at Calcutta. For each group the index number is calculated by taking the arithmetic average of the items included. Weighting is introduced indirectly by taking more than one quotation for important items in a group. Thus 'cereals' group includes 4 varieties of rice and only one each of wheat, barley, maize and oats.

WHOLESALE PRICE INDEX NUMBER (WPI) BASE 1993-94

Issues

The Wholesale Price Index (WPI) series with base 1993-94 is compiled by the Office of Economic Adviser (OEA), Ministry of Industry, on weekly basis, based on the price quotations collected by the official as well as non-official source agencies in respect of 435 selected items/commodities identified in the basket of the index. As the concept of wholesale price has assumed various connotations and has been put to different uses by the source agencies, it becomes difficult to identify which price i.e. producer/ wholesale/retail is being collected by an agency. Owing to wide variety of sources, centres, and specifications and due to practical compulsion of collecting data on voluntary method, it is difficult to maintain the uniformity of concept of wholesale price in collection of price data. In many cases these prices correspond to farm-gate, factory-gate or mine-head prices; and in many other cases they refer to prices at the level of primary markets, secondary markets or other wholesale or retail markets. The Ministry of Agriculture has defined wholesale price as the rate at which a relatively large transaction of purchase, usually for further sale, is effected. As per OEA, wholesale prices represent transactions at the primary stage, which broadly correspond to producer's prices. In actual practice, the primary sales are not always held at ex-farm, ex-mines or ex-factory. Sometimes the sales are held ex-warehouses and in such cases the price quotations may include an element of the cost of transportation from the farm, mine or factory to warehouse. In the trade transactions, the terms of delivery may include the cost of transportation up to the point of consumption. With such variation in the concept of price, it is difficult to say what exactly WPI is measuring and it is posing serious problem for policy planners and researchers.

The official measure of inflation in the Indian economy is based on WPI. As WPI measures the price change at the level of either the wholesaler or the producer and does not take into account retail margins, thus it represents the production side and not the consumption side. For true measure of inflation, it is necessary to measure the changes in the prices only for the final goods, thus making the present WPI an improper measure of inflation.

It seems that the voluntary system of primary data collection on weekly basis is becoming unsustainable as the economy changes its character and levers of control. Some of the criticisms against WPI are as under:

- Divergent connotations of the concept of wholesale price
- Changes in quality of products
- Capturing shift in structure of economy
- Non-inclusion of Services Sector
- Weak price data collection mechanism

An attempt should be made to include prices of services, at least for those which could be collected regularly, such as rent, telephone, water, railway (possibly also road transport), banking and finance, medical, education and insurance. Data on user charges on these could be obtained either through sample surveys or directly from the concerned government establishments. In this context, the Working Group on revision of WPI, under Prof. S.R. Hashim, Member, Planning Commission had made categorical recommendation that Services Price Index should be developed, initially as a complement to the WPI, once it had established its robustness. The OEA, after having obtained the approval of government to create a Business Service Price Index, constituted a Sub-group of the Technical Advisory Commitee (TAC) on prices for the purpose of advising on the methodology for the preparation of such index.

Further, WPI is neither a wholesale price index nor a producer price index; it is something in between. One of the options could be to construct separately producer price index and market price index. The feasibility of collection of both i.e. the producer prices and the market prices in respect of all the selected commodities of the basket for arriving at the ratios between the two, in the year of revision of the base may be explored. These ratios would act as benchmark indicators for forwarding the prices in future years. There is a need to revise the WPI at shorter intervals to reflect changing behaviour of industrial production structure. Changes in tariff structure and removal of barriers together with liberalisation of foreign capital has altered the industrial structure. In the eventuality of having available.

Besides the attempt at the national level, different States and Union Territories are also collecting price data and compiling wholesale price indices on different base years. For instance SSB, Assam is compiling WPI with base as old as 1953, Tamil Nadu base 1970-71, West Bengal with base 1980-81. Further, States are compiling indices for different sub-groups such as agricultural commodities, manufactured items or both. The number of items in the basket of the various States also differs significantly. Since the indices being compiled by the various States lack in uniformity in base year, item basket, periodicity, method of compilation and the sources of data, thus making it impossible to undertake any analysis of regional/State level wholesale price variations being reflected by such indices.

Suggested Solutions

(a) The need to develop a Service Price Index, as recommended by the Working Group on Revision of WPI under Prof. S.R. Hashim, Member,

Planning Commission, initially as a complement to the WPI, requires no emphasis. It should be merged with the WPI, once it has established its robustness.

(b) At the national level, there is a need to have a producer price index but on account of inherent problems in collection of data for producer price, WPI is being compiled as a proxy to the producer price index. Due to limitations in the mechanism of voluntary price data collection, the present WPI is neither reflecting the movement of wholesale prices nor the producer prices. The immediate requirement is to make at least the existing WPI consistent within itself. Further, the endeavour should be to move towards the producer price. The feasibility of collection of both i.e. the producer prices and the market prices in respect of all the selected commodities of the basket for arriving at the ratios between the two, in the year of revision of the base may be explored. These ratios would act as benchmark indicators for forwarding the prices in future years. Most of the countries have the practice of compiling the Producer's Price Index and there is no concept of WPI.

There is a need to bring uniformity in terms of base year, number of items, data sources, etc. In wholesale price indices being compiled by the various States/UTs in order to make any meaningful analysis of regional variation in prices of wholesale transactions. It would be preferable that all the State WPIs should have the same base year or around that, as that of all-India.

EXISTING PRICE COLLECTION MECHANISM

Issues

The data on prices are regularly collected by Central and State Government Departments/agencies for varied purposes. These data basically form the source of different information compiled in various forms in accordance with specific needs by various agencies. Though all efforts are being made to ensure the correctness and reliability of price data being collected by various agencies by introducing multi-tier supervision, yet the quality of data have been questioned at various forums on account of variety of reasons, some of them are:

- Involvement of multiple data collection agencies;
- Use of varying concepts and definitions;
- Non-existence of an exclusive field agency;
- Non-standard specifications;
- Repetition of prices due to non-response; and
- Meagre honorarium for data collectors.

This question had been addressed at the highest forum of Committee of Secretaries, which expressed a concern over the multiplicity of agencies being involved in collection of price data and suggested that there was a need for convergence of data collection mechanism. In this context, a Sub-Group of TAC on Statistics of Prices and Cost of Living (SPCL), under the Chairmanship of DG and CEO, NSSO with OEA, Ministry of Industry as Member Secretary has been constituted to explore the possibility of convergence of price data collection mechanism. Based on the discussions, the Office of Economic Adviser is preparing a draft report to strengthen the wholesale price collection mechanism. The sub-group has also taken up the issue of speedier electronic transmission of price data from various data collecting agencies.

There is a need to unify the system of price data collection in such a way that the proposed mechanism should also take into account the requirements of not only national but also the State level CPIs and WPIs. As there is no legislation of collection of price data at present, the feasibility of bringing it under the umbrella of Collection of Statistics Act, 1953 may be explored.

Suggested Solutions For development of a convergent price data collection mechanism, the following steps are required:
- Better coordination between the State and the Centre;
- Perfect coordination among the data collection agencies along with demarcation of their jurisdiction;
- Uniformity in concepts and definitions;
- Introduction of checks and validations;

The proposed system could be a bottom-up approach and enable to throw a reliable data at the State level for compilation of various price indicators. One copy of the Price Collection Schedule in respect of items included in the basket of all India indices may be sent to the central agencies. Similarly, price data on items required for compilation of State level indices may be sent to the respective State/UTs agencies. The proposed system would enhance the reliability of data by using uniform concepts and definitions, avoid involvement of multiple agencies and would result in optimum use of resources.

The index numbers of wholesale prices of rice and wheat with agricultural year 1981-82 as base are compiled on a weekly basis by the Directorate of Economics and Statistics. Price quotations from 95 representative markets are utilized in respect of rice and 43 markets in respect of wheat. A simple arithmetic mean of the price relative for all the markets gives the index number of wholesale price for the commodity for the State while all-India index numbers are computed as weighted arithmetic mean of the State index numbers. Presently the DES compiles monthly all-India index numbers of wholesale prices of various agricultural commodities, manufactured articles and agricultural inputs. Data on wholesale prices of 96 commodities and retail prices of 39 agricultural commodities are compiled with base year 1981-82. But commodities included in the index vary from State to State depending upon the importance of the individual commodities in the different States.

Also, instead of index numbers, price relative of commodities are published for these centres. These centres are wayside railway stations. Prices are collected through station masters, whose work is supervised by the Inspector of Railways Labour. Labour Bureau now publishes all India Consumer Price Index-Industrial Workers (1982 = 100), Urban Non-Manual Employees (1984-85 = 100) and Agriculture Labour (1986-87 = 100). Latest information is as in Table 21.5).

Table 21.5 All India Consumer Price Index Numbers

	Industrial workers (Base: 1982=100)		Urban non-manual employees (Base: 1984-85=100)	Agricultural labourers (Base: 1986-87=100)
	Food index	*General*	*General index*	*General index*
1	*2*	*3*	*4*	*5*
Average of Months				
1986-87	141 *	137 *	115 **	572 $
1987-88	154 *	149 *	126 **	629 $
1988-89	169 *	163 *	136	708 $
1989-90	177	173	145	746 $
1990-91	199	193	161	803 $
1991-92	230	219	183	958 $
1992-93	254	240	202	1076 $
1993-94	272	258	216	1114 $
1994-95	297	279	232	1204 $
1995-96	337	313	259	234
1996-97	369	342	283	256
1997-98	388	366	302	267
1998-99	431	414	340	296
1999-00	446	428	352	208
Last Month of				
1986-87	142	138	117	573 $
1987-88	156	153	129	658 $
1988-89	169	163	138	729 $
1989-90	178	177	149	736 $
1990-91	207	201	169	858 $
1991-92	241	229	192	1046 $
1992-93	253	243	205	1053 $
1993-94	281	267	222	1175 $
1994-95	311	293	244	1300 $
1995-96	339	319	264	237
1996-97	373	351	291	262
1997-98	401	380	312	284
1998-99	445	414	337	293
1999-00	446	434	357	306

Table 21.5 All India Consumer Price Index Numbers (Contd.)

| 1 | Industrial workers (Base: 1982=100) | | Urban non-manual employees (Base: 1984-85=100) | Agricultural labourers (Base: 1986-87=100) |
	Food index	General	General index	General index
1	2	3	4	5
1999-00				
April	431	415	341	295
May	437	419	344	298
June	438	420	346	301
July	443	424	350	304
August	447	426	352	308
September	451	429	353	310
October	462	437	357	315
November	462	438	357	316
December	450	431	354	311
January	444	431	355	307
February	442	430	355	306
March	446	434	357	306
2000-01				
April	450	438	362	307
May	452	440	364	310
June	454	442	366	310
July	457	445	370	310
August	454	443	370	308
September	454	444	370	306
October	459	449	375	305
November	NA	450	NA	306

*		The new series of CPI for industrial workers with 1982 base has been introduced w.e.f. October, 1988. The earlier series on base 1960 = 100 has been simultaneously discontinued. The conversion factor from the new to the old series is 4.93 to regard to the General index, and 4.93 to regard to the General index, and 4.98 in regard to the Food index.
**		The new series of CPI for urban non-manual employees with 1984-85 base was introduced w.e.f. November, 1987. The earlier series on base 1960 = 100 has been simultaneously discontinued. The conversion factor from the new to the old series is 5.32.
$		Old base 1960-61 = 10C
NA		Not available
Note:	1.	Annual figures are yearly averages of months.
	2.	The new senses of CPI for agricultural labourers with 1986-87 (July 1986 to June 1987) base was introduced w.e.f. November, 1995. The earlier series on base 1960-61 (July 1960 to June 1961) has been simultaneously discontinued. The conversion factor from the new to the old series is 5.89.
Sources:	1.	Labour Bureau, Simla for consumer price indices or industrial workers and agricultural factors.
	2.	C.S.O. for consumer price indices for urban non-manual employees.

Index Number of Parity between Prices Received and Prices Paid by the Farmers

Index numbers of parity between prices received and prices paid by the farmer are available for the States of Assam, Kerala, Orissa, Punjab and West Bengal. These index numbers suffer from a number of limitations which certainly vitiates inter-State comparability. The crop coverage of the indices of prices received is inadequate in a number of cases and may not be fully representative of the movement in prices received by the farmer, the basis of assignment of weights for the different commodities in the index of prices received also differs from State to State. In some cases, the weights are in proportion to the value of production during the base period. Similarly, in the index of domestic expenditure, the weights in most cases are based on family budget of a limited number of rural families which cannot be considered representative for the entire States. The retail prices utilized for the index of domestic expenditure are in many cases urban prices of a few markets only. The items included in the index of cost of cultivation and their weights are generally approximate, being based on data from a few farms.

With a view to effecting improvements in the existing series of index numbers and to enable other States to initiate these index numbers, the Technical Committee on Construction of Agricultural Index Numbers in India reviewed the technical details and made far reaching recommendations for improvements in the scope, coverage and methodology of the existing series.

Consumer Price Index Numbers for Non-Manual Employees

Of late, the need for such a series was felt which would bring out the changes in conditions and levels of living of the middle class population. In an effort to bridge the gap, the Central Statistical Organization conducted in 1958-59 a Middle Class Family Living Survey. This survey covered nearly 36,000 families of non-manual employees in 45 cities and towns.

In 1964 the first volume of the report on the middle class family living survey was published which discussed the number, size, income distribution and expenditure of middle class families, employment and service conditions thereof. This report also discussed the origin, purpose, scope, design and organization of the Survey, schedules, concepts and definitions used, etc. In 1966, the second volume of the Report was published which discussed the food consumption and nutrition, health education, housing and welfare of the middle class families. This was the first venture in this field attempted to cover so many concepts of the conditions and levels of living of any section of the population in the country. The Survey provided the basic material for deriving the weighting diagram needed for the construction of manual consumer price index numbers for non-manual employees in 45 selected urban centres.

, The selection of the centres was made with due consideration to their administrative importance, middle class concentration and regional representation. The number of centres allotted were broadly according to the size of urban population of different States as in 1951. National and State capitals and other large cities with a population of 5 lakh and above had enjoyed the priority.

The index for these centres covered about 180 priceable items of goods and services and have been grouped into the following five main groups. These groups have been further divided into 23 sub-groups. The five main groups are as under:

1. Food, beverages and tobacco.
   (Cereals; pulses; oils and fats; meat, fish and eggs; milk and milk products; condiments and spices; vegetables; fruits; sugar; non-alcoholic beverages; prepared meals and refreshments, pan-supari and tobacco).
2. Fuel and light.
3. Housing.
4. Clothing and bedding; footwear.
5. Miscellaneous.
   (Medical care; education and reading; recreation and amusement; transport and communication; personal care and effects; household requisites; others, etc.)

Prices

For the purpose of construction of retail price index numbers, prices are collected every month in respect of 180 items from 36 shops in Kolkata and Mumbai, from 24 shops in each of the nine centres, viz. Hyderabad, Pune, Nagpur, Ahmedabad, Kanpur, Bangalore, Lucknow, Chennai and Delhi-New Delhi. In each of the remaining centres, prices are collected from 12 outlets every month. In view of the growing importance of fair price shops and cooperative stores, price quotations are also collected from them in each centre where they exist and due representation given in the index of these quotations along with the open market prices.

Information on house rent is collected through a half-yearly survey of house rents. The survey covers on a repetitive basis, a fixed sample of dwelling (which varies from 60 to 240) occupied by middle class families subject to only occasional substitution from the reserve list.

Specifications have been fixed separately in respect of each item, outlet depending on availability; and identity of specifications maintained in each case as long as the specified variety is available. In cases of lapse, method of substitution for shops and other specification is made use of. This system facilitates coverage of more than one variety in respect of each item while maintaining comparability over time.

Methodology

According to the method adopted for calculation of index numbers for each centre, the price relative for each item is computed by chaining together a series of successive 'links' each representing the average change in the prices of the item as compared with the preceding month. Since January 1968 the links and the price relatives are computed directly with reference to December 1963.

In case of vegetables, fruits and pan leaf the price relatives are obtained by a straight comparison of the average price during the month under reference, with the average price during the base period.

The index for a sub-group is computed as weighted arithmetic average of price relatives of the items included in the sub-group.

The index for a group is likewise computed as weighted arithmetic average of the sub-group indices and the overall index as a weighted arithmetic average of the group indices.

The all-India index is computed on the lines approved by the Technical Advisory Committee on Cost of Living Index Numbers as a weighted average of the centre indices with weights representing the aggregate expenditure of the middle class population which the centre indices are expected to serve.

Allotment of weights is made taking into account the following items:

(a) The economic and administrative policies of a State.

(b) Within a State, each selected centre is regarded as representing a sub-stratum of unspecified geographical demarcation but comprising of an equal share of urban middle class population in the State, excepting in the cities exceeding in size the predetermined equal share of the sub-strata.

(c) The population data of the 1961 Census have been used for determining weights to be assigned at the stratum and sub-stratum levels. The proportion of middle class population in each stratum/sub-stratum has been estimated by using the occupational distribution of the employed population available from the results of the 14th round of the National Sample as occupational distribution was available at the division level: (1) Professional, Technical and Related Workers; (2) Administrative, Executive and Managerial Workers; (3) Clerical and Related Workers; and (4) Sales Workers, which have been regarded as broadly representing the middle class population satisfying the definition of nonmanual activities.

(d) The per capita expenditure of consumption as observed in the Middle Class Family Living Survey has been assumed to be valid for the entire sub-stratum represented by the Centre. The aggregate expenditure of middle class families in each sub-stratum is obtained as a product of the estimated middle class population and the assumed per capita expenditure. The aggregate expenditure at the State level is obtained by summing up the sub-stratum estimates.

Major survey work on the new 2001 Consumer Price Index has been completed, but not lively to be implemented before 2004. The new series is made to effect present day consumption pattern of country's labour force.

CONSUMER PRICE INDEX NUMBERS (CPIs)

Issues

At the national level, there are four Consumer Price Indices (CPIs), namely CPI for Industrial Workers {CPI (IW)}, base 1981-82; CPI for Urban Non-Manual Employees {CPI (UNME)}, base 1984-85; CPI for Agricultural Labourers {CPI (AL)}, base 1986-87 and CPI for Rural Labourers {CPI (RL)}, base 1986-87. The responsibility for compilation and release of CPI (UNME) rests on CSO, whereas the other three CPIs are being brought out by Labour Bureau. These indices relate to different base years and cater to specific segments of the population, and thus can be considered as partial indices. These indices are not oriented to reflect a true picture of the price behaviour, and effect of price fluctuations of various goods and services on the living standards of rural and urban segments of the overall population in the country, over a period of time. As such, there is a need for compiling CPI series, separately for rural and urban population at national level, for which Government's approval in principle has also been obtained. There is also a need to address the issue of integration of CPI (R) and CPI (U) into a comprehensive index at national level.

At present there is no separate CPI for informal and some other major segments like urban and rural poor. The total working population can be broadly categorized into those employed in formal and informal sectors. The penetration of this sector in almost all sectors of the economy has witnessed a surge in employment opportunities. The importance of the informal sector can be gauged from its contribution, which is over two-fifth of the industrial productions and is providing livelihood to more than 16 million persons apart from accounting for a major share in the GDP. The segment of population working in the informal sector is not covered completely by any of the present CPI series compiled at national level. As such, there is need for constructing CPI series, separately for urban and rural informal sector workers. Need has also been felt for compilation of CPI series, separately for rural and urban poor; say for the population at the lowest three or four deciles of the income group. At present, no such series exists.

Different States and Union Territories are also collecting price data and compiling various price indices on very old base years. Against 32 States/UTs, there are only 19 of them, which are constructing CPIs pertaining to any one segment or the other. Among the 19 States/UTs, which are engaged in compilation of CPIs, majority of them have very old base years and there are only 5 States having CPIs with base year

1981-82 or thereafter. For instance, base year is as old as 1939 and the latest being 1988-89. There is a significant variation among the base years of different indices being compiled by a State. Further, there is a diversity not only on the segments of population for which CPIs are being compiled, but also on the number of representative items included in the item basket and data sources. Information on price data collected and price indices compiled by various Central Ministries/Departments along with periodicity is given in Table 21.6.

At present separate Family Living Surveys (FLS) are being conducted for the preparation of weighting diagrams for the national level CPIs. A national question arises whether there is a need to conduct separate FLS or the requisite data for compilation of all the weighting diagrams at national level and if possible for the State level CPIs also can be met through a single comprehensive survey.

The States/UTs may present their considered views on the following issues:

- Need for a Comprehensive Survey by the central agency to derive weighting diagrams for different CPIs with common base year:
- Whether the proposed Comprehensive Survey should meet the requirements of all-India CPIs only or both all-India as well as States with break-up such as rural/urban, informal/formal etc.
- Do not need to compute at State/UT level also, all the four national level CPIs and proposed CPI (R) and CPI (U)?
- Willingness on the part of States/UTs to shoulder the responsibility of price data collection required for compilation of State level indices.

Suggested Solutions

(a) Instead of conducting multiple surveys, there is a case for undertaking a comprehensive single survey to cater to the needs of not only the existing national level (CPIs, proposed CPI (Rural) and (Urban), but also of State level CPIs. The sampling design should be developed in such a way that apart from meeting the requirements of construction of weighting diagrams at the national level, the State level requirements with rural and urban breakup may also be fulfilled. The various concepts such as household, family and other technical details being used in the four existing series may be resolved before deciding on the comprehensive survey. The proposed comprehensive survey would also facilitate the compilation of all indices with same base year and with uniform concepts and definitions both at national and State level. It is expected that the proposed comprehensive survey might have a slightly larger sample size for preparation of weighting diagrams at State level but it would be cost effective as compared to separate surveys being in vogue at present.

(b) The CPIs being compiled by some of the States varies not only in base year but also in item basket, periodicity and sources of data used. There is a need to bring uniformity of methodology in the compilation

Table 21.6 *Details of Price Data Collected, and Price Indices Compiled, by Various Central Ministries and Departments*

Dept./Ministry	Price Data	Periodicity	Price Indices	Periodicity	Related Publication

1. Directorate of Economics and Statistics, Department of Agriculture and Co-operation, Ministry of Agriculture	1. Wholesale prices of agricultural commodities
	2. Retail prices of selected agricultural commodities
	3. Farm harvest prices of selected agricultural commodities
	4. Retail prices of 37 agricultural commodities selected centres in different states
		Weekly
		Weekly
		Annual
		Month-end
			None	None	1. Daily Bulletin of Wholesale Prices of Food Grains and Sugar
					2. Weekly Bulletins:
					  a) Wholesale Prices of Selected Commodities
					  b) Retail Prices of Essential Commodities
					3. Annual Publications:
					  a) Agricultural Prices in India;
					  b) Bulletin on Food Statistics
					4. Quarterly Bulletin on Sugar Situation in India
					5. Farm Harvest Prices of Principal Crops in India

2. Labour Bureau, Ministry of Labour	1. Retail prices for various consumer items relating to Industrial workers, collected by State Directorates of Economics and Statistics and Labour Commissioner offices in some states 2. Rural retail prices for compilation of CPI(AL) and CPI(RL) collected by FOD, NSSO	Weekly/Monthly Monthly	1. CPI(IW); Base 1982 = 100 2. CPI(AL); Base 1986-87 = 100 3. CP(RL); Base 1986-87 = 100 4. RPI of 31 essential commodities	Monthly Monthly Monthly Monthly	1. Indian Labour Journal; Monthly 2. Press release; CPI(IW), CPI(AL) and CPI(RL); Monthly 3. Labour Intelligence; Monthly 4. Report on CPI Numbers; Annual 5. Indian Labour year book; Annual 6. Indian Labour Statistics; Annual

Table 21.6 Details of Price Data Collected, and Price Indices Compiled, by Various Central Ministries and Departments (Contd.)

Dept./Ministry	Price Data	Periodicity	Price Indices	Periodicity	Related Publication
3. CSO, Min. of Planning and Programme Implementation	Retail price data collected by FOD, NSSO	Monthly	CPI(UNME)	Monthly	1. Monthly Abstract of Statistics 2. Statistical Abstract of India; Annual
4. NSSO, Ministry of Planning and Programme Implementation	1. Rural retail prices of 260 items from 603 villages; 2. Retail prices of selected goods and services from 59 urban centres	Monthly Monthly	None	None	None
5. Office of Economic Adviser Department of Industrial Policy and Promotion, Ministry of Industry	Wholesale prices of agricultural commodities and products, specified varieties/grades of selected manufactured products/ industrial items are collected through state DES and other govt. agencies	Weekly	WPI	Weekly and monthly	Press release: i) Index Numbers of Wholesale Prices in India; ii) Weekly and Monthly Reviews of WPI; iii) Printed bulletin on Index Numbers of Wholesale Prices in India.

Table 21.6 Details of Price Data Collected, and Price Indices Compiled, by Various Central Ministries and Departments (Contd.)

Dept./Ministry	Price Data	Periodicity	Price Indices	Periodicity	Related Publication
6. NBO, Ministry of Urban Affairs and Employment	Prices of building materials and wage rates of building construction labourers in 250 centres through state governments	Quarterly	1. Residential Building Cost Index (BCI) for Delhi 2. Building Cost Indices (BCI) compiled by some states are sent to NBO	Quarterly	1. Quarterly Bulletin on Building Material Prices and Wages 2. Prominent facts on Housing
7. Office of the Coal Controller	Price data of coal	Monthly	None	None	1. Monthly Bulletin on Coal Statistics; 2. Annual Coal Statistics 3. Coal Directory in India; Annual
8. Indian Bureau of Mines, Ministry of Steel and Mines	Prices of selected minerals, metals in domestic and foreign markets	Annual	None	None	Indian Minerals Year-Book
9. Reserve Bank of India	Spot prices of gold and silver (Based on the information of Bombay Bullion association)	Daily	1. Indices of Security prices, Base '80-81 2. Indices of yields on shares	Monthly Monthly	1. RBI Bulletin 2. Weekly Statistical Supplement of RBI Bulletin

Table 21.6 Details of Price Data Collected, and Price Indices Compiled, by Various Central Ministries and Departments (Contd.)

Dept./Ministry	Price Data	Periodicity	Price Indices	Periodicity	Related Publication
10. DGCIS, Ministry of Commerce	Prices of slected major commodities, which are important as regards foreign trade, eceived from different customs organisations throughout the country	Monthly	1. Unit value and quantum indices 2. Price indices for fiscal years of exports and imports; 3. Indices of imports and exports	Quarterly and Annual Annual Quarterly	1. Foreign Trade Statistics of India; Monthly 2. Indian Trade Journal; Weekly 3. Selected statistics of the Foreign Trade of India
11. Office of the Textile Commissioner, Ministry of Textiles	1. Prices of yarn and fibres 2. Prices of various kinds of cloths	Weekly Monthly	None	None	1. Basic Textile Statistics 2. Compendium of Textile Statistics
12. Department of Consumer Affairs, Min. of Food and Consumer Affairs	Wholesale and Retail prices of 12 essential commodities from 50 selected centres	Daily	None	None	None

Consumer Price Index

The Consumer Price Index is an indicator of the cost of living at a particular point of time. Chart I shows the annual average growth in the cost of living index—consumer inflation—in select countries during two periods, covering the decade ending 1990 and the eight years thereafter. There are countries which able to reduce the average growth rates of inflation in 1990-98 as against that in 1980-90. As usual, the advanced nations were able to keep prices in check whereas certain Latin American countries with economic crises suffered uncontrolled price rises.

Prices have remained under substantial control in Japan, its average annual growth rate of cost of living index dropped to 1.1 per cent in 1990-98 from 1.7 per cent in 1980-90. Likewise, Canada, the U.K. Italy and the U.S. were able to keep the growth rates of their indices at much lower levels in 1990-98 as compared to the earlier decade.

Among the developing countries, Mexico could bring the average yearly price increase down to nearly 20 per cent against a whopping 74 per cent in the earlier period. Similarly, Argentina had a phenomenal success in bringing down the rate from 390 to 13 per cent. But Brazil had its problems and the average growth in the cost of living index shot up to 333 per cent from 285 per cent.

Indonesia and India had higher average growth rates of consumer prices at 11.2 per cent and 9.7 per cent in 1990-98 against 8.3 and 8.6 per cent in the previous decade.

Chart II shows the changes in food price index. These indices follow closely the cost of living index. Pakistan had a higher growth in its food index than the cost of living index in 1990-98. In India too, the food index was slightly higher than the cost of living index in the same period.

Chart II

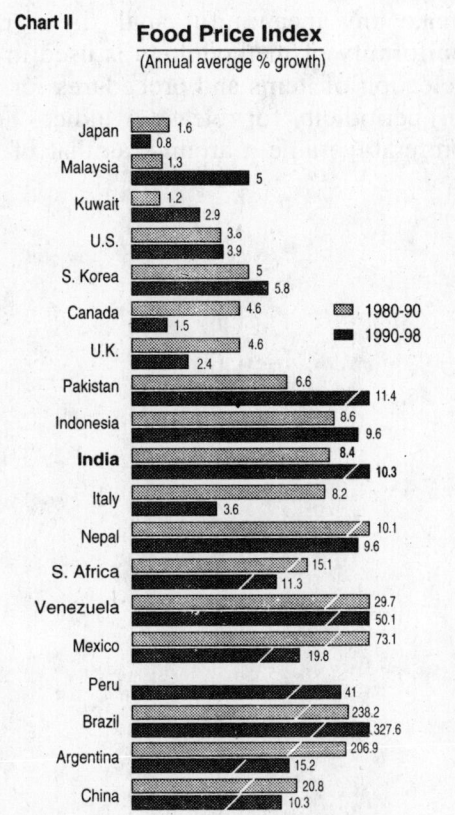

Food Price Index
(Annual average % growth)

1980-90 / 1990-98

- Japan: 1.6 / 0.8
- Malaysia: 1.3 / 5
- Kuwait: 1.2 / 2.9
- U.S.: 3.0 / 3.9
- S. Korea: 5 / 5.8
- Canada: 4.6 / 1.5
- U.K.: 4.6 / 2.4
- Pakistan: 6.6 / 11.4
- Indonesia: 8.6 / 9.6
- **India**: 8.4 / 10.3
- Italy: 8.2 / 3.6
- Nepal: 10.1 / 9.6
- S. Africa: 15.1 / 11.3
- Venezuela: 29.7 / 50.1
- Mexico: 73.1 / 19.8
- Peru: 41
- Brazil: 238.2 / 327.6
- Argentina: 206.9 / 15.2
- China: 20.8 / 10.3
- Russian Fed.: 207

Chart I

Cost of Living Index
(Annual average % growth)

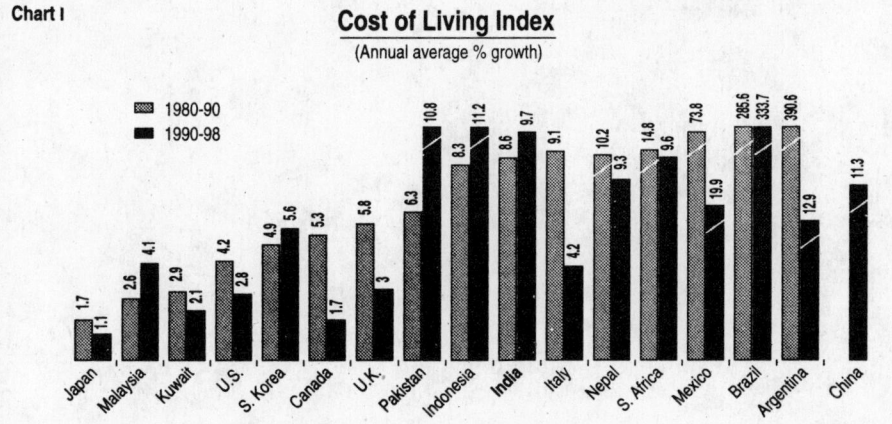

1980-90 / 1990-98

- Japan: 1.7 / 1.1
- Malaysia: 2.6 / 4.1
- Kuwait: 2.9 / 2.1
- U.S.: 4.2 / 2.8
- S. Korea: 4.9 / 5.6
- Canada: 5.3 / 1.7
- U.K.: 5.8 / 3
- Pakistan: 6.3 / 10.8
- Indonesia: 8.3 / 11.2
- India: 8.6 / 9.7
- Italy: 9.1 / 4.2
- Nepal: 10.2 / 9.3
- S. Africa: 14.8 / 9.6
- Mexico: 73.8 / 19.9
- Brazil: 285.6 / 333.7
- Argentina: 390.6 / 12.9
- China: 11.3

Source: World Development Indicators, 2000

of price indices being attempted by the various States/UTs in order to make any meaningful analysis of regional variation of prices. The uniformity of methodology is used in the context that (i) the criteria for selection of items and procedures for preparation of weighting diagram, (ii) periodicity for release A indices and (iii) choice of base year should preferably same a around, as that of all India.

22

Indices of Area, Cropping Pattern, Agricultural Production, and Crop Yield

The following series are available for the index numbers of agricultural production in India:
1. Ministry of Agriculture.
2. FAO Series.

A few common features of the above series may first be noted. All indices are related to the gross production of crops obtained from the 'Crop Estimates' or the 'Area and Production of Principal Crops in India'. All indices are annual. Individual commodities are classified into groups and in addition to general index, group indices are also available in all the series. For every year, first, the provisional indices are calculated, based on production figures given in the final crop estimates. These are later revised when the revised crop estimates become available next year. The formula used in the construction of all the above three index numbers is that of Laspeyer as given below:

$$P_{01} = \frac{P_1 q_0}{P_0 q_0}$$

where
P_{01} = Price index number of the current year
P_1 = Current year price
q_0 = Base year quantity
P_0 = Base year price

Foodgrains are included in all the series. The coverage for non-food crops varies slightly for different indices. The method of determination of weights is the same in the first two series. The FAO method of determining weights is a little different. Various series are described below.

MINISTRY OF AGRICULTURE SERIES

In 1949, a series of 'All-India Index Number of Agricultural Production' covering 19 principal agricultural commodities for which estimates of

531

production were then available, was initiated with the quinquennium ending 1938-39 as the base. In view of the extended number and coverage of the crop estimates during later years, a revised series of index numbers was issued in 1954 with the base 1949-50. The index which in the earlier years covered 19 commodities, covered 28 crops divided into two main groups and six sub-groups. The crops are:

(a) Foodgrains:
  (i) Cereals—
      Rice, jowar, bajra, maize, ragi, wheat, barley and small millets.
  (ii) Pulses—
      Gram, tur, other pulses.
(b) Non-foodgrains:
  (i) Oilseeds—
      Groundnut, sesamum, rape and mustard, linseed, castor.
  (ii) Fibres—
      Cotton, jute, mesta.
  (iii) Plantation crops—
      Tea, coffee, rubber.
  (iv) Miscellaneous crops—
      Sugarcane, pepper, tobacco, potatoes, ginger, chillies.

In principle, the index of agricultural production should cover all agricultural crops and also livestock products. But as reliable annual estimates of production of minor crops and livestock products are not available, the present series has been confined to 28 crops listed above. Efforts are being made to obtain regular and reliable estimates of production of as many additional agricultural commodities as possible and the question of inclusion of more commodities in the Index is to be reviewed quinquennially. For a study of trends in area under crops and agricultural productivity all-India index numbers of area under crops and productivity were issued in August 1962 with the same base and coverage as for the index numbers of agricultural production.

In view of the importance of index numbers of agricultural production and other items for planning and policy formulation and the multiplicity of uses to which these are being put at the national and international levels, it was felt that a deeper examination of the various problems involved in the construction of different series was necessary. Accordingly a Technical Committee was set up under the chairmanship of late Dr. V.G. Panse. The Committee reviewed the technical details of these indices and made recommendations for improvements in the scope, coverage and methodology of the series. The Committee further recommended the intensity of a number of new series of index numbers, such as index numbers of net area sown, cropping pattern, cropping intensity and productivity per hectare. In the light of these recommendations, the Directorate of Economics and Statistics issued a revised series of index numbers of area under crops, agricultural production, etc. in 1972. Details of revised series are discussed below briefly.

Base Period

Agricultural production is greatly affected by uncertain factors like rainfall, temperature, floods, etc. and is, therefore, subject to large fluctuations from year to year. As such for study of trends in area, production, etc. the base period should generally be broad based by taking an average of a number of years instead of a single year. Taking into account the various criteria, triennium ending 1961-62 was selected as the base period for the all-India series in accordance with the recommendation of the Central Advisory Committee in Statistics and also of the FAO. This was later revised to triennium ending 1969-70 and all the existing series are with this best.

Coverage

During recent years a number of additional crops has been covered under the system of crop estimation. To make the all-India series more representative, their coverage has been enlarged. The revised series cover 38 croups divided into two main groups and eight sub-groups. The crops included are:
  I. Foodgrains
    (i) Cereals—Rice, jowar, bajra, maize, ragi, wheat, barley and small millets.
    (ii) Pulses—Gram, tur and other pulses.
  II. Non-Foodgrains
    (i) Oilseeds—groundnut, sesamum, rape and mustard, linseed, castor, cotton seed, safflower, nigerseed and coconut.
    (ii) Fibres—cotton, jute, mesta and sannhemp.
  III. Plantation crops
    Tea, coffee and rubber.
  IV. Condiments and spices
    Pepper, ginger, chillies, turmeric and arecanut.
  V. Fruit and vegetables
    Potatoes, bananas and cashewnut.
  VI. Miscellaneous crops
    Sugarcane, tobacco and guar.

The above crops account for nearly 94 per cent of the total gross cropped area in the country.

Area under Crops

As area under crops can be added hectare by hectare, no explicit weights have been given to different crops for computation of sub-group, group and all-crop indices. These have been calculated directly from the area under sub-groups, group and all-crops in different years. There is thus implied weighting in proportion to the area under individual crops to the total area under all-crops in the base period.

Cropping Pattern

Weights are assigned to individual crops in proportion to the value of yield per hectare during the base period.

Yield

Current year's area under individual crops are used as weights.

Agricultural Production

Average prices in the base period have been used as weight coefficients.

The prices used for the weighting diagrams of various indices are harvest prices or wholesale prices during the peak marketing period in the Primary Markets. Base period prices and value weight of different crops are given below.

Concept of Production. The concept of production utilized in the index of agricultural production is essentially that of gross production of crops, no allowance being made for wastage or seed. It may be mentioned that the FAO series of index numbers of agricultural production are also essentially based on gross output but that organization deducts quantities of crops, milk and skimmed milk utilized as animal feed, whether they come from domestic or import sources. This is done to avoid double counting which would occur if foodgrains credited to the food crop production are fed to livestock and the resultant livestock products are included in the index. This situation does not arise in the case of the present series since livestock products are excluded from the scope of the index of agricultural production.

Methodology The changeover during the last decade or so from the traditional method of reporting area and production of crops to the method of complete enumeration in the case of area and to crop estimation survey for estimation of yield rates, and also the increase in reporting area, have taken place progressively in respect of different crops in different States. To provide for these changes in coverage and methods of estimation, the index numbers of area under crops, yield, agricultural production, etc. are constructed by the chain-base method under which the area/production/yield, etc. of a crop during a year is expressed as a relative of the corresponding area/production/yield in the preceding year, based on the same coverage and methods of estimation. These relatives for each crop are linked to the base year through the intervening chain relatives to give the area/production/yield, etc. index for the crop.

The application of chain-base method involves two basic assumptions which are:

  (i) the variation in production/area/yield in the non-reporting areas is the same as that in the reporting areas in the aggregate; and
 (ii) the relative variation in the figures of yield/production based on crop-estimation surveys is the same as that based on the traditional method of crop estimation employing eye-appraisal and normal yield figures.

The practical implications of (ii) above are that for the transitional year, that is, when the method of estimation undergoes a change, the estimates of production/yield should be available on the basis of both the traditional method and the crop-estimation surveys.

The formulae for the existing index series are as under:

$$\text{Index of area under crops} = \frac{\Sigma a_{ij}}{\Sigma a_{i0}} \times 100 \qquad (1)$$

$$\text{Index of net area sown} = \frac{N_j}{N_0} \times 100 \qquad (2)$$

$$\text{Index of cropping intensity} = \frac{\Sigma a_{ij}}{\Sigma a_{i0}} \left| \frac{N_j}{N_0} \times 100 \right.$$

$$= \frac{\Sigma a_{ij}}{\Sigma a_{i0}} \times \frac{N_0}{N_j} 100 \qquad (3)$$

$$\text{Index of cropping pattern} = \frac{\Sigma c_{ij}\, y_{i0}\, P_{i0}}{\Sigma c_{i0}\, y_{i0}\, P_{i0}} \times 100$$

$$= \frac{\Sigma \left(\dfrac{a_{ij}}{\Sigma a_{ij}}\, y_{i0}\, P_{i0} \right)}{\Sigma \left(\dfrac{a_{i0}}{\Sigma a_{i0}}\, y_{in}\, P_{i0} \right)} \times 100$$

$$= \frac{\Sigma a_{ij}\, y_{i0}\, P_{i0}}{\Sigma a_{ij}\, y_{i0}\, P_{ij}} \times \frac{\Sigma a_{i0}}{\Sigma a_{ij}} \times 100 \qquad (4)$$

$$\text{Index of yield} = \frac{\Sigma a_{ij}\, y_{ij}\, P_{i0}}{\Sigma a_{ij}\, y_{i0}\, P_{i0}} \times 100 \qquad (5)$$

Index of productivity per hectare of the net area

$$= \frac{\Sigma a_{ij}\, y_{ij}\, P_{i0}}{\Sigma a_{i0}\, y_{i0}\, P_{i0}} \left| \frac{N_i}{N_0} \times 100 \right. \qquad (6)$$

Index of agricultural production

$$= \frac{\Sigma a_{ij}\, y_{ij}\, p_{i0}}{\Sigma a_{i0}\, y_{i0}\, p_{0i}} \times 100 = \frac{\Sigma P_{ij}\, P_{ij}}{\Sigma P_{i0}\, P_{i0}} = \frac{\Sigma \dfrac{P_{ij}}{P_{i0}} \times P_{i0}\, P_{i0}}{\Sigma P_{i0}\, P_{i0}} \qquad (7)$$

where
a_{i0} = Area under the ith crop in the base period
a_{ij} = Area under the ith crop in the ith year
N_0 = Net area sown in the base period
N_j = Net area sown in the jth year

$$c_{i0} = \frac{a_{i0}}{\Sigma a_{i0}}$$

$$c_{i0} = \frac{a_{i0}}{\Sigma a_{ij}}$$

y_{in} = Yield per hectare of the ith crop in the base period
y_{ij} = Yield per hecate of the ith crop in the jth year
P_{i0} = Price per unit of the ith crop in the base period
P_{i0} = Production of the ith crop in the base period
P_{ij} = Production of the ith crop in the jth year

LINKING OF NEW SERIES WITH OLD SERIES

In order to maintain continuity in the index numbers of area under crops, agricultural production and yield, the new series has been linked with the old series by suitable conversion factors for the base period in respect of individual crops.

Due to enlargement in the coverage of the revised series, a few new sub-groups have been introduced. However, index numbers for the new crops are not available for the period prior to 1959-60. To provide continuity in the sub-group and group indices, as far as possible, the crops in the old series have been re-grouped to provide indices according to new sub-groups like fruits and vegetables, condiments and spices and miscellaneous crops. The procedures for working out the sub-group, group and all-crops indices of area, production and yield are indicated below:

Area under Crops   As no explicit weights are assigned to individual crops, the sub-group, group and all-crops indices have been reworked with triennium ending 1961-62, keeping the coverage as in the old series for the period prior to 1959-60.

Agricultural Production   Individual crop indices on the revised base have been combined into sub-group, group and all-crops indices taking the revised weights for the triennium ending 1961-62, keeping the coverage as in the old series for the period prior to 1959-60.

Yield Methodology for working out sub-group and all-crops indices has undergone a change. To provide a comparable series, indices for the period prior to 1959-60, sub-group, group and all-crops-indices have been reworked by giving current year's area weights to individual crop yields, in accordance with the revised methodology.

The revised series are published in 'Agricultural Situation in India' and 'Estimates of Area and Production of Principal Crops in India'.

INDEX WITH 1981-82 BASE

Series of index numbers, as of base triennium ending the agricultural year 1969-70, was evolved on the basis of recommendations made by the "Technical Committee on Index Numbers Relation to Agricultural Economy", set up in 1965 under the Chairmanship of the late Dr. V.G. Panse. The details regarding construction of the present series are discussed briefly below:

Base Period

Area and Production of different crops vary considerably from region to region and over time depending upon weather conditions, spatial and temporal distribution of rainfall, level of various inputs application and other unpredictable factors such as intensity of drought, floods, etc. In order to have a 'normal' year as the base period. Usually an average of three to five years is taken. The revised series of index numbers, triennium ending the agricultural year 1981-82 was selected as the base.

Keeping these in view, A Technical Committee was constituted under the Chairmanship of Economic and Statistical Adviser in May, 1985 to suggest an appropriate base period, composition of crops to be included and the new weighting diagram. The Technical Committee after consideration of various alternatives recommended to take triennium ending 1981-82 = 100 as the base period. It had also suggested to include new crops like soyabean, sunflower, garlic and onion in the new series.

Coverage

The index numbers cover 46 crops under two main groups and eight sub-groups. The crops and groups are listed below:

Foodgrains

  (i) Cereals: Rice, wheat, jowar, bajra, maize, ragi, barley and small millets (Crops except rice and wheat constitute the sub-group coarse cereals).
  (ii) Pulses: Gram, tur and other pulses.

Non-foodgrains

  (i) Oilseeds: Groundnut, sesamum, rapeseed and mustard, linseed, castorseed, safflower, nigerseed, soyabean, sunflower, coconut

and cottonseed. (The oilseed crops except coconut and cottonseed constitute 9 oilseeds for the new series).
  (ii) Fibres: Cotton, jute, mesta and sannhemp. (Jute and mesta constitute a sub-group).
 (iii) Plantation crops: Tea, coffee and rubber.
 (iv) Condiments and spices: Pepper, ginger, garlic, chillies, turmeric, arecanut, coriander and cardamom.
  (v) Fruits and Vegetable: Potato, Onion, banana, cashewnut, tapioca and sweet potato.
  (v) Misc. Crops: Sugarcane, tobacco and guarseed.

Weighting Pattern In order to combine the production indices of various crops, their base year values are used in a weighting diagram. Such a problem does not arise for the index numbers of area, as area under various crops are additive crop by crop. The value coefficients of crops have been adopted from the Central Statistical Organisation's National Income returns and these are based on farm harvest prices or wholesale prices in primary markets during the peak marketing season.

Methodology

Let
1. a_{ij}—the area under ith crop in the jth year.
2. a_{io}—the area under ith crop in base year period.
3. p_{ij}—production of ith crop in the jth year.
4. p_{io}—production of ith crop in the year period.
5. y_{ij}—yield of ith crop per hectare in jth year.
6. y_{io}—yield per hectare of ith crop in base year period.
7. w_i—weight of ith crop

$$= \frac{\text{value of the } i\text{th crop in base year}}{\text{value of all selected crops in base year}} \times 100$$

8. P_{io}—Price per unit of the ith crop in the base period.
9. N_i and N_o are the net area sown, respectively for the jth year and the base year.

Individual crop indices are calculated as below:

(a) Index number of area $= \dfrac{a_{ij}}{a_{io}} \times 100 = IA_{ij}$

(b) Index number of production $\dfrac{p_{ij}}{p_{io}} \times 100 = \dfrac{a_{ij}y_{ij}}{a_{io}y_{io}} \times 100 = IP_{oj}$

(c) Index number of yield $= \dfrac{IP_{ij}}{IA_{ij}} \times 100$

For sub-groups and groups of crops the indices are as below: (summations are over the crops suffix i)

(a) Index number of area $= \dfrac{\Sigma a_{ij}}{\Sigma a_{io}} \times 100$

(b) Index number of Production

$$= \dfrac{\Sigma \text{ Value of current year's crop with base year's price}}{\Sigma \text{ Value of base year's production of } i\text{th crop}} \times 100$$

$$= \dfrac{\Sigma a_{ij}\, y_{ij}\, P_{io}}{\Sigma a_{io}\, y_{io}\, p_{io}} \times 100$$

$$= \dfrac{\Sigma w_i\, IP_{ij}}{\Sigma w_i}$$

(c) Index number of field

$$= \dfrac{\Sigma a_{ij}\, y_{ij}\, P_{io}}{\Sigma a_{ij}\, y_{io}\, P_{io}} \times 100$$

The index numbers for the individual crops are calculated on the chain base method so as to account for the changes in concept/coverage in crops estimation.

In addition to the above, a few other index numbers, primarily related to land use, are also computed and are as below:

(i) Index number of net area sown $= \dfrac{N_i}{N_o} \times 100$

(ii) Index number of cropping intensity

$$= \dfrac{\text{Cropping intensity in the current year}}{\text{Cropping intensity in the base year.}} \times 100$$

(iii) Index number of cropping pattern

$$= \dfrac{\Sigma c_{ij}\, y_{io}\, p_{io}}{\Sigma c_{io}\, y_{io}\, p_{io}} \times 100$$

$$\text{Where} \quad c_{io} = \frac{a_{ij}}{\Sigma a_{ij}}, \quad c_{io} = \frac{a_{io}}{\Sigma a_{io}}$$

(iv) Index number of productivity per ha. of net area sown

$$= \frac{\Sigma a_{ij} \, y_{ii} \, w_i \, / N_j}{\Sigma a_{io} \, y_{io} \, w_i \, / N_o} \times 100$$

Computation of Growth Rates

The average annual growth rates have been calculated by fitting and exponential function.

$$Y^t = ab^t$$

to be observed time series data

Where (i) Y_t stands for the observation (area, production, yield index number for a crop) in the time-point.

(ii) 'a' and 'b' are the parameters, which are estimated by the least square method, and

(iii) $b = \left(1 + - \dfrac{r}{100} \right)$

Therefore, $r = (b - 1) \times 100$ gives the average growth rate in the form of percentage per annum.

THE 1993-94 BASE

Since the C.S.O. has now changed the base for national accounts to 1993-94, base in the Agricultural Production Index has also been changed accordingly. This is the first time that statewise Index Nos. for all the States have been released for the years from 1993-94 to 1998-99 in the publication Index of Agricultural Production Area and Yield, July 2000 issued by the Directorate of Economics and Statistics. Methodology for the same is given below. Basic data about index numbers of these series are given in Tables 22.1 and 22.2.

Base Year

The base year of the present series of state "Index of Area, Production and Yield in Agriculture" is chosen as the Triennium Ending (T.E.) 1993-94 as a way of updating the base to a recent year and to be in harmony with the other series of indices such as Index of Industrial Production, Wholesale Price Index and the series of National Accounts Statistics. Since area and production in agriculture fluctuate a great deal from one year to another year, the average of area/production over the

Table 22.1 All-India Compound Growth Rates of Area, Production and Yield of Principal Crops

(Base: Triennium ending 1981-82=100)

(Percent per annum)

Crops	1949-50 to 1997-98*			1949-50 to 1964-65			1967-68 to 1997-98*		
	A	P	Y	A	P	Y	A	P	Y
Rice	0.77	2.67	1.89	1.21	3.50	2.25	0.62	2.85	2.27
Wheat	2.21	5.47	3.18	2.69	3.98	1.27	1.51	4.59	3.04
Jowar	-0.71	0.82	1.55	0.99	2.51	1.49	-1.43	0.40	1.86
Bajra	-0.16	1.66	1.82	1.08	2.34	1.24	0.86	0.99	1.87
Maize	1.16	2.40	1.22	2.67	3.88	1.18	0.09	1.85	1.76
Ragi	-0.41	1.19	1.61	0.84	3.08	2.22	-1.07	0.69	1.78
Small Millets	-2.19	-2.01	0.18	-0.30	-0.2	0.09	-3.93	-3.28	0.67
Barley	-3.24	-1.41	1.88	-0.64	-0.28	0.36	-4.89	-2.47	2.55
Coarse Cereals	-0.55	1.07	1.53	0.90	2.25	1.23	-1.36	0.59	1.91
Total Cereals	0.48	2.89	2.03	1.25	3.21	1.77	0.01	2.86	2.39
Gram	-0.64	0.06	0.70	1.64	2.66	1.00	-0.53	0.15	0.69
Tur	0.97	0.81	-0.16	0.57	-1.34	-1.9	1.40	1.37	-0.02
Other Pulses	0.49	0.93	0.44	2.06	1.28	-0.77	0.20	1.44	1.24
Total Pulses	0.16	0.55	0.44	1.72	1.41	-0.18	0.13	0.91	0.75
Total Foodgrains	0.41	2.50	1.70	1.35	2.82	1.36	0.03	2.59	1.98
Sugarcane	1.84	3.07	1.21	3.28	4.26	0.95	1.76	3.11	1.98
Groundnut	0.99	1.84	0.84	4.01	4.34	0.31	0.41	1.68	1.26
Sesamum	-0.21	0.96	1.17	0.14	-0.32	-0.46	-0.61	1.57	2.19
Rape & Mustard Seed	2.19	4.29	2.05	2.97	3.35	0.37	2.68	5.38	2.63
Sunflower +							13.21	12.39	-0.73

Table 22.1 All-India Compound Growth Rates of Area, Production and Yield of Principal Crops (Contd.)

(Base: Triennium ending 1981-82=100)

(Percent per annum)

Crops	1949-50 to 1997-98*			1949-50 to 1964-65			1967-68 to 1997-98*		
	A	P	Y	A	P	Y	A	P	Y
Soyabean +							22.79	24.68	1.53
Nine Oilseeds	1.45	2.82	1.19	2.53	3.12	-	1.84	3.74	1.80
Total Oilseeds	1.23	2.77	1.14	2.67	3.20	0.30	1.41	3.60	1.70
Cotton	0.28	2.56	2.28	2.47	4.55	2.04	0.17	2.84	2.67
Jute	0.49	1.70	1.21	3.00	3.50	0.49	0.29	2.27	1.97
Mesta	-0.20	0.43	0.63	6.21	7.97	1.66	-1.96	-0.66	1.33
Jute & Mesta	0.31	1.49	1.07	3.88	4.31	0.70	-0.3	1.79	1.72
Total Fibres	0.26	2.40	2.12	2.71	4.56	1.88	0.07	2.68	2.56
Potato	3.67	5.81	2.07	4.38	4.28	-0.11	3.34	5.80	2.38
Tobacco	0.27	1.94	1.68	1.66	2.79	1.10	-0.31	1.77	2.08
Non-Foodgrains	1.27	2.98	1.39	2.44	3.74	0.89	1.42	3.35	1.74
All Crops	0.62	2.68	1.60	1.58	3.15	1.21	0.38	2.88	1.99

Provisional for non-foodgrains and all crops

Nine oilseeds include groundnut, castorseed, sesamum, rapeseed & Mustard, linseed, nigerseed, safflower and soyabean.

Total oilseeds include nine oilseeds, cottonseeds and coconut.

Growth rates for the period from 1970-71

Growth rates of Area.   Growth rates of Production.   Growth rates of Yield.

Table 22.2 All-India Compound Growth Rates of Area, Production and Yield of Principal Crops

(Base: Triennium ending 1981-82=100)

(Percent per annum)

Crops	1967-68 to 1997-98*			1967-68 to 1980-81			1980-81 to 1997-98*		
	A	P	Y	A	P	Y	A	P	Y
Rice	0.62	2.85	2.27	0.77	2.22	1.45	0.52	3.06	2.52
Wheat	1.51	4.59	3.04	2.94	5.65	2.62	0.81	3.57	2.73
Jowar	-1.43	0.40	1.86	-1.15	2.04	3.22	-2.60	-1.02	1.63
Bajra	-0.86	0.99	1.87	-1.15	-0.38	0.77	-1.07	1.87	2.97
Maize	0.09	1.85	1.76	0.01	0.02	-	0.34	2.73	2.38
Ragi	-1.07	0.69	1.78	0.91	3.38	2.45	-2.55	-0.48	2.12
Small Millets	-3.93	-3.28	0.67	-1.18	-0.81	0.38	-5.67	-4.76	0.97
Barley	-4.89	-2.47	2.55	-3.88	-2.72	1.21	-4.67	-1.72	3.10
Coarse Cereals	-1.36	0.59	1.91	-1.03	0.67	1.64	-1.96	0.50	2.30
Total Cereals	0.01	2.86	2.39	0.37	2.61	1.70	-0.30	2.79	2.57
Gram	-0.53	0.15	0.69	-0.55	-1.02	-0.48	-0.22	1.09	1.31
Tur	1.40	1.37	-0.02	0.38	0.56	0.19	1.13	0.32	-0.80
Other Pulses	0.20	1.44	1.24	1.05	-0.13	-1.18	-0.49	1.24	1.73
Total Pulses	0.13	0.91	0.75	0.44	-0.40	-0.67	-0.17	1.04	1.06
Total Foodgrains	0.03	2.59	1.98	0.38	2.15	1.33	-0.28	2.58	1.40
Sugarcane	1.76	3.11	1.33	1.78	2.60	0.8	2.12	3.47	1.32
Groundnut	0.41	1.68	1.26	-0.31	0.64	0.96	0.67	2.44	1.76
Sesamum	-0.61	1.57	2.19	-0.32	-0.31	0.02	-1.24	1.39	2.66
Rape & Mustard Seed	2.68	5.38	2.63	1.26	1.50	0.23	3.98	6.78	2.69
Sunflower +	13.21	12.39	-0.73	-1.11	-3.77	-2.71	13.99	15.59	1.41

Table 22.2 All-India Compound Growth Rates of Area, Production and Yield of Principal Crops (Contd.)

(Base: Triennium ending 1981-82=100)

(Percent per annum)

Crops	1967-68 to 1997-98*			1967-68 to 1980-81			1980-81 to 1997-98*		
	A	P	Y	A	P	Y	A	P	Y
Soyabean +	22.79	24.68	1.53	38.28	44.32	4.31	15.65	19.03	2.93
Nine Oilseeds	1.84	3.74	1.80	0.34	1.09	0.85	2.88	5.33	2.27
Total Oilseeds	1.41	3.60	1.70	0.26	0.98	0.68	2.35	5.36	2.30
Cotton	0.17	2.84	2.67	0.07	2.61	2.54	0.72	3.97	3.23
Jute	0.29	2.27	1.97	1.23	2.06	0.81	-0.36	2.02	1.01
Mesta	-1.96	-0.66	1.33	1.78	4.24	2.41	-3.64	-1.93	1.78
Jute & Mesta	-0.30	1.79	1.72	1.39	2.48	1.13	-1.14	1.46	1.37
Total Fibres	0.07	2.68	2.56	0.19	2.53	2.31	0.45	3.63	3.13
Potato	3.34	5.80	2.38	4.29	7.78	3.35	3.06	4.53	1.42
Tobacco	-0.31	1.77	2.08	-0.08	2.22	2.30	-0.44	1.45	1.90
Non-Foodgrains	1.42	3.35	1.74	0.94	2.26	1.19	1.98	4.45	2.10
All Crops	0.38	2.88	1.99	0.51	2.19	1.28	0.31	3.23	2.24

Provisional for non-foodgrains and all crops

Nine oilseeds include groundnut, castorseed, sesamum, rapeseed & Mustard, linseed, nigerseed, safflower, sunflower and soyabean.

Total oilseeds include nine oilseeds, cottonseeds and coconut.   Growth rates for the period from 1970-71.

Growth rates of Area.   Growth rates of Production.   Growth rates of Yield.

TE 1993-94 is taken for determining the base level of area/production against which the area/production of the succeeding years is to be compared.

Weighting Diagram

The weight of a commodity for the production index is taken as the average production of the commodity in the TE 1993-94 and the national average price of the commodity during 1993-94 as obtained from the National Accounts Statistics. This has been done to fix the base production as its average level by eliminating the cyclical variation and to evaluate the production with the same price for all states in view of wide variations observed in the state prices.

Coverage

The index numbers of agriculture commodities cover 46 crops under two main groups and eight sub-groups. The crops and groups are listed below:

Foodgrains

  (i) Cereals   Rice, wheat, jowar, bajra, maize, ragi, barley and small millets. (Crops except rice and wheat constitute the sub-group coarse cereals).
 (ii) Pulses   Gram, tur and other pulses.

Non-foodgrains

  (i) Groundnut, sesamum, rapeseed and mustard, linseed, castorseed, safflower, nigerseed, soyabean, sunflower, coconut and cottonseed. (The oilseed crops except coconut and cottonseed constitute 9 oilseeds.)
 (ii) Fibers   Cotton, jute, mesta and sannhemp. (Jute and mesta constitute a sub-group).
(iii) Plantation crops   Tea, coffee and rubber.
 (iv) Condiments and spices   Pepper, ginger, garlic, chillies, turmeric, arecanut, coriander and cardamom.
  (v) Fruits and vegetables   Potato, onion, banana, cashewnut, tapioca and sweet potato.
 (vi) Other crops   Sugarcane, tobacco and guarseed.

Methodology

Let 1. a_{ijk} the area under ith crop in the jth year in kth state.
    2. a_{iok} the area under ith crop in base year period in kth state.
    3. P_{ijk} production of ith crop in the jth year in kth state.
    4. P_{iok} production of ith crop in base year period in kth state.
    5. W_{ik} weight of ith crop in kth state.
    6. P_{io} price per unit of the ith crop in the base period.

For the state k and for the year j, individual crop indices are calculated as below:

(a) Index number of area $\quad = \dfrac{a_{ijk}}{a_{iok}} \times 100 = IA_{ijk}$

(b) Index number of production $\quad = \dfrac{p_{ijk}}{p_{ick}} \times 100 = IP_{ijk}$

(c) Index number of yield $\quad = \dfrac{IP_{ijk}}{IA_{ijk}} \times 100$

For any sub-group G of commodities, the indices are for the year j and state k are as below:

(a) Index number of area $\quad = \dfrac{\Sigma a_{ijk}}{\Sigma a_{iok}} \times 100$

The state index is obtained by including all the items of the state in subgroup G where the summation is taken over items in G.

(b) Index number of production $\quad = \dfrac{Ep_{ijk}\, p_{io}}{Sp_{iok}\, p_{io}} \times 100$

(c) Index number of yield $\quad = \dfrac{\text{Index number of production}}{\text{Index number of area}} \times 100$

The FAO Index

The Food and Agricultural Organisation of the United Nations is compiling and publishing index numbers of agricultural production for various countries, including India. These are published in the FAO Production Year Book. Earlier base period for the Indian index 1969-70, has now been changed is 1989-91 = 100. The index number relates to gross production of a large number of commodities, divided into 11 groups. These groups are grains, starchy roots, sugar, pulses, oil crops, nuts, fruits, vegetables, livestock and livestock product, fibres and others. Crops and milk used as feed in livestock production are deducted to avoid double counting. In addition, allowances are made for seed.

The weighting system adopted is fairly complicated. The commodity weights are world prices. These commodity weights are calculated in terms of gold francs per metric ton and then converted to wheat relative price—the price of wheat being 100 gold francs per metric ton in 1936-38. Weights are assigned on the basis of such commodity prices expressed in terms of wheat. The world prices are used in the preparation of index numbers to make possible international comparisons.

23

State Index Numbers Relating to Agricultural Economy

Just like the all-India index number of agricultural production, area under crops, agricultural productivity. farm harvest prices, agricultural wholesale prices, etc. a number of States are also publishing various index numbers concerning their respective States.

AGRICULTURAL PRODUCTION

Considering the importance of similar indices at the State level for appraisal of trends in their agricultural production, the States were requested in 1955 to undertake construction of index numbers of their agricultural production on the lines of the all-India series. Besides Uttar Pradesh which was already constructing this index with 1948-49 as the base, Andhra Pradesh, Assam, Bihar, Gujarat, Kerala, Madhya Pradesh, Tamil Nadu, Maharashtra, Karnataka, Punjab, Rajasthan and West Bengal also started their series. They followed essentially the same concepts and definitions and methodology as was adopted in the all-India series, yet there were and still are a few variations with regard to the base, coverage and group and sub-group classification of crops. These variations are discussed in this chapter.

BASE PERIOD

The States of Andhra Pradesh, Assam, Bihar, Gujarat, Maharashtra, Punjab and West Bengal adopted in conformity with the all-India series, the agricultural year 1949-50 as the base, while the base adopted was the agricultural year 1952-53 in Kerala, Madhya Pradesh and Karnataka, the triennium ending with 1949-50 in Tamil Nadu and the quadrennium ending with 1955-56 in Rajasthan. The choice of a different base by the States from that of the all-India series was guided either by the lack of basic data for the year 1949-50 or the abnormality of that year from the point of view of agricultural production in the States. The series of index numbers in U.P. continued with the year 1948-49 as the base. The latest series of State

Index Number of Agricultural Production relates to a least period as triennium ending 1969-70 conforming with All-India index.

The question of adoption of a suitable base for the State series of index numbers agricultural production was, *inter alia*, discussed during the Ninth Conference of Central and State Statisticians held at Jaipur in December 1960. The Conference recommended the selection of a post-States reorganization year as the base so as to avoid inaccuracies that might have entered in the statistics of production of crops of individual States for the earlier years as a result of this reorganization. It was further desired that the base year should be, as far as possible, normal from the point of view of agricultural production and prices and should preferably be a landmark in the planning stages such as the base or the beginning of a Plan. In the light of these considerations the agricultural year 1956-57 was recommended as the base, and all the States except Rajasthan, Orissa, Uttar Pradesh and West Bengal have constructed their revised series of index numbers with this year as the base. Rajasthan and Uttar Pradesh still continue their series with the old base. Orissa has adopted 1952-53 as the base as 1956-57 is considered to be an abdormal year in that State. Other States and Union Territories are still in the process of finalizing their series or revising their old series.

Method of Construction and Weighting Diagram

The conference also emphasized the need for uniformity in concepts, definitions, base period, etc. in the State series so as to obtain a proper appraisal of the progress in the field of agriculture in the different States on a comparable basis. Accordingly, a note laying down broad criteria governing the selection of crops for inclusion in the index method of construction, weighting diagram, etc. were prepared in the Ministry of Food and Agriculture in consultation with the Central Statistical Organization and sent to the States in June 1961 for their guidance. However, some State series still differ from the all-India series not only with regard to the base period as already discussed, but also with regard to the method of construction, crop coverage and nature of prices used for evaluating the production, for the purpose of weighting diagram. While most of the States follow the chain base method for the construction of the index numbers, Gujarat and Uttar Pradesh adopt the fixed base method. In U.P., the prices used for evaluation of production for the purpose of weighting diagram are the wholesale prices prevailing during the harvest season, and not the farm (harvest) prices as employed in the all-India and other State series.

Coverage and Classification of Crops

Some of the crops covered by the all-India series are not included in the series for individual States because of their lack of importance in the States concerned. Similarly certain crops not included in the all-India series, are included in the individual State series because of their importance in these States. The area accounted for by the crops included in the State series is more than 90 per cent of the gross cropped area in all the States except Orissa, Punjab and Rajasthan where the coverage is limited to 70 to 80 per cent of the cropped area mainly due to non-availability of reliable production data for the excluded crops.

There are some variations between all-India and State series with regard to grouping of crops also. In U.P., group indices are constructed for 'food crops' and 'cash crops', whereas in the all-India series as well as in other State series the group indices are constructed for 'foodgrains' and 'non-foodgrains'. The States of Andhra Pradesh, Tamil Nadu and U.P. compile index numbers for individual crops under the sub-group 'small millets', but not for the group as a whole. Coconut is generally included in the 'oilseeds' group and it has been so included in Kerala and Tamil Madu, but in Karnatka it is included under the 'miscellaneous' sub-group. In U.P., gram has been included under the 'cereals' sub-group and not in the 'pulses' sub-group as has been done in the case of all-India series and other State series.

AREA UNDER CROPS AND AGRICULTURAL PRODUCTIVITY

The index numbers of area under the principal crops are based on the revised estimates issued in the Crop Estimates from time to time. However, since these estimates become available with a time lag of more than a year, index numbers for the latest two years are based on the 'Final' and 'Partially Revised' Estimates.

The index number of agricultural production divided by the index number of area gives more or less a measure of gross agricultural productivity. To obtain an index number of productivity, it may be necessary to base the index number of area on 'net' area sown and not on 'gross' area. But, as 'net' area under individual crops is not available, the index of gross productivity has been worked out from 'gross areas'.

Following the methodology of the all-India indices of area under crops and agricultural productivity, Andhra Pradesh, Gujarat, Kerala, Madhya Pradesh, Maharashtra, Karnataka and Punjab are also constructing similar State indices with 1956-57 as the base and covering the same crops as included under the index numbers of production.

On the lines of the revised all-India index numbers of net area sown, area under crops, cropping intensity, cropping pattern, yield, productivity per net hectare and agricultural production issued in 1972 with triennium ending 1961-62 as base, State Governments have also started compiling their State series. These series will provide a good basis for inter-State comparisons in agricultural growth.

FARM HARVEST PRICES

Only Madhya Pradesh has been compiling the index numbers of its harvest prices with 1952-53 as the base. The series cover 22 principal crops divided into two main groups, viz. foodgrains and non-foodgrains and four sub-groups, viz. cereals, pulses, oilseeds, and miscellaneous crops. The farm (harvest) prices utilized in the construction of this series are according to the new connotation in respect of Mahakoshal region and according to the old connotation up to 1956-57 and new connotation thereafter in respect of Madhya Bharat, Vindhya Pradesh and Bhopal regions. According to the new connotation, the farm (harvest) price is defined as the average wholesale price at which a commodity is disposed of by the producer at the village site during its specified harvesting period. In each district the weekly farm prices of the principal crop are collected from 10 representative village markets for all the weeks of its harvesting season and a simple average pooled over the centres and all the weeks in the season gives the district average farm price for the year. According to old connotation the district farm (harvest) price is the wholesale price ruling at the district headquarters market on the last day of February in the case of kharif crops and on the last day of May in the case of rabi crops. The State farm (harvest) price of a commodity is the weighted average of all the available district farm (harvest) prices, the weights being its total production in the districts. The average farm price of each commodity for the State as a whole for any year is expressed as a price relative of the corresponding price with preceding year. The price relative thus worked out is linked to the price in the base year through the intervening chain relatives to give the price index for the crop. The weighted arithmetic average of such price indices of different commodities is taken to give the index numbers for sub-groups and groups and all commodities, weights being assigned to the different commodities in proportion to the total value of their production in the base year, the production itself being evaluated at the State average farm price.

WHOLESALE PRICES OF AGRICULTURAL COMMODITIES

The index numbers at all-India and State level of wholesale prices of rice and wheat are compiled on a weekly basis by the Directorate of Economics and Statistics. The agricultural year 1955-56, the last year of the First Five Year Plan, is taken as the base, as in that year the level of agricultural price was more or less normal, and the availability of the price data was also quite satisfactory. Price quotations from 95 representative markets are utilized in respect of rice and from 43 representative markets in respect of wheat. Average annual price for each market for the base year is computed by taking the arithmetic mean of the weekly wholesale prices for all the weeks during the base year. For each selected market price relatives are computed every week by taking the average wholesale price of the commodity in the base year as 100. A simple arithmetic average of the price relatives for all the markets gives the index number of wholesale price for the commodity for the State. All-India index numbers are computed as weighted arithmetic mean of the State index numbers, weights being proportional to the volume of marketable surplus of the commodity in each State.

The States of Bihar, Kerala, Karnataka, Punjab and Uttar Pradesh are, also compiling index numbers of wholesale prices of agricultural commodities. The base adopted is the agricultural year 1952-53 in Bihar and Kerala, the financial year 1952-53 in Karnataka and Punjab and the agricultural year 1957-58 in Uttar Pradesh.

The commodities included in the index vary from State to State depending upon the importance of individual commodities in the different States. Besides important cereals, pulses, oilseeds, fibres and other miscellaneous crops, some States have included other agricultural products and industrial raw materials. The commodities included account for about 90 per cent of the cropped area and about 90 per cent of the produce marketed in Karnataka and about 87 per cent of the annual value of the total agricultural production in Punjab.

In Bihar, Mysore, Punjab and Uttar Pradesh the weekly prices utilized in the index are the wholesale prices as prevailing on Friday. In Kerala, on the other hand, month-end wholesale prices are used. In Karnataka, the prices are exclusive of sales tax, market transportation charges while in Punjab the Mandi auction prices as on Friday of the week are used.

In Bihar, the weights are assigned to individual commodities in proportion to the value of their average out-turn during the triennium ending 1949-50 evaluated at the prices prevailing in 1952-53. In Kerala, for all commodities except rice, sugar and cashewnut, weights are assigned in proportion to the value of their production. For rice and molasses, weights are assigned in proportion to the value of consumption estimated by sample surveys. For cashewnut value of production and imports are taken into account. The value taken relates to the base year for all commodities. In Karnataka, weights have been assigned to individual commodities in proportion to the value of quantities marketed during 1958-59 evaluated at the prices prevailing in the base year. In Punjab, the weights have been assigned to individual commodities in proportion to the value of production in the base year. In Uttar Pradesh, weights are used at two stages: (a) centre-wise weights for working out the index for the State for each commodity, and (b) commodity-wise weights for working out the general weighted index for the State. Weights for a centre in respect of each commodity are based on the value of its production during the base year. weight for a commodity is the total value of its production in the State as a whole.

In Bihar, monthly price for any commodity is arrived at as simple average of the weekly prices for each centre. A simple average of the monthly prices at different centres gives the average price for each commodity. The average monthly price of each commodity is expressed as a percentage of the corresponding price in the base year to give the commodity index. In Kerala, the monthly price of a commodity for each centre is expressed as a percentage of the corresponding price in the base period. The commodity index is calculated as the simple arithmetic mean of price relatives at various centres. In Karnataka, the current weekly price of a commodity or a variety of a commodity is expressed as percentage of the corresponding base year price for each market. A simple average of these price relatives for the markets and varieties gives the commodity index. In Punjab and Uttar Pradesh, the quotations for prescribed varieties of commodities from selected markets are converted into price relatives of corresponding prices in the base year. The commodity index is calculated as the simple arithmetic average of centre-wise price relatives. The subgroup, group and general indices in all the States are arrived at by taking the weighted arithmetic average of the individual commodity indices.

AGRICULTURAL WAGES

The States of Madhya Pradesh and Andhra Pradesh are regularly constructing and publishing the State Index numbers of agricultural wages with 1960-61 and 1958-59 respectively as the base, while some other States are finalizing their schemes in this regard.

As regards the scope and coverage, the index of agricultural wages in Madhya Pradesh covers 72 centres (one or two villages in each district), while that in Andhra Pradesh covers 60 centres (three villages in each district). The categories of labour covered are: (a) skilled labour— carpenter, blacksmith and cobbler, and (b) agricultural labour—field labour, herdsmen and others. In Madhya Pradesh the field labour is further divided into: (i) ploughman, (ii) sower and transplanter, (iii) weeder, (iv) reaper and harvester, and (v) other agricultural labour. Except for ploughman, herdsman and skilled labour, each category is further divided into: (i) man, (ii) woman and non-adult.

In Madhya Pradesh, for each type of agricultural labour in a district, the wage in the base year is calculated by averaging all the monthly wages of all the reporting centres and that in each subsequent month by averaging the wages in all the centres. The latter is then expressed as the percentage of the former to give the wage relative for the type for that month. These relatives are, however, calculated only for those types which are employed in that month. The wage relatives of different types are averaged to give the wage relative for the category and the categorywise wage relatives are further averaged to give the overall wage relative in the district for the month. The weights have been assigned to the different districts in proportion to the population of earners and earning dependents under the class of cultivating labourers in the district. The State has been divided into a number of agricultural zones, and to obtain the index for the month for a particular zone, the weighted average of the wage relative of different districts is worked out. The State index is calculated at the weighted average of zonal indices.

In Andhra Pradesh, the average wage rate for each district in respect of different categories of labour is calculated as the simple arithmetic mean of the wages prevailing at the three centres in the district during the month. The average wage rate for each category of skilled labour for the State is calculated as a simple arithmetic mean of the district wages. In the case of different categories of agricultural labour, on the other hand, the wage rate for the State is obtained as the weighted arithmetic mean of the district wage rates, weights being proportional to the rural agricultural labour population, in the districts according to 1951 Census. The base year average wage rates are calculated as the simple average of the monthly wages. The current monthly wage rate for each category of labour is expressed as the percentage of the base year average wage rate to give the wage relative. The index number of wages of skilled labour is worked out as the average of wage relatives of carpenters, blacksmiths and cobblers. The simple average of wage relatives of different categories of agricultural labour is taken as the index number of agricultural wages.

PARITY BETWEEN PRICES RECEIVED AND PRICES PAID BY THE FARMERS

Earlier, the State Governments of Assam, Kerala, Orissa, Punjab and West Bengal were compiling the Index of Parity between Prices Received and Prices Paid by the Farmers. Surveys for collection of basic data for working out the weighting diagram for this index are at present in progress in the States of Bihar, Madhya Pradesh, Karnataka and Punjab.

The base period adopted is the calendar year 1944 in Assam, agricultural year 1952-53 in Kerala, August 1939 in Orissa, August 1938 to July 1939 in Punjab and calendar year 1939 in West Bengal. West Bengal also constructs indices with three other base periods, viz. calendar year 1948 previous year, and previous month.

Index Numbers of Prices Received

The commodities included and weights assigned to them are determined on a joint consideration of their marketed surplus and availability of price data. In Assam the weights have been assigned to the different commodities in proportion to the value of their marketed surplus based on the Rural Economic Survey conducted in 1949-50 in the plain districts of the State; in Kerala in proportion to the value of production during the base period; in Orissa in proportion to the average value of the marketed surplus during 1936-37 to 1938-39; in Punjab generally in proportion to the value of marketed surplus of the commodities during 1938-39; and in West Bengal in proportion to the average value of marketed surplus of the commodities during the period 1947-48 to 1950-51. The price data used in the construction of the index relate to wholesale prices in Assam, Kerala, Orissa, and Punjab. In West Bengal monthly indices are based on the monthly wholesale prices and annual indices on the farm harvest prices.

The method of construction of the index numbers of prices received is the weighted geometric average of the monthly prices relatives for individual commodities in Assam, Orissa and West Bengal. In Kerala a simple arithmetic mean of the prices of the different centres in a district gives the district price. The district prices are weighted with district production figures in 1956-57 to obtain the State average price. Weighted geometric mean of the State price relatives of different commodities gives the index. In Punjab, a simple average of the fortnightly prices gives the monthly price of a commodity. A weighted geometric average of the monthly price relatives of the commodities gives the index.

Index Numbers of Prices Paid

Index Number of Domestic Expenditure The various items of consumption included in the State series of Assam, Orissa and Punjab account for 70 to 80 per cent of the total cash expenditure and are fairly representative of the total domestic expenditure. In Kerala, the average cost of living index for 12 centres with the base changed to 1952-53 is taken to represent the index of domestic expenditure.

The weights are based in Assam on the results of the enquiry into domestic expenditure for rural families conducted in 1948-50 in the plain districts; in Orissa on the tentative estimates of expenditure of an average agricultural family; and in Punjab and West Bengal on the family budget surveys conducted during 1939-40 and 1944-45 respectively.

The prices used in the construction of the index are weekly retail prices in Assam and West Bengal and monthly retail prices in Orissa and Punjab. Generally the weighted geometric average of the monthly price relatives of individual commodities is taken in all the States to obtain the overall index of domestic expenses.

Index of Farm Cultivation Costs Items of cost included in the compilation of this index include seeds, labour, depreciation, rent and interest, etc. Weights have been assigned on the basis of enquiries into cost of cultivation conducted in the States of Assam, Orissa, Punjab and West Bengal. In Kerala, the weights are rough, as no enquiry has been conducted to determine the weights for items of farm cultivation cost. The index numbers of the cost of cultivation are calculated in all the States by taking weighted geometric average of the relatives for individual items.

CONSOLIDATED INDEX OF PRICES PAID

The index number of prices paid by the farmers is constructed by taking the weighted geometric average of the indices of domestic expenditure and farm cultivation costs, weights being proportional to the expenditures on domestic and farm accounts to the total expenditure.

INDEX NUMBER OF PARITY

The index number of parity between prices received and prices paid by the farmers is calculated by taking the ratio of the index of prices received and the index of prices paid by the farmers multiplied by 100.

LATEST POSITION

Latest position regarding various types of price data being collected by different states is given in (Table 23.1) and Index Numbers being prepared by them in (Table 23.2).

QUALITY AND LIMITATIONS OF DATA BASE

Current data available from the States on production and prices suffer from a number of limitations viz., (a) non-availability of species-wise production and prices, (b) incomplete coverage of reporting of production, (c) the non-availability of data on production and prices of most of the minor forest products, (d) lack of adequate data on prices, and (e) time lag.

The forestry products have a lot of variability with regard to their quality and the prices even vary within the same species. Depending upon the climatic and other factors, trees belonging to the same species may belong to different quality classes. The products of these various quality classes may also fetch prices which are largely varying from one quality class to another. Thus, for proper evaluation of forestry products, it is necessary to have the production as well as price data, not only species-wise but also quality/class-wise for the same species. However, under the present system of reporting of forestry statistics, many SDFs are reporting a single figure for production and a single price against that volume. This has a telling effect on the quality of the estimates. Another major drawback of the available statistics of production is that their is no way to check its completeness. The data availability position on the minor forest products needs considerable improvement. As far as possible, the State governments should collect data on production as well as prices of all such products which are important for their states so that economic value of the MFPs can be worked out. The data position with regard to various inputs for this sector is also very weak.

Comprehensive studies are required to be undertaken by the State Forest Departments for estimating the various norms that are used for calculation of domestic product from forestry sector, viz. TTMs, material inputs, unrecorded removals etc. As has already been highlighted, these norms vary from state to state. Thus state-wise estimates will help in improving the national product and related aggregates to a large extent.

The scope of present day forestry has gone beyond the traditional forest areas. Programmes of social forestry, farm forestry, agro-forestry, etc. are being implemented on a massive scale with public participation. Several international agencies like Swedish International Development Agency, World Bank, FAO, etc., are funding these programmes in addition to large scale investment by Government of India. Since a substantial portion of this money is going into the private hands and owing to the economic nature of this activity, lot of income is being generated. However, there is no proper recording of the output of timber, fuelwood,

Table 23.1 Details of Price-Data Collected by States and Union Territories

State/UT		Price-Data	Periodicity
1. Andhra Pradesh	1.	Retail prices of 64 essential commodities	Weekly
	2.	Prices of 48 non-food items	Monthly
	3.	Wholesale prices of 125 items of livestock, livestock products and feeds	Monthly
	4.	Wholesale prices of 30 agricultural commodities	Monthly
	5.	Prices of building material	Quarterly
	6.	Farm harvest prices of agricultural commodities	Kharif and rabi
	7.	Daily agricultural labour wages from 66 centres	Monthly
2. Arunachal Pradesh	1.	Retail prices of 85 essential food items	Fortnightly
	2.	Retail prices of 82 non-food items	Monthly
	3.	Prices of 12 essential commodities sold at Fair Price shops	Monthly
	4.	Rates of service charges of 10 items from 12 markets	Quarterly
3. Assam	1.	Urban and rural retail prices	Weekly/ Monthly
	2.	Wholesale prices of food and non-food items	Weekly/ Monthly
	3.	Prices of building materials	Quarterly
4. Bihar	1.	Farm prices of all crops	Seasonal
	2.	Retail prices of consumer items agricultural commodities	Weekly
5. NCT of Delhi	1.	Retail prices of 74 food and other items	Weekly
	2.	Retail prices of 42 items	Monthly
	3.	Wholesale prices of agricultural and other commodities	Weekly
	4.	Building material rates and wage rates	Quarterly
6. Goa	1.	Retail prices of essential items of food, fuel and light	Weekly
	2.	Retail prices of items pertaining to middle class non-manual employees	Monthly
7. Gujarat	1.	Wholesale and retail prices of selected agricultural items	Fortnightly
	2.	Retail prices of six types of iodised and non-iodised salt	Monthly

Table 23.1 Details of Price-Data Collected by States and Union Territories (Contd.)

State/UT	Price-Data	Periodicity
8. Haryana	1. Retail consumer prices	Weekly/ Monthly
	2. Rural retail prices	Fortnightly
	3. Retail prices of essential commodities	Weekly
	4. Wholesale prices of agricultural commodities	Weekly
9. Himachal Pradesh	1. Retail prices of sixteen essential commodities	Weekly
	2. Wholesale and retail prices of selected commodities	Fortnightly
	3. Prices of livestock and poultry	Half-yearly
10. Jammu and Kashmir	1. Retail prices of essential commodities	Weekly
	2. Wholesale prices of agricultural commodities	Weekly
11. Karnataka	1. Prices of 20 selected commodities	Weekly
	2. Wholesale and retail prices of 110 agricultural commodities	Fortnightly·
	3. Harvest prices of agricultural commodities	Kharif, rabi and summer
	4. Prices of building materials	Quarterly
12. Kerala	1. Wholesale prices of 38 agricultural commodities	Daily
	2. Retail price of essential commodities	Daily and Monthly
	3. Retail prices of food items	Weekly and Quarterly
	4. Retail prices of agricultural commodities	Weekly
	5. Wholesale prices of coir and husk	Weekly
	6. Wholesale prices of agricultural commodities	Fortnightly
	7. Retail prices of farm products	Monthly
	8. Wholesale and retail prices of salt	Monthly
	9. Retail prices of essential non-food items	Monthly
	10. Retail prices of forest products	Quarterly
	11. Prices of building materials	Quarterly
	12. Retail prices of 1059 ayurvedic items	Annual
13. Madhya Pradesh	Wholesale prices of 290 agricultural commodities	Monthly

Table 23.1 Details of Price-Data Collected by States and Union Territories (*Contd.*)

State/UT	Price-Data	Periodicity
14. Maharashtra	1. Urban retail prices of 84 essential commodities from 31 centres	Weekly
	2. Rural retail prices of 59 essential commodities from 75 centres	Weekly
	3. Wholesale prices of essential commodities from 28 district HQs., and 10 chemical fertilisers from 30 centres	Fortnightly/ Monthly
	4. Retail prices of 30 important commodities from 59 centres	Monthly
15. Manipur	1. Retail prices of essential commodities and services from District HQs.	Monthly
	2. Retail prices of livestock and livestock products from district HQs.	Monthly
16. Meghalaya	Retail prices	Weekly/ Monthly
17. Mizoram	1. Retail prices of essential commodities, and prices of food and non-food items from urban towns	Weekly/ Monthly
	2. Retail prices of food and non-food items from Aizwal centre	Weekly
	3. Wholesale prices of 23 items from six urban centres	Monthly
18. Nagaland	1. Wholesale and retail prices of essential commodities	Weekly
	2. Rates of service charges from 9 centres	Weekly
19. Orissa	1. Rural retail prices	Fortnightly
	2. Farm harvest and wholesale prices of agricultural commodities	Weekly
	3. Prices of livestock and poultry	Monthly
	4. Prices of meat, egg and milk products	Fortnightly
	5. Prices of animal by-products	Quarterly
20. Punjab	1. Retail prices from all district HQs.	Weekly
	2. Retail price of 70 items for working class population	Weekly
	3. Retail prices of 82 items from six centres	Monthly
	4. Rural retail prices of 44 items from one village in each district	Monthly
	5. Wholesale prices of 49 commodities from 4 centres	Weekly

Table 23.1 Details of Price-Data Collected by States and Union Territories (Contd.)

State/UT	Price-Data	Periodicity
21. Rajasthan	1. Retail prices of 49 essential commodities	Weekly
	2. Prices of building materials and wage rates of construction labourers	Quarterly
	3. Prices of livestock and livestock products of 61 items from 31 Dist. Hqs.	Weekly
22. Sikkim	NA	NA
23. Tamil Nadu	1. Wholesale and retail prices from 96 centres	Daily
	2. Wholesale prices from Chennai city	Monthly
	3. Wholesale and retail prices for Chennai city	Weekly
24. Tripura	1. Retail prices from Batala and Maharajganj	Weekly
	2. Retail and wholesale prices at sub-divisional HQs.	Fortnightly
	3. Rural retail prices from 168 markets	Monthly
25. Uttar Pradesh	1. Urban retail prices	Monthly
	2. Rural retail prices	Monthly
	3. Prices of building materials	Quarterly
26. West Bengal	1. Prices from Calcutta	Weekly
	2. Prices from 20 urban centres	Fortnightly
27. Lakshadweep	Prices of essential goods and services	Monthly
28. Dadar and Nagar Haveli	Farm harvest prices of agricultural commodities	Weekly
29. Daman and Diu	Retail prices of 97 commodities	Weekly
30. Andaman and Nicobar Islands	Retail prices for food and non-food items	Weekly
31. Chandigarh	None	None
32. Pondichery	Wholesale and retail prices of important essential commodities	Weekly

pulpwood etc. from these privately owned forests. The quantity of out turn from this sector of forestry may be partially covered under estimates of unrecorded production. However, a need is felt for proper recording of production and other aspects of these programmes. This would, no doubt, improve the data base for national product estimation, but at the same time provide sufficient information for monitoring purposes.

Table 23.2 Details of Price-Indices Collected by States and Union Territories

State/UT	Price-Indices	Periodicity	Others indices
1. Andhra Pradesh	1. WPI of agricultural commodities 2. CPI(IW) for six centres; Base 1982	Monthly Monthly	IIP; Base 1970; Monthly
2. Arunachal Pradesh	None	None	None
3. Assam	1. WPI; Base 1953 2. CPI(R) for Plains District; Base 1944 3. CPI(IW) for Digboi centres; Base 1960 4. Index for farm harvest prices; Base 1970-71 5. Index number of parity between prices received and paid by farmers; Base 1944	Monthly Monthly Monthly Annual Monthly	1. IPP; Base-1970; Annual; 2. Index no. of agricultural production; Base 1981-82; Annual; 3. Index of Mineral production; Base 1970; Annual
4. Bihar	1. WPI for Agricultural commodities 2. CPI for Patna, Muzaffarpur and Dehri-on-Sone; Base 1939	Weekly Weekly	None
5. Delhi (NCT)	None	None	IIP; Base '80-81; Quarterly
6. Goa	CPI; Middle class non-manual employees; Base 1982-83	Monthly and Quarterly	IIP; Base 1975; Quarterly/Annual
7. Gujarat	Index numbers (Price relatives) for wholesale and retail prices for 8 selected agriculture items; Base 1970-71	Monthly	IIP; Base 1970; Annual

Table 23.2 Details of Price-Indices Collected by States and Union Territories (Contd.)

State/UT	Price-Indices	Periodicity	Others indices
8. Haryana	1. WPI of agriculture commodities; Base 1980-81	Monthly	1. IIP; Base 1985-86;
	2. CPI of essential commodities for rural sector; Base 1988-89	Monthly	2. Index number of agriculture
	3. CPI(IW) for 6 centres; Base 1982	Monthly	
	4. Weighted index numbers of harvest prices of harvest prices of Agriculture commodities; Base 1980-81	Annual	
9. Himachal Pradesh	None	None	None
10. Jammu and Kashmir	None	None	None
11. Karnataka	1. WPI for 33 agricultural commodities	Monthly	IIP; Base 1980-81; Annual
	2. CPI(IW) for 12 centres; base 1987-88 = 100	Monthly	
	3. Price index (Rural and Urban); Base 1970	Monthly	
	4. Index numbers for farm harvest prices of	Annual	
	5. Index numbers of building materials	Annual	
12. Kerala	1. WPI for manufactured items of organised and un-organised sector; Base 1952-53	Monthly	1. IIP
	2. CPI for 92 essential commodities	Monthly	2. Wage index of agricultural labourers
	3. Parity index of 45 agricultural commodities; Base 1952-53	Monthly	
13. Madhya Pradesh	CPI(W) for Gwalior; Base 1960	Monthly	IIP; Base 1980-81; Annual

Table 23.2 Details of Price-Indices Collected by States and Union Territories (Contd.)

	State/UT	Price-Indices	Periodicity	Others indices
14.	Maharashtra	1. CPI (R); Base 1982 2. CPI (U); Base 1982	Monthly Monthly	None
15.	Manipur	Farm harvest price index of principal crops	NA	None
16.	Mizoram	RPI for essential commodities	Monthly	None
17.	Meghalaya	None	None	None
18.	Nagaland	CPI for 3rd and 4th grade government employees; base 1981-82	Monthly	None
19.	Orissa	None	None	None
20.	Punjab	1. WPI (Weighted/un-weighted) 2. CPI (Working class); Base 1987 3. Index for cost of construction of residential building	Monthly Monthly Quarterly	1. IIP; Annual Base 1975-76; 2. Index for agricultural production
21.	Rajasthan	WPI for 22 centres in respect of 114 commodities; Base 1952-53	Weekly/ Monthly	IIP; Base 1970; Annual
22.	Sikkim	NA	NA	NA

Table 23.2 Details of Price-Indices Collected by States and Union Territories (Contd.)

	State/UT	Price-Indices	Periodicity	Others indices
23.	Tamilnadu	1. WPI; Base 1970-71 2. CPI(IW); Base 1982 3. CPI(U); Base 1970-71 4. CPI(R); Base 1970-71	Monthly Monthly Monthly Monthly	IIP; Base 1981-82; Monthly
24.	Tripura	CPI (Middle Class) for Agartala; Base 1961	Monthly	None
25.	Uttar Pradesh	1. WPI; Base 1970-71 2. CPI(U) and CPI(R); Base 1970-71 3. Agricultural parity index for U.P.; Base 1970-71	Quarterly Quarterly Annual	1. IIP; Base 1970-71; Quarterly 2. Index of wage rate for rural labourers; base; 1970-71 3. Index; Cost of construction for Class IV employees; Base; 1980-81.
26.	West Bengal	1. WPI of agricultural commodities for Calcutta; Base 1980-81 2. CPI(U) for 21 urban centres including Calcutta; Base 1960	Monthly Weekly/fortnightly	IIP; Base 1980-81 Quarterly
27.	Lakshadweep	CPI; Base 1975	Monthly	None
28.	Dadar and Nagar Haveli	None	None	None

Table 23.2 Details of Price-Indices Collected by States and Union Territories *(Contd.)*

	State/UT	Price-Indices	Periodicity	Others indices
28.	Dadar and Nagar Haveli	None	None	None
29.	Daman and Diu	NA	NA	NA
30.	Andaman and Nicobar Islands	None	None	None
31.	Chandigarh	None	None	IIP
32.	Pondichery	None	None	IIP; Base 1980-81 Quarterly

FISHING

Coverage

The activities covered in the fishing sector are (i) commercial fishing in (a) ocean, coastal and offshore waters and (b) inland waters, that include catching, tackling and gathering of fish from rivers, irrigation and other canals, lakes, tanks, fields inundated tracts etc., (ii) subsistence fishing in land waters and artificial ponds, (iii) gathering of sea weeds, sea shells, pearls, sponges and other ocean and coastal water products and (iv) fish curing viz., salting and sundrying of fish.

Methodology and Source Material

The GVA from this sector is estimated by using the production approach. This involves the estimation of the total value of output at factor cost and deducting therefrom the various inputs at purchasers' prices which are used in the process of production. The data on production, prices and disposition of fish are supplied by the State Fisheries Departments (SFDs).

Estimates at Current Prices

Value of Output

Marine Fish Data on estimated landings of marine fish, prices and value of fish catch are directly obtained from the SFDs of maritime states/union territories. For the estimation of marine fish production almost all maritime states are following some kind of statistical sampling design except the state of Karnataka, where complete enumeration method is followed. The states of Tamil Nadu and Maharashtra are following multistage stratified sampling designs involving stratification in space and time viz., landing centres and days respectively. Gujarat is following a stratified systematic sampling procedure. Kerala has adopted a stratified two stage sampling design with marine districts as the strata.

Inland Fish The data on inland fish production are also supplied by the SFDs except in the case of Assam and West Bengal where production estimates are prepared by the respective DESs. As in the case of marine fish production, various approaches are adopted by the states for the estimation of inland fish production. By and large the estimates are prepared on the basis of market arrivals of fish or on the basis of surveys conducted in selected landing centres. However, some states like Karnataka, Madhya Pradesh, Tamil Nadu and Uttar Pradesh have taken up surveys under a centrally sponsored scheme for standardising the methodology of estimation of inland fish production. In West Bengal and Assam the inland fish production estimates are based on consumption data. For example in Assam the estimates are based on the consumption norms and the estimated fish consuming population available through 38th round Jan.–Dec. 1983 of NSSO. The per-capita monthly consumption norms of dry as well as fresh fish as available from the NSSO for rural and urban areas have been used for estimating the annual consumption. These consumption estimates are adjusted for imports/exports for arriving at the state production. The bench mark estimates are projected for the subsequent years using the annual estimated population.

Subsistence Fishing Direct estimates of production from subsistence fishing i.e., fish caught by non-professional fishermen are available from a few states only viz., Himachal Pradesh, Kerala, West Bengal, Andaman and Nicobar, Madhya Pradesh, Manipur and Mizoram. However, the inland fish production estimates supplied by Haryana, Punjab, Orissa, Tripura, Goa, and Gujarat are inclusive of subsistence fishing. Some of the SFDs have attempted to estimate the subsistence fish production through some ad-hoc enquiries. Data collected through local enquiries by SFD Karnataka, show that value of subsistence fish forms 12.5 per cent of the value of output of inland fish in the state. In the case of Tamil Nadu and Uttar Pradesh, the corresponding percentages suggested by the DESs in consultation with the SFDs are 2.5 and 8.7 respectively. The percentage of 12.5 being at the average level, is presently adopted for the remaining states for which no independent information is available.

For working out the value of output, the average annual auction prices of marine fish (species wise) collected by the SFDs at the landing centres along with production are made use of. The inland fish prices reported by the SFDs are generally the assembling centre prices. These are duly adjusted for TTMs so as to conform to producer prices. The subsistence fish is evaluated at the inland fish price, unless otherwise provided.

Fish Curing Most of the maritime states are resorting to the allied activities of fish curing which include salting and sun-drying. The quantities and prices of fish let-in and let-out for fish curing and the value of salt used are by and large available on an annual basis from the SFDs.

Value of Input

In the absence of any data based on scientific studies, it has been assumed after consultation with the Joint Commissioner of Fisheries, that in the case of marine fish and inland fish, the operational costs and repairs and maintenance form 10 per cent and 6 per cent respectively of the corresponding value of output. Operational costs broadly include expenditure on boats (mechanised and non-mechanised), trawlers, liners, fishing gears, gillnets, trawlnets, castnets, traps, other bagnets, consumption of diesel oil etc. In the case of subsistence fishing, an allowance of 1 per cent of value of output is made (arbitrarily) for operational costs and repairs and maintenance.

Other Products Data on producer prices and value of output in respect of gathering of pearls, chanks, oysters, sea-weeds, lime-shells, sea-shells etc., are not available. However, estimates of GVA by these activities are available for a few states like Kerala, Tamil Nadu, Gujarat, Andaman and Nicobar Islands and Pondicherry on annual basis. For the remaining states the estimates are arrived at, by multiplying the estimated number of persons engaged in these activities with the corresponding value added per person. The estimated number of persons are arrived at by moving the 1981 census working force data using the compound growth rate observed between 1971 and 1981 censuses. As regards the value added per person, the estimate of Kerala is used for other maritime states. For the landbound states, the value added per person is arbitrarily taken as one third of that in Kerala.

Estimates at Constant Prices

The current catch of marine fish, inland fish and subsistence fish are valued at 1980-81 prices for the estimation of the output at constant prices. Similar treatment is given to data on fish curing also. The value of pearls, chanks etc., at current prices is deflated by the ratio of output of marine fish at constant prices over current prices to arrive at the value at constant prices. The same proportions of expenditure on operational costs and repairs and maintenance to total output as for estimates at current prices have been used to obtain corresponding estimates of value added at constant prices.

Quality and Limitations of Data Base

Statewise annual estimates of production of fish are available from the various SFDs. As already mentioned most of the states are following scientific procedures for the estimation of marine fish production. However, due to differences in procedures of sampling, the estimates of various states are at different levels of efficiency. It is high time for the SFDs to adopt a uniform procedure for the estimation of marine fish production. The sampling design developed by the Central Marine Fisheries Research Institute should serve as a standard for this purpose. Unlike marine fish production estimates, the inland fish production estimates prepared by the SFDs are based on very crude methodologies. As regards subsistence fishing, no reliable data are available and the methods followed for the estimation at state level are very tentative.

The data on collection of pearls, chanks, weeds etc., on a regular basis are available only for a few states. The estimates of this activity for other states are prepared on the basis of working force and approximate measure of per person value added.

No appropriate official mechanism exists in the states for collecting reliable data on the activity of fish curing. Maharashtra is carrying out some enquiries on sample basis for estimating the utilisation of fish for various purposes. Gujarat through its SFD is collecting utilisation data from district offices and quantity of fish cured from the manufacturers of fish meal etc. Kerala SFD collects data on quantity and value of fish cured/dried in the state periodically through their field staff. Tamil Nadu is resorting to the application of fixed ratios for arriving at the quantities of fish let-in and let-out.

The proportion used for preparing estimates of operational costs and expenditure on repairs and.maintenance is not based on any scientific enquiries. Some information on expenditure on repairs, maintenance of boats and nets by types, average cost of boats, number of boats etc., available with the states have been analysed. The results show wide variations amongst states and a meaningful ratio at national level could not be arrived at for adoption.

NATIONAL ACCOUNTS STATISTICS

Committee on Regional Accounts

The state accounts statistics are an extension of the system of national accounts to the regional level. These comprise of various accounts indicating the flows of all transactions within a time period between the economic agents constituting the state economy and their stocks. These accounts include various items like total output of economy, the intermediate expenditure, state domestic product, factor incomes, consumption expenditure, capital formation, capital stocks, consumption of fixed capital, etc.

The most important aggregate of the state accounts is the state domestic product (state income). The state income can conceptually be prepared by adopting two approaches, namely, income originating and income accruing. In the Income originating approach, the measurement corresponds to income originating to the factors of production physically located within the geographical boundaries of state and represents net value of goods and services produced within the state. The income accruing approach relates to the income accruing to the normal residents of a state. Since in this approach one measures the income that become available to the residents of a state, it provides a better measure of the welfare of the residents of the state. Due to non-availability of data on inter-state flows of goods and services, compilation of estimates of state income on income accruing concept is not possible. Compilation of other aggregates and state accounts is also problematic, due to the absence of requisite data, particularly on the inter-state flows of incomes. These issues had been gone through by the Committee on Regional Accounts (RAC), set up by the Government in May 1972. The RAC submitted its First Report in 1974 and the Final Report in 1976. A number of recommendations were made in these Reports by the Committee, which aim at developing a set of consolidated accounts for the States.

The Government of India in May 1972 set up a Regional Accounts Committee (RAC) with the following terms of reference:

- to consider and advise on the levels (state, district or other regions) at which accounts should be prepared;
- to devise a system of regional accounts and standard supporting and supplementary tables for adoption by all the states;

- to suggest measures for building up regional accounts in the country taking into consideration the availability of data and requirements of Central and State Governments; and
- to examine the concepts, definitions, and classifications for preparation of regional accounts and to lay down guidelines.

The RAC in its First Report, submitted to the Government in November 1974, recommended a set of Standard Tables mainly to meet the immediate requirements of the policy makers at the regional level. The committee submitted its second and final report to the government in September 1976. In the final report, Committee recommended the System of Regional Accounts (SRA) consisting three consolidated accounts:

Consolidated Accounts of the Region
1. production account
2. income and outlay account
3. capital finance account

Household Accounts
1. Income and outlay account
2. Total consumption and income of the population

Accounts of State and Local Governments
1. production account of state government departmental enterprises
2. production account of state government non-departmental enterprises
3. income and outlay account of state government administrative departments and departmental enterprises
4. income and outlay account of state government non-departmental enterprises
5. capital finance account of state government non-departmental enterprises administrative departments and departmental enterprises
6. capital finance account of state government non-departmental enterprises

A consolidated list of recommended Tables and Accounts is given at Annex-I. The reports also describe the concepts, coverage and method of estimation of various aggregates appearing in the Accounts and Standard Tables. Further the reports deal with major gaps in the existing data system and makes recommendations for the collection of essential statistics required for satisfactory measurement of regional income and related aggregates and construction of the recommended SRA. The committee felt that an accounting framework for the states can be recommended, but there is little point in recommending one for regions smaller than states, like district.

Since the submission of the Reports by the RAC, the work on estimation of state income has improved and expanded in different states. Currently, almost all States/UTs are compiling estimates of state domestic product (SDP), following the income originating approach, both at current and constant prices. The States/UTs follow the same base year adopted for national accounts statistics for the constant price estimates, which currently is 1993-94. These estimates are put in the form of standard tables as recommended by RAC. A consolidated list of States/UTs who are compiling the SDP estimates is placed at Table 23.3. Some states are also preparing district level estimates of domestic product. A consolidated list of States/UTs who are preparing district level estimates is placed at Table 23.4. The district domestic product estimates compiled by the States are not based on district level databases, but are built-up by allocating the state level estimates using some indicators. A few States/UTs are also preparing the estimates with rural-urban break-up. The methodology adopted by different states is not strictly uniform, being primarily dependent on the type of data available with them. However, none of the states appear to have been preparing the complete accounts as per the recommendations of the SRA.

Table 23.4 States Preparing District Level Estimates

S.No.	State/U.T.	Commodity Producing Sectors	All Sectors
1	Andhra Pradesh	Yes	Yes
2	Arunachal Pradesh	Under Progress	No
3	Assam	Yes	No
4	Bihar	Yes	Yes
5	Haryana	Yes	Yes
6	Karnataka	Yes	Yes
7	Kerala	Yes	Yes
8	Madhya Pradesh	Yes	Only for the year 1995-96
9	Maharashtra	Yes	Yes
10	Rajasthan	Yes	Yes
11	Tamil Nadu	Yes	Yes
12	Uttar Pradesh	Yes	No
13	West Bengal	Yes	Yes

Summary Status of Compilations

As per the recommendations of the Regional Accounts Committee (RAC) in their final report submitted to Central Statistical Organisation (CSO) in 1976, the States and Union Territories were advised to prepare a few sets of accounts and supporting tables. During the time elapsed. Directorates of Economics and Statistics (DES) of States/UTs, under the advice/guidance of CSO and Advisory Committee on National Accounts,

Table 23.3 Status of Regional Accounting System of various States/UTs

State	Supporting Tables																				
	1	2.1	2.2	3.1	3.2	4.1	4.2	5.1	5.2	6	7	8.1	8.2	9	10	11	12.1	12.2	13	14	15
Andhra Pradesh	Y	Y	Y	Y	Y			Y	Y		Y					Y	Y		Y		Agri
Arunachal Pradesh	Y	Y	Y	Y	Y			@	@							Y			Y		
Assam	Y	Y	Y	Y	Y				Y							Y	Y		Y		Y
Bihar	Y	Y	Y	Y	Y						Y					Y	Y		@		Agri
Goa	Y	Y	Y	Y	Y						Y								Y		
Gujrat	Y	Y	Y	Y	Y						Y					Y	Y				
Haryana	Y	Y	Y	Y	Y			Y	Y							Y	Y	Y	Y		Agri
Himachal Pradesh	Y	Y	Y	Y	Y			Y	Y		Y					Y	Y		@		
Jammu & Kashmir	Y	Y	Y	Y	Y																
Karnataka	Y	Y	Y	Y	Y			Y	Y		Y					Y	Y		Y		Agri
Kerala	Y	Y	Y	Y	Y			Y	Y		Y					Y	Y				Y
Madhya Pradesh	Y	Y	Y	Y	Y			@	@		@					Y	Y		@		Agri
Maharashtra	Y	Y	Y	Y	Y			Y	Y		Y					Y	Y		Y		
Manipur	Y	Y	Y	Y	Y																
Meghalaya	Y	Y	Y	Y	Y											Y	Y				
Mizoram	Y	Y	Y	Y	Y																Y
Nagaland	Y	Y	Y	Y	Y																
Orissa	Y	Y	Y	Y	Y			Y	Y		Y					Y	Y	Y	Y		
Punjab	Y	Y	Y	Y	Y			Y	Y		Y					Y	Y	Y	Y		Y
Rajasthan	Y	Y	Y	Y	Y											Y	Y	Y	Y		Y
Sikkim	Y	Y	Y	Y	Y																
Tamil Nadu	Y	Y	Y	Y	Y			Y	Y		Y	Y				Y	Y		Y		Y
Tripura	Y	Y	Y	Y	Y																

Table 23.3 Status of Regional Accounting System of various States/UTs (Contd.)

State	Supporting Tables																				
	1	2.1	2.2	3.1	3.2	4.1	4.2	5.1	5.2	6	7	8.1	8.2	9	10	11	12.1	12.2	13	14	15
Uttar Pradesh	Y	Y	Y	Y	Y	Y	Y	Y	Y	Y	Y									Y	Y
West Bengal	Y	Y	Y	Y	Y	Y	Y	Y	Y	Y	Y								Y	Y	Y
Union Territories																Y					
Andaman and Nicobar Islands	Y	Y	Y	Y																	
Chandigarh	Y	Y	Y	Y	Y																
D & N Haveli																					
Daman & Diu																					
Delhi	Y	Y	Y	Y	Y						Y					Y	Y		Y		
Lakshadweep																	@				
Pondicherry	Y	Y	Y	Y				Y								@			Y		

Y: Yes
@: Under Progress, Agri: Only for agriculture

have been trying to implement the recommendations, to the extent data is available. In brief the achievements are:

(a) All the States and UTs, with the exception of D and N Haveli, Daman and Diu and Lakshadweep, are preparing the estimates of GSDP and NSDP.

(b) The State/UT of Andhra Pradesh, Assam, Bihar, Haryana, Karnataka, Kerala, Madhya Pradesh, Maharashtra, Rajasthan, Tamil Nadu, Uttar Pradesh, and West Bengal are preparing the SDP estimates by areas (districts) by commodity producing sectors only and out of which the States/UTs of Andhra Pradesh, Bihar, Haryana, Karnataka, Kerala, Maharashtra, Rajasthan, Tamil Nadu, and West Bengal prepare the district estimates for all the sectors. The State of Arunachal Pradesh is in the process of preparing district level estimates.

(c) The States/UT of Andhra Pradesh, Bihar, Goa, Gujarat, Himachal Pradesh, Karnataka, Kerala, Maharashtra, Orissa, Punjab, Tamil Nadu, Uttar Pradesh, West Bengal and Delhi are preparing the Economic and Purpose Classification of the Expenditure of Administrative departments.

(d) The States of Andhra Pradesh, Assam, Gujarat, Haryana, H.P., Karnataka, Kerala, M.P., Maharashtra, Meghalaya, Orissa, Punjab, Rajasthan and Tamil Nadu are preparing the estimates of Gross Fixed capital Formation (GFCF). No UT is preparing the GFCF estimates.

(e) None of the States/UT except Tamil Nadu (that too only at current prices) is learnt to have been preparing the—Consumption Expenditure.

(f) None of the States are preparing input-out tables.

(g) The States of Andhra Pradesh, Assam, Gujarat, Haryana, H.P., Karnataka, Kerala, M.P., Maharashtra, Meghalaya, Orissa, Punjab, Rajasthan and Tamil Nadu are preparing the estimates of Gross Fixed capital Formation (GFCF). None of the UT is preparing the GFCF estimates.

(h) None of the State/UTs appear to have been preparing the Consolidated Account of the Region and accounts for Household sector. However, the States of Haryana, Himachal Pradesh, Kerala, Madhya Pradesh and Tamil Nadu are preparing the complete accounts of Public Administration and Local Bodies. Where as the States/UT of Andhra Pradesh, Manipur and Rajasthan prepare the accounts of only Public Administration and the States/UT of Gujarat, Karnataka, Tripura and Pondicherry are preparing the Public Sector Accounts relating to administrative departments only.

Current Issues

State Domestic Product For the purpose of compiling the SDP estimates, the major data gaps appear to be the absence of certain key datasets at State level, namely,

- cost of cultivation studies for most crops
- index of industrial production
- wholesale price index
- consumer price index
- corporate sector statistics
- benchmark surveys of enterprises
- annual surveys of enterprises
- indicators to extrapolate the estimates based on five-yearly benchmark surveys
- local bodies

Cost of Cultivation Studies   The cost of cultivation studies are conducted by the DESAg through the agricultural universities. The number of crops covered in each state are very few and the sample size (about 10,000) is too small to give reliable estimates. The time lag in the release of the results of these studies is of the order of 3 years. For generating the input structure of different crops in each state/UT, it is necessary to conduct large scale sample surveys on inputs of agricultural crops, rather than the current practice of "studies" and the work needs to be entrusted to a professional organisation like the National Sample Survey Organisation (NSSO). This would enable coverage of most crops in all the states, a manifold increase in the current sample size and reduction in the time lag in releasing the estimates.

Index of Industrial Production   Most states/UTs do not have a database on the industrial production in their states. The ASI is the only source of data on industrial activity in the states. With the ASI being annual and the time lag in the availability of its results being about two years, there is no data on the current industrial production scenario at state level. While, there is an IIP at the national level, the absence of a corresponding index for the states is a major data gap. The development and maintenance of an IIP by each State/UT, would lead to an enormous improvement in the SDP estimates. The State/UT IIP could be used to prepare the Advance and Quick Estimates of SDP and would also act as a cross-check to the ASI results. The States could consider using the frame/database of Directorates of Industries or/and the Central Excise authorities. While the weights for different industry/commodity groups at state level could be taken from the ASI results, the monthly production figures collected either directly or from the database of the central excise authorities, from a fixed sample (with suitable adjustments for new units, information on which is available with the above mentioned two organisations) would enable the states to have an IIP for their states.

Wholesale Price Index   The weekly wholesale price index (WPI) at national level is compiled on the basis of the weighting diagram generated from the ASI results and a limited number of quotations received voluntarily from the industries. The state agencies are the source for the wholesale prices of agricultural commodities. The compilation of this index requires very small manpower, once a simple worksheet on a personal computer is developed, as total number of quotations are not many. Since the states are the source for agricultural commodities, it may not be difficult to identify few industries and collect information from them and compile a wholesale price index (to begin with on monthly basis).

Consumer Price Index   The problem on the consumer price indices (CPI) at state level is not as serious as in the case of WPIs. Firstly, most states have an index number of consumer prices and secondly, the all India CPIs are released for various centres of the country, from which the price quotations are collected. Nevertheless, since the CPIs are used for current price estimates of domestic product for a few items at dis-aggregated level, it is desirable that the states review/introduce the CPIs. The coverage of the rural population in the state-specific index numbers of consumer price needs to be discussed. The all India sample of villages in consumer price index number for agricultural labourers is inadequate. The situation in different States needs to be documented in this connection.

Corporate Sector Statistics   For most services sectors, the GDP estimates are derived separately for the corporate sector, on the basis of the RBI's company finance statistics. The same source is also used for generating domestic product estimates for the corporate sector segment at state level. However, since the size of the sample is considered too small even at national level to give reliable estimates at industry-group level. At state level, the estimates are not considered scientific even at aggregate level, much less at the sectoral level. If states manage to compile corporate statistics (the number of corporations may not be many in a single state) on the basis of the frame available with the Regional Registrars of Companies, even once in five years, the quality of SDP estimates will considerably improve.

Benchmark Surveys of Enterprises   Presently the benchmark surveys of enterprises are conducted once in about 5 years, by the CSO/NSSO. In future these surveys will be carried out by the NSSO. The states also participate in these surveys with a matching sample. The results generated by the NSSO are not considered reliable at state/detailed industry-group level. However, if the state and centre samples are pooled (copies of the filled-in NSSO schedules could be obtained from the NSSO regional offices located in the states) and analysed by the states, there would be significant improvement in the quality of the SDP estimates, which are based on these benchmark surveys (mostly the unorganised manufacturing and services sectors). The problem of getting plausible estimates of value added per worker from small-scale enterprises that do not maintain accounts requires attention from survey methodology point of view.

Annual Surveys of Enterprises   The major data gap in the GDP or the SDP estimates is considered to be the absence of annual surveys of enterprises (with the exception of registered manufacturing). This has also been identified so by the RAC in 1970s. However, due to various reasons (particularly attributable to lack of resources), the annual surveys of enterprises have not found a place in the statistical system of the country. However, it may be possible to conduct these annual surveys of enterprises by using a fixed sub-sample of the benchmark sample (Such a recommendation was also made by the RAC) and collecting information on about five items, namely, employment, production/total receipts, salaries and wages, capital expenditure and changes in stocks. The problem of "deaths' in the enterprises could be overcome by assuming that the proportion of "deaths" in the fixed sample and the population is same. For the new enterprises, which come into existence, a correction factor could be applied on the basis of information on number of enterprises (for any segment of the enterprises for which such information is available) commencing economic activity in the state, from the State Directors of Industries or the District Industries Centres.

Indicators to Extrapolate the Estimates Based on Five-Yearly Benchmark Surveys   Currently, for the purpose of preparing annual GDP and SDP estimates on unorganised manufacturing and services sectors, various indicators are used to extrapolate the benchmark estimates (for example, in the case of unregistered manufacturing, the IIP). However, it is essential to have a reliable set of proxy indicators and ensure that data is available on them on annual basis. The introduction of annual surveys on enterprises stated in the above para, would generate the database required for extrapolating the benchmark estimates.

Local Bodies   There are large number of local bodies in each state and since they get grants from the state budgets and also generate their own resources (for example, Municipalities), it is necessary that their budgets/accounts are analysed and expenditures are properly accounted for in the SDP/GDP estimates, as also under other expenditure categories of national accounts. Currently the estimates of local bodies are prepared on the basis of grants shown in the state budgets, which implies that resources generated internally by these bodies are not covered. At the CSO level, it may not be possible to analyse these local bodies' budgets and efforts have to be initiated only at the state level. Appropriate inclusion of local bodies' expenditures in the state accounts will show a correct picture of the public sector component.

State Income, Disposable Income, Saving and Net Lending from Other Regions   The compilation of state income (following the income accruing approach) and other aggregates, requires data on inter-state flows of income and net lending from other regions, besides the estimates of consumption expenditure of households and non-profit institutions serving households (NPISH). At this juncture it may be difficult to collect the data on these items, with the exception of consumption expenditure of households and NPISHs. Even for this aggregate, the approach followed for all-India estimates (the commodity-flow) may not hold good at state level, as this approach again requires inter-state movement of goods and services.

Capital Formation, Capital Stock and Consumption of Fixed Capital   Currently, some states are compiling estimates of gross fixed capital formation (GFCF) by assets and industry for the public sector, while few states are also compiling the GFCF estimates for the whole state economy. Since estimates of construction and machinery equipment are already compiled for the SDP estimates, it may not be difficult to compile GFCF estimates at state level, with certain assumptions. The CSO has provided necessary technical guidance from time to time on the compilation of GFCF at state level. Currently the CSO is organising five Regional Workshops for imparting training on the concepts of 1993 SNA, constant price estimates, rebasing and linking of SDP estimates and capital formation. Once the states start compiling the GFCF estimates, a database on this could be developed, which in the long run, will be used for compiling the estimates of capital stock and consumption of fixed capital.

Involvement of State Governments in Type-studies for updating Rates and Ratios   A number of rates and ratios, which are being used in the estimation process of national accounts, are based on surveys conducted long back and as such they might have lost their relevance-to-day. For instance some of the rates and ratios were derived from the following surveys:

- NSS Survey on Grass and Fodder yield estimates was conducted in the year 1950-51;
- NSSO survey on Livestock inputs was conducted in 1974-75; and
- Yield rates of meat by products are based on DMI studies conducted during 1955-60.

Therefore there is an urgent need for updating these rates and ratios. It is suggested that type studies on relevant subjects may be conducted in order to update the different rates and ratios. As these are essentially State subjects, the States are requested to participate in these type studies in updating these rates and ratios.

Appointment of Expert Groups   The States of Karnataka and Rajasthan have recently constituted Expert Groups to look into the various aspects relating to improvement of the estimates of SDP and expenditure aggregates. Such expert groups could be constituted by other states as well. However, the CSO looks after these issues in consultation with the Advisory Committee on National Accounts in respect of both national and state accounts.

Need for Resources   Improvement in the quality of SDP estimates and other aggregates requires introduction of various surveys and development of database, besides availability of adequate trained personnel. All these require resources and importance needs to be attached to state income estimates. Without providing adequate resources, it may not be feasible for the states to come up with improvements in the state income estimates. In most states, only a skeleton contingent of staff have been given the responsibility of compiling the SDP estimates, which barely manages to put together the annual estimates. The State Income Units in various states need to be augmented with qualified personnel. This could be done by the DESs by re-deploying the staff appropriately.

24

National Income from Agriculture

CONCEPT AND METHODS OF ESTIMATION

As all of you are aware, national income is a measure of the totality of all goods and services that the economy produces for the consumption of its nationals or for the expansion of their existing productive assets to be used for further production. As the different units of production and the different measures of services are not directly additive because of differences in units of measurements, the measure has to be expressed in value terms. To get the correct measure it is to be ensured that the total value to products is counted without duplication, i.e. the value added at each stage of further processing is only taken into account while measuring the total.

The national income of a country can be measured in its three phases of production, income generation and final utilization. These three phases are circular in nature. It begins at the production stage where the productive units engage capital and labour and turn out goods and services, the total measure of which gives the national product of the country. This production process yields some money income which is distributed by the productive units to the two factors of production, viz. labour and capital. The totality of this distribution gives a measure of national income or distributive shares of national product or national income by factor shares. This money income received by the two factors of production is either spent by the labour in purchase of goods and services by households or in acquiring more capital and increasing physical assets of the productive units both by households and the producers. Thus the national income can be measured by following any one of three alternative approaches, viz. production approach, income approach and expenditure approach. The national income by definition is equivalent under each of the three alternative approaches. For a complete analysis of the economy it is desirable to measure national income by all the three approaches simultaneously. However, in most of the developing countries, adequate data are not available to derive national income estimates through all the approaches separately.

In India a combination of the three approaches is used for different sectors of the economy in arriving at the most plausible estimate of national income. For the primary sector, viz. agriculture, livestock, forestry and fishing (excluding irrigation), the production approach is used. This involves estimation of gross value of products and by-products and ancillary activities and deduction of value of inputs of raw materials, services and consumption of fixed capital in the process of production to obtain the net value added. The prices to be used for evaluating production are the prices received by the producers or prices paid at the first point of transaction. Only for irrigation, income approach is used. The gross value added from the operation of Government irrigation system is obtained as the sum compensation of employees, interest payments, operating surplus and maintenance provisions, the details of which are available from the Central and State Government budgets. The estimates of gross value added are then needed for consumption of fixed capital to obtain the corresponding net value added.

National income is generally measured at prices prevailing during the year or in other words at current prices. When calculated over a number of years the changes in national income would, therefore, include implicitly not only the effect of the changes in the quantum of production over the period but also changes on account of fall or rise in prices. For a proper measurement of the economic welfare of the people or growth of the economy it would be necessary to eliminate the effect of change in prices by working out national income/product/expenditure at constant prices. The system of national income estimates would, therefore, include measures both at current and constant prices.

EARLY DATA

No regular estimates of national income were available in India before 1948-49. Some of the estimates formulated by individual scholars and one by the Ministry of Commerce for the year 1945-46 are presented in Table 24.1. A comprehensive study about national and per capita income in India was also undertaken by M. Mukherjee. In the absence of reliable data, he made an attempt to indicate tentatively the growth of per capita income in India for the period 1857-1957. The year 1857 was taken as the initial point because in this year following the mutiny, the administration of the country was taken over by the British Crown. He approached the problem by making use of the existing estimates of national income as far as possible, supplemented by a freshly constructed series to cover the earlier half century for which the existing national income data are not adequate.

It may be rather difficult to compare these different estimates, but one thing which comes out clearly from their study is that the share of agriculture in the national output of India has tended to decline over the last 70-75 years. The broad procedure adopted by various workers in this field, for computing the value of agricultural output has been more or less the same. But difficulties faced by all of them have been the non-availability of sufficient data on output as well as prices of agricultural commodities.

Table 24.1 Estimates of National Income—India

Sl. No.	Estimate by	Year	Total income in Rs. abja*	Per capita income Rs.	Contribution of agriculture in Rs. abja*	per cent	Coverage
1	Dadabhai Naoroji	1867-68	3.4	20	2.6	77	for most of British India
2	Baring Barbour	1882	5.3	27	3.5	67	for British India - all non-agri. Income assumed to half of agricultural income
3	Curzon	1897-98	6.7	30	4.5	67	"
4	W. Digby	1898-99	4.3	18	2.8	67	for British India
5	F.J. Atkinton	1895	8.8	39.5	5.6	63	"
6	Wadia and Joshi	1913-14	12.1	44	8.6	70	"
7	Vakil and Muranjan	1910-14	17.7	58.5	11.1	64	for the whole of India
8	Findlay Shirras	1921	26	107	17.1	66	for British India
9	Shah and Khambatta	1921-22	23.6	74	21	89	for the whole of India
10	V.K.R.V. Rao	1925-29	23	78	12.9	57	for British India
11	R.C. Desai	1931-32	16.9	62	9	53	for the whole of India
		1931-32	28.1	82.5	-	62	for British India
12	Ministry of Commerce	1945-46	62.3	198	27.4	44	for British India

*abja = 100 crores = 10⁹

Source: Tenth International Conference of Agricultural Economists (Mysore, India, 1958). J.P. Bhattacharjee (ed). *Studies in Indian Agricultural Economics,* Indian Society of Agricultural Economics, New Delhi, 1958.

NATIONAL INCOME COMMITTEE

The National Income Committee set up by the Government of India in 1949 produced, for the first time, national income estimates for the entire Indian Union. The estimates along with the methodological details were published in the *First and Final Reports of the National Income Committee* (Ministry of Finance, 1951 and 1954). The Committee encountered several problems of estimation mainly due to the many gaps in the statistical field. Subsequently to improve the empirical data base for measuring national product and related aggregates special efforts were made from time to time for a comprehensive review of all available data both published and unpublished. The first results of these efforts were presented by the Central Statistical Organization (CSO) in the *National Income Statistics—Proposals for a Revised Series of National Income Estimates*, 1955-56 to 1959-60 (CSO, 1961). These proposals were discussed in detail at a Seminar especially organized for the purpose and in the light of the comments and suggestions made by the experts in the field of national income. Several follow up studies were undertaken. The results of these studies along with the revised series of national income were published in *Brochure on the Revised Series of National Product 1960-61 to 1964-65* (CSO, 1967). The revised series had also a new base year (1960-61) for the constant price estimates, the base period of the earlier estimate being 1948-49.

Simultaneously with the revision of estimates of national product, attention was paid to the preparation of the related aggregates like capital formation and saving. Such estimates for the period 1960-61 to 1965-66 were brought out along with the details of the methodology adopted in two special brochures, viz. (1) *National Income Statistics—Estimates of Capital Formation in India*, 1960-61 to 1965-66 (CSO, 1969) and (2) *National Income Statistics—Estimates of Saving in India*, 1960-61 to 1965-66 (CSO, 1969). To meet the demand of the users regarding details of estimates of national product etc. a special supplement, viz. *National Accounts Statistics*, 1960-61 to 1972-73—*Disaggregated Tables* (CSO, 1975) was also brought out. This publication gives the disaggregated tables on outputs, inputs and value added by industry groups, private consumption expenditure by object and saving and capital formation by types for public, private corporate and households sectors and covered the period 1960-61 to 1972-73. The publication includes the data at current prices for the period 1960-61 to 1972-73 whereas for the constant (1960-61) price series the details are given for the complete period beginning in 1950-51.

The coverage of the annual *National Accounts Statistics* (NAS or alternatively, White Paper) has been extended gradually to incorporate the estimates of capital formation, saving, private consumption expenditure, factor incomes and the disaggregated tables. The deliberations of the Standing Advisory Committees on 'Collection of Data for National Income' and 'Compilation and Analysis of National

Accounts', helped in this process of gradual augmentation of the scope and coverage of the annual NAS. The annual publication on national accounts besides including the estimates, has an introductory write-up giving a brief analysis of the results and highlighting the more important aspects of the behaviour of the Indian economy over the recent past. The latest issue of NAS published in July, 2000 contains data up to 1998-99.

The new series of NAS with the base year 1993-94 was introduced in 1999 replacing the earlier series with the base year 1980-81. Thus, the estimates in the various statements given in the NAS 1999 and NAS 2000 are from 1993-94 and onwards. Estimates for the earlier years as per the new series are being worked out by the CSO and will be brought out in a separate publication. However, a table giving the main macro-economic aggregate for the years 1950-51 to 1998-99 as per new series at current and constant (1993-94) prices is included in the NAS 2000 publication as a special statement.

The NAS, at the outset gives an overview of national economy along with the summary tables of GDP and National Income, performance of agriculture, indices of industrial production at 2-digit level, GDP by broad sectors, price indices, private final consumption expenditure, domestic saving, and capital formation. The NAS is divided into five parts. Part I gives detail tables of the macro-economic aggregates and population, average annual growth rates, price and quantum indices, relationship of national income and other aggregates, consolidated accounts of the nation and performance of public sector. Part II covers gross and net domestic product by economic activity, their percentage distribution and percentage growth. Private final consumption expenditure by object and classified by type of goods including their percentage distribution, domestic saving by type of institutions, capital formation of type of assets and by type of institutions, gross capital formation by industry of use, net capital stock by type of institutions and by industry of use are given in Part III. Part IV covers public sector transactions. Other than details of aggregates like value added, consumption expenditure, saving, capital formation, this section presents the economic accounts separately for administrative departments and departmental and non-departmental enterprises. Purpose-wise details of both current and capital expenditures of administrative departments have also been presented in this section. Finally, Part V contains the disaggregated statements which inlcude domestic products and value of output from agriculture and allied activities livestock, forestry and logging, fishing, mining and quarrying, manufacturing, electricity, gas and water supply, construction, trade, etc. railways and transport, communication, banking and insurance, real estate and allied sectors. There are also statements on set factor income from abroad, financial assets and liabilities of the household sector, gross fixed capital formation by type of assets and by type of institutions and detailed external transaction accounts.

A few special statements are also given at the end of this White Paper. These include (i) macro-economic aggregates and population,

(ii) depreciation as provided in the books of accounts, (iii) value of output and domestic product from livestock sector, (iv) update of advance estimates of national income for 1999-2000, (v) quarterly estimates of GDP, (vi) net domestic product in rural and urban areas.

The estimates prepared annually use the latest available data collected from different sources. To ensure the use of the most recent information (e.g. point estimates from occasional sample surveys) it becomes necessary from time to time to introduce minor revisions in the method of estimation followed. Such changes are generally indicated briefly in the annual White Paper as and when they are introduced. The present volume gives comprehensive methodological details in respect of the estimates as presented in *National Accounts Statistics*, 1970-71 to 1977-78 (CSA, 1980) were as follows:

The publication was divided into seven broad parts. The first part covered national product and the measurement of value added in each of the sectors (industry groups) was discussed in detail in fourteen different chapters. Within each of these sectors, details were presented separately for each of the sub-sectors for which separate estimates were prepared. The extent to which the industry groups could be sub-classified depended primarily on the availability of data. Following the chapters on individual industries there were two separate chapters devoted to Working Force and Net Factor Income from Abroad. The estimates of working force were used for the measurement of base year value added in a number of unorganized sectors for which the usual product approach became impracticable. The measurement of net factor income from abroad was essential for estimating net national product which was the algebraic sum of the former and the aggregate net domestic product. The discussions on net national product in Part I was followed by the methodological details in respect of national income, i.e. factor incomes, national expenditure covering domestic saving, capital formation and private consumption expenditure and national accounts. Part II was concerned with factor incomes, Part III dealt with consumption, saving and capital formation, Part IV dealt with Public sector, Part V was concerned with consolidated Accounts of the Nation, and Part VI dealt with the method followed for preparing 'Quick' estimates of national product and related aggregates. In order to cover the subject exhaustively, a chapter had also been added giving the Glossary of the Main Terms used in NAS or generally in the literature on the subject. This come as the Part VIII of the volume.

In general, each chapter was divided into three Sections. Section I dealt with the details of the coverage of the sector in terms of economic activities included. Section II dealt with the methodology followed and the source material used for the preparation of the estimates at current and constant prices. Section III made an assessment of the reliability, objectivity and the current status of data which were collected from the various sources and also undertakes an overall appraisal of the estimates.

Revision of the national income estimates is a common practice even in countries with better or more up-to-date data base and is linked with availability of basic data. The estimates of national product and related aggregates for this country undergo revisions as and when complete/revised data become available. The methodology of preparation of the estimates is also modified from time to time to utilize fresh data in respect of each sub-sector as and when they become available. The past estimates for more recent years, are revised annually at the time of the issue of the fresh estimates. However, depending on the availability of data the process of revision does not always end with annual changes but sometimes, extend over a large number of preceding years. This generally happens for the estimates in respect of the unorganized sectors where 'bench mark' estimates are based on periodic survey results or on 'bench mark' data like the decennial or quinquennial censuses. Thus, revision of past estimates becomes often necessary, when fresh surveys are conducted and is undertaken after a number of years because of the lag between the period of reference of the surveys and the date of availability of the results.

A comparison of such revisions over a number of years and their analysis would not enable a better judgment of the levels of these estimates but also help in developing suitable methods of short-term forecasting. An examination of such estimates of net national product for the past few years suggests that the overall effect of the revisions in the estimates is not large. At the sectoral level, however, the extent of revision is substantial in some cases and further the revisions are in either direction (i.e. either reduces or increases the value level). In the case of the primary sectors, revision of the basic data (with the arrival of final forecasts and fully revised figures of agricultural production) mainly account for the variation in the estimates. For sectors like manufacturing, on the other hand, there are often gaps in basic data (e.g. non-availability of ASI results) at the time of preparations of the first set of estimates. In the case of public administration and defence, railways and communication, the estimates are revised as and when the budget estimates are replaced by the 'actuals' or 'revised'. In the case of the unorganized sectors, on the other hand, the measurements are often based on limited available data on indicators or on past trends at the time of preparation of the first set of estimates. These are subsequently revised when data from fresh surveys/type studies become available.

Such comparisons of estimates can be undertaken also for major components of expenditure like final consumption expenditure and capital formation as well as for saving. Since the estimates of private final consumption expenditure and capital formation are obtained by the commodity flow method, all revisions in the estimates of national product which are due to the availability of fresh data on production of commodities will naturally affect estimates of these aggregates. Further, these aggregates would, also be affected by revisions in the data either on exports/imports or the trade and transport margins. As regards saving, as the measurement of financial saving is mostly based on current data, it is affected only marginally because of the use of the fresh information. This, however, is not true for household saving in physical assets the revisions wherein are linked with the revisions in the estimates of capital formation.

In view of such revisions in the estimates as and when fresh data become available it is worthwhile to attempt a broad assessment of the extent to which the estimates of domestic product are based on direct current data. This will be particularly pertinent if estimates for one of the more recent years are used for evaluation. The proportion of direct current data implicit in the estimates will vary between years particularly in the unorganized sectors. The proportion is likely to be higher for those years for which bench-mark data become available. This, for example, would be true for the estimates for 1991-92 for all such sectors for which either 1991 Census results on population/working force or data from RBI All-India Debt and Investment Survey, form one of the basis for the estimates. This will affect the proportion of inputs in agriculture, own account capital formation in the household sector for this year and domestic product in trade, unorganized transport and services sectors.

Considering the year 1988-99, the sources of data of output and input have been examined for each of the sectors from the point of view of not only their current status but also their direct relevancy. In sectors like agriculture, mining and registered manufacturing, the extent of current data in use can be measured without any difficulty as the data used for estimation are of direct relevant nature. In case of sectors like construction and trade, the problem of evaluation of the quantum of current data used in estimation raises problems. For example, in the case of construction, though current data are available on input of five specified construction materials, sufficient data of current nature are not available on proportions of input of other materials and of labour. In the case of trade, the bench mark estimate is taken forward using the total value of marketed output of commodity producing sectors which it is assumed is a measure of quantum of goods handled. Also current data on proportions of total output marketed and trade and transport margins are available annually for a few items only. In the case of such sectors, since the indicators used for preparing the estimates are current but are of indirect nature, two alternative proportions have been worked out. In the first alternative for these sectors, only the estimates for the public and private corporate sectors for construction and public sector for trade have, therefore, been considered as based on current data. Alternatively however, for these sectors the proportion of current data used for the estimates have been determined according to the current nature of the indicators (i.e. the proportion of value of five specified construction materials in total value of construction and current nature of the value of marketed commodities in the total value of goods handled.) This approach gives two alternative estimates of the overall proportion which can be assumed to give the range.

Using such criterion the estimates for the share of net domestic product based on direct current data for 1993-98 has been presented in Table 24.2. Examples of current data in the case of agriculture are figures of actual output of responding States. The production of agricultural crops based on area are not treated as direct current data even if the area estimates are available for the current year. Also, annual estimates of all livestock products are excluded from the list of current data even though current data on milk yield rates separately for cows and buffaloes are available for many of the States. Similarly, the use of the index of production of specified groups of commodities in the registered manufacturing sector for carrying forward/backward the bench mark estimates in the corresponding industries in the unregistered manufacturing establishments has not been considered as current data base even though the bench mark estimates in such cases are based on direct current data. For each sector where value added method is used for measurement of domestic product, the shares of current data in output and input have been combined using the total values under the respective categories as weights to obtain the overall proportions for value added.

In the case of private final consumption expenditure and capital formation, estimates are prepared using the commodity flow approach and as such estimates of the portion based on direct current data will be directly related to that of domestic product. Estimates of saving, contrary to this situation, are based on independent set of data on financial instruments. Direct current data for items like currency, shares and debentures, provident fund, deposits, advances, etc. are available with hardly any time lag except for local bodies and branches of foreign companies. Since, the contribution of local bodies and branches of foreign companies is negligible in the context of household or public or corporate sector saving, the estimates of financial saving can be taken to be based on direct current data available from different sources.

$$V_i = \frac{\alpha_i x_i + \beta_i y_i}{x_i - y_i} \tag{1}$$

where i represents the sector, V_i' the value added based on direct current data, x and y respectively total output and α and β corresponding percentages based on direct data. Alternatively this share V_i' can also be obtained using the formula.

$$V_i = \frac{\alpha_i x^1 + \beta_i y_i}{x_i - y_i} \tag{2}$$

588 Agricultural Statistics in India

Table 24.2 Net Domestic Product by Economic Activity
(percentage distribution) (at 1993-94 prices)

Industry	1993-94	1994-95	1995-96	1996-97	1997-98	1998-99	1993-94	1994-95	1995-96	1996-97	1997-98	1998-99
1	2	3	4	5	6	7	8	9	10	11	12	13
1. Agriculture, forestry & fishing	32.9	32.5	30.3	31.4	29.9	31.1	32.1	32.4	30.0	30.7	28.7	28.8
Agriculture	30.2	29.8	27.8	28.9	27.3	28.4	29.6	29.8	27.5	28.3	26.3	26.6
Forestry & logging	1.6	1.5	1.4	1.3	1.2	1.2	1.4	1.5	1.4	1.3	1.3	1.3
Fishing	1.1	1.2	1.1	1.1	1.5	1.4	1.1	1.1	1.1	1.1.0	1.0	1.0
2. Mining & quarrying	2.1	2.0	1.9	1.8	2.0	1.7	2.0	2.2	2.1	2.0	2.1	2.0
3. Manufacturing	14.9	15.6	16.4	15.8	14.8	13.7	14.7	15.4	16.4	16.2	15.8	15
Registered	9.4	10.1	10.7	10.3	9.4	8.7	9.4	10.0	10.8	10.6	10.2	9.6
Unregistered	5.4	5.5	5.7	5.5	5.4	5.0	5.3	5.3	5.6	5.6	5.6	5.4
4. Elect. gas & water supply	1.3	1.5	1.5	1.3	1.3	1.3	1.2	1.3	1.4	1.3	1.4	1.4
5. Construction	5.6	5.4	5.5	5.5	6.1	6.1	5.4	5.4	5.4	5.2	5.4	5.4
6. Trade, hotels & restaurant	13.8	14.1	14.7	15.1	15.0	14.4	15.1	14.2	15.2	15.2	15.1	15.3
Trade	13.1	13.3	13.9	14.3	14.2	13.5	14.5	13.5	14.4	14.3	14.2	14.4
Hotels & restaurants	0.8	0.7	0.8	0.8	0.9	0.9	0.6	0.8	0.9	0.9	0.9	0.9
7. Transport, storage & communication	5.4	5.5	5.5	5.7	6.1	6.1	6.2	5.5	5.8	5.9	6.2	6.3
Railways	1.0	1.0	1.0	0.9	0.8	0.7	1.0	0.9	1.0	0.9	0.9	0.9
Transport by other means	3.3	3.3	3.3	3.5	3.8	4.0	4.1	3.4	3.4	3.5	3.5	3.5
Storage	0.1	0.1	0.1	0.1	0.1	0.1	0.1	0.1	0.1	0.1	0.1	0.1
Communication	1.1	1.2	1.2	1.2	1.3	1.3	1.0	1.2	1.3	1.5	1.7	1.9
8. Financing, insurance, real Estate & business services	11.5	11.3	11.8	11.1	11.4	11.3	11.2	11.4	11.5	11.5	12.3	12.3
Banking & insurance	5.7	5.9	6.6	6.2	6.5	6.2	5.6	5.8	5.9	6.1	6.8	6.8
Real estate, ownership of Dwellings & business services	5.8	5.4	5.1	4.9	5	5.1	5.6	5.7	5.5	5.4	5.5	5.5

Table 24.2 Net Domestic Product by Economic Activity (Contd.)
(percentage distribution) (at 1993-94 prices)

Industry	1993-94	1994-95	1995-96	1996-97	1997-98	1998-99	1993-94	1994-95	1995-96	1996-97	1997-98	1998-99
1	2	3	4	5	6	7	8	9	10	11	12	13
9. Community, social & Personal services	12.5	12.1	12.4	12.4	13.4	14.4	12.1	12.0	12.2	12.0	13.0	13.5
Public administration & defence	5.6	5.3	5.4	5.3	5.8	6.4	5.5	5.2	5.3	5.1	5.6	6.0
Other services	6.9	6.8	7.0	7.2	7.6	8.0	6.6	6.8	6.9	6.9	7.3	7.5
10. Net domestic product at Factor cost (1 to 9)	100	100	100	100	100	100	100	100	100	100	100	100

where $\alpha_i x_i + \beta_i y_i$ is value added based on direct current data and $x_i - y_i$ is the total value added for sector i. Now, for every sector (i),

$$\frac{\alpha_i x_i + \beta_i y_i}{x_i - y_i} - \frac{\alpha_i x_i + \beta_i y_i}{x_i - y_i} = \frac{2x_i y_i(\alpha_i - \beta_i)}{x_i^2 - y_i^2} \tag{3}$$

Since $x_i > y_i$ and also that generally a larger percentage of output than of input is based on current data, the value of equation (3) will in general be positive. However, the percentage of value added based on direct data in the second alternative works out to more than 100 for sectors where

$$\frac{\alpha}{\beta} > \frac{y}{x}$$

In view of this the results of the first 'alternative, i.e., equation (1) have only been used for the present exercise which may be said to give the lower bounds of Vi' for each of the sectors.

AGRICULTURE AND ALLIED ACTIVITIES

Coverage

The economic activities included in this sector are: (i) growing of field crops, fruits, nuts, seeds and vegetables, (ii) management of tea, coffee, and rubber plantations, (iii) growing of trees on farm lands and village common lands, (iv) agricultural and horticultural services on a fee or on contract basis such as harvesting, baling and threshing, husking and shelling, preparation of tobacco for marketing, pest destroying and spraying pruning, picking, packing and operating irrigation systems (including those operated by government), and (v) ancillary activities of the cultivators such as transportation operations[1] and activities yielding rental income from farm buildings and farm machinery and interest on agricultural loans. In India, agriculture and livestock production generally go together and it is not possible to separate the various inputs like livestock feed, repairs and maintenance costs, consumption of fixed capital, etc. into those used for agricultural products and livestock production. As such breeding and rearing of animals and poultry including private veterinary services, production of milk and milk products, slaughtering, preparation and dressing of meat, production of raw hides and skins, eggs, dung, raw wool, honey and silk worm cocoons, hunting and trapping are included in the sector. Irrigation services are also included under this activity.

Methodology and Source Material Estimates at Current Prices

The contribution to domestic product from agriculture, livestock and allied activities except government irrigation system is estimated by using the production approach which involves estimation of the gross value of products and by-products and ancillary activities and deduction of the value of inputs of raw materials, services and consumption of fixed capital in the process of production to obtain the net value added. For irrigation an income approach is used and the total incomes generated as a result of providing the irrigation services is measured. Separate estimates of gross value of output for agricultural crops and livestock production are prepared while gross/net value added (GVA/NVA) estimates are worked out for the activity as a whole. Sources of data on agriculture output/input and prices are given in Tables 24.3 and 24.4. Information regarding statewise price differentials and trade margins is given in Tables 24.5A and B.

Table 24.3 Agriculture and Allied Activities: Source for Data on

Item	Source
1. Principal crops[2] and indigo, opium, sweet potato, cashewnut, tea, coffee and rubber	*Estimates of Area and Production of Principal Crops in India (DESAg).*
2. Cashewnut	Directorate of Cashewnut, Cochin.
3. Tea	ASI, Tea Statistics (Tea Board).
4. Mango, citrus fruits and grapes	Marketing Reports (DMI), *Indian Agricultural Statistics* (DESAg).
5. Miscellaneous un-specified crops[4]	*Indian Agricultural Statistics* (DESAg).
6. Stalks and straw	*NSS Report No. 32, Some Aspects of Cost of Cultivation of different Crops,* 5th to 7th Rounds: 1951-52 and 1952-53 (NSSO, 1960) (Parts I to III), NSS Report No. 65, *Tables with Note on Animal Husbandry*, 11th Round: 1956-57 (NSSO, 1962), SSBs.
7. Sticks (arhar, sesamum and cotton)	State Agriculture Departments.
8. Jute sticks	State Development Office
9. Bran and sticks	*Report on the Marketing of Rice in India*, 1955 (DMI).
10. Sugarcane (crushed)	*Agricultural Situation in India* (DESAg).
11. Sugarcane (for seeding, chewing, juice making etc.)	Marketing of Gur, 1961-62, unpublished (DMI, 1962).
12. Cane trash	Fertilizer Statistics (Fertilizer Association of Indian).
13. Grass	NSS Report No. 65, Tables with Notes on *Animal Husbandry*, 11th Round: 1956-57 (NSSO, 1962).
14. Industrial and fuel	*Timber Trends and Prospects in India*, 1960-75 (Ministry of Agriculture, 1952).
15. Lemon grass oil	SSB, Kerala.
16. Foodgrains procured by govts.	*Bulletin of Food Statistics* (DESAg).
17. Proportion of paddy milled	*Report of Rice Milling Committee* (Ministry of Food and Agriculture, 1955).
18. Livestock (numbers)	*Quinquennial Livestock Census.*

Table 24.3 Agriculture and Allied Activities: Source for Data on (*Contd.*)

Item	Source
19. Yield of milk	Institute of Agricultural Research Statistics (IARS); Animal Husbandry Deptts. of States; *Ninth Quinquennial Livestock Census*, 1961 (SSB, AP.); Sample Survey by SSB (W.B.)
20. Utilization rates (milk)	DMI; SSBs; ILC (1961).
21. Yield rate (meat)	DMI; IASRI; Animal Husbandry Deptt. (U.P.); SSB (Bihar)
22. Slaughtered animals	DMI
23. Hides and skins	DMI
24. Eggs and poultry meat	IASRI; Poultry Egg Production and its per capita availability in *Indian Journal of Animal Production*, Dec. (ICAR, 1972); ILC, Animal Husbandry Departments of some States.
25. Wool and hair	IARS; Animal Husbandry Deptts. of some States; ILC; DMI (1961-62, 64); DMI (1958-59 unpublished).
26. Dung	IASRI; Animal Husbandry Deptt. of some States.
27. Increment in Livestock	ILC.
28. Other livestock products	DMI (1957, 61).
29. Silk worm cocoons honey	Central Silk Board; Khadi and Village Industries Commission.
30. Hunting and trapping	DESAg; Forest Research Institute and Colleges, Dehra Dun.
31. Seed rates	NSS Report No. 32; Marketing Reports (DMI); Studies on Cost of Cultivation (DESAg) State Govt.
32. Manure	*Fertilizer Statistics; Farm Management Studies* (DESAg); NSS Report No. 140 *Tables with Notes on Some Aspects of Agricultural in India* (Rural), 11th Round: 1956-57 (NSSO, 1969).
33. Diesel oil	ILC, SSBs.
34. Electricity	Central Electricity Authority.
35. Irrigation charges	Budget documents.
36. Repairs and maintenance	*All India Debt and Investment Survey*, 1971-72 (RBI) AIDIS, 1971-72, NSS Report No. 136, *Tables with Notes on Capital Formation* (Urban) 17th Round: 1961-62 (NSSO, 1968).
37. Consumption of fixed capital	AIDIS, 1971-72; SSBs, ILC, NSS Report No. 136, *Tables with Notes on Capital Formation* (Urban) 17th Round: 1961-62 (NSSO, 1968).
38. Pesticides	Fertilizer Association of India.
39. Cost of livestock feed	*Population and Food Planning in India* (Baljit Singh, 1947) (for percentage of each cereal fed to cattle), NSS, Report No. 65, Tables with Notes on Animal Husbandry, 11th Round: 1956-57 (NSSO, 1962); DMI; Oilseeds in India, 1954-55 (DESAg, 1955); ILC.

Table 24.4 Agriculture and Allied Activities: Source of Data on Prices of Outputs and Inputs

Item	Source
1. Individual crops for output and input as seed) .	Weekly bulletins of wholesale prices (statistical supplements to State gazettes); DESAg; SSBs.
2. Small millets, pulses, etc. (individual prices not available)	Same as (1) above NSS Report No. 32.
3. Arecanut	Indian Central Arecanut Committee.
4. Rubber	Market prices (Kerala); Plantation Enquiry Commission Report on Rubber.
5. Lemon grass oil	SSB, Kerala.
6. Fodder crops	NSS Report No 32, Some Aspects of Costs of Cultivation (Parts I to III), 5th to 7th Round: 1951-52 and 1952-53 (NSSO, 1960).
7. Straw	SSBs.
8. Cotton sticks	State Agriculture Deptt. (Punjab and TN).
9. Jute sticks	Indian Central Jute Committee.
10. Bagasse	ASI (1966).
11. Rice Bran	DESAg; SSBs.
12. Grass	SSBs (Haryana, Kerala, M.P., Punjab, Rajasthan, Delhi and Manipur).
13. Livestock products	Same as (1) above and *A Note on Urban Distribution on Margins* (Indian Statistical Institute, unpublished); DMI (1961); Central Silk Board; Khadi and Village Industries Commission.
14. Procurement price	*Bulletin of Food Statistics.*
15. Hunting and trapping	DESAg; Forest Research Institute and Colleges, Dehra Dun.
16. Rice milling charges	*Price Spread of Rice Studies in Costs and Margins,* 1959-60 (DMI, 1961).
17. Manure	*Fertilizer Statistics*; Farm Management Studies by DESAg; NSS Report No. 140; SSBs.
18. Cost of repairs and maintenance	All India Debt and Investment Survey, 1971-72 (RBI, AIDIS); NSS Report No. 136, *Tables with Notes on Capital Formation* (Urban) 17th Round: 1961-62 (NSSO, 1968).
19. Cost of livestock feed	*Population and Food Planning in India* (Baljit Singh, 1947) (for percentage of each cereal fed to cattle); NSS Report No. 65, *Tables with Notes on Animal Husbandry,* 11th round: 1956-57 (NSSO, 1962); DMI; *Oilseeds in India,* 1954-55 (DESAg, 1955) ILC.
20. Market charges	*Rural Credit Survey,* 1951-52 (RBI, 1954) *Marketing Report on Meat* (DMI, 1955); *Marketing Report on Milk and Butter* (DMI, 1957).
21. Electricity charges	Central Electricity Authority.

Table 24.4 Agriculture and Allied Activities: Source of Data on Prices of Outputs and Inputs (Contd.)

Item	Source
22. Cost of pesticides and insecticides	Pesticides Association of India.
23. Cost of diesel oil	State govts; ILC; Indian Oil Corporation.
24. Consumption of fixed capital	AIDIS, 1971-72; SSBs; ILC; NSS Report No. 136, Tables with Notes on Capital Formation (Urban), 17th Rounds; 1961-62 (NSSO, 1968).

Table 24.5A—State-wise Price Differentials and Trade Margins for Milk and Ghee/Butter

State	Rural price as per cent of urban price of milk	Percentage share of producer in wholesale price of ghee/butter
1. Andhra Pradesh	79	94
2. Assam	86	91
3. Bihar	67	91
4. Gujarat	83	94
5. Jammu & Kashmir	82	91
6. Karnataka	79	86
7. Kerala	79	90
8. Madhya Pradesh	77	94
9. Tamil Nadu	79	90
10. Maharashtra	83	94
11. Orissa	69	94
12. Punjab	85	96
13. Rajasthan	80	94
14. Uttar Pradesh	83	94
15. West Bengal	69	91
16. Delhi	84	94
17. Himachal Pradesh	84	91
18. Manipur	63	83
19. Tripura	69	83
20. A. & N. Island	69	90

Value of Output

Agriculture   In respect of the sub-sector agriculture proper, the estimates of value of output are prepared separately for 78 crops/crop-groups. These 78 crops/crop-groups are broadly divided into three categories, namely, principal crops, crops other than the principal crops and by-products. The estimates of value of output for the 49 principal crops are

Table 24.5B—Price Differentials and Trade Margins for Livestock Products Other than Milk and Ghee/Butter; All-India

Item	Rural price as per cent of urban price	Percentage share of producer in wholesale price
1. Meat	84	100a
2. Other meat products	—	90
3. Eggs	85	90
4. Hides and skins	—	90
5. Poultry	—	95
6. Wool	—	95

[a] In case of Maharashtra and W.B. the share of producer in the wholesale price has been taken as 90 per cent.

Source: NSS/MRS/unpublished paper of A. Sanyal and N. Chattopadhyaya.

prepared using the production figures compiled by the DESAg and the prices relating to the peak marketing period prevailing in the primary market centres provided by the state DESs. The estimates of value of output of crops other than the principal crops are based on the area estimates provided by the DESAg and the production data provided by various Boards, National Horticulture Board (NHB) and the State DESs. The estimates of value of output for by products are based on the data obtained from the results of CCS.

Livestock The estimates of value of output for the livestock sector are prepared separately for the items, milk, meat group, eggs, wool and hair, dung, silk-worm cocoons, honey and increment in livestock. The value of output of these products is estimated utilising the figures of production finalised by the TCD (milk, egg and wool) and made available by the DAHD and the price figures furnished by the State DESs. In the case of meat group, which comprises meat (including edible offals and glands and poultry meat), meat products (fats, legs, head, etc.) and by-products (hides, skins, guts, blood, bones, horns, hoofs, etc), the production figures are estimated with the help of yield rates and number of slaughtered animals, furnished by the State AHDs. The estimates of other meat products and by-products are based on the number of slaughtered animals and fallen animals, wherever applicable, and the corresponding yield rates available from various reports of Directorate of Marketing and Inspection (DMI), Ministry of Agriculture. The estimates of poultry meat are prepared in terms of number of adult fowls and chickens slaughtered using the information on utilisation of eggs and chickens survived. The estimates of dung are prepared on the basis of the results of ISS. The utilisation rates of dung used as manure and used as fuel are based on some adhoc norms, which in turn was based on the information supplied by the Department of AHD. In the case of silk and honey the output figures of silk worm cocoons by types, namely, mulberry, tasar, ericot and muga and honey are available with Central Silk Board and Khadi and Village Industries Commission (KVIC), respectively. The estimates of increment in livestock population are estimated by extrapolating the population figures available from the successive ILCs. The state weighted average prices required for estimating the value of output for both agriculture and livestock products are supplied to the CSO by the state DESs.

Inputs

The inputs of agriculture sector are divided into 11 items, namely, (i) seed, (ii) organic manure, (iii) chemical fertilisers, (iv) current repairs, maintenance of fixed assets and other operational costs, (v) feed of livestock, (vi) irrigation charges, (vii) market charges, (viii) electricity, (ix) pesticides and insecticides, (x) diesel oil and (xi) imputed bank charges. Data on seed rates are available from the CCS as well as the state Agriculture Departments and the reports of the DMI. In the case of organic manure, it is assumed that the output of dung manure in the livestock sector is equivalent to the organic manure input in the agriculture sector. The estimates of value of chemical fertilisers consumed are arrived at by using the figures of material-wise distribution of chemical fertilisers published by the Fertiliser Association of India and the retail prices. The estimates of current repairs, maintenance of fixed assets and other operational costs are based on the results of all-India Debt and Investment Survey (AIDIS), which is conducted once in 10 years. The livestock feed comprises of roughages and concentrates. The roughages include cane trash, grass, fodder, stalks, straw, etc., while concentrates are oil cakes, crushed pulses, grains, grams, rice bran, husk, oil seeds, gur, etc. The entire production of fodder, cane trash and grass and 95 per cent of production of stalks and straw in the agriculture sector are considered to be consumed by the livestock population. Adjustment is made towards the consumption of these items by the animals which are not directly connected to agriculture sector. The estimates of concentrates fed to livestock are largely based on the feed rates collected under the 30th round of NSSO in 1975-76, studies conducted by the IASRI as well as by the state DESs. The estimates of irrigation charges are based on the information available from the state irrigation departments. The estimates of market charges are arrived at by conducting a special study with the help of state DESs and the DESAg, covering various agricultural and livestock commodities and several primary marketing centres. These market charges as proportion of value of output are assumed to be constant during a period of few years and are therefore, not revised every year. Whereas the estimates for electricity and pesticides and insecticides are based on the information received from the Central Electricity Authority and the Pesticides Association of India, the estimates of diesel oil are prepared using the norms available from the CCS and the figures of number of diesel engines and tractors available from the state DESs. The estimates of repairs and maintenance are prepared using the norms available from the AIDIS. The imputed bank charges for the agriculture sector is estimated on the basis of data on loans and deposits of the agriculture sector.

Estimates of Factor Incomes

For estimating the domestic product by organised and unorganised sectors, the domestic product from the government irrigation system, non-departmental enterprises and crop production in plantation crops of tea, coffee and rubber covered in private corporate sector, has been treated to be in the organised sector. Rest of the economic activities are assumed to be covered under the unorganised sector.

Agriculture The public sector component, which consists of government irrigation system, is estimated from the budget documents and the annual reports of the non-departmental commercial undertakings. The private sector component (which consists of private corporate sector and the unorganised sector), is broken into three segments, namely, plantation crops, crop production excluding plantation crops and animal husbandry. The estimates for the private corporate sector are derived from the Company Finance Studies conducted by the RBI. However, it may be noted that these studies are based on a sample size of about 2000 companies and the results are prone to errors at sectoral level, where the sample size is even smaller. The estimates of factor incomes for crop production (excluding plantation), which is treated as the unorganised segment of the sector, are prepared using data contained in the CCS (for components other than interest) and the AIDIS (for the component interest).

From the results of the CCS, the net value added, compensation of employees, for casual and attached labour, family labour, rental value of owned land and rent paid for leased land are estimated, state-wise/crop-wise. These estimates are aggregated by using area under the crop in states/crops, as weights. From the aggregated figures, ratio of factor incomes to the NDP are built up and the factor incomes for the agriculture sector are derived.

Livestock The estimates of factor incomes (comprising the compensation of employees and mixed income) for the livestock sector are based on the results of the NSSO survey conducted on animal husbandry during Aug 56 to 57 (11th round, Report No. 65 Tables *i*th notes on Animal Husbandry). From this report, the estimates of service charges in the form of compensation of employees per cattle has been worked out for the year 1955-56. This norm, together with the livestock population for the current year, cattle equivalent ratios and the index of wages of agricultural labourers are used for deriving the estimate of compensation of employees for the current year. The estimated mixed income of the self employed is derived as a residual from the estimated net domestic product of the livestock sector.

Quarterly Estimates of GDP

The quarterly agriculture production estimates of different crops are specially compiled by the Directorate of Economics and Statistics, Ministry of Agriculture (DESAg) for the purpose of quarterly GDP estimates This is done by apportioning the season-wise/state-wise/crop-wise production into various quarters on the basis of "harvest stage approach", utilising the Indian Crop Calendar, 1998. The harvest stage approach (i.e. to record the output of the crops in the quarters in which it is harvested) assumes that the entire production of a particular state/season/crop occurs in the harvesting period, which is documented in the Indian Crop Calendar, 1998.

For the current year, the annual estimates are based on those released by the DESAg at quarterly intervals of time which in turn are based on sowings and crop assessments reported by the SASAs. The DESAg makes available the quarterly agriculture production estimates to the CSO with a lag of three months. By adopting this method the total estimated agriculture production during the four quarters of a financial year (April to March) will be different from the one relating to the agriculture year (July to June). However, for national accounting purposes, the CSO has been taking the total crop production of an agriculture year as such for the corresponding financial year. Therefore, in order to ensure consistency between the quarterly GDP estimates and the annual GDP estimates, the agriculture production estimates in the four quarters of a financial year are adjusted on a priority basis so that the total of four quarters production in the financial year becomes the same as the total production in the agriculture year.

In the case of livestock sub-sector, quarterly estimates of production of livestock products are available for the two major livestock products, namely milk and egg and also for wool, from the Department of Animal Husbandry, Ministry of Agriculture. These estimates are compiled through special tabulations of the schedules of Integrated Sample Survey (ISS), season-wise.

The crops/livestock products for which the quarterly production data is available are rice, wheat, jowar, bajra, barley, maize, Ragi, small millets, gram, tur, urad, moong, masur, khesari, moth, kulthi, peas and beans, other kharif pulses, other rabi pulses, groundnut, sesamum, rapeseed and mustard, linseed, castorseed, safflower, nigerseed, coconut, sunflower, soyabean, cotton, jute, mesta, sanhemp, blackpepper, dry chillies, dry ginger, turmeric, arecanut, cardamom, coiander, potato, tapioca, garlic, sweet potato, banana, onion, sugarcane, tobacco, guarseed (all these crops are principal crops), milk, egg and wool.

For preparing quarterly estimates of the benchmark year (1996-97), the crops and livestock products for which quarterly production estimates are available, the value of output of each such item during 1996-97 has been apportioned into the four quarters of 1996-97, on the basis of the quarterly production (based on harvest approach) of the items during

1996-97. For the remaining crops and the livestock products for which the quarterly production data is not available, the values of output of these crops for the year 1996-97, are apportioned equally into all the four quarters of 1996-97.

As regards estimation of the value of inputs of agriculture sector, the annual input-output ratios of the previous year at aggregate level are assumed to be constant for all the quarters of the year. Using constant input-output ratio and the value of quarterly output of the agriculture sector mentioned above, the values of inputs are estimated for the respective quarters. The quarterly GDP estimates are then obtained as the difference of quarterly estimates of output and material inputs.

Capital Formation in Agriculture

Capital formation in agriculture sector is measured as expenditure incurred on construction activities and acquisition of machinery and equipment by the various institutional sectors namely, government, corporate, non-profit institutions serving household and households engaged in the agricultural sector. The estimates of capital formation in agriculture are prepared separately for the institutional sectors. The public sector, which includes govt. Departmental Commercial Undertakings (DCU) and Non-Departmental Commercial Undertakings (NDCU) component essentially, consists of portion of government irrigation system. Information about this is available from the budget documents of various states and UTs and annual reports of the DCU and NDCU. The estimates are prepared separately for the construction and machinery and equipment. As regards corporate sector component, the information on the construction activity and machinery and equipment is obtained from the annual reports of the Tea, Coffee and Rubber Board besides the information which is available from the sample studies of corporate sector conducted by the Reserve Bank of India. The household sector information is available only through the decennial survey "All-India Debt and Investment Survey (AIDIS)" which provides information on the fixed assets of the households for agricultural activities. The estimates of construction machinery and equipment are thus made for the base year on the basis of the results of the latest AIDIS. The estimates for subsequent years are obtained by moving the base year estimates with the help of appropriate physical indicators (value of output of agricultural crops, population of livestock and value of production of machinery and equipment as and price indices. Another component relating to the increment in the livestock is also taken as a part of machinery and equipment under capital formation.

Capital Stock and Consumption of Fixed Capital The estimates of capital stock are built up utilising the information on the capital formation and following the perpetual inventory method (PIM) approach making use of also information on the average life of various assets. The estimates of consumption of fixed capital (CFC) are made on the basis of the estimates of capital stock and average life of the various assets.

Requirements of Data for the Compilation of National Accounts

For the purpose of preparing the value of output, data is required, state-wise, for (i) all the 78 crops on area, yield, (ii) livestock population, (iii) production of each of the livestock products and (iv) average prices prevailing during the peak marketing period in primary marketing centres in the case of agricultural commodities and first places of transactions in the case of livestock products. In respect of inputs, data is required separately for each of the inputs. Data is also required on all agricultural activities which are not operated in land holdings, like back-yard/foreyard production, mushroom culture, floriculture, cut and dried flowers and other parts of plants, medicinal plants and herbs, plants grown in glass houses. These activities are not being captured in the land revenue records and also the Economic Census and the follow-up surveys conducted by the CSO do not cover agricultural activities. Further, information relating to the value added products produced and consumed within the households are also required to be included in the estimation of GDP.

For the purpose of Input-Output Transactions Table (IOTT) and Factor Incomes prepared by the CSO, data is required on item-wise material inputs and outputs of each individual crop and also the expenditure made towards the repair and maintenance of the machinery utilised in each of the crops, rent, imputed rent on account of own land, interest and wages paid to hired labour and imputed wages for family labour.

The quarterly estimates of GDP demand more information both in terms of frequency (four times each year) and timeliness with regard to the production of agricultural crops on quarterly basis.

The national accounts statistics (NAS) are compiled based on internationally accepted concepts and definitions and agreed standards, which are recommended from time to time, by the international agency, the United Nations through System of National Accounts (SNA), first introduced in 1953 and revised subsequently in 1968 and 1993. In 1993, United Nations Statistical Commission has adopted the latest revised version of the SNA, popularly known as 1993 SNA, which was prepared under the auspices of the Inter Secretariat Working Group on National Accounts (ISWGNA) comprising the Commission of the European Communities (Eurostat), International Monetary Fund (IMF), Organisation for Economic Cooperation and Development (OECD), United Nations (UN) and the World Bank (WB). 1993 SNA retains the basic analytical framework of 1968 SNA and is a much more comprehensive system harmonising other major statistical systems, like Balance of Payments Statistics and Government Finance Statistics of the IMF. It recommends preparation of sequence of accounts for all the institutional sectors into which the economy has been divided, namely, (i) non-financial corporations, (ii) financial corporations, (iii) general government (iv) households, and (v) non-profit institutions serving households. Several satellite accounts including the environmental accounts have been recommended. Production and assets boundaries of the 1993 SNA have been enlarged. As per the extended production boundary the production of the households for own-account consumption, illegal and underground production are required to be reckoned with in the national accounting framework. To meet these requirements, data is required by institutional sectors, particularly, the agricultural household sub-sector. The data requirements for the purpose of preparation of (i) Production Account, are value of output, including output for own final use and inputs; (ii) Generation of Income Account, are GVA and factor incomes; and (iii) Capital Account, are acquisitions, less disposals of new or existing tangible fixed assets (farm building and other structures, machinery and equipment, cultivated assets-plantations, trees and livestock-that are used repeatedly or continuously to produce products), major improvements to tangible non-produced assets, including land, costs associated with the transfer of ownership of non-produced assets and changes in stocks (work-in-progress on cultivated assets, materials and supplies and others). At present the NAS is compiled following broadly the recommendations of 1993 SNA, to the extent feasible from the point of view of data availability. The Statistics Division of the Food and Agricultural Organisation (FAO) has recently developed a System of Economic Accounts for Food and Agriculture.

Data Availability in the Context of Above Requirements

In the case of 49 principal crops/crop-groups, estimates on area and yield are available without any time lag. Among the non-principal crops, data on production and prices are available from the NHB. However, the sources of NHB data and the method of compilation are not known, as crop-cutting experiments are not conducted by any agency on these horticultural crops. For crops like other oilseeds, other cereals, etc., only area figures are available from the DESAg alongwith the LUS. Price statistics are available from both the DESAg and the State DESs. Whereas the data on prices from the DESAg is in the form of quotations and fewer centres, the same from DESs are the state weighted average prices and are based on price data collected from larger number of centres. For estimating the area under kitchen garden in foreyard/backyard in rural areas, the results of NSSO survey on operational holdings are used. In the case of livestock products, estimates of milk, egg and wool are available from the DAHD with a lag of about two years, which are generated from the ISS. Estimates of meat and no. of slaughtered/fallen animals are available from the State AHDs/DESs and that of livestock population from the DESAg/State AHDs from the results of livestock censuses. Estimates of silk, honey and evacuation rates of dung are available from the respective Boards/state AHDs from the results of ISS. In respect of inputs, data is available with a lag of about 3 years from the results of the CCS, State DESs, State agriculture departments, Central Electricity Authority, Fertiliser Association of India and Pesticides Association of India, with certain gaps, listed in Part 5. For estimating the value added from the operation of government irrigation system, government budgets contain the relevant information. Information on farm machinery and equipment for certain reference years is available from the agricultural census/input survey, livestock census and AIDIS.

Data Gaps

Estimates of Production   Major data gaps in the agriculture sector relate to yield estimates of crops other than the principal crops. Although some of the states have initiated a Scheme for "Crop Estimation Surveys on Fruits and Vegetables and Minor Crops", to estimate the yield rates of fruits and vegetables as well as minor crops, the same is not being done in all the states. In the case of grass and fodder, the estimates are based on very old yield rates, relating to 1952-53. The estimate of area under grass is also based on very old norms based on LUS. A major data gap in the agriculture sector is with respect to separate data on many minor crops as well as crops which have recently been taken up on large scale as commercial crops. Another major data gap is with reference to the production of mushrooms, high valued minor crops and other parts of plants, medicinal herbs. It is possible that most of these are not being covered in the present estimates of production as they are likely to be carried out in areas other than the farmlands. Being missed in production statistics, these relatively new areas of cultivation may not also be covered in the estimation of GDP, since the Economic Census and follow-up surveys do not capture agricultural activities. There is a possibility that other ancillary activities, like cut flowers and dried flowers and other parts of plants may also do not figure in the estimation of GDP, due to this.

In respect of livestock products, reliable estimates of production are available for three major products, namely milk, egg and wool, although the time lag of these estimates is of the order of two years. In the case of meat, the estimates of yield are not generally based on any scientific techniques, although some states are generating the estimates using the ISS results. Besides no reliable estimates of number of animals slaughtered in places other than the slaughter houses like unorganised slaughter houses, religious slaughters, etc., are available. The estimates of yield rates of meat products and by-products are based on the DMI studies done in 1960s. In addition, there is no data on number of fallen animals and these are estimated using DMI 1961 studies on the subject. In the case of poultry meat, the estimated number of fowls, ducks killed and average meat yield per bird are not available. These are based on some very rough norms and results of few studies conducted by IASRI. The estimates of hair and bristles suffer due to lack of scientific studies on the yield of these items. The present estimates are based on DMI 1958, 1961 and 1962 studies. The evacuation rates of animals in terms of dung, and its utilisation as manure and for fuel purpose too are based on a limited study conducted by few states and coordinated by the

Department of AHD in 1984-85. However, some of the states are able to generate presently the evacuation rates of dung from ISS results. In the case of estimates of increment in livestock, the estimates are based on successive ILCs and using extrapolation techniques. The ILC is unfortunately not conducted at the same time by all the states. Besides, if the reference period happens to coincide with a drought year, as happened in the case of 1987, the estimates for the subsequent years based on extrapolation would totally go awry. This technique also does not take into account the present conditions, like death of animals due to natural calamities. Therefore, there is data gap to the extent that there are no reliable estimates of livestock population on annual basis due to lack of information on the annual data on number of deaths of different categories of animals due to natural calamities in different regions.

Inputs   In the case of inputs, the seed rates of crops other than those for which CCS is being conducted, relates to NSS 1951-52 and various marketing reports of DMI. Even the CCS is not conducted in all the states and norms of neighbouring states are applied to the states where CCS is not being done. This is a major data gap as different states have different farm and soil conditions. In the case of chemical fertilisers and pesticides and insecticides, instead of the consumption figures, the estimates are being prepared using the dispatch figures. The estimates are very weak as far as the feed of livestock is concerned. The benchmark estimates of production of fodder and grass are based on NSS, 1955-56 survey. The estimates of yield rates of stalks and straws other than those available from CCS are based on NSS 1951-52. The estimates of quantity and percentage of different components of concentrates consumed per cattle are based on NSS 1975-76 survey and studies conducted by IASRI. The itemwise consumption of roughages and concentrates consumed by different categories of livestock is not available, which is essential both for the construction of input-output transaction table as well as reliable estimates of livestock feed. Such data separately for rural and urban areas will help in evaluating the value of output of animals used in sectors other than agriculture and livestock. The data on operational costs and repair and maintenance is very weak. The estimates of repair and maintenance are based on rough norms based on AIDIS conducted once in ten years. The annual estimates are, therefore, very weak due to the absence of annual indicators. Based on limited data available on operational costs of livestock products, it is assumed to be 0.25 per cent of value of output. The data on market changes of livestock products is also not available.

Prices   In respect of prices, ideally, these should relate to the first point of transaction, at which income accrues to the producer. Unfortunately, such data is not available and estimates are usually based on prices prevailing in the primary marketing centres. Further, the actual quantity of transactions at different prices levels give accurate estimates of value of output. In the absence of these, the output of a district is treated as transacted at the average price prevailing in different primary marketing centres during the peak marketing period in a district. Even the assumption of bulk of transactions of agricultural commodities taking place in the peak marketing period may not hold good in the present economic conditions of farmers, as some of them have the capacity to withhold agriculture production till they get higher prices for their commodities. In the case of milk, due to its peculiar nature of marketing, separate data on prices is required in respect of co-operative marketing federations and milk sold directly, which is presently not available. Reliable estimates of prices of meat products, dung used as fuel and dung used as manure and various categories of animals, are not available.

Factor Income For estimating the contribution of different factors in the generation of income, namely, land, labour, capital and entrepreneurship (which respectively generate rent, including imputed rent on account of owned land, compensation of employees, including that of family labour, interest and profits), data required in detail on these is not available. Although, data is available from CCS with considerable time lag, no such details are available as far as livestock sector is concerned. The Department of AHD's surveys on cost of inputs and ISS collect data on these aspects, but unfortunately, the same are not being tabulated. In order to implement the System of National Accounts, 1993 (1993 SNA), which, interalia, recommends preparation of sequence of accounts for various institutional sectors like household, non-profit institutions serving households, non-financial corporations, financial corporations and government, data in detail is required on factor incomes cross-classified by type of institutions, particularly for the agricultural households.

Quarterly Estimates of Production Quarterly estimates of agricultural production required for the preparation of quarterly GDP estimates are presently not available. Indeed it is a difficult task as crop calendar do not follow quarterly system but ways and means required have to be devised to accomplish this. This currently available estimates of quarterly agricultural production are based on Indian Crop Calendar, 1998.

Environmental Accounts For compiling the environmental accounts information relating to the imputed cost for degradation and depletion on the non-produced natural assets like soil and water etc. are not available, but required to be generated. initially this may require extensive research work to be initiated at a place like IASRI with the co-operation of the agricultural universities.

Capital Formation for Agriculture It has been observed that in recent past capital formation in agriculture has been declining particularly in the public sector. The public sector agriculture is mainly the government irrigation activity and it is a fact that the capital formation in agriculture in the public sector has been declining.

Whereas capital formation in public sector in totality for all industries has been rising, the capital formation in agriculture has been declining.

Views have been expressed by some researchers that from practical point of view the capital formation in agriculture as estimated in the national accounts is not a good indicator for assessing the development of agriculture for estimated growth. What is important for agriculture sector is that the capital formation for agriculture. Thus for example if capital formation has taken place for providing rural electrification, it is not the capital formation in agriculture but certainly it is for agriculture. Likewise, the capital formation which takes place in the activity of construction of rural roads providing connectivity of village and town for the use of the farmers to take their produce from the farm site to the marketing centres is not capital formation in agriculture but certainly it is capital formation for agriculture. Also one could argue and give examples like capital formation, which take place in the fertilizer industry, which are not the capital formation in agriculture but certainly the capital formation in the fertilizer industry. However, this capital formation is for the exclusive use, of the agriculture sector as the fertilizer is totally meant for the agriculture sector. Similar arguments could be made for the capital formation which take place in the pesticides industry, herbicide industry, agriculture implements manufacturing industries, and so on. In short the concept as explained above, capital formation for agriculture is more relevant for the understanding of the development of agriculture sector rather than the capital formation in agriculture. If we see the numbers on the capital formation in various activities mentioned above which are meant for the total use of agriculture sector, we observe that the capital formation for agriculture has not declined but has in fact been rising in the part in Indian economy. There is a need to develop such useful concept and macro-aggregates for explaining the economic activities more explicitly and meaningfully. It is also necessary to organise requisite data for compiling such macro-aggregates.

Other Aggregates   Information on the consumption expenditure of the household engaged in the agricultural activity, per se, not available as such are though the consumption expenditure information is available by rural and urban areas. There is no information on the income distribution as it has not been possible to conduct household income and expenditure surveys as yet. Pilot studies conducted by NSSO have indicated that it is not feasible to collect reliable information on the income. Also information on the saving of the household engaged in the agricultural activity is not available purely because the information on the income and expenditure is not available. Saving information is available only at the economy level for various institutional sectors and not by economic activity.

QUALITY OF AGRICULTURAL STATISTICS

Area Estimates

According to the findings of the ICS, during 1995-96, TRS statements were submitted in time after completion of Girdawari in 28 per cent (in autumn), 41 per cent (in winter), 41 per cent (in rabi) and in 30 per cent (in summer) of the sample villages. The traditional reporting system of agricultural statistics (the village patwari) is perceived to be overburdened with other jobs.

In some important states (A.P., Haryana, J & K, H.P.), Girdawari (recording of area under different crops, by the patwaris) is undertaken only twice a year (Table 24.6) in the months of October and April. This could result in under-enumeration of crop-acreage in respect of 3rd and 4th crops in these states, if the established procedures are not followed.

Table 24.6 Number of Enumerations Undertaken in Different States

States	No. of Enumerations
Assam, Bihar, Orissa, Tamil Nadu and West Bengal	4 (Early Kharif, Kharif, Rabi and Summer)
Gujarat, Karnataka, Kerala, Madhya Pradesh, Maharashtra. Punjab, Rajasthan, Uttar Pradesh	3 (Kharif, Rabi and Summer)
Andhra Pradesh, Haryana, Himachal Pradesh, Jammu and Kashmir	2 (Kharif and Rabi)

The Scheme of ICS observed large scale under-enumeration in the acreage of crops. The ratios of estimates of crop area at all-India level based on supervisory check under ICS (A-IV) and the entire of state primary workers (A-III) in the corresponding sampling units of ICS, presented in Table 24.7 below, shows extent of area under-enumeration, particularly with reference to the major crop like rice, wheat, jowar, bajra, barley and gram.

Table 24.7 Extent of Area Under-Enumeration (A IV/A III) Based on ICS Results

Crop	1995-96	1994-95	1993-94	1992-93	1991-92
Rice (Kh)	1.1824	1.2252	1.1319	1.2102	1.2339
Rice (S)	1.4022	1.2686	1.0957	1.1675	1.1788
Jowar (Kh)	0.9864	1.0413	1.0229	1.0668	1.0140
Jowar (R)	1.0419	1.1178	1.1194	1.0481	1.0575
Bajra	1.0422	1.0374	1.0123	1.0372	1.0054
Maize	1.0823	1.3204	1.1148	1.0589	1.0547
Ragi	1.0113	0.9796	0.9872	1.0892	1.0853
Wheat	1.0934	1.1318	1.1580	1.1275	1.1619
Barley	1.0000	1.3773	1.1317	1.2174	1.3591

Note: A-III denotes estimates of area based on patwari's entries
A-IV denotes estimates of area based on Supervisor's entries
Both the entries refer to the same sample villages covered under the ICS

Yield Estimates The above stated weaknesses in the agricultural statistics system are perhaps responsible for the large scale revisions that are now taking place in the estimates of foodgrains released at various points of time, during the last few years. The estimates of foodgrains released at various points of time, since 1993-94, show that the range of estimates is 179-184 million tonnes for the year 1993-94, 185-192 million tonnes for the year 1994-95, 193-180 million tonnes for 1995-96 (largest variation in any year), and 191-199 million tonnes for 1996-97. The range of estimates for the year 1997-98 and 1998-99 are 192-194 and 195-203 million tonnes, respectively. For the year 1999-2000, the range of estimates is 199-209 million tonnes.

The weaknesses of agriculture statistical system also reflect sometimes in the data not conforming to auxiliary evidence, like the data on procurement and exports. In 1998-99, while the foodgrains production fell from 199.44 mn. tonnes to 192.43 mn. tonnes (– 3.5 per cent), the procurement (under central pool) has risen from 21.3 mn. tonnes to 27.0 mn. tonnes (between July 1, 1997 to July 1, 1998), registering a growth rate of 26.8 per cent. Looking at the main commodities of rice and wheat, the inconsistency in the estimates emerges clearer. During the year 1997-98, the production of rice has gone up by 0.57 mn. tonnes from 81.73 mn. tonnes from 81.73 mn. tonnes in 1996-97 to 82.30 million tonnes, thus registering a marginal growth of 0.7 per cent. However, the procurement of rice in the same period had risen by 21 per cent, from 12.0 mn. tonnes to 14.5 million tonnes. In the case of wheat, while the production had declined to 65.90 mn. tonnes in 1997-98, from 69.35 mn. tonnes in 1996-97 (a negative growth rate of 5.0 per cent), the procurement had risen to 12.65 mn. tonnes in 1997-98 from 9.30 mn. tonnes in 1996-97 (registering a growth rate of 36.0 per cent).

The CSO uses the data provided by the NHB and the states on horticultural crops. In respect of these crops, the data for the principal crops comes from the DESAg, those covered under the pilot scheme "Crop Estimation Surveys on Fruits and Vegetables and Minor Crops" (which is in operation in select states and for select crops) from the state DESs and the rest from the NHB. Although for the crops for which the NHB provides the data, the state DESs also provide certain information. There is large discrepancy in the two sets of data. Whereas the source agencies for the NHB are the state horticulture boards/horticulture directorates, the estimates provided by the DESs are on adhoc basis.

Prices Although the CSO uses the price data furnished by the State DESs, there is no system of auditing of these data for the sake of consistency and comparability of data across the states. There is a tendency on the part of some of the states (whole per capita income is around the all-India average or below) to under-report price data, since the devolution of central funds, to some extent, depends on the estimates of state domestic product.

Cost of Cultivation Studies The CCS although termed as a "Study", is in fact a large scale sample survey. The conduct of the survey involves sampling design, selection of scientific sample and canvassing of schedules and collection of data. This survey also requires adoption of uniform concepts, definitions and procedures. In this background, it is felt that the association of different agricultural universities (which are primarily research institutions) is not proper. These universities do not have the proper infrastructure or expertise to conduct large scale sample surveys, being primarily academic and research bodies, and collect statistics from the surveys or generate quality reports timely and quickly. Due to these weaknesses in the operation of CCS, data on some of the inputs is not usable in the compilation of national accounts. This is because the estimates of some of the inputs (eg. fertilisers) made at all-India level, using the data of CCS, show much higher than the total availability of the commodity in the country. The other weak areas of CCS relate to the time lag in the release of results (which is of the order of 3 years) and the absence of region wise estimates.

Livestock Statistics The results of Livestock Census also suffer from many inconsistencies. The states do not conduct Livestock Census, simultaneously or within a reasonable time-frame. The time lag in the availability of results is quite large. The reports of livestock census released from time to time have several inconsistencies. The livestock statistics are considered to be quite weak in comparison to the crop statistics. Particular reference in this context is with reference to the production of meat and meat by-products and inputs of livestock sector.

FORESTRY AND LOGGING

Coverage The economic activities considered include: (i) forestry (gathering of uncultivated forest products, charcoal burning carried out in the forests and the like), and (ii) logging (felling and rough cutting of trees, hewing or rough shaping of poles, blocks, etc.) and transportation of the logs up to the permanent lines of transport. The forest products are classified into two broad groups, viz. (a) major products comprising industrial wood (timber, round wood and match and pulp wood) and fuel wood (fire wood and charcoal wood), and (b) minor products, comprising a large number of heterogeneous items such as bamboo, sandal wood, charcoal, lac, etc.

Methodology and Source Material Estimates at Current Prices The domestic product is measured following the 'production approach'.

Volume of Major Products For major products, State-wise data on quantities exploited and royalty value are released annually in *Forestry in India* by DESAg in a mimeographed form. For recent years for which information is not available from DESAg, production and wholesale prices (inclusive of trade and transport margins) data at assembling centres are obtained from the Chief Conservator of Forests in each State.

For estimating the value of output of major products, the recorded production is evaluated at producers' prices at the State level. The producers' prices are estimated by adjusting the wholesale prices for trade and transport margins which are determined from the details available in the *'Timber Trends Study for the Far East, Country Report for India'* (Inspector General of Forests, 1958).

The available evidence shows that considerable quantities of industrial and fuel wood escape official recording. A rough estimate of the extent of under reporting/illegal removals of major forest products for the year 1957-58 is given in the 'Timber Trends and Prospects in India, 1960-75' (Ministry of Food and Agriculture, 1962). On this basis an allowance of 10 per cent of the value of recorded production is made to cover all such unrecorded production for major forest products.

Value of Minor Products   Information on the minor products available is in the form of royalty value or contract fee realized by the government and not the economic value of output of these products. The reported figures are therefore adjusted to arrive at their economic value. The value of output is therefore worked out indirectly from the royalty value using the ratio of the total value of output (recorded and unrecorded) to royalty value of the major products. However, to the extent data on production and prices of different categories of minor forest products (e.g. charcoal in Kerala and A.P., bidi leaves and sandalwood in A.P., bamboo in A.P. and U.P. and resin in H.P.) are available, their value is estimated separately and included in the total.

Value of Inputs   The inputs under this economic activity refer to operational costs and expenditure on repairs and maintenance of roads and other assets. Information on purchase of commodities and services for government forests are available from the budgets of the State governments and union territories. On the basis of these details, the total value of operational costs, and repairs and maintenance is taken to be 4 per cent of the value of output. Using similar details from the budgets, expenditure on consumption of fixed capital is estimated at 1 per cent of the total value of major and minor forest products.

Estimates at Constant Prices   In the case of major forest products (industrial wood and fuel wood) for which information on physical output is available, State-wise constant price estimates of the value of output are obtained by evaluation of State level of output by the corresponding base year (1993-94) prices. For minor forest products for which data on the value of output only are available, the method of deflation is used to estimate the value of output at 1993-94 prices. The relevant index is the weighted average price index of major forest products specially constructed for the purpose using the 1993-94 production figures as weights. The State-wise weighted annual average prices per unit of industrial wood and fuel wood are worked out given the data on physical production and value of output. The same proportions of value of operational costs, repairs and maintenance and consumption of fixed capital to value of output as for estimates at current prices are used to obtain estimates of gross and net added values at constant prices.

Concluding Remarks

The importance of statistics of area, production and yield of crops, their reliability and timeliness assume utmost importance to the planners, administrators, policy makers and research workers. Though the system of agricultural statistics, which has been evolved over a period of time and is a decentralised one, has generated the agricultural data base for meeting the requirements of various users quite satisfactorily; nonetheless it needs to amplify its scope further to make available the information on account of changing economic scenario and ensure quality in terms of timeliness and reliability.

The database of agriculture sector is relatively adequate, vis-a-vis, that of the livestock sector. However, with the emergence of new areas and techniques of cultivation, data is required on these areas so as to include them in the estimates of value of output of agriculture. These relatively new areas are the horticulture, mushroom cultivation, herbs, medicinal plants, backyard/foreyard cultivation, etc., which may or may not be taking place on farmlands.

There has been some deterioration in the quality of area statistics in the recent years, the reasons of which are generally attributed to many factors. The central agencies show helplessness in the matter on the plea that agriculture is a state subject, ignoring the fact that statistics is a concurrent subject. This allows collection of statistics even on state subjects by the central departments.

The schemes for generating advance estimates are also apparently not fully functional, as brought out by the results of the ICS and the substantial revisions that are taking place in the agriculture production estimates in the recent years.

Similarly, absence of a central data base on prices of agricultural commodities, has resulted in our inability to cross-check the prices data maintained by the states, resulting at times in under or over estimation of value of output of agriculture sector. The tendency of under-reporting of price data is particularly in evidence from some of the states whose per capita income is below or around the all-India average per capita income, since the devolution of funds to some extent depends on these estimates.

The data provided by the NHB is used for estimating the GDP, in respect of those crops/states which are not covered under the principal crops or under the scheme "Crop Estimation Surveys on Fruits and Vegetables and Minor Crops". The states also provide information on such crops, but they are substantially lower than those provided by the NHB. Since the Ministry of Agriculture is the administrative ministry for the crop statistics, standardisation of the procedures of data collection on horticultural crops need to be put in place. Since the scheme "Crop

Estimation Surveys on Fruits and Vegetables and Minor Crops" is in position for a long time it is suggested that the DESAg should release the estimates of fruits and vegetables covered under this scheme, as part of the principal crops, by suitably extending this scheme to all states or integrating these crops with the principal crops.

The data gaps in livestock sector, however, are quite serious. The CCS gives substantial information for estimating the factor incomes, for agriculture sector but the manner in which it is being conducted, the role of agricultural universities and the time lag in the release of results, need a relook. Similarly, system of the livestock census needs a thorough review and possible revamp.

India is considered to have an excellent and widely acknowledged and recognised agricultural statistical system. We must restore the credibility of the system and monitor this system continuously to ensure that it continues to be one of the best systems in the world. The recent evidences of a tendency of deterioration in the quality of agricultural statistics needs to be stemmed immediately. Several Committees went into the inherent technical deficiencies in the generation of agricultural statistics in the past few years.

The Working Group for the Ninth Plan headed by Secretary (Agriculture) and the Expert Group On Crop Forecasting And Advance Estimation have made several suggestions to improve the agricultural statistical system. To begin with both the Groups identified lack of professional statistical expertise in the DES as one of the bottle-neck areas. One of these Groups went to the extent of suggesting the setting up of a Standing Committee for reviewing and bringing improvements on regular basis in the system of crop statistics in India and creation of a National Centre for Crop Forecasting to be exclusively manned by ISS officers and located in the Department of Agriculture and Cooperation, but outside the purview of the DES. It is essential that the recommendations of these Groups are considered immediately for implementation.

The needs of the Indian agricultural statistical system must be given prime importance. If the system requires competent statistical expertise (as stated by the Expert Groups) the same must be provided to it. All other considerations and issues, which are at the cost of the System, must be put aside.

25

Weather Systems and Weather Forecasting in India[1]

INTRODUCTION

India is one of the few countries in the world to have a large spectra of whether events having spatial scale of less than 1 km to more than 1000 km and temporal range of less than an hour to more than a week. Different parts of the country experience different kinds of weather conditions which constitute the local climatology of that particular place or region. Understanding and prediction of weather systems are the challenging fields of the applied physical sciences. Meteorological Department in the country was one of the first scientific departments which started scientific research on weather systems as early as in 18th century. Indian monsoon is a field of active research all over the world as it is a unique weather event which covers several oceans and continents but depicts its characteristic phase over Indian sub-continent. The monsoon rains are crucial for agricultural production in the country as most parts of the country depend on this rain for day-to-day agricultural operations. Tropical cyclones over the Indian region are considered as the most deadliest, not merely due to its intensity but because of a unique combination of its intensity, population density and design (slope) of Indian coastal areas. Thunderstorms in certain parts of the country are highly furious.

Orographical (geography) features of certain parts of the country modulate the impact of weather systems. Most of the weather systems have two basic atmospheric components: moisture (rain) and winds. Quantity of moisture content and force of winds in the systems decide their intensity. The winds are closely related to an invisible atmospheric component: surface pressure. Lower the atmospheric pressure, stronger are the winds in the systems.

---

[1]Authored by Akhilesh Gupta, this paper was read at the National Workshop on Improvement of Agricultural Statistics, June, 2001.

While majority of the weather systems are disastrous to lives and property, a few of them (particularly low intensity systems) are highly beneficial as they provide much needed rain water, necessary for livelihood of all living beings including agriculture. The weather systems are the carriers of water from Ocean to land and act as natural water purifying plants. They also transport air from lower latitudes to higher latitudes as a part of general circulation. Some of the systems like thunderstorms/hailstorms etc are helpful in maintaining the electrical field of the earth's atmosphere. Thunderstorm converts atmospheric nitrogen into nitrous compounds (through lightening) which are brought down to the ground through rain. This rain is very useful for the growth of plants and therefore have great relevance to agriculture.

Prediction of weather systems over the Indian region therefore assumes considerable importance. Several organisations are engaged in developing techniques for prediction of these systems. There has been good progress in recent years in this field.

BASIC ELEMENTS OF WEATHER

There are six basic elements of atmosphere which decides weather over a place. These are: temperature (maximum and minimum), pressure, humidity, wind (speed and direction), cloudiness and rainfall.

Surface Temperature The term "temperature" is normally being referred to as the temperature of surface air layer at a height of 4.5 ft (normal height of human being including children). The measurement of temperature is made through a mercury thermometer kept inside a wooden chamber called "Stevenson screen". Common man is generally concerned with the maximum temperature which is attained around 2 p.m. during the day time and the minimum temperature which occurs a few minutes after the sun rises in the morning. There is a general misconception in the public that maximum temperature which is attained around noon. The reason for occurrence of maximum temperature nearly 2 hours later than noon, is that although maximum solar radiation is received at ground around noon, it takes about 2 hours for the ground and the ambient air to get heated up to their threshold level. Similarly the misconception that minimum temperature occurs around midnight, is not true as the ground gets cooler and cooler throughout the night until sun rises when it starts getting fresh solar radiation.

The diurnal (maximum and minimum) variation of temperature is mainly due to day and night cycle (spinning of earth around its axis). Apart from diurnal cycle, temperature has seasonal cycle (winter to summer and again winter through spring and autumn) which is due to rotation of earth around sun.

The Sun is the ultimate creator of all weather systems and atmospheric motion. The genesis of entire range of weather systems is caused by the diurnal and seasonal changes in the temperature. A simple concept of formation of weather system can be explained as follows: High temperature causes the ambient air to become lighter and hence its upward motion. This causes fall in surface pressure. To fill the vacuum created by fall in pressure, air from surrounding areas rushes (increase in surface winds) into this place. The cycle continues and intensifies with time.The upward motion of air causes condensation (humidity) of moisture (formation of clouds) and finally precipitation of moisture as rain (after saturation). While such a simplistic mechanism of the formation of weather system does not occur in the atmosphere as it is, it clearly depicts the role and the inter-relation of various elements in this process.

Surface Pressure   The surface pressure is defined as the weight of air column above a unit surface area. The fall in surface pressure described above can be explained as follows When the air at the surface is heated up, it becomes lighter and therefore rises upwards. It then pushes the air immediately above in the air column. The air at the top most part of air column (as the top of troposphere) moves horizontally outside the column and thus the total weight of air in the particular column becomes less than surroundings. This obviously causes fall in surface pressure. When such a process occurs in a larger area (more than 100 km) instead of an air column, a low pressure area forms. The air from surrounding areas rushes towards this area (from high pressure to low pressure) and hence this low pressure area becomes the region of upward motion. This obviously makes this area as the region of stronger winds, cloudiness and precipitation.

Humidity   The moisture in the atmosphere is very important and perhaps the deciding factor for the development of a weather system. The humidity is the measure of moisture content in the air. Relative humidity is defined as the ratio of weight of water vapours to that of dry air expressed in percentage. A saturated air is expected to have 100% relative humidity.

Surface Winds   Wind is defined as air in motion. The winds blow because of difference in atmospheric pressure between two places. Steeper is the pressure gradient, stronger is the wind.

Cloudiness   As explained above, the clouds form due to condensation of water vapours. Normally condensation takes place on the dust and nuclei of atmospheric pollutants. Clouds are of several types and are categorised into three main categories, viz, Low, Medium and High clouds, depending on their height from the ground. Deep convective clouds associated with thunderstorms have strong vertical motions and are hazardous to aircraft flying.

Rainfall   Rainfall is the ultimate product of most of the weather systems. When the air in the atmosphere gets fully saturated and starts loosing its moisture holding capacity due to various reasons, water droplets fall towards the ground in the form of rain.

SPATIAL SCALES AND TEMPORAL RANGES OF WEATHER SYSTEMS

Weather systems form in different spatial scales. These scales are:

- Micro (less than 1 km)
- Meso (1–100 km)
- Synoptic (100–100 km)
- Planetary (100–10,000 km)
- Climate (> 10,000 km)

The life cycle of the weather systems depends mainly on their spatial scales. Larger the spatial scale or extent of the systems, longer is their life. Similarly larger the scale, better is their forecasting (and also the temporal range of forecasting).

SIMPLICITY AND COMPLEXITY OF INDIAN REGION

The Indian region is considered as unique and perhaps one of the most complex regions in the world. It has two monsoon seasons-SW and NE monsoons; two cyclone seasons-Premonsoon and Post monsoon. The Indian sub-continent is covered by sea from three sides-south (Indian Ocean), east (Bay of Bengal) and west (Arabian Sea) and by Himalayan ranges on its northern side. Both Sea and Himalayan areas have very little meteorological observations which makes the diagnosis of the weather systems difficult. Almost whole of the country comes under tropical belt where sudden development of localized weather systems is very common. This poses further complexity in the forecasting of systems and associated weather. Some of the coastal regions of the country are very prone to storm surges due to tropical cyclones. Nevertheless, there are several simplicities also in the Indian region. For example, tropical cyclones are less intense and have more straight direction of movement as compared to other regions. Monsoon over the country is a well behaved event as in nearly 87% of the cases, the monsoon is expected to be normal or excess. Hence, in only 13% of the cases, the monsoon is likely to fail (below normal rainfall).

WEATHER SYSTEMS IN DIFFERENT SEASONS

Winter

Although the country receives most of its annual precipitation during monsoon period, the precipitation during winter over North-west India plays very important role for building and replenishment of water resources in the western Himalayas. The weather systems responsible for ushering in winter rainfall over these areas are popularly known as Western Disturbances (WD). The WDs as their name suggest approach Indian sub-continent from west in the form of a trough in the upper and middle tropospheric westerlies. These moving troughs give rise to formation of closed cyclonic circulations in the lower tropospheric level and often at the sea level chart over Iran, western Pakistan and North India. It is generally believed that the westerly troughs and associated lower level cyclonic systems originate in the Mediterranean or the West Atlantic region, with secondaries developing over the Persian gulf either directly or as a result of the arrival of low pressure systems from SW Arabia. It is well known that the western disturbances occasionally deepen when they come over the Indo-Pak area, particularly over Rajasthan and Punjab. One of the reasons assigned to this intensification is the cooperative feed of relatively moist air from the Arabian Sea or from the Bay of Bengal and the Central parts of India. However, there is another school of thought that the dynamic effects and not the advection of air masses of different temperature and density are responsible for fall in pressure at any locality. Severe winter storm is considered as one of the major natural disasters in some of the countries of higher latitudes. The biting cold winds, snowfall and blowing snow associated with such systems can cause havoc over large areas. The extra-tropical systems travel in the form of waves in upper tropospheric westerlies. The magnitude of these waves is of the order of 20–30 deg. Lat.

Monsoon

The period during June to September is considered as Monsoon season in India. Monsoon is the most spectacular event over the Indian sub-continent as it gives widespread rains over the entire country. For a country like India which is mostly agrarian having large area under rainfed crop, monsoon rains play crucial role for its economy. The most interesting fact about the monsoon is that it comes without fail every year and strikes the country on nearly same time (1st June). The origin of monsoonal circulation is in the southern hemisphere over the South Indian Ocean, Winds from a latitude of 30 deg. S crosses the equator, moves along eastern coast of Africa, turns towards Indian peninsula and spreads over the entire sub-continent as it takes another turn from Northeastern states of India. The important weather systems which originate within the monsoonal circulation include: Monsoon Depressional/Lows over the head Bay of Bengal, Onset Vortex over Arabian Sea, Offshore vortices off west coast of India, Mid-tropospheric Cyclone over South Gujarat and adjoining North Arabian Sea, etc. The normal quantity of monsoon rainfall over the country is 88 cm.

The India Meteorological Department issues long range forecast for South-west monsoon season rainfall. The highlights of this year's forecast are as follows:

(a) In 2001, the rainfall for the South-west monsoon season (June to September) for the country as a whole is likely to be normal, thus making the year 2001 the 13th normal monsoon year in succession. The normal is defined as rainfall within ± 10% of its long period average.

(b) Quantitatively, the rainfall over the country as a whole for the 2001 South-west monsoon season (June to September) is likely to be 98% of its long period average with an estimated model error of ± 4%.

(c) Over the three broad homogeneous regions of India, the rainfall for the 2001 South-west monsoon season is likely to be 100% of its long period average (LPA) over North-west India, 96% of the LPA over the Peninsula and 100% of the LPA over North-east India with an estimated model error of ± 8%.

The National Centre for Medium Range Weather Forecasting (NCMRWF) issues medium range weather forecast (3-10 days in advance) twice a week to the farmers of the country through its 81 Agrometeorological Advisory Service (AAS) Units located in different parts of the country. It also issues weekly forecast to Ministry of Agriculture, Govt. of India through Crop Weather Watch Group on every Monday. The forecast include location specific quantitative forecast for 6 meteorological parameters, viz., Clouds, Rainfall, Wind Speed, Wind Direction, Maximum temperature and Minimum temperature. While the average skill of the forecast during winter season is as high as 88%, during monsoon the skill is about 67%.

Pre-Monsoon and Post-monsoon

The most important meteorological event during Pre and Post monsoon periods over the country is the Tropical Cyclones. Tropical cyclones are one of the nature's most violent manifestations and potentially the deadliest of all meteorological phenomena. It is unique combination of violent winds, heavy rainfall, mountainous waves and abrupt sea. The casualty figures associated with major cyclones in the Indian sub-continent in the recent past: 2,00,000 and 1,31,000 in Bangladesh in 1971 and 1991, 10,000 and 1000 in 1977 and 1990 in Andhra Pradesh (India), give an idea about its enormous destructive capability. The word 'Cyclone' was coined in 1848 by Henry Piddington, President of the Marine Counts, Calcutta (India), the word being derived from the Greek word for a snake as the air flow in these storms resembles them.

The Indian sub-continent is the worst affected part in the world so far as associated death tolls are concerned. Though the cyclones of this region are considered to be much weaker in intensity and smaller in size as compared to other regions, yet the number of deaths in the region is highest in the globe. Much of this is contributed by the relatively dense and poor economic condition of the coastal population, shallow bottom topography and coastal configuration and also due to reluctance of the people to vacate the area under cyclone threat. As they evolve from a loosely organised state into mature, intense storms, they pass through several characteristic stages. The four important stages of storm development were defined as, tropical disturbance, tropical depression, tropical storm and hurricane. There are some variations in the definition and names of these stages of storm's intensity in one region to other. In the Indian region, these stages are divided into six categories depending on the maximum sustained surface winds associated with the system. These are given in Table 25.1.

Table 25.1

SN	Category of System	Maximum Sustained Surface Winds
1.	Low (L)	Less than 17 kt (31 kmph)
2.	Depression (D)	Between 17 and 27 kt (between 31 and 49 kmph)
3.	Deep Depression (DD)	Between 28 and 33 kt (between 50 and 61 kmh)
4.	Cyclonic Storm (CS)	Between 34 and 47 kt (between 62 and 88 kmph)
5.	Severe Cyclonic Storm (SCS)	Between 48 and 63 kt (between 89 and 117 kmph)
6.	Very Severe Cyclonic Storm (VSCS)	Between 64 kt and 119 kt (between 118-220 kmph)
7.	Super Cyclonic Storm (SUCS)	120 kt and more (221 kmph and more)

Tropical cyclones have roughly 1000–2000 km diameter with an "eye" at the centre surrounded by an "eyewall" which is the most active and damaging part of the cyclone.

Thunderstorms, hailstorms, duststorms (Andhi), tornadoes etc. are some of the names of smaller scale weather systems which generally occur during pre-monsoon period of March-May. These systems are normally localized in nature and have spatial extent ranging from less than a km (tornado) to 100 km. These systems form either due to local heating or as a part of larger system. A number of tornadoes of less then a km size are seen to be forming within a 100 km size tropical cyclone. The eastern and north eastern parts of the country experience most devastating thunderstorms/hailstorms activity during March-May.

FORECASTING TECHNIQUES

The weather forecasting is done in the following categories of temporal ranges:

- Nowcasting   (a few hours in advance)
- Short Range   (upto 3 days in advance)
- Medium Range   (3-10 days in advance)
- Long Range   (more than 10 days to season in advance)
- Climate Prediction   (one year to centuries in advance)

There are three broad categories of techniques used for weather forecasting in the world:

- Synoptic or Subjective
- Statistical
- Dynamical

Synoptic Prediction of Weather Systems This is the most traditional method of prediction which basically involves considerable skill of the forecaster. The basic approach for such a technique is to make detailed diagnosis of the prevailing system and its environment with the help of available meteorological observations and predict its future behaviour based on the past experience of the forecaster keeping in mind normal pattern of rainfall and other parameters associated with such a system. As the method is highly subjective, the skill of the forecast varies considerably from one forecaster to an other. However, as it is the simplest method of prediction which does not involve any sophisticated device like computers, etc; it has been so far used widely all over the world.

Statistical Methods The basic approach of the statistical techniques is to use historical data to formulate some sort of prediction algorithm by which the behaviour of the system over some future time interval is found to be statistically related to some current parameters, environmental or otherwise. The long range prediction of monsoon rainfall is done using a statistical model. The parameters which are most significantly related to monsoon rainfall (based on past data) are utilized in this model to predict the performance of monsoon over the country. While statistical techniques are less expensive and easy to use as they consumes less computer resources as compared to sophisticated dynamical models, their greatest weakness is that unusual behaviour of events are less likely to be predicted by such methods.

Dynamical Methods This is the most advanced method of prediction as these are basic dynamical and physical laws of the atmospheric motion. This method is highly computer intensive. Some of the most powerful computing systems such as Super Computers are used for prediction of weather by these methods. The prediction by dynamical method depicts movement and intensification or weakening of the weather systems in the simulated atmosphere. The biggest obstacle in using such a method is the non-availability of observed meteorological data over the data sparse regions e.g., ocean and mountains. Moreover these methods require unlimited computing resources and highly fine mesh atmospheric models for adequate simulation of weather systems. Another limitation is that the dynamical methods are not very successful for prediction beyond a week period. With the recent advances in computing technology and availability of fine mesh models, several centres in the world have been able to predict the systems with good accuracy. In India, the National Centre for Medium Range Weather Forecasting (NCMRWF), New Delhi is making concerted efforts to provide accurate prediction of weather events over the country using dynamical techniques. The Centre was first in the country to acquire a Super Computer Cray XMP/216 in 1988.

26

Small Area Statistics

INTRODUCTION

Consequent upon the 73rd and 74th Amendment of the Constitution, an Expert Committee on Small Area Statistics was set up by the Department of Statistics to examine additional data requirements for decentralised planning, the capability of the present statistical system to meet these requirements and to recommend modifications if necessary. Besides this, implementation of the National Agricultural Insurance Scheme would also call for such data requirement. Both these aspects have been examined here.

The term "Small Area" is technically interpreted as a small segment of a population determined in terms of any criterion, not necessarily geographical. Thus a village or a municipal ward are examples of small geographical areas, whereas "females belonging to poor scheduled caste households in a district is an example of a "Small Area", based on socio-economic considerations. A broader term than "Small Area" is "Small Domain" which is also frequently used. The word "small" is used in a relative sense. Generally speaking, a segment of population is considered to be "small" if reliable estimate of parameter of the segment cannot be obtained through standard sample survey techniques. Techniques for obtaining small area statistics from large scale sample surveys combined with supplementary information from other sources have been developed in recent years using various assumptions and models.

There are three broad methods of compilation of data: (1) second hand from administrative records or other studies, (2) and (3) first hand by direct collection through complete enumeration (census) or sample surveys. Statistical data are subject to two kinds of errors—sampling and non-sampling, of which the second is more serious. The universal experience is that the total error (sampling plus non-sampling) in an efficiently conducted sample survey is much smaller than the total error in complete enumeration (which in this case refers to non-sampling error only). For small area statistics, one would however have to depend, by and large, on complete enumeration as professional expertise required to conduct a single survey efficiently is not likely to be available in villages or local centres of administration. Usually, large scale sample surveys conducted on an all-India or even at the level of a State by themselves would not be able to produce reliable small area statistics. But in recent years, new statistical methodologies have been developed and tried successfully in advanced countries like Canada and the USA to combine sample survey data with data obtained from other sources to obtain reliable estimates for small areas.

Information remotely sensed from satellites have been cost effectively utilised to obtain information about agriculture, human habitation, natural calamities etc. for small areas. The data implications of the 73rd and the 74th Amendments were examined by the committee with the help of the National Institute of Rural Development (NIRD) document on the suggested detailed functions of various tiers (District or Zone/Block or Panchayat Samiti/Gram Panchayat) for the list of 29 items included in the Eleventh Schedule. This was done by the Sub-Group on Panchayati Raj.

An in-depth examination of the capabilities of the existing system was rendered difficult in the absence of information on the varying types of statistical set up at the District/Block/Villages in different States and their functions. The discussions and recommendations of the Committee were based on the broad pattern which possibly obtains in most States and the knowledge of the specific pattern in some States represented in the Committee.

There is a scope and need for greater coordination between line Departments and statistics Departments in the matter of data collection/ compilation in order to save the expenditure and effort. Creation of additional posts at the ground level may not be a feasible proposition on account of the vast numbers of units involved (2 lakh Gram Panchayats, 5000 Panchayats, 5000 Panchayat Samities, 500 Zilla Parishads). Instead, it may be more useful to provide tools (e.g. computers) to reduce drudgery and improve efficiency of the statistical functions.

The specific variables on which Small Area Statistics are to be generated are fairly extensive in coverage. But the requirement in specific geographical areas may be different and, therefore, some minor additions or omissions may have to be made to the suggested list (Table 26.1).

SUB-GROUP ON METHODOLOGY OF SMALL AREA STATISTICS

This sub-group was constituted to explore various methodologies for generating small area statistics on the basis of central sector NSS sample survey data and suggest the appropriate methodologies for different types of small area statistics. The sub-group attempted to define 'small area' as a "domain which is too small for application of the conventional estimation procedures but much larger than that relating to village-level statistics." There are clearly two ways of generating estimates at any specified local area level. Either the information is collected through primary data collection or collated from various sources where data have

Table 26.1 List of Data Requirement

---

1. Demography (annual)
   — Distribution of population by age, sex and social group
   — Distribution of population by employment status
2. Land (decennial)
   — Area by land-utilisation
   — Area irrigated by source
   — Size-distribution of operational holdings
3. Livestock (decennial)
   — Count of domestic animals
4. Distribution of villages by distance from nearest available facility
   — primary school
   — secondary school
   — primary health centre
   — community health centre
   — hospital
   — registered medical practitioner
   — sources of safe drinking water
   — railway station
   — bus route
   — ferry ghat
   — all weather road
   — bank
   — post office
   — cooperative society
5. Literacy rate by age, sex and social group
6. Employment and unemployment by social-group and sex
7. Consumer expenditure
   — Distribution of persons by monthly per capita consumption expenditure
   — Average per capita expenditure by social group

In addition, data from other central surveys like, Sample Survey on Health and Sanitation (ICMR) and All India Educational Census (NCERT) could also be used.

already been collected Due to wide spectrum of data needs these types of data should obviously be limited to some basic indicators which are essential for local area level planning. The other approach may be to obtain small level estimates through the results of large scale sample surveys by using "small area estimation techniques" (TSAS). In recent years, several TSAS have been developed based on assumptions and models and have been successfully used in several areas. Sample surveys are usually planned for obtaining estimates at somewhat higher level like States, Districts, etc. The parameters to be estimated in such surveys are those on which data collection is somewhat intricate involving qualitative aspects of data collection and cost aspects which may be effectively tackled through cost effective sampling technique. Some examples of such large scale surveys are several household surveys of

NSSO, crop estimation surveys of Ministry of Agriculture, etc. The estimates of these surveys can be scaled down to small area levels utilising several small area statistics techniques. However, such techniques require additional information from different sources such as censuses, registers, etc. The information to be generated at village Panchayat and municipality levels will help in utilisation of 'SAS' techniques for generation of various small area level estimate from vast amount of information generated through various countrywide survey conducted by NSSO and other Central and State level agencies.

It is also felt that in small domain estimation "traditional" or "direct" methods that utilize sample observations specific to respective domains alone are not often very fruitful because of smallness of the domain-specific sample-sizes. So, indirect estimators that involve sample values within respective domains as well as some or all of the those outside the domains plus external data may often be gainfully employed. There is a body of techniques available for obtaining reliable estimates at lower levels using the large scale survey data together with auxiliary information from other sources. The rationale behind the later is that some or all domains may have similar features which may encourage "borrowing strength" across "similar domains" by way of improving upon the direct estimators. Methods such as Synthetic methods, Generalized Regression methods, and their modifications, Empirical and Hierarchical Bayes methods, etc. make use of postulated models which reflect "similarity of domains". Since the efficacy of any such technique is strongly dependent on the tenability of the assumptions about the domain features on which it is based, it is imperative to empirically examine its applicability in a given context based on live data gathered from a large survey research organisation like NSSO. The Sub-group, however, felt that, for the present, generation of district-level statistics was the only feasible alternative.

The Sub-group identified the subjects from the list suggested by the Sub-group on Panchayati Raj on which information may be feasible to obtain at the district level from NSSO, using the recently developed techniques of estimation of small area statistics and suggested that a pilot project for estimation of district level totals from NSS data be taken up immediately jointly by professional statisticians from the SDRD of NSSO and teachers and researchers from the Applied Statistics Unit of ISI. Also, some pilot studies using remotely sensed data might be taken up by IASRI.

The Sub-group felt that the basic data needed for decentralised planning would by and large have to be collected by local agencies under the supervision of the respective State Directorates of Economics and Statistics. The Central Statistical Organisation should ensure comparability of such data. A small Area Estimation Division in CSO and a Methodological Cell for small area estimation in the SDRD should be set up. There should be provision for the participation of outside experts in these exercises.

PANCHAYATI RAJ SYSTEM

Basic data collected by Gramsevak, Patwari (village revenue officer), Health official, teacher, etc. at the village and household levels as part of their duties should be consolidated in the prescribed format by one of these officials who should be specially designated and compensated for additional work. This official should send the data to the block office. The database should be maintained separately for each village/gram panchayat. For that purpose the statistical set up at the block level would have to be strengthened—not necessarily by creating additional positions but to the extent feasible, through reallocation of responsibilities of line officials. The data so collected should be maintained separately for each village as defined under the panchayati raj system under two heads: (i) village statistics, and (ii) register of households for each village.

The work would involve a one-time massive effort to create the base line village and house-hold database and thereafter periodic updation of the database on an annual basis. For the one-time effort additional resources would have been provided in the Ninth Five Year Plan. For the continuing efforts of updation of database, an appropriate system would have to be carefully designed and implemented with close cooperation of the State Directorates of Economics and Statistics. The above database should be maintained at the block level. But a copy of information relating to constituent villages should be available at the respective gram panchayat office. At the gram panchayat level, the gramsevak or the patwari should be made responsible for compiling information (both village statistics and register of households) collected by all agencies and forwarding this to the block office. No official solely for this purpose needs to be posted. Additional remuneration should be paid to the official for the above work.

At the block level there is need for an official fully devoted to statistical work. He should be provided with support in the form of computer hardware and software necessary for data entry and retrieval. He should be given adequate training for this purpose. The Ministry of Rural Development should strengthen the statistical set up at the block and the gram panchayat level. The support for strengthening may be in the form of finances for computing facilities, training, and payment of remunerations. The National Informatics Centre (NIC) maintains a network of computers with nodes at Headquarters of all districts. The role of the NIC is to provide computerised facilities for storage and communication of statistics rather than collection, analysis and interpretation of statistics. The NIC had already revised a district database in collaboration with district authorities and claims to have successfully implemented it in a number of districts. The Committee therefore recommended that to the extent feasible the national statistical system for Small Area Statistics should make use of the NIC network of computers for transmission of statistics from district headquarters to the state and national headquarters, but the main responsibility for collection, editing, storage, analysis, interpretation and dissemination of information should be borne by the national statistical system as suggested in this report.

METHODOLOGICAL ISSUES

Small Area in the Context of the Sub-group

While initiating the technical discussion of the meeting, the Chairman briefly stated the terms of reference of the sub-group. He informed the members that the data requirements for decentralised planning were being examined by another sub-group formed for this purpose. The main task of the present sub-comittee was to explore various methodologies for generating Small Area Statistics on the basis of National Sample Survey data. In the context of the terms of reference of the Sub-group, he explained, *small area* would mean a domain that is too small for application of the conventional estimation procedures but much larger than that relating to village-level statistics. It was felt that, for the present, generation of district-level statistics was the only feasible alternative.

District-Level Estimation from NSS Data

The need for basic data at lower levels, viz. block/municipality/panchayat level, are increasing for Decentralised Planning. It is presumed that the required data could be collected through local-level surveys or complied from administrative records. The likely problem with these data is that of comparability of the estimates owing to adoption of varying concepts, definitions and coverage by the local bodies.

At present, it is difficult for any central agency to ensure adoption of standardised concepts and methodologies used by the local bodies, as there is little or no means to control them. The only way to judge the quality of data generated by the local bodies then is to institute a system of cross-examination by a central authority. For assessment of quality of the estimates, the central authority would require an independent set of data at lower levels than what is available at present.

The National Sample Survey Organisation (NSSO) may play an important role for this purpose. The NSSO generates estimates on a number of socio-economic parameters at regular intervals, although the estimates are generally presented for larger domains, like State or all-India. There is, however, a body of techniques available for obtaining reliable estimates at lower levels (small area estimation) using the large scale survey data together with auxiliary information from other sources. These techniques of small area estimation have been successfully used the Statistics Canada for Canadian Labour Force Survey. Also composite estimates, using essentially the same techniques, have been made over many years by the U.S. Bureau of the Census, notably in connection with monthly Current Population Surveys and monthly surveys of retail sales.

With these techniques, estimation from NSS data may be extended to district, sub-regional or regional level. For a common characteristic, the district level estimates obtained by aggregating the local level estimates that can be compared with the corresponding district level estimates from the NSS data. This may not only provide a basis for assessing the reliability of the local-level estimates but also gives NSSO a chance to introspect for any unreasonable estimate.

Statistical Techniques for Small Area Estimation

In formulating development plans for local areas under the three-tier panchayati raj, data needed may be compiled from administrative records or through local surveys. A new methodology has recently been developed for obtaining estimates for small areas from data based on nationwide large scale sample surveys. When a survey is undertaken to cover a large population the available survey data are often sought to be utilized (along with other auxiliary information) to estimate characteristics of its various non-overlapping domains.

In small domain estimation "traditional" or "direct" methods that utilize sample observations specific to respective domains alone are often very fruitful because of smallness of the domain-specific sample-sizes. So, indirect estimators that involve sample values within respective domains as well as some or all of those outside the domains plus external data may have similar features which may encourage "borrowing strength" across "similar domains" by way of improving upon the direct estimators. Literature around this is growing quite fast and the newly emerging methods such as Synthetic methods, and their modifications, Empirical and Hierarchical Bayes methods, etc. make use of postulated models which reflect "similarity of domains". Since the efficacy of any such technique is strongly dependent on the tenability of the assumptions about the domain features on which it is based, it is imperative to empirically examine its applicability in a given context based on live data gathered from a large survey research organisation like NSSO.

Identification of District-Level Information Derivable from NSS

The Convenor placed before the Sub-group the list indicating the subject coverage of the required village-level data prepared by the Sub-group on Panchayati Raj. The Sub-group examined the list with a view to identifying the subjects on which information may be feasible to obtain at the district level from NSSO, using the recently developed techniques of estimation of small area statistics. The list is given below:

Pilot Study: A Project Proposal

The sub-group recommends that a pilot project for estimation of district level totals from NSS data be taken up immediately jointly by professional statisticians from the SDRD of NSSO and teacher and researchers from the Applied Statistics Unit of ISI. The project would be carried out by voluntary efforts of the participants and would not require additional funding. NSSO would of course have to provide the basic survey data to the project team. It is presumed that computer facilities would also be provided free of cost by NSSO or ISI. The sub-group suggests that in the first phase of the project, methodology for estimation of some of the parameters at the district level should be developed based on data from Schedule 3.0 of the 47th round of NSSO, for each district of West Bengal.

The accuracy of the district level estimates so obtained could, at a later stage, be assessed through field/administrative records/Census '91 data. The 47th round of NSSO was carried out during July–December 1991. The estimates obtained by using the small area estimation techniques can thus be compared with the available Census data. Moreover, a follow-up survey of the two selected districts may also be taken up for evaluation of the small area estimates. An important technique for study of habitation patterns, land utilisation, cropping patterns, etc. is to make use of remotely sensed data. At IASRI, some pilot studies have been carried out in this direction. Prof. Srivastava showed an interest in carrying out pilot studies for which a proposal needs to be developed.

Administrative Arrangements for Continuing Studies within the Department of Statistics

The sub-group felt that the basic data needed for decentralised planning would by any large have to be collected by local agencies under the supervision of the respective State Statistical Bureaus. However, to make the collected data comparable, uniform concepts and definitions, standards of reliability and procedure for collection and presentation of data would have to be introduced and implemented. The CSO would have to bear this responsibility. For this purpose, a division for small area statistics may have to be created within the CSO. To assess the reliability of small area statistics collected locally, district level estimates from NSS data should be prepared using modern techniques of small area estimates from large scale sample surveys. The methodology—through theoretically sound and tested in some developed countries—has not yet been extensively used in India. There is need for adopting these methodologies to suit Indian conditions and only the NSSO, with collaboration from ISI and other statistical research organisations, is capable of undertaking the responsibility. The sub-group recommends that a Methodological Cell for small area estimation should be set up within the SDRD of the NSSO in which there should be provision for participation of outside experts.

NEEDS OF NATIONAL AGRICULTURAL INSURANCE SCHEME[1]

Background

Crop insurance offers insurance against fluctuations in the output of a crop from one year to another or from one crop season to another. The insurance provides a safeguard against crop failures as a result of natural

---

[1]A.K. Srivastava and Anil Rai, Paper read at NSS Golden Jubilee Celebrations, Bangalore, March 2001.

calamities like drought, floods etc. Crop yield estimation attains a central role in any crop insurance plan since crop fluctuations/failures are measured as a deviation of crop output from the normal yield. Current crop yield estimates as well as the crop yield rates for previous years are needed to work out the deviations in crop output.

In the available literature on crop insurance, the indemnity assessment at individual level and for a unit area level has been debated at a considerable length. Without going into details of advantages and limitations of the two approaches, it may be mentioned that a scheme based on the individual approach may be the most appropriate and in a sense ideal but it is impracticable due to the fact that the assessment of crop yield at the individual level poses practical difficulties. The area unit in a crop insurance scheme could be Community Development (CD) Block/tehsils/taluks etc. Ideally, the area unit should be homogeneous from the stand point of a crop insurance scheme based on area approach. An area is homogeneous if the annual crop cut estimates for a majority of the farmers in the area move together above or below their own normals. Thus homogeneity of an area is defined in relation to the crop risk. "For a crop insurance scheme based on the homogeneous area approach all that is needed is a delineation of agroclimatic regions, small enough to be homogeneous in the sense that the annual crop experience of a majority of the farmers in the area accords and coincides with average experience of the area and large enough to have an adequate data base of annual crop cutting experiments to enable the determination of the normal yield and estimating annual average yields with reasonably small statistical error". In the present context. Gram Panchayat (GP) has been identified as an area unit to be considered in NAIS, and therefore, reliable estimates of crop yields at GP level become essential.

In the present agricultural statistics scenario, crop yield/production estimation, for most of the principal crops, is available at district/block level. The method of crop estimation has been through crop cutting approach. The estimation at small area levels such as village panchayat has not been attempted so far. At present, nearly 5 lakh crop cutting experiments are being conducted in the country through General Crop Estimation Surveys (GCES) scheme. In recent years, there have been questions and criticism regarding the quality of data obtained in the crop estimation surveys. Qualitative checks on crop estimation surveys are provided by specialised supervision through a scheme 'Improvement of Crop Statistics (ICS)' which is conducted by National Sample Survey Organisation (NSSO). There has been a general feeling that increasing the crop cutting experiments is likely to be too heavy a burden on the present data collection infrastructure in crop estimation surveys, particularly in view of the findings of ICS scheme, which indicates large amount of Non-Sampling Errors.

Number of Crop Cutting Experiments Required for Crop Yield Estimation at Gram Panchayat Level

In the past, for block level estimation, 16 crop-cutting experiments per crop had been suggested. This had been on statistical considerations in view of the inherent variability in crop yield estimates available at block level. Recently an analysis of data for crop yields for paddy crop as available from two districts of Orissa revealed that coefficient of variation (cv) of crop yield estimates at Gram Panchayat levels, was at least 20 percent. For this amount of variability and for 95 percent precision level of the estimates, the required sample size at Gram Panchayat level should be at least 8 to 10 crop cutting experiments. Thus, if reliable Gram Panchayat level estimates are needed at least 8 to 10 crop-cutting experiments should be conducted in each Gram Panchayat for each crop. It is likely that this requirement will increase the total sample sizes of crop cutting experiments manifold (estimated to be around 74 lakh), which would increase the Non-Sampling Error considerably and may have its obvious impact on the quality of data in GCES.

An Alternative Suggestion for Crop Yield Estimation: Small Area Estimation Approach

In recent years, there have been a lot of developments in the field of small area statistics. In this approach the estimates obtained through sample surveys for a larger area level are scaled down to smaller area levels, through the use of additional ancillary information available from various sources. The basic rationale in this approach is that certain assumptions/models are conceptualised which are assumed to hold good at small as well as large area levels. Such models/relationships are utilised for scaling down the estimates to lower levels. In this particular situation, some ancillary information at Gram Panchayat level may be generated, which is not necessarily based on crop cutting approach and this information may be utilised to scale down the crop yield estimates obtained through GCES at district/block level for developing Gram Panchayat level estimates. To be more specific, information about the crop area and crop yield obtained from other sources such as farmers' appraisal using well tested structured questionnaires obtained through random sampling approach has been found to perform satisfactorily in many practical situations. Studies conducted in several African countries (Verma, Merchant and Scott; Longacre Report, 1988) suggest that such estimates as obtained through farmers' appraisal are in close agreement with the actual production figures as obtained by the whole field harvest. Studies conducted at IASRI also revealed a fairly high degree of correlation between the farmers' estimate and the estimates obtained through the crop cut approach. However, in crop insurance scenario, it is apprehended that farmers' appraisal is likely to be affected qualitatively in view of interest of the stakeholders at Gram Panchayat level. On the other hand this information, if used judiciously, only to workout (say) proportions for scaling down the estimates of crop yields of GCES series is likely to minimize the effect of stakeholders interest. It is realised that the farmers' estimates are likely to be influenced by the interested parties but it is expected that the proportions are free from such effects provided farmer's behaviour in underestimation/overestimation is consistent over the entire area. This approach is, in fact, a standard small area estimation technique known as Synthetic method of estimation. The method has got wide application in different areas particularly in demographic studies because of the availability of stable ratios like birth rates, death rates etc. from various population censuses. Its application in the field of agriculture has, however, been relatively limited. The technique has not been experimented on a large scale in agriculture and hence it is suggested that the above approach may be tried on a pilot basis in few selected areas before it may be adopted at the national level. It may also be mentioned that to start with, even though we may have limited ancillary information to be used but in due course of time as more and more information is generated regarding area, production and productivity of crops as well as regarding irrigation, variety etc. at Gram Panchayat level, the method has enough flexibility to utilise these information for more reliable estimation. Consequently, the Gram Panchayat level estimates will be more precise in due course of time. In future, even if some information is available from remotely sensed data at village level, it may also be utilised in the small area estimation approach.

In order to conduct farmer appraisal survey at Gram Panchayat for yield estimation, the frame for selection of fields as available from village records (Khasra register) may be used. In case records for current year are not available, the records for previous years may be used and updating may be done for a larger sample which may then serve as a frame for selection of fields for farmers' appraisal. The information to be collected in the inquiry at the village level will be area under various crops, area irrigated etc. while those from the selected cultivators will include farmers' estimate on yield besides the area, irrigation status, various inputs, soil type etc. at the field level.

The cost incurred on data collection in this approach will be substantially less than the existing crop cutting based approach.

Salient Features

The proposed plan has the following important features:

- The method of data collection is based on farmers' appraisal as well as other ancillary information available at GP level.
- The yield estimates developed through this approach are to be used only for generating correction factors for scaling down the estimates of GCES based on crop cutting approach and not to be used as yield estimates as such.
- The approach if adopted is not likely to affect the existing system of GCES adversely.
- Data collection is likely to be much cheaper, as such, the reduction in the number of selected cultivators may not be required.

- Data may be collected through an alternative agency utilising village officials/resources e.g. unemployed youth etc. who can be paid on per questionnaire basis.

Procedure for Estimating Average Yield at Gram Panchayat Level

The proposed approach for estimation of data collection is primarily based on the availability of information regarding production at higher level i.e. block, tehsil or district through usual GCES. This may be indicated here that the assumption regarding the availability of information regarding area under a particular crop at all levels has been made while developing this proposal. The procedure can be implemented without affecting the quality of usual GCES by following the steps given below:

Step 1 Formation of frame of survey numbers separately for each notified crop under crop insurance scheme in a given season in a gram panchayat through area enumeration records such as Girdawari of the previous year. The process of formulation of frame may be started approximately three weeks before the current season harvesting period.

Step 2 Make the separate list of the survey numbers for each crop covered under crop insurance scheme.

Step 3 Select 10 survey numbers by circular systematic sampling scheme and identify owner/owners. Verify whether in the selected survey numbers the crop grown is same as in the previous year. If so, retain that survey number in the sample, otherwise, replace it by next survey number from the list and verify again. Repeat the same procedure till 10 survey numbers for each crop are selected in the sample.

Step 4 Collect detailed information from the selected farmers of the corresponding survey number of each category before 2 weeks of expected harvesting time of each crop grown by the farmer.

Step 5 Collect the farmers estimate from all the farmers covered under step-4 for each crop within 3 days after harvest of crop.

Step 6 Calculate the average yield of each crop of Gram Panchayat (GP) as equation (1) of estimation procedure.

Step 7 Calculate total production of each crop of GP through farmer appraisal with the help of equation-2 of estimation procedure.

Step 8 Calculate estimated production for each crop in the Gram Panchayat as given in equation-3 of estimation procedure.

Step 9 Calculate estimated adjusted production for each crop in the Gram Panchayat given in equation-4 of estimation procedure.

Step 10 Calculate adjusted estimated average yield for each crop in the Gram Panchayat given in equation-5.

The above estimation procedure is explained through an example, in which part of the data from Rohtak district of Haryana has been taken for illustrative purpose.

Estimation of Adjusted Crop Yield at Gram Panchayat Level

Let

V = No. of Gram Panchayats (V.P.) in a block

N_{ij} = No. of farmers growing jth crop in ith Gram Panchayat

n_{ij} = No. of selected farmers growing jth crop in ith Gram Panchayat

y_{ijk} = Farmer's appraisal of production for kth selected farmers growing jth crop in ith Gram Panchayat.

a_{ijk} = Area of kth selected farmer for jth crop in the ith GP.

A_{ijk} = Area of kth farmer belonging to jth crop in ith GP.

A_{ij} = Total area of ith V.P. under jth crop.

$Y_{j(G)}$ = Total estimated production of jth crop through GCES.

The average yield of the GP for jth crop can be obtained by

$$Y_{ij(R)} = \frac{y_{ij}}{a_{ij}} A_{ij} \quad \ldots \tag{1}$$

where, $y_{ij} = \dfrac{1}{n_{ij}} \displaystyle\sum_{k=1}^{nij} y_{ijk}$

$$a_{ij} = \frac{1}{n_{ij}} \sum_{k=1}^{nij} a_{ijk}$$

$$A_u = \frac{1}{N_{ij}} \sum_{k=1}^{Nij} A_{ijk}$$

The total estimated production of the jth crop in the ith GP is given by

$$Y_{ij(P)} = A_{ij} y_{ij(R)} \quad \ldots \tag{2}$$

The total estimated production of the jth crop in the block through farmer's appraisal is

$$Y_{j(P)} = \sum_{i=1}^{V} A_{ij} Y_{ij(R)}$$

The estimated proportion of the jth in ith GP is

$$P_{ij(P)} = \frac{Y_{ij(P)}}{Y_{j(P)}} \quad \ldots \tag{3}$$

The estimated adjusted production of jth crop in ith GP can be given by

$$Y_{ij(AP)} = p_{ij(p)} Y_{j(G)} \quad \dots \tag{4}$$

Now the estimated average yield of jth crop in the ith GP can be obtained as

$$Y_{ij(AP)} = \frac{Y_{ij(AP)}}{A_{ij}} \quad \dots \tag{5}$$

Hence, the average adjusted crop yield for a GP can be obtained by equation (5)

Example Consider a block consisting of 19 Gram Panchayats. Tables 26.1 and 26.2 present the calculation of estimated average yield at Gram Panchayat level with the help of farmer's appraisal using crop estimates available at block level through GCES. The example is based on data collected in a study conducted in Rohatak district of Haryana for wheat crop, year 1997-98. The example is only illustrative in nature.

Table 26.1

Column No.	Description
1.	Identification particulars of Gram Panchayat
2.	Farmer's appraisal estimates in Qt./ha.
3.	Area under wheat crop(ha.) in panchayat
4.	Estimated production (Qts.) based on farmer's estimates.
5.	Production proportions based on farmer's estimate
6.	Estimated production (Qts.) of Gram Panchayat using GCES estimates

AVAILABLE SMALL AREA ESTIMATION PROCEDURES

A survey population U is supported to be divisible into a large number D of non-overlapping parts called "domains" of various sizes. Let the size of the dth domain U_4 be N_4 and the population size be N. Let x, y, z, etc. be variables with values x_i, y_j, z_j, etc. for the dth individuals of U and X_d, Y_d etc. over the enite population. Suppose a sample s of size n is suitably drawn from the population using available knowledge of relevant data procured from various sources like past censuses, official publications and registration-cum-administrative documents. Usually N and n are both large. But the number N_d of sampled individuals, S_4 may vary appreciably across the domains and be quite small for many of the domains. The domains with low values of n_4 are 'small domains'; if the domains relate to geographical divisions of the population they are the 'small areas'. Suppose

Table 26.2 Estimated Average yield (Qt./ha.) of Gram Panchayat using GCES

1	2	3	4	5	6	7
1	13.6	1800	24480	0.0166	27208.74	15.12
2	29.8	2644	78791.2	0.0534	87573.9	33.12
3	28.4	2200	62480	0.0423	69444.52	31.57
4	42.3	1240	52452	0.0355	58298.72	47.02
5	40.2	3560	143112	0.097	159064.42	44.68
6	28.12	3620	101794.4	0.068	113141.22	31.25
7	16.5	840	13860	0.0094	15404.95	18.34
8	29.69	2200	65318	0.0443	72598.87	33
9	30.2	2684	81056.8	0.0549	90092.04	33.57
10	40.2	3528	141825.6	0.0961	157634.62	44.68
11	41.7	1620	67554	0.0458	75084.11	46.35
12	30.47	1884	56405.48	0.0389	63804.36	33.87
13	34.9	2688	93811.2	0.0636	104268.15	38.79
14	23.4	3924	91821.6	0.0622	102056.78	26.01
15	26.8	2348	62926.4	0.0426	69940.68	29.79
16	30.98	1756	54400.88	0.0369	60464.84	34.43
17	37.9	3076	116580.4	0.079	129575.39	42.12
18	44.6	2360	105256	0.0713	116988.68	49.57
19	21	2884	60564	0.041	67314.95	23.34
Total	590.76	46856	1475489.96	1.0000	1639959.94	656.62

Total production of the block through GCES = 1639960 Qts.

our object is to use the sample observations on y values to estimates Y and also Y_d for various value of D (= 1, ... , D).

Corresponding to any estimator formula employed for Y using y_j for i in s one may use an analogous one for Y_d using y_j with j only in s_d. Such a 'Direct' estimator t_d, say, for a 'small domain' or 'small area' total may not be good enough because the 'level of aggregation' involved in t_d may be too inadequate.

A reasonable way to improve upon t_d is to 'borrow strength' and employ an 'Indirect estimator' for it using y_i values not only for j in s_d but also for j outside s_d but within s. Let us illustrate, denoting by y, x the sample means of y, x over units in s and by y_d, x_d those over units in s_d.

If N_y be used to estimate Y a 'direct' one for Y_d may be $N_d y_d$ and an 'indirect' one may be N_{dy}. If the ratio estimator $X.y/x$ is suitable for Y, a 'direct' one for Y_d may be $X_d, y/x$. Similarly one may employ an 'indirect' regression estimator as well. While borrowing strength from outside the domains while estimating the total or the mean of a particular domain one may not use y values for the entire sample as in N_{dy} and $X_d y/x$ above but may better use them only for sampled units in those domains which seen to have at least certain features common with the domains under consideration.

To rationalize 'borrowing' from outside a domain one needs to postulate statistical models which seem plausible and may stand 'diagnostic' tests for plausibility. But 'small area' estimation necessarily involves borrowing from outside the domain of interest.

In employing a regression estimator for a small domain total or mean a usual practice is to estimate the regression co-efficients using sample values of the variable of interests and of the regressor (s) for individuals in the domains of interest and in all 'similar' domains. Sometimes it is possible to rationalize the use of an estimator for a small domain total (or mean) which is a 'weighted' sum of a 'direct' estimator and an 'indirect' one. Sometimes the 'weighting' also leads to a 'convex' combination of the two.

We may also emphasize that our concern is 'simultaneous' estimation of totals (or means) of a large number of domains. From James and Stein's (1961) works we know that the 'sample mean vector' for the 'population mean vector' for a p (≥ 3) dimensional normal population is 'inadmissible' and it can be improved upon by a simple alternative. In the present context if $(e_1, \ldots e_d \ldots e_D)$ is an initial vector of estimators for $(Y_1 \ldots, T_d, \ldots Y_D)$, then 'James Stein's improved estimator is $(e_1^x, e_d^x \ldots e_D^x)$ where $e_d^x = (1 - D - 2/e^d_2)$ x e_d, $d = 1, \ldots D$, under appropriate normality assumptions. This e_d can be interpreted as a 'empirical Bayes' (EB, pan) estimator for $Y_d (d = 1, \ldots D)$. Starting with any estimator t_d for Y_d also it is possible to derive, under appropriate model postulations, simple EB estimators which turn out to the 'convex' weighted linear combinations of 'Direct' (t_d itself) and 'Indirect' estimators (derived from t_d) for domain totals (or means).

A Bayesian approach with normal priors enables one also to apply the well-known Kalman filtering technique to derive improved estimators for 'time-specific' domain totals (or means) respectively using domain estimators derived in the 'past'.

Currently popular 'iterated simulation' techniques called Gibbs sampling, Giddy-Gibbs sampling, metropolis-Hastings techniques etc. are being effectively used to derive Hierarchical Bayes estimators as well as domain parameters.

Some adjustment techniques are also available to constraint the 'domain' specific statistics derived in manners above so that 'when they are aggregated across domains, the aggregation matches the estimators derived directly for the domain which is the union of the component domains. This is called level consistency'.

The main concerns are the following:

1. To find appropriate regressors which may be used in the formulate for regression estimators.
2. To identify 'domains' which may be deemed alike when using 'indirect' estimators.
3. To justify models needed to employ 'model-motivated' estimators.

So intensive and continuous research by us seems essential, to be able to correctly employ in practice the emerging estimation procedures.

The formulae are not presented in this 'preface' to 'Small Area Methods', they may be separately listed.

27

Internet Based Data Exchange Systems[1]

INTRODUCTION

With the thrust on higher growth in food grain production and other agricultural commodities, increase in productivity and optimal use of resources in agriculture has received special emphasize all through the process of the development since independence. The efficient use of available resources to maximize production and productivity requires comprehensive and reliable information on various facts of the agriculture. Hence the improvement in the existing agricultural information system is essential for better planing of agriculture resources and for evolving development strategies. Informatics development for sustainable agricultural development requires coordinated inter-sectoral approach and application of appropriate Information Technology (IT). In this chapter we discuss the development of IT applications, the networking of the Directorate of Economics and Statistics and its field offices and connectivity to State Agricultural Statistical Agencies (SASAs), State Agriculture Departments, State Revenue Departments, and State Planning Departments, which are involved in agricultural statistical information collection and information exchange.

NICNET BASED AGRICULTURAL INFORMATICS AND COMMUNICATION (AGRISNET)

In view of the recommendations of ISDA-95[2] and various sub-groups for formulation of the Ninth Plan in the agriculture sector, the Department

---

[1]Presented by Brij Bhushan and others at the National Workshop on "Improvement of Agricultural Statistics" organised by the Directorate of Economics and Statistics, Ministry of Agriculture, held on June 13-14, 2001, at New Delhi.

[2]ISDA-95: National Conference on "Information for Sustainable Agricultural Development" (ISDA-95), organised by National Informatics Centre, in collaboration with the Ministry of Agriculture and the Ministry of Rural Development, 25-26 May, 1995, Vigyan Bhawan, N. Delhi.

of Agriculture and Cooperation (DAC), Ministry of Agriculture, has formulated Information Technology Plan, to establish "Agricultural Information System Network (AGRISNET)" in collaboration with NIC, during the Ninth Plan. This Plan envisages networking of the various directorates and field offices of the Department of Agriculture and Cooperation, State Agricultural Departments, District Agriculture Departments, and Block Agriculture Offices, with the state-of-the-art INTERNET technology. The Department has formulated Central Sector as well as Centrally Sponsored Scheme to implement the IT Plan.

The IT Plan recommends (i) the state-of-the-art IT infrastructure to establish AGRISNET as the INTERNET over NICNET, (ii) development of databases and information systems for decision support for evaluation, monitoring and policy formulations, (iii) human resources development, (iv) multi-media based training and demonstration of transfer of technology to strengthen Farm Research and Education using broadcast VSATs, and (v) special interest groups in respect of subjects, problems, programmes, schemes, etc., and above all, to make Indian Agriculture on-line for INTERNET and INTRANET access through AGRISNET nodes. AGRISNET Nodes are envisaged to be established at

- DAC Hqrs (Krishi Bhawan),
- DAC attached offices and its regional offices,
- DAC subordinate offices and its regional units,
- DAC Public Sector Undertakings (NSC and SFCI) and sub-units,
- DAC autonomous organizations,
- Apex cooperative organizations,
- State agriculture departments,
- NCT/UT agriculture departments,
- District agriculture offices [520 +], and
- Block agriculture offices [5000 +].

"Network-centric" applications using data warehousing techniques, expert systems and knowledge bases, GIS technology, RS technology, and Internet/Intranet web technology, will be made available in AGRISNET nodes.

INFORMATION TECHNOLOGY—AN APPRAISAL

Information Technology (IT) is a multidisciplinary field emerging from computer technology, software technology, database technology, and communication technology. Government of India considers "Information Technology (IT) as an agent of transformation of every facet of human life which will bring about a knowledge based society in the 21st Century"[3]. Database Technology has migrated from hierarchical to network in 1960s, network to relational in 1970s, and now from relational

---

[3] Report of the National Task Force on "Information Technology and Software Development", Government of India, 1998.

to object-relational with web-enabling capabilities over INTERNET/ INTRANET access.

Informatics Network plays an important role in the information flow from the implementation level to the planner at Macro (national) level, Macro-meso (region more than one state) level to Meso (state) level, and Micro (District, Block and Village) level. Information is taking advantage of (i) Multi databases (Federated and non-Federated databases), (ii) information system research and development methodology, (iii) relational-object methods, (iv) knowledge base and expert systems, (v) Geographical Information System (GIS) technology, (vi) Model bases, (vii) Distributed query capabilities over INTERNET/INTRANET.

In the National Workshop on "Improvement of Agricultural Statistics" held in June 2000 we discussed features of various kind of databases, data models and GIS systems. Multi-database system is one that allows users to access and modify data items resident in many heterogeneous environment in various nodes which are being connected by networks. Federated database system is a collection of cooperating database system that are autonomous and possibly heterogeneous. Distributed database system and query system continues to be an extensive area of research. Knowledge Base Management system is a computer system that manages the knowledge in a given domain or field of interest and exhibits reasoning power to the level of a human expert in this domain. Data warehousing systems have become a key component of information technology architecture. A data warehouse is a structured extensible environment designed for the analysis of non-volatile data, logically and physically transformed multiple source applications to align with business structure, updated and maintained for a long period, expressed in simple business terms, and summarized for quick analysis.

Internet is a computer network made up of thousands of networks worldwide. No one knows exactly how many computers are connected to the Internet and this number in the millions is increasing at a rapid rate. There are organizations which develop technical aspects of the Internet and set standards for crating applications on it, but no governing body is in control. Internet backbone, through which Internet traffic flows, is owned by private companies.

All computers on the Internet communicate with one another using the Transmission Control Protocol/Internet Protocol (TCP/IP). Computers on the Internet use client/server architecture. The remote server machine provides files and services to the user's local client machine. An Internet user has access to a wide variety of services:
- E-mail,
- file transfer,
- search and retrieve vast information resources,
- interest group membership,
- interactive collaboration,
- multimedia displays,

- real-time broadcasting,
- e-commerce,
- EDI (electronic document interchange),
- E-governance,
- news,
- chat, games, entertainment, etc.

The World Wide Web (WWW) is a system of Internet servers that supports HyperText to access several Internet protocols on a single interface Almost every protocol type available on the Internet is accessible on the Web. This includes e-mail, FTP, Telnet, and Usenet News, and HyperText Transfer Protocol, (HTTP). The WWW provides a single interface for accessing all these protocols. This creates a convenient and user-friendly environment. It is no longer necessary to be conversant in these protocols within separate, command-level environments. Because of this feature, and because of the Web's ability to work with multimedia and advanced programming languages, the WWW is the fastest-growing component of the Internet.

The operation of the Web relies primarily on HyperText as its means of information retrieval. HyperText is a document containing words that connect to other documents-may be located somewhere else on the Internet. These words are called links and are selectable by the user. A single HyperText document can contain links to many documents. In the context of the Web, words or graphics may serve as links to other documents, images, video, and sound links need not follow a logical path. WWW contains a complex virtual web of connections among a number of documents, graphics, videos, and sounds. Producing HyperText for the Web is accomplished by creating documents with a language called HyperText Markup Language (HTML).

The servers hosting the HTML documents with specific designs are the web sites and contain information of the owner's choice. The static web pages contain fixed information and are required to be updated whenever changes are desired by the owner. The dynamic web pages can handle interactive queries and have a back and database.

E-mail, allows computer users locally and worldwide to exchange messages. Each user of e-mail has a unique mailbox address to which messages are sent. Messages sent through e-mail can arrive within a few seconds. A powerful aspect of e-mail is the option to send non-ASCII files, known as binary files, which may be attached to e-mail messages. These files are referred to as Multimedia Internet Mail Extension (MIME), and was developed to help e-mail software handle a variety of file types. For example, a document created in Microsoft Word can be attached to an e-mail message and retrieved by the recipient with the appropriate e-mail program. Many e-mail programs, including Eudora, Netscape Messenger, and Microsoft Outlook Express, offer the ability to read files written in HTML, which is itself a MIME type.

Telnet is a program that allows to login to computers on the Internet and use online databases, library catalogues, chat services etc. To Telnet to a computer, one must know its address. This can consist of words (agries.delhi.nic.in) or numbers, (164.100.191.12). The most common Web-based resources available through Telnet are library catalogues. A link to a Telnet resource may look like any other link, but it will launch a Telnet session to make the connection. A Telnet program must be installed on your local computer and configured to your Web browser in order to work.

FTP stands for File Transfer Protocol. This is both a program and the method used to transfer files between computers. Anonymous FTP is an option that allows users to transfer files. FTP sites contain books, articles, software, games, images, sounds, multimedia, course work, data sets etc.

e-mail discussion groups offer to people worldwide to communicate via e-mail. Topic-oriented forums distribute discussions by e-mail. Probably the most common program is the listservs. A great variety of topics are covered by listservs, many of them academic in nature. When you subscribe to a listservs, messages from other subscribers are automatically sent to your mailbox. You subscribe to a listerv by sending an e-mail message to a computer program called a listserver. The program handles subscription information and distributes messages to and from subscribers. You must have a e-mail account to participate in a listserv discussion group.

Usenet is a global electronic bulletin boards system in which millions of computer users exchange information on a vast range of topics. The major difference between Usenet News and e-mail discussion groups is that Usenet messages are stored on central computers, and users must connect to these computers to read or download the messages posted to these groups. Usenet itself is set of machines that exchanges messages, or articles, from Usenet discussion forums, called newsgroups. Usenet administrators control their own sites, and decide which (if any) newsgroups to sponsor and which remote newsgroups to allow into the system.

Data security is an important issue while discussing the webenabled IT applications. For years, hackers have had resources available to them to help them learn how to get into your systems, destroy your work, and read your private or proprietary information. They even have places that they go to trade system accounts, your accounts with other hackers. Information need to be protected from unauthorized modification or destruction through password protection and data encryption. Computers need to be protected from virus threat also to protect the invaluable information. Frequent/on-line scanning using latest version of antivirus software, avoiding diskettes used on other, possibly infected PCs, avoiding opening of attachments of mails from unknown sources may help in protecting the data from the virus. Frequent backup, safety measures against hazards is a must.

Improvement in technology and reduction in the hardware cost in past few years has made internet access within reach of masses. The high speed PCs and modems have made it possible to download images, videos. Cable TV is likely to provide very high speed internet connections. Palmtops—particularly simputer is a low cost computer with a modem is suitable for transaction processing involving low volume of data.

INFORMATION SYSTEMS IN DES

Directorate of Economics and Statistics (DES) of the Ministry of Agriculture is responsible for collection, compilation and processing of agricultural statistics in the country. Development of Agricultural Statistics and Agro-economic Research assumes great significance in the country for formulation of agricultural policies and programmes on production, procurement/distribution, marketing, export/import, etc. DES has made Institutional arrangement with the State Departments of Agriculture, State Agricultural Statistical Agencies (SASAs), State Agriculture Departments, State Revenue Departments, and State Planning Departments, for Information Collection in order to facilitate formulation of National Policies and Programmes to achieve rapid agricultural growth. DES also collects information on Agricultural Situation in the country periodically through its Regional Offices. The main thrust, at present, is to improve the timeliness, coverage and quality of agricultural statistics and research required for decision making on various policy issues and planning purposes. DES operates the following schemes to strengthen agricultural statistics in the country:

Central Schemes
- Cost of Cultivation of principal crops
- Crop estimation Surveys of Fruits, Vegetables and Minor Crops
- Agricultural Census and Input Survey

Centrally Sponsored Schemes
- Establishment of Agency for collection of Agricultural Statistics
- Improvement of Crop statistics
- Timely reporting of estimates of Areas and Production of principal crops

DES Collects, Analyses and Disseminates Information on
- Crop production (Area, Production and Yield)
- Land use statistics
- Cost of cultivation of about 26 crops
- Wholesale prices
- Retail prices
- Market arrivals of agricultural commodities, etc.

DES collects, on Weekly Basis
- the wholesale prices from 620 Markets in respect of 153 commodities,
- retail prices of about 78 commodities from 222 centres,

- retail prices on 15 items of food articles and 43 items of non-food articles from 83 urban centres.
- data on market arrival from villages, in respect of 26 major commodities from 2375 markets.

DES also collects, on daily basis, prices of 12 commodities including cereals and sugarcane, from 261 markets. DES has set up its Market Intelligence Units (MIU) in the following locations:

- Eastern Region: Calcutta, Bhuvaneswar, Shillong, Patna
- Northern Region: Delhi, Lucknow
- Western Region: Jaipur, Mumbai, Bhopal, Ahmedabad
- Southern Region: Hyderabad, Bangalore, Thiruvananthapuram, Chennai

ESTABLISHMENT OF AGRICULTURAL ECONOMICS AND STATISTICS NETWORK (AGRIESNET)

The Ninth Five Year Plan Working Group on "Improvement of Agricultural Statistics" under the Chairmanship of Dr. B.B.P.S. Goel, Director (IASRI), suggested to establish a Close-User-Group on NICNET linking various Central/State Departments/Organisations and Field Units of DES involved in producing Agricultural statistics, in order to facilitate the improvement in analysis and transmission of Agricultural Information. This involves networking of (i) State Agricultural Statistical Agencies (SASAs), (ii) State Agriculture Departments, (iii) State Revenue Departments, (iv) State Planning Departments, (v) Departments of Agricultural Economics located in various State and Central Agricultural Universities, (vi) ICAR Institutions dealing with Agricultural Economics and Statistics (NCAP, IASRI, IVRI, NDRI, CIFE, NBSSLUP), (vii) District Level Bureau of Economics and Statistics (596), (viii) Central Water Commission and Central Ground Water Board of the Ministry of Water Resources, (ix) Agro Economic Research Centres, (x) Cost of Cultivation Study Centres (16).

DAC has already formulated a Centrally Sponsored Scheme for strengthening of information technology applications, creation of databases and IT network in the States, NCT and UTs, and this scheme is in different stages of approval. DAC has already approved its Central Sector Scheme (DACNET) to network and establish LAN in the Directorates and its Field Offices.

Department of Agriculture and Cooperation has established a high speed Local Area Network (LAN) in Krishi Bhawan and Shastri Bhawan, with about 750 nodes with Internet Access capabilities NICNET services which include Internet Services, Database Services, Workflow applications, Information Kiosk, etc. are made available over the LAN. NICNET Based Telecommuting Services are provided to all officers of the rank of Joint Secretary and above of the Department. NIC has established Mail Servers and Internet based Video Conferencing in DAC. With this video conferencing facilities, DAC has the infrastructure to conduct video

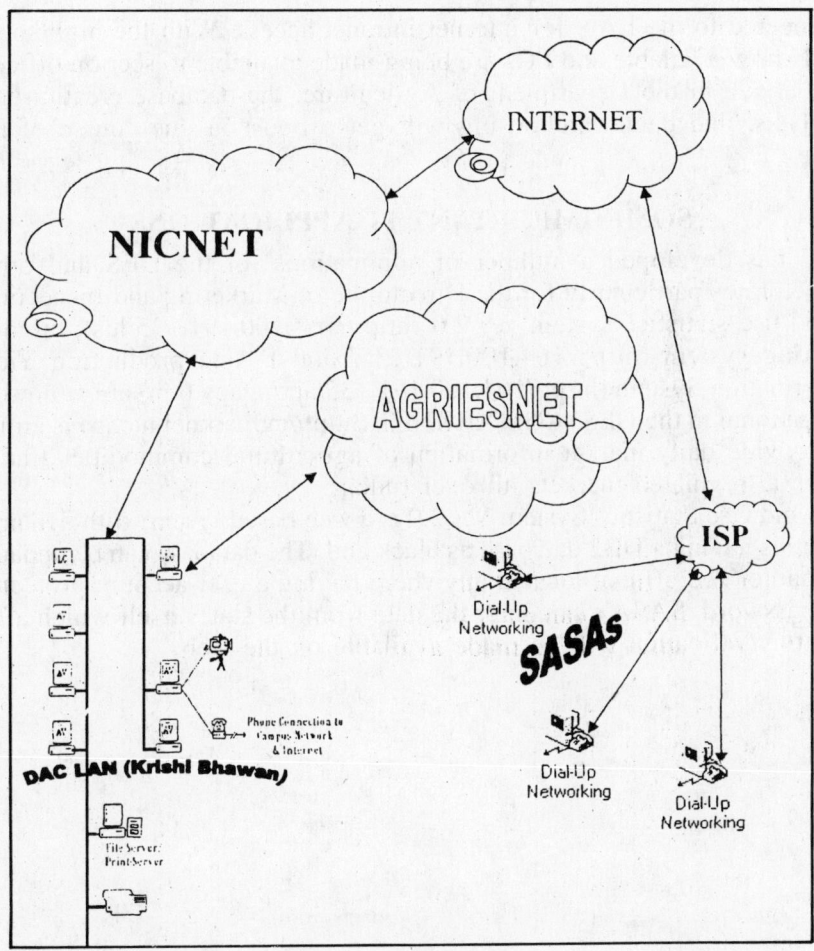

Fig. 27.1 AGRIESNET: A Close user Group of Agricultural Economics and Statistics Information

conferencing from Krishi Bhawan with the State Departments of Agriculture, State Agricultural Statistical Agencies (SASAs), State Agriculture Departments, State Revenue Departments, and State Planning Departments located in the State Capitals. In state capitals, the video conferencing facilities are operational at State NIC Offices.

In the Directorate of Economics and Statistics (DES), NIC has established mail and database servers with about 80 terminals for email and database access and is operational since 1997. This facility was made available to DES from NIC budget on the request of the Economic and Statistical Advisor to strengthen and facilitate database creation and dissemination. DES has also provided PCs to its various divisions and connected to the LAN for internet intranet access. With the high speed LAN now available and PCs are being made available to section officers and above in the Department of Agriculture, the database creation and analysis, and data warehousing will get a boost in due course of the time.

SOME IMPORTANT IT APPLICATIONS

NIC has developed a number of applications for the DES and other directorates particularly for the Directorate of Marketing and Inspection. Land use statistics system ver 2.0 (http://164.100.191.135/lus), circular posting system (http://164.100.191.135/eands) Area production Yield Information System (http://164.100.191.135/apt/pgapy.htm) are at present operational in the DES. AGMARKNET (http://agmarknet.nic.in) is aimed to provide daily market information of agricultural commodities traded in 7000 regulated markets all over India.

Land Use Statistics System Ver 2.0 is a web based system with dynamic features having a DB2 database as black end. The database can be updated by authorized official located anywhere having a user account protected by password. SASA's can enter the data from the states itself which after scrutiny/validation will be made available on the web.

28

Research Priorities in Agricultural Statistics[1]

INTRODUCTION

India can be justly proud of its system for collecting and disseminating statistical information on social and economic life of the country. At the time of Independence, a rudimentary apparatus was in place; but its scope and content were limited and patchy. The last five decades have witnessed a sea change: there are now sizable organizations, staffed by professionals, at the Centre and in the State governments, and in many of the ministries, to collect data on practically all important aspects of the economy and society. Considerable progress has been made in extending coverage, refining and standardizing concepts, improving procedures, speeding up processing and publication. We have seen the widespread use of sample surveys and the creation of a specialized, autonomous National Sample Survey Organisation. As a result, a lot more information, of greater detail and coverage, is now available in the public domain than was the case at the time of Independence. Interaction between data gathering agencies and users has been fostered and in many cases institutionalized. Data and data-based analysis figure increasingly in debates on public policy. And this has stimulated critical discussion among professionals on the content, availability and interpretation of data. All this adds up to an impressive and commendable achievement. But one must also take stock, on this occasion, of several serious lacunae in the statistical system.

India is one of the developing countries which laid considerable emphasis on development of agricultural statistics to meet her planning needs soon after gaining independence. An extensive overview of the available agricultural statistics in the country, the gaps still existing and specific suggestions for improving the quality of agricultural statistics

---

[1]Based on paper read by the author at the Annual Conference of the Indian Society of Agricultural Statistics held in Lucknow.

are available in a published form[2]. Although the publication is almost a decade old, the issues raised therein and suggestions for improvement are still, by and large, valid. This tends to suggest that further follow-up action to remove the existing gaps and improve the quality of available statistics has not made much headway in recent years.

In this paper we would focus our attention mainly on agriculture sector. Two types of problems would be highlighted for a few selected sub-sectors of agricultural statistics which deserve urgent consideration. The first type of problem (type A) concerns unreliability and poor quality of statistics and the second type (type B) highlights the major gaps still existing which need to be filled on a priority basis. The Type A problems are becoming more serious in recent years due to the fact that the quality of statistics generated through laid down procedures seem to be deteriorating in certain areas[3]. It is urgent that the factors responsible for the deteriorating and poor quality of available agricultural statistics are carefully identified and remedial steps are taken to make them useable for development planning. This might call for operation research.

The type B problems have to be dealt with first by evolving a suitable cost-effective method of data collection within available resources and thereafter carrying out in-depth analysis of collected data using modern computing technology to make the results available in time to the planners/policy makers and other users of such statistics. Constraints of resources, both physical (particularly professional and technical manpower) and financial, are often cited as the main cause of the two types of deficiencies. However, lack of strong political will and administrative support to enforce timely implementation of feasible action programmes seems to be also equally responsible for the present state of affairs.

In the following sections we would discuss priority areas of research under three broad heads linked to agricultural statistics. These are: Production, Inputs and Utilisation. We will not go into the details of the present system of data collection with regard to area and yield rate as these are readily available[2]. It is worth mentioning that, in order to improve the timeliness and quality of crop area statistics, two schemes were introduced in the early seventies, viz. the Timely Reporting Scheme (TRS) and the Scheme for Improvement of Crop Statistics (ICS). We would like to highlight the problems under each of them.

PRODUCTION

Crop Area Statistics

Type A Problems First, there has been considerable degeneration in the quality and timeliness of data. In agriculture, for example, land use and

---

[2]Bansil, P.C.: *Agricultural Statistics in India*, Third Edition, 1984.

[3]Rao, V.R.: "Statistics for Rural Development - An Agenda for the Nineties", Technical Address, Indian Society of Agricultural Statistics. 20-22 February, 1993.

crop area statistics used to be completed by village officials as the basis for collecting land revenue. As land revenue became less important and the tasks assigned to village officials became more diverse and demanding, the quality of land use and cropping data suffered. The situation has been aggravated by the abolition of traditional patwaris/karnams, and the weakening of periodic inspection of these records by higher-level officials. Crop yield estimates are based on sample crop-cutting experiments. While the sampling design is done scientifically, the responsibility for conducting the measurements in the sample plots is distributed between several departments. A supervision and sample verification mechanism is in place, but its effectiveness has become a matter of some concern.

There are serious doubts today about the net sown area in the country and its distribution among different crops. There is, over the years, considerable deterioration in the working of the systems which are presently in vogue. It is said that with the increasing range of functions entrusted to the patwari, the girdawari has tended to receive low priority. Another reason attributed to this qualitative deterioration is the reported increase in his workload in the wake of the introduction of many rural development programmes. The fact is that the patwari system, the so-called steel frame of the Land Use Statistics, is really not functioning due to lack of interest of the main functionaries. There is a significant change in land values and hence the attitude of the Patwari. He being the custodian of land records, and quite familiar in the manipulation of such records, his main attention today is on land transactions. It seems that, in villages around major towns where land values have sky rocketed, this village functionary and his immediate bosses (who are supposed to supervise the basic records) are not bothered about the thankless job of maintaining correct land records. We have observed this sacred 'Lal Kitab' (Land Record Register) not having been updated in District Karnal (Haryana)[4] for 5 years. An analysis of the performance of the TRS based on the findings of the ICS scheme also reveals a disturbingly high degree of negligence in carrying out the girdawari, thereby casting doubt on the overall reliability of crop area statistics[3].

A new method of estimation through Remote Sensing Operations which has proved to be quite successful in other parts of the world, has also been introduced in India recently. According to press reports there is an underestimation of around 20-25 percent in the officially declared cropped area. This has made the users now skeptical about the acreage estimates hitherto available.

The scheme for computerization of land records would be very useful in a situation like this. A pilot project in this regard was started by the then Ministry of Rural Development in 1987-88 and a sum of over Rs. 600 million was spent two years back. (Information on physical progress

---

[4]Bansil, P.C.: "District Agricultural Plan, Karnal", Techno Economic Research Institute, (Memeo), 1990.

is not known according to Annual Report of the Ministry of Rural Development 1993-94). If a fool proof system of land transfers is adopted and the Patwari is no longer directly involved in it, he will perforce, be paying due attention to his basic job of maintaining correct land records. It may also be advisable that all the patwaries are given a short training course at the time of recruitment about the importance of these crop data series and how to maintain them properly[5]. It would also be worthwhile to introduce some incentive schemes for efficient Patwaries.

There are two publications of the Directorate of Economics and Statistics, Ministry of Agriculture (DES-Ag) dealing with data on area under different crops-Indian Agricultural Statistics (IAS) and Area and Production of Principal Crops (APPC). The latest issue of the former (IAS) relates to the year 1989-90 for state level and 1988-89 for the District level crop wise data; the Latest issue of APPC relates to 1997-98. During the course of our studies, we have come across with quite a number of anomalies in the statistics published in these two documents. There is an urgent need to reconcile the observed discrepancies. The time-lag in the publication of these data should also be reduced.

Area Under HYV

Type A Problem With regard to area under High Yielding Varieties (HYV), although the Ministry of Agriculture does not publish the data on area under HYV, such information is given in the 'Fertilizer Statistics' brought out by the Fertilizer Association of India with a time lag of about two years. But the information is, often very unreliable. There are instances of India where estimates of HYV area under a certain crop in some of the states are shown to be more than the total area under the crop in the State during that year. Even otherwise, none of these data are based on any actual field surveys—the existing methodology being not free from bias and other deficiencies. Our studies in District Karnal, Haryana, revealed that hardly 4 percent of the total wheat seed was supplied by the government and as much as over 50 percent was purchased by the farmers from the market. Based on these data it could not be vouched that area under HYV is 100 percent under wheat[3].

Irrigation Statistics

Type B Problems With the spread of the new technology, it is not enough to know about the extent of net sown area and its distribution among crops. Although basic data on cropwise irrigated and unirrigated areas are known, much more information is needed about the quality of irrigation. There are large chunks of so called irrigated area where the farmer is not using fertilizers. This has possibly a direct relation with the

---

[5]One of our studies - Management of Religious Lands in Haryana undertaken in 1992 revealed that the Patwari did not know even the definition of Institutional lands.

quality of irrigation. The available, statistics on area irrigated do not throw any light in this regard. This was not an important aspect of the development strategy before the introduction of the present technology. But today just the concept of irrigation is not enough. For this purpose it is important to know, whether in a particular field, under major or minor irrigation, adequate water is available for this water intensive technology at appropriate times. The case of recent diversion of area under wheat to rape and mustard in Rajasthan and UP is a clear indicator of inadequate availability of water for wheat.

It can be established on the basis of data published by Ministry of Water Resources/Planning Commission and the Ministry of Agriculture under Land Utilisation Statistics that there is an area of 20 million hec. (representing more than 30 percent of the present irrigated area) for which potential has been created but it is not being utilised. Precise information about the location of such areas even at the District level is not known[6].

In the case of minor irrigation it is necessary to clearly spell out the areas going out of use. Examples of govt. tubewells in UP not working for long periods may be cited in this regard.

As regards area under HYV, it is important to know about the particular variety of the HYV seed being used. There have been a few scattered studies in some of the villages where wide differences in the yield rate have been found under more or less similar soil, water, fertilizer use and even management practices. This may be due to variations in seed varieties being used.

There being hardly any scope for any extensive agriculture, the future of Indian agriculture depends on intensification. If so, need for detailed information on the aforementioned critical aspects can hardly be over stressed.

Under the present scheme of crop cutting surveys, a good deal of data to cover all the gaps mentioned above are being collected in most of the states on a regular basis all over the country. What is required is to improve the quality of these data by a system of proper supervision and ensure indepth analysis of the collected data and timely dissemination of statewise results.

Yield Rate

Type A Problems Yield rate for a crop is largely based on random sample crop cutting surveys called General Crop Estimation Surveys (GCES)[2]. Around 350, 000 crop-cutting experiments are conducted every year to estimate the yield rates of major crops. GCES covers both the temporary and permanently settled areas for all the States/U.Ts. For fieldwork, part-time services of the state revenue and agricultural staff

---

[6]Bansil, P.C.: *Journal of Indian School of Political Economy*, July - Sept, 1994.

above the rank of the patwari are utilised. The ICS check consists of visiting a sub-sample of GCES at harvest time and verifying that the field staff follows the correct procedure in carrying out the experiments. Around 30,000 experiments are supervised, half by the NSS staff and the remaining half by the staff of the State Agricultural Statistical Authority.

These experiments are based on sound scientific principles with a built in system of checks and supervision. But as regards quality of data under GCES, the situation is quite unsatisfactory. This is amply brought out by the ICS scheme. An analysis of ICS findings of GCES survey were conducted properly in only 60 percent of the cases and the rest had one defect or the other. The quality of performance was uniformly poor over the years and seasons with further decline in recent years. In some states (e.g. Haryana, Maharashtra, Rajasthan) one half to two thirds of the experiments supervised did not meet the prescribed standards. The defects were of a serious nature in 8-10 percent of the cases - mistakes in selection and location of the experimental plot and weighment of produce. It was reported that in a substantial proportion of cases, the field staff was not either supplied or they did not use essential equipment such as measuring tapes and weighing scales for recording the data[3].

Type B Problem There is no disaggregation of yield rate estimates below the District level. It is understood that IASRI had initiated a project for developing appropriate methods of estimating average yield and production of principal crops at block level. A feasible method needs to be evolved on a priority basis. This will go a long way in micro-level agricultural planning.

Production of Cotton, Plantations, Spices, Cashew, Lac

Type A Problems There has been considerable improvement in the production data in respect of major crops like foodgrains, sugarcane, oilseeds and jute, etc. but there is hardly any explanation in respect of the confusion for cotton. There· are as many as 4-5 estimates being floated by different agencies to suit their interests. This is most unfortunate for such a strategic commodity which provides raw materials for one of the most important industry in the country. No solution has been found till today to sort out the issue. Again crop estimates for some commodities-plantations, spices, cashew, lac, are being made by different agencies which create a lot of difficulty in using them. This should probably be the responsibility of a single organization like DES-Ag. If need be, necessary additional resources should be provided to them, so that not only the quality of data is improved, but the existing time lag for various publications is also reduced.

Production of Fruits, Vegetables and Livestock Products

Type A Problems As for the information regarding fruits, vegetables and live stock products, less said the better. If we look at the available area under fruits and vegetables, one comes across a number of gaps and anomalies. Such apparent discrepancies should be removed. Since fruits have been assuming greater importance as protective food for the people in the country and for exports, it is desirable to have a reliable data series in this respect.

Production of Minor Oil Seeds

Type B Problems The position regarding minor oilseeds is very deplorable. Hardly any information is available about them, although the future potentialities of oil availability lie only here. The nine major oilseeds including the newly introduced soyabean and sunflower will not be able to meet the existing and future demand gaps, under the existing technology. According to one of our studies[7], we have an exploitable potential of over 3 million tones of vegetable oils from the various types of oil-bearing trees. The future requirements of vegetable oil in the country will have to be met by the industry rather than agriculture. Same is the position with regard to a number of other minor crops.

From the above scenario, it may be pointed out that the issues with regard to production estimates which need urgent attention are:
1. Patwari system has to be improved and discrepancies between the available publications removed.
2. Improvement in the timeliness of publications.
3. Harmonisation of the available data from different sources and ensure in-depth analysis of the same.
4. Disaggregation of production data of principal crops below the District Level.
5. Inclusion of a large number of minor crops in regular crop estimates.

INPUTS

Production and land productivity have a direct bearing on physical inputs as well as, on management practices. The inputs include fertilizers, seeds, pesticides, irrigation, machinery, etc.

Fertiliser Statistics

Type B Problems There are a lot of data gaps in respect of all these major inputs and a number of assumptions are being made at present to arrive at various types of conclusions. Taking the specific case of fertilizers, the quantity distributed during the two different seasons is assumed to have been consumed during the season. Nothing is known about the dry as well as areas in the assured rainfall regions separately. Some adhoc surveys have been conducted in this respect. The Fertiliser Survey of the NCAER

---

[7]Bansil, P.C.: "India's Crisis in Vegetable Oils", Monthly Commentary on Indian Economic Conditions, Vol. XXIV, No. 8.

is about 20 years old and is of little use to provide an answer to the completely changed ground situation as it exists today[8]. Input Surveys also are being conducted quinquenially as a part of agriculture aim at collection of detailed data on the structure of agriculture.

Although from 1970-71 onward the Census is based on complete enumeration, the Input Survey was conducted for the first time in 1976-77 with only 2 percent sample of villages, increased the sample size to 7 percent during 1986-87. A comparison of the data as released by the Input Survey and Ministry of Agriculture shows that the fertilizer consumption figure given by the Ministry is 0.8 million tonnes (10%) more than the Survey results at the all India level, with much larger differences at the state level. Apart from such wide differences, there is a very big time lag between the survey and the final report-the latest such report available today being for 1986-87 only. Moreover, for purposes of micro planning, such data are required at the District or even below the District level. In the absence of such data all our calculations and international comparisons do not really cut much ice. It is reported that half of the irrigated area in Haryana is not fertilized. Precise quantitative and even qualitative information in this respect is not available[9].

At higher levels of land productivity (as we have in certain selected pockets and areas), micronutrients play an important role. Hardly anything is known about them. In certain pockets of the country fertilizer use is in excess of the absorptive capacity of the soil and this results in soil degradation instead of improving land productivity[3]. In this context, it may be stated that it is most important for India to understand that fertilizers alone are not an answer to the expanding requirements of food and fibre. Organic manures of all types have received only a lip service. According to our study[10] there is a potential of over 16 million tonnes of NPK in the country from organic manures. Information in this area is still sketchy and incomplete.

Mechanisation

Type B Problems   Information on the number of tractors, etc. in the country, is being collected along with other agricultural implements as a part of the Livestock Census every 5 years. Besides some of the known basic deficiencies in these censuses and some of the glaring gaps are:

a. It is not possible to compute any annual series.
b. It is difficult to compute data on the basis of tractor capacity in the country.
c. Practically nothing is known about the qualitative aspects of mechanization, such as the number which needs servicing and can

---

[8]It is understood that a second such survey was conducted a few years back, but for some mysterious reasons, it has never be published.

[9]Bansil, P.C.: "Indian Agriculture at Cross Roads", *Facts For You*, May 1984.

[10]Bansil, P.C.: "Agricultural Planning for 700 Millions in India", 1971.

be put back in the field, how many would have gone out of use and so forth. Only subjective estimates are available based on arbitrary norms. Empirical studies in the area are lacking. This is a serious lacuna in a country like India where agricultural finance is not only shy, but also limited.

d. Information with regard to availability of service facilities for machinery—service stations, public or private, are conspicuous by their absence. This neglected area calls for appropriate investigations.

Such gaps in data should be taken care of in future livestock census/ surveys.

UTILISATION

This would cover post-harvest losses, private stocks, human and livestock consumption after taking into account wastages, marketing, etc.

Post-Harvest Losses

Type B Problems What happens to various agricultural commodities particularly perishable ones like livestock and horticultural products is anybody's guess. Even with regard to major commodities-foodgrains, very limited and quite often unreliable information is available regarding private stocks, interstate movements as well as market arrivals, etc. Although there is a network of regulated markets, 6809 in number, the trader, to avoid taxes, does various transactions outside the normal channels with the result that we are not able to have a correct picture of market arrivals/marketed surpluses, etc. Even otherwise the modernization and commercialization of agriculture currently under way is closely linked with the efficient functioning of the market system for which, dissemination of market information is an essential prerequisite. The system, therefore, requires careful nurturing in the future to cope with the emerging demand and to facilitate market-led growth.

There is hardly any empirical study available in respect of post-harvest losses of major crops as well as minor commodities which are gaining importance. Estimates of losses for horticulture crops vary from 30 to 50 percent. Even with regard to post-harvest losses of foodgrains, there is virtually no system of collecting such information, starting from the field where the grain is harvested, till it comes along the line, is anybody's guess. Certain case studies should be taken for systematic collection of such data for selected commodities so as to suggest suitable remedial measures to minimize the post-harvest losses of many high value crops.

Stocks

Type B Problem Data on private stocks are not available. They are arbitrarily assumed to remain constant in the preparation of food balance sheets. There is an urgent need to take up case studies to fill this data gap.

Consumption

Type B Problem Consumption data are a major component of the development strategy, but the available information in this regard is rather scanty. While some sort of estimates are being made from year to year at the All India Level (Food Balance Sheets), nothing is known at the state and below the state level. Food Balance Sheets are based on quite a few arbitrary assumptions.

Other two sources of consumption data are NSSO and National Nutrition Monitoring Bureau (NNMB). NSSO collects such data annually in value terms. Quantitative data were earlier collected quinquennially. Recently quantitative data are also being collected annually, but on the basis of a thinner sample. It is, therefore, rather difficult to constitute comparable annual series. NNMB has a very small sample and does not cover even the whole country. In both the cases, data series are not available below the State level. Whatever is produced has to be efficiently utilized. In the case of foodgrains, an allowance of 12.5 percent is being made rather arbitrarily for feed, seed and wastages. There is no empirical basis for this. We conducted one pilot study under the sponsorship of the Planning Commission which showed that this was less than 10 percent for the most progressive region, Punjab, Haryana and Western U.P, where livestocks were properly fed[11]. The confusion about the utilization pattern of foodgrains is of such a high order that demand projections for 2000 AD-only 5 years ahead-vary from 196.0 to 240.0 million tonnes[12]. When the system today cannot absorb more that 180.0 million tones and public sector stocks have already crossed an all time high of 36 million tones higher demand projections seem to be doubtful. A major grey area in the whole of this exercise relates to foodgrains being used for feed. This is one of the most crucial areas which have been left out of research/ investigation.

Suggestions for Improvement

NSS sample should be reconstituted in such a way that disaggregated estimates for homogenous zones comprising a small number of districts in each state is possible. An attempt in number of districts should first be made on a pilot basis by pooling the State and central Samples. NSSO may also be requested to cover the other two major gaps private stocks and wastages in one of their rounds. Problems faced will then have to be analysed and arrangements made to collect such data at a regular interval basis. It would also be necessary to undertake a critical study of all the various consumption data series available from different sources and suggest how these could be synthesized.

---

[11]Bansil, P.C.: "Feed, Seed and Wastage Rates in Foodgrains - A Regional Study", TERI, 1989 (Memeo).

[12]Bansil, P.C.: "Demand For Foodgrains by 2000 AD", *Facts For You, 1995* and *Indian Farming*, November 1995.

The two most difficult areas are livestock feeding and interstate movement of foodgrains. With regard to livestock feeding, 'recall method' as under NSSO will not be of much help. There is an urgent need for conducting in depth case studies in the different regions by whole time investigators staying in selected villages. It is not everything that the livestock feeding system in India is very much different as compared with other parts of the world. Major part of meat other than poultry is a by-product of the livestock industry. Majority of animals, particularly cows, yield less than 2 to 2.5 kg of milk per day. Neither it is economical nor possible to give them concentrates or even foodgrains. Major part of the so called waste grains including kitchen waste is again fed to livestock. There is then a double counting in this respect as well. Routine surveys will not be able to deal with each such complicated situations.

With regard to interstate movement of foodgrains, the possible solution appears to be an analysis of the records of a very large number of market committees. Some sort of mandatory regulations may be necessary for proper maintenance of these records.

NEWLY EMERGING AREAS

Environment Statistics

Type B Problems Worldwide concern about environmental balance and protection against degrading practices was expressed at the recent United Nations Conference on Environment and Development (Earth Summit) as well as at the global conventions on climate change and biodiversity which preceded the Conference. The World Development Report 1992 has drawn particular attention to the need for the investment in the stabilization of soil conditions, the protection of forests and the reha-bilitation of environmentally degraded areas. Technological advances, while accelerating growth in agriculture, have also created pollution and other forms of environmental degradation.

These perceptions set new challenges for the statistical systems. It will be essential for systems to generate environment indicators at the macro level to monitor environment health in order to aid policy-making and development administration. The identification and establishment of suitable methods of collecting and interpreting environment statistics will need adequate emphasis. Statistics on ecology, which relates to the study of the dynamics of interaction between populations of plants, animals, trees, pests, fertilizers, pesticides and so on, requires multi-disciplinary involvement. It is a growing discipline and has good potential for fisheries harvesting policies, optimal forestry management, animal nutrition and epidemiology, pest control management and so on. Such models are becoming important tools for predicting the results of inter-action between populations and the adoption of policies for encouraging interactions that are beneficial and controlling those that are not.

India should address the aforesaid tasks in a systematic manner through a long-term statistical development programme. Priority ecological problems should be identified and attempts made to collect relevant data and develop indicators and models wherever feasible. This would also enable the identification of data gaps and statistical problems and indicate the direction of further development[13].

Statistics on Women in Agriculture

Type B Problems Statistics on women in agriculture and rural development are generally scanty. Women perform a variety of tasks in the rural household including sharing in agricultural operations as well as handling and processing of agricultural produce. They tend the domestic animal and participate in any enterprise concerning them. Because of their role in the rural economy, there is a growing interest in statistics related to women. Efforts are necessary to generate the required data and indicators on a systematic basis. Census of population and agriculture and other ongoing household survey programmes, with minor adjustments or expansion, could provide most of the required statistics with the desired level of disaggregation in a cost-effective manner.

Poverty

Type A Problems Few people in India follow the debate on poverty any more. In part this reflects a shift of priorities: information technology, the booming stock market, the boom in consumer durables, all make far bigger headlines today than three decades ago, when poverty dominated. But an additional reason for reduced public interest is the plethora of contradictory data from different sources. The Indian statistical system once had a fine reputation for being world class.

But today's data have so many flaws and differ so widely depending on which source you look at that the most basic facts are matters of statistical dispute. You can claim that poverty is rising, falling or stagnant, and than quote a sheaf of data to support any of these views. When experts have no precise idea what is happening, layfolk cannot be blamed for losing interest.

The Central Statistical Organisation produces the National Accounts System (NAS) data on gross national product and other big macro measures of the economy. On the other hand the National Sample Survey Organisation provides micro-measures of the economy through surveys on consumption, education and much else. Between the two, these organizations once produced data that were the envy of the Third World. Today they seem among the most confused in the Third World.

---

[13]S.K. Mitra: "Statistics in Food and Agriculture in Asia and Pacific", *FAO, Quarterly Bulletin of Statistics*, Vol. 6,1993.

Data on consumption are vital: they determine the poverty ratio and much. We cannot expect consumption estimated by the macro approach of the CSO and the micro approach of the NSSO to tally exactly: some variations are inevitable. But over the years the variations have grown so wide as to become farcical.

The NSS data suggest that the poverty headcount ratio - proportion of people below the poverty line-has stagnated since 1990. However, if we look at total consumption measured by the National Accounts System (NAS) and apportion it according to the income distribution revealed by the NSS, it shows the poverty ratio has fallen steadily in the 1990s. The two sets data tell completely different stories. Food consumption is absolutely basic to poverty. Look at the chart on food consumption. NSS data suggest food consumption per person has been declining steadily. But NAS data shows that grain availability-production plus net imports minus changes in the government's buffer stock - has been rising sharply. Now, consumption and food availability defined in this manner should be equal. Yet the two data sets move in opposite directions.

Quinquennial NSS surveys ask people if they get two square meals a day, and the proportion of such people is rising over time (it was 92 percent in 1993). Yet the same NSS data show falling food consumption per head, not just among the poor but in every single category. Apparently less food goes with fuller stomachs. This is not absolutely impossible. Growing mechanization has decreased manual work in agriculture and construction, so workers need fewer calories. Increased travel by bicycles and buses means that people are walking less, and this again reduces calorie needs. So perhaps people can eat less and yet be more prosperous. The mystery remains, how can the rising food production measured by the NAS vanish into thin air? Maybe additional cereals are being fed to chickens and cows. But this seems insufficient to explain the growing data gap.

There was a time, back in the 1960s when consumption measured by the NSS and NAS were roughly the same. In some years, NSS data actually showed higher consumption than NAS data. But in recent years consumption measured by the NSS has dropped steadily compared with the NAS figures which make up our GNP. Either the NSS is right, in which case India is in dreadful shape, or else the NAS is right, in which case we are in good shape. Critics of liberalization dutifully trumpet the NSS data to prove that poverty has stagnated in the 1990s.

Defenders of liberalization prefer to point to booming GNP data. Clearly we need to go to other sources for a reality check. One such is the National Council for Applied Economic Research, which conducts its own household surveys. The NCAER surveys 300,000 people, far more than the annual NSS sample of 20,000. And although NSSO staff look down on the NCAER's methodology, it is far from clear whether this snobbery is warranted. The NCAER poverty line is somewhat higher than the government's. The poverty ratio as measured by the NCAER has fallen steadily from 58.8 percent in 1989-90 to 49.0 percent in 1995-96. This is in line with the poverty trend as measured by the NAS, but flatly contradicts the trend suggested by the NSS. Data are also available on the wage rate of unskilled agricultural labour, adjusted for inflation. The real agricultural wage rate rose on average by 2.4 percent per year between 1990-91 and '97-98. This again suggests declining poverty.

Finally, look at an indicator that will make more sense to a lay reader. The sale of TV sets has increased from around 4 million per year in 1990, colour TV sales are now as high or fractionally higher than black and white sales. This suggests that an increasing number of people are being promoted from the ranks of the poor to the non-poor. Whether or not our people are getting poorer, our statistics unquestionably are. So, instead of simply talking of structural adjustment of the economy, we need to embark on structural adjustment of our statistical systems. Only then will we know what is actually happening in the economy.

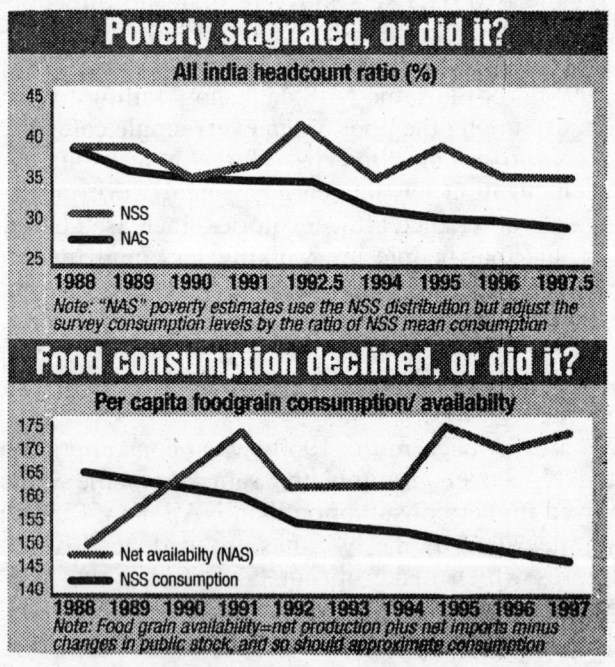

CONCLUDING REMARKS

There are a large number of agencies-official and non-official as well as international-which are collecting/compiling primary data. There is no agency at the Central/State level that has any access to these data. A major part of such data compiled by various organizations is labeled as 'Official' and is not available to research workers and prospective users DES-Ag for example, compiles valuable data on rainfall for each State and sub-region annually, but these are not released. Even 'cost of production' data are not available after 1987-88. It is felt that all types of data collected/compiled at public cost should not be the personal property of anybody. According to Parikh[14], one reason can be the 'dog in the manger' attitude of data producers. They are too preoccupied with their routine duties to undertake in-depth analysis of the data in new and imaginative ways. They would like to do it and some of them have the competence but not the time. There is also vested interest in sitting on the collected data so that the possessors of these data can make use of them for their personal gains.

We feel that a complete inventory of all types of agricultural data being collected/compiled by different organizations should be prepared on a regular basis and supplied to a designated central body say IASRI / NCAP etc. It should be made available at a nominal cost -both hard copies and diskettes to the users.

The tendency for user agencies in government to ask for more information, on more items and at a high level of disaggregation also needs to be checked. It is fashionable to ask for district or even block level estimates without being clear about the kind of specific questions sought to be answered and the information (in terms of content and precision) needed for the purpose. There is little concern about the effect of expanding the scope and the scale of these surveys on costs and on data quality. Unfortunately, the use of data-based analysis as an input to policy, though increasing, remains weak. This has serious consequences: the demand for data is indiscriminate; the relevance and utility of data are not subject to critical scrutiny by users, nor is there much feedback to the data gathering agencies on these aspects; and there is little pressure on data-gathering agencies for improving quality and reliability.

Top managers of government agencies, in particular, should be encouraged to apply their minds more systematically to work out the data needed for various purposes, define their content more precisely and specify periodicity, disaggregation and level of precision with due regard to costs. The possibilities of utilizing data already collected and available in the statistical system should be explored before taking up fresh surveys. There is an enormous scope for more detailed tabulations (including cross tabulations) and analysis of existing data. And in planning fresh surveys, a distinction needs to be made between "staple" data required to be generated at regular intervals on a comparable basis and those which serve special infrequent needs. While the former is properly the function of the NSSO, the latter can be commissioned as required by universities, research organizations and other agencies.

Users outside government have several complaints concerning lack of information on data sources and of getting access to the actual data.

---

[14]Kirit S. Parikh: "Statistics. A Key Technology for Development—How well have we used the key", *Statistical Association Bulletin*, Calcutta, June 1995.

Thanks to the efforts of the Indian Econometric Society, the societies of agricultural and labour economics and other professional bodies, publications giving details of sources and limitations of data on various aspects are available to non-government researchers. The Guide to Official Statistics published by the government is also a valuable source. Some official agencies- notably the CSO-not only have non-official experts on their technical advisory committees but also publish details of data sources, concepts and methodology underlying their estimates as well as the nature and rationale of changes made from time to time. (This unfortunately is an exception rather than the rule.)

The more serious problem is that even if uses know what data is generated and where, getting hold of the data is a problem. Part of the reason is that all data are not published for public dissemination either on request or for a price. Inadequate publicity given to government statistical publications and the poor arrangements for their sale and distribution are serious problems. Efforts by organizations like the ICSSR, the FPW Research Foundation and the CMIE to collate and disseminate published data help to some extent. But a much larger and better-organized effort to expedite this process is essential. The idea of a data network mooted by the ICSSR is meant for this purpose.

Access to unpublished data, especially primary data, is more of a problem. Users complain about this. But it has to be recognized that the possibilities of mapping, analysis and interpretation based on published tabulations are not effectively exploited by researchers. In fact, they have not even scratched the surface of these possibilities. Nevertheless, it is true that certain kinds of analysis would need additional tabulations and/or access to primary data. Considerable bodies of primary data (e.g. individual census slips; schedules of various NSSO inquiries, corporate balance sheets, public financial institutions), have been computerized and this practice is spreading. Until recently, government agencies were reluctant to take up fresh tabulations sought by researchers. Apart from a tradition of secretiveness in government, lack of computer capacity and high cost are also contributory factors. But the attitude is changing: the Freedom of Information Act is a sign of this. The Department of Statistics and the NSSO are also more willing for wider and freer sharing of unpublished tabulations and primary data. There is reason for optimism that the government will approve this policy.

But this is not sufficient to ensure wide and easy access to users all over the country. The creation of a wide network of regional data banks, where unpublished tabulations and unpublished primary data can be stored for ready access, is essential. Non-official organizations serving users must find the resources and be equipped to organize and manage data centers in a progressively competent manner. Moreover, the propensity to corner data is by no means limited to government: after all, control of information could be a source of immense power. This must be effectively checked in any non-governmental initiative. We need to create an environment in which the culture of free sharing of data will flourish.

Finally, a good statistical system must be credible, timely and adequate. Unfortunately, the Indian statistical system, as it is now, suffers from serious deficiencies in relation to credibility, timeliness and adequacy. There is thus the need to find ways and means to address these short-comings this would probably involve looking at major items of data and suggesting how the methodology adopted, the sources from which the data are collected and time taken to process and make available data to the public, can be improved.

Credibility is a fundamental attribute of any set of data. This, in turn, rests on the methodology adopted as well as the sources from where the basic data is collected. Methodology is important as it is as not always possible to collect data through the census method. Sample surveys are the next best alternative. But these must be based on sound sampling techniques if the scope for error is to be minimized. Regarding the need for consistency in data drawn from different sources one could look at the divergence in consumption expenditure estimated through National Sample Survey and National Accounts System which has been the cause of endless controversy regarding the percentage of population below the poverty line.

29

Miscellaneous Statistics

Besides the various types of statistics dealt with in the preceding chapters, we propose to discuss here few other topics which are relevant from the view point of agricultural statistics.

RAINFALL

The primary source of information for rainfall data is the Director General of Observatories, Pune who compiles data collected by various observatories spread throughout the country. The annual publication of the Directorate of Economic and Statistics—Estimates of Area and Production of Principal Crops in India (summary tables)—provides data for the current year regarding actual and normal rainfall figures. The information is provided season-wise with regard to actual and normal rainfall and the whole year is divided into the following four seasons:

1. South-West monsoon   Ist June to 30th September.
2. Post-monsoon   Ist October to 31st December.
3. Winter monsoon   Ist January to 28th February.
4. Summer or pre-monsoon   Ist March to 31st May.
5. Annual rainfall   Ist June to 31st May.

Annual Statistical Abstract of the CSO also publishes these data.

All this information is provided for each of the 35 rainfall divisions into which the country has been divided. Monthly rainfall data are also provided for all the divisions separately indicating annual, normal, and percentage departure in each case. For a proper understanding of the rainfall data it maybe of interest to learn what is considered as excess, normal, deficient or scanty which is explained below:

Excess—120 per cent or more of normal.

Normal—81 to 119 per cent of normal.

Deficient—41 to 80 per cent of normal.

Scanty—40 per cent or less of normal.

CROP CALENDAR

Information relating to the agricultural operations in progress in the different States from month to month is presented in 'Indian Crop

Calendar' issued by the Directorate of Economics and Statistics (DES), with the appropriate background information relating to soil, rainfall, climatic conditions, etc. This information is drawn from a variety of sources, official and non-official.

The principal information giving the calendar of important agricultural operations in each State is given in two tables. The agricultural operations are broadly divided into four categories:

  (i) Preparation of the soil;

 (ii) Sowing and transplanting;

(iii) Growing and maturing, and

(iv) Harvesting and threshing.

The crops in respect of which these operations are in progress in each State and in each month are given and the exact type of operation is described in the first table, the same information is presented crop-wise in respect of rice, wheat, jowar, gram and pulses, barley, cotton, jute, sugarcane and oilseeds. The nature of the operations carried out in each State and in each month in respect of each of these crops is described briefly.

The duration of the sowing and harvesting seasons is also given in a separate table in respect of the principal crops, rice, wheat, barley, ragi, jowar, bajra, maize, sugarcane, groundnut, castorseed, cotton, jute and tobacco, in each of the States. The sowing and harvesting seasons in some of the countries are also given in respect of rice, wheat, barley, maize, sugarcane and cotton. These are also illustrated in the form of charts.

As regards soils, the area of occurrence, characteristic and suitability for cultivation of the important soils of India are given on an all-India basis. The soil classification covers alluvial black, red, laterite and lateritic, mountain and hill, terai, arid and desert, peaty and other organic matter. This is compiled from an article on 'Soils of India and Soil Survey' by S.P. Ray Chaudhri published in Indian Farming, March 1946, State-wise details of the type of soil and their distribution are also given in respect of a few important soil-types. In the absence of a scientifically planned soil survey the information given is of a tentative character.

The data on climatic conditions cover main climatic seasons in India and their characteristics such as low and high pressure, direction of winds, rainfall and others. The year is divided into four seasons— monsoon (June to September), post-monsoon (October and November), winter or north-east monsoon (December to February) and pre-monsoon (March to May). Additional information regarding normal seasonal rainfall, actual annual rainfall for ten years, in selected rainfall divisions of India is also given in the crop calendar. Approximate starting and closing dates of monsoon rains are also indicated. Data on annual normals of temperature and relative humidity at selected centres in the different States based on the information extracted from the Memories of the Indian Meteorological Department (XXII-1913-21) are also published:

Under crop seasons and rotations, the following information is included:

(i) Duration of climatic seasons;

(ii) Crop seasons;

(iii) Double cropping patterns;

(iv) Important crop rotations;

(v) Season and duration (in months) of principal crops; and

(vi) Crop years.

Miscellaneous information given in the Brochure covers natural regions, sub-regions and divisions of India, natural divisions of States of India. Due dates of release of crop estimates, relative importance of principal crops in each State and estimates of area under principal crops as given in successive forecasts, expressed as percentage of the final revised estimates are also given. A glossary of English, vernacular and botanical names of crops is added at the end of the crop calendar. Some of the information given in this crop calendar has become out of date. A revised edition containing later information is being brought out by the Directorate of Economics and Statistics.

INDIAN AGRICULTURAL ATLAS

Indian Agricultural Atlas issued by the Directorate of Economics and Statistics gives the most important agro-economic data relating to the country in the form of maps and diagrams. This pictorial Atlas covers a wide field and gives information regarding population, rainfall, temperature, soils, sown area, irrigated area, forest area, current fallows and other uncultivated land, total area, total yield and yield per acre of important crops, livestock population and number of agricultural implements; share of each State is also indicated in the maps and diagrams. The Atlas also gives the world position regarding area, production and yield per acre of rice, wheat, sugarcane, jute and cotton.

NUMBER AND SIZE OF CULTIVATORS' HOLDINGS

The data on holdings can be built from the village records maintained in the temporary settled areas. There are a number of surveys which give information about the pattern of distribution of land in the rural sector both at the all-India and State levels, the characteristics of the economy of household with different size of holdings, the pattern of employment and wages of agricultural labourers and the incidence of tenancy. Many of the surveys are national in scope, while a few, notably Farm Management Surveys, Studies of the Programme Evaluation Organization and those of some of the Universities relate to specific areas.

The NSS surveys of agricultural holdings in their eighth round, the Agricultural Labour Enquiry, the All-India Rural Credit Survey, the Farm Management Investigations and the Akola Survey into the Cost of Production, provide partial information. Data on operational holdings were also collected by the NSS as part of the socio-economic surveys in the 8th, 16th, 17th and 26th rounds which provided estimates at the all-India and state levels. Realizing the need to provide such data at a lower levels for effective planning, an agricultural census was undertaken in 1971-72 with 1970-71 as the reference year. The data were collected on complete enumeration basis in States having basic revenue records and through sample surveys in States where land records are not maintained. The second agricultural census was carried out with 1976-77 as the reference year. Subsequent censuses had been carried out during 1981-82, 1986-87 and 1991-92.

One of the lacunae of the agricultural censuses has been that these could provide information on open tenancies only, since concealed tenancies are not mentioned in the land records and it was the method of retabulation from land records which was adopted in the censuses. Thus it was not possible to get correct information in regard to operational holdings. Unless the tenancies are regulated and, in particular the rights of all the crop shares are correctly recorded, it will be very difficult to improve the present situation. A study conducted by the Techno Economic Research Institution on Reverse Tenancy in Haryana provides all the details for that state.

DISTRIBUTION OF LAND

The National Sample Survey have collected information of and holdings in their eighth and subsequent rounds. Detailed information is available on the size of holdings, etc. both on household ownership holdings and household operational holdings. Some information is given on tenure holders. The National Sample Survey Report No. 30 'Report on Land Holdings (Operational Holdings in Rural India)' and No. 36, 'Report on the Ownership Aspect of Land Holdings, Rural Sector' also contain useful data on land holdings based on the Eighth Round Survey.

State-wise figures of average size of cultivator's holdings for different categories of families such as agricultural owners, agricultural tenants, agricultural workers, non-agriculturalists and all families are published in 'Rural Man-Power and Occupational Structure' issued by the Ministry of Labour based on the second stage of the First All-India Agricultural Labour Enquiry. Data on utilization of cultivator's holdings are also included in this publication. The Report on the Second Agricultural Labour Enquiry also gives data on the land holdings. Some information on cultivated holdings is also available in the All-India Rural Credit Survey Report of the Reserve Bank of India. The Third Five Year Plan gives information regarding the levels at which ceilings on agricultural holdings have been prescribed or proposed in different States. This Report also contains State-wise data on distribution and size of holdings based on the 'Census of Land Holdings and Cultivations' carried out in 1954-55 in all the States except Assam, West Bengal and Jammu & Kashmir and the Union Territories of Manipur and Tripura.

In response to the World Food and Agricultural Organization (FAO)'s Programme of Agricultural Census, 1960, the last land holdings enquiry was carried out by the National Sample Survey (NSS) in its 16th round (July 1960 to June 1961). The survey was continued in the 17th round (September 1961 to July 1962), also with a view to obtaining dependable estimates at the regional level by pooling the area of both the rounds. Results covering various aspects of land holdings especially characteristics of the household holding (ownership and operational) and area under different crops in agricultural holdings were published in NSS Report No. 162—Tables on Some Features of Land Holding in Rural Areas— issued by the Cabinet Secretariat.

Apart from the problem of inordinate time lag in the publication of these data, which is common to many other elements of agricultural statistics, a major problem with the available data in this field is the lack of comparability in concepts and coverage. For instance, in some surveys though the entire country is covered, the focus is only on size, distribution of ownership and operational holdings together with information on irrigation, size of households, etc. But the cropping pattern and output are not covered at the same time. On the other hand, farm management surveys deal with almost all aspects of the farm economy but they have a limited geographical coverage and are not repeated often enough.

OWNERSHIP AND TENANCY

Details of ownership and tenancy are available with a fair degree of accuracy from the village records and other revenue settlement records. A large scale change in the pattern of ownership and tenancy is taking place in most of the States on account of land legislation measures, like zamindari abolition, ceilings on holdings and consolidation of land holdings. There is need to process and analyze the data already available in a comprehensive form. A scheme for computerisation of land records is already in operation and has been discussed in detail elsewhere in the book.

LAND REVENUE AND AGRICULTURAL INCOME TAX

From 1947-48, land revenue statistics, which previously formed part of the Indian Agricultural Statistics, issued by the Directorate of Economics and Statistics are being published in a separate publication entitled 'Indian Land Revenue Statistics'. This gives State-wise and district-wise figures of: (i) fully assessed area for which figures are available, (ii) total revenue from land excluding cesses, (iii) population of fully assessed area, (iv) total revenue from land per head of population, (v) land revenue assessed on fully assessed area, (vi) incidence per acre of land revenue on fully assessed area, and (vii) land revenue assessment per head of population of fully assessed area. Each State and district is classified according to the nature of tenures and settlement, viz. raiyatwari, zamindari or village communities, temporarily settled or permanently settled.

While utilizing these statistics, the following points may be kept in view:

(i) The statistics of land revenue assessment, etc. are collected annually in Assam, Madhya Pradesh, Punjab, Jammu & Kashmir, Karnataka, Rajasthan, Gujarat, Kerala, Delhi, Himachal Pradesh, Manipur, Tripura and Andaman and Nicobar Islands. These are collected quinquennially in Andhra Pradesh, Bihar, Maharashtra, Tamil Nadu, Orissa, Uttar Pradesh and West Bengal. The statistics contained in this publication cover only the reporting areas in each State and relate to the latest year for which they are available in each case.

(ii) The data relate generally to the agricultural year ending 30th June except in the case of some States for which the period covered is different. The statistics covered for a year generally include both the kharif crops and therefore inter-State comparisons are vitiated.

The statistics covered for a year generally include both the kharif and rabi crops and therefore relate to the year ending with the harvesting of rabi crops.

(iii) The types of land revenue in the different States have been grouped under the following three heads:

(a) Zamindari and Village Communities (temporarily settled);

(b) Zamindari permanently settled; and

(c) Raiyatwari.

Under the Zamindari or Village Community, temporary or permanent system of settlement, revenue is assessed by the State, temporarily or permanently as the case may be, on an individual or community holding an estate and occupying the position of an intermediary between the State and the ryot. Under the raiyatwari system, the revenue is assessed on individuals who are the actual occupants or are accepted as representing the occupants of the holdings. Under both these systems there may be rent paying sub-tenants.

(iv) Since the data for all the States do not refer to a uniform period and to the same type of land tenure(s) it is not possible to work out all-India revenue and incidence of land revenue per head of population or per acre of land. The data given in the tables represent only the assessment that is the actual realizable demand in respect of the year concerned and do not take into account either the collection of arrears for past years or the amounts remaining uncollected at the end of each year.

The Report of the Taxation Enquiry Commission, 1953-54 (Vol. III) issued by the Ministry of Finance (Department of Economic Affairs) also gives background information on land revenue systems and other information along with information on proportion of receipts from land revenue to total revenue and share of land revenue in total tax revenue of Part 'A' States (former Provinces). It also gives information on receipts from agricultural income tax in different States from 1940-41 to 1954-

55, rates of tax in different States, and effect of agricultural income tax on agricultural incomes. The Report of the Finance Commission, 1957 also gives some data on land revenue and agricultural income tax. Latest information on Land Revenue and Agricultural Income Tax is provided in the various issues of the Reserve Bank of India Monthly Bulletins which is reproduced in Indian Agriculture in Brief being issued annually by the D.E.S.

AGRICULTURAL PRICES

Fairly detailed, comprehensive and reliable data on wholesale prices of agricultural commodities are available in India. This is largely the result of the basic framework laid down by the Agricultural Prices Enquiry Committee 1954 (Chairman: P.N. Thapar). Not only the reporting agencies were specified in the different markets but the concepts and nature of the quotations to be reported were also laid down. The DES through its market intelligence staff also maintains a close watch on the reporting of the prices. In India, there are about 7,255 regular wholesale markets with 4,742 sub-markets besides over 22,000 periodical markets or shandis held bi-weekly, weekly or fortnightly in rural areas. Of the total number of the wholesale markets, 2,333 have already been regulated and the scope of regulation is being gradually extended to others. At important markets whole-time price reporters have been appointed under the Scheme for Improvement of Market Intelligence.

At the State level, the work regarding collection and reporting of prices and other market intelligence is looked after by Marketing Departments/Directorates in most of the States. Arrangements for supervision and training of price reporting agencies at centres other than those for which data are reported to the Government of India, need to be strengthened.

At the Centre the DES obtains telegraphically daily wholesale prices of foodgrains in respect of 140 markets covering primary, secondary and terminal markets. Weekly wholesale prices are collected from about 621 markets in respect of 7,153 agricultural commodities. Daily retail prices of foodgrains are collected from over 90 centres and weekly retail prices of agricultural commodities from 7,222 centres. Weekly data on market arrivals and stocks of 714 agricultural commodities are also reported from 2,375 markets spread all over the country. The DES also, collects lots of other market intelligence but the same are not published regularly.

Further improvements in market intelligence should be in the following directions:

(i) Emphasis so far has been on current information. To improve the usefulness of price and other market intelligence, efforts should be made to issue periodical reports on outlook for future to provide material for advance action to forestall local shortages, scarcities or glut.

(ii) Market intelligence for pulses, edible oils, important fruits and vegetables, minor oilseeds and condiments and spices should be organized on the same lines as for cereals and fibres.

(iii) The study on costs and margins should be extended to more centres and crops.

(iv) All the regulated markets in the country should be made reporting centres for price collection. The State should have a larger number of centres than that at present for their own use.

(v) Whole-time technical reporting agencies should be set up in all the important wholesale markets according to a phased programme.

(vi) The scope of market news service should be extended gradually so as to increase the number of market and commodities in respect which market news is disseminated by the All-India Radio and through other media.

The DES collects periodical information regarding prices prevailing in important world markets for a few important agricultural commodities entering into the import export trade. There is, however, considerable time lag in the availability of the data. The coverage of the commodities and centres is also not adequate and needs to be enlarged. We suggest that the whole question of the scope and coverage of the foreign market intelligence should be reviewed in consultation with the Ministry of Commerce and adequate arrangements should be made for their systematic collection. The help of Indian Embassies and High Commissions abroad and foreign Embassies and High Commissions situated in India may be taken wherever necessary in collecting up-to-date information.

With regard to stocks, the only complete and reliable data that are at present available are those relating to stocks of foodgrains held by the Government in their own godowns, or godowns of the Food Corporation of India. In the case of cash crops like cotton and jute, data on stocks held by trade are available. Some data are also available with regard to stocks pledged with the banks. The market arrival returns also give some data on stocks, but these are not very reliable. It is necessary to improve the availability of data on the stocks with farmers, consumers and various agencies such as wholesalers, retailers, etc. Even with regard to storage accommodation, although information regarding the total storage constructed by different agencies is available, its occupancy by commodity and period is not available. This information should also be collected.

MARKETED SURPLUS

The quantum of marketed surplus, and the pattern of its disposal is changing with the economic development of the country. Some scattered and sketchy information on this aspect is available in the Marketing Reports. Besides the fact that there is practically no scientific basis behind these figures, they can at best give an idea of the position as it existed when the particular Report was being prepared. Changes in this respect are taking place rapidly. All types of planning about transport, storage and even reserve stocks, etc. depends upon the accuracy of information of this nature.

During the 1958-59 season when the market prices of foodgrains were on the whole found to be not in keeping with the level of production obtained in the year, the Directorate of Economics and Statistics, Ministry of Food and Agriculture conducted a special inquiry through the Agro-Economic Research Centres and the Farm Management Centres, to have an idea of the market arrivals of foodgrains during the 1958-59 season. The Report entitled 'Report on Market Arrivals of Foodgrains—1958-59 Season' was published towards the end of 1959.

Based on the information supplied by their Marketing Inspectors, spread all over the country, the Directorate is also publishing in the various issues of their monthly journal 'Agricultural Situation in India' data about market arrivals of different foodgrains, Estimates of marketed surplus of wheat for the important wheat growing States are also being published.

STOCKS

Data on stocks and reserves of foodgrains relate only to government stocks and off-take from the same. These are published annually in the 'Bulletin on Food Statistics', since 1949. The position before that year is given in the "Indian Food Statistics, 1949'.

As regards cash crops like cotton, jute, etc. information is also available on stocks held by trade. Annual Balance Sheets of some of the important commodities are being published by the Directorate of Economics and Statistics in their 'Commodity Series'.

FEED, SEED AND WASTAGE RATES

There is at present no information available on any scientific basis about the quantity of foodgrains being used for purposes of feed and seed and that being wasted. Some rough estimates were formulated long back by the Agricultural Marketing Adviser, Percentages of different foodgrains allocated to these different heads as calculated by the Marketing Adviser are given in Table 29.1. Applying these percentages to the annual gross production of different foodgrains over a number of years, a net figure of $12\frac{1}{2}$ per cent was arrived at. For all official calculations, this is the formula being adopted to arrive at the figure of the net consumption of foodgrains.

None of these three items is in any way related to the gross production. Seed, for example, is related to the area under the crop. Wastage rates, if at all, are related to the condition and type of storage available and the quantities of marketable surplus entering the market. Similarly feed rates have a direct relation with the programme of animal husbandry and poultry development. As set formula like the one in use at present is of little value for planning purposes, suitable statistical information has to be developed in these respects.

Table 29.1 Feed Seed and Wastage Rates in India

(Percentage of production)

Commodity	Feed	Seed	Wastage	Total
Rice (paddy)	2.1[a]	6.4	1.1	6.7
Wheat	Negligible	82.7[b]	3.0	15.6
Barley	1.2	72.1[b]	2.0	22.7
Jowar	2.6	3.0	5.0	10.6
Bajra	4.1	2.7	5.0	11.18
Maize	1.0	3.3	5.0	9.3
Ragi	1.2	2.3	5.0	8.5
Small millets	2.1	2.3	2.5	6.9
Gram	12.0	49.1[b]	2.0	18.7
Other pulses	5.0	5.0	2.5	12.5
Potatoes	—	70.8[b]	17.0	—
Groundnut (in shell)	—	12.0	—	12.0
Sesamum	—	2.3	—	2.3
Fruits	—	—	25.0	25.0
Sugarcane (gur)	3.0	6.6	—	15.0

[a]Absolute figure (thousands tonnes).

[b]Ib per acre.

Source: Agriculture in Brief, third edition, 1957, p. 62, Directorate of Economics and Statistics, Ministry of Food and Agriculture.

CAPITAL-OUTPUT AND COST-BENEFIT RATIOS

The overall allocation to agriculture within the total plan outlay is at present determined mainly on the basis of the aggregate costs of the different schemes included in the State and Central Plans. But once the rate of increase in national income in any given Plan is known and the share of agriculture is also determined, the investments necessary for achieving this increase could be estimated fairly accurately by using the capital output ratio technique. Precise coefficients of such capital-output ratios for investment in agriculture have not yet been worked out although some sporadic attempts have been made to determine them in isolated fields of programme.

In formulating and even determining the consistency of any Plan, the technique of input-output or inter-industry table is generally adopted in advanced countries. Under this technique the contribution of agriculture to other sectors of the economy is worked out as also the contribution of the latter to the former. An attempt is thus made to secure balances between and within different sectors. Similarly, within agriculture, inter-industry tables are worked out for different sub-heads of development such as livestock, fisheries, forestry, etc. Such studies are being initiated in India. Efforts in this direction need intensification.

Data on cost-benefit ratios of different schemes are required for determining their *inter se* priorities. The question of relative investment to be made in major and medium irrigation on the one hand, and minor irrigation on the other, can be decided, among other things, on the basis of cost-benefit ratios. Similarly, the relative contribution of irrigation and fertilizers to the national target of agricultural production might also be determined on the basis of cost-benefit ratios.

An attempt was made in 1958 by the Ministry of Food and Agriculture to collect relevant information from States regarding costs and benefit from different types of minor irrigation schemes on the basis of experience of the first three years of the Second Plan. Broadly, the information collected included nature and costs of work, particulars of assistance, dimensions and capacity of works, area benefited and additional production expected from the area benefited. Such studies are necessary for other schemes also.

DEMAND PROJECTIONS

Exercises on demand projections made from time to time particularly in the formulative stage of various plans relate to foodgrains in particular and also other agricultural commodities like oilseeds, cotton, jute and plantation crops, etc. For determining the future food requirements, it is customary to make use of the income elasticity coefficient. This approach can no doubt serve as a most scientific method to determine the future food requirements atleast for a short period. But we have in the country at present a large amount of data with regard to income/expenditure/quantity elasticity for various food items. Whatever the validity of these coefficients, they try to establish a relation between increases in the household consumption expenditure and the portion of it which is expended by the average consumer on the commodity concerned. For demand projections we are hardly interested in the expected value of the amount to be spent on the commodity. Our requirements are to work out the estimated increase in the quantity consumed because there is quite a big price differential in the qualities of the consumed commodities.

If a poor man today is spending Rs. X on quantity Y of rice, with a 100 per cent increase in his income he might very well be spending Rs. 2X if the income elasticity of rice is 1. But the actual quantity consumed by him may be far below 2Y because there is a greater likelihood of his shifting from an inferior to a superior variety of rice where the cost per unit of the superior variety may be much higher than that of the inferior one.

If the total demand for foodgrains is projected on the basis of some such income/expenditure elasticity formula, the position becomes still worse because it will not reflect the substitution of fine by coarse grains which is a normally expected phenomenon all over the world. Prices of coarse grains are invariably lower than those of rice and wheat. From whatever sketchy data of quantity elasticity are available, it goes to prove that quantity elasticity is invariably much lower.

Looking at the methodological problem, we observe that a number of limitations have to be kept in view in using elasticity coefficient as a tool for projecting demand:

1. The coefficient of income elasticity is derived by analysis of expenditure behaviour of a family belonging to different groups in a given set of relative prices.
2. Income elasticity of demand at a given time holds true over longer periods when it is assumed that tastes and habits of population do not change over time.
3. The slope of expenditure curves (i.e. those correlating to expenditure and income) may be different at different levels of income.
4. It can also be reasonably assumed that the pattern of distribution of total expenditure at different levels of income cannot remain the same.
5. Change in the pattern of distribution of purchasing power amongst various sections of population is another factor which might render the available elasticity coefficient as inapplicable for the future.

All the limitations mentioned above involve serious complications to adopt the income elasticity approach for determining the future levels of demand particularly over a longer period. While it might be all right to assume that the general price level will not affect the model when both income and expenditure are assumed to be calculated at a constant price, it is impossible to think that the relative prices as between the various items of food or for that matter between food as a group, textiles or footwear, etc. will continue to have the same relationship between them. This would mean that there is a need for a comprehensive study on price elasticities for different commodities. At present, unfortunately, there is hardly any study available which throws a useful light on price elasticities.

Studies on demand projections also suffer from the available lacuna in the basic reliable data regarding the present consumption levels of horticulture and animal husbandry products in the country. The consumption of even different types of cereals as between the rural and urban sectors as well as in the different regions is also not precisely known. Practically nothing is known about private stocks and inter-State movement of various commodities. This information could have usefully been deployed to form a correct estimate of the existing consumption patterns in the country. For any useful study of demand projections, it is also essential to have an idea about savings, national income, household income and State income separately for rural and urban sectors. Efforts have got to be made to make such data available.

Gaps in availability of information required in connection with the estimation of demand for different agricultural commodities may be summarized as in Table 29.2.

Table 29.2 Gaps in Data Needed for Demand Projections

Items	Level at which estimates are needed	Agricultural commodities for which information is required
Population growth	Rural and urban sectors separately	—
Savings	"	—
National income	"	—
Household income	"	—
State income, State-wise	"	—
Income or expenditure elasticity	All-India, regions and States	All commodities for which demand estimates are to be made
Quantity elasticity	"	
Price elasticity	All-India and regions	Substitute goods.
Private stock	"	All commodities.
Inter-State movement of commodities	"	Major commodities covering all modes of transport
Consumption	All-India, separately for urban and rural sectors	Rice, wheat, other cereals, pulses, vegetable oil, etc.
Production	All-India, regions and States	Fruits, vegetables, meat, fish, egg, milk and milk products.

INPUT-OUTPUT RELATIONS

In addition to data on the spread of key inputs and the technology associated with them, sound agricultural planning requires reliable data on the responsiveness of yield of different crops to various inputs individually, in combination and under different agro-climatic conditions. The crop cutting surveys provide estimates of yield per unit area in irrigated and unirrigated land in different States. A large volume of data relevant to the estimation of input-output relations is generated by the various all-India crop improvement programmes of the ICAR. The simple fertilizer trials conducted as part of national demonstration programme have accumulated a vast body of information on yield responses to fertilizers. On the basis of these yardsticks the response of major crops to irrigation and fertilizers in irrigated and unirrigated conditions has been evolved. In general, these yardsticks relate to the effect of particular inputs on yield. However, in the case of high yielding varieties, a composite yardstick intended to reflect the additional production from the application of the recommended package of inputs and management practices has been evolved.

Although in sheer volume, the information on input responses is impressive, yet there are several serious deficiencies. First the data relating to pulses and non-foodgrain crops are relatively sparse. Second, there is a serious dearth of experiments relevant for estimating water-yield relationship (in particular the effect of quantum and timing of water on yields), and interaction between moisture conditions and fertilizer responses. Third, since the yield responses of inputs are significantly influenced by the genetic property of seed, this consideration has become all the more important with the evolution of new high yielding varieties for many crops—it is essential to have information on input-output relation for different seed varieties. Some efforts have been made to collect variety specific response data, particularly for fertilizers, in the case of some cereal crops. But these need to be greatly enlarged and made more systematic. Fourth, wide variations in the response to fertilizers even within apparently homogenous agro-climatic conditions makes it difficult to derive meaningful estimates of average responses. The utility of data for estimating average responses could be greatly enhanced by compiling data on the base fertility status of the control plots and by allowing for larger range of fertilizer application than is currently in vouge. Fifth, the available data on responses to plant protection and other so-called improved practices is extremely meagre. There seems to be very little systematic large scale experimentation to provide the basis for reliable estimates of responses. Sixth, one needs data on input responses and production functions under actual farming conditions. To the extent input responses are a function of quality of management, it is possible that the responses in average farming conditions differ substantially from those estimated from research station data or under control demonstrations conditions. As of now, there is no way of knowing whether there are differences, much less whether these differences are significant and whether they get narrowed as the farmers learn and master the new technology. This information has important bearing not only in making more realistic projections of input absorption but also in identifying the factors which make responses under average conditions lower than what is technically possible so that the necessary corrective measures can be planned. Finally, as the average dosage per hectare of nitrogen, phosphorus, etc. are increased, micronutrients in the soil will get exhausted. This aspect has to be looked into carefully.

PRIVATE AGRICULTURAL INVESTMENT

Apart from investment in the agricultural sector by the Government, substantial investment in land improvement, irrigation facilities, farm implements, etc. is made by individual farmers. Data on that part of this investment that if financed by credit obtained from institutional sources, are in principle available in the records of lending institutions. But data on such investment out of farmers's own resources are available only in the Rural Credit Surveys of Reserve Bank of India and no annual data on a continuing basis are being collected.

RURAL CREDIT SURVEY REPORT

The Reserve Bank of India conducted a Rural Credit Survey during November 1951 to August 1952, in 75 selected Districts spread all over the country. Being a 'Policy-oriented' survey, it was planned and conducted in a manner so as to provide some factual basis for proper formulation of recommendations relating to rural credit, rather than providing any State/national estimates of various economic characteristics. The data collected by the Survey, however, included farm expenses along with other items. In respect of expenditure, data were collected on average cash and total expenditure on seed and manure, cash expenditure on fodder, 'other cash expenditure' and cash and kind expenditure on wages. In the absence of any relatively firmer information of all-India validity, some use can be made of the results in this report.

BENCH MARK SURVEY REPORTS

The Programme Evaluation Organization of the Planning Commission has conducted a number of Bench Mark Surveys in some of the selected blocks. Among other items information has also been collected on capital formation in agriculture. As these surveys are mostly local in character with centres hardly representing the country or even the State and with their primary objective other than the investigation of cost of cultivation, the data collected by them are also of very limited use.

TRADE IN AGRICULTURAL COMMODITIES

Indian official trade statistics arise in the first place out of compilations made in the course of administration of customs laws such as those relating to taxation of goods entering and leaving the country and secondly from compilations made by various Government Departments for their own use such as returns received from Railways on which statistics of inland trade are based. These statistics cover only a small section of the total field of exchange of goods moving along certain specified channels of trade.

Statistics regarding foreign trade in agricultural commodities, especially foodgrains, are almost complete and detailed break-up of the quantity and value is available in the publications of the Department of Commercial Intelligence and Statistics. All useful data about foodgrains are also published by the Directorate of Economics and Statistics in their Bulletin on Food Statistics: an annual publication.

INLAND TRADE

The position is, however, different with regard to inland trade. When a complete system of food control existed, movements of principal foodgrains were easy to obtain. With the lifting of the controls, the situation has, however, changed and there is practically no information available regarding the trade taking place at various levels. An important gap in the inland trade statistics is the lack of information on the movement of agricultural commodities within the same State or principal trade blocks. For cotton the quantity of raw cotton imported (exported) by rail and river into (from) each internal block of the State or area (to) each external block and other internal blocks of the State or area is given in 'Cotton Trade Statistics'. Trade blocks for each commodity or a group of commodities will be different and data in respect of trade between these will be quite valuable.

Data on inter-State Movement of foodgrains by rail and river are collected and published by the Director-General of Commercial Intelligence and Statistics. With the development of roads and road transport, the inter-State movement of foodgrains by road has assumed great importance. To obtain a complete picture of the extent of inter-State movement of foodgrains, the data on their movement by motor vehicles and other modes of transport, namely, carts, head-loads, etc. also need to be collected. The Directorate of Economics and Statistics in the Ministry of Food and Agriculture, had organized a scheme to collect data on inter-State movement of foodgrains by motor vehicles. Up to February, 1967, the scheme was in operation in the States of Bihar, Maharashtra, Assam, West Bengal and Punjab (erstwhile). In view of the various restrictions imposed on the movement of foodgrains from time to time it was observed that it would not be possible to continue the scheme in all the States. Hence, with effect from 1st March, 1967, the scheme was discontinued in the States of Assam, Bihar, Maharashtra and West Bengal. At present, this scheme is in operation in the States of Haryana and Punjab. But data on road movement of foodgrains are not being published.

Trade statistics that are now being compiled and published may be classified as follows:

1. Foreign Trade
   (*a*) Sea and air-borne trade with foreign countries.
   (*b*) Trade across land frontiers.
2. Inland Trade
   (*a*) Rail and river-borne trade.
   (*b*) Coastal trade.

The publications furnishing the respective information are:

1. *Accounts Relating to the Foreign Trade and Navigation of India*—Monthly.
2. *Annual Statement of the Foreign, Sea-borne Trade of India*.
3. *Accounts Relating to Inland (Rail and River-borne) Trade of India*—Monthly.
4. *Accounts Relating to the Coastal Trade and Navigation of India*—Monthly.

Recently, several important changes in the coverage, content, periodicity, trade classification, pattern of presentation of statistics, etc. have been introduced in these publications.

Important gaps in the inland trade statistics may be enumerated as follows:

1. Value of the commodity in movement is not shown.
2. Only 66 commodities are covered at present, and quite a large number of others are left out.
3. In the case of river-borne trade, the statistics cover only the trade carried by two steamer companies between three trade blocks.
4. The movements reported by the Railways relate to freight traffic only. The passenger parcel traffic is excluded.
5. Nothing is known about the trade carried by road—lorries or carts—and country craft.
6. As for the air-borne trade, although the trade is carried on by organized agencies, the required trade data are not published in any form excepting the total freight carried. The commoditywise breakdown of the goods traffic are not being maintained by the Director-General of Civil Aviation.

The whole question of improvements in the inland trade statistics was raised as far back as 1933 in the Report of the Committee on 'Amplification of Inland Trade Statistics' under the Chairmanship of John Mathai. But no improvement has so far been possible. The matter was again discussed at the Tenth Conference of Central and State Statisticians, in December, 1961. Various agencies concerned with the collection of such data have agreed to take necessary action in the matter.

During recent years, with the development of road transport, inter-State movement of agricultural commodities has assumed considerable importance. Efforts are, therefore, being made to organize the collection of data on inter-State movement of foodgrains by motor vehicles.

INTEGRATED SYSTEM OF AGRICULTURAL SURVEYS

A large variety of data on different aspects of agriculture are being collected at present. The needs for collection of data are expanding faster than the rate at which improvements in statistics are taking place. The modernization of Indian agriculture as envisaged through the agricultural planning technique would need the collection and compilation of a large quantity and variety of data with different periodicities. Obviously, all the data cannot be collected every year nor is this needed. For example, data on the structure of holdings need not be obtained every year as these do not show significant annual variations. Quinquennial censuses based on complete-enumeration or sample surveys will serve to throw light on the changes in the structure and characteristics of holdings. For meeting the data needs in the sphere of agriculture referred to in the different Sections, the best approach is to device an integrated system of agricultural surveys covering both current agricultural surveys and periodical agricultural and livestock censuses. The integration essentially consists in combining, wherever feasible, surveys with the common sampling units and staggering the programme of collection of data over a period of five years, taking up a major group of items each year. Sample surveys can be superimposed on complete-enumeration enquiries both for checking up the reliability of the data and for providing additional information. The agencies for the collection of data can also be employed rationally by combining different surveys. Primarily four types of surveys need to be undertaken, viz:

(i) those with fields as the unit.
(ii) those with holding as the unit,
(iii) those with livestock holding as the unit, and
(iv) cost of production enquiries.

All these together can form National Agricultural Surveys.

In the case of the surveys with field and holding as units the items to be canvassed would relate to:

(i) improved seeds,
(ii) fertilizers and manures,
(iii) irrigation, drainage and soils,
(iv) plant protections, and
(v) cultivation practices and extension. These can be covered by rotation over a period of five years.
(i) characteristics of holdings as in the agricultural census;
(ii) data required for production and utilization accounts;
(iii) debt and investment of savings;
(iv) employment, unemployment, underemployment, labour force and labour inputs; and
(v) food consumption and nutrition.

These items can be covered in different years. In the field of animal husbandry, the five-year programme should successively cover:

(i) quinquennial livestock census with a sample survey for the additional particulars about breeds and age-composition;
(ii) milk and milk products;
(iii) poultry and poultry products;
(iv) wool; and
(v) meat and meat products and hides and skins.

Changes in livestock numbers and also in the output of products other than the main product under survey in a particular year can be studied every year. The cost of production surveys should also be conducted in a phased manner taking up for study different crops and animal husbandry products during the different years. Some of the integrated agricultural surveys can be dovetailed into the agricultural surveys being conducted under the auspices of the NSSO.

As techniques of agricultural planning are improved, a continuous appraisal of the resources of agricultural holdings will be necessary. It is possible to secure this information by obtaining data on selected characteristics in respect of a rotating sample of holdings continuously, year after year. This rotating sample may form a sub-sample of the main sample selected for the annual survey of holdings envisaged under the National Agricultural Surveys. This method is known as the Perpetual Inventory Method. This development should be kept in view in the future agricultural statistics system of the country.

The surveys with the field as a unit can be combined with the crop-cutting surveys at present carried out in different States under the technical supervision of the NSSO. Even at present there is provision for giving information on the various inputs in the preliminary return to be furnished by the primary agency immediately after the field is selected for crop-cutting. This information is at present not being tabulated. By reviewing the scope of the return and modifying it to provide details of information required each year, and tabulating the data collected, very useful information on the various inputs can be collected at a very little extra cost.

After reorganization, the NSSO even at present has a phased programme for collection of information on different items as part of socio-economic rounds as under:

(i)	Population, births, deaths, disability, morbidity, fertility, maternity, child care and family planning	once in ten years.
(ii)	Debt and investment and capital formation	,,
(iii)	Land-holdings and livestock enterprises	,,
(iv)	Employment, unemployment rural labour enquiry and consumer expenditure	twice in ten years
(v)	Self-employment in non-agricultural sector	,,

The five groups of subjects cited above would cover, in all, seven rounds of a year each out of the ten-year programme. The remaining three years out of a decade have been kept open for undertaking surveys on subjects unexplored so far as also to accommodate special requests from the Central and State Governments. Thus a system of phased collection of information on various items has already been adopted by the NSSO. The essential difference is that the ultimate sampling unit in the socio-economic surveys of the NSSO is the household. For agricultural purposes, what is needed is the operational unit of cultivator's holding. It is, however, possible to establish the relationship between the operational holdings and household holdings and collect the relevant information through the NSSO.

Reference has been made to the surveys with the livestock holding as a unit in Section 8. We recommend that the various integrated surveys which we have referred to might continue to be carried out by the agencies responsible for the different subjects as at present. What is, however, needed is that there should be adequate arrangements for technical coordination and guidance. We suggest that the Governing Council of the NSSO should examine this question further.

Thus, the tendency to organize a fresh survey whenever any information on a new item is required should be discouraged. Hereafter, there should be the annual crop surveys/livestock surveys/fisheries surveys which should provide all the related information required at yearly intervals. Other information required at periodical intervals should be fitted into the quinquennial agricultural censuses or sample surveys/livestock census/ fishery census or into the cost of production enquiries. These could be ultimately developed into a system of National Agricultural Surveys. Information on any other items not covered by these surveys should be collected through the National Sample Surveys whenever possible.

In this approach of integrating the various sources of information, it would be important to visualize the role of computers, a modern technology, which has made revolution in data collection. The information on each household, village or a region is not only to be collected but should be appropriately coded and punched on cards to be stored serially with all the other data on computer tapes. By storing such vast amount of data, computer software and hardware can enable one to develop various formats which could be useful for planners and policy-makers.

RESEARCH STATISTICS

Till recently, research work in agriculture was handicapped by the absence of a unified record of experimental data in the country to serve as a reference and guide for future experimentation. IASRI has filled up this gap by preparing the National Index of Field Experiments which is a collection of all relevant details of several thousands of scientifically planned and conducted agricultural experiments in the State and Central institutes. The index contains a wealth of information for the research and development workers in the country and helps them in planning their future programme. The data collected under the project are also being made use of to undertake research studies of agricultural and statistical interest. For example, studies on the effect of irrigation on crop yields and its interaction with other factors such as fertilizers, varieties, seed cultural practices, are in progress.

As already referred to earlier, to meet the needs of the data for planning, etc., the IASRI has developed appropriate statistical methodology for estimation of yield of various crops including condiments and spices and fruit crops. The feasibility of employing sample survey techniques in the fields of animal husbandry and marine fisheries has also been successfully demonstrated for adoption on regular basis by the States.

With the introduction of high yielding varieties during recent years, an acute need was felt for an objective assessment and evaluation of the programme. IASRI initiated sample surveys for assessment of HYV programme in 1968-69 with the objective of collecting reliable data on the extent of cultivation of high yielding varieties, the yield rates of these varieties and comparable estimates of local varieties and extent of adoption of improved agricultural practices recommended for high yielding varieties in these districts. The coverage of the surveys was extended to 88 districts spread over 15 States by 1971-72. The results of these surveys have thrown light not only on the actual achievement under the High Yielding Varieties Programme but also provided a sound and realistic basis for agricultural planning, policy formulation and target setting at the State and national levels. The scope of these surveys, however, needs to be extended to provide information on the local factors and problems contributing to low or high yields in different regions to serve as the basis for accelerating the pace of agricultural development.

The results of agricultural experiments conducted at various research and experimental stations may not be strictly applicable to farmer's fields. Experimentation on cultivators' fields, therefore, is necessary before making recommendations for adoption. Such experiments have to be representative of the range of cultivators conditions, fairly simple and scientifically rigorous so that valid scientific data become available for making recommendations. IASRI has developed suitable designs for such experiments and at present these experiments are being adopted on a large scale all over the country.

Cost of production studies in agriculture present special difficulties as production is largely in the hands of small and illiterate cultivators who do not keep any accounts. IASRI has developed suitable statistical techniques for carrying out large scale studies for estimation of cost of production of principal crops and livestock products. Efforts should be made to evolve suitable techniques for estimation of cost of production of important fruits and vegetables also.

In the field of animal sciences, IASRI has collected and analyzed large bodies of data pertaining to breeding of cattle, buffaloes, sheep and goats. These studies have provided useful information on the inherited economic characteristics which form the basis for preparing efficient breeding plans for the future. The Institute has also been helping research workers with suitable experimental sampling plans and appropriate techniques of analysis of data.

During recent years the demand for fertilizers has been gradually increasing. However, as a result of the recent fuel crisis, serious shortages in supply of fertilizers are being experienced not only in India but in the developed countries in the western world. In this context an important field which needs to be attended to, relates to the optimum use of fertilizers in relation to crop production. The work regarding determination of optimum dosages of fertilizers for different crops in different regions already being done by IASRI needs to be expanded.

Consequent upon the increasing tempo of agricultural and animal husbandry research, new types of statistical problems are being thrown up. To tackle the various research problems, to coordinate and supervise the programmes of statistical surveys and schemes sponsored by IASRI in the various regions of the country and to expand the programmes for training in agricultural statistics, it is necessary that the Institute should be suitably strengthened.

DERIVED STATISTICS AND INDICATORS OF AGRICULTURAL ECONOMY

Several derived statistics and indicators of the agricultural economy are being currently worked out and published by the different Central and State Government Organizations with a view to meeting various requirements such as for studying the trends over time in respect of area, yield, production, productivity and prices, etc. and that for studying the comparative performance of different regions in regard to their agricultural development.

The main derived statistics comprise the different agricultural index number series and growth rates, though a number of other derived statistics are also being made use of for various purposes in the field of agriculture. These index number series have been constructed after making due allowance for changes in the coverage and methods of estimation due to which the absolute figures of area, yield and production, etc. are known to be unsuitable for study of trends over time. We have reviewed the current status of such derived statistics and indicators of the agricultural economy with a view to effecting improvements in their quality. This review has revealed that although a number of improvements have been introduced in regard to agricultural index numbers through implementation in part of the recommendations of the Technical Sub-Committee on Index Numbers set up by the Ministry of Agriculture and Irrigation under the chairmanship of V.G. Panse in 1965, there is still scope for further improvements. Likewise, although the available information in regard to some of the other derived statistics serves the present day needs, improvements need to be affected in the case of others.

Revised series of the all-India index numbers of area under crops, net area sown, cropping intensity, cropping pattern, crop yields, productivity per hectare and agricultural production with the triennium 1993-94 ending as base are being compiled and issued by DES in the light of the recommendations of the Technical Committee. At the State level, index number series are being issued by the State Governments. Revised series on the lines of the all-India series have recently been compiled for all the states and union territories till 1996-97. All-India and State series of index numbers should be published every year with the minimum possible time lag.

In order to provide ready basis for comparison of the productivity of different regions, index numbers of gross agricultural output per hectare and per agricultural worker for different crop regions of the country were issued only once, viz. for the 3 year period ending 1958-59. These index numbers should be issued periodically, say once in every 5 years, in future.

In regard to growth rates in agriculture, State-wise studies carried out by the DES covered the period up to 1998-99 with the base year T.E. 1993-94.

Information regarding crop-wise input-output relationships in relation to size of holdings is needed by research workers, policy makers and administrators. The available data based on farm management surveys are out of date. A Comprehensive Scheme on the Cost of Production of Principal Crops has been sponsored by the DES. Technical coefficients should be worked out on then basis of these data and the results analyzed to provide up-to-date data on input-output relationships.

For the preparation of commodity balance sheets, information is needed not only on the estimates of output as it leaves the farm but also in terms of the processed commodity and the by-products. Thus in the case of paddy, data are needed on the milling ratios to give separate estimates of output of rice and by-products like husk and bran. In the case of sugarcane which is consumed in different forms, e.g. in the form of cane for chewing or juice, raw sugar, refined sugar and *khandsari*, separate estimates of output of these processed forms and cane utilized for each purpose are needed. The available information in this regard for oilseeds, vegetable oils, sugarcane, cotton, jute, milk and other livestock products is mostly based on old surveys and as such has become outdated. Fresh surveys, therefore, need to be conducted in a phased manner so as to make these data up-to-date.

While the estimates of national income including the contribution of agriculture to national income are published by the Central Statistical Organization (CSO), there is need for compilation of National Accounts for Agriculture both by household and commodity disposition. Analysis of this type of data for the agricultural sector should be done by the DES in close collaboration with the CSO.

One of the basic difficulties in the introduction of the crop insurance schemes has been the absence of reliable data on variability in yields of different crops for smaller areas. Now that data on crop yields are available for a long period of time, these should be analyzed periodically to provide a basis for fixation of insurance premia for different crops/ regions.

STRENGTHENING COORDINATION BETWEEN THE MINISTRY OF STATISTICS AND PI AND STATES/UTs

For optimum utilisation of resources, methodological correctness. uniformity of concepts, definitions, etc. and timely compilation and dissemination of quality data, greater co-ordination and co-operation between the centre and the States/UTs is essential. It may be recalled that the Ministry of Statistics and PI used to organise a Conference of Central and State Statistical Organisations once in every two years. The last such conference was held in 1992 after which only regional conferences/ meetings with the States/UTs were organised by the Ministry of Statistics and PI. The need for such a co-ordinating/participatory mechanism at the regional level has been actually felt and has been echoing in the statistical community in recent years. Some States have already expressed their desire for an increased participation in the national statistical system, especially in evolving suitable methodologies for data gaps in different sectors, data processing, joint fieldwork and conduct of regular training programmes. Maharashtra has, for example, expressed the desire for greater centralised control of Ministry of Statistics and PI on the data collecting agencies for uniformity in concepts, definition, coverage and improvement in the quality of the fieldwork. Pondichery has likewise suggested a technical wing for standardisation of definitions, preparation of technical studies, etc. Other states have also desired to get help and participation from the centre.

Taking these factors and the strategic role that needs to be played by the Ministry of Statistics and PI into consideration. It is desired that States/UTs may give their views/suggestions on the following issues:

- the kind of mechanism required to have better coordination between Centre and States/UTs
- revival of the Conference of Central and State Statistial Organisations as organised in the past
- revival of standing committees/working groups on technical matters between centre and states

States Statistical Service and Exchange of Central and State Statistical Cadres

In most of the States there is no organised cadre for statistical personnel and the DESs have little control over the vertical and horizontal mobility of the statistical personnel across State Departments. This has its impact on the continuity of work and motivation of the personnel, especially since statistical activities are manpower intensive and statistical expertise cannot be acquired overnight without intensive training and exposure. Some of the States are seized of the problem and it was felt necessary that an organised State Statistical Cadre be formed in the States, say, on the line similar to the Indian Statistial Service at the Centre. Even in the Centre, there are some statistical posts that are operating in isolation with no opportunities for horizontal mobility. And this might affect adversely the motivation and morale of the statistical machinery. Thus the States/UTs/Central Ministries may give their views on:

(i) need for an organised State Statistical Cadre comprising all statistical posts in the States
(ii) integration of all Group A posts of the central Ministries carrying out statistical activities into the Indian Statistical Service
(iii) interaction and participation of Central and State Statistical Cadres on critical posts so as to have a wholesome opportunity of exchange experiences for improvement of the overall statistical system

Human Resource Development and Training

In some states about 90% of the staff were recruited before 1970 and in most of the cases it was not possible to provide them with required training on recent development in statistical techniques and computer orientation. Therefore regular training and refresher programmes need to be evolved at National as well as State level for statistical personnel. The State/UT authority might look into the feasibility of performing this role. They may also give their views on the requirement in this regard from the Ministry of Statistics and PI. In order to conduct regular training programmes for the Central and State statistical personnel, the need for establishing a national training and research institute may be commented upon.

Participation of States in Conducting Censuses

A number of censuses are being conducted in the country like Agriculture Census, Livestock Census. Population Census, Economic Census, etc. The need for conducting Censuses to collect statistics required for micro level planning and inter-spatial and inter-temporal statistical analysis from the information generated from these Censuses cannot be over emphasised. In order to achieve this goal, timely generation of reliable data is a prerequisite. However, some States/UTs have faced certain difficulties while conducting these censuses. States/UTs may therefore give their views on the type of problems they generally face while conducting these censuses and suggestions for improving the situation.

Improvement of Information-flow from Primary Level

The recent democratic decentralisation process initiated by the 73rd and 74th amendments give greater responsibilities and powers to the Panchayats and Nagar Palikas as the third tier of governance. This affords a new window of opportunity for local planning, effective implementation and monitoring of various social and economic development programmes in the country. Micro level planning needs in the context of decentralisation necessitate maintenance of decentralised database on population size and its characteristics apart from information on some basic indicators. It requires systematically building Local Area Statistical database on some core statistics from smallest localised statutory units, viz. the Panchayats and the Nagar Palikas. Keeping this purpose in mind, action is to be taken for development of basic data sets required at the village/block/district level. The scope of decentralised planning has more or less been limited to coordination and collection of local level statistics and administrative data. The main problem with administrative data is their poor quality, often caused by non-uniformity of concepts, definitions and procedures in different states and areas. On the other hand, the data from population censuses become available only after considerable time lags. Since the resources availble at the local statistical level are limited (if not non-existent), there is a need to enhance it for fortifying the decentralised planning machinery. in order to make the system responsive and effective to these needs, the existing Block and District level statistial set up will need to be suitably upgraded with apporpirate infrastructural facilities. The Data Bank operations can also be automated at the Block level with inter-networking within the State level institutions. States/UTs may like to suggest the feasible mechanism for establishing this.

Timely Release of State-Sample Data of NSS Surveys

Considerable resources are expended by the States/UTs in the annual NSSO Rounds and it is observed that there is considerable delay in data processing and subsequently in final outputs being ready for release. Delays in data processing by the States/UTs negate the huge effort put in data collection in the field. As an illustration, as far as the 50th round (1993-94) is concerned, even after 7 years, only 4 States have either released the report of the state sample data or have completed the report preparation. Data processing is still in progress in most of the states. For the 54th Round (Jan-June, 98), only one State has completed the data processing.

There is a need, therefore, to reduce the time lag in bringing out the survey results so that the repots/results can be used for planning and other micro-analytical purposes. Effects have to be made towards cutting down the inordinate dealy in data processing and bringing out the reports on the state sample within a stipulated time frame, say, within one year of completion of the survey. States/UTs may identify the problems faced by them in processing the data, and give their views/suggestions on the steps to be taken to ensure supply of state sample data as per the stipulated time frame. Centre may like to provide software/training available with them for this purpose.

SOCIO-ECONOMIC STATISTICS

General Population Characteristics

Basic Population Related Statistics at the Local Area Level

The democratic decentralisation process initiated by the 73rd and 74th amendments, gives greater responsibilities and powers to the Panchayats and Nagar Palikas as the third tier of governance offers a new window of opportunity for local planning, effective implementation and monitoring of various social and economic development programmes in the country. Micro level planning necessitates maintenance of decentralised database on population size and its characteristics apart from information on some basic indicators. It requires systematically building statistical database on some core statistics from smallest localised statutory units viz. the Panchayats and the Nagar Palikas. The following steps in this direction may be deliberated upon:

- Identify a minimum list of population characteristics and other indicators, which need to be maintained at the Panchayat level and develop a mechanism to integrate data available from different sources. The periodicity of updating of each variable may be decided depending upon its relevance, viz. monthly, quarterly, annually etc. It should be the responsibility of the local bodies to update these characteristics as per the specified periodicity. A system to verify the information on a minimal sample basis should also be evolved to ensure the quality of data.

• For maintaining this list a copy of the abridged house-list which gives the building number, census house number, use of census house, and the name of the head of the household and other details available in the abridged house-list along with national map prepared for 2001 census may be made available at village Panchayat to serve as the basis for local area planning as also for periodic updating.

• The basic list including house list available with the Panchayats be permitted for sale at a prescribed price to the users. The revenue thus generated may be made available to the Panchayats to enable them to raise funds for developmental works and to ensure their involvement in the exercise. Legislative provisions needed to carry out the above exercise may be enacted.

• The basic information thus collected should be displayed prominently on a black board in the Panchayat Office to serve important purpose of development activities at that level.

• A suitable mechanism by involving Panchayats, the state statistical agencies, district and state administration, and lastly the Central Government may be evolved for upward movement of this core statistics to build statistics at the block, district, state and national levels on a periodical basis with the least time lag.

In order to implement the above scheme of work, combined efforts of the agencies in the Central Government (Ministry of Home Affairs, Ministry of Health and Family Welfare, Ministry of Rural Development and Ministry of Statistics and PI), State Governments (Administrative Wings, Planning Departments and DESs, Local Affairs Departments) and Local Bodies are needed. Small Committee of Experts comprising representatives from the above agencies may look into the feasibility of this project.

Development of Unique Geo-Codes for Districts, Blocks and Villages

There is an increasing demand for timely and reliable data on socio-economic sector at Local Area Level. Information about different sectors is generated by different agencies. It is necessary to integrate them uniformly and published the same at the Local Area Level. Towards this end, attempts should be made to develop uniform area codes for districts, blocks and villages at the national level, which should facilitate identification of every village and urban blocks. These codes should include, as a part, geo-codes necessary, which should be sufficient to locate them in a map. Similarly, all houses in the country should be given a unique permanent number, which should be used by all agencies, government or non-government; and should not be changed without the authorisation of appropriate authority. The numbering system should be flexible enough to accommodate additional numbers for new houses.

All the developed countries and some developing countries, are providing each adult individual citizen of the country a social security number, which is also an identity number and is being used for purposes of revenue collection, taxation, analysis of social statistics, crime, commerce etc. With the advancement of computer technology, it is possible to develop within the next 3–5 years a system of providing social security number for all individuals in the country. The Election Commission has been issuing photo identity cards and numbering of electorates and with a slight modification of the same system, a social security number or a citizen identification number can be provided to each citizen of the country.

Health and Family Welfare Statistics

Strengthening of Civil Registration System and Sample Registration System

The health of the citizens is a matter of serious national concern. A healthy population is a development goal by itself though it is an important ingredient for overall social and economic development. In India, though the life expectancy at birth has significantly increased, the morbidity levels are quite high and the levels on nutritional deficiency and anaemia remain also quite high. The health statistics yield indicators for regular and systematic assessment of the health status of the population, on the efficacy and impact of various health policies, strategies and programmes implemented and if needed redesign the programmes at the local level. Health related data for any population should provide insights in the following three areas.
- State of health of the population (morbidity and mortality),
- factors influencing the health of the population (socio-economic conditions), and
- services rendered for controlling the factors (preventive services) and for treating health ailments (curative and rehabilitative).

At present estimates of birth rate, death rate, infant mortality rate and other related fertility and mortality indicators are available only at State level through Sample Registration System (SRS). There is a strong demand and need to generate these rats at district and below district levels. With the present sample size of SRS, it may not be possible to generate district level estimates. Even the estimates of infant mortality rate for small States/UTs are not reliable due to the small sample size. The Civil Registration System (CRS), which is capable of providing not only district but also lower level vital rates, is deficient in most of the

States/UTs. In spite of demands for publication of absolute number of births, deaths, infant deaths etc. from SRS, such figures are not being published.

Due to non-availability of vital rates at lower levels, proper monitoring of various health and family welfare programmes is not possible: The future planning at district level becomes deficient due to non-availability of these data. Thus, the registration of births and deaths should be made the responsibility of the Panchayats in rural areas and the municipal bodies in the urban areas by necessary legislation, if required. The Panchayats should register all births within 14 days and all deaths within a week. It should also be made obligatory and not mandatory, for the Panchayats to record all marriages including the age at marriage of the bride and the bridegroom though the rituals may be performed according to the local customs or religion.

Strengthening the Health Management Information System

Health Management Information System (HMIS) introduced in the country on a trial basis has a good potential for improving the efficacy of the health system but has not succeeded completely in its objectives due to various reasons. The system should be modified suitably on the basis of the past experience and should be strengthened. As extensive data are being collected by various agencies and compiled, there exist various problems, deficiencies and gaps. The data reported from the states suffer from deficiencies such as non-reporting, under-reporting, variable coverage from month to month hence, not amenable to statistical analysis. In order to improve the HMIS, it is suggested to:

- Systematic steps should be taken to rationalise and minimise the number of records and registers maintained by the peripheral health workers viz. ANMs, public health inspectors, etc. so that the paper work gets reduced to the essential minimum with relevant quality standard. Identify minimum data set on which data from grass root levels should be regularly collected along with their periodicity.
- There is need for computerisation of the administrative records of all specialised hospitals and general-purpose hospitals both in public and private sectors. Incorporate ICD-10 Coding System for Medical Records for generating morbidity/mortality data.
- Evolving a mechanism to collect the data at the grass root level and its upward movement to the district, state and the national level. For doing this, it is imperative to modernise the methods of data collection, transmission, and processing. Integration and reinforcement of the existing statistical set-up at the District. State and Central level health agencies are essential to have timely and reliable health statistics. There should be separate staff at District Statistical Office for the maintenance of health information.
- The system needs to be revamped and reinforced to include the information from the private sector health facilities integrated

approach for capturing statistics on health and Indian System of Medicines and Homeopathy.

Improving Statistics on Causes of Deaths and Maternal Mortality Rate at Disaggregated Levels

At present, survey on causes of deaths being conducted by the Office of RGI provides some data on causes of deaths. However, because of laymen reporting of causes of deaths and limited sample size, the quality of data from this survey is very poor. Due to this, even there is no estimate of Maternal Mortality Rate (MMR) available for the country and States. The National Family Health Survey (NFHS) conducted during 1992-93 provided estimates of MMR but only at the national level. The present surveys on the subject are, therefore, unable to meet the data requirements at the district and below and become a serious handicap in planning the preventive action at these levels. It is, therefore, suggested that:

- There should be a procedure for medical certification of the cause of death at least on a sample basis throughout the country regularly, in order to have a better understanding of causes/factors underlying the deaths in the country.
- There should be a system for immediate reporting of deaths due to certain diseases, like cholera, polio, malaria, diphtheria etc. to take immediate preventive and curative action.
- Morbidity Surveys using a household approach should be conducted at regular intervals.
- Social consumption/expenditure incurred on medical treatment or availing health facilities should be captured more comprehensively from the NSS's Consumer Expenditure Surveys The pooling of State sample may also be done to get better and reliable estimate even at district level.
- The statistical system in all hospitals and dispensaries should include certain basic information on each patient and they should furnish certain basic information on the inpatient and outpatient statistics to the statistical system.

Frame of Medical Practitioners, Hospitals, etc.—Need for Legislation

Presently health statistics is based on the data mainly coming out as an offshoot of the administrative data collection and compiled in the Government health sector only. In the last few years, the Private Sector has entered in a big way in providing health facilities, particularly in the urban areas and is contributing significantly in meeting the basic health facilities and other specialised medication and diagnostic services. However, there is no systematic way to tap any information arising out of these private health centres. There is no body with whom they are required to register and therefore, there is no information on even the numbers of these health facilities in a given area. There is need to have an enabling legislation making it compulsory registration for setting up specific types of health facility with a statutory body and also encourage these agencies to provide data necessary for policy initiatives and interventions.

Information on all the hospitals, medical practitioners of various systems, allopathic, homeopathy, ayurveda, siddha, etc. should be compiled and a directory of institutions and personnel made available at the district level with their locations identified by the geo-codes. These directories should be updated every two years. The basic information with these agencies could be integrated with the existing HMIS for building up an improved database on health services.

Education Statistics

Improving the Availability of Educational Statistics, its Quality and Timeliness

The system of collection and compilation of educational statistics in India needs a lot of improvement in order to become capable of providing sufficiently reliable statistics on various essential items without much time lag. At present, the problems faced by the system that have led to deterioration in the quality of educational statistics, are broadly as follows:

* Data gaps-non-availability of data on some important items;
* Poor reliability of data-lack of consistency between data on the same items obtained from different sources;
* Time lag-delays in making the statistics available to users;
* Weak infrastructure, inadequate staff and equipment for collection and processing of data at all levels;
* Lack of co-ordination between different data collection agencies; and
* Low priority given to educational statistics.

Present system of collection of educational statistics suffers from non-availability of information about un-recognised institutions and their activities, age-grade matrix of students, children not attending school, expenditure and finances of private institutions, detailed information about the teachers, e.g. qualification, age, sex, subject taught etc. The record keeping in the schools is very poor which could be due to non-availability of relevant registers, untrained teachers to maintain them, lack of supervision etc. Further, as the information is to be collected from a large number of schools located all over the country, the availability of information is generally delayed and remain mostly incomplete, apart from its poor quality. There are multiple agencies collecting information directly from the schools, colleges and Universities, which prescribe different formats and time for supply of information and thus create confusion. In this background, the following suggestions are made for filling the data gaps, improving the quality and timeliness of data:

- The un-recognised schools/institutions are not covered in the official statistics collected at present, as the Department of Education has no control on such institutions. However, since educational statistics remain incomplete without the statistics of such institutions, some minimum data on enrolment and teachers should be collected from them annually along with other educational data. Necessary legal provision should be made to make it mandatory for all such institutions to supply the needed data to Education Department.
- At present, data on age of primary students is collected for DPEP districts under EMIS established for DPEP, but the quality of data is generally poor. It is suggested that data on expenditure incurred by parents and guardians on education should be collected through social consumption surveys conducted by NSSO once in 5 years. The data on income and expenditure of private institutions should be collected through sample surveys of such institutions once in 5 years.
- At present, only meagre data is collected on teachers, which gives information only on number of teachers by sex and SC/ST, for different types of institutions. It is suggested that the questionnaire should have provision for collecting data on individual teachers (their age, sex, qualifications, subjects taught etc.) so that detailed information on teachers can be made available on distribution of teachers by age, sex, qualifications, etc.
- Household data on children attending or not attending school should be collected annually from the village education register, as a part of micro-planning exercise. The school enrolment data should be compared with the data on school attendance supplied by households at the village level itself to remove discrepancies.
- The main results of large-scale surveys that provide educational data, such as those conducted by NCERT and NSSO should be available in published form within a year of the data of reference and the detailed results within 2 years.
- All-India Educational Surveys by NCERT should be regularly conducted once in 5 years.

Development of Database of Institutions and Computerisation of Data

India has developed a large infrastructure in the field of education since independence. As per 1997-98, there were 6,11,000 primary schools, 1,86,000 upper primary schools, 76,000 high schools, 26,000 higher secondary/intermediate colleges, 7199 art, science, commerce colleges, 458 engineering colleges, 769 medical colleges and over 125 Universities/ Deemed universities. In India more than one sixth of its population is engaged in the pursuit and promotion of education when we take into account 180 million students, 4.5 million teachers, one million educational institutions. Therefore, there is a need to develop a database of these institutions preferably at each district of the country. Each institution should be assigned a unique code, which will facilitate its identification and retrieval of information. This will help in retrieving the data not only for the district as a whole, but for blocks, clusters of villages and for individual schools. When computerisation of data is undertaken in all the districts and use of Internet for regular flow of data from district to state and from district/state to national level is made effectively, this will reduce the time-lag automatically, but also do away with the system of supplying state level compiled statistics on forms such as ES1, ES2, etc., which are used at present.

Infrastructure for Collection of Educational Statistics

The entire infrastructure for collection of educational statistics, from the national level down to the district and block levels is quite weak and needs substantial inputs, both financial and manpower, for upgrading the quality and coverage of educational statistics. Apart from improvements desired at the central level the infrastructure at the States and districts also needs to be strengthened by redeploying the existing resources of staff, computers and other facilities. It is suggested that invariably, an Educational Statistics Unit should be created in all the States at the district level on the pattern of the DPEP to take the role of meeting the data requirements in the field of education upto the district level. The agencies involved in the states and the districts should take full advantage of the Information Technology in the data compilation and analysis to improve the timeliness, validity and reliability of data. Adequate funds should be provided to them to purchase required hardware and software and necessary connectivity for transmission of information should be provided. For rural areas, a village-based data system should be developed in which all educational facilities existing in the village and data on non-school going children, literacy etc. should be compiled and maintained in a Village Education Register.

Labour and Employment Statistics

Response, Quality, Availability and Timeliness of Labour Statistics

The labour statistics is collected under various statutory provisions like Factory Act, Payment of Wages Act, Minimum Wages Act, Plantations Labour Act, Motor Transport Workers Act, Shops and Commercial Establishment Act, Industrial Employment (Standing Orders) Act, Workmen's Compensation Act, Maternity Benefit Act, Trade Unions Act, Industry disputes Act, Collection of Statistics Act, the Employment Exchanges (compulsory notification of vacancies) Act, etc. On voluntary basis, the statistics is also collected in respect of industrial dispute, closures, layoffs and retrenchment. In addition, surveys/studies are also conducted to assess the working condition of labour, minimum wages, occupational wages, rural labour enquiry, Working Class Family Income and Expenditure, Annual Survey of Industries, etc.

The Labour Statistics suffers from poor response, poor quality and time lag in submission of returns, which leads to delay in submission of consolidated information to the Labour Bureau from the States. Time lag has been of the order of upto 16 months and in certain cases returns have not been submitted to the Labour Bureau for years together. Further, the information received in the Bureau is of poor quality, as the State Government staff is not properly trained for collection and compilation of statistics. The Labour Bureau faces a series of problems, in the process the data quality suffers greatly. The following suggestions are given for improving the situation:

- The Labour Bureau should strengthen its on-going programme for training of staff both from the State Government as well as from the agencies receiving the return. The States may also start such training programmes for staff of agencies supplying information/returns to them.
- The industrial and other establishments are presently required to submit a large number of Returns statutory/non-statutory to the Central and State Governments under provisions of various Labour Enactments. This becomes a major irritant in the collection of data, as it requires huge resources on the part of the establishment. The returns are sometimes complicated, thus there is need to simplify and consolidate various returns. In the liberalized economic environment, this will be a forward step and will find great favour from the industry.
- A number of concepts have been defined differently under different labour enactments. To quote a few examples like 'family', 'wages' are defined differently in different Acts. This leads to confusion among the data users and also data comparability is affected. For the sake of uniformity in the collection and dissemination of labour statistics, it is necessary that variety of definitions for a single concept be avoided. Ministry of Labour in consultation with the States may identify such differences and arrive at uniform definition on various concepts, if necessary, amendments in the labour enactments may be made to bring about the uniformity.
- A regular system of meeting with business/manufacturers associations may be taken up to orient them about the returns to be submitted under various statutory and other provisions. As most of the labour statistics is collected, as per Statutory Acts, non-submission of returns by agencies on time should be treated as per law.

Use of IT for Networking and Creation of Data Bank on Labour Statistics

There is a need for labour networking so that online data is available by connecting Labour Bureau not only with the various Divisions of Ministry of Labour and LEM Division of the Planning Commission but also with the Labour Departments of the State Governments. Since a number of

States have already computerized their data, it is necessary to make the Bureau a nodal agency to bring into the main networking of States and other organizations engaged in labour research/compilation of statistics. Ministry of Labour in consultation with the States may decide to systematically plan and implement the whole idea of creating a network— LABOURNET and data bank. All Employment Exchanges in the country should also be computerised and linked through the network to share the vacancies and employment seekers.

Environment Statistics

Co-ordination Among the Data, Producers and Users of Environment Statistics

Environment Statistics is a newly emerging area of statistical discipline and with the worldwide concern for environment protection and sustainable development, the demand of the data on environmental variables has been growing rapidly. Data on many issues are either not being presently captured or only partially available. There is need to strengthen the statistical machinery of the agencies responsible for collecting information on air pollution, water pollution, deforestation, soil degradation and environment etc. The following suggestions are given for its improvement:

To assess the data needs on environment, its availability and deficiencies, the coordination with various agencies is desirable. The CSO at the Centre and the DESs in the States should coordinate with the agencies producing environment statistics on the well recognised parameters, viz. Flora, Fauna, Atmosphere, Water, Land/Soil and Human settlements. Presently there is no coordinating agency at States, Therefore, to improve the collection, compilation and dissemination of Environmental Statistics, a separate Cell may be created in each State Directorate of Economics and Statistics.

Natural Resource Accounting

The United Nations System of National Accounts, 1993 has recommended the preparation of natural resource accounting as the satellite accounts for measuring the environmental damages consequence of the developmental activities. When a system for data collection is established and adequate data is made available for compiling the integrated Green GDP, the satellite accounts should be compiled even by the States.

Gender Statistics

The States should make suitable arrangement for collection of gender-based information in respect of all socio-economic variables. In addition, information on crime, atrocities against women, violation of rights particularly of women etc. needs to be compiled and published periodically.

Poverty and Levels of Living

Considerable work on assessment of levels of living of the population has been made by the Consumer Expenditure Surveys conducted by NSSO and by the National Accounts System. Estimates on levels of poverty obtained from these two sources vary considerably. The following suggestions are given for improving the estimation of poverty and levels of living:

- An appropriate methodology needs to be evolved for conducting household income surveys in India. Pilot studies should be continued till an appropriate methodology is evolved. Attempts should also be made to collect longitudinal data on household income, consumption and other indicators of level of living.
- The results of an on-going pilot survey on reference period should be utilised to decide whether 'the last week' should be chosen as the reference period in place of 'the last month', which has been used for more than four decades. Data collected in recent NSS rounds show that if 'last week' was chosen in place of 'last month'; NSS estimates would move closer to NAS estimates.
- There is urgent need to pool the results of the Central and State samples of NSS to generate region-specific estimates, with the aim to arrive at district level estimates using small area estimation techniques.
- To provide the basis for government subsidies and support to the poor, identification of below poverty line should be done utilising easily ascertainable/verifiable criteria covering different facets of level of living. The items of information relate to (i) incidence of starvation (e.g. Whether members of the household get two square meals a day throughout the year) housing conditions, (iii) stocks of clothing and warm clothing, bedding and footwear (e.g. whether each female member has two saris/garments) (iv) whether young children are going to school, (v) literacy and education of earning members. (vi) occupations of earners (e.g. whether any members is engaged in begging) and unemployment and (vii) income generating assets etc.

30

World Agricultural Statistics

GENERAL

General world agricultural statistics are available in the following publications:

I. Statistical Yearbook—Issued by the United Nations
II. Production, Trade Yearbooks Issued by the Food and Agriculture Organisation (FAO)
III. Yearbook of Forest Products Statistics Organization of the United Nations.
IV. United States Department of Agriculture, (USA)
V. The State of Food and Agriculture, FAO.
VI. World Economic Survey—Issued by the United Nations
VII. Economic Survey of Asia and the Far East—Issued by the United Nations
VIII. Monthly Bulletin of Statistics—Issued by the United Nations.
IX. World Bank.
X. Other International Agencies.

UNITED NATIONS STATISTICAL YEARBOOK

This publication is intended to continue the work of the Statistical Yearbook of the League of Nations in providing a convenient and comprehensive summary of international statistics. The scope of this volume is somewhat broader than the League of Nations Statistical Yearbook which ceased publication in 1945. The aim of this book is to show for the various countries over the period covered (generally 1978-1979 in the 1980 issue), continuous time series which are as nearly comparable internationally as the available statistics permit. Where necessary, any lack of comparability in the data is indicated in the notes.

The statistics included in this publication in the sphere of agriculture are index numbers of agriculture production, production of wheat, rice, rye, maize, barley, oats, groundnuts, cottonseed, linseed, soyabeans, potatoes, tea, coffee, cotton, wool and milk. It also gives figures of livestock population, production of roundwood and natural rubber, fish catches, number of whales caught and oil produced. Data regarding production of meat, butter, cheese and sugar; exports of palm and palm oil, palm kernels from important producing countries are also given.

Except where otherwise stated, the data for the agricultural tables are furnished by the Food and Agriculture Organization of the United Nations (FAO).

A short note explaining the scope and nature of the figures shown usually accompanies the tables. In some instances, it has been thought desirable to give more lengthy explanatory notes at the beginning of a chapter. In using and interpreting the data given in the various tables, the notes referred to above should be carefully read.

FOOD AND AGRICULTURE ORGANISATION (FAO)

Production Yearbook

This book contains figures of total area, classified into land area, agricultural area (arable land and land under tree crops, permanent meadows and pastures), forested land, area unused but potentially productive, built-in area, wasteland and other areas for each country.

A table giving figures of irrigated arable land and land under tree crops is included in the yearbook. Unless otherwise indicated, data related to arable land and land under tree crops receiving the necessary water supply, in addition to precipitation, by artificial irrigation schemes, thus excluding land receiving water by uncontrolled floods and irrigated permanent meadows and pastures. Definitions, wherever possible, are given in the footnotes. In general, figures refer to irrigable land rather than to land actually cultivated under irrigation in any particular year, and they cover land irrigated by canals, tanks, wells, artesan bores and sprinklers, either all the year round or only during the dry season. These figures are not comparable internationally since definitions of 'irrigated land' vary widely from country to country.

The yearbook also furnishes country-wise figures of total population, agricultural population and population engaged in agricultural occupations (for both sexes and for males separately). The agricultural population is generally defined as all persons who depend upon agriculture includes all economically active persons engaged principally in agriculture and their non-working dependents. The accuracy of data is highly variable. In several areas, no comprehensive and reasonably reliable population count has been made recently and the estimates given for them are largely conjectural. In view of the fact that for several areas of the world, the size of the population is unknown or uncertain, the regional and the world totals must be regarded as approximate estimates only. The estimates relate to present boundaries except when otherwise noted.

Detailed figures of area, production and yield per hectare of various crops are given. The crops dealt with are wheat, rye, oats, mixed grain, millet and sorghum, rice (paddy), sugarcane, sugar, sugar beets, centrifugal sugar (raw value) and non-centrifugal cane sugar, potatoes, sweet potatoes and yarns, cassava, onions, tomatoes, dry beans, dry peas, broad beans, chick peas, lentils, apples, pears, plums and prunes, cherries peaches, apricots, grapes, raisins, citrus fruit, dates, figs, bananas, pineapples, olive and olive oil, palm kernels and palm oil, soyabeans, groundnuts, cottonseed, linseed, rapeseed, sesame seed, sunflower seed, copra, hard fibres, natural rubber, etc.

It also furnishes livestock numbers by major species, ie. horses, mules, asses, cattle, pigs, sheep, goats, buffaloes, camels and poultry and production of meat (beef and veal, pork, mutton and lamb), milk, butter, cheese, condensed and evaporated milk, dried milk, wool, etc. Data on milk yield, gross food supplies, food supplies for direct human consumption and net food supply per person are also available. The data on food supply are based on national balance sheets, a statistical method which starts from the data of total food production, trade and movement in stocks; makes appropriate deductions for the amounts used for the animal feed, seed and non-food purposes; and so arrives at the estimated quantity of food and nutrient supplies available at the retail level for a given yearly period, usually July to June. These food balance sheets are, however, subject to certain limitations which are enumerated in the notes given for respective tables in the Yearbook.

This publication also contains data on production and consumption of fertilizers and number of tractors (crawler and wheel) used in agriculture and for all purposes. Statistics of prices of various crops and livestock products are given in detail. The type of price given in each case is indicated in the footnote to the tables. Index numbers of general and agricultural wholesale prices, cost of living and retail food prices, prices paid and received by the farmers, etc. Besides, index numbers of agricultural production are also given.

Except when otherwise stated, the data are based on figures supplied by Governments through questionnaires, or taken from publications and reports to the UN and to the FAO. When official figures are not available, data taken from the reliable unofficial sources are used.

Area and crop production statistics for the Northern Hemisphere pertain generally to the harvests of the spring, summer and fall of the year stated, but for the more southernly regions of this Hemisphere, they represent harvests continuing into the early part of the following year; for the Southern Hemisphere, these data relate to the crops harvested in the later part of the year indicated and the first half of the following year. In accordance with this definition the split year annotation has been omitted from the table. Figures for crop areas refer generally to harvested areas. Position of Indian Agriculture in the World can be computed from this publication (Table 30.1).

Table 30.1: India's Position in World Agriculture-1997

Item	India	World	India's Share%	Rank	Next to
1. AREA(million ha.)**					
Total area	329	13387	2.4	Seventh	Canada, U.S.A, China, Brazil, Australia, Russian-Fed
Land Area	297	13048	2.3	Seventh	U.S.A, China, Canada, Brazil, Australia, Russian-Fed
Arable land	163F	1382	11.8	Second	U.S.A
Irrigated area	57F	242	23.6	First	
2. POPULATION (million)					
Total	960	5849	16.4	Second	China
Agriculture	541	2564	21.1	Second	China
3. ECONOMICALLY ACTIVE POPULATION (million)					
Total	420	2827	14.9	Second	China
Agriculture	256	1302	19.3	Second	China
4. CROP PRODUCTION (million tonnes)					
Cereals	223	2096	10.6	Third	China, USA
Wheat	69*	610	11.3	Second	China
Rice	123*	573	21.5	Second	China
Coarse grains	31	914	3.5	Fifth	USA, China, Brazil, Russian, Fed
Potatoes	19F	295	6.5	Sixth	China, Russian-Fed, Poland, USA, Ukraine
Total pulses	15	58	25.9	First	
Groundnut	8*	30	26.7	Second	China
Tobacco leaves	0.56F	8.24	6.8	Third	China, USA
Rapeseed	7	35	20.0	Second	China
Coffee (green)	0.21*	5.56	3.8	Ninth	Brazil, Colombia, Indonesia, Mexico, Ethopia, Uganda, Vietnam, Gautemala
Sugarcane	265	1241	21.4	Second	Brazil
Tea	0.79F	2.73	28.9	First	
Jute & Allied Fibres	1.72F	3.27	52.6	First	
Cotton(lint)	2.9*	19.7	14.5	Third	USA, China

Table 30.1: India's Position in World Agriculture-1997 (Contd.)

Item	India	World	India's Share%	Rank	Next to
5. LIVESTOCK NUMBERS (million head)					
Cattle	209	1334	15.7	First	
Buffaloes	92*	167	55.1	First	
Camels	1.52F	1950	7.8	Third	Somalia, Sudan
Sheep	56*	1064	5.3	Third	Australia, China
Goats	121*	703	17.2	Second	China
Chicken	343*	13413	2.6	Seventh	China, USA, Brazil, Russian-Fed, Mexico, Indonesia
6. IMPLEMENTS ('000 numbers)**					
Tractors-in-use	1400F	26345	5.3	Fourth	USA, Japan, Italy
"7. VEGETABLES, FRUITS, MILK and EGGS (million tonnes)"					
Vegetables (including Melon)	54.97F	595.56	9.2	Second	China
Fruits (excluding Melon)	37.13F	429.45	8.6	Third	China, Brazil
Milk	72	546.64*	13.2	First	
Eggs	1.61*	51.76	3.1	Fifth	China, USA, Japan, Russian Fed

Note :   F   FAO estimate
　　　　　*   Unofficial Figure
　　　　　** Figures relate to 1996
Source :   1   FAO Production Year Book 1997
　　　　　2   Agricultural Statistics at a Glance, 2000, Directorate of Economics and Statistics, Ministry of Agriculture, Government of India."

Trade Year Book

This book furnishes up-to-date trade statistics in food and agricultural commodities, which are enumerated below:

Cereal and Cereal Preparations—Wheat, wheat flour, rye, barley, oats, maize, rice, sorghum, millets and other cereals.

Fruits—Oranges and tangerines, other citrus fruit, bananas, apples, grapes, pears, coconuts, raisins, currants and dates;

Vegetables—Potatoes and onions;

Sugar—Sugar;

Coffee, etc.—Coffee, tea, pepper, hops, cocoa beans;

Feeding Stuff for Animals—Oilseeds, cakes and meal;

Beverage and Tobacco—Wine, tobacco;

Oilseeds and Nuts—Groundnuts, copra, palm, kernels, soyabeans, linsead, cottonseed, castor beans, rapeseed and mustard seed, sesame.

Vegetable Oils—Linseed oil, soyabean oil, cottonseed oil, groundnut oil, olive oil, palm oil, coconut oil, palm-kernel oil, sunflower-seed oil, castor oil;

Livestock—Cattle, pigs;

Livestock and Dairy Products—Fresh meat, prepared and canned meat, milk, butter, cheese, eggs, liquid and powdered eggs;

Fibres—Cotton, silk, wool, jute, flax, hemp, sisal and other agave fibres;

Rubber—Natural rubber.

The trade figures relate generally to calender year except when otherwise stated.

The statistics furnished are based on official figures obtained either from questionnaires or from Government publications. Where such statistics are not available, estimates have been framed. Limitations as to the general comparability of the data, method used to secure fairly comparable statistical treatment for individual commodities, and problems resulting from changes in customs territory are given in the general notes and in the commodity and country notes given in the publication.

Yearbook of Forest Products Statistics

The Yearbook of Forest Products Statistics gives a review of the salient features of the world situation during the year under review regarding removals of roundwood; world trade in wood products; production and trade of sawnwood, plywood and pulp; and teak logs. The yearbook also furnishes comprehensive world statistics of total removals of coniferous and broad-leaved wood classified into industrial wood (sawlogs, veneer logs and logs for sleepers; pulpwood and pitprops; other industrial wood) and fuelwood. Statistics of exports by destination and imports by origin of roundwood classified into sawlogs and veneer logs, pulpwood and pitprops are reported for two years.

Statistics of processed wood given in the yearbook include production, imports, stocks and apparent consumption of coniferous and broad-leaved sawnwood, plywood and sleepers. Figures of production, consumption, exports and imports of wood pulp are reported in detail. Data on production of pulp products and world trade in forest products, per capita consumption of forest products and land area and area under forests are also given in details.

Figures in this publication, as in other FAO publications, are those supplied by reporting Governments. World and regional tables include estimates for non-reporting countries.

Yearbook of Fishery Statistics

The FAO Yearbook of Fisheries Statistics gives the available recorded and estimated figures of catch and landings in selected countries by species groups. The values and quantities of landings, disposition, preserved and processed commodities are also given. Statistics on production by countries and by-products are also given in details. National statistical tables on fishing craft, broken down by categories characteristic of each country, are also given separately. Besides, data on catch of whales, production of whale oil, sperm oil, whale liver, etc. are also available in details.

Food Outlook

The FAO's bi-monthly Food Outlook reviews the world situation on cereal (including rice), supply and demand, current production and prospects, trade, carryover stock, fertiliser data, export prices and freight rates. The bi-monthly also covers oilcrops, pulses, sugar and meat. FAO also prepares background documents for the meetings of the Intergovernmental Groups on Rice, Coarsegrains, Tea and Tropical Horticultural Products. These provide useful current information, mostly at the regional and global levels. Similarly the annual Commodity Market Review (CMR) provides economic data for the past few years with reasons for the variation and changes as well as some forecasts. The CMR covers many commodities such as cereals, rice, pulses, oilseeds, oils and oilmeals, beverages, sugar, bananas and citrus, tea, livestock and milk products, agricultural raw materials such as natural rubber, cotton, jute fishery and forestry products. FAO also prepares periodically medium term Projections for Agricultural Commodities. Projections for the period 1997-2005 have just been finalized. All these publications can serve as a useful source of market intelligence. Now most of the material is also available on the Internet as part of the FAO World Wide Web. The FAO Global Information and Early Warning Service had already been approached to include in their periodicals mailing list, the name of the Assistant Director, Trade and Business Section, DAPO, MAOI.

The State of Food and Agriculture

This annual publication on the 'State of Food and Agriculture' contains a comprehensive world review and outlook, which covers information on agricultural production, changes in stock, demand for agricultural products, food supplies and consumption and international trade in agricultural products. It also gives information on farm prices and incomes, consumer prices, sales, agricultural policies and development plans. The special feature of this review is the commodity survey and outlook on commodities like wheat, coarse grains, rice, sugar, meat, eggs, dairy products, fishery products, fats, oils and oilseeds, fresh fruit, dried fruit and wine, cocoa, cotton, coffee, wool, jute, hard fibres, rubber, forest products, etc.

Every year the survey gives a comprehensive discussion of a special subject of topical interest.

The statistical tables annexed to this publication have general statistical information on world production and exports of major commodities for the last five years. These also give information on production, exports and imports of major commodities, separately for Western Europe and USSR, North, America, Oceania, Latin America, Far East, Near East, Africa, etc. Statistics are also available on total catch of fish, variability of production and yields of selected products by regions, food supplies available for human consumption, etc.

Selected Indicators of Food and Agriculture Development in Asia-Pacific Region

The latest issue (seventeenth 1989-99) released in October 2000 presents data on selected items for the years 1989-1999, except some tables which provide information for the period 1988-98. Most tables show two types of information: annual figures for 1989, 1996, 1997, 1988 and 1999 and the average annual growth rate for the period 1989-1999. The indicators are grouped under the following headings: Agricultural land and population, agricultural inputs, production indices, staple food crops, edible oil crops, horticultural crops, fibre, other crops, livestock, agricultural trade, fisheries, forestry, nutrition and other indicators. Countries of the region are shown under two groups: "Developing countries", and for comparison purpose, figures relating to "Rest of World" are also presented.

FERTILISERS

Fertiliser Statistics, an annual issue of the Fertiliser Association of India, is the most reliable source for all types of data (national/international) on fertilisers in the section dealing with world fertiliser statistics, various types of data are compiled from the following publications.

1. Fertiliser statistics yearbook, FAO.
2. World Fertiliser Consumption statistics, Paris.
3. International Fertiliser Industry Associations, Paris.
4. International Energy Agency.
5. OCED Economic Outlook.

World Economic Survey (UN)

This is a book on world economy and contains statistics on food and agricultural situation. It is divided into two parts. Part I deals with investment trends and policies; Part II contains current economic developments. The information is given in the form of notes and articles along with statistical data, wherever necessary. Statistical tables give information on indices of producer prices of selected agricultural commodities in nine Western-European countries, major foodgrains, etc. Information is also given on imports and exports of selected agricultural goods, output of selected agricultural machinery in USSR, indices of agricultural production and output of major agricultural products, etc.

Economic Survey of Asia and the Far East (UN)

This book contains statistical data for ESCAP countries, etc. regarding indices of crop production and plan targets, production, gross exports and prices of export commodities, production and trade in cereals, apparent consumption of cereals, commodity imports and exports, etc. The chapters on production and foreign trade included in this book give information on food trends and agricultural production, and individual commodity trends on foreign trade.

Monthly Bulletin of Statistics (UN)

In the sphere of agricultural statistics this Bulletin furnishes detailed information on forestry, trade, wages, prices. On forestry it furnishes figures of production of natural and synthetic rubber for calender months or monthly averages for different countries of the world based on information supplied by the Secretariat of the International Rubber Study Group (London). It also furnishes data on monthly production of meat, milk, butter, cheese, wheat flour, cotton yarn, woven cotton fabrics, wool yarn, etc. for previous years from 1954. Index numbers of wholesale prices of farm products of animal and vegetable origin such as grains, vegetables and fruits, livestock, poultry, dairy products, etc. and index numbers of wholesale prices for different countries of the world with 1953 as base are given on annual basis from countries of the world with 1958 and with monthly figures for the latest year.

This bulletin contains national wholesale price series for selected commodities which are important in international trade. The agricultural commodities dealt with are as follows:

Food—Bacon, beef, butter, wheat, flour, rice, maize, coffee, cocoa, tea and sugar.

Crude materials—Wool yarn, cotton yarn and fabric, hides, rubber, bumber, wood, pulp, wool, jute, cotton, flax.

Oils and fats—Fats, vegetable oils.

COUNTRY SERIES

Important statistical data in respect of various countries are published by the respective Governments of the countries concerned. The publications discussed are as under:

(i) Statistical Abstract of the United States issued by the U.S. Bureau of the Census.

(ii) Annual Abstract of Statistics issued by Her Majesty's Stationery Office, London.

(iii) The Canada Year Book issued by the Dominion Bureau of Statistics, Canada.

(iv) Sri Lanka Year Book issued by Department of Census and Statistics, Colombo, Sri Lanka.

Statistical Abstract of the United States

The Statistical Abstract of the United States presents in a single annual volume important summary statistics on the industrial, social, political and economic organization of the United States and includes a representative selection from most of the important statistical publications of the United States. In the sphere of agriculture, this Abstract gives detailed statistics on irrigation, drainage and soil conservation, number and acreage of farms, land utilization, value of farm property, farm labour, farmers' marketing and purchasing associations. It also gives indices of volume of farm production by major groups of products and prices received and prices paid by farmers. Data on imports and exports of agricultural products are also furnished. Statistics of acreage, production and value of crops, number of domestic animals and poultry on farms, average prices of crops and livestock, etc. are also given. Data on forests and forest products and fisheries are also published.

The United States Department of Agriculture also brings out annually another publication entitled 'Agricultural Statistics' which gives more important series of statistics concerning agriculture and closely related subjects. A supplement to the farm income situation, 'Farm Income' is also brought out by the US Department of Agriculture.

Annual Abstract of Statistics (UK)

This abstract for the United Kingdom gives detailed statistics on area and climate, acreage and production of crops and grass, estimated yield per acre, number of cattle, sheep, pigs and poultry on agricultural holdings, horses grazed on agricultural land, agricultural tractors, machines and implements in use, sales of farm products and forest area. It gives details of fishing fleet and landings of fish.

Statistics of volume and value of imports and exports and wholesale and retail trade are also available in this publication. In the sphere of price statistics, the Abstract furnishes annual average prices of agricultural prices, indices and prices of dairy cows, store stock and feeding stuffs, etc.

The Commonwealth Economic Committee, London, also brings out a quarterly, 'Tropical Products' which contains statistics relating to production, trade, stocks, prices, etc. of cocoa, spices, vegetable oils and oilseeds, etc.

The Canada Year Book

Agriculture, including stock raising and horticulture, is the most important of the primary industries of the Canadian people. In addition, agriculture provides the raw materials for many Canadian manufactures, and its products in raw or manufactured form constitute a very large percentage of Canadian exports. The Chapter on Agriculture, included in this Year Book furnishes comprehensive statistics on income from farm products and farming operations, field crops, livestock and poultry, dairying, fruits and vegetables, other principal farm products, prices of agricultural produce, food consumption and miscellaneous statistics.

Statistics on forestry and fisheries are also given in separate chapters.

The Dominion Bureau of Statistics, Canada, also bring out biennial supplements to the 'Canadian Statistical Review' which contain more detailed statistical information on the above-mentioned items. Besides, the Bureau also bring out their monthly catalogues which give statistics on commodities like eggs, sugar, fruits and vegetables, etc. 'Agriculture Abroad' brought out by the Department of Agriculture, Canada contains information on developments in Agricultural policy in various counties.

COMMODITY SERIES

Besides the general country series giving agricultural statistics for different countries of the world certain publications devoted exclusively to individual commodities are also issued by international organizations as listed below:

1. International Agreements, Councils and Groups.
2. Commonwealth Economic Committee Reviews.
3. United States Department of Agriculture (USA).

International Agreements, Councils etc.

All these Agreements, Councils and Groups (listed below) are concerned with Trade in the respective commodity and have valuable information on Production, prices, trade and allied issues.

International Coffee Agreement (ICA)
International Cocoa Agreement (ICCA)
International Sugar Agreement
The International Wheat Agreement, 1986.
The International Jute Organisation (IJO)
The second International Rubber Agreement (INRA II)
International Tropical Timber Organisation
International Meat Council (IMC)
International Dairy Products Council (IDPC)
International Group on Tea (IGT)
International Group on Bananas
Intergovernmental Group on Rice
Intergovernmental Groups on Oilseeds, Oils and Fats.
Integovernmental Group on Meat (IGM)
Sub-Group on Hides and Skins
Intergovernmental Group on Jute, Kenaf and Allied Fibers
Sub-Group of Sisal and Henequen Producing Countries
Intergovernmental Group on Hard Fibres
Intergovernmental Group on Wine and Vine Products

Commonwealth Economic Committee Reviews: Commodity Series

The Commonwealth Economic Committee in London is bringing out annually very useful publications in their commodity series. These series cover Fruits, Grain Crop, Plantation Crops, Meat, Dairy Produce, Industrial Fibres and Vegetable Oils and Oilseeds. There is an independent volume for each of these commodities which reviews the chief statistical data of world production, consumption, trade and prices for the commodity concerned. Appendices to each volume analyze Government Legislation, International Agreements, Tariffs, etc. affecting production and marketing in the main exporting and importing countries. The volumes for 2000, for example, would cover the information up to the year 1998-99 and provide comprehensive statistical information in respect of each of the items discussed above for a period of 6 to 7 years.

Besides the above commodity series, FAO, United States Department of Agriculture and other sources have issued series of comprehensive studies reviewing production and trade developments, etc. in individual commodities, as follows:

1. The Wheat Review, issued by the Dominion Bureau of Statistics (Agricultural Division), Canada.
2. The Wheat Situation, published by Economic Research Service, US Department of Agriculture.
3. Commonwealth Economic Committee Grain Bulletin.
4. The National Food Situation, published by Economic Research Service, US Department of Agriculture.
5. The Sugar Situation, published by Agriculture Marketing Service, United States Department of Agriculture.
6. The Cotton Situation, published by Economic Research Service, United States Department of Agriculture.
7. The Wool Situation, published by Economic Research Service. United States Department of Agriculture.
8. Commonwealth Economic Committee Wool Intelligence and Fibres Supplement.
9. The Tobacco Situation, published by Agricultural Marketing Service of United States, Department of Agriculture.
10. Tea-Trends and Prospects, issued by the Food and Agriculture Organization of the United Nations.
11. Fats and Oils, issued by the FAO.
12. Rice, (FAO).
13. Meat and Livestock, (FAO).
14. International Rice Commission Newsletter, December (FAO).
15. Tropical Products Quarterly, published by the Intelligence Branch of the Commonwealth Economic Committee, London.

United States Department of Agriculture (USDA) Current World Market and Trade Reports

The World Market and Trade reports (listed below) provide the latest analysis and data on a number of agricultural commodities, outlining the current supply, demand and trade estimates both for the United States and for many major foreign countries. These reports are released in paper format at the U.S. Department of Agriculture at 3:00 on their release day.

Cotton: World Markets and Trade

Dairy: World Markets and Trade

Dairy, Livestock and Poultry: Trade and Prospects

Dairy Monthly Imports

Fishery Products Circular

Grain: World Markets and Trade

Livestock and Poultry: World Markets and Trade

Oilseeds: World Markets and Trade

Sugar: World Markets and Trade

Tobacco: World Markets and Trade

Tropical Products: World Markets and Trade

U.S. Planting Seed Trade (April 1998) (May 1998) (June 1998)

Wood Products: International Trade and Foreign Markets

World Agricultural Production

World Horticultural Trade and U.S. Export Opportunities (Early Release)

World Horticultural Trade and U.S. Export Opportunities (Full Release)

Socio Economic Data

The following organisations of the United Nations bring out in their annual reports country-wise data on all types of socio economic indicators-demography, health, education, sanitation, infrastructure, employment, etc.

1. United Nations International Drug Control Programme (UNDCP)
2. United Nations Population Fund (UNFPA)
3. United Nations Development Fund for Women (UNIFEM)
4. United Nations Information Centre (UNIC)
5. United Nations Educational, Scientific and Cultural Organisation (UNESCO)
6. United Nations Children's Fund (UNICEF)
7. International (ILO) Labour Organisation
8. World Health Organisation (WHO)
9. International Committee of the Red Cross (ICRC)
10. International Centre for Genetic Engineering and Biotechnology (ICGEB)
11. Asian Development Bank
12. World Bank
13. United Nations Development Programme (UNDP)

ON-GOING SOURCES OF INFORMATION AND STEPS PROPOSED TO IMPROVE ACCESS TO EXPORT INTELLIGENCE

Sources of Information

Sources of intelligence on international agriculture trade markets are numerous and varied. Access to some of the trade intelligence is easy and much of it is also available free of cost or involves little expense. This includes generally the information put out by the International Agencies and some Governments and/or other organizations. However, some essential and important intelligence concerning export crop markets, generally disseminated by private agencies, such as commodity news service firms, international trading companies and large traders, are available on subscription. The subscription rates for trader's publication/ newsletters vary from less than US$ 100 per annum for some to very high fees for others. A considerable amount of useful information about export market intelligence is available on the Internet, both free and at price. Moreover, this information can be obtained much more quickly than in the printed and published form. Two most important basic index on Market Information Sources available through the Internet include (1) ITC Index to Internet Sources of Trade Information and (2) Michigan State University, "Market Information Sources Available through the Internet: Daily to Yearly Market and Outlook Reports, Prices, Commodities and Quotes." Their URL, i.e. addresses on the web sites, are as follows:

1. http://www.intracen.org/itc/inbase/itc3-6htm.
2. http://www.aec.msu.edu/agecon/fs2/market-information.htm.

The ITC's Index to Internet Sources of Trade Information is divided into ten main categories. These include (1) press Agency News, (2) Trade Publications with Bibliographic References, (3) Company Registers, (4) Full-text Trade Publications, (5) Market Research, Norm and Standards, (6) Trade Fairs and Exhibitions, (7) Price Information and Exchange Rates, (8) Tariff Information and Trade Regulations, (9) Public Tenders and Trade Opportunities and (10) Statistics. This web site offers access to 1,300 information sources and is updated systematically. The database is also available in a printed version.

The Michigan State University compilation provides a guide to different sources of market information available on Internet. It is arranged into two sections: (I) Introduction and (II) Internet Sources of Market Information. The section II consists of five sub-sections, described below:

(1) *Market Reports and Prices*   This sub-section covers all sites which offer market data and information from daily closing prices to weekly, monthly and yearly market reports. They differ by the information data banks and reports provided at each Internet site, by their sources of information, by the regions covered or by commodities. This Market Reports sub-section cover five areas: (i) USDA market wire service, agricultural marketing service, and economics and statistics system, (ii) international and world markets, (iii) Africa, (iv) within the United States of America, and (v) specific commodities such as maize, soyabeans, fruits and vegetables, pigs, cattle and cotton. Main periodicals from which price information is available are (i) The Public Ledger Weekly published and distributed by Agra, Europa, London. (ii) Tokyo Market Situation Report. (iii) The Straits Times, Singapore.

(2) *Market, Exchange and Quotes*   This sub-section pertains to exchanges and boards of trade in the US and Canada relative to agricultural market, with particular attention given to grains;

(3) *Links and Other Sources*   This sub-section catalogues the better web sites for starting a general search for agricultural and market information on the Internet.

(4) *E-mail and Discussion Groups*   It groups the mailing lists, which offer reception of monthly USDA reports to open discussion of the market.

(5) *Weather, Farm journals and a Currency and Unit Converter*   Up-to-date market related weather information, satellite images, agricultural news and foreign currency and weight conversions.

In addition to the above-mentioned two sources, a number of Universities in US have useful sites on the Internet on the international agricultural export markets. These include Market News from Oregon State (via University of Arizona: Worldwide information organised by state and country): and USDA-AMS market news by the University of Florida. Based on the review of the information available on the Internet and the printed form, most important sources for the Myanmar export markets are described below and are also listed in Table 30.2.

International Trade intelligence can broadly be classified in two groups viz. (I) geographical coverage such as for (a) country export markets, (b) regional markets and (c) global or world market and (II) by time span. The later category includes three types, i.e. (i) the current and /or the previous year, (ii) medium term covering 3–5 years and (iii) time series or historical data. Although Myanmar is not a significant player in the international market, for expansion of it's foreign exchange earnings from agricultural exports that is must for the country in the future, it needs all types of trade intelligence. It has been classified the published information on international is now available free on the Internet. However, the priced information on international commercial trade and other relevant material can be obtained either by ordering through an electronic trade and other relevant material can be obtained either by ordering through an electronic subscription via the Internet or by subscription for the printed reports and material.   .

One of the most important and primary sources of current export market intelligence is the Reuters daily "Commodity Service". They provide this service through a dedicated satellite signals, on a basis of a monthly subscription plus the cost of installation. This service can be arranged from the Reuters Office in Bangkok (Thailand). Since October 1999 Reuters has also started: "Agrimarkets service" through the Internet. This services provides a continuous up-to-date information on developments and events of the world agriculture market, including comprehensive prices, both physical and exchange and a fourteen days historical news. The basic package includes access to non-fee liable (delayed) agricultural data from the following exchanges: Amsterdam Agricultural Exchange, Chicago

Table 30.2 Major on-going Sources of Export

Category I: Information available free-of-cost

A. Thailand

1. Weekly Market Review: Wholesale and Export Prices of agricultural commodities
   Source: Centre for Agriculture Information
   (Kasetsal University Campus)
   Department of Agriculture:
   Tel. 2824765: 9405407

2. Rice Report: Weekly
   Source: Rice Committee, Board of of Trade Bangkok (Thailand)

3. Rubber Market Situation (Monthly)
   Source: Rubber Research Institute
   (Kasetsat University Campus)
   Department of Agriculture
   Tel Nos. 5797557 and 5794184:

4. Rice price quotations
   Daily Newspaper: Bangkok Post.

5. Thai Rice Economy
   http://www.thrice.org/rice/inded.html

B. USDA World Agricultural Outlook Board (WAOB) and Foreign Agricultural Service (FAS)

6. WAOB: Outlook Reports on world agricultural supply and demand estimates for Rice, Grains, and World Agriculture.
   http://www.usda.gov/wab/wasde/wasde.htm
   Cost per year for a set of printed reports on each commodity is $ 27.50

7. FAS: World market reports on Grains, fruits, sugar, cotton and tobacco: plus Trade Circulars.
   http://www.fas.usda.gov/commodity/html
8. FAS: General Market Reviews
   http://www.fas.usda.gov***
9. USDA Agricultural Attache's reports
   http://www.usda.gov/scripster/AttaliceRep/html

C. International Organizations Food and Agriculture organization

10. Food Outlook: (Bi-Monthly)
    http://wwwfao.org/giews

11. Commodity Market Review
    http:/www.fao.org/waicent/faoinfo0

12. Medium-term Prospects for Agricultural Commodities: Projections to the Year 2005

13. Annual Production Year Book, Vol. 53, L998
14. Quarterly Bulletin of Statistics
15. Annual Trade Yearbook
    Vol. 52. 1998
    http://www.fao.org***

16. Agricultural Marketing
    http://www.fao.org/waicent/faoinfo/agricult/ags/ags.htm

The International Rice Research Institute
17. Rice Web
    http://www.ricceweb.org

Table 30.2 Major on-going Sources of Export (Contd.)

UNCTAD, Geneva (Switzerland)

18. Monthly Commodity Price Bulletin Covers export prices of major commodities, with about two months lag.

19. Handbook of international Trade and Development Statistics: Gives time series data.

Food and Agricultural Policy Research Washington, DC

20. Agricultural Outlook Report: Covers projections to the year 2003/2004 http:/www.ssu.missouri,edu/ssu/FAPRI/reports/195/Intr/outlook.htm

The World Bank: Washington DC

21. Pink Sheet Monthly Commodity Price http://www.worldbank.org.html.iecep/pink.html

CIMMYT (International Centre for Maize research (Mexico)

22. World Maize Facts and Trends Reports http://www.cimmvt.cgir.org/publications/htm

23. World Commodity Price Updates

Malaysian Rubber Board, Kuala Lumpur:

24. Official daily and annual average International physical prices for all varieties of rubber, as well as data on exports, area and production of rubber in Malaysia. http://www.cimmyt.cgir.org/publications/htm

Singapore Commodity of Exchange

25. Daily price quotations for physical quantities of different agricultural commodities including rice rubber, coffee and others. http://www.sicom.sg.html

Universities and Research Organizations web sites

D. Universities and Research Organizations web sites

26. USDA-AMS Market News Service http://www.ams-usda.gov/marketnews.htm

27. University of Florida: http://gnv.ifas.ufl/~marketing.html

28. The Louisiana State University Library http://www.lib.lsu.edu/bus/agbus.html

29. One Globe Market, Ottawa, Canada

ttp://www.oneglobe.com./agriculture/resources.htl

Category II: Priced Information

30. Reuters "Commodity 2000" News Service Provide comprehensive and most valuable information and nation markets developments for major commodities: (for cost see Appendix: II)

US Department of Agriculture: Washington DC

Quarterly Outlook reports on
32. Rice
33. Oil Crops
34. World Agriculture

Table 30.2 Major on-going Sources of Export (Contd.)

31. Reuters Agrimarkets Services through Internet
    Provides news and price covering the Agrimarkets.

    Monthly subscription for Agrimarkets US$ 175. Extra cost are charged for subscribing "real-time" market data.
    http://www.reuters.com/inform/agrimarkets/agrisatic.html

Cost per year for a set of each report US$ 27.50
http://www.usda.gov/publications/usda.hmtl

35. Rice Year Book: Price not known
    http://www.usda.mannlib.cornell.edu/usda/usda/html

UNCTAD/GATT: International Trade

36. Daily market New Service (MNS)
    The service covers rice, and other products mentioned in the text.
    http://www.intracen.org/itc.services/mns2.htm
    (Service available on subscription).

International Rubber Study Group:

37. International Rubber Digest (Monthly)

38. Rubber Statistical Bulletin: (Monthly)

39. Annual Outlook for Elastomer
    http://www.irsg.org. Subscription is necessary.

40. Agra Europe (London)
    The Public Ledger (weekly)
    Contains news, comments and features including a comprehensive price section
    Annual Subscription Pround Sterling 280. Also available to subscribes on the Internet.
    http://www.public-ledger.com

41. London Rice Brokers's Association weekly Circular
    Annual subcription Pound Sterling 75
    Address Jackson Son & Co. (London) Ltd.
    4 St. George's Yard, Farnham, Surrey GU 7LW (England):
    E.Mail: rice@lrba.com

42. Business Time, Singapore (Daily Newspaper)
    Annual subscription in Yangon: US$ 460-It is also available on-line
    http://business-time.asial.com.sg

43. The Asia Wall Street Journal
    Covers closing price quotations for a number of commodities for North America and London Markets.
    http://awsj.com

44. The Economic Times, New Delhi (India)
    Daily newspaper can be subscribed in New Delhi. Annual subscription US$40.-It covers wholesale prices for cereals, pulses and a number of other commodities, for a number of local wholesale markets in India.
    http://www.economictimes.com

45. Far Eastern Economic Review
    Weekly published every Thrusday. Based on Dow Jones information it gives commodity prices with lag of about three weeks
    Annual subscription in Yangon: US$ 160
    http://www.feer.com

Table 30.2 Major on-going Sources of Export (Contd.)

46. AGRA Food Asia: Monthly
Covers Policy, Market Review, Trade,
Investment and Economic trends for
the countries in the region.
Annual subscription;
Pound Sterling 465.-
Address for subscription:
AGRA Europe 25 Ferant Road,
Tunbridge Well, Kent TN2 5JT (UK):
Tel. 0044-11892-533813:
Fax: 044-1892-524593;
Home page on the World Wide Web:
http://www.agr.food.news.co
Agra Net Internet services is free
and exclusive only to weekly
subscribers.

The World Bank, Washington DC (USA)
47. Global Commodity Markets-
Quarterly Printed in mid-January,
April, July and October Regular
Quarterly subscription: Reports
(Printed Only)   US$ 495/annual

Full Service Subscription Report
(printed and electronic) with electronic
Monthly update: US$ 465
Mail Order: The World Bank,
P.O. Box 7247-7956,
Philadephia PA 19170 (USA)
Pre-paid order on
e-mail: book@worldbank.org.

48. Asia Pacific Agribusiness Report (Monthly)
Newsletter: Covers trade and agribusiness developments in the region; include
2 special reports in each issue; Publisher Asia Letter GRoup GPO Box 8061,
Hong Kong: Tele No. 852-526-2950 Annual Subs. US$ 240.-

49. Cargill Newsletter: Singapore:
Weekly
Reviews market developments in
major agricultural commodities in
Asia Region:
Publisher, Cargill International
Trading Pvt. Ltd., Singa;ore:
Annual sub: US$ 750 (ad-hoc.)

Economic Intelligence Unit: London
(UK)
50, Rubber Trends: Quarterly
Annual subscription: £ Sterling 495.-
http://www.eiu.co
Publication accessible to those clients
who have paid for an Internet
subscription

The International Advisory Cotton Committee
51, Monthly reports on supply and use of cotton by country and
IACC Cotton Price Index.
Http:/www.icac.org/icac.english/main.html
Monthly reports are available on subscription. The rest of the site that contains
reports, graphs and most is available in pdf format (Adobe acrobar reader).

Board of Trade, Chicago Mercantile Exchange, Commodity and Monetary
Exchange of Malaysia, London Financial and Futures Exchange, Kansas
City Board of Trade, MATIF, New York Board of Trade, Sydney Future
Exchange, Winnipeg Commodity Exchange. The monthly subscription for
the basic package is US $ 175. Extra costs are changed for obtaining "real-
time" market data i.e. current prices from some of the Exchanges mentioned
above. Reuters offers free access to its Agrimarkets Service for 14 days
trail. To obtain access to this service the agency or the firm has to register.
Upon expiry of 14 days trail period, the service can be accessed only on
payment of subscription.

Among the national sources, several agencies in Thailand put out regularly weekly, fortnightly or monthly market reviews covering both the national and international markets. Thailand is a leading exporter of agricultural commodities in the region and also imports some of these commodities from Myanmar mainly through informal border cross trade. The above-cited reviews can be of considerable use for Myanmar's export market information system. Most of these reviews can be obtained free of cost, by requesting in writing to the issuing authority concerned in Bangkok. However, most of these reviews are available in Thai language and will need to be translated in the local language.

Next the Reuters Commodity and Agrimarkets services, is The Public Ledger: World Commodities, a weekly published and distributed by Agra Europa (London) Ltd. It provides a much useful information including news, comments and analysis for a larger number of markets and agricultural commodities. It also contains a comprehensive International Commodity Price Section. It is available in the printed form as well as on the Internet to its subscribers. Its annual subscription of Pound Sterling 280, as mentioned above, is being arranged from the current TCP funds. Also, a good deal of current information on commodity markets is readily available in the National Daily Newspapers. For example, Business Times Singapore, a daily newspaper (also available Online), offers a great variety of market information on commodities. It gives data on daily FOB Thai rice prices (covering several varieties) as well as prices for many more agricultural commodities varying from sugar, palm, coffee and rubber for LIFFE, Rotterdam to New York CBOT and Singapore.

The other national source of information includes the USDA World Agricultural Outlook Boards reports on the World Agricultural Supply and Demand Estimates for major commodities. These reports are available free on e-mail. However, printed reports are available on subscription. Also the US Foreign Agricultural Service (FAS) offers regularly reports on current commodity analysis on world market and trade for different commodities. The World Situation and Outlook reports on rice, grains, sugar, tobacco and tropical fruits are of interest to Myanmar. FAS General Market overviews provide valuable information about some important export markets. These are not available on the Internet, but have to be ordered from the US Trade Assistance & Promotion office. However, commodity information as analysed by FAS is available to the public. Current commodity reports and Pages on the World Web include (i) World Market & Trade Circulars, (ii) World Market Short Trade Reports and (iii) Archives of FAS's available circulars.

Moreover, reports of the US Agricultural Attaches covering 130 countries including important agricultural importing and exporting countries in various regions, are of considerable importance. In their Annual Grain and Feed reports the Attaches review the situation for the current year and the outlook for the next year for the country of their assignment e.g. on Pulses for Myanmar. These reports are one of the valuable sources of export crop market information. The US Department of Agriculture in Washington D.C distributes these reports free, with a time lag, on request to the interested parties. FAS Global Reports as well as its Attaches' reports can be accessed through the Internet Agricultural Attaches. Reports especially for China, India, Indonesia, Japan, Korea Republic, Malaysia, Philippines and Thailand are of interest to the Myanmar. Singapore Rubber Commodity Exchange provides information on daily quotations for physical and futures. Also a few major trading companies/traders dealing in rice, maize, and natural rubber, bring out market reviews/newsletters. These include Agra Europa (London) weekly, The Public Ledger: World Commodities, Cargill Singapore Weekly Newsletter, Monthly Asia Pacific Report, and Monthly Agra Asia Food. However, these are available on subscriptions. A weekly London Rice Brokers Association Circular deals with developments in rice producing countries and price quotations. Its annual subscription is Pound Sterling 75 and is available only in a printed form. Information on rice prices for US, Thai and world are available at the latest web site of Michigan State University's guide mentioned above. A Thai national has a web page on the Thai Rice economy.

The World Bank offers commodity price data in their analysis and forecast sections in the "Pink Sheet". These monthly reports contain price data on rice, grains, oils and fats and agricultural raw material for the last three months, three quarters and the last three years. It can be accessed free on the Internet. Since January 1999 the Bank's new quarterly publication Global Commodity Markets is published in January, April, July and October. Each issue is available in both print and electronic form, but at a price. These quarterlies give price forecasts for 46 primary commodities, for the next three years and for 2005 and 2010. It also contains detailed market reviews for 27 major commodities and the newly expanded sections cover global and regional indices. Although subscription is necessary for full copy of the Quarterly, the summary and the featured article can be viewed on the Internet.

Agricultural Policy Research Institute brings out outlook reports in the U.S. agricultural sector and international commodity markets. One of their reports contains recent baseline projections to the year 2003/2004 and covering many comodities in U.S. and world trade. Their data are available in spreadsheet form as well as graphics.

The International Trade Centre's Market New Service (MNS) provides regular news and prices information on world markets for products is included in the MNS currently covers the major markets for rice, fruits and vegetables, cut flowers, tropical and ornamental plants, common spices and other products. For rice the MNS provides weekly price quotations for 15 different varieties and qualities (of South East Asian origin) in world market. For fruits and vegetables weekly price quotations are given for 72 tropical and off-season products in selected European, Middle Eastern and North American markets. Historical price data, over the last three to five years on individual products are also made available on request. The MNS price and market information is a useful tool for farmers, exporters, importers, banks, export promotion agencies, ministries etc. This service is, however, available on an annual subscription payable separately for each individual item. Also the ITC has recently established two web sites on fresh fruit and vegetables. These sites provide an interactive matchmaking tool for exporters and importers of fruits and vegetables worldwide. These sites are freely accessible for developing countries and the transition economies. In due course of time Myanmar export promotion agencies should take advantage by establishing insertion and updates services as they do not themselves have yet access to Internet.

The CIMMYT offers a variety of publications. Of particular interest are on the World Maize Facts and Trends reports and the World Commodity Market Prices updates, which include selected grains, fertilizers, oil prices and freight rates.

The International Cotton Advisory Committee provides cotton information, including supply and use of cotton by country, world cotton price index, as well as many background papers, graphs and trends. The monthly market information and monthly updates are available on subcription. The rest of its site on the World Wide Web on the Internet is free.

For national rubber the Malaysian Rubber Board issues Daily fob International prices for RSS, SMR and framgate Latex Prices. The Board's Home Page on the Internet also contains data on acreage, production of natural rubber in Malaysia, Annual Average Price of RSS1, RSS3 and SMR20 as well as Export of Natural Rubber from Malaysia. All this information is available free on the Internet. The International Rubber Study Group (IRSG) in London puts out a number of monthly and ad-hoc reports. Its home page provides all the information on the material available with the Group but non-member countries have to subscribe the publications or order them from the IRSG's office in London. A Quarterly Rubber Trends, issued by the Economist Intelligence Unit, London (UK), is another important source of information. In addition, a few weeklies such as Far Eastern Economic Review and the Asia week provide international prices for agricultural commodities However, the prices reported are out-dated.

Time series data on international agricultural trade, that cover information on export crop markets of interest to Myanmar, are being compiled by FAO, UNCTAD, USDA and ITC, and it is distributed free among member governments and/or interested parties. These data are also available through the Internet FAO compiles and distributes a detailed international agricultural trade data for the entire major internationally traded commodities covering all countries in the world. The information is contaied in annual publications, and is also available on the CDs as well as through the Internet facility. The publications containing time series data can serve only as a background information, since there is generally a two years time lag. As regards the future outlook, FAO prepares periodically a medium terms projections. The FAO's latest projections relate to the period 1997 to 2005. The Government of Myanmar can obtain, by requesting in writing to various agencies, all these publications free, which are currently not being received by various Government Trading Agencies. Subscriptions will have to be renewed for The Public Ledger and the Business Times. Also, till access to the Internet is allowed, Myanmar embassies in major markets such as London, New York, Singapore, Thailand might conceivably be able to organise a regular facsimile transmission of the latest prices and conditions for the Myanmar major export crops.

Internet and Electronic Commerce

The Internet is the most important technological event to have hit the world economy for the fast ten years. Internet represents a key to trade information exchange and to the development of the Electronic Commerce (so called E-commerce). Electronic commerce covers the prodution, distribution, sale or delivery of goods and services by electronic means. Internet use worldwide is growing fast. Estimates of the value of global Internet Commerce ranges from 1.3 percent to 3.3 percent global gross domestic product. The intensity of the Internet use roughly reflects levels of economic development. Canada, Nordic countries and the United States adopted Internet technology most rapidly. However, many developing countries such as Republic of Korea, Hong Kong Special Administrative Region of China, Singa;ore and Taiwan Province of China have now almost caught up with early adopters. In developing countries across Southeast Asia, Argentina, Brazil, China and some Island States such as Barbados, Fiji and Tonga uptake of Internet has also been growing rapidly since 1996.

Using the Internet to lower communication costs and reduce time-to-market for goods and services makes it very valuable medium for agencies and firms engaged in international trade. Its ability to deliver information of almost any sort in digital format at lower cost offers significant efficiencies that the trading agencies and firms can pass on to importers and customers in the form of lower prices. Electronic commerce will in due course become ubiquitous as developments to make-the Internet more useful and seamless increase. At the same time access through Television and mobile phones and other wireless devices will increase its power as a business, trade and consumer tool Internet use and electronic commerce are expanding rapidly in food products sector, encompassing market monitoring and promotion, electronic networking of producers, processors, traders and consumers and scanner-based software systems for tracking consumer preference and demand. However, commodity markets are currently in the early stages of moting to an Internet use. Web sites are developing fast in Asia and Latin America. Already in several Asian and Latin American countries, trade development organisations and exporters of agricultural commodities such as rice, pulses, maize, soybean and natural rubber, have set up their websites.

31

Conclusions and Recommendations

Agriculture is a vital sector of economy even among highly industrialized countries and much care and expenditure are devoted to the compilation of agricultural statistics. In India agriculture forms by far the most important economic activity and the need for a comprehensive and reliable system of agricultural statistics has a correspondingly greater emphasis. In the past, the collection of agricultural statistics was merely incidental to the collection of land revenue which formed the principal source of finance to the Governments. Apart from other users like the primary producer, trade and industry, the Government itself was directly interested in the compilation of detailed agricultural statistics for its use in the day-to-day administration of land revenue. This special feature of Indian agricultural statistics was having both favourable and adverse effects on their accuracy and comprehensiveness.

The precise scope of agricultural statistics is not easy to be defined. Broadly, however, a comprehensive system of agricultural statistics should include quantitative information on all items directly or indirectly connected with production, processing, distribution and utilization of agricultural commodities including livestock and fisheries. Specifically these include: (i) statistics of land utilization; (ii) agricultural production including livestock and fisheries; (iii) statistics of costs and prices; and (iv) agricultural population which constitutes number and size of holdings, composition of agricultural population, details of ownership and tenancy, agricultural machinery and power, etc.

We have examined in the previous pages how agricultural statistics have reached a stage of maturity. From among the developing world India can boast of having sufficiently dependable statistics for agriculture. Even then there are quite a number of shortcomings—both quantitative and qualitative. After examining the shortcomings of the available data, it was considered necessary to provide a detailed picture of various recommendations made by the National Commission on Agriculture on the subject. The Planning Commission and other Government agencies are conscious of the problems and it can be hopefully assumed that India will in the near future, be in a position to have the most reliable data on agriculture so as to meet the planning needs of the country.

It would not be out of place to mention here that instead of showing an improvement, the quality of crop data has deteriorated and not much progress has been made with regard to livestock and horticulture data system. Most of the recommendations given at the end of this chapter are the same after nearly two decades back as in the third edition. Now that preparations are in progress for the Tenth Plan, it would be extremely important that necessary corrective steps are taken to raise the level of agricultural intelligence to meet the 21st century challenges.

SHORTCOMINGS OF AVAILABLE DATA

The current agricultural statistics do not fully meet the needs of planning and suffer from a number of defects. Efforts have been made to improve the quality and contents of these statistics. The main defects existing and improvements effected so far can be discussed broadly under the following heads:

   (i) Gaps in coverage,
  (ii) Lack of uniformity in definition and classification,
 (iii) Defects in tabulation and processing,
 (iv) Defects in primary reporting agency
  (v) Defects in supervision, inspection and checking, and
 (vi) Lack of proper planning and coordination.

Gaps in Coverage

  (a) Gaps in geographical coverage, and
  (b) Gaps regarding the availability of statistics in respects of certain items.

(a) Agricultural statistics, as stated earlier, are available in respect of 93.3 per cent of the total geographical area in the country and for the remaining 6.7 per cent of the total area, estimates are not available. Since most of the non-reporting areas are not cadastrally surveyed, difficulties are experienced in collection of agricultural statistics in those areas. In the non-reporting areas which have been surveyed, there does not exist any primary reporting agency for crop reporting.

During recent years some of the State Governments have been persuaded to take up cadastral survey of agriculturally important areas and to set up primary reporting agencies wherever these do not exist. It is felt that in non-reporting areas, land use classification can be obtained on the basis of aerial photographs coupled with broad topographical survey on the ground. In fact, in some hilly areas aerial photographs have already been taken and what is necessary is a proper interpretation of these photographs.

(b) There are some gaps in respect of the production statistics of minor crops of commercial importance and protective foods like fruits and vegetables. Statistics of crop yields separately for irrigated and unirrigated areas are not available in most of the States. The use of sample survey techniques for collection of these data can be made with success. In fact, the IASRI on the basis of a series of pilot investigations, has been able to develop a suitable sampling technique for obtaining reliable estimates of the extent of cultivation of fruits. Similarly techniques for estimating the extent of cultivation of vegetables have been developed by the IASRI.

Detailed information on cultivators' holdings were not available till the Agricultural Census (1971) when such data were collected for the first time throughout the country at a point of time.

With respect to the statistics of livestock products no data are regularly compiled. Although estimates of some important products like milk, egg and wool are obtained on the basis of sample surveys, the techniques of which were evolved by the IASRI, these do not cover all products. Moreover the surveys for any particular product are not undertaken in all the States to provide estimate on an all-India basis for any year. Steps are being taken to overcome this drawback. Unless estimates are obtained for all the livestock products and on a regular basis, it cannot be said as satisfactory.

Reliable information on extent of fodder cultivation and yield of fodder crops is not available. Instructions have been given to States to record area under fodder crops in village records. Suitable sampling technique for estimation of yield of fodder crops has now been developed by IASRI.

The available statistics in the field of agricultural economics are scanty. It is essential to collect reliable data on cost of production of principal crops and livestock products, utilization of agricultural inputs and produce etc. Efforts are made to fill in some of these gaps in agricultural statistics.

Lack of Uniformity in Definition and Classification

Available statistics are not only of some degree of accuracy in different states, but are sometimes not comparable due to lack of uniformity in definition and classification adopted.

There was considerable divergence in methods adopted for recording areas under mixed crops. In some States, while enumerating field sown with more than one crop, the gross area covered by the mixture used to be recorded, totalled up for the whole district and then allocated between component crops according to the fixed ratio prescribed by the State authorities. In certain States the allocation of the areas of the mixed crops to components used to be made at field itself on the basis of eye-estimation, but this is not satisfactory as the estimates are often influenced by the relative stand of the crops rather than the relative seed rates. In case of certain mixtures where one crop forms a very small fraction, for instance like wheat and linseed, the minor component is generally disregarded at the time of enumeration, although some adjustments are made at the final stage in the acreage of component crops.

The condition factor which gives the condition of the crop in any year in relation to the normal crop is expressed in some States in annawari notation. But the *anna* equivalent of the normal crops is not the same in all the States. While the normal crop is represented by 12 *annas* in some States, it is denoted 13.3 *annas* in a few States and even 16 *annas* in other States. The methods used for working out the average condition factor for the district and State are not uniform.

With the introduction of short-duration varieties of crops, the sowing and harvesting seasons have undergone a change in many areas particularly under irrigated conditions. Normally, two or three crop inspections are done in a year in different States. In some States there is no provision for inspection during summer season, and as such the late sown summer crops are not recorded.

The procedure of estimation of area under bunds between fields is not uniform in all the States. In some parts, the narrow bunds are included in the total cropped area and no provision is made while working out cropped area whereas in some States a certain proportion varying from 2 to 5 per cent is deducted from cropped area. The lower limits for recording crop acreage are not uniform from State to State. In some States, the area, if it is less than 1/40th of an acre, is neglected, whereas in other States the lower limits 1/20th of an acre.

In order to remove the above defects, uniform standards, definitions and concepts have been evolved for adoption by various States, although these have not been fully implemented.

Defects in Tabulation and Processing

A lot of useful information is available at the primary source; but these are not tabulated and processed properly and as such are not of much use for utilizing for developmental purpose. For example, data are recorded in some States about sources of irrigation but it is not correlated with the number of area holdings irrigated from these sources. It is only in Jodhpur unit of Rajasthan where the 'berewar' (well) statement is prepared to assess the irrigation capacity of each well and to ascertain whether the land classed as irrigable from that well was covered by its capacity or not.

Information regarding transfer of agricultural property is recorded in Mutation Register for each village by the primary reporter in some States; but this is not consolidated beyond tehsil level and as such no figure for the State level is available.

Data regarding ownership holdings is compiled in some States to show the area under different tenure and the incidence of land revenue per hectare and per head of population. But similar statement in respect of cultivators' holdings was not made till recently when agricultural census was organized and detailed information on cultivators' holdings was made available.

Defects in the Primary Reporting Agency

Data on agricultural statistics collected in the villages are not often reliable on account of defects in the primary reporting agencies. Due to a number of reasons, the Patwari does not devote the time and attention that is needed to the collection of agricultural statistics, resulting in inaccuracies in recording and delays in submission of return. The main reason of inaccuracy in the reporting is the large geographical jurisdiction and increase in the work load of the primary reporter. Being the only Government official in the village, he has to undertake multifarious duties connected with various departmental and developmental schemes. As such, he gets little time to devote to the proper collection and compilation of agricultural statistics. He usually has no instructions as to the priority to be given to the different enquiries and hence he takes all the work in the same routine manner, showing indifference to collection of statistical data. In order to remove the existing defects in the primary reporting agency and to improve the accuracy of agricultural statistics, recommendations have been made by the Technical Committee on Coordinations of Agricultural Statistics (TCCAS). The recommendations made are: (i) to revise the qualifications and conditions of employment of a primary reporter, (ii) to give them special training in collection of various statistics, (iii) to reduce the jurisdiction of each primary reporter wherever it is in excess; and (iv) to reduce the number of crop inspections where it is more but each inspection is to be made more thorough. States are taking steps progressively to implement these suggestions, particularly in appointing more reporters and thereby reducing the jurisdiction of each primary reporter. A training programme was organized in 1954-55 under which selected Tehsildars or officers of equivalent level from all the States were trained in Delhi and these officials imparted training to primary reporters in their respective States.

Defects in Supervision, Inspection and Checking

The supervision of the work of the primary reporters is exercized by the Tehsildars and revenue Inspectors in the temporarily settled States. Such supervisory staff is expected to visit a certain number of villages under his jurisdiction in the normal course of his tour and inspect the work of the primary reporters. In the midst of his administrative duties he is unable to devote desired attention to the supervision work and as a result the primary reporters neglect in their work. Moreover, the methods of supervision and checking are not rationalized. For instance, tour programmes of the Inspecting Officers are intimated well in advance to all the Patwaris so that the Patwaris know the villages which will be inspected. They try to maintain proper records only for these villages without paying much attention for records in respect of other villages. If, on the other hand, surprise visits would be paid and the villages chosen for inspection and fields in respect of which the entries were to be checked, would be selected at random, the Patwaris would be forced to exercise greater care in their work.

The Tehsildars and Revenue Inspectors are not able to exercize adequate supervision mainly due to the fact that their jurisdiction is very large and the work-load other than the inspection is too heavy. Their jurisdiction needs to be reduced.

Lack of Proper Planning and Coordination

Another defect in the system of collection and compilation of agricultural statistics is the lack of proper planning and coordination among different agencies collecting data. In regard to certain items, data are collected by different agencies independently and there is wide difference in the sets of figures. For instance, with respect to cotton, there was wide discrepancies between the estimates of production prepared by trade agencies and by the Indian Cotton Development Board. Similarly in the case of tea, coffee and rubber, the estimates of production framed by the Indian Tea Board, the Indian Coffee Board and Indian Rubber Board respectively differ from those received from the State Governments. In respect of tobacco, there used to be difference in the two estimates, one based on data collected by the Central Board of Revenue through the Excise Department and the other by the State Governments. Three independent agencies viz. Ministry of Agriculture, Central Board of Agriculture and Ministry of Water Resources require irrigation statistics for their departmental work. Although the scope and coverage are the same, a large discrepancy is observed among their figures. Effects are being made to examine the causes of discrepancies between different sets of figures and suggestions have been made for bringing about coordination in the different agencies collecting the data.

Duplication

In some States, revenue department is responsible for collection of agricultural statistics whereas in others, department of agriculture is the nodal agency for the purpose. Still in certain other States, State Agricultural Statistics Authorities (SASAs) are the nodal agencies either for all agricultural statistics or for selected activities only. Horticultural statistics is collected by horticulture department and so on. Table 31.1 indicates the departments in different States who have the role of SASA.

In some states, different agencies attempt to gather the same statistics which lead to inconsistencies. Such multiplicity of agencies has led to lack of coordination and absence of time schedule for collection and dissemination of agricultural statistics. In the role of a nodal agency for laying down procedures and standards on agricultural statistical system, it is essential on the part of States to do away with the multiplicity of agencies, to harmonize standards for quality and timeliness and play a

Table 31.1 States and Departments having the role of SASA

Planning (Economics and Statistics)	Agriculture	Revenue
1. Andhra Pradesh	1. Gujarat	1. Madhya Pradesh
2. Assam	2. Haryana	
3. Bihar	3. Himachal Pradesh	
4. Jammu & Kashmir	4. Maharashtra	
5. Karnataka	5. Orissa (for remaining crops)	
6. Kerala	6. Punjab	
7. Orissa (for 13 crops)	7. Uttar Pradesh	
8. Rajasthan	8. West Bengal	
9. Tamil Nadu		

professional, proactive role for ensuring and enhancing the credibility of statistics. Though there exists High level Coordination Committees for Agricultural Statistics in various States, not much seems to have been done to address this issue. The SASAs may follow what can be summarised as "Thou shalt have one datum in only one place at only one time".

Parallax Between Official Estimates and Trade Estimates

There is a divergence between official estimates of oilseeds and corresponding estimates released by COOIT. There is a parallax between the two series of estimates in the sense that there is a uni-directional divergence between the two sets. The extent of divergence is more pronounced when there is a bumper production of oilseeds in the country. Conversely, the extent of divergence is low whenever the production is low.

With a view to identifying reasons of divergence between the two set of estimates, orders to constitute two regional committees in the state of Andhra Pradesh and Madhya Pradesh were issued on 3.2.2000. In these regional committees, the state of Karnataka, Tamil Nadu, Gujarat, Maharashtra and Rajasthan besides the states of Andhra Pradesh and Madhya Pradesh were representing. However, the first meeting of these regional committees is yet to be convened.

The official estimates of cotton production are generally lower than that of the trade estimates. There has been the problem of reconciling the estimates of Cotton Advisory Board, trade vis-a-vis official estimates. The State Agricultural Statistics Authorities of southern, western and central regions of the country, where the divergence in the estimates is of large magnitude, are called upon to take such steps as to reduce the divergence.

Refinement of Methodology for Preparation of Advance Estimates

The shelf life of advance estimates may be very short in the sense that these estimates become redundant once the final estimates are available. Nonetheless, their utility as inputs in the process of policy making can hardly be over-emphasised. Therefore, preparation of advance estimates calls for as much scientific approach as final estimates command. However, in reality, we undertake expensive and meticulously drawn Crop Cutting Experiments before making the final estimates but pay precious little attention to preparation of advance estimates. It is observed that some of the states prepare advance estimates simply by adding the reports received by them from District Collectors who have the tendency to under report advance estimates year after year. For making an objective assessment of likely coverage of area, production and yield, it is essential to have a system similar to CWWG in place in the states.

Timeliness

Delays in Furnishing of Estimates

The centre depends on SASAs/ State Agriculture Departments etc. for having the holistic view on the crop husbandry. For this purpose, it is essential that States furnish the requisite returns for making crop-wise assessment of production scenario to enable us to make important policy decisions. However, it is observed some of the States do not furnish the advance, final and fully revised estimates of area, production and yield of various crops in time.

The following schedule, as given in Table 31.2, for furnishing the returns by SASAs/ State Agriculture Departments to DES, New Delhi has been drawn :

Table 31.2

Estimates	Season	Due Date
First advance estimates	Kharif	15th September
Second advance estimates	Kharif and rabi	31st December
Third advance estimates	Kharif and rabi	15th March
Fourth advance estimates	Rabi	15th June
Final estimates	Kharif	31st March
	Rabi	31st August of the succeeding agriculture year*
Fully revised estimates	All seasons	31st January of the succeeding agriculture year@

* Final estimates for 2000-01, for instance, are to be furnished by 30th September, 2001.
@ Fully revised estimates for 2000-01, for instance, are to be furnished by 31st January, 2002.

The estimates of area and yield are usually not received from the States as per time schedules resulting in delay in finalisation of these estimates at all-India level. It will be appreciated if SASAs/ State Agriculture Departments accord due priority to the need for timeliness in flow of statistics.

Delays in TRS

The timely reporting scheme (TRS) has the principal objective of reducing the time lag in making available area statistics of major crops besides providing sampling frame for selection of crop fields for conducting Crop Cutting Experiments. Under the scheme, Patwari is required to complete the Girdawari on a priority basis in 20% of the villages and submit the village crop statements to higher authorities by stipulated date for preparation of advance estimates of area under major crops. The TRS sample of villages also selected in such a way that entire non-permanently settled States are covered over a period of five years.

In a sub-sample of TRS sample villages, an independent agency of supervisors carries out physical verification of Girdawari work under ICS scheme. The main purpose of ICS scheme is to monitor the performance of the primary reporting agency in the TRS and EARAS villages. The findings of ICS during 1995-96 to 1998-99 is summarised in Table 31.3.

Table 31.3 Submission of Crop Statements by the Patwari

Percentage of villages	*Season*	*1995-96*	*1996-97*	*1997-98*	*1998-99*
Statement submitted by due	Kharif	41	44	4	45
date after completing Girdawari	Rabi	41	36	41	43
Statement submitted without	Kharif	11	11	10	9
completing Girdawari	Rabi	11	11	8	9
Total Statements submitted	Kharif	77	78	80	78
for processing	Rabi	80	79	78	77

It is noted from the above table that
* Village crop statements are submitted by due date after completing Girdawari in about 45% of cases only.
* Patwaries submit crop statements to the processing centres without completing the Girdawari in around 10% of the villages.
* Village crop statements are received at the processing centres in about 78% of the villages.
* Despite existence of a well established and time tested scientific crop statistics system in the country, there are certain data gaps and shortcomings. The primary village level agency, namely Patwari

involved in the collection of area statistics in many cases is over-burdened with multifarious activities which leads to neglect of area enumeration work in terms of late recording or non-recording as well as wrong totalling.

Adequate

Non-availability of Yield Estimates by Key Inputs With the existing size of crop cutting experiments, the district level yield estimates are obtained with a standard error of 5 to 6 percent. If the objective is to obtain block level estimates for decentralised planning, the sample size of experiments needs to be raised. Also, separate yield estimates for irrigated/ unirrigated, fertilized/ animal operated areas are not possible through pre-stratification of sample because of small number of crop cutting experiments. The absence of such statistics hampers the process of micro level planning, monitoring and evaluation of developmental schemes. The potential of post-stratification for generating some yield statistics on finer details of inputs needs to be explored.

Under Estimation of Contribution of Agriculture Sector due to non-capturing of Emerging Activities With the development of agriculture and modernisation, several new short duration and summer crops are being grown. These are generally not covered in the Land Record manual for Girdawari. Further in some of the states, the collection of land revenue has been discontinued for certain categories of farmers. This has also affected collection of area statistics. The need is, therefore, felt to have a long hard look on the manual for Girdawari so that this gap can be bridged effectively in the grass root data generation exercise. Besides, it is perceived that contribution of agricultural sector to GDP is under estimated essentially due to non-capturing of emerging activities of floriculture, tissue culture and mushroom culture.

Advance Estimates of Potato and Onion Though there exists a system of working out advance estimates of crop production, none of the horticulture crops are covered in such a system. An attempt had been made to include onion and potato in the advance estimates crops in 1996. However, this system is yet to get streamlined due to several factors. The area under potato and onion is small in comparison to other crops covered for the advanced estimates. However, in view of their sensitivity to consumption basket, it was decided to include these crops in the list of the crops for preparing advanced estimates for 1997-98. All the States were communicated to report the advance estimates of area and production of onion and potato regularly. For the purpose of advance estimates of major crops, States are called upon to take steps to conduct ad-hoc crop inspection (Girdawari) and gather the impression of the crop condition through the conventional 'Annawari' method. It is not certain if the States have taken measures to cover potato and onion in such crop assessment.

SUMMARY OF RECOMMENDATIONS

Important recommendations for the improvement of agricultural statistics made in this chapter are indicated below:

1. The coverage of land utilization and crop statistics should be extended to the entire geographical area of the country. Ad hoc estimates of land utilization should be prepared in respect of the non-reporting areas on the basis of aerial photographs, broad topographical survey and other available information.

2. The Patwari agency should continue to be responsible for collection of basic agricultural statistics. The jurisdiction of the Patwari should be reduced whenever it is excessive. Intensive supervision through normal revenue and statistical staff should be organized over his work of area enumeration.

3. The method of complete enumeration for collection of basic agricultural statistics should be introduced in the States of West Bengal, Orissa and Kerala in a phased manner.

4. Refresher training should be imparted to the Patwari and the Kanungos in the methods of collection of agricultural statistics at periodic intervals.

5. The States should adopt the revised basic and abstract land record forms and concepts and definitions and the procedures for recording of area under mixed crops recommended by the Committee on Improvement of Agricultural Statistics.

6. Crops like soyabean may be brought within the scope of crop estimation system.

7. The sampling design for crop-cutting surveys should be reviewed with a view to introducing stratification according to irrigated and rainfed areas and according to high yielding and local varieties of crops.

8. The Timely Reporting Scheme which is in operation in 17 States, should be extended to the remaining States.

9. Each State should review the sowing and harvesting seasons of different crops, at the district level, and revise the period of crop inspection where necessary so that all crops including, late sown summer crops are covered.

10. Steps should be taken to reconcile the variations between the different sets of estimates for crops like cotton, tobacco, pepper, cashewnuts, etc. issued by different agencies.

11. The DES should prepare qualitative reports on crop and weather conditions on the basis of reports from Block Agricultural Development Officers at the block level and Chief Agricultural Development Officers at the district level which could be later developed into advance estimates of crop production.

12. The scope of the pilot investigations being carried out by the IASRI for developing advance estimates of crop production on the basis of biometric measurements of the crop during its growth

should be extended to other crops and the results utilized on a field scale as soon as the requisite techniques are evolved.

13. The Committee on Improvement of Agricultural Statistics (CIAS) should be activated to consider new proposals for improvement of agricultural statistics and to review from time to time the action taken on its recommendations. The scope of the Committee should be widened to cover livestock, fisheries and forestry statistics also.

14. At the present stage of development of remote sensing techniques, their use in crop estimates has certain limitations. The DES should however keep in touch with the developments in the field.

15. Situation and outlook reports covering area, production, prices, market arrivals internal and external trade, stocks, etc. should be prepared and issued in respect of principal crops.

16. Adequate arrangements should be made in each State for collection of statistics of area under important fruits and vegetables.

17. A census of fruit trees should be conducted once in every five years.

18. Sample surveys for estimating the yield rates and production of fruits should be conducted for one or two crops every year in rotation in accordance with an all-India programme. For vegetables, pilot investigations should be conducted by the States and IASRI in important growing areas.

19. To collect the data on prices and arrivals of fruits and vegetables, full time staff should be provided in all the important city fruit markets.

20. Methodological investigations should be carried out to standardize the data collection techniques for estimating cost of cultivation of fruits.

21. Statistical units should be created in the State Horticulture Departments or agricultural statistics sections to look after the work of horticultural statistics. A separate cell may be created in DES to coordinate the data collected by the States.

22. Standard concept and definitions of terms used in irrigation statistics should be adopted uniformly. Reconciliation of the figures reported in LUS and Irrigation Progress Reports should be done by the planning unit at the district level.

23. Source-wise classification of irrigated area should be amplified to give separate figures for major, medium and minor sources and from surface and ground water sources.

24. A census of irrigation sources should be undertaken along with the Agricultural Census once in five years. Special irrigation surveys on the number of wells and their utilization may be undertaken by other States.

25. Annual administration reports of State Irrigation Departments should be published every year together with comprehensive

statistical data in standard proformas. These data should be consolidated at all-India level and published annually.

26. Statistical units should be provided in the State irrigation Departments for collection and analysis of irrigation statistics.

27. Livestock census should be undertaken simultaneously in all States and Union Territories. While the complete enumeration census may be confined to the broad classification of cattle and other livestock and poultry, details regarding breeds, sex, etc. should be obtained through sample surveys. The practice of having a post-enumeration check by an independent agency should be revived.

28. Advance reports on the livestock census results should be brought out within a few months of its completion on the basis of advance tabulations on sampling basis.

29. The methodology of integrated surveys for obtaining estimates of output of livestock products and numbers spread over a period of five years should be finalized quickly. Till then, sample surveys for estimation of production of milk and other livestock products should be conducted on a priority basis. System of periodical release of all-India and State estimates of livestock products should be introduced.

30. Weekly wholesale and retail prices of livestock, livestock products, livestock feed and fodder, market arrivals of major livestock products and monthly production of livestock feed should be collected regularly.

31. The Directorate of Marketing and Inspection should carry out fresh surveys to collect up-to-date information on marketing of major livestock products and proportions of these products converted into various indigenous products such as butter, ghee, cheese, etc.

32. Standard proformas for collection of information on various items in respect of dairy plants, slaughter houses, bacon factories, poultry dressing plants, feed manufacturing plants, bone digesters, etc. should be prescribed.

33. Quarterly district livestock situation reports containing information relating to season, incidence of disease, availability of animal feed and fodder, etc. should be developed.

34. The District Animal Husbandry Officer should have the help of requisite computational and other staff, to help him in the collection, compilation and submission of various types of livestock statistics. At the State level, the Director of Animal Husbandry should have a full-fledged Statistical Division for collection, compilation, analysis and dissemination of all animal husbandry statistics. This Division should be under the charge of a fairly senior statistician not below the rank of Joint Director of Animal Husbandry. An economist of a suitable rank should also be provided in this Division for economic analysis of various projects and undertaking evaluation studies.

35. The major dairy plants should have an economist on their staff to render advice on economic problems.

36. At the Central level, the Statistical unit in the Animal Husbandry Division of the Ministry of Agriculture and Irrigation should be considerably strengthened. An economist should also be provided in this unit.

37. The IASRI should continue to handle methodological research and pilot investigations in the sphere of livestock statistics. Similar methodological studies should also be taken up by agricultural universities with financial assistance from the Centre.

38. An integrated survey should be designed to enable all-India and State-wise estimates of marine fish catches to be obtained with a reasonable degree of precision.

39. Appropriate methodology for estimation of inland fish production including catches from captive fishery resources should be made available to the State Governments for implementation.

40. Data on fishermen population, fishing crafts and tackle; inland water resources, biological and research statistics, prices, etc. should be collected regularly.

41. Census of fishing craft, tackle and nets should be conducted independently of the livestock census by the State Fisheries Departments under the overall technical control and guidance of the Fisheries Division of the Central Ministry of Agriculture.

42. Inland fisheries resources should be surveyed periodically specially with reference to geographical, physical, chemical and biological factors and classified accordingly.

43. A continuous survey of marine fisheries resources should be undertaken to collect information on various biological characteristics such as growth, recruitment, mortality, etc.

44. Registration of small mechanized boats below 25 GRT should be introduced to enable maintenance of up-to-date statistics of number of such boats in operations as also to keep a watch on the growth of mechanization of boats.

45. In the case of larger vessels above 25 GRT data regarding operational details and performance should be collected and analysed systematically.

46. State Departments of Fisheries should collect reliable estimates of seed fish on a regular basis.

47. Data on producers' wholesale and retail prices 'for standard varieties and predetermined specifications and other market intelligence in regard to fish should be collected.

48. Every State should have a strong statistical unit in the Fisheries Department to deal with all aspects of fisheries statistics. At the Central level, the Fisheries Statistics Unit in the Fisheries Divisions should be strengthened. An economist should also be added to this unit at the Central and State levels.

49. The Statistical Units in the Central fisheries institutes like the Central Marine Fisheries Research Institute, Central Inland Fisheries Research Institute and Central Institute of Fisheries Technology should be strengthened. For the work of economic evaluation, etc. the assistance of an economist should also be provided to these institutes.

50. Efforts should be made to reconcile the differences in the two sets of forest area figures available from Land Utilization Statistics and Indian Forest Statistics. The States should adopt modern classification in the collection of forestry statistics according to functional classification.

51. Suitable procedures should be devised to frame estimates of unrecorded production through sample surveys or otherwise at least once in five years. The possibility of collecting data on timber and fuelwood from agricultural lands through the periodical agricultural censuses should be examined.

52. There is need for verifying the reported figures of output of forest produce in respect of coupes auctioned in standing position, through sample checks.

53. The concept of value of out-turn of forest produce should be clearly defined and should relate to the value at the first point of sale by the Forest Departments.

54. Wholesale prices of major and minor forest products should be collected regularly at fortnightly or monthly intervals and should be included in the scope of index numbers of wholesale prices.

55. Careful analysis of costs of various operations from the stage of plantations to the actual marketing of timber on the basis of economic concepts and usual principles of costing is necessary.

56. Regular data on various aspects of labour employed in forestry should be collected according to uniform concepts and definitions.

57. A Whole-time Forester (Statistics) should be provided in each range for collection of forestry statistics. At the divisional level, the Divisional Forest Officer should be assisted by a Range Forest Officer (Statistics) and a Junior Statistical Assistant for statistical work. At the circle level, the statistical unit should consist of a class II Statistical Officer assisted by requisite complement of Statistical Assistants and Clerks. At the State Headquarters, the Chief Conservator of Forests should be assisted by a Director of Forest Statistics. He should be assisted by requisite number of statisticians.

58. At the Centre, the existing Statistical Unit in the Central Forestry Commission should be developed into a full-fledged Statistical Division and in charge of a Statistician in an appropriate scale.

59. Data on consumption of fertilizers by crops and by size classes of holdings, etc. should be collected through the Comprehensive Scheme for Cost of Cultivation of Crops or through special surveys.

60. Data on seed production and distribution and seed rates of different crops/varieties should be collected and compiled regularly.
61. Data on quantities of pesticides produced, distributed and applied to different crops should be collected systematically.
62. Scope and coverage of foreign market intelligence should be reviewed in consultation with the Ministry of Commerce and adequate arrangements should be made for their systematic collection.
63. For meeting the minimum data needs in the sphere of agriculture, an integrated system of agricultural surveys, covering both the current agricultural surveys and the periodical agricultural and livestock censuses should be devised. Various integrated surveys should continue to the carried out by the agencies reponsible for the different subjects as at present. There should, however, be adequate arrangements for technical coordination and guidance. The Governing Council of the NSSO should examine this question further.
64. The scope of the assessment surveys on High Yielding Varieties Programme being conducted by the IASRI should be extended to provide information on the local factors and problems contributing to low or high yields in different regions to serve as the basis for accelerating the pace of agricultural development.
65. The work regarding the determination of optimum dosages for fertilizers for different crops in different regions already being done by the IASRI should be expanded.
66. The IASRI should be suitably strengthened to tackle the various research problems, to coordinate and supervise the programmes of statistical surveys and to expand the programmes of training in agricultural statistics.
67. Revised series of all-India index numbers of area under crops, net area sown, crop yields, agricultural production, etc. should be issued for all the States. The all-India and State series of these index numbers should be published every year with the minimum possible time lag.
68. The new series of index numbers of harvest (producers) prices as recommended by the Technical Committee on Index Numbers should be initiated as early as possible.
69. The compilation of the revised series on index numbers of parity between prices received and prices paid by the farmer should be taken up by all the States.
70. State-wise and district-wise studies on growth rates in agriculture should be undertaken at more frequent intervals.
71. Technical coefficients for input-output relationships should be worked out on the basis of the data collected during the comprehensive scheme on cost of production on principal crops.
72. The scope for use of computers in the collection, compilation and analysis of agricultural statistics needs to be carefully examined.

A beginning in this regard should be made by transferring the basic data for past years to magnetic tapes for depth studies, easy and timely retrieval and accuracy of tabulation. If found useful, this could be followed up to cover current data also.

73. To reduce the time lag in the availability of agricultural statistics the concerned departments should be provided with printing facilities of their own or a Government printing press should be reserved for the purpose.

74. A bibliography of all printed and cyclostyled reports on different aspects of agriculture including those intended for limited official use should be brought out regularly by a Central agency.

75. One Statistical Supervisor should be provided in each tehsil to supervise the field work of different censuses and surveys, etc. This supervisor should work under the Tehsildar. To improve the accuracy of tabulation, one hand-operated calculating machine should be provided for each tehsil.

76. A statistical unit consisting of a District Agricultural Statistics Officer assisted by one Statistical Supervisor/Assistant and one Junior Clerk/Computer should be provided at the district level. He should work under the proposed Chief Agricultural Development Officers at the district level. One hand-operated calculating machine should be provided to this Unit.

77. At the State level, the existing organization for agricultural statistics should be strengthened. The Head of the State Agricultural Statistics Organization should be a qualified statistician with adequate experience, in an appropriate scale. The Agricultural Statistician should be administratively under the Agricultural Production Commissioner and should be physically located in the same office. He should be assisted by an adequate number of Statisticians, Assistant Statisticians, Economists, and lower staff.

78. At the Centre, the Agricultural Intelligence Division of the Directorate of Economics and Statistics, the National Sample Survey Organization and IARS should be suitably strengthened.

79. Suitable training courses should be developed for periodic training of statistical staff employed in the State and Central Offices.

80. For rationalization of agro-economic research priority areas of research have broadly been spelt out. Institutions having field level staff like the agro-economic research centres, etc. can be entrusted with the type of studies which need collection of information from micro level units. Studies based on secondary data could preferably be arranged at postgraduate centres of research.

81. Postgraduate students of the agricultural universities should be involved in the process of economic investigation, data collection and analysis by including investigational work in the field of agricultural economics as an integral part of the curriculum

prescribed for M.Sc. students in agricultural economics, applied statistics, etc.

82. Research scholarship or fellowships may be arranged at specialized institutions for systematic analysis of the information collected during the village surveys by the agro-economic research centres so as to provide an insight regarding the growth and development process of Indian economy. The cadre authority administering the Indian Economic Service and Indian Statistical Service should, in consultation with the Ministry of Agriculture, select eligible and competent candidates for these fellowships.

83. Farm management studies provide a lot of useful information and should be continued.

84. All important institutions engaged in agro-economic research should be represented on the Coordination Committee for organization of micro-economic studies in the field of agricultural economics.

85. The Research Division and the Economic Policy Cell of Directorate of Economics and Statistics should be strengthened.

Appendices

Appendix 1
Territories of Reorganized States—1956

Reorganized States	Territories as constituted under the States Reorganization Act, 1956.
1. Andhra Pradesh	Andhra plus the following portions of Hyderabad: Hyderabad, Medak, Nizamabad, Karimnagar, Warangal, Khammam, Nalgonda and Mahbubnagar districts; Alampur and Gadwal taluks of Raichur district; Kodangal and Tandur taluks of Gulbarga district; Zahirabad taluk (except Nirna circle), Nyalkal circle of Bidar taluk and Narayankhed taluk of Bidar district; Bichkonda and Jukkal circles of Deglur taluk of Nanded district; Mudhol, Bhiansa and Kuber circles of Mudhol taluk of Nanded district and Adilabad district (except Islapur circle of Boath taluk, Kinwar and Rajura taluks).
2. Assam	
3. Bihar	Bihar except Purulia sub-district of Manbhum district (excluding Chas thana, Chandil thana and Patamda police station of Barabhum thana), Kishenganj sub-division of Purnea district which lies to the east of Mahananda district and the portion of Gopalpur thana of Purnea district which lies to the north of the national highway in the said thana and that portion of the said thana which is occupied by the said highway.
4. Bombay	Bombay State excluding Bijapur, Dharwar and Kanara districts and Belgaum district (except Chandgad taluk) and Abu Road taluk of Banaskantha district plus Aurangabad, Parbhani, Bhir and Osmanabad districts; Ahmadpur, Nilanga and Udgir taluks of Bidar, district; Nanded district (except Bichkonda and Jukkal circles of Deglur taluk and Mudhol, Bhiansa and Kuber circles of Mudhol taluk) and Islapur circles of Boath taluk, Kinwat and Rajpura taluks of Adilabad district of Hyderabad; Buldana, Akola, Amravati, Yeotmal, Wardha, Nagpur, Bhandara and Chanda districts of Madhya Pradesh; Saurashtra and Kutch.
5. Kerala	Travancore-Cochin excluding Agastheeswaram, Thovala, Kalkulam and Vilavancode taluks of

Trivandrum district; Shencottah taluks of Quilon district plus Malabar district (excluding the island of Laccadive and Minicoy) and Kasaragod taluk of South Kanara district of Madras.

6. *Madhya Pradesh*   Madhya pradesh except Buldana, Akola, Amravati, Yeotmal, Wardha, Nagpur, Bhandara and Chanda districts plus Madhya Bharat (except Sunel tappa of Bhanpura tehsil of Mandasaur district); Sironj sub-division of Kotah district of Rajasthan; Bhopal and Vindhya Pradesh.

7. *Madras*   Madras plus Agastheeswaram, Thovala, Kalkulam and Vilavancode taluks of Trivandrum district and Shencottah taluk of Quilon district of Travancore-Cochin.

8. *Mysore*   Mysore State plus Belgaum (except Chandgad taluk, Bijapur, Dharwar, and Kanara districts of Bombay; Gulbarga district (except Kodangal and Tandur taluks), Raichur district (except Alampur and Gadwal taluks), Zahirabad taluk excluding Nirna circle, Nyalkal circle of Bidar taluk and Narayankhed taluk) of Hyderabad State; South Kanara district (except Kasaragod taluk and Amindivi Islands); Killegal taluk of Coimbatore district of Madras State and Coorg State.

9. *Orissa*   Orissa.

10. *Punjab*   Punjab PEPSU.

11. *Rajasthan*   Rajasthan except Sironj sub-division of Kotah district, plus Ajmer, Abu Road taluk of Banaskantha district of Bombay State and Sunel tappa of Bhanpura tehsil of Mandsaur district of Madhya Bharat.

12. *Uttar pradesh*   Uttar Pradesh.

13. *West Bengal*   West Bengal plus Purulia sub-district of Manbhum district (excluding Chas thana, Chandil thana and Patamda police station of Barabhum thana), Kishenganj sub-division of Purnea district which lies to the east of Mahananda river and the portion of Gopalpur thana of Purnea district which lies to the north of the national highway in the said thana and that portion of the said thana which is occupied by the said highway.

14. *Jammu & Kashmir*   Jammu & Kashmir

15. *Delhi*   Delhi

16. *Himachal Pradesh*   Himachal Pradesh

17. *Manipur*	Manipur
18. *Tripura*	Tripura
19. *The Andaman &* *Nicobar Islands*	The Andaman & Nicobar Islands
20. The Laccadives, Minicoy and	The Laccadives, Minicoy and Amindivi Islands (previously forming part of Milabar and South Kanara district).

BIFURCATION OF BOMBAY STATE, 1960

The Bombay Reorganization Bill designed to reconstitute the existing Bombay State as two separate States was passed by both Houses of Parliament and received the assent of the President on 25th April, 1960. According to this Act, the new State of Gujarat comprises: (a) the districts of Banaskantha, Mehsana, Sabarkantha, Ahmedabad, Kaira, Panch Mahals, Baroda, Broach, Surat, Dangs, Amreli, Surendranagar, Rajkot, Jamnagar, Junagarh, Bhavnagar and Kutch; (b) 50 villages in Umbergaon Taluk of Thana district; and (c) 156 villages of Nawapur, Nandurbar Akkalkuwa and Taloda taluks of West Khandesh. The remaining parts of the erstwhile Bombay State constitute of State of Maharashtra as from the 1st May, 1960.

The two States of Maharashtra and Gujarat as constituted under the Bombay Reorganization Act, 1960 share the geographical area of the former Bombay State in the proportion of 62.1 and 37.9 per cent respectively. The area of Maharashtra is nearly 29.55 million acres higher than that of Gujarat. Maharashtra has a slightly more than proportionate share of Net Area Sown and Total Cropped Area. Forests are largely concentrated in Maharashtra whereas Gujarat has more than double the are under the category 'Not Available for Cultivation' compared to Maharashtra.

The two States share the 'Net Irrigated Area' and 'Total Irrigated Area' in almost the proportion of their geographical area though there are considerable variations in the extent of irrigation under different crops.

PUNJAB REORGANIZATION ACT, 1966

According to the 'Punjab Reorganization Act, 1966' the territories of the newly demarcated States and Union Territories are as under:

(i) *Haryana*   This State shall comprise the following territories of the erstwhile State of Punjab, namely:

(a) Hissar, Rohtak, Gurgaon, Karnal and Mahendragarh districts;
(b) Narwana and jind tehsils of Sangrur district;
(c) Ambala, Jagadhri and Naraingarh tehsils of Ambala district;
(d) Pinjor Kanungo circle of Kharar tehsil of Ambala district; and
(e) The territories in Manimajra Kanungo circle of Kharar tehsil of Ambala district specified in Appendix I.

(ii) *Chandigarh* This Union Territory shall comprise such of the territories of Manimajra and Manauli Kanungo circle of Kharar tehsil of Ambala district in the erstwhile State of Punjab as are specified in Appendix II.

(iii) *Himachal Pradesh* The following territories in the erstwhile State of Punjab shall be added to the existing Union Territory of Himachal Pradesh:

(a) Simla, Kangra, Kulu and Lahaul and Spiti districts;
(b) Nalagarh tehsil of Ambala district;
(c) Lohara, Amb and Una Kanungo circles of Una tehsil of Hoshiarpur district specified in Part I of Appendix III.
(d) The territories in Santokhgarh Kanungo Circle of Una tehsil of Hoshiarpur district specified in Part I of Appendix III;
(e) The territories in Una tehsil of Hoshiarpur district specified in Part II of Appendix III; and
(f) The Territories of Dhar Kalan Kanungo circle of Pathankot tehsil of Gurdaspur district specified in Part III of Appendix III.

(iv) *Punjab* The reorganized States of Punjab shall comprise the territories of the erstwhile State of Punjab other than those specified against (i) to (iii) above, Reorganized Punjab shall thus comprise Amritsar, Bhatinda, Ferozepur, Jullundur, Kapurthala, Ludhiana, Patiala districts and parts of Ambala, Gurdaspur, Hoshiarpur and Sangrur districts of the erstwhile Punjab State, which have not been transferred to Haryana, Himachal Pradesh and Chandigarh.

Source: Haryana, Punjab, Chandigarh and Himachal Pradesh—Agricultural Statistics issued by the Economic and Statisical Adviser, Ministry of Food, Agriculture, C.D. and Cooperation, Government of India.

I

Territories transferred from Manimajra Kanungo circle of Kharar tehsil of Ambala district in the existing State of Punjab to the new State of Haryana.

1. The following Patwar circles:
Bhareli
Batawar
Barwala
Majri
Kalka.

2. So much of the territories of the following Patwar circles have not been transferred to form the Union Terrotory of Chandigarh:
Manimajra
Mauli
Chandimander

Source: The First Schedule of the Punjab Reorganization Act, 1966.

· II ·

Territories transferred from the existing State of Punjab to form the Union Territory of Chandigarh.

1. The following Patwar circles of Manimajra Kanungo circle of Kharar tehsil of Ambala district:

    Dhanas
    Kalibar
    Kailer
    Dadu Majra
    Kanthala
    Hallo Majra.

2. The following villages of Manimajra Kanungo circle of Kharar tehsil of Ambala district:

Name of village	Hadbast No.	Name of Patwar circle in which village is included
Lahora	348	Lahora
Sarangpur	347	Sarangpur
Khuda Alisher	353	Kansal
Daria	374	
Manimajra	375	
Mauli Jagran	373	
Bara Raipur	374	Mauli
Chota Raipur	232	

3. The following portions, the extent whereof is specified in column 3 of the Table below of the village specified in corresponding entry in column 1 below of Manimajra Kanungo circle of Kharar tehsil of Ambala district:

Name of village	Hadbast No.	Area acquired No. (in acres)
Suketri	376	77.74
Karoran	352	214.59
Kansil	354	199.78

4. The following villages of Manauli Kanungo circle of Kharar tehsil of Ambala district:

Name of village	Hadbast No.	Name of Patwar circle in which village is included
Behlana	231	
Chuharpur	233	Bhabat
Bair Majra	224	Dharamgarh
Nizampur Kumbra	197	Kumbra
Budheri	12	
Kujheri	198	Kujheri
Attawa	199	
Palsora	11	Mataur
Maloya	13	
Salahpur	201	Maloya
Burail	222	
Nizampur Burail	259	Burail
Jumro	260	

Source: The Second Schedule of the Punjab Reorganization Act, 1966.

III

Territories referred to in Para 1 (ii) (d), (e) and (f) of the Introductory Note transferred from the existing State of Punjab to the Union Territory of Himachal Pradesh.

PART I

1. The following Patwar circle of Santokhgarh Kunungo circle of Una tehsil of Hoshiarpur district:—

Name of Patwar circle	Patwar circle No.
Palkwah	60
Pubowal	62
Polian	63
Dulehar	64
Bietan	65
Kungrat	66
Nangal Kalan	67
Nangran	68
Bathu	74

2. The following villages of Santokhgarh Kanungo circle of Una tehsil of Hoshiarpur district:

Name of village	Hadbast	No. and name of Patwar circle in which village is included
Fatewal	460	61 Jakhera
Bangarh	461	
Charatgarh	225	
Khanpur	226	72 Charatgarh
Chhatharpur	227	
Jatpur	245	
Takhatpur	247	73 Santokharh
Santokhgarh	246	
Bathri	476	75 Bathri

3. The following village of Santokhgarh Kanungo circle of Una tehsil of Hoshiarpur district except portions of those villages as have been included in the local area comprising Naya Nagal:

Name of village	Hadbast No.	No. and name of Patwar circle in which village is included
Jakhera	229	61 Jakhera
Malikpur	242	
Binewal	243	69 Kanchera
Majara	248	
Meharpur	230	70 Basdehra
Bhatoli	231	
Basdehra	228	
Ajauli	237	
Puna	244	71 Basdehra
Raipur	218	72 Charatagarh
Sanoli	249	77 Sanoli

PART II
4. Village Kosar forming part of Una tehsil of Hoshiarpur district.

PART III
5. The following villages of Dhar Kalan Kanungo circle of Pathankot tehsil of Gurdaspur district:

Name of village No.	Hadbast
Bakloh	421
Balun	422
Dalhousie	423

Source: Third Schedule of the Punjab Reorganization Act, 1966.

NEW STATES

November, 2000, has acquired a unique distinction. It will be remembered for the birth by caesarean section of three states—Uttaranchal, Jharkhand and Chhattisgarh. There is a great difference between the factors that led to the creation of these and the old ones. The new states are the result of a prolonged struggle mainly for the economic well-being of the people of the areas concerned. Thus with the adoption of the necessary legislation—the Uttar Pradesh Reorganisation Bill, 2000; the Bihar Reorganisation Bill, 2000; and the Madhya Pradesh Reorganisation Bill, 2000—by the Lok Sabha, the Indian Union now has 28 federated units or states.

Why was such a decision taken then? Obviously, because smaller states are easily and more effectively governable. There are greater chances of their speedy economic development. Political compulsions are another explanation.

Uttaranchal, with a population of 70.45 lakh spread over an area of 55,845 sq km, is composed of 13 districts to be governed from Dehra Dun, the capital. These are Dehra Dun, Uttarkashi, Tehri Garhwal, Rudraprayag, Chamoli, Hardwar, Pauri Garhwal, Bogeswar, Pithoragarh, Almora, Nainital, Champawal and Udham Singh Nagar.

Jharkhand, with an area of 79,714 sq km, has to look after the interests of 2.18 crore people. Most of them are among the poorest of he poor, though their state is the richest in mineral resources and has abundant deposits of coal, bauxite, copper, iron, uranium, etc. Most of its 6,500 villages in 18 districts are without roads. The government will be under tremendous pressure to transform the life of the people at the bottom half of the country's development index. This will mean increased mining activity, resulting in the destruction of the forest wealth. Nearly one crore tribals of the state, concentrated in 67 blocks, will resent any programme that affects the already depleted forest cover.

Chhattisgarh is faced with a severe drought and people expect innovative schemes from the Jogi government to alleviate their suffering. The administrative ability of the Chief Minister—whose "first priority would be irrigation and then the tightening of the administrative set-up'—is, therefore, on test immediately.

Jogi is presiding over the destiny of a power-surplus state. It needs for its 1.76 crore people, living in an area of 1,35,100 sq km, only 25 per cent of its total power generation. Chhattisgarh fulfilled nearly 38 per cent power requirement of Madhya Pradesh. To be precise, it has a big surplus of nearly 300 MW which can be used to lunch development projects in the shortest possible time. The new state is also rich in forest wealth. Nearly 75 per cent of the forests of undivided Madhya Pradesh are in Chhattisgarh, whereas the latter has got only 22 per cent population of the parent state. However, there are fewer roads. Building of roads demands special attention.

In these new states, there are a number of similarities. All of them lack a network of roads in their villages. They suffer from an acute shortage of water supply for drinking and irrigation purposes. Electricity is available in plenty, but they have not been able to use it for their industrial and agricultural advancement. Compared to Jharkhand and Chhattisgarh, Uttaranchal is in an uncomfortable position so far as natural resources are concerned. But with the completion of the Tehri dam project, it can generate enough funds to take care of its various socio-economic requirements. Besides this, it has sufficient forest wealth, which will have to be saved from the destructive designs of the mafia. There is great potential to develop the tourism industry. More than all this, Uttaranchalis have been known for being a dedicated and hard-working people. It is a valuable quality and should be helpful in speeding up the growth process. Jharkhand and Chhattisgarh are uniquely placed because of their abundant mineral wealth. They have all the ingredients to make them industrial power-houses of India.

Appendix 2
Concepts and Definitions for Surveys on Fruits and Vegetables

A. FRUITS

1. Three of Bearing Age   A Tree of bearing age may be regarded as a tree which has attained the age at which 95 per cent of the trees are normally expected to bear fruits. The bearing ages for different fruit crops may be taken as follows:

(i)	Guava, plum, apricot, peach, sapota, lime and other citrus fruits	4 years
(ii)	Mango and litchi	5 years
(iii)	Grape vine	3 years
(iv)	Papaya	18 months
(v)	Apple	7 years
(vi)	Pear	6 year
(vii)	Walnut	10 years

It may be noted that the bearing ages as given above are only indicative. The States may suitably modify these ages according to the agro-climatic conditions prevailing in the State.

2. Bearing Tree   The bearing tree is regarded as the one which has attained the bearing age as specified under (1) and has also borne fruits during the season/year under survey.

3. Non-bearing Tree   A tree of bearing age which fails to bear fruits during the season/year under survey due to any reason such as disease, old age, withering of flowers, etc. is regarded as non-bearing tree.

4. Young Tree   Young tree is the one which has not attained the fruit bearing age as yet.

5. Orchard   A compact price of land which it at least 1/10th of an hrectare are in size or is having at least 12 trees planted on it, may be regarded as an orchard.

It may be clarified that in the case of such fruit trees where distance between the trees is quite large say more than six metres as in the case of mangoes, the orchard will be defined according to the minimum number of 12 trees planted in it while, in such cases where the distance is less than six metres as in the case of bananas, papayas, grape vines etc. the orchard will be defined on the basis of the minimum area of 1/10th of an hectare.

6. Stray or Scattered Trees   Trees not planted in orchards, those planted in clusters of less than 12 trees, or those in a piece of land less than 1/10th of an hectare as well as those planted in back-yard of houses, along the roads, river banks empire regarded as stray or scattered trees.

7. Young and Bearing Orchards   A young orchard is defined as the one in which at least 90 per cent of the trees planted have not attained the bearing age during the year under survey, other wise it will be regarded as a bearing orchard.

8. Extent of Cultvation of Fruits   Extent of cultivation of fruits includes:

   (i) Total number of fruit trees categorized as bearing, non-bearing and young;

   (ii) Number of orchards categorized as bearing and young; and

   (iii) Area under orchards.

9. Area Under Orchards of a Given Fruit Crop   In a tract or a region, the sum-total of areas under all orchards in which a minimum number of 12 trees of a given fruit crop are planted or those orchards having area more than 1/10th of an hectare will be regarded as area under orchards of a given fruit crop in the tract. It may be remarked that this area will include all such area occupied by vacant spaces in the orchards mixed crops other than the given fruit crop grown in the orchards, wells, huts and bunds, etc.

10. Net Area under a Given Fruit Crop   Net area under a given fruit crop is defined as the area occupied by trees of the given fruit crop alone excluding all such areas occupied by vacant space, wells, huts and area under mixed crops including area occupied by fruit crops other than the given fruit crop planted in the orchards of a given fruit crop. This area could be obtained by estimating the number of fruit trees planted in the region and average area occupied by a single tree as estimated from average spacing between the trees planted systematically in rows and multiplying these two estimates, i.e. the estimate of number of trees of a given fruit crop by the estimate of average area occupied by a tree of that crop.

11. Average Yield per Tree of Bearing Age   By average yield per tree of a bearing age is meant the average yield per tree of bearing age as specified in (i) in terms of weight as well as count of fruits.

12. Average Yield per Bearing Tree   The average yield per bearing tree is the average yield obtained from trees of bearing age which have borne fruit during the season/year under survey in terms of weight as well as count of fruits.

B. VEGETABLES

1. Vegetable   Vegetable is an agricultural product which is used for human consumption and eaten as raw or in cooked form along with cereals. We may broadly classify different vegetable crops in the following categories:

   (i) Fresh vegetables

   (ii) Root crops

   (iii) Peas and beans.

Note: Onions and gree spice crops are excluded from this definition. The fresh vegetables may be categorized as:

(a) Leafy vegetables include fenugreek (*methi*), *palak*, *cholai*, etc.

(b) Gourds including bottle gourd, bitter gourds, skuash melon and sponge-gourd, etc.

(c) Other vegetables such as lady's finger, cabbage, brinjal, tomato, cauliflower, etc.

Root crops may include potato, arvi, zimik and, etc.

Beans may include green peas, french beans, etc.

2. Vegetable Field   A vegetable field is a compact piece of land in which vegetables are grown either as pure or in mixed form or as intercrops. For the purpose of survey the minimum size of such field in plains should be 0.05 hectare and in hilly areas it should be 0.02 hectare.

3. Mixed Vegetable Field   When in a field, two or more vegetable crops, are sown in such way that it is different to apportion the area under each crop and also, when percentage of any single crop does not exceed 90 per cent of the total number of plants in the field then, such field will be regarded as under mixed vegetables. Vegetables sown in mixed form are harvested more or less during the same period.

4. Pure Vegetable Field   A pure vegetable field is the one in which either a single vegetable crop is sown at a time or the percentage of the number of plants of the main vegetable crop is more than 90.

5. Inter-crop/Support-Crop   Inter-or support-crop is the one which is sown along with certain other field or horticultural crop in a systematic form, e.g. vegetables sown in the vacant spaces in a mango orchard or those sown as support crops in a young orchard. Vegetables which are sown in a mixed form such that when harvesting of one vegetable crop is more or less completed, the harvesting of second crop commences will also be regarded as inter-crop. When sown along with certain field crops, the area will be accounted for vegetables only when the plant ratio of vegetables is at least 25 per cent.

6. Area under a Given Vegetable Crop   The area under a given vegetable crop in a tract is the total of areas of fields sown under that vegetable. The areas under such feilds in which the given vegetable is sown in a mixed from will be regarded as inter-crop as if the entire areas were under that crop.

7. Area Under Vegetables   Area under vegetables may be measured as net area cropped area:

(i) Net area under vegetables is the area under cultivation of vegetables during the given agricultural year excluding area sown more than once.

(ii) Cropped area under vegetables is the total area under all the vegetable fields sown during the year including area sown more than once during the year as well as areas under mixed crop counted as many number of times as the number of mixed crops' sown in the field. Alternatively cropped area may be defined as total of areas under different vegetable crops grown in the agricultural year.

8. Crop-cuting Plot   For the purpose of estimating the production of vegetables, the random plot having a size of 5×5 sq. meters will be regarded as a crop-cutting plot. However, for conducting surveys, in Hill areas where cultivation of vegetables is done on terraces, the size of such plot may be smaller suiting the conditions of the crop.

9. Sowing Date   Sowing date of any vegetable crop will be week and month during which the vegetable seeds are sown in the field or transplantation of seedlings takes place.

10. Period of Harvesting   Period of harvesting of any vegetable crop will be regarded as total period between the first picking and the last picking when, either the crop is completely harvested or the vegetable field is ploughed for sowing the next crop.

11. Vegetable Season   Different vegetables are sown during different periods. In fact, for some of the vegetables, the total sowing and harvesting period may be less than 80 days. It is rather difficult to define the season for each and every vegetable. Sometime, the harvesting and sowing of vegetables in different fields goes on simultaneously. We may broadly divide the year into three seasons, viz. winter season starting from October to February, summer from March to June and rainy from July to October. In order to collect reliable data on the extent of cultivation of vegetables it is necessary to completely survey the selected villages during each of the three seasons. For a given vegetable, its season will be the one in which majority of the crop is harvested.

Appendix 3
Irrigated and Unirrigated Yields

Area per hec. yield kg/ha.

State		Area irrigated	Per cent	Yield irrigated	Yield unirrigated	Per cent diff.
			Rice			
A.P.		3491	94	1507	722	109
Assam		532	24	1398	1122	25
Bihar		1789	33	1066	846	26
Gujarat		138	29	1797	1132	59
Haryana		3349	N.A.	2377	(a)	N.A.
Karnataka		979	21	1768	1370	29
Kerala		664	60	1639	1272	29
Orissa		319	22	1109	901	23
Punjab		119	N.A.	2712	(a)	N.A.
Tamil Nadu		1162	25	2030	1092	86
U.P.		979	21	1355	877	55
			Wheat			
Bihar		1332	71	1219	868	40
Gujarat		449	64	2064	546	278
Haryana		1165	88	2138	1203	78
M.P.		838	25	1442	748	93
Maharashtra		554	46	1072	544	97
Punjab		2545	N.A.	2447	(a)	N.A.
Rajasthan		1245	69	1469	905	62
U.P.		5173	79	1520	920	65
			Maize			
A.P.		53	—	2132	1160	84
Bihar		136	18	1193	901	32
Haryana		270	15	1090	1123	(–) 3
Rajasthan		30	4	1168	670	74
			Bajra			
A.P.		63	N.A.	1321	453	192
Haryana		83	11	812	473	72
Maharashtra		55	9	758	364	108
Rajasthan		(a)	N.A.	(a)	289	—
Tamil Nadu		56	13	1774	746	138
			Jowar			
A.P.	(K)	23.3	—	1232	524	135
	(R)	23.3	—	1650	515	220
Gujarat	(K)	36.0	1	1023	460	122
	(R)	36.0	1	1446	739	96
Karnataka	(K)	123	4	1109	765	45
	(R)	123	6	1030	471	119
Maharashtra	(R)	305	5	943	448	110
Tamil Nadu		112	14	1048	765	156

(a)   Negligible:
(K)   Kharif;
(R)   Rabi

Source: Directorate of Economics and Statistics, Ministry of Agriculture, New Delhi.

Data Base and Procedure in Estimating Value of Output from Agriculture Sector
(at Current Prices)

Name of the crop/ product/by- product	Whether State-wise estimates are prepared	Data base for production (quantity) estimates	Price and their sources	Procedure of estimation
(1)	(2)	(3)	(4)	(5)
Principal Crops				
[a](i) Rice	State-wise estimates are prepared	State-wise forecasts of production based upon crop-cutting experiments brought out by DES-Ag 'Estimates of Area and Production of Principal Crops in India'	State Statistical Bureaus (SSBs) supply wholesale prices at primary markets which are used to calcu- late the State average price	State-wise production is evaluated at the State average price
(ii) Wheat				
(iii) Jowar				
(iv) Bajra				
(v) Barley				
(vi) Maize				
(vii) Ragi				
(viii) Gram				
(ix) Arhar				
(x) Urad				
(xi) Moong				
(xii) Masur				
(xiii) Groundnut				
(xiv) Castor				
(xv) Linseed				
(xvi) Sesamum				

[a]The percentage of area covered, at present, under the crop-cutting experiments is more than 90 per cent for the crops other than ragi (87), arhar (82), linseed (52), sesamum (45), rape and mustard (40), cotton (75), coconut (75), mesta (53), tobacco (69), dry chillies (32), potato (54). In case of urad, moong and masur, the percentage of area covered under crop-cutting experiments is not known.

Appendix 4 *(Contd.)*

(1)	(2)	(3)	(4)	(5)
(xvii) Rape and mustard (xviii) Kapas (xix) Jute (xx) Mesta (xxi) Tobacco (xxii) Dry chillies (xxiii) Potato (xxiv) Tapioca (xxv) Coconut				
2. Small millets	State-wise estimates are prepared	State-wise forecasts of production based upon crop-cutting experiments brought out by DES-Ag 'Estimates of Area and Production of Principal Crops in India'	Price data available for some States (A.P., M.P.). For others 75 per cent of weighted average State-wise prices of jowar, bajra, barley, maize and ragi is used. (NSS Report No. 32, 5th to 7th Round: 1951-52 to 1952-53)	State-wise production is evaluated at the State average price
3. Other pulses	"	"	Price data available for some States (A.P., Bihar, M.P., Karnataka, Rajasthan). For others 75 per cent of weighted average State-wise prices of arhar urad, moong and masur is used (NSS Report No. 32)	"

Appendix 4 *(Contd.)*

(1)	(2)	(3)	(4)	(5)
ᶜ4.	Sugarcane and gur	"	SSBs furnish the prices paid by sugar factories and wholesale prices of gur	Quantity of sugarcane purchased by factories supplied by DES-Ag (Directorate of Sugar), is evaluated at prices paid by sugar factories and so is the quantity used for chewing and juice-making and seeding. The balance of the quantity is converted into gur and is evaluated at gur prices. The proportion of production for chewing and juice-making, seed rates and conversion ratio of cane to gur are based upon DMI report 'Market-

ᵇOnly 40 per cent of the area is covered by the crop cutting experiment and price is estimated on the price relationship norm based upon NSS Report No. 32 'Some aspects of cost of cultivation of agricultural crop' 5th Round to 7th Round.

ᶜArea covered under crop-cutting experiment is 94 per cent. Seed rate and percentage of production consumed in chewing and juice-making are based upon unpublished Report of DMI (1961-62).

Appendix 4 (*Contd.*)

(1)	(2)	(3)	(4)	(5)
				ing of gur (1961-62)' (DMI-1962).
5. (i) Niger-seed (ii) Safflower (iii) Sannhemp (iv) Cardamom (v) Black pepper (vi) Dry ginger (vii) Turmeric (viii) Garlic (ix) Corriander (x) Sweet potato (xi) Gur seed	"	State-wise DES-Ag forecast of production	SSBs supply the wholesale prices at primary markets which are used to calculate the State average price	State-wise production is evaluated at State average price.
6. Arecanut	State-wise estimates- are prepared	State-wise forecasts of production based upon crop-cutting experiments brought out by DES-Ag. 'Estimates of Area and Production of Principal Crops in India'	Directorate of Arecanut and Spices Development provides the wholesale State-wise prices of different varieties of arecanut marketed. These are averaged over the peak marketing periods. Producers' prices are arrived at by making 20 per cent deduction for processing and trade, transport margins	State-wise production is evaluated at State average price.

Appendix 4 (*Contd.*)

(1)	(2)	(3)	(4)	(5)
7. Banana	"	State-wise DES-Ag forecast of production	SSBs supply district-wise wholesale prices. A simple average of these district prices over the peak marketing period is taken as the State average price	State-wise production is evaluated at State average price.
Minor Crops				
8. Indigo	"	State-wise production data obtained from DES-Ag (time lag one year)	SSBs	Current year estimates are obtained on the basis of past trends.
9. Tea	All-India	Data about quantity of processed tea taken from Tea Board and quantity/value of processed and raw tea leaf taken from Annual Survey of Industries (ASI)	Only raw tea leaf constitutes the product from Agriculture. Total production/value of raw tea leaf are directly not available. The proportion of raw tea leaf is available in the latest detailed ASI results applied to the processed tea leaf estimates for the current year	—
10. Coffee	State-wise	State-wise production from DES-Ag	SSBs	
11. Opium	"	Narcotic Commissioner	Narcotic Commission	—

Appendix 4 *(Contd.)*

(1)	(2)	(3)	(4)	(5)
12. (i) Mangoes (ii) Citrus fruits (iii) Grapes	"	Area under these crop is taken from Indian Agricultural Statistics of DES-Ag and the yield rates are taken from the relevant DMI reports relating to 1962-63.	SSBs	—
13. Cashewnut	"	Directorate of Cashewnut Development DESAg	Directorate of Cashewnut Development/SSBs	—
14. Rubber			SSB Kerala supplies the wholesale prices of sheet rubber at Kottayam market which is deflated by 28 per cent to obtain producers' prices (based on Report of the Plantation Enquiry Commission on Rubber 1956, Ministry of Commerce).	—
15. Papaya	State-wise	DESAg	SSBs	
16. Onion	No. separate estimates are prepared due to lack of data from all States. This crop is included under 'other fruits and vegetables'.			—
Unspecified and Miscellaneous Crops				
17. (i) Other cereals (ii) Other oilseeds	All-India	Production Estimates not available; area is given in 'Indian Agricultural Statistics' (DES-Ag)[d]	Prices not available. For 'other cereals' 100 per cent of weighted average value of yield/hectare of jower, bajra, barley, maize	By using data on area and value of production/hectare.

Appendix 4 (*Contd.*)

(1)	(2)	(3)	(4)	(5)

and ragi and for other oil-seeds, 85 per cent of weighted average value of yield/hectare of linseed, sesamum and castor are taken. (Based upon NSS Report No. 32.)

"

Prices not available; value of production/hectare taken as under:

'Other sugars' = 90 per cent of value of yield/hecatre of gur

'Other fibres' = 90 per cent of value of yield/hectare of mesta and sannhemp

'Other dyes' = 90 per cent of value of yield/hecatre of indigo

'Other drugs and Narcotics' = 90 per cent of value of yield/hectare of opium

'Other condiments and spices' = 90 per cent of value of yield/hectare of cardomum, dry chillies, dry ginger and black pepper

'Other fruits and vegetables, includ-' = 100 per cent of weighted average value of yield/hectare of mango,

18. (i) Other sugars
(ii) Other fibres
(iii) Other dyes
(iv) Other drugs and narcotics
(v) Other condiments and spices
(vi) Other fruits and vegetables

"

ᵈArea estimates have 3 years' time lag.

Appendix 4 *(Contd.)*

(1)	(2)	(3)	(4)	(5)
			ing onion' banana, citrus fruits, cashewnuts, potato, sweet potato and tapioca	
19. Fodder	All-India	Production estimates not available; area is given in 'Indian Agricultural Statistics (DES-Ag)	Prices not available	NSS Report No. 65 (1956-57) Tables with Notes on Animal Husbandry 11th Round, provides estimates of of fodder. The production estimates are moved forward on the basis of area and prices on the basis of straw prices.
20. (i) Miscellaneous food crops (ii) Miscellaneous non-food crops	State-wise	Area provided by DES-Ag in Indian Agriculture Statistics	Values of yield/hectare for 1970-71 were provided for Miscellaneous Food Crops by Assam, H.P., A.P., Punjab and U.P. and for 'Miscellaneous Non-food Crops' by A.P., Assam, H.P., Kerala, Punjab, Tamil Nadu, U.P., Haryana. These are moved forward on the basis of Wholesale Price	Area × value of yield/ per hectare.

Appendix 4 *(Contd.)*

(1)	(2)	(3)	(4)	(5)
			Index Number of Agricultural Commodities (Economic Adviser's), For remaining States, Rs. 40.00 per hectare in 1948-49 used by National Income Committee (1954) is moved forward by using the same Index.	
Products and By-products				
21. Farmyard wood (industrial and fuel)	All-India	Not available	Prices of fuel woods and industrial woods are supplied by SSBs/State Chief Conservators of Forests	The production for 1957-58 given in the Report 'Timber Trends and Prospects in India 1960-75', Ministry of Agriculture, 1965 are moved on the basis of change in total area under: (i) miscellaneous tree crops and groves not included in net area sown, and (ii) fruits other than banana and grapes. These are evaluated at the prices

Appendix 4 *(Contd.)*

(1)	(2)	(3)	(4)	(5)
				of fuel wood and industrial woods.
22. Straw and stalks	State-wise	DES-Ag provides data on area under different crops and NSS Report No. 32 gives zonal yield rates of different stalks and straws which are inflated by 14.4 per cent on the basis of NSS Report No. 65	Prices provided by some SSBs; for others NSS Report No. 32 prices are projected on the basis of changes observed in the available data	—
23. (i) Rice bran (ii) Rice husk	State-wise	DES-Ag provides production of paddy and 'Report on the Marketing of Rice in India' (DMI 1955) give yield rates of rice bran and husk/tonne of paddy. Ad hoc wastage allowance at 5 per cent for bran and 25 per cent for husk are made	Prices provided by SSBs	—
24. (i) Cotton sticks (ii) Arhar sticks (iii) Sesamum sticks (iv) Jute sticks	State-wise	Production estimates not available	Prices not available	Production estimates are made on the basis of yield rates provided by some States: cotton sticks (T.N. and Punjab 1960-61), jute sticks (West Bengal 1975-76), arhar sticks (Rajasthan), sesamum sticks (Punjab). Prices are moved forward on the

Appendix 4 *(Contd.)*

(1)	(2)	(3)	(4)	(5)
				basis of index of firewood prices (CSO).
25. Cane trash	State-wise	Production of cane trash is taken as 10 per cent of out-turn of sugarcane (based on 'Fertilizer Statistics', Fertilizer Association of India)	The prices of fodder are used	—
26. Bagasse	State-wise	Production is estimated at 45 per cent of sugarcane and for gur production, 95 per cent of bagasse is used as fuel for gur making and the balance 5 per cent is evaluated only	The average State-wise ex-factory price for 1966-67 (ASI Report 1968) is adjusted on the basis of index of fire-wood prices	—
27. Grass	State-wise	Production not available	Prices received from SSBs (Haryana, Kerala, Punjab, M.P., Rajasthan, Delhi and Manipur) are used for other States the weighted average of the prices of the available State are used	Based on data given in NSS Report No. 65, the rural All-India estimates of out-turn prepaed for 1955-56 together with adjustment for urban areas are moved on the basis of changed and combined areas of pastures and grazing lands, fallow lands etc. The production estimates are allocated

Appendix 4 *(Contd.)*

(1)	(2)	(3)	(4)	(5)
				to States on the basis of State-wise combined area of pastures etc. These are evaluated as per State prices.
28. Tobacco stem	State-wise	Tobacco stem production is taken as percentage of tobacco leaf production which varies among the States	50 per cent of tobacco leaf price	—
		LIVESTOCK		
29. Milk and milk products (i) Milk consumed as such (ii) Ghee (iii) Butter (iv) Lassi	State-wise	The State-wise production of cow and buffalo-milk is estimated separately on the basis of milch animals, proportions in milk and milk yield rates. Surveys conducted by NSSO, States Animal Husbandry Departments IASRI provide data on proportions of milch animals in milk and their yield rates. Regarding goat milk production data on the various constituent factors supplied by DMI are being used for States other than A.P., Tamil Nadu, Karnataka, West Bengal and Pondicherry. Data on utilization rates of fluid milk and conversion ratio of milk into ghee,	Wholesale prices usually for urban areas are supplied by SSBs which are adjusted for rural/urban price differentials and trade margins	The annual estimates of production are prepared by estimating the different categories of animals on the basis of the last 2/3 consecutive Indian Livestock Censuses (ILCs); the proportions of milch animals to milch animals and their yield rates.

Appendix 4 *(Contd.)*

(1)	(2)	(3)	(4)	(5)
		butter and lassi were supplied by DMI in 1968 (unpublished)		
30. Meat and meat products (i) Beaf (ii) Buffalo meat (iii) Mutton (iv) Goat meat (v) Pork (vi) Edible offals (vii) Fat from slaughtered animals (viii) Fat from fallen animals (ix) Heads and legs (x) Guts (xi) Oesophagus (xii) Blood (xiii) Tailstumps (xiv) Useless meat	State-wise	The State-wise estimates are prepared by using data on number of animals slaughtered and yield rates for different categories of animals. The State-wise proportions of slaughtered to the total animals' populations by categories are based on DMI data for the year 1967-68 and information from SSBs in respect of Maharashtra, Delhi and U.P. The yield rates of meat are based on data from DMI in 1972, IASRI (for Tamil Nadu) Animal Husbandry Departments, Uttar Pradesh and SSB, Bihar. The basic data on yield rates of other products are taken from DMI (1968) which also gives proportion of fallen animals.	Wholesale urban price are supplied by SSBs which are adjusted for rural/urban differentials and trade margins.	
31. Hides and skins (i) Cattle hides (ii) Buffalo hides (iii) Sheep skins (iv) Goat skins	State-wise	Number of hides and skins are obtained from number slaughtered and number fallen due to natural death. The estimates of fallen animals given in MR (DMI 1961) are projected by using the animal population of	Wholesale prices obtained from SSBs are adjusted for trade margins	—

Appendix 4 (*Contd.*)

(1)	(2)	(3)	(4)	(5)
32. Wool and hair	State-wise	different categories. The State-wise production is estimated on the basis of number of sheep and the yield rates. The wool yield rate (clipped) per sheep are provided by the surveys (published/unpublished) conducted by IASRI and some State Animal Husbandry Departments. For the State for which these rates are not available, data on yield rates of the adjoining States are used. The number of sheep are based upon ILC data. The 'pulled' wool estimates are based on number of sheep slaughtered, and 'pulled' wool rates taken from relevant MR (DMI 1964).	Prices supplied by the SSBs duly deflated for trade margin are used	—
33. (i) Goat hair (ii) Camel hair (iii) Pig bristle	State-wise	Number of animals are based on the ILC data. The rates for goat hair and pig bristles are taken from relevant MRs (DMI 1961-62) and for camel hair, information received from DMI 1958-59	For goat hair and pig bristles export prices given in 'Monthly Statistics of Foreign Trade in India' are arbitrarily deflated by 20 per cent. Camel hair prices are taken as 45.3 per cent of wool prices on the basis of MR (DMI-1946)	

Appendix 4 *(Contd.)*

(1)	(2)	(3)	(4)	(5)
Eggs and poultry meat				
34. Eggs	State-wise	The estimates are prepared on the basis of State-wise number of layers worked out using ILC data and yield rates of eggs per layer taken from the State Animal Husbandry Deptts, Poultry Surveys and the results of IASRI Surveys available in the article 'Poultry Eggs Production and its per capita avaiability in India' —Indian Journal of Animal Production, Dec. 1972. Allowance for wastage, proportion of eggs for consumption and hatching obtained from these surveys are also utilized	Average wholesale prices provided by SSBs are deflated for trade and transport margins and rural/urban differentials	—
35. Poultry meat	State-wise	Estimates of slaughtered fowls and chickens are derived from poultry (chickens and adults fowl) population in the two consecutive years using ILC data and the estimates of annual hatchings	SSBs provide the prices per slaughtered adult fowl and chicken	—
36. Dung	State-wise	Estimates are prepared using evacuation rates of dung per bovine collected by IASRI/State Animal Husbandry Deptts, during milk production surveys and the number of bovines esti-	Prices for dry dung are provided by SSBs. For dung manure, prices are provided by some SSBs which are also used for	—

Appendix 4 *(Contd.)*

(1)	(2)	(3)	(4)	(5)
		mated on the basis of ILC data. For States for which no survey results are available, the rates pertaining to ad-joining States are used. These estimates are then classified into dung used as manure and dung used as duel using State-wise proportions supplied by IASRI (1972). Dry dung taken as 40 per cent of green dung	which prices are not available	—
37. Increment in livestock	State-wise	Increase in number of different cate-gories of livestock are estimated on the basis of projected population using ILC data	SSBs provide the prices of different categories of livestock	—
		OTHER PRODUCTS		
38. (i) Bones (ii) Horns (iii) Hoofs	State-wise	The yield rates of bones per animal of different category of horns and hoofs from relevant MR (DMI 1957) and (DMI 1961) are applied to the esti-mated slaughtered and fallen animals	Bone prices are provided by SSBs. For horns and hoofs, prices received earlier are moved for-ward by applying price index of meat.	—
39. Silk worm cocoons	State-wise	Out-turn and value estimates provided by Central Silk Board	—	
40. Honey	State-wise	Out-turn and value estimates provided by Khadi and Village Industries Commission	—	

Appendix 4 (*Contd.*)

(1)	(2)	(3)	(4)	(5)
		INPUTS		
41. Seed	State-wise	Crop-wise consumption is estimated on the basis of seed rates made available from various sources viz. cost of cultivation studies (DES-Ag), MR Reports, NSS Report No. 32 and various studies conducted by States	State average prices of the crops are used	—
42. Fertilizer	All-India	Data on material-wise offtake of chemical fertilizers are available in 'Fertilizer Statistics' (Fertilizer Association of India) which is used as a close approximation to the consumption material-wise data	Data on material-wise price are given in 'Fertilizer Statistics'	—
43. Organic manure	All-India	Estimates of consumption are prepared by using data given in NSS Report No. 140 (11th Round: 1956-57) and the Report of Farm Management Statistics (DES-Ag). The base year estimates are projected on the basis of changes in given area sown in each State	The base year prices are moved on the basis of change in dung prices.	—
44. Pesticides and insecticides	All-India	Value of consumption data provided by Pesticides Association of India		—
45. Livestock feed (for animals used in agricul-	All-India	Total cost of feed of all animal is estimated as under: (1) Entire value of fodder, canetrash,	Total cost of feed is distributed between agriculture and non-agriculture sec-	—

Appendix 4 *(Contd.)*

(1)	(2)	(3)	(4)	(5)
tural activities)		grass, rice bran,	tors in proportion to res-	
		(2) 95 per cent value of stalks and straws,	pective number of animals converted into cattle	
		(3) 85 per cent value of cotton seed,	equivalents using cattle.	
		(4) 1 per cent value of rice and wheat per cent value of jowar, bajra, maize, ragi, other cereals,	'Equivalence Scale from 'Economic Effects of Irrigation' by D.R. Gadgil.	
		(Based on *Population and Food Planning in India* by Baljit Singh, 1947).		
		(5) 35 per cent value of gram (based on NSS Report No. 65),		
		(6) 55 per cent value of groundnut oil cake.		
		80 per cent value of lineseed cake, 60 per cent value of coconut cake, 60 per cent value of cotton seed cake.		
		(Based on *Oilseeds in India 1954-55*, DES)-Ag		
		(7) Rs. 1.62 per cattle equivalent of salt, medicines and miscl, feed in salt, medicines and miscl, feed in 1955-56 (based on NSS Report No. 65) are moved on the basis of index number of wholesale price of salt (EA)		

Appendix 4 (*Contd.*)

(1)	(2)	(3)	(4)	(5)
46. Irrigation charges	State-wise	Available in the State budgets		
47. Cost of electricity	State-wise	Data on quantity consumed and price per unit electricity are obtained from Central Electricity Authority		
48. Diesel oil	State-wise	Estimates are prepared on the basis of number of tractors supplied by SSBs and diesel engines (based on Indian Livestock Census Data). The consumption per unit is based on data collected from SSBs	Retail price are supplied by Indian Oil Corporation	

MARKET CHARGES

49. For agriculture	All-India	The ratio of market charges to gross value of output based on *Rural Credit Survey 1951-52* (RBI 1954) is being used.		
50. Livestock (for ghee, butter and meat)	All-India	Data on market charges given in the MR on milk and butter (DMI 1957) and meat (DMI 1955) are used to estimate the ratio of market charges to output. These ratios are assumed to remain unchanged for preparing estimates for subsequent years.		
51. Operational cost of livestock products (towards	All India	Operational cost based on limited data are taken as Rs. 267.92 per tonne for ghee and butter and 0.25 per cent of		

Appendix 4 (*Contd.*)

(1)	(2)	(3)	(4)	(5)
current expenditure on the production of ghee, butter, milk, hides, skins, eggs, poultry, wool, hair, honey, silk-worm cocoons)		the value of output for other products		
52. Current expenditrue on repairs	State-wise	The estimates are prepared separately for: (a), (b), and (c) groups, AIDIS (All India Debt and Investment Survey) (RBI) (1971-72) provide State-wise data on repairs and replacements and one-third of this is assumed to form the expenditure on repairs and maintenance. Regarding: (a), and (b), the capital stock at (1970-71) prices are first prepared and for subsequent years by adding annual figures of net capital formation at (1970-71) prices. The estimates of repairs and maintenance are obtained by applying the proportion of expenditure on 'repairs and maintenance' to the value of Capital Stock which is assumed to remain unchanged. These are adjusted		
(a) agricultural machinery, implement and transport equipment,			—	
(b) non-residential buildings, i.e. farm houses, grain golas, cattle sheds,				—
(c) Other construction				

Appendix 4 (*Contd.*)

(1)	(2)	(3)	(4)	(5)
works, e.g. bunding and other land improvements, wells, other irrigation resources		for price changes to obtain current price estimates. Regarding (c) the point estimates are moved with the help of constant price value added in the unorganized sectors. Adjustment for urban areas are done on the basis of ILC 1972 (urban assets 3.1 per cent of rural assets)		
53. Consumption of fixed capital (a) (b) and (c) as per item 52 above	State-wise	Regarding (a) and (b) consumption of fixed capital is estimated from the value of capital stock and average life of these assets. Average life for (a) is taken as 9 years on the basis of SSBs data and 50 year for (b). In case of (c) the consumption of fixed-capital for 1971-72 is taken as the sum of expenditure on replacement only, i.e. the two-third of expenditure on repairs and replacement and expenditure on major alternations is respect of bundings, land improvements, wells and other irrigation resources. The point estimates are moved with the help of value added in the unorganzied sectors to obtain estimates for		

Appendix 4 (*Contd.*)

(1)	(2)	(3)	(4)	(5)
		subsequent years.		
		FORESTRY		
54. Major products	State-wise	SSBs/State Chief Conservators of Forests (CCFs) provide data on production of Industrial and fuel wood. The estimates of under-reporting and illegtal removals are assumed to be 10 per cent of the recorded production (Report *Timber Trends and Prospects in India*—1960-75) Ministry of Food and Agriculture, 1965)	State CCFs/SSBs provide the wholesale prices which are adjusted for trade and transport margins based on '*Timber Trends Study for the Far East*; Country Report For India' (I.G. of Forests, 1958)	
55. Minor	State-wise	Information is available in the form of royalty value or contract value realized by the Government and not the economic value of output. The value of output is estimated indirectly by using the ratio of the total value of output (recorded and unrecorded) to the royalty value of major forest products. However, information on production and prices for some minor products (resin in H.P., bidi leaves and sandalwood in A.P., etc.) are provided by some State CCFs which are also made		

Appendix 4 *(Contd.)*

(1)	(2)	(3)	(4)	(5)
56. Inputs	State-wise	use of The operational costs and repairs and maintenance are assumed to be 4 per cent of value of output and consumption of fixed capital at 1 per cent		
		FISHING		
57. Marine	State-wise	State-wise data on marine catch are provided by Central Marine Fisheries Research Institute or State Fisheries Departments (SFDs)	State Fisheries Deptts/SSBs provided the price data	—
58. Inland	State-wise	State Fisheries Depts. provide the data of inland catch for all States other than Assam, West Bengal, Bihar for which SSBs provide the estimates	SSBs/SFDs provide the price data	—
59. Subsistence	State-wise	No direct estimates available; derived as some percentage varying from 2.5 per cent to 25 per cent of inland fish output	—	—
60. Inputs and consumption of fixed capital	State-wise	No direct estimates are available. Estimates are being prepared as some percentages of output	—	—
61. Value added from fish curing (salting and sundrying)	State-wise	SSBs/SFDs provide data on quantity and price of fish cured, salt used and fish let-in.		

Appendix 4 *(Contd.)*

(1)	(2)	(3)	(4)	(5)
62. Other products	State-wise	The estimates of net value added are prepared on the basis of persons engaged in such activities (using Population Censuses data) and net value added per worker	—	—

Source: K.C. Seal, Agricultural Statistics and National Income Estimates, Technical Address, December, 1980

Index